Library and Learning Resources
Central Saint Martins College of
Art and Design
Southampton Row
London
WC1B 4AP

SR
Three week loan

late return of this item will incur fines
renew online: http://www.arts.ac.uk/library
renew by phone: 020 7514 8125

54133620

THE ART OF EURIPIDES

In this book, Professor Mastronarde draws on the seventeen surviving tragedies of Euripides, as well as the fragmentary remains of his lost plays, to explore key topics in the interpretation of the plays. It investigates their relation to the Greek poetic tradition and to the social and political structures of their original setting, aiming both to be attentive to the great variety of the corpus and to identify commonalities across it. In examining such topics as genre, structural strategies, the chorus, the gods, rhetoric, and the portrayal of women and men, this study highlights the ways in which audience responses are manipulated through the use of plot structures and the multiplicity of viewpoints expressed. It argues that the dramas of Euripides, through their dramatic technique, pose a strong challenge to simple formulations of norms, to the reading of a consistent human character, and to the quest for certainty and closure.

DONALD J. MASTRONARDE is Melpomene Distinguished Professor of Classics at the University of California, Berkeley. He has published extensively on Greek tragedy and Euripides in particular, including *Euripides: Medea* (Cambridge, 2002) and *Euripides: Phoenissae* (Cambridge, 1994).

THE ART OF EURIPIDES

Dramatic Technique and Social Context

DONALD J. MASTRONARDE

Melpomene Professor of Classics, University of California, Berkeley

CAMBRIDGE
UNIVERSITY PRESS

CAMBRIDGE UNIVERSITY PRESS

Cambridge, New York, Melbourne, Madrid, Cape Town, Singapore,
São Paulo, Delhi, Dubai, Tokyo

Cambridge University Press
The Edinburgh Building, Cambridge CB2 8RU, UK

Published in the United States of America by Cambridge University Press, New York

www.cambridge.org
Information on this title: www.cambridge.org/9780521768399

First published 2010

Printed in the United Kingdom at the University Press, Cambridge

A catalogue record for this publication is available from the British Library

ISBN: 978-0-521-76839-9 Hardback

Contents

Preface   *page* vii
Abbreviations and reference system   xi

1. Approaching Euripides   1
   Pre-modern reception   1
   From the Renaissance to German Classicism   9
   The nineteenth and twentieth centuries   12
   Current debates: tragedy, democracy, and teaching   15
   The approaches and scope of this book   25
   Appendix: a brief guide to Euripides' plays   28

2. Problems of genre   44
   Genre: expectations, variety, and change   44
   Tragedy, satyr-play, and the comic   54
   Generic labels and their problems   58

3. Dramatic structures: variety and unity   63
   Open form and structural strategies   64
   Double structures   68
   Strategies of juxtaposition   77
   A final example: *Orestes*   83
   Open structures and the challenge of tragedy   85

4. The chorus   88
   The chorus and the audience   89
   Limits on identification and authority   98
   The chorus and knowledge   106
   The chorus and moral and interpretive authority   114
   Myth in the choral odes   122

v

Connection and relevance 126
(1) Connection and relevance of the parodos 127
(2) Connection and relevance in the stasima 130
"Not as in Euripides but as in Sophocles" 145

5. The gods 153
Preliminary considerations on Greek religion and the divine 154
The drama of human belief 161
Criticism and speculation 169
Seen gods: prologue gods 174
Seen gods: epilogue gods 181
Unseen gods: inference and uncertainty 195
Conclusion 205

6. Rhetoric and character 207
Rhetoric and its context 208
Ambivalence about rhetoric and the modern 211
Rhetoric, *agōn*, and character 222
(1) *Hippolytus* and *Medea*: expressing world-views 222
(2) *Alcestis* and *Hecuba*: shaping the self 227
(3) *Iphigenia in Aulis* and *Orestes*: instability and self-delusion 234

7. Women 246
Indoors and outdoors 248
Family and city and gendered motivations 254
Women, fame, and courage 261
Misogynistic speech 271

8. Euripidean males and the limits of autonomy 280
Unmarried young males 285
Old men 292
Mature males 297
The deficient hero 304

Conclusion 307
Bibliography 313
Index of names and topics 334
Index of passages cited 346

Preface

It is over twenty-five years since I first contemplated writing (eventually) a general book on Euripides (at the time I had in mind the somewhat perverse title *The Unity of Euripides*). It is over ten years since I began trying to write this book, for which I had by then tentatively adopted the title *The Art of Euripides*, in tribute to the example of my senior colleague Tom Rosenmeyer's *The Art of Aeschylus*. I wanted to write a book that dealt with topics that span most or all of the extant plays rather than one with a chapter on each play; and I hoped to find a middle ground between the formalist studies that I have admired and the social and political approaches that have been so successful and influential in the past thirty years. As things turned out, Tom Rosenmeyer died not many months before I was finally far enough along in my work to seek the reactions of some readers (had he lived, he would have been one), and I began to doubt whether I should keep the allusive title, being all too aware that I could not match the breadth of his reading in the history of drama and dramatic theory or the elegance of his writing. In the end, I kept the title but added a subtitle, "dramatic technique and social context," to declare the two types of concerns that I have attempted to combine (with what success or utility it is left to each reader to decide). The Greek tragedians, like other Greek poets, were consummate craftsmen, innovating and experimenting with the formal elements of their art and reinterpreting the myths and personalities of the traditional heroes with an inextricable mixture of seriousness and playfulness. At the same time, their activity was clearly embedded in the social and political culture in which they operated, and their works reacted to and commented on issues and conflicts present in a broad archaic and classical Greek tradition and in the specifically Athenian tradition of the imperial democracy.

In the chapters that follow, I have approached the corpus from a number of directions, choosing topics that strike me as important and challenging. I did not aim to write a definitive book, and there are surely interesting topics that I have omitted. Even in the topics I have chosen, I have been more interested in exploration and in recognition of variety and even contradiction than in reaching conclusions that can be neatly summarized. I believe that much of what is best in Euripides (and in the Greek tragedians generally) is exploratory and aporetic, and I approach the work in the same spirit. But I am not unaware that what I see and emphasize in analyzing Euripides is unavoidably a product of my own personal and scholarly profile: attending high school and college in the US in the 1960s and reading Greats at Oxford; being receptive to German scholarship of the fifties and sixties (Reinhardt, Ludwig, Strohm, Matthiessen) and American scholarship of the sixties and seventies (Knox, Wolff, the early works of Charles Segal); owing my earliest technical interests to Fraenkel's commentary on *Agamemnon* and Barrett's on *Hippolytus*; and pursuing my career at the University of California, Berkeley.

Because of the pressures of other responsibilities and projects, my work on this book has taken longer than I would have wished. Various chapters were drafted and redrafted over a period of a dozen years. I have worked intensively in the summers of 2007 and 2008 to bring it to completion and I have not always been able to take account of work published in the past few years, since I felt I needed to set a final limit for myself and finish the book before I got any farther past my prime, and the choice was between revising my drafts or almost interminably postponing completion in order to read new publications. I am conscious of the book's shortcomings and difficulties. It is not an introductory book, nor easy to read, since it draws on so many plays, and I do not take up time and paper summarizing plot details (except for some brief summaries at the end of Chapter 1), and I cite a very large number of passages without including the text, requiring the reader to have at hand an edition or translation (with appropriate line numbers) in order to verify my claims or to flesh out concise statements. Nevertheless, I have tried in various ways to make it as accessible as possible to the serious reader who may come to it with knowledge of only a few plays or even may not read Greek. On the other hand, despite the advanced nature of the book in some regards, I may disappoint more expert readers by not engaging more frequently and specifically with the specialized scholarship on Euripides. Since my early formation as a scholar, I have of course learned greatly from the works of important critics like Zeitlin, Foley, and Goldhill, and my ideas have been sharpened and refined by the significant books on individual plays (here I would single out those of Mossman, Allan, and Mendelsohn for special praise). But I was trying from the beginning to come to terms with the chosen topics from a personal perspective based on a long period of reading and teaching and not to write in detail about the trends of scholarship; to do more with the bibliography would have extended the book (and the date of its completion) even more (as it is, I am grateful to Michael Sharp and Cambridge University Press for tolerating the current length).

It is a pleasure to record here my gratitude for the help I have received from many friends. Mark Griffith has been a wonderful colleague for thirty-five years, and I have learned much from his bold and original readings. He read the penultimate draft and, as usual, provided copious brief remarks that guided me toward many improvements. Martin Cropp (whose friendship goes back even further, to our time at Toronto) not only read that same draft and gave helpful suggestions of both a particular and a general nature, but allowed me to see the page proofs of the second volume of the Loeb edition of the fragments (Collard and Cropp 2008b) and a version of its index. Marco Fantuzzi spontaneously offered to read my work, gave suggestions on all but one chapter (the one I revised too late to share with him), and cheered me up when I was suffering self-doubt. Three readers for Cambridge University Press also helped me in important ways to decide on the final shape of the book. My ideas on particular topics have also benefitted from interactions with my students, of whom I want to mention here Luigi Battezzato, Melissa Mueller, and Johanna Hanink. David Jacobson provided another set of eyes to proofread the revised chapters, pointed out passages that could be made clearer, and checked a near-final version of the compiled bibliography. I must emphasize, of course, that these readers should not be assumed to agree with all my views (or my decisions about the final form of the book), and that any errors, omissions, or perversities present in the book are my own responsibility. Versions of various parts of the book were presented as lectures in Berkeley, Pisa, Urbino, Rome, Calgary, and Boulder, and at Amherst, Columbia, Harvard, and a Greek drama conference at Sydney, and students in seminars at Berkeley and Harvard have also heard parts of this study: I thank all my audiences for their kind reception and helpful questions.

Editors and presses have generously given me permission to reuse here material that I have published previously. The versions in this book are sometimes abbreviated, sometimes expanded, sometimes appear in English for the first time, and most have received some degree of revision in wording. Chapter 2 is derived from "Euripidean tragedy and genre: the terminology and its problems," in *Illinois Classical Studies* 24–25 (1999–2000) 23–39. Parts of Chapter 4 appeared in "Il coro euripideo: autorità e integrazione," *Quaderni Urbinati di Cultura Classica* 60 (1998) 55–80 and in "Knowledge and authority in the choral voice of Euripidean tragedy," *Syllecta Classica* 10 (1999) 87–104. Parts of Chapter 5 appeared in "The optimistic rationalist in Euripides: Theseus, Jocasta, Teiresias," in *Greek Tragedy and its Legacy: Essays presented to Desmond Conacher*, eds. M. Cropp, E. Fantham, S. Scully (Calgary 1986) 201–11, in "Euripidean tragedy and theology," *Seminari Romani di Cultura Greca* 5 (2002) 17–49, and in "The Gods," in *A Companion to Greek Tragedy*, ed. J. Gregory (Blackwell: Oxford 2005) 321–32. I am grateful to Banca Intesa, Milan, for providing a high-quality digital image of the volute crater with what is plausibly regarded as an illustration of *Andromache* (Milan, Collezione H. A. (Banca Intesa Collection) 239, attributed to the Ilioupersis Painter) and for giving permission for its use on the cover (and thanks to Oliver Taplin for his help with this). I refer to this image in n. 25 of Chapter 3, and I consider it a good choice for this book for several reasons: it is a fine work that has not been frequently illustrated in the past; it is part of the evidence for Euripides' popularity after his death; it features one of the extant plays that is less often studied; it shows the divine agent in a higher frame above the humans and expresses the close association of Apollo with Orestes in the ambush; and it catches the underhandedness of Orestes' role and the underlying opposition between him and Neoptolemus.

In my drawn-out work on this book, I have benefited from fellowships from the American Council of Learned Societies and the National Endowment for the Humanities, and my progress was also assisted by the fact that my Berkeley department colleagues honored me with appointment to the Melpomene Chair (for which I also want to thank the anonymous donor). Finally, I must acknowledge the patience of my wife Joan, who has had less enjoyment of summer vacations (and weekends) than she should have while I have been completing this book.

Abbreviations and reference system

The names used in the text are an eclectic mix of Latinized versions of the Greek titles and a few English names. Some alternative names not used in this book are listed here. In the footnotes and in parentheses, abbreviated versions (as shown here) are used.

Aeschylus

Persae (= *Persians*), *Pe.*
Septem (= *Septem contra Thebas*, *Seven against Thebes*), *Se.*
Supplices (= *Suppliant Women*), *Su.*
Agamemnon, Agam.
Choephori (= *Libation Bearers*), *Choe.*
Eumenides, Eum.

[Aeschylus]

Prometheus (= *Prometheus Vinctus*, *Prometheus Bound*), *Prom.*

Sophocles

Ajax
Antigone, Ant.
Trachiniae (= *Trachinian Women*), *Trach.*
Oedipus Tyrannus (= *Oedipus Rex*, *Oedipus the King*), *OT*
Electra, El.
Philoctetes, Phil.
Oedipus Coloneus (= *Oedipus at Colonus*), *OC*

Euripides

Alcestis, Alc.
Medea, Med.
Heracleidae (= *Children of Heracles*), *Hcld.*
Hippolytus (= *Hippolytos Stephanias*, the second *Hippolytus*), *Hipp.*
Andromache, Andr.
Hecuba (= *Hekabe*), *Hec.*
Supplices (= *Suppliant Women*), *Su.*
Electra, El.
Heracles (= *Herakles Mainomenos, Hercules Furens*), *Her.*
Troades (= *Trojan Women*), *Tro.*
Iphigenia in Tauris (= *Iphigenia Taurica, Iphigenia among the Taurians*), *IT*
Ion
Helen (= *Helena*), *Hel.*
Phoenissae (= *Phoenician Women*), *Phoen.*
Orestes, Or.
Bacchae (= *Bacchants*), *Ba.*
Iphigenia in Aulis (= *Iphigenia in Aulide, Iphigenia Aulidensis*), *IA*
Cyclops, Cycl.
Rhesus, Rhes.

Fragmentary plays are generally referred to by their Latinized names (but English is used in a few names like *Melanippe the Wise* and *Melanippe the Captive*). References to fragments of Euripides follow the numbering in *TrGF*, which has also been adopted in other recent collections of tragic fragments.

NAMES OF GODS AND CHARACTERS

Most proper names are in Latinized forms, but there are exceptions (e.g., Helios, Thanatos) when Latinization strikes me as too odd.

ABBREVIATIONS

Dindorf   W. Dindorf, ed., *Scholia graeca in Euripidis tragoedias ex codicibus aucta et emendata*. 4 vols. Oxford 1863.

D–K   H. Diels and W. Kranz, eds., *Die Fragmente der Vorsokratiker*. 6th edn. Zurich 1951–52.

K–A   Rudolph Kassel and Colin Austin, eds., *Poetae Comici Graeci*. Berlin and New York 1983–.

LIMC   *Lexicon iconographicum mythologiae classicae*. Zurich and Munich 1981–97.

L–P   E. Lobel and D. Page, eds., *Poetarum Lesbiorum fragmenta*. Oxford 1955.

T Kannicht   Testimonia pertaining to Euripides in *TrGF* vol. V.1, ed. R. Kannicht.

TrGF   *Tragicorum Graecorum fragmenta*, ed. B. Snell, R. Kannicht, and S. Radt. 5 vols. in 6. Berlin 1971–2004.

W   M. L. West, ed., *Iambi et elegi Graeci ante Alexandrum cantati*, 2nd edn. Oxford 1989–92.

Abbreviations of journal titles generally conform to those used in *L'Année philologique*.

Translations are my own, except for two short extracts credited in the footnotes.

CHAPTER I

Approaching Euripides

PRE-MODERN RECEPTION

Modern reception and interpretation of the major authors and literary texts of ancient Greece are heavily conditioned, and often distorted, by the long history of anecdote, criticism, pedagogy, and scholarship that has accreted around them, and there are few authors to whom this applies more forcefully than to Euripides. It is indispensable, therefore, as a preliminary step in approaching the works of Euripides, to take account of the long tradition of reception and judgment to which the plays have been subjected. Such an accounting will reveal several important potentialities inherent in his dramas as well as the agendas and preferences of the various readers and audiences, and it ought to help us move beyond some of the commonplaces that continue to influence the appreciation of his work.

A thorough treatment of the reception of Euripides would require a whole volume to itself. For the purposes of this book, some highlights will have to suffice. We may begin with the earliest stages of that reception, those from antiquity, which have had the longest span of direct and indirect influence: the judgments about Euripides' themes and styles conveyed in comic form in the plays of Aristophanes; the strictures on his dramatic technique that emerge as *obiter dicta* in Aristotle's *Poetics*; the biographical tradition about the poet himself; and the scholia and prefatory material transmitted with select plays in the medieval tradition of the extant plays.

Aristophanes, a younger contemporary[1] who staged his comedies during the last two decades of the tragedian's career, made use of Euripides most intensively in *Acharnians* (425), *Women at the Thesmophoria* (411), *Frogs* (405), and in a minor way in *Clouds* (the extant version is somewhat later than 423) and *Peace* (421). Exploiting a kind of culture war for humor, the

---

[1] Aristophanes' productions date from 427 to 388 and he may have been born around 450–445, whereas Euripides' productions date from 455 to 405 (posthumous) and he is likely to have been born in the period 485–475.

comic playwright fashions an exaggerated and oversimplified contrast
between old and new, assimilating under one grouping Euripides, New
Music, the sophists, Socrates, and the amoralism engendered by intense
internal political strife, prolonged war, and dedication to retaining imperial
power. The Aristophanic portrayal is the earliest source for the idea that in
Euripides (as contrasted primarily with Aeschylus[2]) rhetorical cleverness,
"realistic" costuming, choice of sensationalized myth, and innovative lyric
style diminish the dignity of the tragic genre and fail to produce the proper
edification of the audience, as well as for the idea that Euripides is an
atheist.[3]

From the *Poetics* derive many of the often repeated charges of the defects
of Euripidean dramaturgy: faulty dramatic construction (use of the *deus
ex machina*, Ch. 15; the backhanded compliment about being "most tragic
even if he does not manage other matters well," Ch. 13, which leads many to
apply Aristotle's complaint about lack of probability or necessity in Ch. 9 to
Euripides); the perception of unworthy or unrealistic characterization
(Menelaus and Iphigenia, Chs. 25, 15); the contrast with Sophocles, implicit
when Euripides is cited as an example of the wrong approach, and explicit
with respect to characterization (Ch. 25)[4] and the use of the chorus (Ch. 18).
Curiously, Aristotle's admiration for Euripides' *Iphigenia in Tauris* (Chs. 14,
16) has been much less influential until recent times. Aristotle's opinions
were especially decisive for reception once interest in tragedy was revived in
Western Europe in the sixteenth century. But even though we cannot trace
much direct knowledge of the *Poetics* itself in antiquity, similar judgments
were no doubt conveyed in other works of Aristotle and in those of his
immediate students (especially Dicaearchus and Aristoxenus) and thus had
an impact on the scholarly treatment of Euripides in the Hellenistic and
Roman periods, especially the major Alexandrian scholars, whose views
have left traces in the surviving scholia.[5]

---

[2] Aeschylus is featured most prominently in *Frogs*, but the same contrast is assumed in *Acharnians* 10
and *Clouds* 1365, and presumably in fr. 161 K–A.
[3] For the decisive role of Aristophanes in conditioning subsequent interpretation and criticism of
Euripides, see Snell 1953.
[4] Aristotle (*Poetics* 1460b33–4) ascribes the contrast between idealized characterization in Sophocles and
realistic in Euripides to a statement of Sophocles himself. If this reflects a reality of written transmission (Sophocles is alleged to have written "About the chorus," which some think could have been
about tragic production in general and not simply about the chorus), it is another contemporary
source of reception. But the statement could also have had an anecdotal origin, perhaps involving oral
transmission, so that it could be apocryphal, but still an early perception.
[5] For the importance of the Aristotelian background to rhetorical and literary theories assumed in the
scholia (primarily on Homer and the dramatists), see Meijering 1987.

The biographical tradition for most Greek poets is almost completely unreliable, and the case of Euripides is no exception. Mythical elements enter the lives, especially regarding birth, oracles, and death. Elements of rivalry and one-upmanship are highlighted or invented. Similarities between ideas in the poetic text and the works of other famous men generate allegations of plagiarism, collaboration, or teacher–pupil relationships that probably never existed. Illegitimate inferences are made from statements of characters in the dramas to establish the attitudes or experiences of the poet himself. The exaggerated, fantastic, or humorously malicious details provided in comedy are treated as facts.[6] In the biographical tradition[7] on Euripides we find the claim that his mother was a seller of vegetables (and the opinion that this claim is false); that he tried his hand at painting, or at competitive athletics, before becoming a poet; that he was student of Prodicus, Socrates, and Anaxagoras; that he was socially aloof and unpopular with his fellow-citizens; that he composed his plays in a lonely cave on Salamis overlooking the sea;[8] that his dramas about adulterous women were inspired by his personal experience of two adulterous wives; that Athenian women at the Thesmophoria festival discussed condemning him to death; that he was torn to pieces by dogs (or by women). It is easy to see how some of these details come from a comedy, from well-known myths, or from Euripides' own plays, and scholars have long acknowledged that most of what we read in the *Life of Euripides* or learn in other anecdotes is not to be taken seriously, but there is always some residual pull of the framework of perception suggested by the biographical tradition, especially where it overlaps the Aristophanic characterization, so that many still approach Euripides' relationship to his contemporary intellectuals and artists and to his civic community in the light of that unreliable tradition.[9]

Following the lead of Aristophanes and Aristotle, Hellenistic scholars found fault with various Euripidean strategies and techniques, especially on grounds of deviation from proper tragic decorum and lack of "necessity" in construction of scenes or speeches. An implicit contrast with Sophocles often seems to

---

[6] On the characteristics of the lives of ancient poets see Fairweather 1974, Lefkowitz 1979 and 1981.

[7] The major sources are a life prefixed to the plays in the medieval manuscripts, an extended notice in the Byzantine encyclopedia called the *Suda*, and a section of Aulus Gellius (*Noctes Atticae* 15.20). For these and other testimonia see Kannicht, *TrGF* 5:1.39–45, Kovacs 1994: 1–141 (with English translation).

[8] The cave on Salamis where Euripides was believed to have worked has been identified and contains various dedications, showing it was a place of pilgrimage in postclassical times: one cup has Euripides' name inscribed on it in lettering of the Roman period. See Lolos 1997; Blackman 1998: 16–17; Sauzeau 1998.

[9] On Euripides as an Athenian citizen, see Stevens 1956.

operate in such evaluations, and it is possible that Didymus, the great compiler of Hellenistic literary commentary in the age of Augustus, was decisive in shaping the content and tone of the surviving scholia to Euripides.[10] Other judgments found their way into the prefatory materials[11] that accompany the select plays: two short extracts of aesthetic evaluation accompany *Phoenissae* (one somewhat appreciative, the other complaining of unnecessary or undramatic parts); the characters in *Orestes* are condemned for their ethical shortcomings ("all are bad except Pylades" – an unjustified exception); the material accompanying *Alcestis* and *Orestes* notes a resolution more suitable to comedy or satyr-play than tragedy (relying on the crude assumption that all tragedies end in disaster or death); the extant *Hippolytus* is praised as correcting what was "unseemly and deserving of condemnation" in the other version Euripides wrote. In the early reception of Greek tragedy in the Renaissance, when command of the Greek language (especially poetic idiom) was rare, the literary judgments of the scholia and prefatory material were taken very seriously and strongly influenced what was said about the plays and the poets.[12]

If we now turn from these earliest sources of literary and philological interpretation to later ones, we find that the reputation of Euripides in the Hellenistic and Roman periods was actually complex and conditioned by the different contexts of reception. For the general educated public, he rapidly became a cultural icon of wisdom and skill. One theme of Euripides' biography in the Peripatetic tradition reflected in Satyros[13] is the failure of

---

[10] Elsperger 1908; Meijering 1987.

[11] These prefatory supplements to the poetic text fall into three broad categories: (1) a one- or two-sentence summary of the play's action together with basic information about the production (year, accompanying plays, ranking in the dramatic competition) and the play (scene, composition of chorus, speaker of prologue); (2) an epitome of the play in a long paragraph, often as much about the antecedents of the action as posited in the play or narrated in the prologue as about what happens in the play itself; (3) miscellaneous other comments (some pertaining to rhetorical qualities, some to questions of authenticity or dependence on another version) or mythographic information. On the first type see Achelis 1913, Zuntz 1955: 129–31 (with references to other discussions), Barrett 1964: 153; on the second type, see especially Rusten 1982, Rossum-Steenbeek 1998, with references to earlier discussions; for examples of the third type, see the prefatory matter accompanying *Med.*, *Phoen.*, and *Rhesus*.

[12] These ancient judgments are still taken more seriously than they ought to be, especially the ones in the prefatory material that have been attached to the name of Aristophanes of Byzantium (second century BCE). In my opinion, this ascription results from a process of accretion, and the literary judgments do not actually go back to that scholar, who may have been responsible only for the standard factual details about the original production.

[13] On a fragmentary papyrus book-roll recovered from Egypt, we have tantalizing scraps of a bizarre "life" of Euripides in dialogue form by Satyros of Callatis (third century BCE). The papyrus is re-edited with an extensive commentary, including good observations on the biographical tradition of Euripides, by Schorn 2004.

his contemporary Athenians to appreciate him adequately as the innovative intellectual and great artist that he was. The tradition may in fact have exaggerated this motif as part of a tendency of later historians and scholars to denigrate the Athenian democracy of the fifth century. The positive counterpart to such denigration of Athens was the claim to cultural authority made for the Macedonian dynasties by writers who passed on and elaborated the anecdotes about Euripides' residence in Macedonia at the end of his life as well as by scholars performing the bibliographic and editorial work at the Alexandrian Library (which claimed, truly or not, to possess the Athenian state copies of the plays of the three great tragedians).[14] On the other side of this competition for ownership of a cultural icon, the Athenians of the later fourth century made no differentiation between Euripides and Sophocles and Aeschylus when they recognized them as sources of wisdom and national pride in their orations, honored them with statues in the new stone-built theater, and accorded special treatment to their reperformed texts.[15]

Although in his own lifetime Euripides won only four first prizes in (perhaps) twenty-one productions at the Great Dionysia,[16] after his death he quickly eclipsed all other fifth-century dramatists in the performance repertoire. As time went on, performances included not only more or less fully staged complete plays, but virtuoso performance of excerpts with new music and dance. Among early papyri of tragedy, many are not from full texts of the plays, but from selections or anthologies that must reflect the performance tradition.[17] Moreover, for the fourth century there is tantalizing evidence of Euripides' popularity and influence in the fragments of comedy. Among the subset of known comic titles that match those of known tragedies, a remarkable number are Euripidean titles.[18] We often

---

[14] See Revermann 1999–2000, Battezzato 2003, Hanink 2008.
[15] See Wilson 1996 (esp. 315–16); on the symbolic significance of Lycurgus' decree requiring actors to follow the accepted texts of the great three, see Scodel 2007.
[16] He won for the fifth time posthumously. The entry in the *Suda* says that Euripides produced plays in twenty-two years all together. It cannot be determined whether this total is based on a count of didaskalic notices (and if so, whether the count applies only to the Great Dionysia or whether possible productions at the Lenaea are included – but most of the ancient scholarly references to tragic competitions are to the Dionysia) or by someone who considered eighty-eight plays to be genuine and divided that total by four. On the number of plays and productions, see Collard and Cropp 2008a: xi–xii; Kannicht *TrGF* V.77–80; Kannicht 1996; Pechstein 1998: 19–29 and in Krumeich *et al.* 1999: 400–1.
[17] The nature of the Ptolemaic papyri of Euripides is the subject of a work in progress by Susan Stephens (presented at Berkeley in spring 2009).
[18] Euripidean titles that also occur as titles of comedies in the late fifth and in the fourth century: *Aegeus* (Philyllius), *Aeolus* (Antiphanes, Eriphus; cf. Aristophanes' *Aeolosicon*), *Alcmeon* (Amphis, Mnesimachus), *Andromeda* (Antiphanes), *Antiope* (Eubulus), *Auge* (Philyllius, Eubulus), *Bacchae*

cannot be sure that Euripides' plays inspired all of these instances, since
some titles are known to have been used by Sophocles or other tragedians as
well. Nor do most fragments permit us to see how the comedy may have
exploited a tragic play (did the heroic characters of the original also appear in
the comedy? How extensively were the tragic characters, tragic plot-motifs,
or parodied passages deployed throughout the complete comedy?).[19]
Nevertheless, such reception of Euripides in Middle Comedy will have
been one mechanism for reinforcing his stature with the theater audience
and may have provided an auxiliary path for the adoption in New Comedy
of plot-motifs like rape, exposure, and recognition and of conventions like
the prologue monologue. In addition, scholars can discover allusions to or
parodies of Euripidean passages or expressions in both Middle and New
Comedy.[20] Although it is possible that by the time of Menander many
tragic allusions may have been recognized by the audience as typically tragic
rather than specifically Euripidean,[21] this general perception in itself attests
to the canonical status his works and his style had attained within the
century after his death.

The gnomological tradition and the citation of Euripidean lines by cultured
authors indicate a high prestige value for some degree of (even indirect)
familiarity with the classic writer. Euripides' authority manifested itself also
in the way mythographers followed or reported his versions of myths, even
when modern scholars have concluded that Euripides' versions were innovative, even eccentric, at the time his plays were written. It was a major mark of
Greek educated culture to show familiarity with a wide range of myths, so as to
be able both to understand allusions in art, literature, and performances and to
make appropriate display of one's knowledge. Such familiarity came in part
from direct knowledge of reading texts, at school or in the home, and
Euripides is, after Homer, the poet most commonly represented in the scraps
of ancient books that have accidentally survived from antiquity, mainly in
Egypt. But more often this cultural training derived not from detailed knowledge of an extensive range of classic texts, but from mythographic handbooks
and collections of stories,[22] such as the so-called epitomes or "Tales from

(Diocles, Antiphanes), *Bellerophon* (Eubulus), *Cretans* (Apollophanes, Nicochares), *Danae*
(Apollophanes, Sannyrion, Eubulus), *Erechtheus* (Anaxandrides), *Ion* (Eubulus), *Ixion* (Eubulus),
Helen (Alexis, Anaxandrides, Philyllius), *Medea* (Strattis, Antiphanes, Eubulus), *Meleager*
(Antiphanes, Philetaerus), *Mysi* (Eubulus), *Oedipus* (Eubulus), *Oenomaus* (Antiphanes, Eubulus),
Orestes (Alexis), *Peliades* (Diphilus), *Phoenissae* (Aristophanes, Strattis), *Polyidus* (Aristophanes),
Protesilaus (Anaxandrides), *Philoctetes* (Strattis, Antiphanes), *Phoenix* (Eubulus), *Chrysippus*
(Strattis). In addition, note that both Axionicus and Philippides wrote plays entitled *Phileuripides*.
[19] See, in general, Hunter 1983: 28–30; Nesselrath 1990: 188–241 and 1993; Casolari 2003.
[20] See, for example, Arnott 1996: 62–3.   [21] Porter 1999–2000: 172.   [22] Cameron 2004.

Euripides" ascribed (falsely, it appears) to Dicaearchus of Messene (Sicily). Numerous papyrus fragments give evidence of the popularity of this collection, and it was a source both for later mythographers and for the epitome included as "hypothesis" to each play in the medieval tradition of select plays.[23]

The educational system, especially training in rhetoric, displays a second strand of this broader reception. Some of the positive comments about Euripides are based on admiration for the tragedies not as dramas or literary representations of emotion-stirring events,[24] but as sources for gnomic statements and examples of rhetorical technique. Thus the prefatory material to *Andromache* comments favorably on the style of the prologue speech, on Hermione's speeches in the first episode (one evidencing "royal stature" and the other being "not badly framed"), and apparently on Peleus' speech as well; *Phoenissae* is "full of many fine gnomic statements." Quintilian leaves undecided whether Sophocles or Euripides is the better poet overall, but effusively explains why Euripides is far more useful to the person training himself for oratory (*Inst. orat.* 10.1.66–8 = Eur. T 145 Kannicht). Rhetorical skill and the abundance of gnomic sayings are chief points in Dio Chrysostomus' recommendation of Euripides to a politically active man seeking greater proficiency in oratory (*Orat.* 18.6 = T 147 Kannicht: see further T 146, 148, 196, 197). Incidents and speeches from tragedy could serve as inspiration for rhetorical practice, as for instance in the *progymnasma* (exercise) of Libanius (a prolific author from Antioch in Syria, fourth century CE) that paraphrases and expands the speech of Menoeceus about willingly sacrificing himself to save his city (*Phoenissae* 991–1018; Libanius *progymn.* 11.22). Indeed, if one asks why *Hecuba*, *Orestes*, and *Phoenissae* emerged as the Euripidean triad, that is, as the plays most likely to be read and studied in the Byzantine "system" of higher education, one must weigh not only the popularity of these plays in the performance tradition (for which there is evidence in the case of the latter two) and the range of important mythography that is covered by the set (embracing Troy, Thebes, and Argos), but also the speeches and gnomes that would have been prized in the rhetorically oriented education of the late Roman period. Euripidean excerpts also loom very large in the anthology of gnomic wisdom of Stobaeus from the fifth century CE, and such collections must go back many centuries, even perhaps to the fourth century BCE.

---

[23] Rossum-Steenbeek 1998. On the disputed ascription to Dicaearchus, see Mastronarde 1994: 140 n. 1.

[24] There are, however, also appreciations of the pathos of Euripides: in the prefatory material to *Medea*, the opening is praised for being "very pathetic" at the same time that the artful composition (*epexergasia*) of the nurse's speech is admired; *Phoenissae* is also called "very pathetic," apparently as a positive evaluation.

In contrast to the appreciation that Euripides received as a general cultural authority and as a model for rhetorical skill, a more critical attitude flourished in scholarly and philosophical contexts. Philological commentary aspired to a relative ranking or comparison of the three tragedians; biography and anecdote sought juicy material; scholars paraded their expertise by finding fault with the famous poet on specific points of style; and scholars or teachers promoted a particular ethical and artistic decorum by condemning his deviations from their preferred norm. We can observe how the scholia to Sophocles preserve many comments praising his dramatic construction and characterization while those to Euripides more often contain criticism on these counts. Although this contrast goes back ultimately to the influence of Aristotle and his Peripatetic followers, it is likely that the prominence and preservation of such comments in the scholia reflect the agenda of the Roman period, from Didymus in the Augustan age onward.[25] In the renewed "Greek classicism" aligned with Roman imperial rule, cultural authorities such as Dionysius of Halicarnassus were eager to distance themselves from the popular tastes and political disorder of the Hellenistic period and to give higher status to purity of language and style and to canonical works from the fifth and fourth centuries. Scholars and schoolteachers could thus enhance their own standing by subverting the popular preference for Euripides and by demonstrating their skill at detecting weaknesses in his works.

Somewhat akin to such philological commentary is the reception of Euripides among Hellenistic philosophers. It was surely with Euripides' *Medea* in mind that the Stoic Chrysippus began a long tradition of using Medea's killing of her children as an illustration of the harmful triumph of emotion over reason. Fragments and passages of Teles, Favorinus, Epictetus, and Plutarch show that Polyneices in *Phoenissae* was a standard example used in arguments against the false valuation of exile in conventional morality.[26] Epictetus also cites the power-hungry Eteocles for his incorrect judgment about what is the greatest of goods. The culturally familiar and

---

[25] Meijering 1987 often suggests that such judgments of Euripides are survivals of the commentaries of Aristophanes of Byzantium; but Aristophanes' authorship of these opinions is no more secure than the ascription to him of literary critical comments in the prefatory material to plays (n. 12 above). Even if the judgments were taken from Aristophanes, it is significant that they were selected and preserved as the scholiastic comments were compiled and reduced during the Roman and early Byzantine period.

[26] There is some precedent for this use of Euripides in Aristotle, as in *EN* 1110a28 ("what compelled the Euripidean Alcmeon to commit matricide seems ridiculous"), 1167a32–4 ("but whenever one person wants himself [sc. to rule exclusively], like the characters in *Phoenissae*, people engage in civil strife"), and Aristotle uses Euripidean lines to illustrate points (e.g., *EE* 1244a10, *EN* 1136a11, 1142a2, *Pol.* 1277a19), but not in the combative way typical of later diatribe. For Medea see Gill 1983 and 2005, Dillon 1997; for Epictetus' use of the sons of Oedipus, see Mastronarde 2009: 65, 462.

authoritative texts are thus selected to provide effective negative examples for those challenging their listeners and students to follow a more philosophical path in life. Gnomic excerpts on moral and theological themes were likewise of interest to Hellenistic philosophers, either for support of their own views or as alternatives to attack, and Greek patristic texts that quote Euripides probably reflect earlier compilations of key passages on divinity, fate, and the like rather than direct reference to complete plays or a new culling of examples. The fashion of valuing very highly the maxims to be culled from the texts remained strong in the Byzantine middle ages and the Renaissance.[27]

FROM THE RENAISSANCE TO GERMAN CLASSICISM

The ancient sources, particularly the scholia, the lives, Aristotle, and Quintilian, were extremely influential in the first centuries of modern reception, from 1500 well into the 1700s. For instance, to accompany his influential Latin versions of *Hecuba* and *Iphigenia in Aulis* (Paris 1506, Venice 1507, but his work on *Hecuba* probably began a few years earlier), Erasmus translated the hypothesis of the Palaeologan scholar Thomas Magister for *Hecuba*, but wrote his own epitome for *Iphigenia in Aulis*, which had no hypothesis in the manuscript tradition. Some of his choices in his translation of *Hecuba* may perhaps point to use of the scholia (from manuscript sources).[28] The scholia became widely available in 1534 with the edition by Arsenius of Monembasia, and the first Latin translation of the whole Aldine corpus (lacking *Electra*, first available in 1545) appeared in 1541, the work of Dorotheus Camillus, a pseudonym for Rudolf Collin. By the 1550s we begin to see some efforts toward assessment of the individual plays in the context of the Latin translations. The Reformation scholar Philipp Melanchthon was noted for his inspiring lectures on classical authors, and Guilielmus Xylander stitched together, edited, and supplemented translations by Melanchthon to produce a new Latin translation of the full

---

[27] In some Byzantine manuscripts gnomic lines have special marking with marginal symbols or the notation ὡραῖον ("beautiful"), and gnomological compilations were still being made: for instance, *Gnomologium Vatopedianum* (Longman 1959), and the El Escorial and Barberini *gnomologia* (Matthiessen 1974: 38, 45). The first collections of tragic fragments in the Renaissance were essentially gatherings of maxims: Kassel 2005.

[28] For example, *Hec.* 8 πλάκα = *glebam*, 9 φίλιππον = *ferocem*, 16 ὁρίσματα = *Pergama* might reflect explanations in the scholia, but Erasmus had also seen the partial translation of *Hecuba* by Filelfo, who used *glebam, ferocem,* and *moenia* in these three places. The scholia to Euripides were not printed until 1534, but manuscripts of *Hecuba* with at least scholia recentiora are numerous and are likely to have been available to Erasmus. For Erasmus' editions of these two plays, see Waszink 1969.

corpus of Euripides (Basel 1558, with a somewhat revised issue in 1562). Xylander included some sporadic brief comments on particular plays.[29] Contemporaneously, Gasparus Stiblinus (Caspar Stiblin) worked on an even more ambitious edition (Basel 1562, but with a dedicatory letter dated 1559). Stiblinus is now more famous for a utopian political treatise,[30] but his Euripides is significant because it seems to offer the earliest particular assessments of all the plays in the corpus. He produced a new Latin translation of the plays, with the ancient hypotheses also translated before each play. Following each play, he supplies his own preface (*praefatio*) as well as notes (*annotationes*). His approach is in line with the tendency of sixteenth-century writers on poetics (for example, Scaliger, Castelvetro, Sir Philip Sidney) to attempt a reconciliation of Platonic and Aristotelian views of poetry by insisting that poets both delight and instruct, and that representations of morally suspect behavior edify by providing a model of what is to be avoided. Both in his dedicatory epistles (one to the Holy Roman Emperor Ferdinand I and one to his readers) and in his individual prefaces, Stiblinus emphasizes the didactic and moral effects of observing disasters, sufferings, and wrongdoing, and frequently points to the rhetorical skill of particular speeches, in line with Quintilian's advice about the utility of Euripides. As a commentator, Stiblinus drew inspiration from the Donatan commentaries on the comedies of Terence: he divides each tragedy into five acts, following the model of the Terentian comedies and in accordance with Renaissance theory; the structure and topics of his prefaces imitate those of Donatus; and he employs analytic terms that he found in Donatus' work on Terence (*epitasis, catastrophe, paraskeue, praestructio*) to make original observations about dramatic structure. Many of his notes are drawn from the scholia, but he also adduces information and comparative passages from ancient authors,[31] especially prose writers like Plutarch and Cicero on ethical issues. Stiblinus' efforts stand out because philologists editing Euripides in

---

[29] Some relevant remarks are in his dedicatory preface, and others (which might be derived from Melanchthon) precede certain plays, such as *Phoenissae* and *Cyclops*: for the latter, the comment is "this tragedy is the image of some extremely cruel tyrant. I believe the poet may have wanted to describe some Egyptian king or tyrant. By the Satyrs he means fools and imposters (*moriones et impostores*). The play has the general argument that no one is trustworthy to a tyrant, even someone who obeys."

[30] Firpo 1963.

[31] A telling example is Stiblinus' note on *Hecuba* 1261, where he gives a rationalized alternative version of the death of Hecuba: she annoyed the Greeks so much with her insults and curses that they threw her from the mast into the sea. This unusual version is taken from half of a *scholion recentius* on 1261 (I.509.3–9 Dindorf, already published in Arsenius' edition of 1534), where throwing from the mast is confusingly conflated with stoning on land. A similar rationalization, with stoning rather than casting into the sea, is in the Latin Dictys Cretensis 5.16.

this period rarely addressed broader issues of dramatic interpretation, but simply cited or paraphrased what they found in the ancient sources.

Writers on poetic or dramatic theory and commentators on Aristotle's *Poetics* were more likely than editors of the plays to make evaluative comments about tragedies or their authors, although such comments touch on the handling of details more often than on overall impact or meaning or structure. Most repeat the ancient examples without showing any independent judgment, but there are exceptions, like Minturno, Castelvetro, and Daniel Heinsius.[32] By the early eighteenth century, the French, with their own well-developed dramatic tradition, could judge their own best productions more skilful and decorous than the ancient models, as Pierre Brumoy, the author of the first general handbook of Greek drama in a vernacular language, remarked.[33] After 1750, however, German Classicism and Romanticism are the background for major developments in classical philology and also in the literary and cultural interpretation of Greek drama. Along with a better sense of historical contextualization (and clearer differentiation of Greek and Roman traditions), approaches in this period rely on a new idealized sense of "the classical." They imitate and elaborate the ancient tradition when they posit a quasi-biological growth and decay of the genre, in parallel with political trends in Athens and changes in other artistic modes, such as sculpture. Tragedy is thus an art-form crude and underdeveloped in Aeschylus, perfect in its harmony, control, and organic unity in Sophocles, and declining and decadent in Euripides. Aristotle's teleological perspective (*Poetics* 4.1449a14–15: "and after undergoing many changes, tragedy stopped [changing], since it had attained its natural form")

---

[32] Antonio Sebastiano Minturno, *De Poeta* (1559) and *L'arte poetica* (1564); Lodovico Castelvetro, *Poetica d'Aristotele vulgarizzata et sposta* (1576); Daniel Heinsius, *De Tragoediae Constitutione* (1611). For a survey of treatises on poetics in Renaissance, see Weinberg 1961. For reception of Greek tragedies on the stage in this period, see Burian 1997b.

[33] Brumoy 1730. This work contained translations of the plays together with analyses and aesthetic criticism. Brumoy died in 1742, but his book was re-edited and expanded into an almost unrecognizable form in later editions over about 150 years. An English translation appeared in London 1759. Note the following extracts from the introduction: "I do not believe I do an injustice to an age as polished and as enlightened as our own when I say that in the very period when the taste for theater performances has been purified to an extreme degree by the great geniuses who have worked in the theater, people have had little knowledge of, and people now know almost nothing any longer of, the Greek theater. To be sure the little which survives for us is still the delight of certain curious persons whom the study of the Greek language has not repulsed; but their number is very limited, and in their sphere one does not always prevail a taste equal to their erudition, as if these two things were rarely combined …" [Moreover, the French theater has reached such a height that people feel it is unnecessary to look elsewhere.] "The favorable opinion of the present theater, which people enjoy and which depicts our manners, has caused the neglect of knowledge of the theater of the past, which costs too much toil and which holds too little interest."

is obviously important as a source, but the criticisms provided by
Aristophanes also find wholehearted acceptance in this scheme, which is
well illustrated in the works of the brothers Schlegel.[34] The belief that there
existed at a certain moment of Greek or Athenian culture a "classical"
balance and perfection goes hand in hand with the conviction that peoples
and races are characterized by distinct psychological and cultural traits
carried in their blood and preserved by purity of descent. This was already
an ancient attitude, but it received strong development and pseudo-
scientific support in the nineteenth and early twentieth century.
Euripides' decadence can then be viewed not only as a matter of quasi-
biological senescence in the genre, but also as a personal betrayal of the
purest cultural norms and values.

The charges against Euripides taken over from Aristophanes and developed
by critics like the Schlegels reappear in a striking form later in the nineteenth century when Friedrich Nietzsche, in *The Birth of Tragedy* (1872),
elaborates his fantasy of a lost perfect musical culture combining both the
Dionysiac and the Apollinian.[35] This essay has many distinctive features,
such as indebtedness to the metaphysics of Schopenhauer and a schematic
view of stages of alternation between Apollinian and Dionysian moments in
the history of Greek religion, culture, and poetic and musical art, and it also
reflects Romantic notions, such as the essentialist assumption of inherent
ethnic/racial qualities and the belief in the non-intellectual origins of
genuine art. What Nietzsche has to say about Euripides himself, however,
is mostly a continuation or extension of the previous traditions: for instance,
Euripides' rationalism and devotion to intelligibility and clarity
(Sections 10, 12), his realism (Sections 11, 17), his affinity to Socrates
(Sections 12–15), his betrayal and dismantling of traditional myth and the
previous tragic approach to it (Sections 10–11). Nietzsche echoes the early
nineteenth-century idea that Euripides experimented with tragedy in a
desperate attempt to win the favor of an audience ill disposed toward
him, but then modifies this view, making the striking claim that
Euripides wrote to please only two viewers – himself and Socrates
(Section 11). This was an important impetus to theories that posited that

[34] See F. Schlegel 1794a, 1794b, 1795–97, 1798, 1815; A. Schlegel 1809; Jacobs 1798: 335–422; and the
discussions of Snell 1953, Behler 1986, Michelini 1987: 3–11.
[35] For a full discussion see Silk and Stern 1980.

Euripides wrote in such a way as to convey one impression to the masses while signaling a quite different meaning to a small group of intellectuals.[36] Nietzsche's description of the Euripidean prologue and divine epilogue as epic elements different in kind from the dramatic-lyric elements in between them (Section 12) likewise addresses a problem that has exercised many later critics and suggests one of the common approaches (insisting on the separability or otherness of these parts of the play). Nietzsche's view of Euripides is not wholly consistent. At one moment, for rhetorical effect, he speaks of Euripides as killing tragedy, but then partly absolves him as an individual by declaring him to be only the mask of a new divine force, Socratic aestheticism (Section 12). Similarly, when decrying Euripides' approach to the chorus and to characterization, he is honest enough to concede that Sophocles also already reflected in his use of the chorus a breakdown of the Dionysian basis of tragedy (Section 14) and that Sophocles introduced psychological refinements that began to move tragic characters away from the eternal types that Nietzsche considered proper to genuine tragedy (Section 17).

In defense of Euripides, throughout the nineteenth century, and much of the twentieth, many critics reacted to the widely accepted picture of a decadent Euripides by emphasizing one or another aspect of the oeuvre, particularly any aspect that would have a strong resonance in the critics' contemporary culture. The modern novel, the theater of Ibsen or Shaw, and the rise of the discipline of psychology influenced those who saw realism or psychological depth as the main goal of Euripidean drama.[37] The struggles between church and science found their echo in the approaches that made Euripides a would-be educator of the people in the latest science and philosophy, a proponent of a Greek Enlightenment, or an anti-clerical rationalist.[38] The experience of massively destructive or divisive wars made it attractive to emphasize anti-war themes in Euripides. All such approaches latch on to something that is in the plays, but fail to examine the applicability and ambiguity of their chosen terms, treating (for instance) "realism" or "character" as self-evident concepts that meant the same in antiquity as they do now, and they suffer from the partiality inherent in any narrowly focused lens of interpretation.

[36] See n. 38 below.
[37] For fuller discussion of the period from 1800 to the 1980s, see Michelini 1987: 3–51.
[38] The idea of Euripides as a "philosopher on the stage" (σκηνικὸς φιλόσοφος) has ancient roots (T 166a–169 Kannicht). Euripides' espousal of and intention to promote "modern thinking" were central to the interpretations of, e.g., Hartung (1843) and Nestle (1901). A similar assumption is made in the dual audience approach of so-called Verrallism, in which the rational view is a message to be understood only by a select few of the large audience: Verrall (1895). On Verrall and his influence on several later critics, see Michelini 1987: 11–19, 22–8.

The longstanding views just described continue to be influential, especially among non-specialists. Among professional scholars of Greek tragedy,
their limitations are, in general, well recognized. Three general kinds of
approach have been particularly prominent and productive in the scholarship of the past fifty years: formalism, structuralism and semiotics, and
several flavors of historicism. The first of these embraces the stylistic and
formal studies that have heightened our awareness of various conventions of
language, dialogue, extended speech, and scenic composition.[39] Formal
studies of this kind go back much farther than fifty years, but many earlier
specimens presupposed an evolutionary scheme of growth, perfection, and
decline, and thus tended to look at Euripides in terms of ossification of
formal elements or predominance of pathetic effects over organically integrated expression of emotion. From the 1950s onward, however, there has
been a greater tendency to recognize variety and creativity in the use of
conventional forms and to resist, to some extent, the temptation of seeing
linear development as a key to interpretation (and chronology). The
importance of the study of forms and conventions is twofold. First, it
reveals the complexity of tragic art as a form that comprises both elements
that are conventional to the genre and not to be read as personal to a
particular playwright and elements that are unconventional and idiosyn-
cratic. Second, it reinforces the lesson that modern terms of reference
cannot be simply carried over to the Greek plays, that we must take account
of the intricate interweaving of the conventional with the particular elements unique to a speech, to a character, or to a scene, even if this makes
interpretation more difficult or indeterminate.

Structuralism and its offshoots have proven to be well suited to Greek
tragedy as well as to other Greek texts. Binary oppositions were embedded in
many structures of the Greek language and were often exploited in their
social, political, and philosophical thinking. Human and bestial, civilized and
uncivilized, Greek and non-Greek, male and female, free and slave – these are
only some of the major themes explored in tragedies and fruitfully analyzed in
the scholarship of the last several decades. Broader applications of semiotics
have illuminated various symbolic meanings of space (inside and outside, up
and down, city and countryside) and the body (integrity and permeability,
openness and concealment, variations of dress and appearance).[40] The

[39] Major examples are Ludwig 1954, Strohm 1957, Matthiessen 1967, Schwinge 1968, Kaimio 1970 and
1988, Jens 1971, Taplin 1977 and 1978, Bain 1977 and 1981, Mastronarde 1979, Halleran 1985. The best
of earlier work: Schadewalt 1926, Kranz 1933.
[40] Some prominent examples: Segal 1965, 1970, 1971, 1982; Zeitlin 1985, 1989, 1996; Padel 1990.

deconstructive turn in criticism has successfully highlighted the strains of language and meaning and the collapse of difference that tragedies typically develop in the representation of transgressive and destructive events.[41] Some critics of earlier generations recognized similar contrasts, polarities, codes, and ambiguities, but the scholarship of recent times has sharpened previous perceptions in a helpful, systematic way.

The third major impetus in recent work on tragedy comes from the complex of historicizing and contextualizing methods and interests identified with marxism, feminism, ritual studies, gender studies, cultural studies, and the like. Again, these approaches sometimes reinforce perceptions that can be found already in earlier scholarship; but they have brought new or enhanced attention to matters of class, political ideology, gender relations, and constructions of personal and social identities.[42] All of this brings a deeper and richer contextualization for the interpretation of Attic tragedy, counteracting in a welcome fashion the long-engrained habit of applying transhistorical or transcultural assumptions about "the tragic" or "character." But like any advance, this one has not come without risks of distortion or exaggeration, and one of the key issues in this first decade of the twenty-first century is how to balance the claims of those who emphasize that Attic tragedy was tightly embedded in the social and political structures of democratic Athens with the claims of those who argue that tragedy had aims and appeals that went beyond the boundaries of its civic setting.

CURRENT DEBATES: TRAGEDY, DEMOCRACY, AND TEACHING

The increased attention to the social and political contexts of Greek tragedy is the more important trend in recent criticism, but it is salutary to recall that many specific claims about the intimate connection of tragedy at Athens to the democratic political structures of the imperial city are still uncertain. For example, there is the question of the dating of the official incorporation of tragic performances into a major civic religious festival, the Great Dionysia. The competitive tribal organization of the dithyrambic choruses at this festival can have begun only after the Cleisthenic reforms created the ten new tribes of the democratic system in 507 BCE or shortly thereafter.[43] Moreover, it seems

---

[41] For example, Pucci 1980, Goldhill 1986, Goff 1990, Pelling 2000.
[42] For example, Foley 1985, 2001, Loraux 1987, 1990, Zeitlin 1996, Griffith 1998, 2001, 2005a, 2005b, Wohl 1998, McClure 1999.
[43] For the organization of the Great Dionysia and the competitions within it, see Pickard-Cambridge 1988, Goldhill 1987, Csapo and Slater 1995.

likely that the record-keeping which preserved the results of competitions did not reach farther back than the advent of the new democratic system, since in later Greek sources the information and guesses about sixth-century productions are decidedly inferior.[44] So the suggestion has been made that production of tragedies at the Great Dionysia began only with the democracy.[45] But ancient sources[46] date the placement of tragic performance in this festival about thirty years earlier, under the tyrant Peististratus and his family, and this is perfectly plausible. Tyrants at Athens and elsewhere were patrons of poetry and performance, and creation or reorganization of large festivals was a useful policy for tyrants, creating greater status for the tyrant and his city and offering benefits of the tyrant's leadership (entertainment, sacrificial meals, social cohesion, a share of the prestige) to the wider population. Likewise, it is uncertain how far we can extend the notion of a congruence between being a member of the audience at the Great Dionysia and being a citizen of the democracy. There are certainly some continuities between civic spaces and civic "rituals" and those of the theater: for instance, the placement of important city officials and priests in front of other spectators – the *prohedria* or "privilege of front-row seating" – is paralleled in other civic and festival contexts. But was the theater audience in the fifth century arranged as a more precise reflection of the structure of the citizen body by the assignment of wedges of the seating to separate tribes? This practice is attested later, but cannot actually be proven for the fifth century, and it is circular to believe in such fuller congruence because one believes there is something especially democratic about the festival.[47] The same uncertainty applies to the question whether women (specifically the wives and daughters of citizens) were present in the audience of tragedy or not. The evidence is ambiguous, but seems to me to favor (by a slight margin) their presence, and it seems problematic to posit that tragedy addresses Athenian adult male citizens so specifically and so intrinsically that this tenet itself influences one to settle the question on the side of exclusion of women.[48]

---

[44] Much of the surviving information about the names of poets and plays, years of productions, numbers of productions and victories ultimately goes back to a compilation of records in the city archives (or perhaps sometimes recorded on public monuments) carried out in the fourth century BCE. We cannot tell whether this compilation depended on the researches of Aristotle and his students or whether it preceded that work. See Pickard-Cambridge 1988: 71–4, Csapo and Slater 1995: 19–20, 40–3.

[45] Connor 1989, West 1989.

[46] *TrGF* I, 1 T 1–3 (testimonia about Thespis, from the Marmor Parium, Eusebius, and the *Suda*).

[47] For different reservations about the democratic affiliation of tragedy, see Rhodes 2003 and Kurke 1998.

[48] The classic statements of the opposing views are Henderson 1991 (for the presence of women) and Goldhill 1994 (cf. Goldhill 1997); for the evidence see also Csapo and Slater 1995: 286–7.

The relation of tragedy to civic religion and to political and class structures is, in fact, quite hard to pin down. Through the placement of tragic performances within festivals of Dionysus sponsored by the city or demes, there are obvious points of contact both with the experience of civic religious practices and with the articulation and display of the political order. On the religious side, the dramatic festivals that sponsored tragedies also involved processions, sacrifices, prayers, and other performances that were more overtly marked as Dionysian. Comedy and satyr-play were marked as such by features like the phallic costuming, the emphasis on revelry and drinking wine, and the flouting of everyday proprieties. Dithyrambic choral performances at the Great Dionysia were similarly marked by the integral connection of the word *dithyrambos* with Dionysian cult and perhaps by direct address to or summoning of the god within some of the choral songs.[49] The Athenian political system, on the other hand, was implicated in many preliminaries and accompaniments of the tragic performance, including the role of the city's eponymous archon in organizing the Great Dionysia, the choregic system [50] serving tragedy and comedy as well as the great tribal competitions in the men's and boys' dithyrambs, the requirement that the chorus members be citizens, the civic proclamations and displays occurring in the theater, and the tribe-based and sortition-based system of civic judging of the competitors.[51] These factors condition, but do not necessarily predetermine or constrain how the playwrights and the audience think of the functions and meanings of the tragedies themselves. From early on, tragedy draws on, appropriates, and competes with older genres of poetry and performance that are the shared property of many Greek communities, so that the playwrights were probably conscious of a wider intellectual and cultural horizon than that which is specific to the Athenian democracy. By the end of the fifth century, tragedy is well on the way to becoming the "international" (that is, panhellenic

---

[49] It appears, however, that at least some choral dithyrambs contained no such element of Dionysiac address (Bacchylides 15, 18); the disputes in antiquity about whether some poems were dithyrambs or paeans also indicate how choral poems with mythological narratives might fail to give obvious clues to the divinity honored by the performance (for instance, Bacchylides 17, with a minimal final address to Apollo and no paean-cry, is transmitted among dithyrambs, but is likely to be a paean). For the problems of classification created by the elimination of specific address to a god or of tell-tale ritual cries, see Käppel 1992, Zimmermann 1992, Rutherford 2001: 90–108.

[50] The wealthiest citizens of Athens, in annual rotation, were compelled to underwrite various public expenses for both military and festival activities sponsored by the city: this service is called "liturgy" (λειτουγία) in its original Greek sense. Support of the costuming and training of choruses, both those for the tribal competitions in dithyramb and those for dramatic performances, was a particularly prominent form of liturgy, known as *chorēgia*. See Wilson 2000.

[51] Goldhill 1987, Csapo and Slater 1995: 103–21.

rather than specifically Attic) institution it clearly is from the fourth century to the end of classical civilization.[52] In many regards, it is a form of mass entertainment eliciting increasing professionalization of skills in acting, singing, musical accompaniment, scenery, props, and theatrical architecture and machinery. We cannot assume that the theater of Aeschylus' generation was understood in the same way as the theater of the last third of the fifth century, and, similarly, explanations based on the reconstructed origins of the genre or the festival or frameworks derived from the analysis of political ideology in the earlier generations of the fifth century are not necessarily valid when we are looking at the majority of the surviving plays of Sophocles and Euripides.

One Marxian approach sometimes applied in studies of classical culture exploits the notion of literature or public spectacle as a cultural institution that works to evoke in the members of the audience a set of positions and identities that articulate and reinforce the structures of power and hierarchy in the society.[53] Applied to Attic tragedy, this approach can be used with various degrees of flexibility and with different assumptions about the consciousness of the participants and "founders" of the institution, and disagreements about these assumptions are partly responsible for the dis-connection between the arguments of some proponents and opponents of social and political interpretations.[54] The state-sponsored performance can be read as addressing the democratic Athenian (that is, free male) citizen and appealing to or justifying the main ideological constructs of the imperial democratic state: the equality of those in citizen status; the exclusivity of this status and its clear distinction from and superiority to other statuses, such as those of the metic, the "citizen" woman, the non-citizen free woman, the slave, the Greek foreigner, and the non-Greek foreigner; the primacy of the interests of the collectivity of citizens over those of an individual or of a family; the superiority of Athenian civilization and the justice of Athenian hegemony. The destruction of great individuals and the ruin of dynastic houses would then be popular themes for tragedy because they inculcate or echo shared views of the rightness of current arrangements and of the shortcomings of traditional aristocratic ways, while dramatization of gender conflicts would serve as negative examples suggesting *ex contrario* the naturalness and validity of the controls and hierarchy that are in place.

[52] Easterling 1994, Csapo and Slater 1995, Dearden 1999, Csapo 2004b, Taplin 2007: 4–7.
[53] Some of the most important and influential variations on this kind of interpretation are to be found in Goldhill 1987, Hall 1989 and 1997, Croally 1994, Seaford 1994, Griffith 1995, Cartledge 1997.
[54] Cf. the debate between Griffin 1998 and Goldhill 2000 or Seaford 2000.

There is much to be learned from such an approach, and it fits well with the perception of the external links of tragic performance to civic institutions and with the fact that there are other, more specific, links within tragedy to contemporary events and issues. For instance, there are analogies of content between suppliant-drama and real political decisions about whom to protect and whom to take as an ally in the dangerously unstable situation of rival hegemonic alliances, or between tragic arguments about burial and treatment of captives and real decisions about self-restraint vs. brutality in the context of the vague but important principles of the "laws of the Greeks" or "laws of the gods" or "laws of mankind." Moreover, there are obvious similarities of form between the opposing speeches in tragedy and those in the court and the assembly as arenas of public discourse and debate, while the techniques and styles of argument develop in parallel in drama and in civic life.

On the other hand, there are countervailing elements in tragedy that cannot be taken to endorse the status quo or Athenian democratic ideology in any simple way. Dramatic genres provide a polyphony of voices, and in Attic tragedy the polyphony entails contrasts and contests not only between major characters, but also between major characters and humble, usually anonymous characters, and between major characters and the collective body of the chorus.[55] Traditional aristocratic values are indeed subject to interrogation in tragedy (but they were already so in Homeric epic and some archaic poetry), but they are also often treated as valid and admirable, and the values expressed and acted on by humbler characters, slaves, and women frequently match or are borrowed from the aristocratic tradition of honor, reciprocity, and fame (*timē, charis, kleos*). So there is often a negotiation or adaptation or extension of the aristocratic rather than a rejection of it. The *chorēgia* itself provided an authorized outlet for elite display that gratified and benefitted the wealthy *chorēgos* at the same time that it served and entertained the democratic community as a whole.[56] We ought to view the negotiation of class structure and class conflict in tragedy as similarly complex and flexible. The heroic characters may be transgressors or may

---

[55] On the chorus see further Chapter 4 below. For good discussions of issues of hierarchy and the leaders vs. the led, see Griffith 1995, 1998, and 2005a.

[56] The flexibility or ambiguity of status extended to the members of choruses as well: on the one hand, they could view themselves and be viewed by others as relatively "elite" because they had the musical and physical education to make them eligible for participation in the chorus (and I assume that the choruses of drama, especially those serving in a tragic tetralogy, required higher levels of talent and skill than other choruses); on the other hand, while serving in the chorus, the members placed themselves in a relatively subordinate position, under the patronage of a more prominent and wealthy individual. For discussion, see Wilson 2000: 75–6, 128–30.

be seduced by overconfidence and fierce ambition for primacy, and they may be destroyed. But the Greek audience, it can be argued, engages in a changing and multiple relationship with such figures, involving both identification and alienation, both admiration and disapproval. One interpretation of the spatial dynamics and conventional performance patterns of the tragic chorus (for which I will offer arguments in Chapter 4) is that these elements generally emphasize the division between the elite agents and sufferers, with their strength of resolve and capacity for decision and action, and the anonymous collective group, with their more cautious approach to life, their peripherality or exemption with respect to real responsibility and real consequences. The chorus is in part an internal analogue of the external audience, and the capacity of the chorus to vary its stance along a spectrum between admiration and alienation, approval and condemnation, suggests that a similar variability of response could be expected of the external audience.

One of the most hotly and perennially debated issues related to our understanding of the position and function of tragedy within the Athenian city-state is whether and in what ways these plays are instructive, and if they are, whether this instruction is individual and moral or collective and political. There is, first of all, the paradox that so many of the external framing elements of the performance within the festival of the Great Dionysia affirm the democratic system and put on display its success and power, but that tragedy itself is best understood as interrogating values, both traditional and contemporary. Such interrogation is both a continuation of one function of earlier poetry and an outgrowth of the specifically Athenian democratic atmosphere of personal freedom, speech open to all (*parrhēsia*), and interactive political debate. In the case of Old Comedy, we can use the concepts of carnival and the grotesque to gain some purchase on the temporarily anarchic and transgressive aspects in a genre patronized by the city-state, and even so there is continuing debate about the degree to which the transgression is bracketed off and thus tamed by its frame within the festival and within the genre, leaving the realities outside the frame unaffected.[57] In the case of tragedy, there is a similar careful framing of the "transgressive" event (killings, violations of social and familial order) by means of the conditions of performance and conventional structures of the genre, while the mythic material brings the added effect of a distinctive separation in time and space and modality, so that the interrogation of values is not felt to be too direct. Moreover, alternative viewpoints are

[57] See Goldhill 1991: 167–222, Edwards 1993, Platter 2006.

juxtaposed in satyr-play, comedy, and choral dithyrambs, so that the extremes and the instability highlighted in the tragic world are also in a sense contained or rendered less absolute by the existence at the same festival of such alternatives.

The possibility exists that at some point the Athenians, or influential political leaders, consciously decided the city would sponsor tragic performances in its festival because they wanted the citizens' cherished assumptions to be scrutinized and challenged in order to strengthen the critical awareness of the citizen body and create more thoughtful participants in the deliberations and activities of the city. Yet the politically powerful rarely want people to engage in such scrutiny and independent judgment. And even if the "founders" or "sponsors" did view tragic performance in this way, that does not necessarily entail that the playwrights took the same view of their role. The scrutiny and challenge found in tragedy can equally well be understood as an outgrowth of the religious and social functions of poetic performance, not exclusive to tragedy: by narrating, revisiting, and revising the stories of the heroes, poetry offers images and models of the operations of the world and the conditions of human life, instilling a mixture of inspiration and caution, celebration and consolation, humility before the gods and pride in human achievement, and reshaping and reinventing traditions about the shared past of the audience, their ancestors, and their institutions. Tragedy, of course, interacts with the specifics of its Athenian context as well, and in important ways, but that is not all that it does, and thus I believe that it is too limiting to assume that the implied audience is the Athenian male citizen rather than a larger range of the community, both within Athens and outside it. If there is a religious element in such self-scrutiny and contemplation of insecurity, one might regard it as a Dionysiac element, since Dionysus is "a complex figure composed of, and associated with, polarities such as god/man, man/beast, male/female, sanity/madness, joy/terror, wild/mild or foreign/indigenous,"[58] but it can also derive from Greek religion as a whole.[59]

---

[58] Henrichs 1990: 258.
[59] There have been and are scholars who would argue that the Dionysian connections of tragedy are accidental rather than intrinsic: see Else 1967 and more recently Friedrich 1996, Scullion 2002. On the whole, however, although one may still be unsure how central the Dionysiac mysteries or Dionysiac possession were to the practices of the late fifth-century tragedians and performers and to their audience's understanding of the dramas, Dionysian origins and various types of Dionysian connections seem secure. For a variety of views on the Dionysiac aspects of Greek tragedy, see Segal 1982, Henrichs 1984, Winkler and Zeitlin 1990, Bierl 1991, Seaford 1994 and 1996, Zeitlin 1996, Easterling 1997b, and the papers in Csapo and Miller 2007a.

The "teaching" function of tragedy has also been hard to describe in a way that meets general acceptance.[60] On the one side, those who emphasize only the psychagogic effects of tragic drama and the various emotions and pleasures a performance may give an audience reduce the richness and complex suggestiveness of the plays.[61] At the other extreme, those who take the tag "poet as teacher of his people" too literally may turn the tragedian into a writer of ephemeral political allegories or a prophet of the failure of the Sicilian Expedition or a champion of progressive ideas.[62] It is essential to consider again the background of the poetic tradition as well as to take account of the controversies over education in the last third of the fifth century. Since the sixth century, Greek poets were traditionally referred to as "wise" (*sophos*), and it is useful to analyze the elements that go into this designation in the tripartite way adopted by Mark Griffith.[63] He delineates three senses. First, poets are wise because they display and reformulate the inherited "wisdom" and values of their culture, expressed more openly in traditional maxims (*gnōmai*) and more indirectly in stories (*muthoi*). Second, poets are wise because they learn and carry a mass of (supposedly) factual knowledge, such as the names of peoples and places, genealogies and aetiologies. And, third, poets are wise/clever because they are masters of the techniques and adornments of their craft, including meter, music, specialized language, and artful arrangement of words. Clearly, the first sense is the most important one for the question of the instructive function of tragedy. Within this type of wisdom, some lessons are conveyed quite directly, as in maxims spoken in the poet/performer's voice in Pindar or Bacchylides or advice offered in sympotic elegiacs; but other lessons are conveyed less explicitly, as by the myths embedded in choral lyric. The instructive application of the myth may be made partially clear by the way in which it is framed, but the frame sometimes interprets only one aspect of the myth, and at times gives very little guidance at all, leaving it up to the audience to infer analogies and applications. When choral myth is divorced from such a frame or proportionately overwhelms any framing, the "lesson" of the story is even more indeterminate or in need

---

[60] The overall approach to the plays' didactic function espoused by Gregory 1991 has struck many reviewers as less convincing than the individual perceptions in the analysis of the plays she handles. The most subtle presentation of the case for the didactic functions of tragedy is offered in Croally 1994: 1–69 and 2005.

[61] A skillful example of this type of approach is Heath 1987b.

[62] On the school of historicizing readings that involve political allegory, see the just assessment of Michelini 1987: 28–9, agreeing with Zuntz 1955 and 1958. For Euripides as champion of progressive ideas, see, e.g., Hartung 1843–44 and Nestle 1901.

[63] Griffith 1990: 188–9.

of supplementation from the audience's familiarity with the genre and from their cultural knowledge. Moreover, the "lesson" may be very general and banal ("this is the way the world works"; "gods are strong and humans are weak"), yet the specific shaping of the story may evoke a momentary enhancement of awareness and expansion of human sympathy.

As drama, tragedy dispenses with the voice of the poet and lets the characters and the story speak for themselves. Sometimes voices within the drama will draw specific lessons either in the form of (ignored) warnings or as commentary after the fact. But such voices may have different degrees of authority for the audience and may suffer from some partiality in their interpretation. Again, the shifting process of interpretation on the part of the audience, involving an expanded awareness of complexity and conflict, is probably more significant as "instruction" of the audience than any particular gnomic observation. One way to associate this process in the audience with the specific Athenian democratic context is to suggest that it served as a valuable mode of "instructing" the Athenians in the arts of politics and law within their political system, where, for instance, rapid but thoughtful assessment of different opinions and narratives was a key skill required of the citizen male in the council, the assembly, the courts, and other gatherings (such as at the deme level).[64]

But let us step back for a moment to the contemporary or slightly later evidence about tragedy. The contemporary passage constantly cited is the debate between "Aeschylus" and "Euripides" in Aristophanes' *Frogs*. At *Frogs* 1008–10, "Aeschylus" challenges "Euripides" to answer the question "For what reason should a poet be admired?" The latter answers: "For clever skill (*dexiotēs*) and for [sound] admonition (*nouthesia*) and because we make men better in the cities (*en tais polesin*)."[65] The fact that Aristophanes makes both his characters agree on the civic didactic function of their poetry does not authorize the inference that real poets (or real audience members) all agreed on this point (or agreed on what it is that poets "teach"), since these are fictional figures created for Aristophanes' own purposes. In this scene, the specificity of what the poets teach is, in my view, a strong pointer to the satirical nature of this representation. As we saw above, poets traditionally provided instruction on many levels, but perhaps most importantly on a very general cultural level. In the second half of the fifth century, the sophists and other intellectuals who were making explicit the boundaries,

<hr/>

[64] See again Croally 1994 and 2005.
[65] Note as well what "Aeschylus" says at *Frogs* 1054–5 : "Little children have a teacher who advises (*phrazei*), while those who are of [adult] age (*hoi hēbōntes*) have poets."

methods, and insights of their *technai* were engaged in a contest for authority and acceptance, not only with each other, but with the existing cultural
traditions of education and training. An important consequence of this
contestation is that the defenders of the traditional ways were induced to
argue in response for their own authority and importance. In framing this
counterargument, some of Aristophanes' contemporaries went too far and
made excessive claims. Plato reflects this problem in his portrayal of the
rhapsode Ion, who insists (when pressed and led on by Socrates) that he has
learned from Homer specific skills of use to military officers (*Ion* 540d–1b),
rather than claiming merely that Homer provides general guidance on the
protocols of interpersonal relationships and the importance of good counsel
and effective communication with one's peers. The satirical aspects of the
Just Argument in Aristophanes' *Clouds* also reflect an exaggerated position
taken by a representative of the traditional ways in strong opposition to the
new educational currents.[66] Within *Frogs* we find "Aeschylus" citing
Homer's usefulness to generals and soldiers in the same way as Plato's
Ion,[67] while "Euripides" prides himself on having taught Athenians to
pay attention more acutely to their household management (971–9). The
claim "to make the people better in the cities" (*Frogs* 1009–10) cannot be
considered completely untainted by the general context of the comically
exaggerated argument. It, too, reflects the overspecification to which the
arguments about education fell victim in this period. Of course, poetry may
make people better, but in what sense of "goodness" are they better? And
what of "in the cities"? (Note that this does not say "in our city" or "in our
democracy," but rather "in their [respective, potentially different] cities.")
Can this really be taken to reflect the fact that tragedy primarily appeals to
the audience-member as a citizen, or is it rather a narrowing of the goal that
suits Aristophanes' plot, which seeks a poet to save Athens from its decline
and decides the contest at the end with a specific political riddle, the kind of
advice that even most proponents of the civic educational force of tragedy
do not think that tragedy gives?

   Plato, a younger witness than Aristophanes, but still one who as a boy and
teenager presumably attended the theater during the final decade of the
activity of Sophocles and Euripides, does not consider the tragedians
explicit teachers in the way the famous passage in *Frogs* suggests. He is

---

[66] Compare, too, the specific instruction ascribed to Euripides by the woman who denounces him in
Aristophanes' *Women at the Thesmophoria* 389–428.
[67] *Frogs* 1034–6: "What source was there for Homer's gaining honor and fame except this one, the fact
that he taught useful things – arrangements of troops, displays of valor, and armings of warriors?"
(*taxeis, aretas, hopliseis andrōn*).

not, of course, an unbiased witness, because he is offering an iconoclastic alternative to the traditional mode of Greek education and to traditional notions of citizenship, and thus is at pains to criticize and supplant a source of authoritative traditions cherished by the Athenians (and also increasingly by other fourth-century cities). In the *Republic* and *Laws*, Plato assumes that tragedy does teach things to the audience, but he does not consider this an explicit process or even intentional on the part of the poets. For him, the problem is that poetry seductively moves and shapes the audience's souls, rendering them more vulnerable to uncontrolled emotion, and he fears that the audience may model their own behavior on that of the heroic characters, even when the latter are acting in an unmanly or impious manner. It is not that the poets intend their audience to do so, but that they lavish adornments on the stories that sweep the audience along.[68]

THE APPROACHES AND SCOPE OF THIS BOOK

In the chapters that follow, I hope to demonstrate the usefulness of an approach that is eclectic, flexible, and wary of totalizing interpretations. Some of the general axioms of this approach may be crudely enumerated here. (1) Tragedy as a genre participates in a continuing tradition of poetic craft and of serious illustration and exploration of human character and social relations, investigating the order or disorder of the world humans inhabit by retelling and modifying traditional stories in a new form. While some issues are inflected in tragic representation in a particularly Athenian way, the ambitions of the poets and the interest generated by their dramas extend well beyond narrowly Athenian or democratic concerns. (2) Tragedy

---

[68] The strong psychagogic influence of tragedy and the need for the good member of the audience to submit to it are implied by a famous statement ascribed to the sophist Gorgias (82 B 23 D–K): "Tragedy (is) a deception in which the deceiver is more just than the non-deceiver and the deceived is wiser than the non-deceived." The evidence of Aristotle's *Poetics*, however, is better left aside in the debate about "teaching." He wrote at a couple of generations' remove from the fifth-century theater, and so those who believe he is radically wrong about tragedy's purposes and effects can well argue that he simply did not understand the political and social significance of the genre in the lifetime of Euripides. In Aristotle's theory, the poets' intentions are directed to shaping the plot and contriving the words and rhythm and music to attain a certain effect. Shaping the plot involves attention to probability and necessity, to the universal, and to the relation of ethos to action. The audience derives various pleasures from watching or reading tragedy, and one is the pleasure involved in recognizing the universal patterns. But the main pleasure has to do with the evocation and purging of pity and fear, or whatever one takes *katharsis* to be; in the most generous interpretation (which may be reading too much into Aristotle) this *katharsis* is a valuable training of the moral sensibilities and thus good for intersocial relations in a community, but it is not implied that the poets know that they are aiming to provide such training, nor that Aristotle's intends such training to be applied to any particular kind of political community.

in the fifth century was an ever-evolving genre, and it is unjustified to posit an ideal fixed form. Neat reconstructions of musical and artistic history must always be treated with caution and skepticism, and awareness of the agenda that lie behind each ancient or modern theorist's take on the problem. Thus, we must resist Aristophanes' and Plato's idealized histories of musical style, which pit the decadence of late fifth-century forms against the ideal simplicity and sobriety of an imagined past. Equally, we must not slavishly follow Aristotle's preference for organic unity and rationally ana- lyzable chains of probability or necessity. And we need to question theories of "the tragic" that have often tyrannized interpretation by enforcing a search for consistent decorum, harmony, and grandeur (or for Dionysiac ecstasy and ritual energy). (3) Drama is inherently a multivocal representa- tion, and none of the voices in it have absolute authority, transparency, or reliability for an audience in its efforts to interpret what it sees and hears. Tragedies may present important areas of ambivalence, impasse, or open- endedness in their scrutiny of psychological, ethical, and social issues. (4) Attic tragedy exploits many different conventions of style and presentation and freely mixes elements of realism or psychological depth with artistic contrivance, stylization, conventionality, and the needs of communication in an engaging and effective way to the external audience. (5) Our evidence for the variety of style, tone, and subject-matter in fifth-century tragedy is seriously deficient. At least a thousand different tragedies were written (perhaps by some fifty individual poets) and performed in Attika during the fifth century, of which we have in complete form only thirty-one tragedies written by only three or four poets.[69] It is therefore prudent to avoid any overconfidence in simple generalizations drawn from what sur- vives. (6) Attempts to characterize the three great tragedians in sharp

[69] 1,000 tragedies: theoretically, the Great Dionysia alone would require 900 tragedies, but this total would be increased somewhat by instances in which the fourth play was also a "tragedy" (that is, had a chorus of humans and not a chorus of satyrs). This substitution occurred in 438 with Euripides' *Alcestis* (on my policy of treating this along with the other plays rather than as belonging to a separate "prosatyric" genre, see pp. 55–7 below; for the speculation that *Alcestis* was not the only instance of this practice, see p. 56 n. 33). The total would be decreased somewhat by any reperformances (Aeschylus' plays are supposed to have been allowed reperformance in the festival after his death). There were also tragedies produced at the Lenaea festival and at some of the local Dionysia festivals in demes around Attika, and it is likely that some of these were original plays (some by playwrights not yet deemed worthy of being allotted a chorus at the Great Dionysia) rather than works from the major festival. Fifty tragedians: in the listing in *TrGF* vol. I, the tragedians numbered 2 through 49 apparently produced plays in the fifth century; a few of these are doubtful, but there must have been other playwrights whose names have not survived. Thirty-one surviving plays by three or four authors: six by Aeschylus, one (*Prometheus*) by Aeschylus or an unknown author, seven by Sophocles, and seventeen by Euripides (a corpus of nineteen dramas, minus the satyr-play *Cyclops* and the tragedy *Rhesus*, which I believe to be a fourth-century work and do not discuss in this book).

contradistinction to one another run the risk of homogenizing the oeuvre of each one. Doing so is as harmful to the appreciation of Sophocles as it is to assessment of Euripides. In terms of world-views and motivations and the like, there is a great deal that is shared across the genre, and the differences are sometimes a matter of gradations along a spectrum rather than of polar opposition. My discussions attempt to keep in view the larger context of Aeschylean and Sophoclean drama, where appropriate. (7) Since there is much more evidence in the case of Euripides (more complete plays surviving, comprising a greater proportion of his output, as well as more supplementary information provided by quotations, papyrus fragments, and epitomes), the variety of his oeuvre is widely recognized, although it is not always given enough prominence in works that discuss an individual play or a small group of plays, especially those best known to the contemporary "educated public." In the chapters that follow, I try to draw on all the plays. Finally, (8) character presentation, causation, world-view, and other factors are strongly conditioned in each particular tragedy by plot-type and story-pattern, and therefore we may not find consistency across all the surviving examples. In other words, the ambitions and interests that we infer for the "implied author" of one Euripidean play need not match or agree with those that we infer for the "implied author" of another Euripidean play.

Since not every reader of this book will be familiar with all the plays referred to in my discussions, I provide as an appendix to this chapter a brief guide to the plots of the plays of Euripides, with references to the most helpful recent commentaries and to a few important discussions. More advanced readers can skip this, but I have included it in the hope that it will make some parts of this book more accessible to less advanced readers. The remaining chapters of the book address a variety of topics in Euripidean dramatic art, usually with some preliminary attention to background issues followed by detailed discussion of particular examples drawn from all the extant tragedies and, where useful, from the remnants of lost plays. Chapter 2 presents some of the problems related to generic definition, arguing that we must not either limit or overdefine our response to particular plays by the assumption of a clear and consistent definition of "tragedy" or of other dramatic genres considered to be "not tragic." Chapter 3 discusses structural strategies, in particular the use of "open" structures, mirroring and reversal, and juxtaposition as alternatives to the tight organic form admired by Aristotle and his followers. Chapter 4 covers the chorus, first addressing the relation of the tragic chorus to the tradition of Greek choral poetry and the issues of status, knowledge, and authority, and then surveying the use of myth in the chorus, connection and relevance of choral songs, and Euripides' general preference for a less emotionally engaged choral contribution within his dramatic structures. Chapter 5 takes up the topic of theology and the gods in Euripidean tragedy: after some preliminary considerations, it turns to the represented drama of human belief and doubt and the dramatic functions of criticism of the gods or speculation about the nature of divinity, and then studies examples of the operations of the gods, both seen (in essence, prologue and epilogue gods) and unseen, in the action of the plays. Chapter 6 addresses problems of rhetoric and character: after starting from general considerations of what it means to speak of "rhetoric" in Euripides and in his fifth-century context, it proceeds to evaluate representations of cultural ambivalence about rhetoric and the modern and finally to examine the interaction of rhetoric, character representation, and character formation, especially in the formal debate scenes. The final pair of chapters addresses some issues of gender and the nature and efficacy of human agency in the dramas. Chapter 7 concentrates on female figures: after reviewing the alignment (or lack of alignment) between gender and spatial relations to indoors and outdoors and between gender and relations to household and city, it explores some examples of appropriation of "male" values of fame and courage by female characters and concludes with a discussion of misogynistic speech. Chapter 8 turns to male figures to study their styles of action and degrees of success or failure, explaining some of the differences in terms of age status and plot-type and highlighting the limitations on autonomy that are typical of the tragic genre but also often accentuated in Euripides' treatment of human action.

APPENDIX: A BRIEF GUIDE TO EURIPIDES' PLAYS

The studies in the following chapters refer to the seventeen complete surviving plays of Euripides and a number of the lost plays partially known from fragments and indirect testimony. This guide is intended to make these discussions somewhat more accessible to those who are not already thoroughly familiar with the corpus and to offer selective references to helpful commentaries, books, and articles. (More advanced readers will want to skip this appendix.) In addition to the works cited, the reader should assume that there is relevant information in major books on Euripides that cover all or most of the plays.[70] Large-scale reviews of

---

[70] For a sampling of older perspectives see in particular Hartung 1843–44, Pohlenz 1930 and 1954, Grube 1941, Norwood 1953, Kitto 1961. For the last forty years, consult Conacher 1967, Burnett 1971, Di Benedetto 1971, Lesky 1983, Aélion 1983 and 1986, Foley 1985, Michelini 1987, Gregory 1991, Rabinowitz 1993, Assaël 2001, Morwood 2002, Matthiessen 2002, Hose 2008.

Euripidean bibliography are also available.[71] The most reliable "close" English translation of the full set of tragedies is available in Kovacs 1994–2002. Many other relatively modern translations may also be useful, provided they allow reference to the standard line numbering by which passages in Euripides are conventionally cited.

Alcestis[72] (known performance date 438)[73] presents the day on which Alcestis, wife of Admetus (king of Pherae in Thessaly) and mother of his children, dies in fulfillment of a promise to die in place of her husband. This promise had been made at an unspecified earlier time, after Admetus was granted the privilege of finding a substitute as a favor by Apollo, who had been well treated by Admetus when serving in his house as a punishment imposed by Zeus. Admetus' father and mother had refused their son's request for a substitute. In the prologue, Apollo explains the background, tries to dissuade Thanatos (Death) when he arrives to collect Alcestis' life, and finally foretells that Alcestis will be saved from death by an arriving guest. Alcestis' farewell to her household and family is first reported to the chorus of old men from the community, then the family appears before the house and Alcestis makes her final request (that Admetus not marry again nor give his children a stepmother) and last farewells, then dies. Admetus promises never to remarry and indeed never to enjoy any form of celebration again. Heracles arrives on the way to one of his labors; he sees that the house is in mourning and tries to go elsewhere for hospitality, but Admetus conceals the identity of the deceased and insists that Heracles lodge with him and enjoy hospitality as if no mourning were going on. As the funeral procession leaves the palace, Admetus' father, Pheres, arrives to pay his respects to the dead woman, but an acrimonious argument ensues between father and son. While the chorus and the funeral party are away, a servant emerges to complain of Heracles' drunken celebration within the guest-chambers; Heracles himself emerges, criticizing the servant's gloomy demeanor, but is then informed of the true state of affairs and resolves to win Alcestis back from death. Admetus returns with the mourning chorus and recognizes that accepting the substitution of Alcestis has left him in a shameful position. Heracles returns with a veiled woman who he says is a prize he won in a contest, and he insists on entrusting her to Admetus while

---

[71] Hose *et al.* 2005, Cambiano *et al.* 1996: 415–33. Convenient lists for individual plays follow the discussion of each play in Matthiessen 2002.

[72] Commentaries: Dale 1954, Conacher 1988, Parker 2007; select studies: Burnett 1965, Rivier 1972–73, Gregory 1979, Buxton 1985, Lloyd 1985, Dyson 1988, Segal 1991, 1992, 1993.

[73] All performance dates are, of course, BCE. On the chronology of the plays and the kinds of evidence used for it, see Mastronarde 2002b: 3–5, Cropp and Fick 1985, Collard and Cropp 2008a: xxix–xxxii.

he proceeds on his labor. Admetus reluctantly takes the woman by the arm and finally looks at her face, and she is Alcestis (silent for ritual reasons).

Medea[74] (known performance date 431) takes place several years after the Argonautic expedition, when Medea and Jason have two young sons and are living in Corinth, in exile from Jason's native city of Iolcus in Thessaly. In the prologue, Medea's nurse explains that Medea is desperately distraught and resentful because Jason has just married the daughter of Creon, king of Corinth. Medea's complaints and curses are heard from inside and some Corinthian women of the neighborhood arrive to express sympathy. Medea emerges to address them in full control of herself and proceeds to win their favor and consent to keep silent if she finds a way to punish her enemies. Creon arrives to order her into immediate exile with her sons, to forestall any violence against his daughter. Medea persuades him to allow her one more day to prepare for exile, and after he leaves tells the chorus she will get her revenge before leaving, but is not yet sure of the best way to do so. Jason arrives to offer Medea help in exile, but she denounces him in a formal speech of accusation, to which he replies by explaining the motivation of his new marriage and the benefits it will bring to his sons. Aegeus, king of Athens, arrives next, receives from Medea a promise of help to cure his childlessness, and promises to protect her if she makes her way on her own to Athens. Medea reveals to the chorus a plan to kill the princess through poisoned gifts carried by her sons and then to kill her own sons to torment Jason and save them from possible revenge from the Corinthians. She dupes Jason into believing she has recognized the wisdom of his new marriage and induces him to take their sons with the fatal gifts to the princess. Once her sons return from their mission, Medea wavers between her eagerness for revenge and her desire to spare her sons, but decides on revenge. A messenger reports the death of the princess and her father. Medea goes in to kill her sons, and their cries are heard just before Jason enters, hoping to rescue them from angry relatives of Creon. Medea appears above the building in a winged chariot lent by her grandfather, the sun; she and Jason exchange hostile words, and Medea predicts his lonely future death before escaping.

Heracleidae[75] (estimated performance date *ca.* 430) tells how the Athenians championed the children of the dead hero Heracles against

[74] Commentary: Mastronarde 2002b; select studies: Schlesinger 1966, Burnett 1973 and 1998: 192–224, Easterling 1977, Knox 1977, Bongie 1977, Pucci 1980, Boedeker 1991 and 1997, Kovacs 1993, Clauss and Johnston 1997, Foley 1989 and 2001: 243–71, McDermott 1989, Griffiths 2006.
[75] Commentaries: Wilkins 1993, Allan 2001; select studies: Zuntz 1955, Mendelsohn 2002; see also Roselli 2007.

persecution by the Argive king Eurystheus. Iolaus, nephew and helper of Heracles, now an old man, tells in the prologue of the wanderings of the underage children under the protection of Heracles' mother, Alcmene, and himself. The girls are inside the temple of Zeus at Marathon with Alcmene; the boys are with Iolaus as suppliants at the altar outside it. An Argive herald arrives and tries to drag Iolaus from the altar, but a chorus of local Athenian old men arrives in response to his cries and soon thereafter the Athenian king Demophon (with his silent brother, the co-regent Akamas). The herald argues that the suppliants are still subjects of Argos and that the Athenians risk war if they do not give them up; Iolaus counters that they are no longer subjects of Eurystheus and deserve protection as suppliants and that the Athenian kings as sons of Theseus have a special tie to the children of Heracles, since the two heroes were friends. Demophon accepts the suppliants. Soon he returns to explain that an oracle calls for the sacrifice of a well-born virgin for success in the coming war with Argos and that he cannot ask that any of his citizens offer a child for this purpose. The eldest daughter of Heracles emerges from the temple and soon volunteers to be the sacrifice, in order to save her family and ensure that the Athenians defeat the Argives. Next, a servant arrives to say that the eldest son of Heracles, Hyllus, has also collected an army to participate with the Athenians in the war against Eurystheus. Iolaus, despite his old age and weakness, insists on going to the battle, leaving Alcmene in charge of the suppliants. A messenger brings news of the defeat of the Argives and the capture of Eurystheus by Iolaus, who had been rejuvenated after a prayer to the gods. The captive Eurystheus is brought before Alcmene, who insists she will have him killed, rejecting admonitions that this is improper treatment of a captive already spared. Eurystheus accepts his fate and promises that his tomb in Attika will provide protection in the future.

Hippolytus[76] (probable performance date 428)[77] tells of the fatal passion of Phaedra, daughter of Minos, wife of Theseus, and mother of his legitimate sons, for the youth Hippolytus, illegitimate son of Theseus by an Amazon. She and Theseus are dwelling temporarily in Trozen (where Hippolytus normally resides) and during Theseus' temporary absence from home Phaedra is trying to starve herself to death. In the prologue the goddess Aphrodite reveals that she is punishing Hippolytus, a devotee of

---

[76] Commentaries: Barrett 1964, Halleran 1995; select studies: Knox 1952, Segal 1965 and 1993, Frischer 1970, Zeitlin 1985, Goff 1990.

[77] On the controversy whether the surviving *Hippolytus* is really the second of the plays of this title that Euripides composed and was thus produced in 428, as ancient scholars inferred, see Gibert 1997, Mastronarde 2002b: 4 n. 13, Collard and Cropp 2008a: 467–8, 471.

the virgin goddess Artemis, for his neglect of her and that she has instilled desire for the youth in Phaedra to bring about his ruin. Returning from hunting, Hippolytus leads a secondary chorus of his attendants in hymning Artemis and then scorns the advice of an old servant who warns him to acknowledge Aphrodite as well. A chorus of local women arrives to inquire about Phaedra's health. Phaedra is brought outdoors at her own request by her nurse and attendants and speaks indirectly of her desire in frenzied lyrics that are not understood by the nurse. The nurse, after repeated efforts, extracts from Phaedra the reason for her desire to die. Phaedra then explains to the chorus why death is the best way to avoid shame for her family and herself. The nurse tries to dissuade her from this viewpoint, arguing that it would be better and natural to give in to her desire. After Phaedra angrily rejects this view, the nurse pretends to adopt a different tactic and goes indoors alone. Soon it is clear that the nurse approached Hippolytus indoors; Hippolytus rushes out, reviling the nurse, Phaedra, and all women, and then leaves the stage. Phaedra decides to commit suicide at once, but protect her name and her children's honor by leaving a letter for Theseus accusing Hippolytus of rape. Theseus arrives just after Phaedra has hanged herself, reads the letter, and curses his son. Hippolytus arrives, fails to convince Theseus of his innocence, and is sentenced to immediate exile. A messenger soon brings news that as Hippolytus rode his chariot away from Trozen, a bull appeared from the sea, crazed his horses, and caused him grievous injuries. As Theseus waits to confront his dying son, Artemis appears to accuse Theseus of haste and injustice and explain the true situation. Hippolytus is brought back barely alive and makes his farewells to Artemis and his father, forgiving Theseus for causing his death.

Andromache[78] (estimated performance date *ca.* 425) opens with Andromache, the widow of Hector, a suppliant at the altar of Thetis in Phthia (Thessaly) before the house of Neoptolemus, son of Achilles. Since the fall of Troy she has been the concubine of Neoptolemus and has borne him a son. Now he has been married for a while to Hermione from Sparta, daughter of Menelaus and Helen, who has not yet borne a child. In the prologue, Andromache explains that she is a suppliant because, during a temporary absence of Neoptolemus to visit Delphi, Hermione has summoned Menelaus to help her kill Andromache and her son. A servant woman who had been a slave in Hector's house at Troy agrees to carry a

---

[78] Commentaries: Stevens 1971, Lloyd 1994; select studies: Burnett 1971: 130–56, McClure 1999: 158–204, Allan 2000, Hesk 2000: 64–84.

message to Neoptolemus' grandfather, the aged Peleus, to appeal for his help. A chorus of local women arrive to express their sympathy. Hermione emerges and accuses Andromache of making her sterile with drugs; Andromache defends herself and stays at the altar. Menelaus enters, reporting that he has discovered where Andromache hid her son and offering to let her son live if Andromache herself gives up her asylum and accepts death. Once Andromache does so, Menelaus reveals that he will kill the son as well. Peleus arrives just as bound mother and son are being led to slaughter, frees them, and drives Menelaus away. Hermione, now fearing Neoptolemus' return, is restrained from suicide. Hermione's cousin Orestes arrives, pretends not to know what is happening, and accepts Hermione's plea that he rescue her, finally revealing that he knew the situation, has planned to ambush Neoptolemus at Delphi, and wants to marry Hermione once her husband is dead. A messenger brings word to Peleus that Neoptolemus has been killed at Delphi. As he mourns his loss, Thetis appears above, consoles him, and explains that the son of Andromache and Neoptolemus will found a dynasty in Molossia in western Greece.

Hecuba[79] (estimated performance date *ca.* 425–24) takes place during a stop of the Greek fleet in the Thracian Chersonese on its return voyage from Troy. The ghost of Polydorus, youngest son of Priam and Hecuba, speaks the prologue, revealing that he had been murdered by his host, the Thracian king Polymestor, to whom he had been entrusted by his parents, and that the Greek army is about to accede to a demand from the ghost of Achilles (whose tomb is nearby) that they sacrifice Polyxena, daughter of Priam and Hecuba, on his tomb. Hecuba awakens from a troubling dream reflecting Polymestor's presence and is joined by the chorus, reporting the decision of the Greeks to sacrifice her daughter. Polyxena is summoned from inside and told the news, then Odysseus arrives to fetch her for sacrifice. Hecuba attempts to persuade Odysseus to relent, and he refutes her arguments. Polyxena refuses to beg for life, seeing death as more honorable than living on as a slave. Soon the herald Talthybius comes to tell Hecuba of Polyxena's bravery in facing death and invite her to come and attend to the corpse. A servant sent to fetch water for the funeral preparations brings back a body she found washed up on the shore, Polydorus. Hecuba laments for her son briefly until Agamemnon appears. She then appeals to him to assist her in punishing Polymestor for his treachery. He is sympathetic, but does not want to be seen by the Greeks to be helping her. Hecuba then summons

---

[79] Commentaries: Collard 1991, Gregory 1999, Matthiessen 2008; select studies: Heath 1987a, Zeitlin 1991, Thalmann 1993, Segal 1993, Mossman 1995.

Polymestor and his two sons with a false promise of buried treasure and kills the sons and blinds their father. Agamemnon returns in response to the tumult of Polymestor's blind rage and adjudicates a trial scene, accepting Hecuba's case that Polymestor deserved his punishment. Polymestor predicts the deaths of Hecuba, Agamemnon, and Cassandra before being led away.

Supplices[80] (estimated performance date *ca.* 423) is named for the chorus of women representing the mothers of the Seven against Thebes, who are supplicating at the temple of Demeter in Eleusis in order to obtain assistance in retrieving the bodies of their sons, since the victorious Thebans have refused to let their dead enemies be buried. Aethra, the mother of Theseus, is visiting the temple for a ritual and has become the object of their supplication, as she explains in the prologue. Theseus arrives to check on his mother and learns of the supplication; he interrogates Adrastus, king of Argos and survivor of the army of the Seven, and says he will not help him, but Aethra intervenes and Theseus changes his mind. A herald arrives from Thebes, warns the Athenians not to interfere, and in debate with Theseus criticizes the ways of democracies. Theseus refutes him and sends him back to Thebes. Soon a messenger appears to report that the Athenians have won the battle and the corpses are being given proper burial. The remains of the Seven are brought before the chorus, and after a short lyric lament Theseus asks Adrastus to praise the dead, then takes the corpses away for burning. The pyre of Capaneus is to be separate and nearby. Evadne, that hero's wife, appears above (as if on a crag) declaring she will throw herself on her husband's pyre. Her aged father arrives searching for her and she rejects his commands and jumps to her death, leaving him to mourn. The sons of the Seven bring the urns with their fathers' ashes before the chorus, and after more lamentation Theseus is ready to send the Argives home. Athena appears above, requires Adrastus to swear an oath of Argive friendship and gratitude, and makes other arrangements for the future.

Electra[81] (estimated performance date *ca.* 420)[82] presents, like Aeschylus' *Choephori* (of 458) and Sophocles' *Electra*,[83] the vengeance of the youth Orestes against his father's cousin Aegisthus and his mother Clytemnestra

[80] Commentaries: Collard 1975a and 1984; select studies: Zuntz 1955, Burian 1985b, Foley 2001: 36–44, Mendelsohn 2002.
[81] Commentaries: Denniston 1939, Cropp 1988; select studies: Zeitlin 1970, Arnott 1981, Lloyd 1986, Burnett 1998: 225–46, Goff 1999–2000.
[82] On this date instead of the date 413, which used to be widely assumed, see Zuntz 1955: 63–71 and Cropp 1988: l–li.
[83] The date of performance of Sophocles' version is unknown and its relation to Euripides' play has long been debated. See Cropp 1988: xlviii–l.

for slaying his father Agamemnon on his return from Troy. Orestes' sister, Electra, has been married off to a poor farmer far from the city, but the farmer (who speaks the prologue) has not consummated the marriage out of respect for her status. The play takes place at the farmhouse rather than before the palace in town. While Electra goes off to fetch water and the farmer goes to work at a distance, Orestes (with a silent Pylades) appears and explains he is seeking to find his sister for help with his project of revenge. He hides and eavesdrops as Electra returns, singing a lament for her father, and as the chorus of local women arrive to invite Electra to a festival. When Orestes comes out of hiding, he calms her fear by saying he brings a message from her brother. He learns from her the situation (as she sees it) and does not volunteer his identity. The farmer returns and insists the strangers must be invited inside, and an old family retainer (once tutor of Agamemnon) is summoned with a request that he bring food for entertainment of the guests. On his way, the old man has seen signs on the grave of Agamemnon that suggest Orestes may be nearby, but Electra dismisses his inferences and insists Orestes would have come openly, not in secret. But then the old man identifies Orestes, and with his help a plan for killing Aegisthus and Clytemnestra is devised. A messenger reports how Orestes posed as a stranger, got himself invited to the sacrifice Aegisthus was holding in the countryside nearby, and then killed Aegisthus. Aegisthus' body is brought to the farmhouse, and Electra reviles him. Clytemnestra, who had been summoned to help Electra in the aftermath of a supposed childbirth, is seen approaching. Orestes wavers, but Electra insists he must kill her. Electra lures her mother into the house (after a set debate of accusation and defense), where she is soon killed, whereupon both siblings are stricken with remorse. Their lamentation is cut off by the arrival of the Dioscuri on high, Castor gives instructions for the future, and the siblings part for their separate exiles.

Heracles[84] (estimated production date *ca*. 416) dramatizes Heracles' killing of his wife Megara and their children in a fit of madness. Euripides places this event at the end of Heracles' labors rather than before them and creates a crisis in which they are first almost killed by an enemy. Amphitryon, Heracles' human father, is with Megara and three young sons of Heracles at an altar before their palace to protect themselves from Lycus, the new ruler of Thebes who has recently killed king Creon,

---

[84] Commentaries: Bond 1981, Barlow 1996; select studies: Sheppard 1916, Chalk 1962, Kamerbeek 1966, Burnett 1971: 157–82, Ruck 1976, Gregory 1977, Foley 1985: 147–204, Mastronarde 1983 and 1986, Hamilton 1985, Papadopoulou 2005.

Megara's father. Heracles is away on his final labor to the underworld to bring back Cerberus. After Amphitryon explains the situation in the pro- logue, Megara asks whether it is proper to drag out their misery or to accept quick death, and he insists they must wait and have hope. A chorus of sympathetic old men visits the scene. Lycus arrives and threatens to burn them where they are if they do not leave the altar. Megara now persuades Amphitryon that it is more noble to give themselves up now and die a dignified death, and the family is allowed to enter the house to dress for death while Lycus goes away for a time. As the family comes out ready to die, Heracles suddenly enters to save his family, and in a short time Lycus is lured into the palace and killed. As the chorus is celebrating this turn of events, the goddesses Iris and Lyssa ("Madness") appear above the roof to explain that by Hera's will Heracles will now go mad indoors and kill his wife and children. A messenger appears from within to describe what happened, then an unconscious Heracles is brought out on stage tied to a fallen pillar. He awakens and Amphitryon gradually reveals what has happened. Theseus arrives on the chance that Heracles needed help against Lycus, but now debates with Heracles whether suicide is a proper response to what has happened. Heracles decides to live on and departs with Theseus to Athens.

Troades[85] (known performance date 415) begins with the sea-god Poseidon bidding farewell to the sacked city of Troy. Athena arrives to say that the Greek victors have offended her and asks Poseidon to help her punish them with a destructive storm on their voyage home. Hecuba, collapsed in sleep on the stage, rouses herself after the gods depart and summons the chorus of captive Trojan women to join her in lamentation. The Greek army's herald, Talthybius, arrives to fetch Cassandra for Agamemnon and tells Hecuba to whom she and Andromache have been allotted and alludes enigmatically to the sacrifice of Polyxena at Achilles' tomb. Cassandra rushes out of the tent in a frenzy, celebrating her "mar- riage" to Agamemnon as a step toward his destruction back home. She prophesies some of the coming sufferings of the Greek leaders and argues paradoxically that the Trojans have been and are better off than the Greeks. Next Andromache, with her son by Hector, Astyanax, arrives on her way to the ship of Neoptolemus, which is about to depart. But Talthybius returns to tell her that the Greeks have decided to throw the boy to his death from the walls, and he takes the child away. Menelaus arrives to fetch Helen, who has been kept with the Trojan captives. He claims she is to be punished

---

[85] Commentaries: Lee 1976, Barlow 1986; select studies: Scodel 1980, Lloyd 1984, Gregory 1986, Griffith 1990, Croally 1994, Meridor 2000.

when she reaches home. Helen asks to be allowed to defend herself, and Hecuba encourages this, so they deliver a pair of contradictory speeches on motivations and responsibility for the war. The body of Astyanax is brought to Hecuba to prepare for burial, and she laments her grandson. Finally, Hecuba and the chorus are summoned to go to the ships for departure, as the city is fired in the distance.

Iphigenia in Tauris[86] (estimated performance date *ca.* 414) opens with Iphigenia explaining that while all the Greeks believe she was sacrificed at Aulis she was actually spirited away by Artemis and has been serving in a temple of Artemis in the land of the Taurians (on the Crimean peninsula in the north of the Black Sea), acting as a priestess in a cult involving human sacrifice of all strangers captured by the Taurians. She tells of an ominous dream that the audience can recognize as symbolizing the woes of her family in Argos up to the death of Clytemnestra, but she interprets it as meaning her younger brother Orestes is now dead and she will never be able to send him a message to rescue her. When she returns inside temporarily, Orestes and Pylades appear, and the audience learn that Orestes is on a mission commanded by Apollo to take the statue of Artemis from here back to Greece. They do not see an easy way to accomplish this and go back to the shore to await darkness. The chorus of female temple servants arrives and joins Iphigenia in lamentation for Orestes. A herdsman comes to advise Iphigenia that two new victims are to be brought to her and describes their capture (the audience understands they are Orestes and Pylades). When the captives arrive, she interrogates them about affairs in Greece and Argos (and learns that Orestes is not dead after all), but both she and Orestes conceal their true identity. She agrees to let one captive live and return home if he takes a written message to her relatives. After an argument between the friends, it is determined that Pylades will go free and Orestes stay to die. In the conveyance of the letter to Pylades, Iphigenia is induced to recite the contents and the recognition of brother and sister results. They devise a scheme for escape with the statue, with Iphigenia convincing the king that the captives have polluted the statue with their blood-guilt and that the statue and the captives need to be purified in sea-water. A messenger brings back word of the effort of the Greeks to escape and of the possibility that it will fail. As the king prepares to muster forces to recapture the Greeks, Athena appears to stop him and explain what lies ahead for Orestes, Iphigenia, and the statue of Artemis.

---

[86] Commentaries: Cropp 2000, Kyriakou 2006; select studies: Burnett 1971: 47–72, Whitman 1974: 1–34, Mastronarde 1986, Wolff 1992, Wright 2005.

Ion[87] (estimated performance date *ca.* 414) opens with Hermes explaining the secret background: the Athenian princess Creusa was once raped in a cave on the Acropolis by Apollo and concealed her pregnancy and child-birth, leaving the newborn in the cave. The baby was spirited away to Delphi, where he has grown into an adolescent serving as a temple slave at the oracle of his father. Creusa has feared that the baby was killed by wild animals. Creusa and her husband Xuthus (a non-Athenian brought into the family because of his military prowess) have come to consult this oracle (and another) about their lack of offspring. As the lost son is sweeping the temple steps, the chorus of slave women of the Athenian royal house gazes at the decoration of the temple. Creusa arrives and establishes an immediate rapport with the boy, but he advises her not to make an embarrassing enquiry to the god about "a friend" who says she had a baby by him. Xuthus arrives and reports that another oracle he visited on the way declared that they would have offspring. He enters the temple and Creusa departs to pray at altars elsewhere in Delphi. The oracle of Apollo tells Xuthus that the first person he meets on leaving the temple is Xuthus' son, and he meets Creusa's lost son, who after some hesitation accepts his new identity as Xuthus' son and receives the name Ion. When Creusa returns to the scene, the chorus tell her what has happened. She feels betrayed and reveals the secret of her childbirth long ago. With the encouragement of an old family retainer, she plans to kill Ion before he can go to Athens and usurp her house. The old man is sent to poison Ion's cup at the great banquet he is hosting to mark his new status and departure from Delphi. A messenger soon reports that the murder plot has failed and that Ion has found out that Creusa was behind it and has had her condemned to death by local authorities. Creusa takes refuge at the altar when Ion comes to arrest her. Ion is considering wresting her violently from her asylum when the priestess emerges from the temple and gives Ion the items that were with him when he arrived at Delphi as a baby. These serve as recognition tokens for mother and son to acknowledge each other. Ion is about to enter the temple to make certain of the truth by asking Apollo when Athena appears above and reveals the glorious future of the descendants of Creusa and Ion.

Helen[88] (known performance date 412) exploits an alternative tradition that Helen herself never went to Troy, but was safeguarded in Egypt by Proteus

[87] Commentaries: Lee 1997; select studies: Burnett 1962 and 1971: 101–29, Whitman 1974: 69–103, Mastronarde 1975, Zeitlin 1989, Loraux 1990, Lee 1996, Zacharia 2003.
[88] Commentaries: Kannicht 1969, Allan 2008; select studies: Solmsen 1934, Zuntz 1960, Burnett 1960 and 1971: 76–100, Segal 1971, Wolff 1973, Whitman 1974: 35–68, Seidensticker 1982: 153–99, Foley 2001: 301–31, Wright 2003.

during the Trojan War. Helen explains in the prologue that Hera foiled Paris by providing an image of Helen to be fought over at Troy while Helen herself was carried to Egypt by Hermes. She is now claiming asylum at the tomb of Proteus outside the Egyptian royal palace because Proteus' son Theoclymenus, the new king, wants to marry her against her will. She has been saving herself for Menelaus, since the gods told her she would eventually be reunited with him, and she hopes to return to Greece to clear her name of the shame that has been heaped upon it because of the Trojan War. To stop Menelaus from recovering Helen, Theoclymenus has ordered that all Greeks landing in Egypt be killed. Teucer, brother of Ajax, exiled from his home by their father, arrives hoping to consult Proteus' daughter, the prophetess Theonoe, about the new home he is supposed to found on Cyprus. In a conversation that shows the confusion of identity caused by the phantom, he makes it clear how much Helen is hated by all and tells Helen that Menelaus is believed to be dead. Helen laments for Menelaus with the accompaniment of the chorus of enslaved Greek women captives. Helen accepts the suggestion that she ask the prophetess whether Menelaus is really dead, and the chorus goes inside with her. Menelaus arrives on the empty stage, explains his long wanderings and recent shipwreck and appeals for aid from the palace. An unhelpful slave woman answers his knock, warns him of the danger to him from Theoclymenus, and tells him Helen is in the palace (which he finds incredible). Helen and the chorus return from the palace, and a recognition between husband and wife is frustrated by Menelaus' conviction that he has the true Helen in the phantom he fought for at Troy, whom he left with his shipmates at the shore. A messenger from his shipmates tells him the phantom Helen has just announced its true (false) nature and disappeared, and so he accepts that the Helen before him is his wife. Theonoe emerges and the two Greeks plead with her to conceal Menelaus' identity from her brother. She agrees to do so in order to uphold the commitment her father made and not to abet her brother's injustice. The couple then deceives Theoclymenus by claiming that Menelaus has died at sea and that Helen is now ready to marry Theoclymenus if he allows her first to perform funeral rites at sea for Menelaus. Theoclymenus provides a ship, the shipwrecked Greeks commandeer it and sail home. Theoclymenus wants to punish his sister for helping their deception of him, but the Dioscuri appear to stop him.

Phoenissae[89] (estimated performance date *ca.* 411–409) presents the events surrounding the attack of the Seven against Thebes. Jocasta, who in this

---

[89] Commentaries: Craik 1988, Mastronarde 1994, Medda 2006; select studies: Rawson 1970, Arthur 1977, Foley 1985: 112–32, Saïd 1985, Mueller-Goldingen 1985.

version did not commit suicide on learning Oedipus' identity, explains the background in the prologue. Her sons Eteocles and Polyneices had made an agreement to alternate year by year in ruling Thebes, but once on the throne Eteocles reneged and Polyneices married the daughter of Adrastus of Argos and now, with his help, is attacking Thebes. Jocasta has arranged a truce so that she may try to reconcile her sons without a battle. The young Antigone appears on the roof of the palace with a servant to be shown the Argive army in the distance and especially to spot her exiled brother. Polyneices enters, Jocasta sings an emotional aria to welcome him, then inquires about his experiences in exile. Eteocles then joins them, and the negotiation turns into a set debate with two sharply opposed speeches and a third speech by Jocasta urging her sons to relent. They do not, but instead broach the idea of meeting face to face in the battle. In the next scene Creon and Eteocles consult, and Creon advises his nephew to place champions to lead the forces at each gate, while Eteocles gives instructions for the future in case the curse of Oedipus is fulfilled and both brothers die. Creon then receives the prophet Teiresias to learn whether there is an oracle that will help the city win the battle. Teiresias says that Creon's youngest son Menoceus is the only eligible descendent of the Sown Men (born when Cadmus planted the teeth of the dragon he had slain) who can satisfy a divine demand for a human sacrifice to save Thebes. Creon refuses to let his son be sacrificed, but the boy deceives his father and goes to sacrifice himself. A messenger brings news to Jocasta that the main assault of the Argives has been repulsed and most of their leaders killed, but now Eteocles and Polyneices are about to duel each other to settle their quarrel. Jocasta calls Antigone out to join her in trying to stop the duel. Creon comes to fetch Jocasta to help in the funeral of Menoeceus, but she is already gone, and a second messenger now describes the duel, the death of the two brothers, and the suicide of Jocasta over their corpses. Antigone enters with the bodies, singing a lament, and calls Oedipus from the house to hear the news. Creon intervenes to say that Oedipus must go into exile, Polyneices be left unburied, and Antigone marry his surviving son Haemon. Antigone objects, but Creon does not yield on the first two points, although he allows Antigone to renounce the marriage and accompany Oedipus in exile.

Orestes[90] (known performance date 408) presents an innovative view of the immediate aftermath of the killing of Aegisthus and Clytemnestra by Orestes. Orestes has fallen ill from madness induced by the Furies, and the

---

[90] Commentaries: Willink 1986, West 1987, Medda 2001; select studies: Reinhardt 1957 and 2003, Wolff 1968, Burnett 1971: 183–222, Porter 1994, Zeitlin 2003, Griffith 2009.

Argive community is angry about the matricide and is about to try the perpetrators. Orestes is asleep on his sickbed in public before the palace, tended by his sister, who explains the desperate situation in the prologue. Menelaus has returned to Greece just the night before; Helen is already in the palace, and he is expected to arrive soon. Helen emerges to ask Electra to carry offerings to Clytemnestra's tomb on her behalf, but Electra points out how inappropriate this is and suggests that Helen's young daughter Hermione be sent instead, and this is done. Sympathetic women from the neighborhood arrive as the chorus. Orestes awakens, is momentarily lucid, and then believes he is being attacked by Furies and acts out warding them off before regaining his normal state of mind. Electra is sent indoors to rest. In the next episode, Menelaus arrives and Orestes begins to appeal for his help when his grandfather Tyndareus arrives on the scene, reviling Orestes and threatening Menelaus if he should try to save Orestes from punishment. Orestes now defends his actions at length to Tyndareus, and after the old man leaves, makes a fuller appeal to Menelaus for help, but Menelaus is evasive and departs. Pylades arrives, having been exiled by his father, and with his help Orestes heads off to the Argive assembly that will consider his case. When Electra returns from inside at the start of the next episode, a messenger arrives to describe the course of the assembly meeting and the verdict of death by suicide for Orestes and Electra. After the chorus and Electra sing a lamentation of this doom, Orestes and Pylades return. After agreeing on a group suicide, the three decide to make Menelaus suffer too and to kill Helen and use Hermione as a hostage to force Menelaus to save them. Hermione returns and is seized. A Phrygian eunuch from Helen's retinue emerges to deliver a lyric report of the confusing events within (Helen was attacked, but seems to have disappeared). Orestes comes out to scare the eunuch back into the palace. In the finale Menelaus arrives and finds Orestes on the roof with a sword at Hermione's neck and Pylades carrying a torch. Their argument breaks down and Orestes orders the firing of the palace, but Apollo arrives on the crane, showing that Helen has been saved and is being made immortal, and he arranges for Orestes to be released from the death sentence and married to Hermione.

Bacchae[91] (known performance date 405, one year after Euripides' death) presents the prototypical myth of the arrival of Dionysiac worship despite the opposition of a resisting king. Dionysus speaks the prologue, explaining that he has adopted the disguise of a human male leader of a band of

[91] Commentaries: Dodds 1960, Roux 1970–72, Seaford 2001; select studies: Segal 1982 and 2001, Oranje 1984, Foley 1985: 205–58, Seaford 1981 and 1994: 288–301 et passim, Lienieks 1996.

bacchants from Asia Minor who are spreading Dionysiac worship in
Greece. When the Theban princess Semele, daughter of Cadmus, was
pregnant with him, her sisters (Ino, Agave, and Autonoe) denied that the
father was Zeus, and now the young king of Thebes, Pentheus, son of
Agave, denies the new god. But the women of Thebes (including Cadmus'
daughters) have been driven from the city by Dionysiac possession. The
chorus consists of Asian bacchants. In the first episode, the aged prophet
Teiresias arrives to fetch old Cadmus so that they can go dance on the
mountains in honor of the new god Dionysus. Pentheus appears and argues
with them and receives futile warnings. In the next episode the disguised
god is brought on as a captive; Pentheus taunts him, but the god holds his
own in the verbal sparring. After the prisoner is taken inside, the rumbling
of an earthquake is heard, and the disguised god reappears free of his bonds,
reassures the chorus, and waits for the confused and frustrated Pentheus to
come out. A herdsman arrives to describe wondrous events on the mountain, where Pentheus' aunts and the rest of the women of Thebes are
worshipping Dionysus. Pentheus thinks of mustering his army against the
women, but Dionysus persuades him to go alone as a spy upon the
maenads. Pentheus is dressed up as a woman, his mind now controlled by
the god, and he is led away to the mountain by Dionysus. A messenger
reports the tearing apart of Pentheus by his mother and the other women.
Agave, still frenzied, enters with the head of Pentheus on her Dionysiac
wand. Cadmus arrives with the pieces of Pentheus' body that have been
recovered. He helps Agave recover her grip on reality, and they mourn for
Pentheus. Dionysus appears on high as a true god and directs Cadmus and
Agave into separate exiles.

Iphigenia in Aulis[92] (performed posthumously in 405 along with *Bacchae*)
is a problematic text. It appears that the play was incomplete at the time of
Euripides' death and was variously supplemented by producers and actors.[93]
The situation at the outset is that when the Greek expedition intended for
the punishment of Troy was blocked from departure from its assembly
point at Aulis (on the shore of Boeotia opposite Euboea), Agamemnon had

[92] Commentaries: Stockert 1992; select studies: Page 1934, Foley 1985: 65–105, Gibert 1995: 202–55 and
2005, Michelini 1999–2000.
[93] The beginning and end of the play are particularly problematic. The prologue as we have it seems to
be a clumsy conflation of two alternatives, both of which may be post-Euripidean. The last fifty lines
of the extant text shows signs of composition in late antiquity, and the lines that precede these are
unlikely to be by Euripides. There is indirect attestation of a different ending in which the goddess
Artemis appeared. For recent approaches to the difficult task of judging what may or may not be
original, see Günther 1988, Stockert 1992, Diggle 1981–1994: vol. III, Kovacs 1994–2002: vol. VI; Page
1934 is the most important older study.

consented to the sacrifice of his daughter Iphigenia in response to an oracle and had sent a secret message to Argos telling his wife Clytemnestra to send Iphigenia alone to Aulis to be married to Achilles. Agamemnon had then regretted this decision and attempts to send a second letter countermanding the first one. The chorus consists of women visiting from Chalkis to see the spectacle of the Greek army and has limited interaction with the characters. Menelaus stops the messenger carrying Agamemnon's second letter to his wife, reads it, and comes to confront his brother. During their argument about their respective behavior and the propriety of the sacrifice of Iphigenia, a report arrives that Iphigenia is now about to arrive and that Clytemnestra is with her, and Agamemnon concludes the sacrifice is now inevitable. He conceals the truth when greeting his wife and daughter and leaves the scene. Achilles, unaware of the use of his name for the deception about a marriage, arrives seeking Agamemnon and is greeted instead by Clytemnestra. The confusion between Achilles and Clytemnestra is removed when the old man who had tried to carry the second letter tells them the true situation. Clytemnestra supplicates Achilles for his protection of Iphigenia. In the next episode Clytemnestra, with Iphigenia by her side, confronts Agamemnon about his deception, and Iphigenia at first begs to be spared. Agamemnon says this cannot be done and departs again. Achilles arrives in haste to report that the Greeks now all demand the sacrifice and threaten even him if he tries to stop it. Iphigenia interrupts the agitated dialogue of Achilles and Clytemnestra to declare that she has decided to agree to the sacrifice in order to make the expedition possible and to win glory for herself. She departs for sacrifice. From that point, it is not known how Euripides intended to end the play.

CHAPTER 2

Problems of genre

GENRE: EXPECTATIONS, VARIETY, AND CHANGE

From the humorous perspective of Aristophanes' *Frogs*, a critic might say
that Euripides changed tragedy in various ways: among them, he put
tragedy on a diet (939–44), democratized tragedy (948–51), eroticized
tragedy (849–50, 1043–51, 1078–81, 1301–2, 1327–8), feminized tragedy
(949–50, 1043–52), trivialized tragedy (976–91, 1203, 1331–63), rhetoricized
tragedy (841, 892, 954, 1069–71, 1084–6), sophisticized tragedy (892–4,
1471–8, 1491–9). These claims address the ways that Euripides stretched
and deformed traditional aspects of language, tone, structure, and content
in the tragic genre, and these aspects are often the same ones targeted from
postclassical antiquity to the present by critics who exploit the concept of
literary genres either to complain that Euripides has often failed to write
"genuine tragedy" or to gain, in a less judgmental fashion, a fuller appreciation of the variety of Euripides' work. The present chapter is intended to
explore some of the problems of definition and perspective that bedevil
criticism of this kind and to point out the difficulty, and occasional futility,
of trying to apply strict genre terms to the ancient plays.

Before embarking on this topic, it is necessary to consider briefly a prior
question, whether the whole enterprise of genre-criticism is outmoded and
misleading, a relic of an approach that isolates the literary product from the
social, political, and ideological contexts in which it is embedded. As
scholars have become more attuned to the role of tragedy in constructing
the identity of the Athenian citizen, in solidifying the consciousness of
Greekness, maleness, and freedom by exploration of the "other," and in
negotiating the power relations between elites and mass,[1] some have deliberately turned away from an interest in the formal and literary aspects.
There are several reasons, however, why a broader cultural and ideological

---

[1] See for example Goldhill 1986, Winkler and Zeitlin 1990, Griffith 1995, Zeitlin 1996, Cartledge 1997,
Hall 1997.

awareness does not render such an interest obsolete. First, the practice and craft of drama follow a detectable trajectory of increasing professionalization and specialization. Even if we could agree about the perennially disputed origins of tragedy[2] and about how the ideological functions of the rituals and performances of the Great Dionysia were related to the foundation and consolidation of Athenian democracy,[3] and even if we recognize significant political/ideological implications in Aeschylus' *Persae* and *Oresteia* or Sophocles' *Antigone*, it does not follow that these insights are generalizable across the full range of plays and the full course of the fifth century. Theater in the second half of the fifth century was in the process of becoming a partially autonomous institution, pursuing its own interests independent of the imperatives of the city-state, the Great Dionysia, and the Athenian democracy.[4] Second, the playwrights themselves were involved in a competition for attention, authority, and honor of the same sort that had characterized poetry and performance for many generations. To establish their claim, they had to display *sophia* in all its aspects, including manipulation of formal features, artistic embellishments and innovations, and other marks of superior craftsmanship. Third, tragedy's use of mythological subject-matter already bespeaks a transposition of focus from the immediate to the distant, from the particular to the general, and thus opens a space for universalizing concerns such as genre-criticism often entails. Fourth, the testimony of Gorgias, Aristophanes, Plato, and Aristotle indicates that for the audience of the later fifth century, at least, tragic art could be judged in aesthetic and formal terms as well as in other ways; and notwithstanding the distortions caused by Aristophanes' comic stance, by Plato's disapproval of emotion and his rejection of the untidiness of traditional theology, and by Aristotle's virtual elision of the chorus and the gods and his preference for transparent and univocal causation, these witnesses cannot all have been completely blind to the nature and roles of fifth-century tragedy. If some critics of the nineteenth and twentieth centuries made the error of exaggerating the "literary" side of Greek tragedy, this does not justify our falling into the opposite extreme of recognizing only a "non-literary" (political and social) side.

The concept of literary genre, however, is itself problematic, and has been explored in literary and aesthetic theory, especially in comparative literature,

---

[2] The latest major contributions in this field are Sourvinou-Inwood 2003 and several papers in Csapo and Miller 2007a, especially Csapo and Miller 2007b, Kowalzig 2007, Seaford 2007.

[3] See pages 15–20 above.

[4] See, for instance, Taplin 1993 and 2007, Easterling 1994, Kurke 1998; for material on the long history of theatrical institutions see Pickard-Cambridge 1988, Csapo and Slater 1995.

for the past century.[5] One of the useful outcomes of these debates is the recognition of the different uses served by the concept of genre. For the reader or critic situated in the present, genre has an important retrospective function. One looks back over centuries, or millennia, studying literary productions of many languages and societies. In part one may engage in a process of inventory and classification that continues the activities of Aristotle, the Alexandrian librarians, and the late antique rhetorical theorists.[6] The map of genres and species and subspecies demonstrates the variety of human creativity, world-views, and social matrices. All of this need not be problematic. But retrospective comparison may also lead to the establishment of a global category such as "tragedy" or "the tragic," whose primary purpose is perhaps to characterize a distinct world-view, but which secondarily becomes a tool to identify great or idealized specimens and to winnow out or condemn the deviant.

The retrospective approach tends toward a narrowing of focus and a greater clarity of specification. Aristotle gives some impetus to this trend in the prescriptive parts of his *Poetics* and in his interest in the "best kind" of tragedy, but we find coexisting in his study of tragedy a balancing element of descriptiveness. He acknowledges considerable variety, he explicitly says that a change of fortune in tragedy may be either from good to bad or from bad to good, and he makes room for (or leaves unreconciled) inconsistent alternative hierarchies. The anonymous postclassical critics who made negative judgments on the "happy" endings of *Alcestis* and *Orestes* as other than tragic[7] show, however, a fuller commitment to a simplified and narrow definition. Among twentieth-century English-speaking literary critics of Euripides, Kitto and Conacher both show a strong commitment to pursuing their respective classificatory schemes by genres or subgenres, although the degree of sympathy for Euripides' projects is notably greater in the work of Conacher.[8] For critics of a philosophical bent, especially those under the

---

[5] See for instance Guillén 1971: Chapter 4, "On the Uses of Literary Genre"; Rosenmeyer 1985; Vietor 1986; Genette 1986; Conte 1994: Chapter 4, "Genre between Empiricism and Theory"; Barchiesi 2001; Fantuzzi 2004.

[6] E.g., Frye 1957.

[7] In the hypothesis to *Orestes* we read "the play has a conclusion that is more comic" (κωμικωτέραν ἔχει τὴν καταστροφήν), while in that of *Alcestis* we find "the drama is more satyr-play-like because it ends in joy and pleasure contrary to the tragic mode. Both *Orestes* and *Alcestis* are excluded as inappropriate to tragic poetry, since they begin in misfortune but end in happiness and joy, which are more characteristic of comedy" (τὸ δὲ δρᾶμά ἐστι σατυρικώτερον ὅτι εἰς χαρὰν καὶ ἡδονὴν καταστρέφει παρὰ τὸ τραγικόν. [Leo: τοῖς τραγικοῖς V] ἐκβάλλεται ὡς ἀνοίκεια τῆς τραγικῆς ποιήσεως ὅ τε Ὀρέστης καὶ ἡ Ἄλκηστις, ὡς ἐκ συμφορᾶς μὲν ἀρχόμενα, εἰς εὐδαιμονίαν ⟨δὲ⟩ καὶ χαρὰν λήξαντα, ⟨ἅ⟩ ἐστι μᾶλλον κωμῳδίας ἐχόμενα). See n. 34 below.

[8] Kitto 1961 (the first edition was published in 1936); Conacher 1967. Compare also Burnett 1971.

influence of Hegel and of the literary history developed within the German Romantic movement by the Schlegels and others, "tragedy" often becomes a transcultural ideal form, fixed and stable and seemingly epistemologically prior to the works in which it is instantiated. This idealization has been remarkably persistent and still underlies many offhand assessments of scenes, characters, and plays.[9] But the relationship of particular works to a generic category is no longer universally viewed in this way. Instead, instability, dynamism, and indeterminacy have entered the picture. Critics have acknowledged the hermeneutic circle in which the particular works and the generic category are bound; and it is also recognized that definitions may admit the notion of peripheral as well as central features, and the Wittgensteinian idea of definition by "family resemblance" is sometimes invoked.[10]

The other perspective we may apply to considerations of genre is a temporally embedded or prospective one. As often with Greek genres, students of Greek tragedy are positioned in the early phases of what turned out to be a long development in Western and world literature. There is justifiably a lively scholarly interest in the traditions of reception, translation, imitation, adaptation, and appropriation of Greek plays, but I do not accept the view that there is for the literature of the past only a succession of different, equally valid moments of reception. As students of the ancient world we ought, in my view, also to be especially interested in the original context of production, performance, and reception. Not merely for the fairness of our literary criticism of the individual author or text, but also for any approach to understanding the place of Greek tragedy in the cultural dynamics of the Athenian polis and the wider Greek world of the period, we need to consider the "horizon of expectations"[11] shared by the playwrights and the audience – for this is the essence of genre in this temporally embedded perspective. Guillén speaks of genre as "provocation," as the background or context in which each writer explores the vitality and the limits of a form. The genre is thus a (slowly) moving target, a work in progress, not a fixed and rigid form. This is especially true in the Greek tradition, where poets emulate and rival authoritative inventors of various models and feel free to extend and vary what they find in the tradition.[12]

---

[9] For the persistence of the axiom of "the tragic" see Most 2000.
[10] Guillén 1971: 130–1, citing Elliott 1962: 23.
[11] This term derives from the reader-response theories of H. R. Jauss and W. Iser, in which genre-expectations are part of a larger matrix of socio-historical backgrounds shared by author and reader: e.g. Jauss 1982: 88–9, Iser 1978: 96–103, 111–13.
[12] Rosenmeyer 1985.

In recent years, scholars have demonstrated that the Greek musical tradition had a long history of experiment and innovation. The claim that at a certain moment Greek music was stable and simple and "natural" and then became corrupted reflects a particular ideological perspective in a contestation of cultural values.[13] The same long history of continuous experiment and change must apply to tragedy as well. Sophocles and Euripides and a good portion of their audience in any specific year in the second half of the fifth century had themselves lived through changes in the style, construction, performance, and physical setting of tragedy. Furthermore, tragedy was embedded in multiple systems that promoted change and experimentation. In the widest context of the Greek poetic tradition, especially those parts that featured mythic narration, all poets were engaged in a contest for authority, a competition of *sophia* involving the adaptive interpretation and extrapolation of a multiform tradition.[14] In the more local context, the Athenian democracy of the fifth century was a constantly evolving experiment, a society in which citizens were free to propose that things be done differently than before, that new procedures be developed to face new conditions and new opportunities. Finally, in the narrower context of the tragic festivals, competition itself must also have been a spur to constant innovation and differentiation.

The *Frogs* may give the impression that people – or some particular persons – had a clear idea of what tragedy should be and that Euripides was not meeting the standard. Yet Aristophanes' comedy, here as elsewhere, relies on stark contrasts that facilitate parody and sharpen humor. The simplifications that occur in comic debates are not far removed from those that are prevalent in contemporary "hot-button" cultural debates manipulated by political parties, where it is in the interest of one or both antagonists to pretend that an issue is clearer or a definition more narrow than it is in the actual usage of the society as a whole. In addition, the very concept of the classical, of perfect harmony, balance, and decorum, of the uniformly *spoudaion* ("serious, valuable"), is a construction created to satisfy certain needs and to contest alternative views. It is often a mirage, a retrojection into the past of the desire for order (often for hierarchy) felt by those who feel acutely its lack in their present. As Selden has noted in another connection, an emphasis on fixed boundaries and clarity of definition is in fact a polemical stance, an insistence that literary production mirror the hoped-for stability of a fixed social order and thus reinforce that order.[15]

---

[13] See, e.g., Csapo 1999–2000 and 2004a, Wilson 1999 and 2003.   [14] See, e.g., Griffith 1990.
[15] Selden 1994. For an earlier consideration of the trap of devotion to the classical, see Johnson 1970.

Aristophanes is engaged in such a polemic in *Frogs*. In a remarkable passage in Plato's *Laws* (700–1) we find a similar wishful retrojection: the Athenian speaker projects on the Athens of the age before Salamis a parallel regimentation of social discipline and musical types, and decries the mutual deterioration and indiscriminate contamination that, in the age after Salamis, affected both the social order and the purity and tastefulness of music. Modern critics who assume too clear a notion of what is "true" tragedy and what is not risk replicating this contrived image of the purity of the genre.

Tragedy, at least as we know it in the fifth century, is inherently a genre of varied form and content. The iambic dialogue sections in relatively short alternating speeches are essentially *sui generis*, although one can find some affinity to earlier poetic forms (short dialogue exchanges in Homer and choral lyric).[16] Of the longer forms of iambic speeches, the narrative passages may exploit the associations of hexameter epic narrative, while the first-person speeches of self-justification, argument, and analysis may recall the Solonic branch of the iambic tradition as well as the more extensive speeches of argument and persuasion (often in pairs) in Homer. The anapaestic and choral parts, however, borrow from or appropriate other genres, such as processional, hymn, formal lament, epinician, wedding-song, etc. What has been identified as the occasional self-referentiality of the tragic chorus, that is, allusion to itself as a body of citizens performing ritual song, depends on the recognition by the theater-audience that the tragic performance alludes to and adapts other kinds of performance in festival and cult.[17] The "dithyrambic"-style odes[18] of late Euripides need not be viewed as a genre-violation, but simply as a new adaptation and extension of pre-existing tendencies in the choral voice. Even the actual *embolima* (choral interludes without relation to the particular plot) of Agathon and later tragic poets may not have struck their audience as a generic boundary violation. Just as we speak of intertextuality to describe the competitive and appropriative stance of different texts within a poetic tradition, so too we may recognize inter-generic play in tragedy not as a violation that marks an abandonment of a fixed genre, but as a key element of the living and changing genre.[19]

---

[16] Compare passages like *Odyssey* 8.382–468 and the opening to the dialogue of Heracles and Meleager in Bacchylides 5.79–92, or the possible conversation in Sappho fr. 137 L–P (if the statement and reply are actually from the same poem).

[17] See especially Henrichs 1994–95.   [18] See below, p. 151 n. 123.

[19] Compare Del Corno 1995. Goldhill 1986: Ch. 10, "Genre and Transgression," relates the variety of tones and genre-features in Euripidean tragedy to the notions of a fractured self and fractured society and to problematics of language and values, and he emphasizes the effect of making the audience aware of itself and of conventions, in the Brechtian manner.

If we imagine ourselves into the position of a member of the audience at the Great Dionysia in the second half of the fifth century, how in fact do we recognize what we see as a tragedy, and what might provoke in us the reaction that something violates the genre or perceptibly suggests to us a different genre? In the archaic and classical period many Greek poetic genres are defined clearly by occasion as well as internal features. An audience recognizes a tragedy by its place in the festival program, by the costumes and masks of the characters and chorus (and perhaps often by the painted decor), by the formality of the language and meter of the iambics, by the mythological identity of the principal characters, by the presence of the chorus (and their accompanying *aulētēs* or piper) and the alternation of episodes and choral songs. Few of these markers show significant variation over time or between different tragedies. If we compare Aeschylus' *Septem* of 467 and Euripides' *Helen* of 412 in these regards, the principal differences are in the relatively minor changes in language and meter. There is some distance between the grandeur and weight of Aeschylus' iambic style and the Euripidean style, lightened by more ordinary words, some prosaic and some colloquial, and by the relative relaxation of the trimeter through frequent resolutions. Yet tragic style is still recognizable as such, and quite different from that of comedy. Metrically, the formality of Porson's Law and the requirement of caesura are maintained, and even the Euripidean resolutions do not go so far as the "split resolutions" or "anapaestic substitutions" permitted in comedy.[20] Verbally, word-order and syntax and morphology are differentiated from those of everyday speech, and metaphor is exploited in the way that is traditional in high-style poetry. And despite some colloquialisms admitted into tragedy by Euripides, even in *Helen* the style is immediately distinct from that of Old Comedy and from actual colloquial spoken Attic. Similarly, in costuming, the occasional "hero in rags" (a device as old as Aeschylus' *Persae* of 472, where Xerxes' tattered garb is a physical display of his defeat and loss of stature) may not be as impressive a sight as the hero in military garb or kingly robes, but the tragic actor is still obviously distinct – generically distinct – from the comic actor with his padding and phallos, and the tragic chorus is likewise distinct from both the comic chorus and the satyr-chorus.

---

[20] Porson's Law strongly limits the occurrence of word-end after the 9th element of the iambic trimeter if it is a long syllable. Caesura is the obligatory word break after the 5th or 7th element of the line (or rarely after the 6th if there is an elision of what would have been the 7th element). A split resolution is the substitution of two short syllables that are parts of separate words for one long element. An anapaestic substitution is the substitution of two short syllables for one short element, which is restricted to proper names in tragedy but is allowed also with common nouns in comedy.

From the perspective of archaic and classical poetry and its audiences, the most important discrimination was not based on plot-type or story-pattern so much as on social and ethical valence, high vs. low, serious (*spoudaion*) vs. non-serious (*phaulon* or *geloion*), the fundamental dichotomy that Aristotle sees as essential to the understanding of the development and nature of tragedy and comedy.[21] The world of myth provided that serious subject-matter. Through many generations of the poetic tradition, the high-style poets – both the composers of epic recitations and of the hexameter hymns and the professional authors of lyric processionals, maiden-songs, wedding-songs, dirges, and the like (who developed the option of incorporating mythic narrative), that is, from Arion and Stesichorus to Simonides and Pindar and the early poets of tragedy – had a wide range of mythic narrative available to them and were also capable of creating new stories. Myth provided both negative and positive exempla, and the mixture of blessing and curse, divine favor and divine rancor, triumph and failure was present in many myths and acceptable in many poetic contexts, since such mixture was a prime characteristic of the Greek conception of human life and of the role of the gods in it. Thus, even if tragedy actually had some original connection to mourning or to extreme suffering or to the anxieties of sacrificial killing or to rituals of the arrival of Dionysus and wine,[22] the poetic traditions amidst which and from which it grew allowed an expansive openness to heroic myth of many kinds. Even if we speculate that, in a period of twenty-five years or so embracing the 430s and 420s, tragedy was in its clearest condition of polarity *vis-à-vis* comedy, as Taplin once argued,[23] and thus showed a strong bias toward tales of destruction and disaster, tragedy's relation to heroic myth ensured that there was also room for stories of achievement, foundation, restoration, rescue, and happy recognition. To put it another way, the *Odyssey*, from the perspective of the fifth century, is a proper model for tragedy because of the social and

[21] *Poetics* 4.1448b24–49a6 διεσπάσθη δὲ κατὰ τὰ οἰκεῖα ἤθη ἡ ποίησις κτλ. ("Poetic composition was split into two in accordance with the composers' own character etc."). I take this to be an important insight even though what Aristotle says cannot have been based on any historical data, but represents instead a theoretical (or one might say "prehistoric") analysis of the history of Greek poetic forms.
[22] The frequent presence of lamentations in tragedy invited the long-abandoned view of tragedy's origin in lamentations for a year-spirit (see the famous critique of Pickard-Cambridge 1927). A possible connection between hero-cult and the commemoration of the sufferings of heroes has been seen in the remark of Herodotus 5.67 that before the tyranny of Cleisthenes the Sicyonians "honored the sufferings of Adrastus with tragic choruses." Burkert 1966 gives the classic exposition relating tragedy to sacrificial ritual. Two quite different modern derivations of tragedy from Dionysiac worship are offered by Seaford 1994 and Sourvinou-Inwood 2003; see also the important discussions in Csapo and Miller 2007a.
[23] Taplin 1986.

ethical level of the main characters. Only from a later perspective is it also to be viewed as a model for comedy, and this applies only when the plot-mechanisms and story-patterns have been transferred to non-heroic characters and the high-style elements have been removed.

Two aspects of Euripides' work have received the most attention when critics speak of his stretching, abandoning, or even "destroying" the traditional genre. First, the unevenness of tone and the mixture of levels of style are contrasted with a putative classical form of tragedy in which these elements are more uniform. This is the basis of many of Aristophanes' comic critiques.[24] Second, many ancient and modern critics have a strong inclination to identify "true tragedy" with the portrayal of a disastrous event affecting a basically sympathetic character and so seek contrasting terms to deal with plots with "happy endings" or "mixed reversals." But both in style and in plot-types, we are scarcely in a secure position to determine the exact degree of Euripidean innovation, because of the loss of so much of the contemporary work that formed the context.

Of the more than 1,000 tragedies produced at the Great Dionysia and the Lenaea in Athens in the fifth century,[25] we have a decent level of knowledge of at most 5 percent. The devastating gaps in our knowledge of the contents of Sophocles' lost plays are an insuperable obstacle to any confidence about the fixity or variability of the concept "Sophoclean tragedy": how would our belief in the centrality of the "heroic temper" of the "Sophoclean hero" be affected if we had his *Aegeus, Andromeda, Atreus,* and *Tereus*? Without such knowledge, any generalization about tragedy in the second half of the fifth century must be hedged with caution, if not in fact abjured. It is, of course, possible that Sophocles was indeed the master of "classicism" and that his dramatic style over a long period of time represented a high consistency of tone, of seriousness, and of dramatic illusion. This fits the late antique view of the perfection of Sophocles' art reflected in the scholia and in the *Life of Aeschylus*,[26] a view that feeds into and is elaborated in the views of German classicism around 1800. It is also the basis of Ann Michelini's attractive interpretation of Euripidean dramaturgy as deliberately "anti-Sophoclean." But it is also possible that Sophocles' work was always more varied than the classicizing tradition

---

[24] On the other hand, Aristotle praises the "naturalness" and "concealment of art" in Euripides' poetic style (*Rhetoric* 3.1405b5–25), and the "smoothness" of his style is commented on by some later authors (T172b, 173, 179, 180 Kannicht).

[25] For this calculation, see Ch. 1 n. 69.

[26] See also Dionysius of Halicarnassus, *de imitatione* II fr. 6.2.10–11 (T146 Kannicht = *TrGF* IV T120) and Dio Chrysostomus *Orat.* 52.15 (T148 Kannicht = *TrGF* IV T123). Dionysius in particular espouses a "classicizing" approach to the authors of the past (p. 8 above).

indicates, that is, that it was not just in late plays such as *Philoctetes* and *Oedipus Coloneus* that he produced works of a very different spirit and construction from *Antigone* and *Oedipus Tyrannus*, the plays that have had such a normative role in shaping the conception of tragedy favored by many critics and most modern readers and viewers. Likewise, it may be that lost tragedies by other contemporary authors also reflected a greater variety, but unfortunately we know nothing really useful about the content and plots of the contemporaries of Aeschylus and early/middle Sophocles. We are thus unable to judge to what degree the neat classicizing arc of development and decline may be a mirage. Even if there is some truth in that image, variety of tone and attitude and mixture of styles are at home in tragedy from the beginning of our record, and it is truer to say that Euripides revived, extended, or extrapolated upon earlier stylistic possibilities with a freedom to be expected in the Greek tradition than that he abandoned something that was clearly and definitely formulated.[27]

The relation of plot-types and plot-outcomes (in the Aristotelian sense of "to good fortune" or "to bad fortune") to the generic status of a play is especially problematic. Critics tend to claim that Euripides is innovating (and perhaps being non-tragic) by adopting and manipulating certain plot-types. In fact, even when we have a complete play to consider, the bare description of the direction of change of fortune and of the outcome presented in the final scene does not tell us all that we need to know about the possible dramatic, emotional, or ethical effects of the play. Such effects may be mixed or contradictory, and one could argue that such mixture or self-contradiction is itself emotionally or metaphysically a key element of the genre of tragedy. Shifts in sympathy, differences of perspective (such as between those of the suffering individuals and those of the observers and survivors), gestures of closure or lack of closure[28] all may cut across the apparent direction of the change of fortune.

---

[27] It is possible to speculate about the presence of a variety of plot-motifs in the lost plays of Aeschylus and Sophocles, but the uncertainties are great and there is often a question whether a particular title is that of a tragedy or of a satyr-play (in a *petitio principii*, some who assign the lost plays to one genre or the other do so on the basis that they cannot imagine a "tragic" enough content to go with the known title and myths: on the problem of identifying satyr-plays from fragments see Sommerstein 2003b, Lopez Eire 2003, Redondo 2003). So one can make guesses about civic, ritual, and cultural foundations (e.g., Aesch. *Aetnaeae*, Soph. *Triptolemus*), possible saving *dei ex machina* (e.g., Soph. *Peleus, Athamas*), non-violent portions of epic (e.g., Aesch. *Argo*, Soph. *Nausicaa, Madness of Odysseus, Niptra*), rescue, release, or happy recognition (*Prom. Luomenos*, Soph. *Tyro* ; see Thummer 1986); miracles of revival or rejuvenation (e.g., Aesch. *Cressae*, Soph. *Manteis*), revenge upon or defeat of a villain (e.g., Soph. *Oenomaus*). For more details see Mastronarde 1999–2000: 30–3 and Wright 2005: 6–55. Apart from the wealth of information in TrGF vols. III–IV, see the useful survey of what Sophoclean fragments tell us about many aspects of his artistic choices in Radt 1991.
[28] For discussion of some closural devices in Euripides see Dunn 1996.

The hypothesis I wish to promote (for the evidence is not sufficient to get beyond hypothesis) is that as a poetic form devoted almost exclusively to heroic myth and arising within the tradition of hexameter epic, high-style choral lyric, and Stesichorean lyric (whether this was choral or not), tragedy had continuously available to it the full range of heroic narratives, including story-patterns of both positive and negative outcome, and allowing tones and overtones of various sorts (including terror, pity, regret, admiration, celebration).[29] Just as tragedy developed over time in the direction of unity of place and unity of time without ever reaching the sort of inviolable rule envisaged by the Renaissance theorists, so, too, it may have developed toward a recognition that a disastrous conclusion and the evocation of pity and fear were fundamental to many effective plays without completely leaving behind the other possibilities. This hypothesis is an alternative to the view that Attic tragedy as a whole, for some defined span of years in Sophocles' prime, was at a peak of sharp definition, restraint, and decorum, differing significantly from a state of greater variety during its preceding developing years as well as from a new efflorescence of innovation and genre-bending in the final decades of the century.[30]

On this view, Euripides' relation to the tragic genre requires careful description. He is not abandoning or corrupting a fixed genre, but exploring the potentialities of a living genre. The concern with questioning, contingency, and double vision that is so prominent in Euripides is to be accepted as properly at home in the tragic tradition. And none of this is to deny the creativity and avant-garde nature of Euripides' work, for example in aspects like self-consciousness of rhetoric, self-consciousness of formal structure, metatheatrical or distancing gestures, the trend toward more personal and domestic themes, including *eros*, and the larger role for women as characters in his plays.

TRAGEDY, SATYR-PLAY, AND THE COMIC

In the two main dramatic festivals of Athens, the Lenaea and the Great (or City) Dionysia, tragic plays shared the stage and orchestra with comedies,

---

[29] The difference between a narrower and a more inclusive conception of tragedy is in some ways analogous to the difference between the content and spirit of Homeric epic and the tone, content, and range of non-Homeric epic (see Griffin 1977). Also analogous, probably, is the classicizing narrowing of the textual tradition of epic and tragedy based on the taste of later generations and on the needs of the educational establishment.

[30] And in the fourth century many playwrights wrote plays of mixed reversal and audiences preferred them, according to Aristotle (*Poetics* 13.1453a30–5, a passage that follows his praise of Euripides because most of his plays end in disaster).

and at the Dionysia (where the vast majority of Euripides' plays were first performed) with satyr-plays as well. It is natural to ask what kind of interaction may have existed between the different genres. Satyr-play is obviously more closely related to tragedy than comedy is: the standard tetralogy of plays contributed by each of the three tragic competitors at the Dionysia consisted of three tragedies followed by a satyr-play, and the satyr-play was performed by the same actors and chorus and underwritten by the same financial backer. The metrical style of the iambic trimeter of satyr-play was closer to that of tragedy than to that of comedy. To judge from Odysseus in Euripides' *Cyclops*, the human figures in satyr-play apparently behaved and spoke with normal decorum, while buffoonery and grossness were left to Silenus, the satyrs, and monster-figures. The costumes and masks of human characters in satyr-play did not differ from those in tragedy: the visually distinctive features of the satyr-play were the chorus wearing the satyr-costume (including a visible phallos) and satyr-mask, the character of Silenus with his special costume, and various ogre-figures (like the Polyphemus of Euripides' *Cyclops*) who would apparently not normally have been seen onstage in a tragedy. The humor, the happy ending, and the more overt celebration of Dionysus in satyr-play can well be viewed as providing relief or decompression after the intensity of the preceding tragedies and facilitating a transition[31] from the world of serious heroic myth to the Dionysiac celebration that would occur outside the theater.[32] Typical motifs in these plays with happy endings included defeat of ogres or villains, liberation from bondage (especially for the satyrs), rescue of maidens in distress through "marriage" with a god or hero, return from the underworld, and discovery of the accoutrements of civilization (such as fire in Aeschylus' *Prometheus Pyrkaeus* or the lyre in Sophocles' *Ichneutae*).

There are two possible grounds for considering that some tragedies may have reminded the audience to some extent of satyr-play. First, the didaskalic record transmitted with *Alcestis* tells us that it was the fourth play of a tetralogy staged in 438, that is, that it took the position normally occupied by a satyr-drama. (It is possible, but very far from firmly established, that this was not the only occasion on which such a substitution took

---

[31] Alternatively, a comedy may have been presented after the tragic tetralogy, providing a further stage of transition. It is uncertain whether comedies at the Great Dionysia had their own day, or were performed last each day, following either a tetralogy or a set of ten dithyrambic choruses. The latter is suggested by a traditional interpretation of the joke in Aristophanes' *Birds* 786–9, but see the note ad loc. in Dunbar 1995: 480–1; see also Csapo and Slater 1995: 107; Pickard-Cambridge 1988: 64–5, 83; Luppe 1972.

[32] On satyr-play and its functions, see especially Seaford 1984: 1–44, Easterling 1997b, Hall 1998, Seidensticker in Krumeich *et al.* 1999:1–40, Voelke 2001, Griffith 2002 and (in press).

place.)[33] Second, the rescues and positive outcomes of satyr-plays would
seem to be a ready model for similar story-patterns in tragedy, so that, for
instance, one might suggest that *Alcestis* shares with satyr-play such features
as a rescue and return from death, the presence of Heracles, a scene of
drunkenness, an ogre-like minor deity (Thanatos, "Death," appears in the
prologue), and a positive outcome. Moreover, any plot in which a hero
travels to a marginal land and rescues a woman from an ogre-like ruler can
be thought of as analogous to myths of quests to the underworld or myths of
overcoming monstrous figures, and since the latter are found in some satyr-
plays one may wonder whether *Iphigenia in Tauris* and *Helen* also reminded
their audiences forcefully of satyr-play. One response to these facts has been to
propose the generic or subgeneric term "prosatyric" with the conviction that
the playwrights and audiences did indeed recognize these features as inherently
satyric and non-tragic.[34]

Many indications suggest that tragedy and satyr-play had a common
origin. The two forms may well have developed over time a sharper
distinction of one from the other by mutual differentiation. But when a
story-pattern is shared, this might be due to descent from a common
ancestor, with all the possibilities of the world of heroic myth, rather than
dependence of the one form on the other. The difference is not so much in
the story-patterns as in the status of the *dramatis personae*. There is a
relaxation or violation of decorum when the half-bestial satyrs and Silenus
are introduced on stage and when other monstrous beings are seen rather
than described in messenger speeches. Similarly, satyr-play takes a more
light-hearted attitude toward heroic values and toward human interactions
with divinity. While it is certainly useful to recognize motifs that are shared
between tragedies and satyr-plays, we cannot be confident that in the
original context of performance these features were so strongly felt to be
distinctive of satyr-play that labeling them "satyric" or "prosatyric" is

---

[33] For speculation about the existence of other Euripidean (and non-Euripidean) fourth plays without a
satyr-chorus, see Pechstein 1998: 13–14, 25–7 and in Krumeich et al. 1999: 400–1; Dale 1954: xix;
Guggisberg 1947: 47–8 (with references to earlier scholars). It is interesting that the part of the
prefatory material to *Alcestis* in which the didaskalic record is given makes no comment like "instead
of a satyr-play"; this could be a hint that for the ancient scholars who had a fuller set of production
records this was not a unique instance, but prefatory material has been so subject to revision and
abbreviation that it is unsafe to put any weight on the silence.

[34] The term is a modern one, already used by Dale 1954: xviii. The prefatory remarks to *Alcestis* (quoted
in n. 7 above) represent an amalgamation of multiple comments: they first say the play has an ending
that is "more comic" (κωμικωτέραν ἔχει τὴν καταστροφήν) and then say that it is "more satyr-
play-like" (σατυρικώτερον), but gloss this term simply with "having a happy ending contrary to the
tragic." See Dale 1954: xl and Sutton 1973 (explaining a confusion that some remarks of the twelfth-
century Byzantine scholar John Tzetzes have created about satyr-play).

explanatory.[35] It is certainly unjustified to suggest that every play with a "happy" ending or some less elevated feature is to be considered as a possible fourth-position play, as if such features could not be found in a play performed first, second, or third in a tetralogy.

Even in the case of *Alcestis*, we unfortunately are uncertain how the "prosatyric" position of the play affected reception. We simply do not know how often, if ever, the audience had seen a fourth play without a satyr-chorus. Does the low number of attested satyr-play titles for Euripides indicate that there were several other occasions where the fourth play was like *Alcestis*, or is it simply that the satyr-plays of Euripides were mostly lost before the collecting activity of the Alexandrian scholars?[36] Did some of the audience know in advance from the *proagōn*, a ceremony preceding the festival, that there would be no satyrs? Did the painted decor provide some hint? Or did the non-satyric character of *Alcestis* become clear only with the entrance of the Pheraean elders, since a satyr-play could have opened with the appearance of the Olympian god Apollo on stage-level and could have included the folkloric rather than high-style mythological character Thanatos? On the whole, given the argument made in the previous section that tragedy probably had considerable variety of theme and plot-type early in and late in, and perhaps throughout, the fifth century, I do not consider it useful to separate *Alcestis* off in a subgenre of its own. Its formal features[37] and dramatic techniques are largely in line with those of Euripides' other plays not believed to have been performed in the fourth position, and for most purposes in this book examples from *Alcestis* are treated as if it were just a Euripidean "tragedy."

Both the surviving plays of Aristophanes and the fragments of lost plays make clear that Old Comedy often quoted, commented on, or alluded to poetry of various genres, and tragedy was an especially suitable subject for such exploitation: as part of the same festival it was well known to the audience, and its high prestige was both a good target for carnivalesque comic attack and an inspiration to vie for similar authoritative stature in the eyes of the audience.

---

[35] Note the cautions of Sansone 1978. [36] See n. 33 above.
[37] The length of *Alcestis* has also been cited as a feature possibly specific to fourth plays. The only extant satyr-play, *Cyclops*, is 709 lines long, and of Sophocles' *Ichneutae* we have papyrus evidence for about the first 450 lines, and this is taken to be more than half of the play. This evidence, combined with Aristotle's remarks (*Poetics* 4.1449a19–21) about tragedy's gradual attainment of its proper μέγεθος ("size" and "grandeur") as it abandoned its more satyric origins, leads scholars to believe that satyr-plays were usually significantly shorter than tragedies. At 1163 lines, however, *Alcestis* is only about 70 lines (less than 6 percent) shorter than Euripides' *Supplices* at 1234 lines, and is probably longer than *Heracleidae* (1055 lines survive, but there are a few lacunae in the text, so it may have run to around 1100 lines – I do not accept the hypothesis that a whole episode of this play has been lost), whereas it is about 450 lines (over 60 percent) longer than *Cyclops*.

The more delicate question is whether the influence and rivalry operated in the opposite direction, with tragic poets taking their cue from comedy. Comic elements in tragedy have been discussed with a fine sense of nuance by Bernd Seidensticker in his monograph *Palintonos Harmonia*, and Bernard Knox famously made a case for regarding Euripides' *Ion* as a "comedy," but there is still ample room for disagreement among scholars.[38] Already in the *Poetics* we find the schizophrenic view that the *Odyssey* is along with the *Iliad* a precursor and model of tragedy, but that it is also, as a double plot, the model for the form of tragedy whose pleasure is more characteristic of comedy than of tragedy.[39] Aristotle's sporadic effort to identify a best form of tragedy, and his use of the term *tragikōtatos*, "most tragic," in his polemic against the audiences or critics who prefer happy endings, betray the same tendency as later retrospective efforts to define a metaphysical core of the tragic genre, that is, toward the marginalization of plays with happy endings. As Knox and Seidensticker acknowledge, there is an anachronism in speaking of Euripides' relation to comedy as a genre: the comic genre to which comparisons are so readily made is that of the Western tradition going back to fourth-century Greece, so that Euripides is a precursor in respect to the relevant points of comparison and not a borrower from a contemporary comic tradition. While it may make sense for us, with a perspective stretching forward from the fifth century, to make these connections, the original audiences were not in a position to do so. From the contemporary perspective of that audience, there were several possible resonances for those aspects of his work that were then or are now felt to diminish the decorum of the high-style mythological tradition: not simply the humorous elements of Old Comedy, but comic elements in Homer and the Homeric Hymns, glimpses of comic foil in Aeschylus' *Choephori* (the nurse recalling her very practical toil over the infant Orestes) and Sophocles' *Antigone* (the guard), and the humor in satyr-play.

GENERIC LABELS AND THEIR PROBLEMS

The term tragicomedy[40] derives from the Latin *tragicomoedia*, apparently an ad hoc comic formation designed for and extant only in the prologue of

[38] Seidensticker 1982; Knox 1970; for reservations, see, e.g., Gregory 1999–2000; Matthiessen 1989–90, Zacharia 1995. See also Sommerstein 2002 on the effective use of "comic" language in tragedy to enhance tragic themes, not to provide any comic relief by evoking comedy.
[39] *Poetics* 4.1448b38–49a2 (*Margites* is to comedy as *Iliad* and *Odyssey* are to tragedy), 8.1451a23–35 (*Odyssey* and *Iliad* have good unified and organic plots, unlike epics about Heracles or Theseus), 13.1453.a30–9 (*Odyssey* is the model for the double plot).
[40] For a few additional terms not considered here see also Fusillo 1992: 271 n. 3, and cf. Canevet 1971, who attempts to describe aspects of Euripidean drama as "baroque."

Plautus' *Amphitruo*, where it refers to the mixture in the same play of characters of different social levels, kings and gods from tragedy and slaves from comedy.[41] The term was taken up in the Renaissance and applied to dramas that in various ways combined features associated in genre-theory with tragedy and comedy, and some theorists included in their lists of examples (on the basis of "happy ending") Aeschylus' *Eumenides* or Sophocles' *Electra* as well as (on the basis of the mixing of figures of different status) *Cyclops* and some Roman comedies.[42] Since the eighteenth century, the theory of tragicomedy has concentrated on the mixture or juxtaposition of characteristic emotional effects induced in the receiving audience, and Seidensticker reasonably arrives at a broadening of the narrow definition developed by K. S. Guthke in his 1968 study of modern tragicomedy: in the tragicomic the tragic and comic elements may be either simultaneous or juxtaposed, and the effect may be either a heightening of the tragic through the comic or a mutual enhancement of the effects of both.[43] This term certainly has heuristic value as we try to describe the special qualities of *Alcestis* or *Helen*, or as we debate the tone of particular scenes such the Iolaus-scene of *Heracleidae* or the Teiresias-Cadmus scene of *Bacchae*, and Seidensticker's preliminary discussion is very scrupulous in acknowledging the potential pitfalls of anachronism and overprecise delimitation of the tragic and the comic. No harm is done if we avoid accepting the myth of the ideal form of tragedy and if we understand the "tragicomedies" as evidence of the richness and flexibility of the Greek dramatic tradition and not as failed tragedies. The questioning and irony that are characteristic of all tragedy are carried on in the double vision that creates such plays,[44] and this category should not be viewed, as it sometimes has been, as a form of tragedy that pulls its punches.

Romantic tragedy is another term that has gained currency in the analysis of happy-ending plays.[45] Again, it is easy to observe retrospectively how features of the later genre of Greek romance are anticipated in plays like *Iphigenia in Tauris* and *Helen*: prolonged wandering from home to exotic locales, shipwreck, separation from and reunion with loved ones, close escapes from imminent death or unwanted marriage, ambiguous oracles

[41] The form *tragicomoedia* is convincingly restored (on metrical grounds) for transmitted *tragicocomoedia* in Plautus, *Amphitryo* 63. Line 59 also ends with *tragico comoedia* or *tragicocomoedia*, where Leo changed to <sit>*tragicomoedia*; but the transmitted reading in 59 should be kept (as two words), and this reading provided the origin of the error in 63: see Seidensticker 1982: 21–2, Schwering 1916–17.
[42] Seidensticker 1982: 25–7.   [43] Seidensticker 1982: 27–45, esp. 36–7.   [44] See Zacharia 1995.
[45] For a consideration of key features of the plays that are usually discussed under this heading, see Fusillo 1992.

and dreams, doubles and disguises, and most of all, for those familiar with the genre, the comfortable sense that all will turn out well in the end, no matter what thrilling reversals and apparent disasters may be experienced on the way to that end. From the contemporary perspective of Euripides' time, however, these motifs look back to the *Odyssey* and other epic tales of quests, to genealogical poetry that incorporates the non-Greek world through stories of exile and foundation and locates the origins of noble clans in the liaisons of gods with mortal women, to stories of ultimate release after suffering, and even to mythical prototypes like the descent and return of Persephone or the triumphs of Dionysus over his captors and persecutors. In addition, the oral tales whose existence Sophie Trenkner posited in her study *The Greek Novella in the Classical Period* probably exploited many of the same motifs, although Trenkner tended to give too much credit to the direct influence of folktale and novella, ignoring the *Odyssey* and other high-style story-telling (such as the lost poems of the Epic Cycle) where some of the same story-patterns could already be found.[46] Romantic tragedy has seemed antithetical to the emotional payoff and metaphysical recognition of contingency that philosophical theories ascribe to "real tragedy," but once again the original context of the plays is rather different. Both Greek religion in general and Dionysiac religion in particular do not present a simple, consistent theology or fixed view of how the gods interact with human life. The Greeks could entertain, among other conceptions, both the idea of cruel and jealous gods and the notion of kindly reciprocity and saving favor from the gods. Both are present in a trilogy like the *Oresteia*, and even in single plays like *Trachiniae* and *Hippolytus* we find not only a "tragic" view of the world, in the narrow sense, but also at least hints of a countervailing view. In *Trachiniae* there is at least an allusion to Heracles' release on the pyre and his deification which, like the action of the whole play, is to be understood as Zeus' will. In *Hippolytus* we find the compensation of memorialization and the constructive cult practice that will guide other young people through the transition that Hippolytus was unable to negotiate, and also the goddess Artemis' personal concern for the youth. Dionysus himself embraces tragedy and comedy, and tragedy and satyr-play, so the themes of release and restoration that we see in romantic tragedy are not unDionysian. Despite a rather strained appeal to Frye's notion of a cycle of modes[47] and an overly biographical/psychological interpretation of Euripides' art, Whitman was correct to note the ritual pattern behind *Helen*

---

[46] Trenkner 1958.   [47] Frye 1957.

and *Iphigenia in Tauris* and to view the move toward synthesis and fulfillment as akin to the structure of some connected tragic trilogies.[48]
   Melodrama is a modern term that originated in French at the turn of the
eighteenth to nineteenth century. The name derives from the regular
incorporation of musical numbers into the performances of what was
considered low-brow theater, but soon came to apply to a genre of play
with a double plot, containing a mixed reversal for the persecuted virtuous
characters and the villain. The opposing characters are drawn in stark
contrast, and motifs such as disguise and unexpected return and reunion
are common, as are spectacular theatrical effects and surprises. For some
critics this term thus overlaps with romantic tragedy or tragicomedy, but it
is probably better to admit in melodrama the more recent connotations of
luridness and extremity of emotion and to differentiate between melodramatic tragedies and plays with a lighter tone and gentler outcome such as
Helen and *Iphigenia in Tauris*. Melodrama was stigmatized for its moralizing and for its strong emotional effects by the critics of a century ago who
championed the new realistic drama, and the application of the term to
Euripidean drama is usually another way to describe his work as non-
classical or non-Sophoclean or not fully tragic (although an unprejudiced
critic might note melodramatic features even in *Oedipus Tyrannus*, taken by
so many theorists as the paradigm of true tragedy).[49] Robert Heilman's
book *Tragedy and Melodrama* discusses the contrast between the two genres
in several ways and defends the place of melodrama in the dramatic
tradition, but throughout his discussion there is undeniably an undertone
of his acceptance of the superiority not only of real tragedy but also of the
audience that wants tragedy.[50] Among the criteria between tragedy and
melodrama frequently cited from his discussion, one is the distinction
between the dividedness of the tragic character and the undivided or
"monopathic" nature of the melodramatic character. This distinction is
not well suited to Greek drama because it assumes a Romantic model of the
individual character. Similarly, the distinction Heilman wants to draw
between tragic motivation from within the major character and melodramatic motivation from without relies on modern (but now challenged)
theories of causation and the will and is not appropriately applied to the
serious drama of the Greeks, where the mysterious interplay of the psychic

[48] Whitman 1974; see also Fusillo 1992, Thummer 1986, Griffith 2008.
[49] See the essays in Redmond 1992, especially the Hauptman 1992 and Sharp 1992.
[50] Heilman 1968; see the brief critique of Michelini 1987: 321–3.

and the demonic is a regular feature.[51] So the term melodrama introduces as
much anachronistic confusion as strict definitions of "the tragic."

In describing the work of Euripides, the terminology of genres is useful as
a heuristic device, for the help it gives us in differentiating various tones and
emotional effects, the mixture and juxtaposition of which is a key to much
of his dramaturgy. The terms give us a convenient way to recognize the
hierarchy of stylistic levels and social situations in Greek life and Greek
poetry and the varieties of story-pattern that are available in myth, folktale,
and poetic narratives. When the terms refer to the high and the low, socially
and ethically and stylistically, to the *spoudaion* and the *phaulon* or *geloion*,
they capture something that had been operative in the Greek poetic
tradition for generations, something to which both playwrights and their
audiences were sensitively attuned in many contexts of life. But when the
terms rely principally on story-patterns and plot-outcomes or on conceptions of personality and causation that are poorly matched to the habits of
thought of the Greek tradition, they are too crude a tool, encouraging a view
of genre that is too prescriptive and that oversimplifies the stemmatics of
intergeneric affinities. The way forward is not to abandon these terms
altogether, but to use them with restraint and self-consciousness and with
respect for the (mostly lost) wealth and variety of the Greek poetic tradition.
For moderns who can observe the multifarious forms and tones and generic
mixtures in contemporary novels, stage-drama, film, and television, there is
no excuse for ignoring the variety in ancient art forms. We must direct our
attention beyond the few plays so often treated as canonical and must
remind ourselves of the constructedness of the idea of the "classical" and
of the idea of "the tragic."

---

[51] For various challenges to nineteenth- and early twentieth-century assumptions about character and
the problematic applicability of such assumptions to Greek drama, see e.g. Jones 1962, Williams 1993,
Gill 1996, Padel 1992 and 1995.

CHAPTER 3

Dramatic structures: variety and unity

In the same way that a narrow and prescriptive concept of genre can do a disservice to our understanding of Euripidean drama, so, too, some prevalent assumptions about structure and unity have tended to encourage a devaluation of Euripides' achievements as a dramatist. The strongest influence, of course, has been exercised by the Aristotelian model of "organic" unity with a tight linear connection by "probability or necessity" from beginning to end of a plot. Aristotle's interest in a hierarchical ranking of artistic possibilities has also played a role, as has his backhanded compliment at *Poetics* 13.1453a29–30: "Euripides, *even if he does not manage other aspects well*, yet appears to be the most tragic of the poets" (emphasis added).[1] In defending tragedy against Plato's strictures, which attack the emotional seductiveness of mimetic poetry and condemn the mimetic artist as lacking true knowledge, Aristotle has a vested interest in emphasizing the intelligibility of tragic plotting in terms of cause and effect and in terms of consistency and appropriateness of character. Aristotle's approach privileges the author of the plot as the creator of a readily readable structure that evokes certain properly tragic responses (pity, fear; also *ekplēxis*, "astonishment"), but at the same time restricts the freedom of such artists. What such an approach tends to underestimate is the opaqueness and difficulty (and at times playfulness) of most Greek tragedies, qualities that present a challenge to the audience and invite a more open-ended process of reception. Some classicizing critics follow up on Aristotle's references to organic unity and make this the ultimate requirement for dramatic composition, idealizing a balance and harmony of elements that they profess to find in Sophocles.[2] Equally troublesome in the long tradition of dramatic criticism is the

---

[1] The Greek is εἰ καὶ τὰ ἄλλα μὴ εὖ οἰκονομεῖ; for a good survey of the meanings of *oikonomia* and related terms in ancient literary criticism see Meijering 1987: 171–210.
[2] See Chapter 1 for the classicizing and Aristotelian approach reflected by critiques of Euripides' *oikonomia* in the scholia, and for the influence of the brothers Schlegel in the modern period.

privileging of the single "hero" as the focus of attention, and of the tragic hero's character as the ultimate vehicle of meaning. Although Aristotle himself gives some countenance to this singular focus in his remarks on *hamartia* (*Poetics* 13), he elsewhere often refers to the plural agents of a plot, and he explicitly subordinates the representation of character to plot.[3] Yet critics bred on Shakespearean tragedy and the nineteenth-century novel have often brought to Greek tragedy assumptions about the overriding interest of one main character and have allowed this preoccupation to govern their interpretation of dramatic structure, so that they detect problems and defects when their expectation is deceived.

OPEN FORM AND STRUCTURAL STRATEGIES

In a descriptive rather than prescriptive poetics of drama, compositional structures can be regarded as falling all along a continuum of possibilities, from a "closed" form with strong representation of overt causal connections and narrow focus on a few main characters to an "open" form in which some or all connections must be supplied by the interpreting audience and in which a multiplicity of agents conflict and collaborate.[4] The closed form, considered by many critics to be more typical of "classical" forms of drama, tends toward concentration and self-containment, creating an impression of totality and unity through a simply organized structure with a single rhythm of rise and fall and through restriction to the deliberate actions of a few figures. The open form tends in the opposite direction, diminishing concentration and hierarchy in various ways. Event (what happens because of outside forces) becomes as prominent as, or more prominent than, action (what occurs because of the deliberate choice of a figure). The number of figures involved in the action is increased and their separate influence on the course of events reduced. The rhythm of complication and resolution is varied and multiplied. The interconnection of the acts or scenes is to be understood by an inductive movement that notes juxtapositions and implicit parallels and contrasts rather than by a deductive movement that recognizes a causal connection in terms of "probability or necessity."

The open structure is not to be viewed as a failed effort at closed structure, but rather as a divergent choice that consciously plays against the world-view of closure and simple order. People are familiar with such open structures in modern novels, films, and television episodes, but when

[3] The classic discussion of objections to this modern privileging of character is Jones 1962: 11–62.
[4] For a clear brief presentation of "open" vs. "closed" forms in drama, see M. Pfister 1988: 239–45.

they turn to antiquity they succumb to the tyranny of a classicistic tradition and apply much more restrictive artistic prescriptions as if they were naturally appropriate. There was, however, no golden age of ideal civic, religious, and artistic uniformity and harmony in the fifth century BCE. The interpretive effort that the open form demands of its audience was not in fact unusual in the context of archaic and classical Greek literature. The traditional use of the mythic exemplum in Pindar and Bacchylides and other choral poets frequently left to the audience much of the work of integration with the surrounding poetic motifs and with the occasion of performance, and in the Homeric epics many similes and digressive narratives likewise demanded an indirect and often subtle interpretive effort. The same was clearly true of many inset stories and anecdotes in the *Histories* of Herodotus. Even in those tragedies most admired for tight organic plotting, the standard juxtaposition of alternating choral odes and dialogue-scenes created an interrupted or punctuated structure. It often required inferential or inductive effort to relate a choral ode to what preceded and followed it, and the spectator's provisional judgment was subject to revision and refinement as the drama continued (this is notably the case in Sophocles' *Antigone* and *Oedipus Tyrannus*).

In the extant remains of Greek tragedy, variety of structural strategy was not solely the province of Euripides. For instance, the use of parallel or mirroring enactments of comparable actions was a common device for engaging an audience's interpretive attention while binding the action together. This was a feature of one kind of trilogy structure, as can be seen in the mirroring between Aeschylus' *Agamemnon* and *Choephori*, for example, in the deceptive confrontation of antagonists at the palace door and in the display of the corpses before the door. It is likely that the lost *Prometheus Unbound* had several aspects that mirrored *Prometheus Bound*, such as the visit of the wandering Heracles to the immobilized Titan, which recalls that of Io in the previous play. For mirroring within one and the same play, we may cite the third and fifth episodes of *Antigone*, where both Creon's young son and the respected prophet Teiresias fail to persuade Creon with an initial admonition, engage in an angry exchange, and depart in enmity (with the chorus using identical half-lines in 766 and 1091 to mark the exits, underlining the mirroring for the audience).

A second example of variety is provided by the frequent portrayal of pairs of main characters or groups of main characters. Aristotle himself refers in *Poetics* 13 to certain "households" that provided the best tragic plots, and in the ancient Greek context membership of a family was often a more important aspect of identity than any sense of individual autonomy. In the past, critics who have approached the Greek plays with an inappropriate sense of individuality and a modern fascination with character have often engaged in fruitless struggles to define the one most important character ("the hero") in plays like *Antigone* and *Hippolytus*, and others have resorted to terms like "diptych structure," as if it is self-evident that a play should feature one central character from beginning to end. Again, the trilogy *Oresteia* shows one way of presenting the travails of a house, focusing in turn on different members and even sending Orestes home several hundred lines before the end of *Eumenides* as the final resolution is enacted within the Athenian polis. *Persae* is a single play with a similar familial (and national) focus, and no priority of focus is to be assigned to Atossa or Darius or Xerxes. Many of Sophocles' extant plays likewise feature pairs or groups: Antigone and Creon in *Antigone*, Deianeira and Heracles in *Trachiniae*, Neoptolemus and Odysseus and Philoctetes in *Philoctetes*. Even *Ajax* is properly appreciated only if one abandons excessive attachment to the "hero" and attends to the whole group of other figures, both friendly and hostile to Ajax.

A third structural possibility that engages the audience in the creation of meaning is juxtaposition. In *Prometheus Bound* there is little probability or necessity in the sequence of arrivals of the chorus, Oceanus, and Io to visit the fettered Titan, but some kind of coherence is built up through the series of dialogues with their gradual process of revelation and emerging defiance. Without any preparation in the first two plays of its trilogy, *Eumenides* introduces Athena and Athens into the resolution of Orestes' problem and tellingly juxtaposes Orestes' supplication at Delphi with his supplication at Athens, and the verbal sparring at Delphi with the trial and process of persuasion in Athens.[5]

A fourth technique that contributes to the coherence of plot and creation of meaning is what might be called mythological depth, that is, allusions to causal events or paradigms that guide the audience to an enlarged view of the particular events of the current plot. Apart from the well-known gradually expanding evocation of the past of the Atreid house in *Agamemnon*, we may mention here the repeated citation of Io's wanderings and release in Aeschylus' *Supplices*, which suggests a paradigm for the Danaids, Io's descendants. In Sophocles' *Oedipus Tyrannus*, the allusions

---

[5] I do not detect juxtaposition of exactly this kind in the extant complete plays of Sophocles. The effect of the series of arrivals of outsiders (Ismene, Creon, Polyneices) to inform or persuade Oedipus in *Oedipus Coloneus* is comparable, but all these entries are motivated by the imminent battle at Thebes and the oracles about the value of Oedipus.

to the solving of the riddle of the Sphinx configure Oedipus' current contest of wits as a repetition of his earlier contest and as a disastrous realization of the special relation of the riddle to his own life: Oedipus is described or seen as baby, healthy adult, and blind man walking with a staff, and his downfall is interpreted by the chorus as exemplary for human life. In *Trachiniae* the monsters slain by Heracles deep in the past come back to compass his death, and Deianeira's experience of terrified and contested maidenhood is relived in Iole's fate. Such a use of mythological depth is perhaps less common in Euripides, but does occur in a play like *Phoenissae*, and mythological depth is reinforced by self-conscious recycling of the tragic tradition in *Orestes*, which alludes so densely to the *Oresteia* and other earlier Atreid dramas, or *Iphigenia in Aulis*, which often alludes forward to the future mythological history of the characters.

Tragic plots can also be constructed out of a combination of typical scene-sequences or story-patterns, or by the distortion of a traditional schema. *Choephori* follows the example of the *Odyssey* in combining a reunion or recognition with a revenge-action, as do the later Electra plays of Sophocles and Euripides. *Trachiniae* is a variation on the disastrous nostos-scheme seen in *Agamemnon*, with Deianeira an unwitting destroyer of her husband. *Oedipus Coloneus* combines standard elements of the suppliant-drama with a form of revenge-action, in which the hero, weak and friendless at the opening of the play, gains stature and value as the action proceeds, and dies with a special connection with the gods and in a situation in which his curse upon his sons is about to reach fulfillment. It is widely recognized that Euripides was extremely creative in the splicing and varying of familiar patterns.[6]

The gradations of structural coherence and structural variety we have just reviewed are not without relevance to the issue of the consistency of audience identification and audience sympathy. Interpretations of Greek tragedy tinged by romanticism or existentialism sometimes assume that a very strong identification of the audience with one main figure is a desideratum of effective serious drama.[7] Greek tragedy, however, is inherently a representation of many voices offering competing viewpoints, and the

---

[6] See in particular Strohm 1957, Matthiessen 1967, Burnett 1971, Burian 1997a.
[7] Like ideas of classical harmony and organic unity, the key importance of the "tragic hero" is an unstated assumption shared by many because it has been well instilled by handbook definitions and early exposure to Greek tragedy in translation in schools. The Greeks themselves recognized the grandeur of the doomed hero (both in literature, as in the *Iliad*, and in cult, as in their worship at hero-shrines and tombs), but, after Hegel, nineteenth-century definitions of tragedy often exaggerate this aspect (e.g., Günther 1885). For an existential inflection to the "hero-worship" approach to tragedy, see Whitman 1951.

competition is not merely between the elite figures of heroic myth, for tragedy also significantly plays off against the elite voices various more humble ones, such as those of the chorus and nameless servants and messengers.[8] It is a mistake to think that the dramatic performances aimed at a univocal response from the varied Athenian audience or even from single viewers. Even a female villain like Clytemnestra in *Agamemnon* may win temporary or grudging sympathy through the virtuosity of her verbal performance and her legitimate appeal to justice. In *Antigone*, shifting and mixed reactions to both the heroine and Creon are a proper response. Many of the most famous characters of Greek tragedy are both great-souled and monstrous. A number of Euripides' plays feature a marked shift from sympathy to revulsion at the end of the play, or other disquieting dissonance. Perhaps Euripides manipulates such shifts more sharply and subversively than do Aeschylus and Sophocles, but the technique may be regarded as an extension of a basic potentiality of the genre to invite the audience to experience a series of differing and sometimes incompatible viewpoints.

DOUBLE STRUCTURES

Our discussion of specific examples of Euripides' structural stategies may suitably begin with examples of dual focus and double movement and mirroring elements. Starting with an admired example of tight structure, we shall then proceed to instances that have often been judged more problematic. The surviving *Hippolytus* is structured around a sharp opposition between Aphrodite and Artemis.[9] The two goddesses appear at separate ends of the play, probably in the same position on the roof of the skene,[10] and they are also represented by two statues on stage (one of which Hippolytus adorns with a garland, the other of which he refuses to honor with a prayer). A prayer to Artemis follows the departure of Aphrodite at 57 and a prayer to Aphrodite precedes the entrance of Artemis at 1283. The goddesses are described in similar terms of pervasive movement (148–50, 447–8, 563–4, 1272–3), and there are echoes between their speeches (such as positive recognition of Phaedra at 47 and 1300–1 and determination to extract vengeance at 21 and 1422). The features just described make the

---

[8] For a good treatment of the process of identification with different characters, even those of different gender or nationality, see Griffith 2001. On the chorus see Chapter 4 below. On named elite vs. humble non-elite characters see Griffith 1995 and 2005a, Hall 1997.
[9] For select bibliography on this play see Ch. 1, n. 76.
[10] While scholars agree that Artemis appears above at the end, there is disagreement about where Aphrodite appears at the beginning; for the view that she appears above see Mastronarde 1990: 275–6.

pairing very emphatic, but they also undermine the antithesis by suggesting traits held in common. A similar opposition within the body of the play, superficially clear-cut but destabilized by echoes and shared themes, applies to Phaedra (female, sexually experienced, indoors, sick, consumed by desire) and Hippolytus (male, virgin, outdoors, healthy and physically active, impervious to desire). Yet Phaedra values nobility and virtue as much as Hippolytus does and engages with him in an implicit dialectic concerning *sōphrosunē* (connoting variously chastity, self-control, and moderation), while Hippolytus is reduced by the end of the play to a quasi-feminized state of physical weakness (his body supported by attendants as Phaedra's was in her first scene) and lyric expression (1347–88). As Phaedra's ethics are challenged by the nurse and as she is forced to worry about her reputation in the eyes of Theseus and others, so Hippolytus' ethics are challenged by Theseus and he painfully finds himself deemed impure and dishonest by his father. Both major figures engage the serious interest of the audience and invite a complex mixture of sympathy and disapproval: Phaedra through her helpless victimization by the goddess and her genuine moral struggle, on the one hand, and through her ultimate weakness before the onslaught of the nurse and her deception of her husband, on the other; Hippolytus through his ideal of purity and the pious fulfillment of his oath, on the one hand, but, on the other, through his inflexible categorization of good and bad, his unperceptive universalization of contempt for women, and his attachment to his unworldly (one might say inhuman) unchanging state, which he retains to the end. If one sets aside any preconception about having a single "hero" and about one character winning a contest for the audience's wholehearted moral approval, the double focus of *Hippolytus* is not a problem but a superbly effective tragic structure. The logical progression from scene to scene, in an Aristotelian sense, is also very strong (although the timing of Theseus' return relies on the convenience to plot that is conventional in effective story-telling). But it is the density of thematic links between scenes and speeches[11] that has made this play one of Euripides' most admired, and the mirroring and duality of so many elements augment the sense of human ignorance, blindness, and entrapment, as well as lending force to the unsettling of certainties.

The double structure of *Heracles* has been more problematic for many critics, and it is instructive to consider why this is so.[12] The doubleness is obvious from the unusual placement of a kind of *deus ex machina* in the

[11] On the speeches in *Hipp.* see pp. 223–6 below.
[12] For select bibliography on this play see Ch. 1, n. 84.

middle of the play. The suppliant- and rescue-action of the first half of the play has just come to an apparent happy ending, with the chorus celebrating the evidence that the gods care for justice and that Zeus acknowledges the obligations of his paternity of Heracles – notions that had been strongly challenged during the earlier scenes. The intervention of Lyssa (a personification of "madness"), spurred on by Iris (representing the absent Hera), causes Heracles himself to complete the destruction of his wife and children originally intended by the usurper Lycus and puts Heracles himself in the position of needing rescue, which is supplied in the second movement of the play by the arrival of Theseus. The parallels between the two parts are created in many ways. The villain of the first part, Lycus, has an invented genealogy that gives him a name etymologically related to Lyssa,[13] so that the two antagonists of Heracles are doublets of each other. Scenic actions make their contribution: the most famous is the mirroring of Heracles "towing" his children indoors at 631–2 and Theseus' towing of Heracles at the end of the play (1424, with repetition of the rare word *epholkides*, "towed vessels"); but there is also the motif of uncovering the head and looking up at the light, urged on the children, veiled for death, by Heracles at 562–4, and on Heracles by Theseus at 1214–27. Most important are the thematic links, especially the theme of friendship/kinship (both aspects are included in the Greek terms *philos/philia*). In the first part, loyal friendship is displayed by those too weak to be of help, while other apparent friends have abandoned the suppliants in their misfortune, and doubts are also expressed about Zeus's ability or willingness to show his friendship/kinship by saving the family. In the second part, Theseus fulfills the duties of a friend and the play ends with recognition of the supreme value of this tie (1425–6). The doubleness of structure is well suited to other motifs of pairs and to the debates of the play, which are similar to sophistic *dissoi logoi* ("double speeches," paired treatments of the same issue from opposite viewpoints). The image of the *diaulos*, a race with two legs, is exploited strikingly by the chorus in 662 and by Heracles in 1102, as he awakens from the unconsciousness that followed his fit of madness. Along with other language in the play, this image suggests the automatic alternation of success and failure in human life, and raises the issue whether change of fortune has any relation to justice and morality. Upon awakening, Heracles wonders whether he has made a second trip to the underworld (1101–4): he had just returned from fetching Cerberus and rescuing Theseus from entrapment

---

[13] The root *luk-*, "wolf", with feminine suffix *-ya* yields **lukya*, which by a process of phonetic adjustment normal in Greek becomes *lussa*.

there, and soon Theseus arrives to save him from this new underworld in return. Among the themes of the argumentative speeches, the significance and value of Heracles' feats and of his choice of arms are discussed in each half of the play. Most important, the nature of hope, courage, and resource-fulness are debated in both parts. After an initial decision to commit suicide Heracles revises his view and resolves to live on, and this process replays and reverses the debate between Megara and Amphitryon in the first part. In that earlier argument, Amphitryon temporarily won the case for endurance and hope but Megara ultimately persuaded him that they must abandon hope and face death without further delay.

Given all these signs of careful design and integration, what accounts for the displeasure of many earlier critics with *Heracles*?[14] The most important factor is the arbitrariness of the intervention on which the plot-structure pivots. Some interpreters have wished to palliate the harshness: some detect subtle signs of megalomania or incipient madness in Heracles before the appearance of Iris and Lyssa; some problematize the violence he has indulged in his labors and extends against the villain Lycus; and some attempt to see in Hera's persecution no more than an ordinary rule of human life that nothing great lasts.[15] It is best to recognize that these are unsatisfactory subterfuges. The challenge for the audience is to accept the difficulty of integrating the two actions and thus to come to terms with the implication – a universe for human life and endeavor that resists ration-alization and moralization, even though it is a natural, even an admirable, human desire to construct order and comprehensibility. The theological implications (discussed in a later chapter)[16] are also far from comforting.

Another variety of double plot is exemplified in *Hecuba*,[17] which com-bines a sacrifice-action related to Polyxena and a revenge-action related to Polydorus. The former is similar to the common pattern of self-sacrifice seen in *Heracleidae*, *Phoenissae*, *Erechtheus*, and *Iphigenia in Aulis*, but Polyxena's voluntary cooperation is not conditioned by the foreseen patri-otic or familial benefit highlighted in the other examples. Both Polyxena and Polydorus are children of Hecuba (and their names share the quality of evoking epithets of Hades, god of the underworld), and Hecuba is present

---

[14] The often-cited complaints are that the play is "broken-backed" (Murray 1947: 112) or an "odious abortion" (Swinburne, as quoted by Verrall 1905: 136; but note that Verrall expresses some caution about whether he recalls this fact correctly, and subsequent scholars have not located the source in Swinburne's writing) or that it "falls so clearly into two parts that we cannot view it as a work of art" (Norwood 1953: 229).

[15] Examples of these three approaches in, respectively, Wilamowitz 1895: II.128–9, Barlow 1981, Grube 1941: 252–6.

[16] See below, pp. 167–9.   [17] For select bibliography on this play see Ch. 1, n. 79.

throughout, but an Aristotelian critic could justifiably say that this is an inferior form of structure, since it merely includes what happens coincidentally within a short time to the same person and not a single action unified by probability or necessity. There are, however, features that interlace the two actions rather than leave them serially juxtaposed. Polydorus foretells the doom of Polyxena, and it is the servant assigned to fetch ritual water from the sea for preparing the maiden's corpse who finds and brings back the corpse of Hecuba's son instead. Without Achilles' demand for Polyxena as his prize, the fleet would not have stopped in Thrace at all: thus the ghost's demand both persecutes Hecuba and allows her to discover and avenge the death of Polydorus. And just as the events of the play deprive Hecuba of two children, Hecuba deprives Polymestor of his two children, an act that may suggest a displacement of her resentment against the Greeks (against whom she can do nothing) onto Polymestor, who would thus be made to pay for Polyxena's death as well.

The whole course of the play develops a dialectic on *charis* (reciprocity or gratitude), *philia* (kinship, friendship) or *xenia* (friendship with a foreigner), as well as the antithesis between Greek and barbarian.[18] As in *Heracles*, the shifting ground of argument and the unstable construction of order provide in *Hecuba* an underlying thematic that links the double movement of the plot. The double structure heightens the challenge to the audience to make sense of the whole. In addition to such thematic linkage, there is also scenic mirroring, specifically in the use of supplication: Hecuba supplicates both Odysseus and Agamemnon, and initially seems as frustrated in her approach to the latter as she was with the former; and Polyxena declines to supplicate Odysseus, whose gesture of avoidance (hiding his hand in his cloak) may be recalled in the later scene when Agamemnon pulls back from Hecuba, in indecision if not outright rejection. The reversal brought about by revenge as well may be reflected in stage-movement, as the weak movement of Hecuba at her entrance (using a staff and the support of attendants, 59–67) and her collapse upon the ground (lasting from the departure of Polyxena at the end of the first episode, 438–40, to the arrival of Talthybius at the beginning of the second episode, 499–502) are perhaps recalled in Polymestor's emergence (on all fours?) from the tent after his blinding (1056–60). At any rate, the verbal (and possibly visual) image of Polymestor as a four-footed beast[19] prepares

---

[18] See Mossman 1995 and the discussion below, pp. 229–34.
[19] *Hec.* 1058–9 τετράποδος βάσιν θηρὸς ὀρεστέρου τιθέμενος ἐπὶ χεῖρα καὶ ἴχνος, "stepping along with the gait of a four-footed beast of the mountain, upon hand and foot."

for the prediction of Hecuba's metamorphosis (1254–79), undermining the apparent distance between victim and avenger.

Another distinctive form of double structure is exemplified by *Helen* and *Iphigenia in Tauris*, two plays with a very similar pattern of recognition/rescue and escape through deception.[20] These dramas again involve a pair or ensemble of main characters, and in each case the set-up of the play features physical danger and psychic distress in figures who are the victims of deception or misinterpretation. In *Helen* the heroine suffers from a bad reputation among the Greeks because of the actions of a phantom double created by the gods, and she is stranded in an isolation that prevents her from defending herself from misjudgment. In addition, Helen is now threatened with a forced marriage (both a physical and a psychic violation) that she is forestalling through supplication. Menelaus arrives in Egypt shipwrecked, at a time when the amorous king has decreed that all Greeks who land in Egypt are to be executed, and the suffering he has undergone to win the phantom Helen and to bring her back to Greece (he has been wandering for years since the fall of Troy, unable to reach home) initially prevents him from acknowledging the real Helen when he meets her and she claims her identity back. Both, then, are the victims of appearances in a monstrous way, human playthings of a world with deliberately manipulative forces. In her play, Iphigenia is also stranded far from Greece with scant hope of return, for the gods have contrived that everyone in Greece believes she is dead, the sacrificial victim of her father at Aulis. Intensifying her nostalgia for Greece and her family is the repugnance she feels at her ritual duty in the local cult of Artemis, the overseeing of human sacrifice of strangers who are captured in the land of the Taurians. On the day of the play's action, moreover, her misinterpretation of a dream about her family exacerbates her misery, since she believes her brother, her one hope, is now dead. Orestes, on the other hand, arrives in this distant foreign country both aware of the mortal danger he and his companion face if captured and in doubt about the purpose of the instruction he has been given by Apollo (is it like the assignments given to other young heroes like Jason and Perseus with the intention that they shall go far away and never return alive?). Orestes and Iphigenia are also victims of a universe unfriendly to human happiness and human beings' control of their lives, although there is somewhat more emphasis in *Iphigenia in Tauris* on the role of human belief and (mis)interpretation in compounding the confusion.[21]

---

[20] On the similarities between these plays, see Matthiessen 1967, Burnett 1971, Whitman 1974; for other basic bibliography see Ch. 1, nn. 86, 88.
[21] See below pp. 162–6.

In both plays, the act of recognition reinvigorates the human agents, changing them from victims of deception or misunderstanding into purveyors of the same. Although *Helen* contains the additional step of obtaining the cooperation of the prophetess Theonoe, sister of the suitor-king, the later scenes of both plays show the reunited pair stage-managing their own escapes and imposing illusion and misunderstanding upon the foreign kings who are obstacles to their return to Greece. Significantly, in both cases the former victims use elements of their own previous suffering. Simply adding a detail to the real story of Menelaus' wandering and shipwreck, Helen contrives, as it were, a phantom husband, drowned at sea, to deflect the king from interest in the real husband present on stage. Likewise, she makes a phantom offer of herself as the king's bride, satisfying the transgressive desire that had made him a new Paris and making him relive the experience of Paris, except that his deception will be short-lived and the rest of the world will know the truth. In *Iphigenia in Tauris*, after Orestes has recognized his sister, he uses the memory or relics of fatal events in their family to persuade Iphigenia to accept his claim to be her brother: the strife between Atreus and Thyestes, the events at Aulis, and the violence with which Pelops won his bride to found the clan. Iphigenia, in her turn, uses the truth of Orestes' matricide and pollution to fashion a deceptive story for the Taurian king. As with Helen and her play-acted funeral ritual, Iphigenia dramatizes a purification in order to get to the seashore and escape. The combination of rescue and escape patterns is thus not simply a juxtaposition of two lively and engaging actions, but reflects an overall conception of an unfriendly and deceptive universe within which humans who are lucky can sometimes see through the veil and take a kind of control of their fortunes.[22] This control is only possible if the characters manipulate the same deceptiveness from which they have suffered, and while there are various ironies about the victimization of barbarians by Greek deceit (especially in the case of the Taurian king, who has elements of the noble savage), critics who have actually sympathized more with the foreign kings and have disapproved of the "immorality" of the Greeks have failed to recognize the metaphysical implications of the dramatic structure (not to mention their ignoring some very unattractive features of the two kings and attending too little to shared beliefs of the Greek audience).

Double structure and double arguments are also obvious qualities of *Andromache*, a play that has generally been neglected as an inferior specimen

---

[22] For the limitation of this control, see below pp. 165–6.

of Euripides' art.[23] In the series of plays of double structure, this is the first case in which the figure for whom the play is named has such a small part in the second half of the play. In Sophocles' *Ajax* and Euripides' *Alcestis*, by contrast, the title characters die well before the end, yet are clearly the focus of attention after their deaths, and Ajax's corpse is a significant presence during the final scenes, while the mute Alcestis returns in the exodos of her play. After her departure with Peleus at 765, however, Andromache probably does not appear again, and if she does, she is oddly treated as a mute character during the mourning for Neoptolemus.[24] Structurally, the two main actions of *Andromache* are linked as similar actions with important reversals. Andromache is a genuine suppliant who comes very close to falling victim, along with her child, to the machinations of Hermione. But she is rescued before the fatal blow can be struck, and Peleus plays the role of a real rescuer. Later, Hermione feels that her life is in danger, but she is only a kind of distorted or failed suppliant: the persecutor is absent and his hostile intentions are only a surmise, and Hermione's first impulse is not towards protected immobility in contact with an altar, but towards thoughts of suicide and uncontrolled movement out of the grasp of her protective servants (820–78). Her actual supplication of Orestes (891–5, 921–3) is a scenic echo of Andromache's supplication of Peleus (572–6), with a telling contrast between Hermione's freedom of movement, allowing her to describe her arms as equivalent to suppliant bands (*stemmata*, 894–5), and Andromache's actual bondage, which limits her to kneeling and to describing her inability to reach her hands to Peleus' chin (573–4). Orestes is then a distorted form of rescuer, in contrast with Peleus: Orestes actually comes to the rescue with his own agenda, which is concealed from Hermione and the audience for the first half of his scene. Orestes is also, unlike Hermione and Menelaus in the first half of the drama, a successful plotter of murder. Finally, the death of Neoptolemus also suggests the same sort of impiety involved in the mistreatment of a suppliant: the hero is attacked when he is praying face to face to the statue in Apollo's shrine (1117), for part of his struggle he stands upon the altar (1123),[25] and he dies close by the altar (1156). Thus the impious act that is often threatened but

---

[23] In the hypothesis to this play we find the phrase "the drama is one of the 'seconds'"; many assume this means "of second rank," that is, "not the best," but this is hardly certain. For bibliography on this play see Ch. 1, n. 78.

[24] On the question of Andromache's absence or presence, see below, p. 132.

[25] The stance may remind an audience of Telephus supplicating on a altar while holding his sword and his hostage, the baby Orestes. For the iconography of Telephus in later vase-painting see Taplin 2007: nos. 75–7, and note that the same posture is used by the artist of the Apulian vase showing

not carried out on the tragic stage, namely a physical attack upon a suppliant who is in contact with a sacred item, is echoed in the analogous crime of a murder carried out not only in Apollo's temple but with the god's connivance.

The argumentative and rhetorical treatments of the proprieties of wifely behavior also interconnect the two main actions of *Andromache*, since this theme appears first in the *agōn* between Andromache and Hermione and then in Hermione's retrospective explanation for her error and her moralizing advice to married men.[26] The chorus' criticism of having two women in the same house widens the theme of marriage beyond the immediate contrast between the Trojan concubine and the Spartan wife. Concurrently, other features of the play raise the question whether this marital *oikos* has another problem besides the rivalry of the women: the misfit of the Spartan wife from the family of the Atreidae with the Phthian son of Achilles. This issue feeds into another overarching theme that is ultimately more important than the gender-based theme – the nature of morality, excellence, and fame. The haughty attitude of Hermione in her first words on stage, the dishonesty of Menelaus, the tirade of Andromache against Spartans (as mythically represented by Menelaus), the deceptive approach of Orestes to Hermione and the scheme of false rumor and ambush that he activates against Neoptolemus – all these details create a bloc of Atreid/Spartan interests that embodies false fame and lack of true virtue. In contrast, Peleus is praised for his heroic exploits in the past and for proving their validity by facing down Menelaus and saving Andromache and the child. The absent Neoptolemus is credited with recognizing the error of his previous behavior and setting out to make due amends. The rescue of Andromache and the flight of Hermione bring about a separation of the bad from the good, and Thetis' instructions at the end of the play affirm the value of the unlikely alliance of Trojan captive and heroic Greek clan, which produces the founder of a new dynasty. This ending also reasserts the importance of (probably unseen) Andromache and her brave efforts to keep Neoptolemus' son alive. The lines of division are even reflected on the divine level, as the morality of Apollo is aligned with that of the matricide Orestes and with his new violence, in opposition to Thetis, whose shrine has had some protective force locally and who can arrange a

Neoptolemus fighting off his attackers at the altar at Delphi, which appears on the cover of this book (Milan, Collezione H. A. (Banca Intesa Collection) 239, attributed to the Ilioupersis Painter; see Taplin 2007: 139–41), which suggests that the association made here is not fanciful.

[26] For further discussion, see pp. 275–9 below and references cited there.

reward for Peleus, but who cannot block the revenge sought by Apollo. The juxtapositions and reversals of structure thus interact with the themes of gender and virtue and the "double discourse" of the formal rhetorical speeches to suggest a shape and direction of the overall action, but the play refuses to privilege one character as focus and a single action as conclusive.

STRATEGIES OF JUXTAPOSITION

Open structures based on juxtaposition are relatively easy to accept as "structures" when the elements of mirroring and reversal are clear, particularly if the doubling in the action is paired with a dialectical or aporetic exploration of key themes in the major speeches and disputes of the drama. Without mirroring or reversal, however, such an open structure may be deemed "episodic" in the Aristotelian sense, offering an accumulation of scenes chronologically ordered and perhaps involving one or more figures in common, but not suggesting a strong "probable or necessary" chain of causation leading from one incident to the next. *Troades*, for instance, has been much admired for its pathos and for its anti-war message,[27] yet its structure is not similarly admired. The play begins with an unusual variation on the prologue-god. A divine monologue is usually employed to let the audience in on facts that they need but which are unknown to the characters,[28] but Poseidon's speech in *Troades* 1–47 contains almost nothing that could not have been introduced through exposition within the words of the human characters and the chorus: there is only the detail that Polyxena has already been sacrificed secretly, which is exploited very briefly at two later points, in Hecuba's misinterpretation of Talthybius' evasive answer

---

[27] This message has often been seen as a direct response by Euripides to the Athenian conquest of Melos and treatment of its inhabitants (Thuc. 5.84, 114–16), but the chronology is difficult. The Melians were under siege for several months from the summer of 416 into the winter season of 416–415; during the winter they surrendered and "the Athenians put to death all the adult males they captured and enslaved the children and women." Yet it is likely that Euripides conceived the play and composed most or all of it before the Melos campaign ended, since poets were selected by the archon at the beginning of the civil year (thus in July 416 for the Great Dionysia festival of March 415) and also matched with actors and *chorēgos* so that recruitment and training of chorus members and other support staff could begin. Moreover, it seems probable that, when requesting a chorus, poets at least informed the archon of the plays to be produced, if they did not in fact show him the scripts. Both the Trojan War story and the brutality of contemporary warfare (which had been exacerbated during the Archidamian War of 431–421) were well enough known to provide inspiration for *Troades* without knowledge of the outcome of the Melian campaign.

[28] See below, pp. 175–6.

about the girl's fate (260–71) and in Andromache's revelation of the truth (619–31). The decisive contribution of the divine scene is postponed to its second part, the dialogue of Poseidon with Athena (48–97). This informs the audience of an important plan for the future after the end of the play: a god-driven storm intended to punish the Greek fleet with death and difficult wandering. Such details are often included in a *deus ex machina* epilogue, and the characters and chorus are thus included among the recipients of the prophetic knowledge. *Troades* has no *deus ex machina*, and displacement of the divine provisions to the prologue casts a pall of unawareness over the human actions within the play, a pall from which the characters are not released at the end. Although Athena says that she wishes "to hearten the Trojans whom I hated before" (65), the "satisfaction" at reversal can be felt only by the audience, not by the Trojans – except for Cassandra, who is treated as raving and is disbelieved even in the argument she claims to make "without Bacchic possession" (365–7, 406–7). The whole scene also activates the motif of abandonment that is then prominent in two choral odes (799–858, 1060–117) and statements of Hecuba and Andromache (469–70, 775–6, 1240–2, 1280–1).

One way to think about the sequence of actions after the prologue of *Troades* is in terms of Hecuba's immobility and powerlessness. In *Prometheus* and *Oedipus Coloneus* we also see immobilized figures of apparent weakness interacting with a series of "visitors," and in those two cases the weak figures paradoxically are revealed to have significant strength and an unsuspected value. Hecuba is a kind of failed exemplar of this pattern. The climax of her apparent strength comes in the *agōn*-scene. After the repeated hammerblows of new misfortunes within the play are piled upon those that preceded the play, Hecuba nevertheless is here shown rising to the occasion, inspired to skillful rhetoric by the opportunity to retaliate against at least one cause of her sufferings and those of her entire city. Although the rhetorical contest contains exaggerations and contradictions that, as usual, leave an audience in some uncertainty, one level of response is probably wholehearted support for the way Hecuba zeroes in on Helen's culpability and asserts human responsibility. Even faced with strong evidence of divine intervention and predetermined fate (suggested by the first play in the Trojan trilogy, *Alexandros*, as well as by the prologue of *Troades* itself), an audience will find it comforting to avoid conscious acceptance of the futility of human endeavor and of human constructs of right and wrong behavior. In other words, Hecuba emerges in the argument as a figure of apparent strength with whom the audience will wish to identify. Yet, unlike the cases of Prometheus or Oedipus, the strength is only apparent.

Euripides provides clues that Menelaus will not carry out his judgment
against Helen, allowing reintegration of the staged events into the Odyssean
story (and indeed the story of all previous versions, as far as we can tell) that
Helen stayed alive as Menelaus' wife. In the end, despite any momentary
identification with Hecuba's cause, the audience must recognize the futility
of her "victory." This failure is the largest manifestation of a pattern shared
by two other developments in the play centered on Hecuba: first, her
temporary illusion that Polyxena is still alive (260–71, 624–5), and, second,
the brief efflorescence of hope in her notion that Astyanax could live on and
refound Troy (701–5), which is immediately squashed by the entrance of
Talthybius (706–9) to announce the child's doom and lead him away from
his mother and grandmother.

Apart from this dynamic involving Hecuba, other links in *Troades* are of a
mainly intellectual or rhetorical nature. There is, to be sure, a sequence of
summonings that creates some impression of mirroring: Polyxena had been
fetched from Hecuba's presence before the play began (260), Casssandra is
summoned to join Agamemnon (294–461), Andromache passes on her
way to Neoptolemus' ship (568–779), Astyanax is summoned to execution
(782–6), and in the end Hecuba herself is summoned to Odysseus' ship
(1269–71). But more important is the variation in the way the major Trojan
roles are heard coping verbally with disaster. Cassandra paradoxically demonstrates that the Greeks have fared worse than the Trojans (365–405).
Andromache argues that the dead Polyxena is better off than she herself is in
her continuing life (630–83). Hecuba herself, both in lyric and in spoken
verse, expresses the gulf between past happiness and current misery and says
farewell to Astyanax, Hector, Troy, and all the others from whom she is
being separated. Hecuba's stance is complicated, as we have just seen, by the
revived confidence of her attack on Helen. Her references to the gods within
that scene swing temporarily away from the sense of disorder and abandonment that pervades the rest of the play. Cassandra's argument and the
attendant prophecy, dismissed as raving by the internal audience (and
that is of course the fated reception of Cassandran prophecy), strike the
audience rather differently, as her predictions square with the poetic tradition they know, and Athena's scheme to punish the Greeks works in the
same direction of undermining their apparent success. When coupled with
the claim of trouble (1126–8) for Peleus and Neoptolemus back in Thessaly
and the implied ineffectuality of Menelaus, the prologue and Cassandra's
speeches make the Greeks (even though mostly unseen) a secondary focus
of interest in the play, as the contrast between victors and defeated
breaks down.

The play that poses the greatest challenge to interpretation, even as an open structure relying heavily on juxtaposition,[29] is *Supplices*.[30] Here too, however, several key themes are shared between disparate sections of the play, and the juxtapositions present the audience with a challenge either to integrate the disputed views about values and choices or to recognize the uncertainty and indeterminacy in human life that even respected cultural norms cannot overcome. The initial movement of the play (through the close of the messenger-episode ending at line 777) has the standard shape and elements of a suppliant-plot, with the temporary distortion that initially the Athenian hero-king Theseus unexpectedly refuses to take up the cause of the suppliants.[31] Theseus himself thus serves as one of the obstacles to be overcome before the problem afflicting the suppliants is solved (87-364). The queen-mother Aethra plays an important role in returning the plot to its proper path, the one cherished in Athenian self-representation,[32] and in general the issue of the relation of the two genders to the city is a significant theme that links disparate parts of this play, as Daniel Mendelsohn has well discussed.[33] The second obstacle is dramatized in the verbal threat of the Thebans conveyed by their herald, who engages in an *agōn* with Theseus (399-597). Finally, the off-stage physical obstacle to recovery of the bodies of the fallen Argives is removed by the Athenian victory in the plain before the walls of Thebes (634-751). Even within the suppliant-action, however, there are dialectical elements of argument that unsettle an audience's judgment. Theseus as "optimistic rationalist"[34] offers in his initial refusal one view of the role of divinity in human affairs and of human moral obligations and later entertains a somewhat different one in accepting the challenge after his mother's admonition. The Theban herald's threat is accompanied by a rejection of belligerence, a praise of peace, and the claim that the Argive attackers were hubristic and therefore hated by the gods. The first theme is echoed later by a chastened and wiser Adrastus, the second is a traditional and well-regarded topos, while the third echoes elements of Theseus' own

---

[29] *Phoenissae* has frequently been referred to as overstuffed (cf. the term παραπληρωματικόν in *hyp. Phoen.* 3 in Mastronarde 1988 (= *hyp.* c in Diggle 1981–94), a unique usage of the adjective in reference to a drama, based on the rhetorical term παραπλήρωμα, "[unnecessary] filler"), episodic, or pageant-like. I do not discuss it here because I have elsewhere written at length about the symmetries, juxtapositions, and key unifying motifs that establish a carefully composed and complex structure: see Mastronarde 1994: 3–11, together with the separate explications in the commentary of each episode and stasimon.
[30] For basic bibliography on this play see Ch. 1, n. 80.
[31] For more on the elements of suppliant-plot and on Theseus' initial refusal, see pp. 216–18 below.
[32] See below, pp. 256–7.   [33] Mendelsohn 2002.
[34] Mastronarde 1986 and pp. 216–17 below.

first reaction to Adrastus' request. The impression created, as often, is that of the contingency and confusion or contradictoriness of values and fundamental constructs of belief.

Incompatibilities of values continue to be brought to the surface in the remainder of the play. Whereas Aethra's willingness to see her son put his life in danger for the glory of Athens exemplifies the civic patriotism encouraged by the public funeral oration and articulated most clearly in the famous speech of Praxithea from the fragmentary *Erechtheus* of Euripides, the various expressions of grief in the last third of the play offer a more personal, almost antipatriotic alternative.[35] In their grief, the Argive mothers of the chorus wish they had never been married and thus never had children (786–91, 822–3). The memory of their dead sons' characters and achievements is apparently no consolation to the chorus, for they follow the praise offered by Theseus and Adrastus in 838–917 with a choral ode that dwells on the bereaved mothers' loss of identity and loss of rootedness in the community and envisions a Niobe-like state of permanent mourning, suspended between life and death (955–89). A reading in terms of patriarchal hegemony might suggest that there is a deliberate contrast between the "good Athenian mother" Aethra, subservient to her son and echoing patriotic constructs of the role of the sexes in the polis, and the chorus, non-Athenian women inadequately supervised by authoritative males and transgressive by their departure from the seclusion of their homes. But to adopt such a one-sided reaction requires suppressing the emotional impact of theatrical representation and choral song shaped by standard ritual themes. It also involves ignoring the identification Aethra feels with the mothers and the cooperation of Adrastus and Theseus in the funeral process. The men prepare the warriors' bodies and exclude the chorus from witnessing the funeral pyres, but the women do view the (wrapped?) bodies before cremation and later see and touch the vessels bearing the bones and ashes, they lament, and they listen to the funeral encomium.[36] In

---

[35] Eur. fr. 360; on the public funeral oration see Loraux 1986; on lamentation as a challenge to the male order of the city see Foley 2001: 19–55.

[36] Some of the elements clearly recall the procedure for the annual Athenian public funeral for the war dead. In that process, the dead warriors were cremated on or near the field of battle and the remains returned to Athens and apparently stored in anticipation of the annual event. (In a standard funeral, the dead body is returned to the home (*komizein*) and washed and dressed by the females of the house.) Then the remains of the dead were set forth (*prothesis*) in a public tent (instead of in the home of the individual, as in a standard funeral). Offerings could be made there by kin. The procession itself (*ekphora*), involving caskets of bones rather than the corpse, went from the tent (instead of from the home) to the burial-place (instead of to pyre and then interment), and it included mourning women. The burial was in a public tomb, rather than the family plot used for other deaths. After interment, the public funeral oration was delivered. In *Supplices*, the oration is out of position, the cremation of

addition, the voicing of this alternative view of parenthood is extended to a male character as well, for Iphis reacts to the suicide of his daughter Evadne and the previous death of his son (one of the Seven) by wishing he had never begotten children at all (1087–91).[37]

The praise of the dead warriors by Adrastus is, on the one hand, a logical extension of the suppliant-action, since the purpose of recovering the bodies is to pay them the honors due to the dead. On the other hand, the praise forms a challenge to the audience, giving them no guidance on how to integrate this positive characterization of the Seven with the earlier condemnations of their foolhardiness and impiety. Those condemnations came not only from the Theban herald, but also from Theseus, who in contrast here invites and accepts Adrastus' encomium and even supplements it with his own compliments to Amphiaraus and Polyneices. One critical reaction to this challenge has been to read the encomium as ironic, parodying the genre of funeral speeches for warriors.[38] But the irony involved here is probably a more general one, at the expense of the human constructs by which we understand character and the connections between character and destiny. As Euripides in other plays exposes the faults and brutality of initially sympathetic characters or uncovers the reasonableness and pathos of initially unsympathetic characters, so here the play seems to be asking its audience to understand that the same persons can have, in one situation, the admirable social and political virtues ascribed to the heroes in Adrastus' speech, and can be, in another situation, the doomed assailants disregarding divine signs and spouting impieties. Moreover, the reversal for an audience lies not only in this view of human character, but in the destabilization of the world-view that gives priority to the strongly political themes of the suppliant-action and the military campaign, since the final third of the play makes prominent several private aspects, before the *deus ex machina* interrupts the ending to insist on a point of interstate relations, a stricter enforcement of Argive gratitude.

The most "episodic" part of *Supplices*, the Evadne-scene (980–1113), stands out structurally because the two characters involved in it, Evadne and her father Iphis, arrive from elsewhere without a summons and interact only with the chorus and each other, not with any of the characters who have participated in the play so far. Such causal and thematic isolation is

the Seven is not carried out on the battlefield, but in Attika (still out of sight of the family), and the procession is partly staged (the sons carry the urns into the presence of the chorus) and partly anticipated as an event that follows the play (return of the Argives to Argos).

[37] See below, p. 295.

[38] Two examples of satirical readings are Fitton 1961 and Smith 1966, but the view was espoused in earlier scholarship too.

unmatched among other named human characters in Euripides. A few anonymous messengers have a similar isolation, but what they have to say always has a bearing on the characters that the chorus and audience have been witnessing. There is here, of course, the connection to Capaneus, who has been named four times previously in the play (496, 639, 861, 934), most recently fifty lines before Evadne's entrance, but the separation of the scene is still striking. One contribution of the scene is to show that although the grief of the chorus of mothers is intense, it can be surpassed. Evadne as a female adopts masculine terms of reference for her demonstration of loyalty, "dying with" her partner, and so takes on the extreme ambition that was displayed by the Seven, and especially Capaneus, in their assault on Thebes. Thus Evadne offers a female version of the warriors while her father Iphis offers a male version of the mourning chorus, adding to the paradoxes already discussed a destabilization of assumed gender norms. This seems to be one kind of meaning created by the paratactic structure in this part of *Supplices*.

A FINAL EXAMPLE: *ORESTES*

Orestes is a suitable play with which to conclude this review of plot constructions, as it illustrates complex structure, a mixture of actions, and a use of mythological depth that is reinforced by self-conscious references to the theatrical tradition.[39] The first part of the play (1–724) is a failed rescue-plot. The position of the threatened siblings Orestes and Electra is partly similar to that of suppliants. They are outside their house (like the suppliants at the beginning of *Heracles*), immobilized by Orestes' sickness, who should perhaps be understood to have collapsed here in the open in one of his fits of guilty raving. They are not in fact yet condemned to death, but are due to be judged on this day and meanwhile are prevented from leaving Argos. The opening movement takes advantage of two similar type-scenes. One is the sleeping-scene (1–210), in which a stricken character is unconscious: this regularly includes elements like the need for quiet and the fear of stirring the sleeper, the solicitude of the chorus or friendly characters, and the awakening of the sleeper. The other is the scene depicting madness or the attack of unbearable pain (211–315): this features disjunction in the dialogue or lyric exchange between the sufferer and another present character, resistance to touch or physical restraint, and eventual restoration of composure and normal dialogue contact. Here these elements contribute to

---

[39] For bibliography on this play see Chap. 1, n. 90.

a build-up of sympathy for Orestes and Electra, as does the contrast provided by the tactless Helen who appears briefly in the prologue (71–131). From Electra's opening monologue onward there is also a build-up of hope, as the siblings look forward to the arrival of their uncle Menelaus as a likely rescuer from their peril. Menelaus, of course, does not provide the help that they desire. In a reversal of the pattern of his frustration in *Andromache*, where he is prevented from harming Andromache and her son by the arrival of old Peleus, here Menelaus is confronted by old Tyndareus, bent on persecuting his grandchildren, and as a result makes an evasive answer to Orestes' plea for help, intending in fact to leave him and his sister to their fate.

The first third of the play displays the sharp contrast between the misery of Orestes and Electra and the undeserved prosperity of Menelaus and Helen, and the failure of rescue is correlated with a betrayal by a *philos*. The middle of the play (725–1097) represents an opposite example of fierce loyalty among *philoi*, and this loyalty affords a second attempt at salvation. Pylades physically supports his weakened friend on the journey to the Argive assembly, where Orestes tries again to plead his own case but fails partly because of the political currents operative in the background and partly because of the excesses of his own rhetoric.[40] The same loyalty infuses the scene following the return from the assembly, as the trio consisting of brother and sister and their cousin Pylades commiserate and plan to die together as the final testament of their bond. But even as this movement seems to reach its logical conclusion with Pylades' insistence on sharing his friends' doom (1085–97), a revenge-plot begins with Pylades' sudden suggestion that they should avenge themselves on Menelaus first, and soon this plot becomes a third attempt at salvation as well (1098–690).

Aeschylus' *Oresteia* is an important intertextual (or for most of the original audience, intertheatrical) reference point for many aspects of *Orestes*. Orestes' vision of the Furies in his episode of madness recalls the end of *Choephori*, where he can see the Furies while no one else on stage can. The two debates in the play recall *Eumenides*. The first, between Orestes and Tyndareus and carried out in front of Menelaus, makes allusions to the famous arguments over the matricide in Aeschylus, and the debate itself can be regarded as a secularization (or de-theologizing) of the famous trial before Athena. The goddess is replaced by the indecisive Menelaus, Orestes speaks entirely on his own, without the direct advocacy of Apollo, and the Furies' role is taken by the old man, with a single angry mask conveying a threat similar to that of the horrible-looking Aeschylean chorus. The second

---

[40] See pp. 243–4 below.

debate, reported by the messenger, contains further allusions, while its outcome matches and contrasts with that in *Eumenides*. The human jurors in Argos are divided in their judgment, but there is a majority for one side, condemnation, and no place for Athena's grace to intervene. Once the revenge-plot begins, the allusions are again to *Choephori*, as the trio of conspirators re-enact the crime for which they have already been condemned, crazily anticipating a different result – praise from all Greece. In *Choephori* Pylades is mute except for three lines which make him a human spokesman for the unseen Apollo. In *Orestes*, Pylades is also a substitute for Apollo: he does not abandon Orestes (as Apollo promises not to do in *Eum.* 64), he stands by Orestes in the trial in the Argive assembly, and he encourages the murder of Helen as Apollo had encouraged that of Clytemnestra. The plotting dialogue is followed by prayers to the ghost of Agamemnon (1225–45) that echo in brief the prayers of the great kommos of *Choephori* 306–509. The chorus of *Orestes* even participates in the plot to some degree by standing lookout with Electra.

The frustration of human endeavor seen in the first two thirds of the play carries over into the finale. The entry into Helen's chamber under false pretenses is successful, but Helen herself is spirited away just before the fatal blow can be struck. Hermione is captured without trouble, but as a hostage does not compel Menelaus' cooperation, or at least not quickly enough. Menelaus' indecisiveness and delays apparently lead Orestes to give up on the negotiation and order the firing of the palace, but this instruction is countermanded by Apollo as *deus ex machina*, in a straining of this convention that is discussed in a later chapter.[41] The multiple movements and paratactic structure of *Orestes* are thus linked by parallelisms and common themes, by continous allusion to the *Oresteia*, and by the deconstruction of rhetoric and values. The interaction of the large ensemble of characters underlines the relative weakness of the separate individuals, and, as in several other plays, the audience's sympathy is first strongly engaged and then confused and repelled.

OPEN STRUCTURES AND THE CHALLENGE OF TRAGEDY

As we have seen, juxtaposition and other features of a more open structure may have an unsettling effect, diverting the audience from a consistent and linear view of the drama unfolding before them and suggesting underlying similarities in contrasting characters or situations. This structural choice,

---

[41] See pp. 192–5 below.

adopted so often in Euripides, may thus reinforce other key features, such as the dialectic of ideas and interpretations created in the rhetorical performances of the characters and the abstraction from consistent emotional involvement often created by Euripidean choral odes, features that will receive fuller treatment in subsequent chapters. The audience is challenged not simply to make sense of the personalities and actions they witness, but to make sense of the swings of their own response.

Many critics have noted the frequency of a "sting in the tail" in Euripidean drama, and it has been recognized that gestures or developments creating a sense of closure at the end of a play may be in competition with other elements that block the sense of closure.[42] Sophocles too, in his (generally milder) way, often denies the satisfying sense of completion that one might expect in a classical, organically unified plot-structure, whether we think of the end of *Trachiniae*, with the harshness of Heracles, the resentment of Hyllus, and the inexplicitness of what might follow on Mt. Oeta; or of *Oedipus Tyrannus*, with the odd shift from Oedipus' self-condemnation and self-isolation to sentimental embrace of his daughters and the lack of a decision about whether he will leave Thebes or not; or of *Philoctetes*, with the sudden intrusion of Heracles and the oblique reference to future impieties at the fall of Troy, which must evoke those of Neoptolemus in particular; or of *Electra*, the abrupt ending of which has fostered unending controversy about the likely response to the moral issues of the revenge. In Euripides we find several variations in the tendency to confuse audience-response through shifts of sympathy. In some plays, the drama works hard in the opening sequences to gain sympathy for a major character, but the character eventually moves in a direction and to a goal that is likely to provoke revulsion: thus most clearly with Medea and Phaedra, but also to some degree with Hecuba. The same applies to Electra and Orestes in both *Electra* and *Orestes*, although in the former the turn toward revulsion is internalized within the world of the play in the agents themselves. In *Heracleidae*, Alcmene's violence and defiance of absent male authorities provide a strong contrast to the behavior of the self-sacrificing daughter of Heracles and even to Alcmene's own previous behavior in the play.[43] In both this play and *Hecuba*, the villain is endowed with special knowledge at the end. Polymestor's prediction that Hecuba will undergo metamorphosis into a dog (*Hec.* 1259–74) is retaliatory, and the bodily change presumably strikes the audience as demeaning or horrible rather than a symbol of any good qualities, although this interpretation continues

[42] See Dunn 1996.   [43] See below, pp. 259–60.

to be debated.[44] Not only does Eurystheus' speech show an unexpected mildness, but his asserted willingness to die is in strong contrast to the messenger's earlier accusation of cowardice (*Hcld.* 813–17), and this willingness and the revelation that his corpse will benefit Athens paradoxically create a minor mirroring of the role and words of the daughter of Heracles. A shift of sympathy in the opposite direction is also possible. Hippolytus, who, in my view, comes across as slightly "inhuman" and blindly intolerant in much of his play, merits pity for his suffering at the end and is impressively generous in his reconciliation with his father. Similarly, Pentheus, who, because of his rashness and blindness, should be seen as a poor specimen of kingship and a poor spokesman for male-centered civic values, must be viewed differently once he has been mockingly deluded by Dionysus and suffered horribly at the hands of his mother, and the love expressed for him by Agave and Cadmus is matched by their open complaints about Dionysus' harshness.

Just as is true of the "sting in the tail," Euripides' use of mirroring, juxtaposition, and other characteristics of a more open form of dramatic composition extends potentialities of the genre that were also exploited in Aeschylus and Sophocles. A more open structure provides excellent opportunities for effects of variety and surprise, but also has the more "serious" effects argued for in this chapter. It presents to an audience a greater challenge to engage in interpretation, to try either to integrate disparate or contrasting elements into a single vision or to acquiesce in the residue of uncertainty, contradiction, and instability that the represented tragic world lays before them. The confrontation of this uncertainty was, for the Greeks, a religious as well as an aesthetic-intellectual experience, and in this aspect Euripides' dramaturgy continues the tradition of the ever-developing genre of Attic tragedy.[45]

---

[44] On this controversy see Gregory 1999: xxxiii–xxxv, Mossman 1995: 194–202.
[45] Cf. Ch. 5, pp. 205–6, Ch. 8, pp. 280, 306.

CHAPTER 4

The chorus

In some fourth-century tragedies the choral parts had apparently become mere interludes dividing the "acts" (eventually the canonical "five acts") in which the named characters performed their scenes without any interaction with a chorus, and such unrelated songs or *embolima* (as Aristotle termed them)[1] had, so far as we know, no relation in content to the actors' scenes. Aristotle ascribed the origin of this practice to the poet Agathon, who was active from about 420 to 399. *Embolima*, according to the same evidence in the *Poetics*, were unknown in the plays of Sophocles and Euripides. Nevertheless, there is evidence in both authors for the gradual reduction of the importance of the chorus, indicated by the smaller proportion of their lines to the total length of the drama, their subordination to particular characters, and other features such as the expansion of actors' songs.[2] Despite this trend, the chorus was still for them an essential part of the performance and of the generation of meaning, as it had been from the conjectured beginnings of the genre. Under the influence of a different remark by Aristotle and some comments in the scholia, Euripides' choral technique has usually been viewed as one aspect of decline from the "true" tragedy of Sophocles, and indeed as preparing the way for the *embolimon* by admitting a distinct looseness of connection and relevance in the content of his choral songs. The aim of this chapter is to survey a number of topics related to the chorus in order to characterize more accurately how the choral parts contribute to Euripides' dramaturgy. The Euripidean chorus in fact shares in creating the instability of perspective and interpretation that is

---

[1] *Poetics* 18.1456a29–30, translated and discussed in n. 79 below. In fifth-century tragedy the choral songs are termed parodos/parodoi (the first song, often partly processional, accompanying the entry of the chorus – except in Eur. *Su.*, where the chorus is present from the beginning) and stasimon/stasima (the songs after the parodos). Later the five acts or (dialogue-)parts (*merē*) might be divided by four interludes marked in some ancient texts simply as "song of the chorus" (*chorou melos*).

[2] On the developments of choral song in tragedy see Kranz 1933, Rode 1971, Csapo 1999–2000, Battezzato 2005.

fostered by many aspects of Euripides' art, but his choral technique lies within the same continuum as that of Aeschylus and Sophocles. The first sections of the chapter consider aspects of the social and ideological functions of the chorus within tragedy, such as the variations in the sense of identification between theater-audience and chorus, the authority of the choral voice, and problems of choral knowledge and ignorance. The later sections look at issues of mythic content and the structural technique of choral odes in their relation to problems of connection and thematic relevance.

In relation to several of the topics of this chapter, two general points deserve particular emphasis. First, it is important to recognize the variety and instability of the choral voice – that is, to understand how it may shift from the "intradramatic" position of a group with a particular fictional identity and status and with plausible psychological motivations and immediate emotional responses to the "extradramatic" position of a collective voice less tied to a particular identity and standing more aloof from the action.[3] Second, it is necessary to recognize that the authority of the choral position is limited and problematic, that there is a competition between factors that lend to the choral voice a special claim upon the audience's attention and agreement and factors that undercut such a privilege.

THE CHORUS AND THE AUDIENCE

One of the most distinctive features of fifth-century Attic tragedy is the counterpoint between the individualized and elite heroes who are the actors and sufferers in Greek tragedies and the anonymous collective voice of the chorus, normally drawn from persons of lower status than the main characters. Since the conflict of individual and collective purposes and the contrast between elite and mass are of heightened interest in the context of Athenian democracy, it is worthwhile to consider whether the tragic chorus has some particularly Athenian or democratic aspects, and whether its collective identity makes some special call upon the audience as citizens. What emerges from a careful consideration is that while the tragic chorus enjoys definite advantages in terms of authority and identification *vis-à-vis* the theater audience, such factors vary significantly in strength from play to play and from moment to moment within a play. Moreover, certain countervailing forces cause the audience to feel itself to be distanced from or superior to the position of the chorus, and thus to regard the chorus

[3] For a more complex classification that attempts to analyze this fluidity by specifying many different positions for the choral voice in a schema of the process of communication, see Calame 1999.

as in some ways "other," as has been argued (a little too one-sidedly) by John Gould.[4]

The first factor which may be considered to contribute significantly to the authority of the tragic chorus is the long history of choral presence in communal events of both public cult and private festivity. In this history, the choral voice has special power both vertically and horizontally.[5] By "vertically" I refer to the communication between the chorus and supernatural powers, especially the gods "in heaven," whereas by "horizontally" I refer to the performers' communication with their human audience. Vertically, the chorus makes a more powerful claim on the attention of the gods than does any single speaker or singer. The group singing in unison (and accompanied by the resonant music of the *aulos*) produces a louder and more penetrating sound, maximizing the likelihood of success in having its message heard by the powers above (or below). The choreographed movements of the group, whether in procession, in circular dance, or in line-and-rank movements within a fixed area, likewise reinforce the attention-holding force of the appeal. The movements may even be considered to have a magical force, compelling epiphany or at least a sympathetic hearing. Even though from a greater distance, the human chorus can hope to perform analogously to the ideal divine chorus, the Muses led by Apollo, that captivates the audience of assembled gods on Mount Olympus.[6]

The horizontal relationship of the performers with the audience of human onlookers is in most contexts conditioned by the fact that the disciplined subgroup that is the chorus is in some sense a selection that presents the community to itself and thus speaks with authority because it articulates shared values. For instance, when a chorus of unmarried girls performs at a festival connected with female rites of passage, their performance enacts on behalf of all girls of like age and status their acceptance of and participation in the social order of the city in which they are destined to become the wives and mothers of citizen males.[7] When young men perform an epinician in a public space, they set the individual victor's achievement in a context of public acknowledgment, revealing not only that they, the victor's closest rivals, are free of envy but that the community as a whole basks in the glory of the victory. Even in a competitive situation, where choruses have a parochial identification (as "men of the Akamantid tribe" in

---

[4] Gould 1996.
[5] See Mullen 1982, Herington 1985, Burnett 1985, Gentili 1988, Lonsdale 1993, Calame 1994–95 and 1997, Bacon 1994–95, Henrichs 1994–95 and 1996.
[6] Cf. *Hom. Hymn. Ap.* 187–206, Pindar, *Pythian* 1.1–12.   [7] See in particular Calame 1997.

the dithyrambic contest of the Great Dionysia, or as "chorus from Delos" at the archaic festival evoked by the *Homeric Hymn to Apollo* 146–76), the full audience may be embraced through a broader identification (as Athenians honoring Dionysus at their most inclusive Dionysiac festival, or as Ionians celebrating a Panionian festival).

The content of choral poems is also important. Historically, choral poems contained a variable mixture of three main kinds of authoritative discourse: performative utterances, gnomic statements, and mythic content. To be categorized with the performative are, on the one hand, what might be called the bardic and directorial content, that is, the self-exhortations that refer to the music and dance or other movements and to the navigation of the path of the song, and, on the other hand, the cultic elements of summons, thanksgiving, prayer for prosperity or protection, and the like. The latter gain significance from, and lend significance to, the vertical and horizontal relationships just described. The former make explicit the beauty, effort, tact, and discipline that make the choral performance a worthy object of attention for both the gods and the human audience.

Gnomic utterances in choral lyric add the weight of traditional wisdom to prayer, or to the impulse to praise, or to the condensation of a particular lesson from a familiar snatch of myth. In the pre-dramatic forms of choral performance, gnomes have unchallenged authority. They invite from the audience renewed assent to inherited, shared wisdom. They demonstrate the acceptance of traditional values by the chorus itself, which is especially significant if the chorus is of children or youths on the brink of adulthood. In such situations, the gnomes accomplish a tactful compulsion of a commonality of judgment, not the separation of perspectives we find in drama, which makes it possible for the audience of tragedy to exercise judgment upon the gnomes of the chorus, just as they do on those of the actors.

Mythic content in choral poetry ranges from extended narrative to brief allusion or example. Although brief traditional cult songs (as well as professional poems written for performance on the spot at Greek athletic games)[8] may often have done without mythic narrative, in the longer odes commissioned well in advance from professional poets myth usually plays some part. The narrative may be firmly encapsulated within a larger frame, for instance as a central *exemplum*, as often in Pindar and Bacchylides and perhaps in Alcman's *First Partheneion*, or the frame may tend toward the perfunctory, with the narrative occupying three-quarters or more of the song. An extreme reduction of the frame is present when the

---

[8] On the genre of shorter epinicians written immediately after a victory, see Gelzer 1985.

narrative seems self-standing until a final prayer or envoi to a god (e.g., Bacchylides 17). Occasionally there may have been no frame at all, as the narrative occupies the entire performance (Bacchylides 18 goes a step farther and turns the unframed narrative into a tiny dramatic dialogue). Unfortunately, some of the most important comparanda for the treatment of myth in tragic lyric are lost to us, for we have virtually no useful knowledge of the hundreds or rather thousands of Attic dithyrambs entered in the competition of tribal choruses of men and of boys at the Great Dionysia.[9] If we had a dozen or two dozen of these extant, along with some didaskalic information to inform us of dating and authorship, we would know a great deal more about the relative frequency of different framing techniques and narrative strategies in the choral lyric most familiar to the audience of tragedy.

Nevertheless, it is possible to claim that all mythic narrative in archaic Greek poetry had an exemplary function. This function is clear enough when the myth narrated concerns the god who is honored by a cult song, or when in other types of song the poet explicitly cites the myth as an example to prove a point. Such explicitness is not, however, universal. When Arion "gave names to" individual dithyrambs (Herodotus 1.23) already in the first half of the sixth century, this seems to mean that he narrated various (non-Dionysian) heroic myths in poems performed at festivals of Dionysus.[10] One could think of this breadth of subject-matter partly in terms of a "secularization" of the song matching the increasing professionalization of the poets, but this is not the whole story. A delightful narrative and consummate skill in performance are assumed to be welcome and pleasing to the god no less than to the human audience, so that beauty and excellence, in poetry as well as in athletics or dedicatory offerings, are suitable "religious" observances within a festival. Even more important, all heroic myth was regarded in a privileged light: it demonstrated important

[9] Similar choral songs were performed at other Attic festivals, and professional poets like Pindar also wrote many choral songs for religious festivals in other Greek communities. So the surviving traces of such songs are only a very small fraction of what existed in the archaic and classical periods.

[10] Ἀρίονα ... ἐόντα κιθαρῳδὸν τῶν τότε ἐόντων οὐδενὸς δεύτερον καὶ διθύραμβον πρῶτον ἀνθρώπων τῶν ἡμεῖς ἴδμεν ποιήσαντά τε καὶ ὀνομάσαντα καὶ διδάξαντα ἐν Κορίνθῳ ("Arion ... who was a kitharode second to none of the poet-performers of that time and who was the first person we know of who composed and named a dithyramb and trained a chorus to perform it in Corinth"); cf. *Suda* s.v. Ἀρίων. Since the word *dithyrambos* is attested two generations earlier in Archilochus (and it is very likely that Herodotus knew that), the "naming" done by Arion is usually assumed to be the act of giving titles to the songs indicating their mythological content (e.g., Pickard-Cambridge 1927: 20–1, Patzer 1962: 17, Lesky 1983: 18); but for the view that the passage means that Arion first extended the term *dithyrambos* to refer to a new kind of choral song, see Zimmermann 1992: 24–5. For the latest speculations about choral and dithyrambic performances in the sixth century, see the contributions in Csapo and Miller 2007a.

aspects of the workings of the world – the relationships of gods and men, the origins of cults, names, and customs, the nature and validity of common Greek practices (guest-friendship, supplication, treatment of the dead). In any cultic setting it was right and proper to illustrate and contemplate such fundamental beliefs, and acknowledgment of them through mythic narrative was as appropriate as acknowledgment of the specific powers of a specific god through a narrative of that god's own actions.

It was the general valorization of mythic narrative as exemplary of essential structures of the world that made it possible for poets to employ myth sometimes without explicit connection to the context of performance. Myths in Pindar may be exemplary of appropriate values (or of their opposites, in negative examples) without there always being a particular correspondence (as older critics of Pindar often wished) between the circumstances of the victor and the details of the chosen myth.[11] Likewise, stories that have "nothing to do with Dionysus" are acceptable in a festival of Dionysus. Myth within choral song thus often involves an effort of interpretation for the audience. It is a sophisticated form of discourse, and the chorus' ability to employ it is another mark of authority. The choral voice appears to have command not only of the vast field of myth but also of the subtle techniques by which mythic narrative is deployed by the professional poets, although this mastery does not preclude either poets or choruses from adopting at times a posture of puzzlement or despair about the mythical events they describe. For their part, the tragedians relied on an audience familiar with the need for interpretation and thus willing to consider carefully how an unobvious myth might be related to the action of the play.

From the inherited moments of authority based on the larger Greek choral and poetic tradition, we may now turn to sources of choral authority connected with the nature of Athenian tragedy itself. Although tragedy depends for its effect on the spectators' emotional engagement with the protagonists (through the sort of "identification" that makes possible Aristotle's pity and fear), there are many ways in which the audience must instead tend to identify with the status and viewpoint of the chorus. The chorus represents an audience within the play and is an intermediary between actors and theatrical audience. This intermediary status is spatial, temporal, and communicative. Spatially, the chorus is most of the time in a

---

[11] On the struggles of critics in the nineteenth and first half of the twentieth century to find greater "unity" or consistency of "relevance" in Pindar's epinicians by detecting allegories or positing biographical details of the poet or victor, see Young 1970.

separate playing region from the actors, the orchestra (*orchēstra*, "dancing place"): this choral region (whether circular or, more likely, rectangular or trapezoidal in the theater of Euripides' lifetime) is enclosed on three sides by the seating area and may have been visually demarcated by a difference in level, if the actor's area was a low platform accessible from the orchestra by a few shallow steps. Numerous scenes in extant plays imply the proximity of the actors to the stage façade and doorway and the separation and distance of the chorus from the façade and the actors, so that the normal spatial arrangement will have been front to back from the vantage point of the middle of the audience.[12] Temporally, the chorus normally comes closest to the theatrical audience itself in the length and continuity of its presence as a witness of the words and action of the play: usually no more than 8 to 10 percent of the total script is covered before the chorus enters, and once present the chorus normally stays until the very end, with departure for any time within the play being exceptional. Moreover, during long stretches of its presence, the chorus must have stood (or knelt or crouched) to face the actors, doing little more than observing and listening in the same way that the audience did. Communicatively, the chorus and its leader are authorized to interact with and react to the actors within the formal conventions of song or chant and (much more restrictedly) of iambic dialogue, while the theatrical audience observes the same events with a range of participation that may have varied from polite contemplation and silent emotion to involuntary gasps, spontaneous hisses, and even, occasionally, the catcalls and heckling of the most boisterous or boorish members. Tragedy's overall respect for the closure of its stage world (for which the term "dramatic illusion" remains the most useful) is clearly distinct from the fluidity or openness to the audience of the stage world of Old Comedy, and this level of closure implies that the authorized or acknowledged behavior of its audience was largely on the silent, contemplative end of the spectrum.

---

[12] The spatial arrangements of the fifth-century theater in which the plays of Sophocles and Euripides were performed are hotly debated, since the archaeological remains from this period are scanty and ambiguous. One issue is whether the orchestra was already a large circle in this period, or whether that form was an innovation of the great stone theaters built in Athens and elsewhere in the fourth century. If the orchestra was not a circle, then it was rectilinear or trapezoidal, similar to the shape known in some small Attic deme theaters of the fifth century. See Moretti 1999–2000 (rectilinear), Wiles 1997 (circular), and Davidson 2005 for a brief summary and basic bibliography. A second issue is whether to assume the front-to-back arrangement of chorus and actors as the norm (as most scholars do) or to posit that the actors routinely performed in the middle of a circle formed by the chorus (for the latter see especially Ley and Ewans 1985, Ewans 1995). If the front-to-back arrangement was the norm, there is still uncertainty whether the stage was demarcated from the orchestra by difference in level (see Mastronarde 1994 on *Phoen.* 846 and 1720–1, MacDowell 1971 on *Wasps* 1341).

The position of the chorus as a group set over against individuals also links the chorus closely to the audience as a collective body. The separation of the individual actors/characters from the group lies at the origin of Attic tragedy and is operative not only in the spatial arrangement just described but also in the conventional structure of alternating dialogue-scenes and songs and in formal features of meter and dialect. Song belongs largely to the chorus, has instrumental accompaniment, and shows dialectic features recalling the non-Attic or panhellenic tradition of high-style choral poetry. Dialogue in iambic trimeter, a spoken rhythm using a poetic form of Attic dialect, is largely the domain of the actors. The audience, for its part, also participates in the theatrical festival as a corporate body, analogous in some ways to the assembly of citizens. Although the audience at the Great Dionysia was more inclusive than that of the assembly, since it included resident aliens and foreign visitors to the city and perhaps children, slaves, and (less certainly) some women,[13] and although we cannot be sure that the system of seating by tribal units was already in use in the fifth century, nonetheless the festival included civic ceremonies and an elaborate judging procedure that made clear to all that the audience as a group represented the collectivity of "the Athenians" with their guests and dependents, set apart from or in judgment upon notable individuals, such as the Priest of Dionysus and other dignitaries in the front seats of honor, the financial sponsors of competing choruses (*chorēgoi*), decked out in their impressive robes and crowns, and the competing poets and actors of the different genres.

In the context of Athenian democracy, the contrast of group and individuals also bears an ideological burden. Sovereignty lies with the group in the Assembly and courts (*ho dēmos, hoi polloi, to plēthos*), while individual office-holders are subject to the examination and judgment of the group. The principles of equality under the law and freedom of speech (*isonomia, isēgoria, parrhēsia*) go hand in hand with social controls that insist that no one seek undue distinction or prominence unless in the service of the community and subject to the scrutiny of the group. The heroic subject-matter of tragedy unavoidably brings with it kings, princes, children, and grandchildren of gods, all characters who pride themselves on high birth and who insist on recognition of special status (*timē*). The Greek audience will therefore have performed a delicate balancing act, on the one hand, admiring heroic characters and sympathizing with their plight and, on the other, viewing some of their excesses as endemic to their claim of superior status, so alien to the democratic ideology. In this context, the audience would

[13] See above, p. 16 with n. 48.

seem to be in a better position to identify with the humbler status of the tragic chorus,[14] which frequently reacts to the words and actions of the protagonists by speaking in favor of moderation or wishing for escape from extremes in their own lives. But since Athenian democratic ideology also strongly valorizes the Greek over the barbarian, the citizen over the non-citizen, the male over the female, and the free over the slave, the issue of audience identification by status is a complex one, to be taken up again shortly, in the next section.

The chorus again provides an internal analogue for the theatrical specta-tors in its conventional status of distanced engagement with the actions affecting the characters, a (dis)engagement realized often in endorsements of moderation, personal apotropaic expressions, and attempts to palliate feuds, and in some cases as powerlessness or indecision. The plays in which the chorus has a major share in the plot, such as Aeschylus' *Supplices* and *Eumenides*, are relatively few and should be regarded as bold experiments rather than as survivals of an early form of "choral tragedy" (which, even if it did actually exist, would not be relevant to the work of Sophocles and Euripides). In contrast, in Euripides' *Supplices* the Argive mothers who form the chorus are not very much more engaged in the action than the normal chorus, since the main burden of articulating their appeal is carried by Aethra and Adrastus. The only difference is that because of their intense emotional involvement in the fate of their sons' corpses these women show a lower degree of reflection and generalization in their songs than most other choruses. The tragic chorus is as powerless as the audience to intervene to forestall a violent deed indoors, even when the action is clearly foreseen and they strongly disapprove of it (as in *Medea*): by convention, the chorus cannot enter the skene-door,[15] and choruses are reluctant even to initiate direct contact with the actors (*Hcld.* 73–119, *Hipp.* 575–80, *Tro.* 462–5). The oath of secrecy, as used in *Medea*, *Hippolytus*, and intrigue plays, is a device that puts the chorus at key points in the same position as the well-behaved members of the audience who would not think of shouting out a warning to either sympathetic or unsympathetic characters within the world of the play. (The obverse of the coin of powerlessness is irresponsibility – discussed later.)

---

[14] See esp. Griffith 1995: 72–81.
[15] See Arnott 1984–85, Pöhlmann 1995. The one extant exception, *Hel.* 385, involves not a chorus interfering with a violent action indoors, but a chorus going inside to hear a prophetic answer to the question whether Menelaus survives or not (this choral curiosity is the internal analogue of the more important external motivation for this staging: the poet wants to bring Menelaus on alone for a kind of second prologue).

Finally, the chorus shares with the audience the status of survivor. With few exceptions,[16] just as the chorus is exempt from the excessive ambitions, enmities, and dangers that confront the protagonists, so is it exempt from the death, bereavement, and exile that often await the individual agents within or at the end of the play's action. The tragic performance allows, or forces, the audience to confront extreme situations, sharp shifts of fortune, violation and questioning of fundamental patterns of society and personal identity. But the violence and the horror are contained and controlled by the aesthetic form of tragic verse and well-defined dramatic forms and by the inherent distance of the represented heroic world as well as by the ordered setting of the festival. Whether the enacted disruption is viewed as part of a Dionysiac liminality leading to reintegration or as a confrontation with the anxiety of sacrificial violence or as a means of purging potentially harmful emotions, the end state for the audience, as usually for the chorus, is a return to everyday life, with its smaller challenges and more gradual pressures. In many plays, the chorus' survival represents the community's survival, as may be claimed for plays like *Oedipus Tyrannus* or *Antigone*, even though many have noted that in the former Sophocles has done nothing to remind us at the end of the play that Thebes must now be freed from the plague and has obscured, by Creon's indecision in the last scene, the notion of Oedipus as *pharmakos* (sacrificial scapegoat) taking the community's sickness away with him. A similar claim about communal survival can sometimes be made in Euripides (for instance, in *Hippolytus* or *Andromache*), but less often and with many qualifications.[17]

One tragic technique that tends to seal the chorus' role as survivor and to grant the choral voice a final impression of privileged authority is the practice of having the chorus utter the final words of the drama. This is clear in cases like *Oedipus Tyrannus* (at least, for those who accept the final anapaests as Sophoclean),[18] *Trachiniae* (with the chorus-leader's final – more contemplative and accepting – lines in counterpoint to the impassioned

---

[16] As noted below, p. 105, the chorus of *Tro.* will be on the Greek ships that the gods plan to afflict with a destructive storm once they depart from shore. The most striking exception (cf. Foley 2003: 15), if it is one, is the chorus of Oceanids in *Prom.*: they bravely refuse to abandon Prometheus when Hermes warns them to depart, although since the play ends with Prometheus describing the earthquake and lightning that engulf him the audience may have no way to infer just how the Oceanids suffer (the chorus could even have scattered in terror, suggesting that they did not suffer as Prometheus did – the staging favored by Griffith 1983: 276–7).

[17] See below, pp. 104–5.

[18] Soph. *OT* 1524–30 have been under suspicion since Ritter 1861: 424–8; the lines are accepted in Lloyd-Jones and Wilson 1990 (cf. Calame 1999: 140), but bracketed as spurious in Dawe 1984.

resentment just expressed by Hyllus),[19] and *Choephori*. In Euripides, *Hippolytus* may be taken as a straightforward case of the same kind, since the chorus summarizes as follows (1462–6): "In common to all the citizens this sorrow has come unexpectedly. There will be repeated bouts of many tears. For the grief-inducing stories of the great have a greater hold on attention." But in general Euripides seems to have reduced or avoided this traditional technique.[20]

LIMITS ON IDENTIFICATION AND AUTHORITY

Let us now turn to the countervailing factors that mark the distinction between the internal audience of the chorus and the external audience of the theater, factors that prevent a facile identification of the impersonated group in the orchestra with the community of citizens. First, there is the very fact of impersonation. Although some scholars believe that one form of pre-tragic dithyramb may have involved impersonation by the dithyrambic chorus,[21] I believe that the invention of tragedy involved two innovations: the definitive separation from the choral group of a solo performer capable of changing roles, and the impersonation by the chorus of a group of human characters from an identified time and place different from the actual time and place of the spectators. The tragic chorus is thus qualitatively different from satyr-choruses, animal choruses, or other ritual choruses involving costuming of some sort. Second, as John Gould has suggested, the language and meter of the chorus are more remote from the idiom of the audience and of civic discourse than are the language and meter of the characters, and

---

[19] I agree with Easterling 1982 in assigning *Trach.* 1275–8 to the chorus.   [20] See below, pp. 105–6.
[21] By "impersonation" here I mean the adoption for the full course of the performance of an identity other than that of contemporary citizen choreuts. When the poems of Bacchylides were first discovered, some thought that the mimetic poem 18 (where half-choruses impersonate Aegeus and a group of his subjects respectively) showed the form of pre-tragic sixth-century dithyramb, but in recent generations the poem's mimetic form is more plausibly taken to be a borrowing from fifth-century tragedy (Zimmermann 1992: 95–7). Pickard-Cambridge 1927: 135 writes of Arion's dithyramb that "it was probably purely lyric; the chorus *may* [emphasis in original] have impersonated some group of characters and been so far dramatic, but there is no proof that they did so." Webster in Pickard-Cambridge 1962: 100–1 removes this statement and declares that the dithyrambs had mimetic satyr-choruses and that impersonation is also proved by the choruses of "padded dancers" shown on archaic vases (see most recently the essays in Csapo and Miller 2007a). Patzer 1962: 121–3 argues that Arion innovated in three separate areas: his dithyrambs were non-mimetic choral poems on heroic myth, he wrote songs for mimetic satyr-choruses (who, he argues, had previously been wordless dancers), and he originated a third type of choral performance (*Urtragödie*) which combined the heroic content of the dithyramb with the mimetic form of satyr-performances. On the problematic phrase in *Suda* s.v. Ἀρίων that credits Arion with being the first "to bring on satyrs speaking in verse" (Σατύρους εἰσενεγκεῖν ἔμμετρα λέγοντας), see Patzer 1962: 54–5, Lesky 1983: 16–17.

this may be taken as an indication of the otherness of the chorus.[22] Third, the ideological alignment of audience with chorus on the axis of collective group versus prominent individual is confused (though not made impossible) by the preference for weak and marginal status in tragic choruses, in contrast to the high valuation in Athenian democratic ideology of the Greek, the citizen, the male, and the free.

In addition, the audience's identification with the chorus and its interpretations is affected by the fact that the audience is, in most respects, in a position of superior knowledge and enjoys the widest perspective.[23] The chorus is indeed privileged as a repository of collective memory of the past, and occasionally the choral voice will sing with an extradramatic prescience that serves the purpose of the poet's manipulations rather than the psychological consistency of the chorus.[24] But regarding the present and future of the events depicted in the play, the chorus cannot attain the level of knowledge that can be claimed for the alert and moderately informed member of the audience. The audience can partially identify with the fears, hopes, and anxieties of a chorus and accept as a guideline the chorus' reaction to the events and to the claims of the speaking actors. But simultaneously the audience feels itself separate from and superior to the chorus, for the audience knows (in most cases, at least) the inevitable outcome of the plot, whether from specific mythological knowledge or from well-trained familiarity with tragic story-patterns and plot-devices, and knows that the chorus speaks from a partial and limited perspective.

The chorus' moral and interpretive stature may also be called into question by its stance toward important actions on the stage, for the conventional limits on choral action may remind the audience that it is an artificial construct of the performance. In some cases a chorus withdraws from participation or is unwilling to make a decisive judgment or to face a harsh truth. An outstanding example of choral withdrawal is found in

---

[22] While it is true that the Athenian audience was very familiar with the language, style, and meter of choral song because of the number of performances they could attend (cf. Goldhill 1996), the significant point for the issue of the "otherness" of the tragic chorus is that choral language is decidedly more distant and artificial in comparison to the language of the iambic parts dominated by the actors, which more strongly called to mind the language and sometimes the subject-matter of public speech in the assembly and courts and also evoked the tradition of the political poetry of Solon.

[23] In my view, this superiority of knowledge is a significant obstacle to interpretations that press too hard on the potential of choral self-referentiality to induce the audience to apply choral statements to their own situation external to the play: in the long-disputed controversy over whether to read "why should I dance?" (τί δεῖ με χορεύειν;) in Soph. *OT* 896 as expressing a position of the author (virtual or real) or the audience, I do not agree with Henrichs 1994–95 or Calame 1999.

[24] Examples are discussed below, pp. 112–14.

Choephori. The chorus takes an extraordinarily active role in the first four-fifths of the play, but when the cries of Aegisthus are heard from indoors, the slave women pull back to the safer distance more usual for a chorus: "let us distance ourselves from the deed that is being completed, so that we may seem to be without responsibility for these evils" (872–4). Ultimately a chorus cannot take responsibility for important action, and its role is often to hold out hope for moderation and harmlessness when the hero and the audience can see only disaster. The futility of this choral stance (as for instance when the chorus of *Septem* advises Eteocles not to fight) lends special stature to the suffering characters who face their danger more directly. The short dialogue at *Trachiniae* 723–30 nicely illustrates the aspect of futility (or blindness or irresponsibility) that may undercut the choral position:

CH. Although it is unavoidable to fear a dreadful outcome,
    you ought not to determine your expectation before the event.
DE. There is in counsels not well taken
    Not even any hope able to procure some confidence.
CH. But in the case of those who slip up involuntarily
    there is a soft and yielding reaction, which you ought to receive.
DE. Such would be the claim not of the one who shares
    in the evil, but of one who does not personally feel the pain.

Deianeira's position cannot simply be regarded as consistent with the fearful outlook already displayed in her prologue-speech, for it is proved accurate by the statements and attitudes of the enraged Heracles later in the play.

It is noteworthy that Euripides goes beyond Aeschylus and Sophocles in weakening the factors that favor identification and authority and exploiting the opposing factors. It has often been noticed how Euripides in his extant plays predominantly employs female choruses, and the issue of the status of the chorus deserves somewhat fuller consideration. There are two broad categories into which choruses may be classified: the chorus may represent the communal group residing in the general location of the action, or the chorus may consist of comrades or dependents of a main character. With their choruses of citizen elders, *Agamemnon* and *Antigone* are good examples of the former, while the female war-captives in *Troades* and kidnapped Greek women-slaves in *Helen* are good examples of the latter. But many variations and mixtures are possible. A chorus of comrades or dependents can still speak for the values of the larger community. The same chorus can share both features (as do the old men in *Heracles*). And in late Euripides there are cases where he seems to be experimenting with avoiding both aspects, representing neither the communal group nor the age-mates or comrades of a major character (*Phoenissae, Iphigenia in Aulis, Bacchae*).[25]

The tragic chorus was most clearly representative of the political community when it consisted of free adult males native to a city, for in classical Athens, as in classical Greek cities generally but with variations in eligibility for various functions, the sovereign group was the male adults of citizen status who participated in government at various levels of organization (deme, tribe, courts, council, assembly) and served in the military. The paradigmatic cases are seen in *Agamemnon, Oedipus Tyrannus*, and *Antigone*, where city elders comprise the chorus. The advanced age of these groups has two advantages: first, there is an assumption of experience and wisdom suitable to counselors of a leader or king; second, age necessitates a marginal role with regard to action, safeguarding the relative distance or non-involvement of the chorus in the critical events. In extant Euripides the chorus of citizen elders is found in only three plays. For *Heracleidae*, a suppliant-play, it is a suitable choice because the burden of protection can be shifted to the king, and the chorus can remain on stage while military action is taken offstage (cf. *Oedipus Coloneus*). In *Heracles*, again a suppliant-play, the theme of old age is exaggerated in a typically Euripidean manner and interacts significantly with the themes of youth and ineffective vs. effective friendship. And in *Alcestis*, the presence of a male chorus despite the domestic subject-matter tilts the interest toward Admetus and the theme of *xenia*, the male guest–host relationship that solves his problem; it also "silences" a female perspective that might challenge the exchange of lives and more sharply criticize the reversals or betrayals perpetrated by Admetus.[26] When younger men form the chorus, they are usually soldiers, clearly dependent on a particular heroic chief, and the military setting shows a community of a different kind from the polis, although analogous themes of mass vs. elite may be deployed. Sophocles' *Ajax* and *Philoctetes* provide examples; but in Euripides there is no certain case of a soldier chorus, although that is one of the two possibilities conjectured for *Telephus*, and his very different choice of a female chorus of sightseers in the army camp in *Iphigenia in Aulis* is noteworthy.

The marginal or dependent status detectable in choruses of old men or soldiers can be portrayed by almost any group of females serving as the

---

[25] Cf. Medda 2005.
[26] Old men as chorus are probable or known in *Antiope, Archelaus, Erechtheus, Cresphontes*, and perhaps *Cretans*; *Telephus* seems to have had either a chorus of soldiers or a chorus of Argive elders. We cannot tell the age of probable or possible male choruses in *Aegeus, Bellerophon, Scyrii, Philoctetes*, nor in *Melanippe the Captive* (if it really had a male chorus).

Table 1: *Choruses in Extant Tragedies*

	Male chorus	Female chorus
Aeschylus	2 (33%)	4 (67%)
Sophocles	5 (71%)	2 (29%)
Euripides	3 (18%)	14 (82%)
anon. *Prom.*, *Rhesus*	1 (50%)	1 (50%)
TOTALS	11 (34%)	21 (66%)

numbers without parentheses or brackets: number of tragedies
numbers in (): percentage of total of plays

Table 2: *Choruses in all tragedies of Aeschylus, Sophocles, and Euripides*

	Male chorus	Female chorus	Undetermined
Aeschylus	14 (41%) [23.3%]	20 (59%) [33.3%]	26 [43.3%]
Sophocles	24 (62%) [25.8%]	15 (38%) [16.1%]	54 [58.1%]
Euripides	15 (36%) [22.4%]	27 (64%) [40.3%]	25 [37.3%]
TOTALS	53 (46%) [24.1%]	62 (54%) [28.2%]	105 [47.7%]

numbers without parentheses or brackets: number of tragedies
numbers in (): percentage of total of plays for which gender known or guessed
numbers in []: percentage of total of known or guessed tragedies

chorus. Even the sea-nymphs who form the chorus of *Prometheus* are clearly divinities of low status, while the mighty Furies of *Eumenides*, exceptional in any case, are portrayed as marginalized by segregation from the heavenly gods and by the shift of cosmic conditions heralded by Apollo's purification and protection of Orestes. One must ask whether preference for a female chorus was not simply a Euripidean choice, but also perhaps a generic feature of tragedy – even a genetic feature, if one follows the speculation that the group of male choristers goes back to a male appropriation of Dionysian maenadism featuring ritual transvestism, as Seaford has theorized.[27] Tables 1 and 2 represent the gender distinction of choruses based on what we may know or guess about lost plays; the numbers are not to be understood as exact, but the ratios are probably suggestive despite a considerable

[27] Seaford 1981 and 1994: 262–75.

degree of uncertainty.[28] When the known and guessed cases are included, the ratios are less one-sided than for the extant plays, but the possible preference for a female chorus seems already present in Aeschylus, and it may be that Euripides carried an existing tendency a little further while Sophocles went against the flow of tradition in preferring male choruses – if in fact he did, since the percentage of undetermined cases is so much higher in his case.

The tendency toward a female chorus seen in Euripides need not have a single cause, but may be related to various factors, as well as to tradition. In all three great tragedians, female choruses are particularly appropriate to domestic conflicts. Aeschylus' choice of household slaves in *Choephori* is striking: in a "tyrannized" Argos there is no room any more for the citizen chorus used in *Agamemnon* or even for sympathetic interest from women outside the house (as in Sophocles' *Electra*). Even so, the slave women articulate the ritual interests of the household and of the dead Agamemnon with great force, identify strongly with the light of freedom brought by Orestes' revenge, and have a more direct participation in the action than is usual for a chorus of either gender. More typical is the chorus of maidens in *Trachiniae*, although Sophocles modulates their identification with Deianeira by having Deianeira draw a sharp contrast between the optimism of their youth and virginity and her own burden of care brought on by marriage and motherhood. In neither *Choephori* nor *Trachiniae* does the gender of the chorus diminish its ability to narrate and to reflect and to articulate communal values.[29] Euripides, however, prefers more domestic and personal themes, more frequently makes a female the protagonist of the action or presents the viewpoints of women, and these traits are relevant because female characters can speak more openly in the presence of women but are expected to be much more restrained in the presence of men from the outside community.[30] The prominent themes of the cost of war and the aftermath of war are also more easily reinforced by a female chorus. Another

---

[28] The relevant titles for Aeschylus and Sophocles are in Mastronarde 1998: 62 n. 11. But I use here a revised list for Euripides based on the information in Kannicht's edition in *TrGF* 5 (also, in Mastronarde 1988 there was a clerical error in the number of indeterminate plays ascribed to Euripides). The fifteen plays with known or guessed male choruses include three extant plays and the following twelve: *Aegeus, Alope, Antiope, Archelaus, Bellerophon, Erechtheus, Cresphontes, Cretans, Melanippe the Captive, Scyrii, Telephus, Philoctetes.* The twenty-seven titles with female choruses include fourteen extant plays and the following thirteen: *Aeolus, Alcmeon* A', *Alcmeon* B', *Andromeda, Danae, Ino, Hippolytus* A', *Cressae, Palamedes, Peliades, Protesilaus, Hypsipyle, Phaethon.* For the uncertainties involved cf. the variations in the lists in Castellani 1991: 15–16, Hose 1990–91: I.22–7, and judgments implicit in the index entries for "chorus" in Collard and Cropp 2008b. See also the lists in Foley 2003: 26–7.

[29] See also Foley 2003: 23 for the suggestion that "by being less linked with a specific political system or set of priorities, female choruses can offer a broader vision of cultural commonalities."

[30] See below, pp. 249–50.

important reason for Euripides' practice is the trend (perhaps growing in tragedy in general in the second half of the fifth century) toward conceiving the chorus as a sympathetic adjunct of the main suffering character – with more female sufferers portrayed in Euripides, more female choruses are to be expected.[31] Hose has also noted that Euripides consistently attaches his chorus to the weaker or threatened party, whereas Sophocles' practice is more varied.[32] It also makes a difference that the chorus' relation is established on entry to the sufferer who is present at the start of the play (more likely to be female because females are tied spatially to the house), and this applies even in plays with dual protagonists or double actions, so that one finds a female chorus in *Hippolytus, Andromache, Electra, Orestes*. This matching of sympathetic female chorus to suffering female character may sometimes serve to keep that character's interests or stake before the audience's mind even when they are absent in the second half of the play, as with Phaedra in *Hippolytus* and Andromache in *Andromache* (observe the more austere choice of Sophocles in *Antigone*, where the heroine has the very limited and grudging sympathy of the Theban elders). In addition, Csapo has plausibly suggested that, because of the Greek ideological assumption that self-control is a masculine (and Greek) virtue, the emotionality of the New Music of the late fifth century was more suitably assigned to female (and Asian) choruses.[33] Finally, Foley notes that the competitive performance context may also have played a role, as the skillful representation of the "other" may have been an important criterion for the best choruses just as versatility and the ability to differentiate roles within the same play must have been highly valued in the actors.[34]

As a corollary of such tendencies, there is a reduction in the use of the chorus to project a communal civic or political voice, perhaps reflective of a

[31] Hose 1990–91: 17–20, Pattoni 1989.   [32] Hose 1990–91: 17.
[33] Csapo 1999–2000: 424–5. The correlation between the modern lyrical style of late Euripidean choruses and the represented gender of the singers was also noted by Kranz 1933: 237 and Castellani 1991; it should be noted, however, that the same modern style was performed by male soloists in the *nomos* and male choruses in contemporary dithyrambs, and these will often, but not always, have been quoting or performing the voices of females (or non-Greek males). One further factor cited in partial explanation of the preference for female choruses (Castellani 1991) is an impulse toward "realism" or "verisimilitude": on this view, the frequency of intrigues of various kinds exerts a pressure to ensure that the chorus is prevented by its status and weakness from intervening in the action, and a female chorus is thought to satisfy this need better than a male one. Yet even a male chorus is often subordinated or marginalized (by dependency, age, and weakness) in such a way as to present no obstacle to intrigue and action within the conventions of the tragic stage, so that this is another area in which Greek drama's gestures toward "realism" should not be overrated and universalized. In plays as separated in time as *Iphigenia in Aulis* and *Medea* the inaction of a female chorus has more to do, I would argue, with convention than with realism.
[34] Foley 2003: 5–7.

weakening of the cohesive forces in Attic society in the final decades of the fifth century. To be sure, even Euripidean female choruses can express communal values or inherited wisdom, along the same lines as the choruses in *Choephori* and *Trachiniae*. But a number of his female choruses are closely dependent on, or tightly identified with, a principal female character, and thus tend to project a more partial perspective, or to echo that character's more private concerns with observations drawn from their own lives. The viewpoint of the community may thus be less in evidence, undermining the consolation of communal survival that might otherwise have been provided by a chorus.

Apart from the issue of status and gender, Euripides also weakens the authority of the choral role in regard to choral survival and choral last words. In general Euripides has reduced the choral contribution in the final scenes of many plays, eliminating both formal dirges involving the chorus and weighty last words from the chorus. In *Medea, Hippolytus,* and *Andromache,* the communities of Corinth and Trozen and Phthia will live on, despite grief at the loss just witnessed, with the terrible events remembered (but tamed) in ritual cult and in repeated song. But the survival of the community at Thebes at the end of *Phoenissae* or *Bacchae* is, at best, implicit because in both cases the chorus is foreign to Thebes and not directly representative of this survival. With the emphasis on the Athenian future of Heracles in *Heracles* one scarcely thinks of the future condition of a leaderless Thebes. The slave choruses of *Hecuba, Troades,* and *Ion* likewise undercut any close identification of chorus as survivors with audience as survivors. Only the slaves of the Athenian royal house in *Ion* can enjoy the outcome of their play. The slaves of *Hecuba* look forward to servitude in Greece, while those of *Troades* are not even assured of survival as slaves, since the gods have agreed, as the audience knows and the characters and chorus do not, that the Greek fleet (on which the new slaves sail) will be devastated on the voyage home.

As for final choral utterances, these are often avoided or weakened in Euripides. There are hardly any other cases to match the relatively specific choral summation of *Hipp.* 1462–6, quoted earlier.[35] In some cases, the

---

[35] Above, p. 98. The chorus of *Hec.* (1293–5) exhorts itself to movement and ends with "for necessity is unbending" (στερρὰ γὰρ ἀνάγκη). The chorus of *El.* (1357–9) offers a general farewell and a comment: "Farewell! Whoever of mortals is able to fare well (be happy) and does not suffer from some misfortune enjoys a blessed fate." The chorus of *Ion* (1619–22) celebrates the happy ending with the generalization: "If anyone's house is tormented by misfortunes, they should revere the gods and have no fear: for in the end, the noble receive the good fate they deserve, while the base, as suits their nature, would never fare well." Compare fr. 446, probably the last lines of the lost first *Hippolytus*: "O blessed hero Hippolytus, what honors you have been granted because of your self-control: there is never any power greater than virtue for mortals, for sooner or later there comes a good recompense for piety."

presence of the *deus ex machina* shifts the weight of authority to that speaker. In other cases the chorus does little more than consent to depart, omitting conclusive reflection.[36] A conclusive choral reflection is found in more or less identical words at the end of several plays: "The dispositions of the gods take many forms; the gods bring many things to fulfillment unexpectedly. What was expected has not been fulfilled, but god found a way for the unexpected. Such is the outcome of this affair."[37] This could be inauthentic, a convention of later performances or of book production. Even if the final tag is accepted as Euripidean, however, it is probably emptied of deep significance by its formulaic nature.[38] This "weakness" of the choral voice at the end of Euripidean plays should be viewed in connection with other aspects that undercut the chorus' involvement and diminish the sense of community that the chorus was traditionally capable of embodying.

THE CHORUS AND KNOWLEDGE

None of the human figures involved in and internally observing the action of a Greek tragedy has the level of knowledge that can be claimed for the alert and moderately informed member of the audience. Among the various members of the original audience, there will, of course, have been different levels of familiarity with heroic legend and with earlier Greek poetry and tragedy, and the poets of tragedy were constantly innovating in larger or smaller details of their treatments of mythic events. Nevertheless, the implied audience of the plays was probably one well versed in a "song culture" of long standing, and Aristotle's famous statement (*Poetics* 9.1451b25–6) about the myths used in tragedy being "known to a few" should not be applied incautiously to the fifth-century audience.[39] The chorus is an internal spectator, and its take on the events and on the argumentative claims of the speaking actors may serve as a guideline for the audience, but despite the several bases of authority outlined in the first

---

[36] Forms of the verb στείχω and other verbs of going are present at *Hcld.* 1053, *Hec.* 1293, *Su.* 1232, *Her.* 1427, *Tro.* 1332.

[37] πολλαὶ μορφαὶ τῶν δαιμονίων, / πολλὰ δ᾽ ἀέλπτως κραίνουσι θεοί· / καὶ τὰ δοκηθέντ᾽ οὐκ ἐτελέσθη, / τῶν δ᾽ ἀδοκήτων πόρον ηὗρε θεός. / τοιόνδ᾽ ἀπέβη τόδε πρᾶγμα: *Alc.* 1159–63, *Andr.* 1284–8, *Hel.* 1688–92, *Ba.* 138–92, cf. *Med.* 1415–19, where the first line is instead πολλῶν ταμίας Ζεὺς ἐν Ὀλύμπῳ ("Zeus in Olympus is the dispenser of many things").

[38] See Mastronarde 2002b on *Med.* 1415–19; the lines are deemed more significant by Roberts 1987 and Kovacs 1987b: 268–9.

[39] On the "song-culture," see Herington 1985; on the competences of the audience, see also Revermann 2006.

section of this chapter, the choral perspective is a partial one, subject to the same deficits relative to the knowledge of the audience as are the perspectives of the characters. For example, the audience of *Agamemnon* is superior to the chorus both in its ability and in its willingness to understand the figurative language of Cassandra (1072–330) as a description of the past and impending murders in the house. No alert member of the audience of *Oedipus Tyrannus* will have shared the deluded expectation of celebration expressed by the chorus in the third stasimon of that play (1086–1109). Such discrepancies of knowledge may contribute a momentary frisson, heightening a sense of pity at the realization of the truth that will soon come to the chorus. But they also have a wider significance in extending the unsettling effect of multiple perspectives, depriving the audience of a voiced perspective that they can automatically follow in order to lighten the burden of trying to make sense of an ethically and emotionally confused story.

The effects of dissonance between audience knowledge and choral knowledge are made stronger in several plays by Euripides' use of the divine prologue. The desire to set the audience explicitly in the priviliged position of observer and interpreter of the plot is, one may argue, one motive for the use of the stereotyped prologue-monologue in Euripides, and the prologue-monologues spoken by divinities have the additional effect of elevating the audience to a much higher plane of awareness, normally of essential features of the outcome and sometimes of important aspects of motivation and causation. In *Alcestis*, for instance, Apollo declares at the end of the prologue that Heracles will exact by force the result which he himself has failed to gain by his attempt to persuade Death (64–71). This prediction, reinforced later by Heracles' own assertion at *Alc.* 840–54 (again in the absence of the chorus), colors all the gnomic admonitions of the chorus about the impossibility of cheating death or returning from the underworld (a theme of the parodos and second and fourth stasima, 112–30, 455–9, 985–90). Particularly noteworthy are the echoes of the parodos in the fourth stasimon,[40] just before Heracles brings Alcestis back onstage. The chorus' position is thus consistently different from that of the audience through most of the play, yet its sincere consolations and encomia still contribute to the bittersweet tenor of this drama's meditation on the importance to life and love of the immutable fact of death. There is one point, however, where the chorus is

---

[40] Note the insufficiency of worship (119–120 ~ 973–5), the futility of seeking far for a cure (112–18 ~ 962–72), Apollo's son(s) – Asclepius and his followers (121–30 ~ 969–72), return from the underworld (124–6 ~ 986), Alcestis as best or noblest (83 ~ 993), the relentlessness of death and Necessity (*apotomos* 118 ~ *apotomou* 982).

made to align itself momentarily with the expectation of a happy ending. In a rather abrupt about-face after the chorus-leader has just reacted with shock to Admetus' reception of Heracles (551–2: "What are you doing? ... do you dare to receive a guest? Why are you being foolish?"), the chorus sings an encomium to the hospitality, piety, nobility, and sense of respect for others (*aidōs*) of Admetus. While the chorus still distances itself slightly from Admetus' behavior, which it views as a special excess, as it were, of the noble (600–3, including "I am amazed at their [the nobles'] wisdom/clever-ness"), it is temporarily confident that some good result will come for a man who has treated Apollo and Heracles so well. This temporary optimism reflects the poet's manipulation rather than psychological realism (little different from the manipulation by Sophocles in his happy odes preceding disasters), but the dramatic effect is meaningfully placed just before the gloom of the debate with Pheres.

Aphrodite's introductory monologue in *Hippolytus* is crucial in providing the audience with privileged knowledge that affects its reception of the rest of the play. As far as the chorus is concerned, the discrepancy is highlighted especially in the parodos, where it immediately reinforces the viewers' perception that the human figures in the play are operating in blindness and ignorance. The second pair of stanzas and the epode (*Hipp.* 141–69) offer a series of possible explanations for Phaedra's silent and voluntary "voyage" toward death, explanations that seem carefully chosen by the poet as inversions of the correct answer. Is she "possessed by a god" (141–4)? Yes, but not by any of those proposed by the chorus. Has some failure to worship Artemis correctly caused her wasting disease (145–50)? No, the failure is Hippolytus' and not hers, and the offended goddess is Aphrodite and not Artemis. Is it the unfaithfulness of her husband that torments her (151–4)? Rather, as the audience can suspect from the prologue and will soon hear from Phaedra, it is her horror at the thought of being unfaithful to her husband. Or if the cause is pregnancy, Artemis is the goddess to call upon (161–9) – yet she has been invoked in prayer, quite in vain, by Hippolytus a moment earlier.[41] As the play proceeds, the chorus' knowledge, along with the nurse's, comes to match that of Phaedra herself; all speak of the baneful power of Aphrodite, but no one realizes the motivation and true target of Aphrodite's assault. The chorus' ability to cite mythic exempla, to yearn for release or escape from human woes, or to agonize over the injustice of what

---

[41] *Hipp.* 155–60 do not present the same mirror-image quality as the surrounding speculations, but introduce the notion of an ill-omened voyage from Crete to the mainland, an idea that returns significantly in the second stasimon at 752–63.

they observe is unimpaired by its deficit in knowledge, but the deficit means
that the audience is left to itself to try to makes full sense of the disaster.

Since the divine prologue of *Troades* informs the audience of the gods'
intention to punish the Greeks on their voyage home, the reproachful tone
of the chorus in addressing the gods' abandonment of Troy (843 "reproach";
1062 "you betrayed"; 1077 "I am in anxious doubt whether you [Zeus] care
for these events") is, of course, slightly ironized by their ignorance. There is,
furthermore, a complex mixture of frustrated wish and prescient truth in
another choral utterance in the third stasimon. This song follows the debate
of Helen and Hecuba before Menelaus. In the final stanza (1100–17), the
chorus imagines Menelaus on his voyage home and prays that he be
deprived of his homecoming by a destroying thunderbolt striking in mid-
sea. The audience's background knowledge of the authoritative tradition
that Helen and Menelaus survived (as in the *Odyssey*) must mark this wish as
futile,[42] just as such knowledge will already have overridden Menelaus'
pronouncement (1053–9) that Helen will be executed back in Greece and
undercut any sense that Hecuba has "won" the debate. The chorus' curse in
fact unwittingly echoes the destructive plans of Athena and Poseidon (77–94),
but Menelaus is one of those known by the audience to have survived the
storm and eventually reached home.

In *Ion*, Hermes is a precursor of the Menandrian prologue gods who
provide the audience with the comforting superior awareness that allows
them to understand the intricacies of the hidden relationships of the
characters and to be shocked or amused at the statements and actions that
arise from the characters' ignorance. The chorus of Creusa's slaves is subject
to the same deficit of knowledge as most of the characters, while Creusa is
slightly superior to other characters and the chorus because for half the play
she alone knows her own experience, although she still lacks the vital detail
that her baby survived and is the young man she meets in Delphi. In the
paired stanzas of the first stasimon (452–91) the chorus prays that the
childless royal couple's consultation of the oracle may have a successful
outcome and sings the praises of having children, rejecting childlessness.
The epode to this pair of stanzas (493–509) then evokes the cave of Pan
where the child of Creusa's "friend" was abandoned, with the contrasting

---

[42] Although Helen is mentioned very indirectly in this stanza (only in the causal clause in *Tro.* 1107–8
and through the periphrasis "having captured <the source of> the shame of a disastrous marriage
[*dusgamon aischos*]" in 1114), an audience may get the impression that she will be on the same ship with
Menelaus. If so, here the chorus' lyric imagination aligns itself with the known tradition and ignores
Menelaus' claim that he appreciates Hecuba's advice and that Helen will therefore not travel on the
same vessel as he (1053–4).

judgment that children born from mixed divine and human parentage never
have good fortune. The audience can perceive that the two topics of the ode
are in fact one. The consultation will indeed bring "fair/abundant children
after a long wait" (470) – in two senses, the fair offspring born long ago
(Ion) and the further offspring finally to be conceived by Creusa and Xuthus
(as predicted by Athena, 1589–94). The chorus itself cannot appreciate this
double meaning, and the second meaning depends on knowledge of the
traditional genealogy, or its understanding has to await Athena's prediction.[43] Nor is the chorus aware of the sting in the proviso "obtain fair
offspring *by pure oracles*" (469–70), since Apollo will in fact be deceiving
Xuthus. And ultimately (in the long-term perspective characteristic of the
gods) Ion, offspring of a mortal woman and a god, will prosper and be
blessed, although the chorus' generalization about mixed parentage seems
borne out by the regrets of the separated mother and child and by the
emotional upheaval and physical dangers that they face, from their limited
human perspectives, in the limited timeframe of the play. The chorus'
ignorance also colors for the audience the indignation and rejection
expressed in the next two stasima (676–724, 1048–105), but there is again
a mixed effect. First, the chorus is right in suspecting deception in the oracle
(685), though wrong about its exact nature. Second, the criticism of Xuthus
as enjoying a private good fortune without sufficient concern for his partner
(699–705, 1099–105) has some force, although the call for a reversal of
traditional songs about unfaithfulness in women (1090–8) is not in fact
supported by the true nature of Xuthus' position, and the contestation of
male vs. female piety is ultimately irrelevant to this case.[44]

Even in tragedies without a prologue god, the playwright has the means
to bring it about that audience knowledge or audience perspective surpasses,
or diverges from, that of the chorus: human characters may give crucial
information in the prologue, or an audience's general knowledge of myth or
of typical story-patterns may be operative. The first technique is seen in

[43] In Hesiod's *Catalogue of Women* (fr. 10a.20–4) Achaius and Diomede as well as Ion are born of
Xuthus and Creusa. In *Ion*, the genealogy as foretold by Athena (1589–94) is modified in a patriotic
Athenian direction: Dorus and Achaeus, ancestors of the Dorians and Achaeans, are the offspring of
Xuthus and Creusa.

[44] Another variation on the divine prologue-speaker who ensures that the audience has the fullest
perspective is the Dionysus of *Bacchae*. The audience is made to understand his disguise, while the
chorus of Bacchants remains ignorant of the true identity of the Lydian stranger until the god's
epiphany at the close (if, that is, Dionysus explained in the lost portion of his speech that he had been
the Lydian stranger all along). Thus their reception of the crucial central scene of the play diverges
from that of the audience, which can sense the terrifying direct manipulation of Pentheus' mind by
the present god.

Iphigenia in Tauris, where Orestes makes his identity and purpose known to
the audience in a second scene before the chorus' entry. The chorus of
Iphigenia in Tauris shares in the title character's premature mourning-song
(143–235) after she misinterprets her dream to imply that Orestes is dead.
The chorus' speculations about the motivation of the Greek strangers who have
been captured (407–21) are not poignant in the same way that the erroneous
guesses in the parodos of *Hippolytus* are. Their reference to seeking wealth
(411–12) will, however, be picked up in the Delphi song (1234–83),[45] and
their comments on human hope (*elpis*, 414–21) have some minor relation to
the important themes of confidence/despair and dreams/oracles.[46]

A general knowledge of myth sets the audience on a different plane from
the chorus in *Andromache*. The myth of the death of Neoptolemus at
Delphi was well known, so that the audience of *Andromache* can already
expect, or at least suspect, when Andromache mentions in the prologue that
Neoptolemus has gone to Delphi (49–55), that he will not live to return to
Phthia. This expectation lends a somber undertone to the chorus' celebration of the resources of noble virtues in the third stasimon (766–802): "there
is no shortage of defensive strength for the well-born" (770–1) will be felt to
be too optimistic a claim by anyone who knows of Neoptolemus' futile fight
against a Delphic mob, and it is strongly challenged by the portrayal of the
helplessness and collapse that strike Peleus a few scenes later. On the other
hand, the chorus' language in 772–6 contains intimations of permanent heroic
cult of which the chorus itself must be unaware. Related to this discrepancy
in awareness between audience and chorus is the pivotal function of the
straightforward ethical calculus of the chorus (eventually the good triumph,
the bad fail: 779–87): the rescue of Andromache just completed by Peleus
illustrates this claim, but the action of reversal that follows shows conversely
the triumph of Orestes in an "ill-famed victory" (778–9).

Comparable ironies beset the positions adopted by the chorus in
Heracles. When the old Thebans in the first stasimon sing of Heracles'

[45] See below, pp. 142–3.
[46] See below, pp. 162–6. *Electra* features a similar structure of revelation to the audience alone in the
second prologue scene, but it is not the ignorance but the confidence of the chorus that is cast in a
special light by the audience's awareness. At 192–7 the women advise that by honoring the gods in
normal cult, not by endlessly mourning, Electra will obtain a change of fortune. In the immediate
context their conventional piety appears correct when juxtaposed with Electra's despair ("no god pays
attention" 198–200), but in fact Electra's lamentations and complaints reinforce her moral authority
over Orestes, who is eavesdropping, and so lead to the completion of the full vengeance she longs for.
In the first stasimon, the chorus displays a similar confidence in the gods when they predict the
punishment of Clytemnestra (483–6), and the audience cannot dismiss this confidence since it knows
that Orestes is present and that he was sent by Apollo (87).

labors as a memorial for the dead hero (357–8) and conclude that Heracles' string of successes has finally come to an end with the Cerberus-labor (425–9), an audience must know that this diagnosis is false. Familiarity with the typical plot-pattern also allows an audience to anticipate the rescue of the suppliants. Yet an audience also knows from the standard stories about Heracles that Megara and her children are unlikely to "live happily ever after," despite the rescue from Lycus. Euripides' plot exploits the chronological/aetiological innovation that the labors of Heracles precede, and are not caused by, his killing of his family, and the Greek audience will have been waiting to see how this innovation would be brought back into line with the common knowledge that he destroyed Megara and her sons. At least some among the audience, alerted by the violent shift of the chorus' attitude between the second and third stasima (637–700, 763–814), may have felt a frisson of anticipation of evil even before Iris and Lyssa rose over the stage-building on the crane (815–21).[47] In contrast, a chorus is revealed as too pessimistic rather than too optimistic in the short anapaestic interlude of *Heracleidae* 701–8. At the least, the original audience probably knew of the story that Iolaus killed Eurystheus in battle, so that it could view with irony the choral admonition that Iolaus' body is weak with age and can give no help in the coming battle. And if the story of Iolaus' rejuvenation is not Euripides' invention,[48] then the irony of "there is no way you will get your youth back" (706–7) will be apparent immediately and not only in retrospect, when the messenger tells of the miracle (849–63).

In the preceding pages we have looked at various limits on the knowlege of the chorus and discrepancies between the awareness of the theater audience and that of the chorus. The chorus in these cases is viewed as enmeshed in the created world of the play, and the audience, positioned apart from that world, can detect the defects of choral knowledge and judgment. Yet the choral voice is variable enough also to reflect a higher level of knowledge, or even an "excess" of knowledge. As privileged commentator, the chorus can narrate myths and perceive in earlier events a distant causation for the current situation. Occasionally, however, the playwright gives to the choral voice a degree of prescience or insight that exceeds what can reasonably be assigned to the chorus if the latter is felt to be strictly in character within the temporal continuum of the action. Sometimes this is a very small detail,

---

[47] See below, pp. 167–8.
[48] It is uncertain whether Pindar assumed his audience would think of rejuvenation when he wrote allusively of Iolaus' triumph (*Pyth.* 9.79–83), and it is disputed whether Aeschylus used this motif in his *Heracleidae* (if it concerned the same general story as Euripides' play). See Wilkins 1993: xvi–xvii.

scarcely noticeable and probably accidental, as when the chorus in *Iphigenia in Tauris* refers in 435–8 to a landmark in the Black Sea as "Achilles' white shore," that is, the White Isle where Achilles was supposed to have lived on after his death at Troy, as described by Thetis in *Andromache* 1260–2. This chorus should not know even that Achilles is dead yet: at any rate, Iphigenia asks whether he is still alive (*IT* 537, 100 lines later). Similarly, the chorus at *Helen* 1126–31 gives details of the ruse of Nauplius[49] that they have no right to know. Elsewhere, the choral voice is being manipulated to foreshadow a later turn of the plot, as in the momentary hopefulness of the chorus in *Alcestis* 604–5 observed above, or the prediction of the chorus in *Andromache* 492–3 that the tables will yet be turned on Hermione. Similarly, when the chorus prays to the Dioscuri at *Helen* 1495–511, they implicitly assume the truth of the more favorable of the two stories about the Dioscuri (*Hel.* 137–42: either they have become gods or they are dead), and the arrival of the *dei ex machina* will soon prove their divine status. The instance in *Andromache* is particularly interesting because of the contrast with the chorus' position in the parodos and because of the ambiguity of the foreshadowing. In the parodos (117–46) the Phthian women advised Andromache to give up her supplication as useless toil and to accept that she is overcome by necessity ("the prevailing power comes/will come [*s' epeisi*] over you [Andromache]," 133), and this phrase is recalled in their next song at 492–3 ("still hereafter a turning [*metatropā*] of these deeds will come over you [*se … epeisin*], lady [Hermione]"). *Metatropā* is a rare noun and its meaning here cannot be firmly pinned down: either "reversal of these deeds," in which case the chorus' prediction is true, for Hermione is later feeling threatened in the way that Andromache has been; or "retribution for these acts," in which case the chorus' prediction is ultimately in vain, for Hermione runs off with Orestes and Neoptolemus is killed.[50]

A greater than justified prescience or perception can also be detected in the two choral songs about love in *Hippolytus*. Their assertion of the

---

[49] The ruse is alluded to by Menelaus in *Hel.* 767, but the details are suppressed by *praeteritio*.
[50] Effects of this kind may be compared to the problematic case of the first stasimon of Sophocles' *Philoctetes* (676–729). After three stanzas imagining the long suffering of Philoctetes, the soldiers assert in the last stanza ("but now," 719) a change of fortune by which Philoctetes will reach home "blessed and great," conducted by the son of noble ancestors, Neoptolemus. It has been debated whether the chorus is to be understood as carelessly forgetful of the plot of deception, or prevaricating in agreement with it, or is fearful that Philoctetes may be able to hear them and so tailors the song for his ears. I think the most likely interpretation is that the choral voice is here exploited extradramatically by Sophocles, foreshadowing both Neoptolemus' later adherence to his noble inherited character and the final return of the hero in glory after the fall of Troy. (Cf. the similar interpretation proposed by Kranz 1933: 221.)

pervasive power of Eros/Aphrodite in 525–64 and 1268–82 is most fully appreciated from the audience's perspective, which includes awareness of Aphrodite's prologue-speech. The two songs both lack a deictic connection to the current situation.[51] Generalizing from the observed misery caused by the force of love in Phaedra's life, the chorus in the first song turns away from the stage character and the individual event: the turn is marked by the opening apostrophe to Eros and the following apotropaic prayer (525–9). After hymnic acknowledgment of the god's power, the second half of the stasimon is taken up with two mythic exempla (Iole and Semele), with a concluding assertion of Aphrodite's power and universality. The chorus' emphasis on destruction suggests a prescient perspective, suited to the ultimate course of the play but not yet quite justified, since despite Phaedra's suffering so far the end of the previous dialogue suggested (deceptively, of course) a way out short of death and ruin. The later song, dividing the messenger-scene from the epiphany of Artemis, much more briefly acknowledges the universal and supreme power of Aphrodite. Since Phaedra herself inferred a personal grudge of Aphrodite against her (725–7), the chorus is entitled to cite the goddess's power here, but the audience can infer a richer connection to the plot.[52] Somewhat similar are details that bear poetic fruit for an audience as the play unfolds but cannot have had such significance for the chorus in character at the moment it sings them. Here we might classify the monster-slaying and gigantomachy motifs of the parodos (184–237) of *Ion*[53] or the allusion to mourning for a dead son (Itys) and to grief in general in the parodos of *Phaethon* (68–70, 93–4 = fr. 773.23–6, 49–50). These cases bear some kinship to the Sophoclean technique of ironic and multiple applications of choral lyric statements, best exemplified by those aspects of the first and second stasima of *Antigone* that ultimately appear more applicable to Creon than to Antigone.

THE CHORUS AND MORAL AND INTERPRETIVE AUTHORITY

The discrepancies in knowledge between the external audience and the chorus (the internal audience) reveal the partiality or fallibility of at least

---

[51] Contrast the Eros ode in Soph. *Ant.* 781–800 (deictic in 793, "this strife").
[52] Theseus is present to hear this song and cannot appreciate the chorus' perspective. Probably an audience is not even to think of what the idle character is supposed to make of this song, but the assertion of the universality of Aphrodite's power is not consonant with Theseus' assumption that the events demonstrate the particular criminal lust of one villain. This song also has an extradramatic quality as part of the chiastic echoing of the opening of the play: see above, p. 68.
[53] Zeitlin 1989; Mastronarde 1975 (with references to other discussions; additional references in the reprint in Mossman 2003).

some of the tragic chorus' utterances. Next, I want to consider to what extent the chorus' moral and interpretive authority may be compromised by the positions it takes. Here again, some examples from Aeschylus and Sophocles may be helpful before we turn to Euripides. The chorus of *Agamemnon* is characterized by a repeated reluctance to face a grim reality. For instance, the old men decline to complete the narration of the sacrifice of Iphigenia (248), excusing themselves on the grounds that they did not witness it (nor, of course, did they witness much of the rest of what they narrate about Aulis). They retreat to doubt and misogynistic dismissal when their lyric imagining of the just punishment of Troy glides into recognition that the Atreidae, too, have much to answer for (355–487). They refuse to admit the conclusion compelled by Cassandra's prediction and their own ears – that Agamemnon has been murdered. The reluctance, almost cowardice, of this chorus is counterbalanced, however, by a strong sense of foreboding and a struggle to understand, and the opposition they offer to Clytemnestra and especially Aegisthus also ensures that an audience will be sympathetic to their position. As mentioned previously, the chorus in *Choephori*, after being extraordinarily active for much of the course of the play, pull back to a safer distance when the cries of Aegisthus show that the murder is in progress: "let us distance ourselves from the deed that is being completed, so that we may seem to be without responsibility for these evils" (872–4). This withdrawal from responsibility prepares for the contrasting positions of Orestes and the chorus at the end of the play, where the chorus tries to look on the bright side while Orestes resolutely acknowledges his isolation and the sufferings he must now face ("You do not see these creatures, but I do!" 1061).[54]

Sophocles' *Antigone* and *Oedipus Tyrannus* offer examples of another kind of undercutting of the authority of the chorus. The multiple references (to Antigone and to Creon) of the first two stasima of *Antigone* (332–75, 582–625), reaching beyond what the Theban elders can on the surface intend, have often been commented on.[55] One might say that their observations here are out of phase with the action of the play, and the same could be claimed for the Eros-ode that follows the exit of Haemon (781–800), since it seems to offer a very skewed and partial interpretation of what

---

[54] See above, pp. 99–100, with the quotation of Soph. *Trach.* 723–30. When a chorus holds out hope for moderation and avoidance of harm while the hero and the audience can see only disaster, the directness with which the hero faces the awful truth invites the audience's admiration, comparable to the admiration the chorus in *Agamemnon* feel for Cassandra (1296–304). Cf. Aesch. *Se.* 677–719.

[55] Griffith 1999: 11–12, 179–81, 218–20, with references to other discussions.

Haemon has tried to do in the previous scene but is much more fitting as an interpretation of his later actions in the cave. In addition, their consolatory myths ostensibly addressed to Antigone after her departure (944–87) are extraordinarily opaque, and their long prayer to Dionysus (1115–54) shares the futility if not the misplaced joy of the notorious odes of premature celebration (*OT* 1086–109, *Ajax* 693–718). When we add to this their lukewarm acquiescence in Creon's decisions (211–22), it might seem to be problematic when in the final scene the chorus observes that Creon has perceived justice too late (1270) and moralizes about "good sense" and avoiding impiety toward the gods. But if we are troubled by this, it is probably mostly because we are treating the chorus too much as a character rather than as a conventional contrasting position within the drama. The confusion and undercutting that affect the choral voice in this play may still have their effect in the end, if an audience recognizes that the simple terms of the traditional maxims that close the play are inadequate to summarize the complex experience offered by this drama. The interpretive skill of the chorus is also challenged in *Oedipus Tyrannus* by the sequence of the second, third, and fourth stasima. The second stasimon (863–910) seems clearly designed to leave an audience uncertain how to pin down the doubts and fears of the chorus at this point: is the attack on *hubris* hypothetical, for contrast to the good striving for the city, or is it aimed at Jocasta, or at Oedipus as they fear he might be revealed to be? If the chorus is attacking Jocasta for impiety, what a remarkable riposte it is to have her emerge immediately to pray to the gods (in particular, Apollo) for help, a prayer cruelly answered at once by the entrance of the Corinthian messenger (911–30). Moreover, the chorus never reverts to the *hubris*-theme, since the next stasimon (1086–109) is based on a deluded expectation of a happy celebration and the fourth stasimon, sung when the full truth is known, views Oedipus' fate as a different kind of lesson, not a tale of wanton insolence and just punishment (1186–222). *Hubris* was a red herring in the struggle toward an interpretation of events.

We may now consider some inconsistencies, reversals, or mistakes in the judgments expressed by Euripidean choruses, and how his choruses relate to the moral issues of a play. The chorus of *Medea* arrives in friendship and sympathy and seems to have already judged that Jason is a betrayer of a god-sanctioned tie: even before Medea refers to Themis and oaths (160–2), the Corinthian women address to Medea (still indoors, not in aural contact) the assurance that "Zeus will prosecute this claim together with you" (157). They can hear Medea include the princess in a curse upon Jason (163), but their concern is to calm Medea herself and to prevent harm to the children[56] and they omit the princess when they next refer to the injustice Medea suffers (Jason as singular offender in 206–7 vs. the plural subject in Medea's phrase at 165 "*they* dare to wrong me"). At 267, in response to the long speech of Medea, the chorus promises its silence, declaring that taking vengeance upon her husband will be just. If it is correct to delete line 262,[57] then Medea would name only Jason in 261 and the chorus' reply would provide an exact response. If, however, 262 is genuine (adding Creon and his daughter as objects of revenge), then there is a mismatch in the response, and already here a significant elision in the chorus' promise, a blindness to the scope of Medea's project. Such blindness, almost a disconnection from the moral problem of Medea's scheme, is certainly present in the first stasimon (410–45). Following a pattern of response exemplified elsewhere,[58] this song begins with a reaction to the first part of the previous episode (Medea's appeal to the women and Creon's threat to Medea), continuing the sympathetic response already given in the anapaestic bridge-passage at 358–63, and it ignores the long rhesis that intervenes, in which Medea clearly states her intention to kill the king and the princess as well as Jason (364–409). Both this stasimon and the next one (627–62) instead remain fixed in the earlier stance of sympathy for Medea and disapproval of the treachery of Jason, providing a suitable frame for the *agōn* between Jason and Medea in the intervening episode and avoiding any forward reference to planned or feared actions. By the end of the Aegeus-episode (663–823), the chorus mobilizes itself briefly in both iambics and lyric to object to the proposal of infanticide: there is still no objection, or even reference to the planned murder of the princess, but the final judgment in the third stasimon (824–65) is that Medea will not be able to carry out the murder of her own children. This judgment of course foreshadows the hesitations in Medea's great monologue (1019–80) and the suppressed regrets of Medea's rhesis before the murder (1236–50), but it is proved wrong by events – another instance of a chorus unable to conceive the extreme of which the tragic characters must be capable. In the fourth stasimon (976–1001), the chorus is already anticipating with resignation the deaths of the princess and the children, spreading pity evenhandedly to the princess, Jason, and

---

[56] *Med.* 182–3: that the chorus should allude to danger to the children either indicates "extradramatic" knowledge put in their mouth by the poet or, perhaps more likely here, means that the chorus is to be understood to have heard from afar Medea's cries in 111–14 or similar cries at an unspecified earlier moment.

[57] As most recent editors of *Med.* do, following the suggestion of Lenting 1819.

[58] On this pattern see below, pp. 136–8. For other points, see also Mastronarde 1998 and the relevant notes in Mastronarde 2002b.

Medea.[59] And resignation is even more evident in the avoidance of direct reaction in the long anapaestic interlude that follows Medea's monologue (1081–115). At the moment of slaughter (1251–92), the chorus is galvanized to (futile) prayer, but its helplessness to affect the action is obvious in the underdeveloped exploitation of the threat to enter the house.[60]

How are we to judge the overall contribution of this chorus? This choral voice seems to be a very mixed entity. There are aspects that are quasi-realistic and in character, such as the claim of an established friendship with Medea and the initial justification of the pledge of silence. Yet in other aspects it stands out that the chorus' reactions to and participation in the unfolding events are extremely partial and sometimes evasive of the moral issues. Early in the play one might say that the chorus has been co-opted by Medea because of her *captatio benevolentiae* and her skill in associating with herself the social disadvantages of the average Greek woman. This would fit well with Medea's string of manipulations of her male adversaries and of her friend Aegeus. The elision of the chorus' consent to the wider scope of Medea's revenge and the ineffectiveness of their later protest may suggest that initial acceptance of the justice of revenge entraps the chorus into going along with the elaborated scheme. The situation of the chorus then parallels to some degree the situation of Medea herself, who kills her children, not (as the nurse initially fears) out of passionate distress at abandonment (in the lyric mode of the prologue and parodos), but through logical steps of plotting (*bouleumata*) conducted in the rational iambic mode, leading her to a conclusion she proves to be unable to resist. But as well as judging the chorus as a character, we may see its utterances as manipulations designed by the playwright to modulate tension and pathos and direct or deflect attention in certain ways (for instance, to underline the weight of Jason's violation of his pledge). The abstraction or distance created by indirect styles of beginning a stasimon, by suppression of key topics, and by general-izing reflection on parenthood, contributes to a muting of pathos. Euripides has it both ways. In some dialogues and rheseis and in amoibaia and arias, he pushes pathos to an extreme, but in other elements (prologue-monologues, extended stichomythias of various kinds, and many choral odes) there is a refusal of pathos. Intense emotional involvement is thus combined with moments of withdrawal in which the audience is reminded of its status as observers, outsiders, interpreters, and enjoyers of the action. Finally, there

---

[59] Note the repetition of the adjectives meaning "wretched, miserable": δύστανος of the princess at 979, 987–8, δύστανε and τάλαν of Jason at 990, 995, τάλαινα of Medea at 997.
[60] Mastronarde 2002b on *Med.* 1275.

may be a third aspect in *Medea*, the dissociation of the community from itself, since the women do not represent solidarity with their own political structure.

From an Aristotelian perspective, one might say that the chorus of *Medea* is not sufficiently integrated. On this view, the failure is viewed as, on one extreme, a result of a lack of skill or experience, or, on the other, as a matter of indifference, a refusal to struggle any further with the "disadvantage" of the conventional requirement of the choral component in tragedy. Indifference seems to be a more likely diagnosis than inability, but even this is too negative a form of explanation. Rather, Euripides' technique shows a positive manipulation that denies to the audience the comfort of choral guidance toward a consistent and comprehensive take on the events they are observing. With regard to the complicity of a chorus, it would be fascinating to have for comparison with *Medea* Euripides' treatment of the chorus in the lost *Hippolytus*, where (it is generally deduced from the evidence of testimonia and fragments) Phaedra behaved more openly and died after Hippolytus, so that the chorus' silence might be more problematic than in the surviving version.[61] At any rate, in the extant *Hippolytus*, the chorus' forced complicity with Phaedra's plot is made easier to understand, as the promise (710–14) is extracted before any notion of vengeance has emerged and that vengeance is only alluded to cryptically in the chorus' presence (721, 728–31). More important, the fatal curse (887–90) is uttered by Theseus even before the chorus can react to the revelation of the accusation in Phaedra's letter. Thereafter, the chorus-leader is allowed to offer veiled cautions to Theseus' quick anger (891–2, 900–1), and the chorus' silence becomes less prominent because Hippolytus' own silence is played out at length before the audience.

In most other cases of choral complicity with violence, the subordination of the chorus to the agent and its sympathy with the agent are adequate justifications. In its songs the chorus of *Hecuba* is not intensely involved in commenting on Hecuba's grief, but the Trojan captives' cooperation with their (former) queen's plan is relied on without explicit request (whereas Medea and Phaedra are outsiders in relation to their choruses). The chorus does not know in advance the nature of the revenge Hecuba intends to exact, and when they see Polymestor enter the tent with Hecuba, they look forward – incorrectly – to Polymestor's just death in the same way that other

---

[61] For discussion of the lost version of the Phaedra-Hippolytus story (*Hippolytos Kalyptomenos* or *Hippolytus Veiled*), fragments with translation, and further references, see Collard and Cropp 2008a: 466–89.

choruses exult in the death of a villain like Lycus or Aegisthus.[62] Their thought of entering the skene to help Hecuba is forestalled by her immediate emergence; and their role and contribution from this point on are minimal. The moral complications attached to the revenge thus concern Hecuba and Agamemnon in particular.[63] The chorus of *Ion*, by contrast, is heavily involved in the plot to kill Ion, as along with the old servant, they relieve Creusa of some of the onus of the plot to poison the youth. The decision not to obey Xuthus' command of silence (752–60) is a striking variation on the standard technique, just as Xuthus' threat of death backing up his abrupt order of silence (666–7) differs sharply from the etiquette that normally applies. The divergence of this instance is partly explained by the master–slave relationship and by gender difference, but an audience probably would still have recalled that cooperative silence is elsewhere requested politely, and is granted or assumed on the basis of pre-existing sympathy. The chorus specifically wishes for the death of Ion before the secret is even revealed to Creusa (720), and it later prays for the success of the poison (1048–60). As recipient of the messenger-speech on the failure of the plot, the chorus admits full complicity and expects full punishment, even referring to the reciprocal harm as "just" (1229–49). This is an extraordinary admission for a chorus to make, possible here only because the situation will be saved by the recognition of Ion's true identity.[64]

The complicity of the chorus in *Orestes* is perhaps the oddest case, but it fits the collapse of social and ethical values that characterizes the action of that play. The chorus is sympathetic to Electra and Orestes in the first part of the play because of his sickness, because of the cruelty of the command of Apollo, and because they are viewed as the last survivors of a grand family that has experienced extraordinary prosperity and disasters. Yet in the middle of the play, in between Orestes' failed arguments to Tyndareus and Menelaus and his failed arguments to the Argive assembly, the Argive women offer a fairly firm judgment against the matricide that Orestes is so desperately trying to justify: "the fair is not fair, when one cuts a parent's flesh" (819–21); "to commit vile crime for a good purpose is an intricate impiety and the madness of men of bad judgment" (823–5). Later, however,

[62] *Hec.* 1023–34, cf. *Her.* 734–48, Aesch. *Choe.* 855–69.
[63] See pp. 71–3 and pp. 229–34.
[64] Partly comparable is the position of the chorus in Sophocles' *Philoctetes*, which participates in the deception and lacks the moral qualms that manifest themselves in Neoptolemus. Contrast the humorous instance in Euripides' satyr-play *Cyclops*: when Silenus lies to Polyphemus, claiming that Odysseus and his men stole the food that he had been selling to them, and swears on the lives of his sons (the satyr-chorus), the chorus-leader speaks up against the lie, swearing on the life of Silenus (270–2), but Polyphemus believes the lie.

Orestes can assure Pylades of the women's cooperation on the basis of friendship (1104), and the implication seems to be that the same fevered and corrupted *philia* that powers the conspiracy of the trio of actors toward a mad repetition of the murder of Clytemnestra with Helen as the new victim also spreads to the chorus. Of course, they assert that Helen deserves the hatred of all other women (1153–4), but the women are then involved in guarding the entrances, entrapping the innocent Hermione, and covering the noise of the attack. In their last sung contribution, the women seem, in a typical choral fashion, to withdraw from participation in the crisis, preferring the course of silence and resignation, leaving the outcome in the hands of the gods (1539–40, 1545–8). Nevertheless, in the following announcement of Menelaus' approach, they once again offer some support to Orestes' position, encouraging him to be quick about securing the palace doors, and they pick up again the earlier contrast between unfortunate Orestes and fortunate Menelaus. If in other late plays like *Phoenissae* and *Iphigenia in Aulis* the chorus may be felt to be rather remote from the action and agents, here it seems swept away into the same folly and corruption.

Although there are, as shown earlier, several instances in which the ethical stance of the chorus is shown to be too optimistic (the third stasima of *Medea*, *Andromache*, *Heracles*, the fourth of *Heracleidae*), the most interesting case of choral involvement in the reversal of perspectives at the close of a play is probably *Electra*. Revenge against Clytemnestra is of course spurred at the critical moment by Electra. She is the one who quashes Orestes' doubts (962–87) and makes a kind of speech for the prosecution before her mother goes inside to her death (1060–99); and she later blames herself in the kommos (1183–4, 1224). But in the first half of the play everyone (including the chorus, and even the humble farmer at 352) assumes that punishment of Clytemnestra is overdue. The young women of the chorus introduce the idea of victory over enemies in the parodos (194–5), and they end both the first and second stasima with prediction or admonition that deserved vengeance awaits the queen (482–6, 745–6). There is a small beginning of pity when the chorus hears the death-cries (1168), but the current of regret that is later confirmed by the Dioscuri is begun by Orestes and Electra in the kommos (1177–232), and the chorus is following their lead when they make their most strongly critical rejoinder (1201–5, addressed to Electra). This reproachful view now has validity, but it betrays an inconsistency and irresponsibility in the chorus – partly an echo of the inconsistency that Euripides builds into his tragic world, and partly a traditional privilege of the choral position, with its mixed nature, serving both intradramatic and extradramatic goals in the artistry of Greek tragedy.

MYTH IN THE CHORAL ODES

The uses of myth and mythic narrative in choral odes are mostly distinct from those to be found in the speeches of the characters of tragedy. A human prologue-speaker may, to be sure, exploit an almost extradramatic position to narrate a wider stretch of myth, including self, family, and others involved in the concatenation of actions. After the prologue, however, most of the narratives of past events in the mouths of characters deal with personal experiences of the characters themselves.[65] Only rarely do the characters appeal to myths to which they and their kin are unrelated.[66] For the main characters, the narratives are personal and still developing. The chorus, on the other hand, is normally a bystander for the unfolding actions on stage and a distanced narrator when turning its attention to the past. Its relationship to the stories told is closer to the temporally disjoined stance that is traditional for a chorus performing without impersonation, which often turns from present invocation, prayer, celebration, or praise to the "once upon a time" of mythic narrative. Choral myth in tragedy is thus predominantly exemplary (whether for consolation or praise or some other purpose) or aetiological/explanatory.

The elements of myth in Euripides' choral songs range from allusive two-line relative clauses to narratives extending over several stanzas. The shorter examples may have very localized effects, simply adding a coloring of the exotic and learned.[67] But broader thematic effects can be conveyed even by brief allusions. The chorus of *Alcestis* touches on the story of Asclepius (127–9), which is relevant both to Apollo's connection with Admetus' house, since the god was made to serve Admetus because he took revenge on the Cyclopes for making the thunderbolts with which Zeus punished Asclepius, and to the overall theme of the (im)possibility of eluding death. A topographical relative clause in *Hippolytus* 738–41 evokes the death of and mourning for Phaethon: the more learned members of the audience will note that, like Hippolytus, Phaethon was a youth of

---

[65] Past events may be cited as a proof of identity (*IT* 811–26), in a revelation of concealed troubles (*Ion* 936–69) or a review of sufferings (*Phoen.* 408–25, 1595–614), or in an explanation of a decision or resource (*Su.* 131–61, *Ion* 985–1017).

[66] Examples include citation of a comparandum for excessive grief and lamentation (Soph. *El.* 145–52) or using a divine example in an *a fortiori* argument (*Hipp.* 451–61, *Her.* 1314–21).

[67] For example, the first stasimon of *IT* exploits short topographic references to Io, Phineus, and Achilles (394–8, 423, 435–7); the Argive mothers signal a connection that ought to justify a god's benevolence when they allude to Io and Epaphus in praying to Zeus at *Su.* 628–9. Additional brief examples: *Su.* 833–6, *Her.* 1016–18, 1021–2, *IT* 1098–102, *Ion* 452–7, *Hel.* 1470–5, *Phoen.* 248, 676–7, *Ba.* 561–4, 598–9, *IA* 757–61, 794–7.

marriageable age overstepping a human limit and consequently destroyed in a chariot and then mourned by maidens.[68]

The longer examples predominantly feature myths from the past of the characters, and thus are in some degree comparable to the great choral odes of Aeschylus' *Agamemnon* and *Septem* that extend the temporal sweep and causal nexus of those dramas. The common motif of the *archē kakōn* ("origin of evils") is explicit in a number of cases, especially in regard to the Trojan War and the internal strife of the Tantalids. In both these complexes of myth it is possible to identify several points at which with hindsight one can say "if only this had not happened, none of the present trouble would have occurred." This compounding of critical precursor events and this overdetermination of causes are traditional elements. Even as the dialogue-scenes of Greek tragedy become more rhetorically and psychologically complex and more fully portray the human dimensions of motive and decision, the choral contribution continues to preserve the tragic sense of human insufficiency by offering a more distant and perhaps "old-fashioned" perspective. The burden of the past, the intervention of the gods, and what one might call the fatal beauty of famous events are kept before the audience's mind as it reacts to and combines the different perspectives offered to it.

The Judgment of Paris is cited as a beginning of evils in *Andromache* 274–92, but the survival of Paris as a baby is also treated in the same ode (293–308) as a starting-point for trouble, as the chorus wishes that Cassandra's advice had been followed and that the newborn had been destroyed.[69] Similarly, in *Hecuba* 629–49, the Judgment of Paris is paired with his cutting of timber for the ship to carry Helen from Greece to Troy. By the time of *Iphigenia in Aulis*, even a brief allusion to the judgment suffices to suggest the fatal event that set a long series of disasters in motion.[70] For the Tantalids, the story of the golden lamb provides the original sin in *Electra* 669–746 and *Orestes* 807–43 (combined with Thyestes' banquet) and *Iphigenia in Tauris* 191–201 (possibly grouped with an earlier event, the chariot-race of Pelops to win his bride, but the text is

---

[68] Other examples: *Hipp.* 748–51 (contrast of the blessed hierogamy of Zeus at the end of world with the misery of human life within the limits of Atlas), *Ion* 723–4 (Erechtheus), *Hel.* 214–26 (birth of Helen as origin of troubles, an *archē kakōn*), *Or.* 1305–10, 1361–5 (Helen to blame for Trojan War), *Ba.* 539–44 (Pentheus as descendant of the Spartoi, a *theomachos* like an earthborn giant).

[69] For the contrary-to-fact wish, compare the choral wish in *Phoen.* 801–11 ("would that Oedipus had not survived exposure on Cithaeron, and would that the Sphinx had never come with her riddle"); this trope is also used by a character, the nurse, in *Med.* 1–6.

[70] *IA* 178–84, 573–89: each time the judgment is paired with the abduction of Helen. See in general Stinton 1990: 17–75.

very uncertain). The most elaborate evocation of multiple past events occurs
in the song cycle of *Phoenissae*, where the audience is reminded of Io and
Epaphus, Cadmus' wanderings from Tyre, the oracle he received, his
slaying of the serpent at the spring, and his foundation of Thebes,
Oedipus' exposure and survival, the attacks of the Sphinx and Oedipus'
polluted success in solving the riddle and marrying his mother, and his curse
on his sons.[71]

In addition to its aetiological function, myth within traditional poetic
genres often conveys praise and a justification for praise, as is seen in hymns
to the gods and in praise poems for human recipients. This function, too,
may operate in tragedy. The narrative of Apollo's term as herdsman in the
service of Admetus (*Alc.* 568–87) supports the laudatory epithets applied to
the royal house at the opening of the stasimon, and the transition back to
Admetus at 588 with *toigar* ("that is why") indicates that this story may also
be heard under the convention of the starting-point motif, although in this
play it is significantly and paradoxically both a beginning of evils (*archē
kakōn*) and a beginning of goods. Praise of Heracles is supported by
reference to his apotheosis and marriage to Hebe (*Hcld.* 909–18) and by a
lengthy catalogue of his successful labors (*Her.* 359–429), while praise of
Peleus is substantiated by the brief mention of his valor against the Centaurs
and in the first sacking of Troy (*Andr.* 790–801).[72]

In a few cases a chorus does not draw its narrative from the history of the
main characters. In three of the odes on the fall of Troy in *Hecuba* and
Troades, the chorus-women's personal involvement in the (very recent)
scenes they narrate is much greater than usual, so that the focus in these
stasima shifts not from the suffering protagonists to their ancestors and
kinsmen, but to a wider group afflicted by the same events. So in *Hecuba*
629–49, which follows Talthybius' report of Polyxena's death and Hecuba's
response to it, the chorus says nothing of Hecuba and Polyxena, but
emphasizes instead personal misfortune (note the opening anaphora "To
me … to me …"), and when they expand their viewpoint at the end of the
song, they include the women of Greece who mourn for the same kinds of
losses. The two stasima that narrate the experience of the final night of Troy
(*Hec.* 914–51, *Tro.* 516–67) have the same exceptional first-person involvement, comparable to that of the chorus of mourning Argive mothers in
Supplices. Whereas some choruses, in a typical apotropaic stance, pray not to

---

[71] For detailed discussion of this song cycle, see Arthur 1977, Mastronarde 1994: 330–1, with further refs.
[72] On the praise of Achilles in the stasimon *El.* 432–88, see below, pp. 139–40.

be a victim of war and others consist of slaves of long standing already inured to their status,[73] the choruses of *Hecuba* and *Troades* are newly enslaved and are noteworthy for the close assimilation of their own current and recent experiences to those of the protagonists. As in the case of the generalizing choral anapaests that follow Medea's great monologue, by turning away from the immediate situation of the lead character and speaking of personal experience, these choral songs create a certain degree of distance and slacken the tension that has just been built up by the previous episode.[74]

Bacchae presents another variation of the use of a choral myth not tightly connected to the suffering protagonists. In this case the disjunction reflects the peculiar relationship of this foreign chorus of Lydian bacchants to the human Theban characters. The chorus' allegiance is to the god Dionysus and to the disguised Lydian leader whom they take to be a human but the audience knows to be the god himself. They have no close tie to Cadmus, Teiresias, or the Theban women on the mountain, and share with Pentheus a reciprocal outright hostility. In their choice of myth, therefore, they turn to Dionysiac themes, referring twice to the miraculous double birth (*Ba.* 88–103 and 519–29), told in such as way as to elide the name of Semele. The part of the story before Zeus's visitation with the thunderbolt is omitted, and she is just "mother" in the first passage (91–2) and her corpse is concealed behind the phrase "from the divine fire" in the second (524). The stanza *Bacchae* 120–34 contains the only other extended mythic narrative from this chorus, and it has the traditional hymnic function of memorializing the origin of one of the god's attributes, the *tympanon* (a small frame drum the size of a tambourine). The mythic references thus combine with the evocation and espousal of Dionysiac worship in establishing the chorus as a group apart, a competing voice among the several approaches to encountering the power of the god.[75]

---

[73] Apotropaic prayers: Aesch. *Agam.* 473–4, *Andr.* 785; slaves of long standing: Aesch. *Choe.*, *Helen*, *IT* (but this chorus does recall the capture of their city and their enslavement at 1106–12).
[74] On *Med.* 1081–115, see above, p. 118 and below, n. 115; for the tendency to slacken tension, see below, pp. 150–1.
[75] In *IA* the identity of this touristic chorus of women from Chalcis does not allow them any local insight into or memory of the Argive dynasty's history; on the relevance of the narrative of the marriage of Peleus and Thetis, including Cheiron's prophecy about their future son Achilles (*IA* 1036–79), see below, p. 141. The chorus of Nemean women in *Hypsipyle* sings in the first stasimon (fr. 753c) of the quarrel of Tydeus and Polyneices at the door of Adrastus at Argos: this elaborates on Amphiaraus' brief mention of the purpose of the expedition in the previous scene (fr. 752h.40), providing more background at a moment in the drama when the baby has not yet died and no danger to Hypsipyle has yet developed.

Several other choral myths drawn from stories unrelated to the main characters have a straightforward exemplary function.[76] The two most problematic non-related myths occur in the two stasima that also provide the most indirect or puzzling connection to the preceding actions: the Delphi ode of *Iphigenia in Tauris* (1234–83) and the Great Mother ode of *Helen* (1301–51). These are discussed in more detail in the next section.

CONNECTION AND RELEVANCE

While the dialogue of the actors of Greek tragedy covers a spectrum ranging from stichomythia (which may convey quick reaction to information, calm interrogation, step-by-step plotting, or sharp confrontation and discord) to extended rhesis (with carefully developed arguments of decision or accusation or self-justification or description), the singing choral voice is inherently capable of both greater emotional expressiveness (in joy or grief) and of more associative structuring, as it employs myths, priamels, gnomes, wishes, and prayers to comment on or react to events in a more reflective manner. The capacity to contrast these two modes of discourse, dialogue and song, is basic to the tragic genre, but with the introduction of second and third actors and the increasing concentration of more and more elaborate action and discourse in the episodes of the drama there is a concomitant reduction in the role of the chorus. As already mentioned at the beginning of this chapter,[77] the development can be traced in the lowering of the proportion of the total script assigned to the chorus, in the tendency toward shorter stasima, in the encroachment of actor's song upon the musical space of the chorus, and in the relation of the content of choral song to its immediate surroundings and the overall themes of the play. In this section I want to consider in some detail the problem of the manner of connection of a choral song to the actions and speeches that have immediately preceded it.

Scholarly concern about the relevance of the choral songs in tragedy has a long history. Aristotle reflects it in his remarks condemning *embolima*,

---

[76] Cf. *Hipp.* 545–62 (examples of destructive love: Iole and Semele); *Hypsipyle* fr. 752g.18–31 (examples of Io and Europa, for consolation); *Med.* 1282–9 (Ino as comparandum for Medea; on some possible subtle effects in the similarities and contrasts between Medea and Ino see Newton 1985, Mastronarde 2002b: 370–1); *Her.* 1016–18, 1021–2 (Danaids and Procne as comparanda for Heracles). Cf. *Ion* 184–218: on the surface, the ecphrastic element seems to mark the fact that the chorus is relatively disengaged and unaware at this early point of the action; but eventually an attentive audience can recognize that the imagery of the mythic elements mirrors key themes of the play (theomachy, disorder vs. order); see note 53 above.

[77] See p. 88 above and the bibliography referred to in n. 2.

interlude songs that have no necessary or probable connection to the play.[78]
A few surviving scholia to the dramatists show that this continued to be
discussed. In a typical contrast, the scholia to Sophocles show traces of
critics at pains to ward off any charge of lack of relevance from the model
classical tragedian, while scholia to Euripides and Aristophanes carry a few
surviving remarks of a critic or critics who decry Euripides' failure to do
what is deemed rhetorically proper with the subject matter of a choral
song.[79] The term used for relevance of thematic connection is *akolouthia*
("the quality of following": much more commonly used in logic, and
sometimes in grammatical treatises to indicate adherence of a particular
form to a system of inflection), while the opposite is referred to with phrases
meaning "not following," "to no point," and "superfluous" (*oute ta akoloutha,
pros ouden, peritta*). Given such hints in the scholia and Aristotle, it is not
surprising that the choruses of Greek tragedy were often not only bewildering
to Renaissance critics but subject to theoretical critique, and that it became
a commonplace to complain about some Euripidean examples.

(1) Connection and relevance of the parodos

Before turning to the stasima, for which the issue of relevance has seemed
most pressing, we may first consider what kind of connection, motivation,
or relevance is evident in the first entry of the chorus and its opening song,
the parodos. Upon entry, the choral group usually explicitly declares its
purpose and its relation to the events or the protagonist(s).[80] The most
common technique in the extant plays is for the entrance of the chorus to be
presented as a spontaneous expression of sympathetic interest or concern.[81]
The sympathy of the chorus is usually evident from the opening words
(through address or question), but *Hippolytus* already contains a type of
indirection that, as we shall see, is more typical of some stasima. Here the

---

[78] *Poetics* 18.1456a27–32: "but for the others [scil. other than (that is, younger than?) Sophocles and Euripides] the sung sections belong no more to the plot than to a different tragedy: for this reason choruses sing interludes (*embolima*) following the example initiated by Agathon. But what difference is there between singing interludes and fitting a speech or a whole episode into one play from another?" (τοῖς δὲ λοιποῖς τὰ ἀδόμενα οὐδὲν μᾶλλον τοῦ μύθου ἢ ἄλλης τραγῳδίας ἐστίν· διὸ ἐμβόλιμα ἄδουσιν πρώτου ἄρξαντος Ἀγάθωνος τοῦ τοιούτου. καίτοι τί διαφέρει ἢ ἐμβόλιμα ᾄδειν ἢ εἰ ῥῆσιν ἐξ ἄλλου εἰς ἄλλο ἁρμόττοι ἢ ἐπεισόδιον ὅλον;)
[79] Sch. Soph. *Ajax* 596a, 1205, *OT* 463; Sch. Ar. *Acharn.* 443, Sch. Eur. *Phoen.* 1019, 1053.
[80] It has often been noted that later in a play even a sympathetic chorus sometimes becomes more remote and somewhat distant from the actors in the topics and emotions of its songs: Kranz 1933: 222; Pattoni 1989: 34.
[81] With the protagonist already on stage: *Andr., Hec., El., Her., Or., Hyps.*; with the stage empty: *Alc., Hipp., Phoen.*; probably *Cresphontes*.

female chorus first evokes the setting of everyday life (communal laundry at a public spring, 121–30) where they first heard the report of Phaedra's fasting to death (131–40). Only in the second pair of stanzas and epode (141–69) does the chorus' purpose of making inquiry and giving advice become evident.[82]

In another group of plays the chorus is either summoned by the protagonist or arrives in response to cries made by an actor.[83] The summonses in *Iphigenia in Tauris* and *Bacchae* are distinct from the others in that the chorus in fact enters to an empty stage.[84] In *Iphigenia in Tauris* this occurs because of the plot-driven need for Iphigenia to go indoors after the prologue-speech (1–66) so that the audience can hear from Orestes and Pylades alone in the second-prologue scene (67–122) and so appreciate the unfolding recognition-plot. In *Bacchae* the disguised Dionysus instructs the chorus of Asian bacchants to enter and perform their musical worship, but himself departs by the opposite entrance-ramp – a technique that not only isolates them from their leader and marks their limited interaction with others, but also gives the chorus more weight as a separate voice in the play.

In *Supplices*, we have the closest possible tie of the chorus to the action because the Argive women are engaged in the ritual of supplication and are already onstage at the opening of the play: their entrance-song is one in name only.[85] Conversely, a few plays exhibit parodoi with a looser connection of the sort that is often ascribed to Euripidean stasima. The

---

[82] Other delayed expressions of particular purpose: *El.* (the chorus arrives to invite Electra to the festival of Hera, and the relevance of this to Electra's situation – that honoring the gods is a means to revenge on enemies – appears only in the antistrophe, in response to Electra's refusal, so that one cannot even be sure that this was the original motivation of the invitation); *Hypsipyle* (the chorus seems to arrive only to inform Hypsipyle of the presence nearby of the Argive army and to invite her to come see it); *Phoen.* (the foreign chorus establishes its concern for the beleaguered Thebans in the second strophic pair of its entrance song: its entry is announced by the old servant departing from the roof and is ascribed to a general panic in the city (196–7); and this chorus has not come to inquire of any particular person – it is the arrival of Polyneices and not any choral inquiry that subsequently moves the action forward).

[83] Cf. *Hcld.* (the summons is a cry for help); *Tro., IT, Hel.* (invitation to join in lamentation); *Ba.* (summons to worship); *Cretans* fr. 472 (the chorus has apparently been summoned for consultation by Minos, whom they address in the first chanted lines of the parodos). *Med.* is comparable, except that its chorus is responding to inarticulate cries and not a summons.

[84] I agree with Kovacs 1994–2002: IV.162–5 and Cropp 2000: 78–9 in assigning all of *IT* 123–46 to the chorus and I assume that Iphigenia re-emerged from the temple after line 123 and before 137, in response to the sound of the chorus' brief hymn to Artemis. For the view that Iphigenia enters simultaneously at 123 and sings 123–5 herself, see Kyriakou 2006: 83–4.

[85] That is, the chorus' entry is "cancelled": it takes place before the opening of the play, as a movement of performers and not as a movement of impersonated characters, in the way that actors' entries may be, especially in plays of supplication. Cf. Collard 1975a: I.17, II.115; Taplin 1977: 134–6.

Athenian slave women of *Ion* enter as sightseers: they express in their first song nothing related to the problematic of childlessness and oracular consultation; even their precise identity is not made explicit until the end of the parodos (231–6), although their first words (184–7: "not just in godly Athens") give a clue. This looseness is partly inevitable, given the secret of Ion's identity and the fact that no human other than Creusa yet knows of her rape and concealed childbirth. Nevertheless, as the play goes on, these slave women prove their close identification with the interests of Creusa and her father's house and have an important role in the plot.[86] The slave women of *Phaethon* enter (unusually, from the skene-door) to carry out chores (as announced by Phaethon himself at the end of the previous scene), but after a priamel on the dawn activities of others, they sing in honor of the impending marriage, explicitly identifying with the fortunes of their masters (*Phaeth.* 63–101 = fr. 773.19–58). The parodos of *Iphigenia in Aulis* uses the same sightseeing motif as *Ion*, but in a manner that produces a much greater dissociation of the chorus from the action. The women of the chorus are from Chalkis and have come solely for the delight of gawking at the assembled heroes and their forces. It is uncertain whether the whole transmitted song is to be ascribed to Euripides.[87] If only the first strophic pair and its epode (164–230, in aeolic meters) are original, what is remarkable is the lack of anxiety in the song, the narrative neutrality of the mention of the abduction of Helen and the Judgment of Paris (themes more judgmentally and emotionally treated in other Euripidean songs, including the first stasimon of this play, 543–89), and the emphasis on the heroes' beauty and adornment, in counterpoint to the political machinations within the army attested in the dialogue scenes. The listing of heroes here (and in the doubtful trochaic portion of the parodos, the "catalogue of ships" in 231–302) might give some sense of the size of the expeditionary force that lies just offstage, constraining the visible actors, but that is a sense that will have to arise almost in spite of the viewpoint of the chorus and the style of its song. The only ominous word in the parodos is the epithet *poluthuton*, "where many sacrifices are offered" (185), applied to Artemis' grove, an irony which the audience, but not the chorus, may appreciate. We have, then, already in the parodos of this play, a much looser conception of choral connection; and subsequently as well this chorus remains unusually aloof from the intrigue being attempted in their presence.

---

[86] Cf. also above, p. 120, on their complicity in the plot; on the meaning of the imagery they use, see p. 114.

[87] On the problem of judging how much of the text of *IA* is truly by Euripides, see Chap. 1, n. 93.

(2) Connection and relevance in the stasima

Once the action of the play is fully under way after the parodos, it is, of course, possible for a chorus to react in song very directly to the last words and actions they have just witnessed, or to look forward expectantly to the outcome or new information that the next entrance is expected to bring (what I will refer to later as a song's "forward tension"). Stasima situated later in the play are often more likely to be strongly mimetic (of grief, fear, or joy) or performative (of specific prayers) and shorter in duration than earlier choral odes.[88] Nevertheless, one principal point of the alternation of the dialogue-episodes of the actors and the danced songs of the chorus is the opportunity to display contrasting levels of involvement, to allow a backing away from the action and from the intensity of involvement of the individual agents, to give room for reflection from a different, often more neutral and distanced perspective. This more reflective mode is well suited to the chorus by tradition, since hymnic invocation of a god, gnomic utterance, and mythic narrative are all strategies for either extending the universe of involved listeners or subsuming the present particular into a wider context. One pattern of choral construction found in many odes by all three tragedians is that which parallels the form of a priamel. The opening of the song thereby directs attention away from the immediate context, marking a break from the dialogue just ended, using narrative or elaborate apostrophizing invocation or striking gnomic claim or even a general puzzlement to force a redirecting and widening of perspective. But by the end of the ode the topic becomes focused on something quite specific in the dramatic situation, and the experienced receiver of choral lyric should view all the preceding as foil to or build-up toward the concluding point.

If one divides stasima very roughly into those with an immediate backward connection to the just-concluded scene and those with a non-immediate connection (or in a few cases no explicit connection at all), the latter outnumber the former in extant Euripides by about 60 percent to 40 percent. But it is more helpful to recognize that there are not just two poles of possibility; there is rather a continuum of possibilities for the degree of directness of connection.

The stasima of *Alcestis* provide a good example of a predominance of immediate connections. The first stasimon (213–37) is a lyric dialogue of uncertainty that is quite similar in tenor to the parodos: even the

---

[88] Some examples: Aesch. *Choe.* 935–71; Soph. *Ajax* 693–718, *Trach.* 947–70, *El.* 1384–97, *OC* 1556–78; Eur. *Med.* 1251–92, *Hipp.* 1268–81, *El.* 1147–64, *Ion* 1229–49, *Phoen.* 1284–307, *Or.* 1353–65 = 1537–48.

apostrophizing elements (prayer to Paean, address to Admetus, urging of the Pheraean populace to wail in mourning) are tightly linked to the impending death of Alcestis. The second stasimon (435–75) is an encomium addressed to Alcestis after her death scene. The third stasimon (568–605) is formally very similar to the non-immediate style of connection. The first three stanzas are dominated by narration telling how Apollo deigned to dwell in Admetus' house, how the god's herdsman-songs charmed even wild beasts, and how Admetus' wealth and power have consequently flourished. At the start of the fourth and final stanza there is a move to the present and to the action that has just taken place ("and now he has received as guest" 597–8). The small feature that preserves this ode's immediacy of connection is the opening invocation of the house (568–9), where the key epithet "hospitable to many guests" (*polyxenos*) and the description of Admetus himself as "open and generous" (*eleutherou andros*) explicitly carry on the theme of the dialogue just ended. The final stasimon (962–1005) has a very direct thematic connection, as it continues the consolation that the chorus began in the *kommos* (or song of mourning shared between chorus and actor: 861–934);[89] but this ode also has a clear structure of generalizing preamble followed by concrete application (984–5, "and you too has the goddess [Necessity] seized").

Extreme forms of non-immediate or inexplicit connections are associated mainly with late Euripides, but the form in general is well attested in his work from the time of *Medea* and *Hippolytus* on (as well as being exploited in Aeschylus and Sophocles). *Andromache* offers several examples. The first stasimon (274–308) follows the verbal confrontation of Hermione and Andromache, which ended with Andromache's defiance and Hermione's threat of another ploy. This ode uses the motif of the "beginning of evils" (*archē kakōn*) explicitly in its opening words, identifying the Judgment of Paris as the origin of great griefs (with an impressionistic narration in the first of two pairs of stanzas). The strophe of the second pair pushes the regret at the unleashing of the chain of unhappy events even farther back, to the failure of Cassandra's effort to have the baby Paris destroyed. Only in the final stanza is Andromache addressed and the conclusion drawn from the regretful survey of the past that both Troy and Greece could have been spared so much suffering. The next stasimon (464–93), following the departure of Andromache and her son into the house in apparent preparation for their deaths, again presents three stanzas of general judgments with a final stanza of specific application. The first stanza stakes out the generalizing moral

---

[89] This *kommos* can also be termed an *epiparodos* (a song accompanying re-entry of the chorus).

positions of the choral first person,[90] with obvious reference to strife within a household, and in the next two stanzas gnomes extend the theme of strife to various walks of life. The final stanza turns to Hermione and her murderous intention and contains the prediction of reversal or punishment discussed earlier.[91] After Peleus rescues Andromache and his great-grandson, the chorus sings the third stasimon (766–802), with two stanzas of entirely general praise of good birth and virtuous behavior (again featuring the choral first person, here in a wish, with gnomes) and an epode addressing and praising Peleus. The connections are implicit: the general judgments are inspired by what the chorus has just observed, and the chorus' belief in Peleus' past glories (791 *peithomai*) is inspired by their just witnessing his current upright behavior. The final stasimon of *Andromache* (1009–46) has the most interesting and difficult relation to its setting. The chorus has just been a very passive observer of the verbal seduction (and rescue) of Hermione by Orestes and has heard Orestes' confident declaration that Neoptolemus will die in Delphi. They obviously sing in a different frame of mind from the confidence in nobility and justice that marked the previous ode. Yet it is a mark of their power-lessness to affect the action (or, if looked at from another direction, their distance from the deadly squabbles of the elite characters) that they do not sing directly of any concern for Neoptolemus' fate and do not contemplate attempting to inform someone of the plot against him. They return to an earlier theme, the similarity of suffering on both sides that the Trojan War has caused, and indeed (as in their interaction with Andromache in the first part of the play) give more space to the pitiful fate of Troy, noting the abandon-ment of the city by its wall-building gods and the doom of the Trojan royal family. Through the repeated verb "have/has gone" (1022 *bebâsin*, 1028 *bebâke*), the song pivots from Trojan woe to the destruction of Agamemnon and then of his wife, and here an implicit connection to the previous scene emerges, for the collocation of matricide and oracle prompts the question "Phoebus [Apollo], how do I [= how am I to] believe (1036 *peithomai*) this?" The implied disapproval of Orestes and Apollo for their role in the matricide should be taken to extend to the plot against Neoptolemus. Together, the chorus' identification of Hellenic grief with Trojan grief and their rejection of Orestes (and by implication of Hermione) make com-prehensible the unmediated sympathetic address to Andromache in "not upon you alone" (1042), although she is not visible at this moment.[92] In

---

[90] See further below, p. 133, for the term "ethical first person."   [91] See above, p. 113.
[92] I remain convinced that Andromache is not present at the end of the play (cf. Mastronarde 1979: 99–101; Lloyd 1994: 153–4); but for arguments in favor of her silent presence see Allan 2000: 74–6.

this play with two contrasting actions and no heroine present at the end, the chorus of Phthian women, through its lyric reflection, performs an important function: they establish both the shared sufferings of the victims of the Trojan War and the propriety of the definitive separation of (virtuous) Phthian interests from (base) Atreid interests. Partly because the chorus has provided this more distanced perspective on the action, the child of Andromache and Neoptolemus who will found a new dynasty is an appropriate focus of Thetis' predictions for the future at the end of the drama.

Against this background of the variety of choral techniques of backwards connection in two complete plays we may now propose a classification of the non-immediate connections into several groups on the basis of their starting points. Although there are a few instances that show overlap between different techniques, it is still helpful to define categories as follows: (1) openings with strongly-expressed gnome or other personal judgment (or, as a related type, an expression of personal longing); (2) openings that refer to the earlier portion of the previous episode rather than to the latest developments; (3) openings that use apostrophe to move sharply away from the closing subject of the previous episode; (4) openings that consist simply of mythic narrative; (5) various generalizing openings that introduce songs lacking an explicit tie-in to the situation, even at the end.

(1) The choral voice is most directly displayed when the opening of the stasimon is a strongly expressed gnome or other expression of personal judgment underlined by a first-person verb of belief, contemplation, or judgment or by a wish involving the first person. The generalization is a reaction to the specifics of the preceding scene, but the particular application is postponed or left implicit. We have already seen this type at *Alcestis* 962 ("I have pursued the higher paths of thought and poetry and considered very many ideas") and at *Andromache* 465 ("never shall I approve," followed by "let my husband be content"), and *Andromache* 768 provides an excellent example of the use of what may be called the ethical first person. In Greek choral poetry, and in many kinds of solo poetry meant for performance in a group setting and capable of being recited by different individuals in different places over a long period of time, the force of many a first-person statement is not to provide biographical insight into the formation and beliefs of a particular individual, but rather to offer, within the collaborative setting of shared meal or shared festivity, an exemplary endorsement of a view that either is traditionally accepted as a shared value or is designed to elicit the agreement of the

group.[93] At *Andromache* 768, the chorus propounds its opinion in the form of a wish: "Either may I not be born or may I be born of noble parents and have a share in a wealthy house." The wish is in the optative, as if still capable of fulfillment, which is not literally the case; but this wish functions as a kind of rhetorical superlative and is equivalent to an impassioned claim that to be born of noble parents and share in a wealthy household is better than anything else ("if I can't have that, better not to be born at all"). Another typical element is illustrated at *Medea* 627–35, where the gnomic claim is expressed directly ("Excessive Eros/Aphrodite is harmful, moderate love is a blessing") and followed by first-person wishes that take an apotropaic form. Apotropaic prayer or wish is a device especially suited to maintaining the distance between the elite individual agents and sufferers on stage and the middling or humble persons of the choral group, and this device is often found in Euripidean choruses and also in Aeschylus and Sophocles.[94] In the second stasimon of *Medea*, rather than explicitly addressing the broken erotic passion of Jason and Medea, the chorus' apotropaic stance glides in the second pair of stanzas to the theme of an exile's helplessness, and this latter theme is then explicitly tied to Medea in the final stanza. These first-person judgments of the tragic chorus may have a double-edged effect in both engaging and limiting a theater audience's sympathy (a complex reaction that is evoked by other aspects of tragic performance as well). On the one hand, they set an example by showing the internal audience imagining itself into the position of the suffering character even if they also wish to be spared themselves. On the other hand, they tend to mark off the sufferers as unusually afflicted: although this may evoke further pity, it also offers the possibility of distancing oneself, as observer, from the dangers and sufferings being portrayed.

    One other example from this category deserves some discussion.[95] The first stasimon of *Iphigenia in Aulis* (543–89) features the loosest connection

---

[93] Typical pre-Euripidean examples are Archilochus 114 W, Pindar *Ol.* 1.52–3, *Pyth.* 11.50–4, Aesch. *Agam.* 757–62.

[94] Apotropaic prayers sung by Euridipean choruses: *Alc.* 976–7, *Med.* 633–52 (two prayers), *Hcld.* 357–60, 926–7, *Hipp.* 364–5, 525–9, 1111–19, *Andr.* 469–70, *Hel.* 361–2, *IA* 554–7, 785–6; cf., e.g., Aesch. *Agam.* 471–4, *Prom.* 526–35, 894–7, Soph., *Ant.* 373–5, *OT* 863–72.

[95] Other examples of non-immediate connection though gnome or personal judgment are *Hcld.* 608–29, *Hipp.* 1102–50, *Her.* 637–700, *Or.* 807–43. In the last of these, the chorus begins with a general explanation of the troubles in the house of Atreus – a variation on the *archē kakōn* motif – and moves through a judgment on the impropriety of matricide to imagining the moment of matricide, with a slight allusion to the countervailing duty of a son to a father (828–9, 842–3). The chorus is thus echoing the *agōn* in the first part of the preceding episode, but omitting any reaction to the immediately preceding Pylades-scene (729–806) and declining to evoke any tension about the coming debate and decision of the assembly (for this omission compare the second type of indirect connection, discussed next).

to its setting found within this category. Here, too, the chorus opens with gnomic wisdom about excessive vs. moderate Eros/Aphrodite and prays for moderation in their own experience of love. But whereas the strophe conceives of human fortune as crucially subject to outside forces that bring good or ill, the antistrophe puts the accent instead on internal qualities – character, upbringing, and individual effort. The relevance of the love-theme then becomes clearer in the epode, with its description of the irresistible love that struck Paris and Helen: "looking into each other's eyes, you [Paris] instilled love [in Helen] and with love were yourself set wildly aflutter" (585–6; much more striking in the concise and alliterative Greek original: *erōta t' edōkas erōti t' autos eptoēthēs*). There may be the implication as well that Paris and Helen do not possess the *aidōs* (virtuous sense of shame) praised in the middle stanza. The themes of this stasimon do have forward relevance: they prepare for the second stasimon (751–800), in which the chorus imagine the war at Troy and capture of the city, for the third stasimon (1036–97), which recalls the marriage of Peleus and Thetis, whose virtue is the antithesis of the folly of Paris and Helen, and for the later dialogue-scenes involving Iphigenia, Clytemnestra, and Achilles. But there is very little in the preceding episode (containing the debates of Agamemnon and Menelaus) that can be seen as prompting the theme of love at this point (at most 382–90, on Menelaus' failure to keep Helen and his eagerness to retrieve a bad wife). Rather, the detachment of the chorus (evident in other ways as well) and its mixed perspective on interpreting human behavior continue the bewildering shifts of position observed in the previous episode and match the tendency of so many features of this play to carry conventions, arguments, and formal structures to extremes. As a result, an audience, rather than being moved from one perspective to another in the course of the play, is left almost helplessly adrift and uncentered.

Similar to the gnomic beginning in the foregrounding of the choral first person are two examples that are suitably treated as byforms of our first category. The second stasimon of *Hippolytus* (732–75) features a famous "escape wish" as a starting-point for choral reaction to Phaedra's exit.[96] She has just stated that she will commit suicide and more cryptically that her death will hurt Hippolytus. The suicide is imagined and interpreted in the fourth stanza of the stasimon, while the third stanza evokes Phaedra's bridal sea-voyage from Crete to Athens as the origin of disaster, as the chorus declares (with hindsight) that ill omens accompanied that journey. As foil to

[96] Barrett 1964 on *Hipp.* 732–4, Padel 1974.

this voyage, the first pair of stanzas conveys a wish for metamorphosis and for flight away from the site of Phaedra's travail, past a site of mourning for Phaethon (destroyed in a doomed chariot-ride, as Hippolytus will be), to the limit of the human world, where the gods enjoy the blessedness of an immortal garden, site of untragic hierogamy. This escape-wish may be viewed as a variation on the apotropaic wishes seen in other stasima, one that conveys an emotional rejection of humanity's subjection to change of fortune and to demonic invasion. The third stasimon of *Bacchae* (862–911), on the other hand, begins with a rhetorical question expressive of the Lydian bacchants' longing for nightlong ecstatic revelry. The rest of the first stanza is taken up with a long simile of a fawn escaping danger from hunters and their dogs: on the surface this suggests the pressure the chorus has felt up to this point from the threats of Pentheus and their anticipation of the joy of relief, but the simile also presents an eerily pretty hunting scene soon to be answered by the gruesome hunting down of Pentheus. The remainder of the song responds to the prediction of punishment that ends the previous episode: the antistrophe and epode contain general claims about divine power and the necessity of respecting it and about the nature of human happiness. These themes carry forward this chorus' role as women exclusively identified with an unquestioning acceptance of Dionysiac worship and free of any other ties of family or civic responsibility. Unlike the previous and the following stasima, this one does not directly name or address Pentheus. It is almost more chilling that the most personal engagement of the chorus with Pentheus here lies in the vague plural "enemies" in the cryptic refrain that follows both strophe and antistrophe (877–81 = 897–901).[97]

(2) A second group of stasima is characterized by the technique of starting with a connection to the earlier part of the previous episode rather than making an immediate link to the dialogue that just ended.[98] In *Medea*, for instance, the famous first stasimon (410–45: "The streams of holy rivers flow backwards to their source") follows a lengthy monologue in which the heroine reveals her deception of Creon and contemplates ways to kill three enemies and escape. Yet the chorus' subject is the moral crisis caused

---

[97] There is some doubt about the textual reading, and even more about its interpretation, but I take the kernel of the sense to be "What better gift from the gods is there among mortals than to hold one's hand in superior power over the head of one's enemies?" For various views see Cropp 1981, Segal 1982: 127 and 2001: 121–2; Seaford 1994: 402–5.

[98] Compare Soph. *OT* 463–512, where after the sharp final exchange between Oedipus and Teiresias (408–62) the Theban chorus steps back and evokes the Delphic oracle reported to them at the start of the previous episode before commenting on the quarrel in the second pair of stanzas.

by Jason's betrayal of his oath and pledge to Medea and the change in gender-relations that this implies. The Corinthian women thus not only reinforce the passionate cries about justice and oaths that they heard from Medea in the parodos (131–213) but also accept and extend Medea's image, offered in her first speech onstage (214–66), of the unfairness of the relative positions of men and women. Remarkably, when they do turn to an application of their general claims in the second strophe, they continue to echo Medea's complaints in the first half of the previous episode and make no mention of the plotting of violence that ended it.[99] At the level of the playwright's manipulation of the audience's emotions and allegiance, this procedure ensures that the theme of Jason's treachery remains very prominent: it is not merely a personal offense against Medea but a more general one against the gods and a Greek cultural institution. Within the world of the play, the chorus' skewed response to the previous episode bespeaks the manipulative power of Medea, who triumphs through clever speech over the chorus as well as over Creon, Aegeus, and Jason (and eventually the maternal side of herself).

The same technique is apparent in the third stasimon of *Medea* (824–65). At the end of the third episode, the chorus-leader does speak forcefully against Medea's just-revealed intention to work her revenge on Jason by killing their two sons (811–18). The following stasimon also addresses this shocking intention, but only in the second pair of stanzas. The praise of Athens in the first strophic pair points back to the earlier half of the previous episode, in which Aegeus of Athens promised Medea asylum (663–763). In general terms, this idealized portrait of Attica should be compared to similar odes of praise found in suppliant-dramas after protection has been offered or after it has been upheld by the repulse of a persecutor.[100] The contrast between the ideal situation claimed for Attica and the disruptions found in Corinth serves as foil to the following disbelieving question "how will such a land accept a child-murderer in its midst?" Through this non-immediate connection, the ode brings to light the irony that Medea will (as the audience knew from familiar local myths) dwell in Athens and suggests that her manipulations may have corrupted even a standard motif of Athenian pride. Again, there is complexity and dissonance in the way the Athenian audience is invited to engage with the actions on stage and the judgments offered by the chorus.

---

[99] On this omission and what I call the moral disconnection of this chorus, see above, pp. 116–19.
[100] For the comparanda and the details of the idealization of Athens, see Mastronarde 2002b: 304–5, 307–11.

One other example from this group deserves short discussion.[101] At *Helen* 1107–64 the chorus' treatment of the waste of lives in war and the unde-served bad repute of Helen responds only to the first half of the previous long episode (528–760) and lacks any reference to the second half (761–1106, the planning for escape and the confrontation with Theonoe). Instead of building up any tension for the intrigue to come, this ode steps back from the progress of the plot and insists on drawing moral conclusions and offering advice on the folly of war. Remarkably, Helen is nonetheless addressed in three of the four stanzas of this stasimon, and perhaps the choral reinforcement of the complaints made by Helen throughout the first half of the play helps ensure that an audience sympathizes with Helen and Menelaus as they turn the tables and become the manipulators instead of the manipulated. Nevertheless, there is a centrifugal effect in the directness of the choral admonition to mankind in 1151–4 ("Senseless are all you men who seek the glory of valor by war and the sharp points of the warrior's spear, foolishly ending your toils in death") and in the avoidance of any return to the most immediate plot-development.

(3) Our third major group of stasima features an opening apostrophe as the distancing factor. In the final stasimon of *Andromache* (discussed above), the invocation of Apollo in 1009 moves the audience insistently back to the Trojan War theme and away from the present threat to Neoptolemus' life. There are two similar examples in *Troades*. In 511–67 the initial invocation of the Muse opens a dirge for Troy that is mainly a lyric narrative of the night of the capture, emphasizing the fatal enjoyment of the last happy music and dance and the last cultic celebration that the Trojans were to experience. With its final allusive reference to the personal fate of the women themselves in "child-nurturing prize of young women" (565–6, implying their concubinage and servitude), this lament for Troy creates a parallel on the group level for both the personal lamentation of Hecuba (472–510) and the other articulations of loss heard from Cassandra and Andromache (and Helen). The stasimon at *Troades* 799–859 (following the exit of Astyanax to his death) evokes the more distant past. The opening is an invocation of Telamon of Salamis, companion of Heracles in the first sack of Troy a generation earlier – complete with flattering reference to

---

[101] The other examples are *Her.* 348–441 (lyric narration of the labors of Heracles presented as funerary encomium, reacting to the claim or concession made in the first half of the previous episode that Heracles is to be considered irretrievably dead; only 430–41 acknowledge that Heracles' kin are about to face death); *Ion* 452–509 (initial apostrophe and prayer for a favorable oracle for the royal couple; only in the epode does the chorus turn to the more recent revelation, the story of the abandoned baby).

Athens and its patron goddess Athena (previously enemy of Troy, and enemy still as far as the chorus knows). The narrative of that previous sack, in the first two pairs of stanzas, seems to serve simply as an echo of the present doom,[102] although the allusion to the divinely built walls at 814 foreshadows the theme of abandonment in the following stanzas. In the second strophic pair, the past is again evoked in the examples of Ganymede and Tithonus, Trojans highly honored by the gods' love, but in more direct contrast with the current abandonment of Troy by the gods.[103] The pithy conclusion that "the affectionate ties of the gods are gone for Troy" (856–7) conveys a sense of total collapse, thus matching the despair with which Hecuba closed the previous episode.

The first stasimon of *Electra* (432–86) begins with an apostrophe to the ships that carried the Greek expedition to Troy many years before the time of the play. At this moment in the play, Orestes' identity is not yet known to Electra and the chorus, and there is little tension for the chorus or for Electra. For its part, the audience can have only a vague sense of what Orestes is feeling and why he is concealing his identity and purpose from his sister. The playwright has almost free choice of choral topic at such a point of the action, but since Electra has just heard long-awaited news of Orestes, one might expect some reference to the crime of Clytemnestra, Orestes' exile, and Electra's sufferings, or earlier troubles of the Atreids. The familial past is, however, held for the next stasimon, and the evocation of the war at Troy focuses, surprisingly, on Achilles instead of Agamemnon. The ode is full of pictorial images, showing no fewer than three stages of Achilles' life (voyage, earlier reception of arms, and by implication his later presence with arms at Troy). The glorification of Achilles carries the audience outward to an idealized heroic world, away from the humble setting of Electra's farm and the unheroic caution of Orestes. Apart from the symbolism of the decorations of the arms,[104] this treatment of Achilles is made more directly relevant by the threefold reference to his relationship to Agamemnon: first neutrally, he was conveyed to Troy "with Agamemnon" (440); then, his father Peleus raised him to be a light for Hellas "for the benefit of the Atreids" (451); and finally, he is fully subordinated to Agamemnon at the

---

[102] Note the grouping of the two defeats at the conclusion of the narrative of the first one (817: "twice, in two rhythmic blows of assault"), and the verbal and semantic echo at stanza ends 818 and 839 (*katelusen aichmā* and *ōles' aichmā*, "the spear destroyed").

[103] It may not be too fanciful to detect an implicit parallel and contrast between Ganymede (and Tithonus?) and Astyanax, another young Trojan prince just snatched away to a much different fate: the former were raised to heaven by their lovers, he is doomed to fall from the height of the walls (note the reminders of the Trojan walls in *Tro.* 814 and 817, and in the metaphorical *epurgōsas* in 843).

[104] O'Brien 1964, Walsh 1977, Cropp 1988: 127–9.

point of transition back to the present situation: the "lord of such spearmen
[as Achilles]" was killed through Clytemnestra's adulterous plot (479–80).
The address to Clytemnestra as "daughter of Tyndaris" at this same point
uses the patronymic frequently applied to Helen, so some hearers may be
reminded of a traditional contrast of Thetis with Helen,[105] an opposition
that would reinforce the disjunction between the brightness of the Achillean
epic world depicted in the song and the gloom of crime and displacement at
Argos. Although there are ominous undertones for an audience (or ways in
which an audience will revise its understanding later), the chorus here
embraces the idealized epic world and concludes with a prediction welcoming, at this point without any qualification, the death of Clytemnestra.[106]
The song thus serves to highlight attitudes and judgments that will be
modified or overturned as the drama goes forward.

(4) Our fourth group of non-immediate connections involves the use of
mythic narrative to open a song that eventually turns its attention to the
immediate situation. We have already seen something close to this in *Alcestis*
568–605 (where the narrative followed an apostrophe to the guest-
welcoming house of Admetus) and a proper example in *Andromache* 274–
308 (Judgment of Paris as *archē kakōn*).[107] Another instance of the *archē
kakōn* motif occurs at *Electra* 699–746, where the starting-point is the
golden lamb contested by Atreus and Thyestes. Two stanzas of allusive
narrative of the human actions are followed by a stanza on the spectacular
celestial consequences of Thyestes' treachery – the reversal of the course of
the heavenly bodies. Here, however, there is no explicit statement declaring
that from this origin come the woes of the royal family. Instead, the fourth
stanza turns to a personal judgment of the chorus, a rather paradoxical one:
"This is the story, but slight is the trust [in its truth] that it wins from me –
that the golden-faced sun altered its hot station, bringing misfortune to

---

[105] Cf. Alcaeus 42 L–P. Euripides exploits the contrast between the couples Peleus and Thetis and Paris
and Helen in the choral odes of *IA*; and in *Andr.* Thetis is a member of the good Phthian family
contrasted with Hermione and the Atreids.

[106] See above, p. 121. Other stasima opening with apostrophe are *IT* 1089–152 (address to mourning
halcyon as foil to the chorus' own song of nostalgia for Greece, followed by a turn to Iphigenia's
anticipated return to Greece; but the chorus loops back in the fourth stanza to its own nostalgia,
wishing in the end to be birds themselves in order to return to the maiden's life they lost) and *Ba.* 519–75
(address to Dirce as symbolic of the Theban community, leading to narrative of the birth of
Dionysus and prediction of eventual acceptance of his cult by Thebes; transition to Pentheus'
opposition and a prayer to Dionysus to stop him, and ending with a yearning evocation of peaceful
Dionysiac worship elsewhere). Cf. also *Ion* 452–516 and *Hel.* 1107–64, which combine initial
apostrophe with the second type of indirect opening discussed above, and *Alc.* 569–605, which
combines apostrophe with the fourth type, discussed next.

[107] See above, pp. 123, 131.

men, for the sake of a mortal dispute. But terrifying stories profit mankind, inducing them to worship the gods." They thus doubt the details of the myth and of the mechanism of divine involvement in human affairs, but still accept that wrongdoers should fear the gods and still assume that gods do concern themselves with punishing human wrongdoing, for the conclusion is a minatory apostrophe to Clytemnestra, echoing that of the end of the previous stasimon (mentioned just above).

A similar pattern of narrative followed by application[108] is to be seen in the third stasimon of *Iphigenia in Aulis* (1036–97), which is sung just after Achilles promises his protection to Clytemnestra. The strophe and antistrophe tell of the famous marriage of Peleus and Thetis and report a prophecy about Achilles' service in the Trojan expedition, given by Cheiron, but conveyed in the ode as the directly quoted speech of a band of Centaurs attending the wedding (1062–75). The glorious marriage provides a contrast to the illicit love of Paris and Helen featured in the epode of the first stasimon (573–89), while the prophecy serves as an anticipatory praise of Achilles, who has just taken on the role of rescuer of a suppliant. The figure of Achilles thus provides a somewhat more direct connection to the previous scene, but the epode (1080–97) turns more explicitly and judgmentally to the fate of Iphigenia, destined for sacrifice rather than marriage.[109]

If the text of *Helen* 1301–68 were not corrupt at crucial points, we could more clearly recognize a similar structure of narrative followed by application in the famous Great Mother ode, often identified as one of the most inorganic or *embolimon*-like in extant Euripides. The narrative begins with a "once upon a time" (*pote* 1301)[110] and covers three stanzas; only in the fourth stanza is Helen addressed and a lesson or admonition directed to her and her situation, in a way that cannot be satisfactorily recovered.[111] This ode occurs at the midpoint

[108] Other examples not discussed here: *Phoen.* 638–89 and 1019–66 (both discussed in detail in Mastronarde 1994). The choice of a non-immediate connection for these stasima (and of a non-explicit one for the first) is consonant with the overall use of the chorus in *Phoen.* They are foreigners who, despite their sympathy for Thebes, bring to the action a perspective that is emotionally distant and temporally long and who keep before the audience's mind the bigger picture and the demonic forces that engulf the characters, who are engrossed in their separate, narrower perspectives.

[109] Diggle marks the epode with his symbol for lines "perhaps not by Euripides" while the previous pair is marked as "perhaps by Euripides." If the strophe and antistrophe stood by themselves, then the relevance of the ode would rely much more on implicit contrasts, between the described blessed wedding and the unmentioned false wedding of Iphigenia. The stasimon would then fall into our category 5 (mythic narrative with no explicit tie).

[110] Cf. *El.* 432, 700, *IT* 1235, *Phoen.* 1026, *Ba.* 521.

[111] For efforts to articulate what the relevance of worship of the Great Mother to the Helen of this play may have been, see Burnett 1960: 155–6; Wolff 1973: 70–4; Kannicht 1969: II.333–5, Hose 1990–91: II.29–33; Allan 2008: 292–5, 306–7, 309–10. One promising opening for the detection of relevance is recognition of the mythic *anodos*-pattern (archetypal form: the experience of Kore) in the plot of

of the deception of Theoclymenus, when it is not yet time to imagine or celebrate Helen's voyage home, as the chorus will do in the next stasimon. The limit case for the group of narrative choral songs is the third stasimon of *Iphigenia in Tauris* (1234–83), which tells of Apollo's conquest and securing of his oracle at Delphi: not only does the story begin without mediation, but the narrative continues to the end of the ode, without any turning back, by a deictic or explicit reference, to the characters and the immediate situation. In the previous stasimon, the chorus had already imagined in advance Iphigenia's successful escape. Now that Iphigenia has gone off to the shore with Orestes and the statue to attempt escape, the tension in the situation of the characters is at its greatest, but this tension is not carried over into or reinforced by the stasimon. Such a relaxation of tension between episodes may be a general Euripidean preference,[112] but here it also provides for a stronger contrast and heightened surprise when it is reported that the escape is in jeopardy. Despite the inexplicitness of connection, the song is not an arbitrary interlude. Oracles and dreams have been an important concern of the human characters, who have struggled with interpretation and with doubt and despair from the opening scenes only to reach some understanding and confidence after reunion.[113] The odd story that Earth once used dreams as a competitive product to cut into Apollo's profits but was blocked by the will of Zeus explains why Apollo can now be trusted and gives an apparently final answer to Orestes' fear that Apollo may have used his oracle to deceive him and get him out of the way. There are also details of the narration that strengthen the parallelism between Apollo and Orestes, who are together rescuing their sisters from the barbaric Taurian cult.[114] Moreover, the violent succession at Delphi narrated here recalls the archaic myth of the *Homeric Hymn to Apollo* and implicitly rejects the pacified version of the succession invented by Aeschylus for the prologue of *Eumenides*: thus the ode contributes to the revision of and rivalry with the *Oresteia* that the play as a whole represents. The humorous and playful aspects of the story make it a light counterpoint

rescue and return, although it still takes a substantial leap to believe that an audience could interpret the reference to Helen's errors (1355–7 and 1368) as applicable to the underlying structural role of *parthenos* (unmarried girl) rather than to the Helen of this plot.

[112] See below, pp. 145, 150.   [113] See below, pp. 162–6.

[114] Apollo kills a female chthonic serpent and is confirmed in his power by the father god Zeus; Orestes kills his mother and is helped by male gods. Gaea resents the injury to her daughter Themis, as Clytemnestra resented the injury to Iphigenia. The myth tells of Apollo as "still a baby" and "in his mother's arms," the same phrases used by Iphigenia in 233–4 of her last memory of her brother. More fanciful points: both cross the sea; Apollo seeks wealth, and the chorus earlier suggested (411–21) that Orestes was seeking wealth in coming to the Black Sea.

to the travails of the humans, in the same way that the Odyssean Demodocus' song of Hephaestus' capture of Aphrodite and Ares treats playfully and in the harmless realm of the divine world the kind of sexual rivalry that is disastrous in human stories such as the *Iliad* and *Odyssey*.

(5) The lack of explicit tie-in just observed in the Delphi ode of *Iphigenia in Tauris* is matched in our fifth category of examples: choral odes that similarly call upon the experienced listeners to make inferences and associative connections for themselves. In these songs, the chorus deflects attention in various ways from the particular to the general or from the individual to the group without concluding apostrophe or explicit application. The three choral odes of *Hecuba* strikingly share this technique and deserve brief discussion here.[115]

The first stasimon (444–83) opens with apostrophe to the breeze that will carry the captives to new homes in Greece, the breeze that is supposed to be forthcoming as a result of the sacrifice of Polyxena – the only implicit acknowledgment of the issue that dominated the parodos and first episode. Although this ode contains several words of enslavement and misery, the first three stanzas also display an assimilation to the native Greek point of view as the women imagine their future participation in ritual acts (hymning Artemis on Delos, weaving images on Athena's robe in Athens) and use honorific epithets of Greek sites. This hybrid viewpoint can in part be ascribed to the Hellenic (and in the second strophe Attic) chauvinism of Attic tragedy, but here it also helps the Athenian audience regard the chorus as survivors whose fate is different from that of the princely main characters of the drama (note esp. 482–3 "exchanging the abodes of Greece for the bedchambers of Hades [= death]").

The second stasimon (629–57) follows the episode reporting Polyxena's death, in particular the speech in which Hecuba reacts with praise and mourning and ends in gnomes about the vanity of satisfaction in wealth and

---

[115] I do not discuss here *Med.* 1081–1115 (strictly speaking an anapaestic interlude rather than a stasimon, but its position is that of a standard act-dividing song preceding a messenger-scene); see Mastronarde 2002b: 346–7 for an analysis of the disjunction between the chorus' concerns and what is actually happening in the play and the suggestion that this tends to create an effect of resignation or helplessness. Other examples are *Hipp.* 525–64 and 1268–82 (already discussed in relation to choral knowledge, pp. 113–14 above). Perhaps *IA* 751–800 belongs here too (if the passage is by Euripides). This stasimon imagines the arrival of the Greek expedition at Troy and the eventual destruction of the city and capture of its women. It is not closely related to the previous scene (Agamemnon's deceptive reception of Clytemnestra and Iphigenia) or the following (the meeting of Achilles and Clytemnestra and the revelation of the plot to them). Instead, almost with the perspective of the theater audience, the chorus takes for granted that the expedition will sail and that Troy will fall; that is, it bypasses any tension or suspense about how the deception and potential resistance to sacrifice will be played out.

honor, contrasting a fortune defined by absence (627–8: "he is most blessed who day by day suffers no evil"). The language of suffering is immediately echoed in the anaphoric opening of the stasimon ("For me was destined misfortune, for me was destined suffering"), but with a clear shift from Hecuba and her family to the general population of Troy, represented by the chorus. The Judgment of Paris (644–6) and his felling of a tree to make a ship to sail to Greece (631–4) are both cited as origins (the *archē kakōn* motif) to explain the common suffering, and this glance back to the voyage that began the shared trouble provides a parallel to the voyage that will end the Trojan story, which was the launching-point of the previous stasimon. The epode even extends the compass of the ruin unleashed by Paris' "private folly" (640) to include bereaved wives and mothers in Greece, with a generosity of perspective that takes us even farther away from the immediate action. The avoidance of reference to Polyxena further isolates Hecuba just before she is to receive the shock of the recognition of Polydorus' body and to realize the meaning of her ominous dream.

The third stasimon (905–52) continues the trend of the first two, filling in more details of the experience of the common women of Troy. It occurs at a point of pause in the intrigue plot, as Hecuba waits for the arrival of Polymestor. The women make no reference to the plot or to Polymestor's crime, but instead at 905 they apostrophize the distant ruins of their sacked and burned city, and then evoke the last night of Troy and their voyage away from the Trojan shore, away from the dead bodies of their husbands. Their final curse upon Helen and Paris, both narrated as a past event (939–46) and reiterated at this moment (950–2), recalls the *archē kakōn* motif of the previous stasimon, so that the series of odes carries some of the traditional force of deepening the mythic and "theological" background of the current suffering. Yet what is striking here is that the original sin is played upon in a rather minor way. While the events of this play can be seen as a further working out of the consequences of Paris' crime, the more prominent impression, perhaps, is that they arise directly from the immediate motives and decisions featured in the action: the demand of Achilles' ghost, the decision of the Greek army, the attitude of Odysseus, the greed of Polymestor, and the exasperated recoil of Hecuba.

The Trojan women of the chorus are certainly sympathetic to Hecuba and the royal family, and they support her vengeance against Polymestor, briefly contemplating entering the skene to assist her (1042–3) before she emerges to forestall such action. But in the choral odes they offer a parallel view: the episodes present the experiences of the queen, while the stasima dwell on those of the whole Trojan populace and the nameless survivors.

This wider perspective echoes but also isolates the helplessness of Hecuba herself, the elite individual who after repeated blows finally reacts with vengeful action. By encouraging the audience's sympathy for nameless sufferers more like themselves, the choral voice may make it easier for the Athenian audience to invest heavily in sympathy for the non-Greek Hecuba (and Polyxena and Polydorus). On the other hand, this choral technique represents a refusal to maintain or reinforce the high pitch of pathos that has been reached within the episodes, as well as a deferral of the acknowledgment of ongoing events. The slight emotional distance so created suggests the overall inability of the chorus to affect developing events. For the audience, this distance provides on the one hand a forceful reminder of their own detached, observing position and on the other an encouragement to regard the action with some equanimity or resignation, as if it proceeds on an inevitable path. Since a more engaged choral contribution might create some tension about what is coming and foster a stronger identification with Hecuba and her actions, this treatment of the choral songs of *Hecuba* allows the audience some separation from the harsh actions and the complex shifts of argument in which the protagonist is involved in the second half of the play.

Euripides' strategies for the construction and thematics of his choral songs are, as we have seen, richly varied. The odes frequently create meaning by association and indirection. The techniques of connection and relevance are founded in the tradition of professional choral lyric, and they fully exploit the hybrid nature of tragic poetry and the differing perspectives and modes of discourse of the characters and the choral group. There are, of course, some choral songs which are highly mimetic and which respond very directly to the immediate developments of the plot. But a high proportion of the stasima instead turn the audience, to a greater or lesser extent, away from the action and demand a shift of engagement, a relaxation of tension, and an effort to contemplate the story and the characters from other angles. The effort required for interpretation or the difficulty of integrating the alternative perspectives contributes effectively to the process by which Euripidean tragedy challenges both the emotions and the intellect of the audience and tends to block a simple view of human experience.

"NOT AS IN EURIPIDES BUT AS IN SOPHOCLES"

The proper comportment of the chorus was of interest to ancient theorists of drama and to the scholars and teachers whose remarks have been filtered down to us in the scholia to the tragedians. One possible reading of

Aristotle's rather insufficient remarks on the chorus in *Poetics*[116] is that he calls for, as an ideal, a close participation of the chorus in the emotional ups and downs of the plot-sequence. Such a preference would seem to valorize the more mimetic and "in-character" contributions of the chorus over the more reflective and indirect ones that are sanctioned both by tragic convention and by the traditional functions of choral song. Perhaps Sophocles' *Philoctetes* would have struck Aristotle as providing an example of the correct use of the chorus, for the soldiers of Neoptolemus who form this chorus are very much part of the deception-plot, their songs are few and short and are shared with actors or closely tied to actors' speeches, and there are no flights of mythic imagination or sustained gnomic struggles. On the other hand, *Oedipus Tyrannus* was obviously a prime example for Aristotle of what a tragedy should be, and that play clearly has a more complex use of the chorus than is found in *Philoctetes*. Traces of the opinions of other theorists seem more in tune with some of the choral conventions we have noted. In the pseudo-Aristotelian *Problemata* (19.48) we find the notion that the chorus is "a concerned friend incapable of action" (*kēdeutēs apraktos*), identifying in *apraktos* a crucial generic limitation.[117] A rhetorical approach to choral decorum may be inferred from surviving comments in a number of scholia.[118] Like

---

[116] The passage on the chorus is *Poetics* 18, 1456a25–32. On the last lines of the passage, concerning *embolima*, see above, n. 78. The first part reads καὶ τὸν χόρον δὲ ἕνα δεῖ ὑπολαμβάνειν τῶν ὑποκριτῶν, καὶ μόριον εἶναι τοῦ ὅλου καὶ συναγωνίζεσθαι μὴ ὥσπερ Εὐριπίδῃ ἀλλ' ὥσπερ Σοφοκλεῖ ("The chorus ought to be considered to be one of the actors, and should be an [organic] part of the whole and should *sunagōnizesthai* not as in Euripides but as in Sophocles"). Most interpreters take *sunagōnizesthai* to mean "participate in the action [of the play] together with [the actors or characters]" and then go on to disagree on how strong and active this participation or assistance is meant to be. For discussion of the disputed details of the lines, see Mastronarde 1998: 67 n. 20, with further references.

[117] The sentence comes in a discussion of the musical modes most suited to choral song, in which the mode most suited to action (*praxis*) is said to be proper to the elite heroic characters and not to the ordinary humans of a chorus: κατὰ δὲ τὴν ὑποδωριστὶ καὶ ὑποφρυγιστὶ πράττομεν, ὃ οὐκ οἰκεῖόν ἐστι χορῷ. ἔστι γὰρ ὁ χορὸς κηδευτὴς ἄπρακτος· εὔνοιαν γὰρ μόνον παρέχεται οἷς πάρεστιν ("But through the hypodorian and hypophrygian modes we take action, which is not proper to a chorus. For the chorus is a concerned friend incapable of action, since it only provides good will to those it attends."). Compare Barker 1984: 202–3. The noun κηδευτής is extremely rare: this is the only instance earlier than a handful of occurrences in Christian authors from the fourth century CE onward in the sense "mourner who attends or cares for a dead body" and one in a late legal text in the sense "legal guardian"; "concerned friend" is my best guess at its meaning here; Barker translates it as "attendant"; in view of the later usage, one could also consider translating it as "mourner," but that seems too narrow. Foley 2003: 14–15, 24–5 has disputed whether *apraktos* is a valid perception. I think that this point may have been exaggerated in the postclassical Greek critics, but still is based on a significant tendency that I would want to say is typical of the genre of tragedy.

[118] Well studied by Meijering 1985. For other possible traces of Greek theories of the chorus, cf. Horace, *de arte poetica* 318–26 with the comments of Brink 1971: 254–60, along with Brink 1963: 43–150 for speculation that Horace's prescriptions reflect the work of the third-century Peripatetic Neoptolemus of Parium.

some of the decorum-based judgments these critics applied to characters and actions, these comments may reflect a sense of strong hierarchy and social restriction that fails to do justice to the less constrained fantasy that was acceptable to the Athenian audience of the later fifth century. In the scholia, the chorus is expected to be sympathetic to the suffering characters, but is also expected to tread a wary line between freedom of expression on the one hand and the modesty and caution of social subordinates on the other. These ancient critics, clearly interested in the educational value of reading tragedy in the schoolroom, also overemphasize the claim that a chorus speaks up for what is just, and even try to save the author from potential criticism by alleging that some choral statements are made "out of the person of the poet"[119] – a claim which should not be accepted in any simple sense.

The key Aristotelian phrase in regard to Euripides and the chorus is the recommendation that the chorus should "share in the struggle" (*sunagōnizesthai*) in the manner exemplified in Sophocles and not as in Euripides. Since this phrase follows on "the chorus ought to be an organic part of the whole," the requirement of *sunagōnizesthai* might be taken as an explication of the requirement of organic connection. The outright lack of organic connection as part to whole is, however, ascribed in the following sentences quite clearly to tragedians other than Euripides. Thus Aristotle seems to be saying either that, without falling on the inorganic side of the contrast between organic and inorganic, Euripides fails to show the same high level of integration of the chorus that Sophocles displays, or that Euripides' manner in having his chorus engage in the action is different from, and (in his eyes) inferior to, that of Sophocles.

The verb *sunagōnizesthai* may suggest either something as active and assertive as joining a contest or battle as an ally with someone else against a third party, or something less active such as providing some form of aid or assistance to a party who is under pressure. The common motif of choral sympathy would suggest that the milder sense is the appropriate one. But as usual with the cryptic concision of *Poetics*, there can be no certainty about this, and it is doubtful whether we should fully harmonize the *Poetics* with the post-Aristotelian pronouncements on the chorus.

More useful, perhaps, for coming to terms with the Euripidean chorus is the effort to get clear about how it differs from the Sophoclean. There are, of course, many similarities that are based on generic demands or tendencies of

[119] The Greek phrase is ἐκ προσώπου τοῦ ποιητοῦ or ἐν προσώπῳ τοῦ ποιητοῦ, found in the Euripidean scholia on *Alc.* 962, *Med.* 823, *Hipp.* 1102, *Or.* 1691.

tragedy, and one can observe that some of the developments of the late fifth-century tragic chorus, such as diminution in number of stasima and encroachment of shared lyric or aria upon choral lyric, are common to Sophocles and Euripides. Taplin once went so far as to say that, *pace* Aristotle, one cannot see much difference in the overall use of the chorus in Sophocles and Euripides, and Kranz thought the contrast applied only to late Euripides, considering his earlier choral technique to be comparable to that of Sophocles.[120] But we can detect some significant differences based on the features studied in this chapter. First, in regard to the non-immediate or indirect type of connection between the episode just concluded and the opening of a stasimon, we noted that Euripides' preference for the indirect was about 60 percent vs. 40 percent (individual plays vary across the whole range of possibilities, and there is no chronological development to be detected). Remarkably, the proportion is no different for Sophocles' extant plays as a group (fifteen instances of non-immediate connection vs. ten of immediate), although it is noteworthy that the proportion for the four plays usually presumed to be earlier (*Ajax, Antigone, Trachiniae, Oedipus Tyrannus*) is higher (12:4) than 60 percent, and for the three plays believed to be late (*Electra, Philoctetes, Oedipus Coloneus*) it is quite the reverse (3:6). For the six certainly Aeschylean plays the ratio is 2:12, showing a decidedly different preference. The smallness of the Aeschylean and Sophoclean samples may be misleading us, but the appearance created by the unreliable sample is that the prevalent use of indirect openings may have been developed in mature tragedy in the middle of the century and that Euripides continued with the technique whereas Sophocles turned away from it late in his career.

Furthermore, in Euripidean stasima with a non-immediate connection, the turn to the here and now very often occurs after two-thirds or three-quarters of the song have passed and very rarely before the first half has been completed. This lopsided proportion is not an innovation, because we find it in the first stasimon of Aeschylus' *Choephori* (585–662, featuring a priamel consisting of mythic examples) and in the famous first stasimon of Sophocles' *Antigone* (332–75) and second stasimon of *Oedipus Tyrannus* (863–910). But this proportion is much more common in Euripides than in Sophocles, for the latter (outside of those two examples) tends to have his chorus declare the connection to present concerns at an earlier point in the

---

[120] Taplin (1984–85) 115; Kranz 1933: 252. Note as well Nietzsche's concession that the alteration of the use of the chorus (from what he imagined to be its original and authentic use) is already visible in Sophocles (above, p. 13).

stasimon.[121] The Sophoclean chorus may thus seem more often to be more grounded in the situation of the play, the Euripidean chorus to be more aloof or approaching the point from a more circuitous route. In addition, Euripides, as we have seen, has a few instances where the direct tie is saved for the very last lines and a few where the tie in not made explicit at all. The Delphi ode in *Iphigenia in Tauris* is clearly different from the first stasimon in *Antigone*, which has the most inexplicit tie-in to the present in Sophocles, and also from the fourth stasimon of that play, which consists almost entirely of mythic exempla, puzzlingly related to the circumstances at hand, but contains apostrophes to Antigone near the beginning and at the very end.

Another distinction is in the use of mythic narrative in the choral parts of tragedy. Again, there are excellent precedents for Euripides' technique in earlier authors. The odes of Aeschylus' *Agamemnon* fill in the earlier stages of the story from the arrival of Paris to the sacrifice of Iphigenia and the reception of the ashes of dead warriors during the years of fighting. The second stasimon of his *Septem* looks back to Laius' disobedience, Oedipus' marriage, and the curse on his sons. The second stasimon of Sophocles' *Antigone* alludes to the generations-long destruction (*atē*) afflicting the Labdacids. But it is noteworthy that in extant Sophocles the mythic and narrative elements are less frequent, less extensive, less inclined to dwell on an originary event in the way that is so frequent in Euripides – only the epode of the first stasimon of Sophocles' *Electra* (on Pelops and Myrtilus) bears a close similarity to the *archē kakōn* motif as found in Euripides. Sophocles' preference is to concentrate on the hero's present dilemma, and so he gives less prominence to the causal chain that runs through long stretches of time. Euripides has a different conception of fractured and inconsistent human agency, and the links to the past are more prominent, though not as authoritative as in the connected Aeschylean trilogy.

Both the above-mentioned features contribute to a greater sense of distance or withdrawal from the action in Euripides, and so do his character-istic uses of apostrophe. Again, apostrophe is quite normal in Aeschylean and Sophoclean odes, as in non-tragic forms of choral lyric. But Euripides' choral apostrophes are more frequent and some are distinctively more remote, as Aristophanes recognized when he parodied them.[122] These

---

121 The turn to the here and now falls in the second of four stanzas in both the first stasimon of *Ajax* (596–645) and the second stasimon of *Ant.* (582–625); within the first stanza of the first stasimon of *Trach.* (496–530).

122 E.g., *Hcld.* 748–50 (earth, moon, and rays of the sun), *Hipp.* 752–3 (Cretan ship that once carried Phaedra to Athens), *Hec.* 444 (breeze that propels ships across the sea), *El.* 432 (ships that sailed to

more artificial addressees make the rhetorical device more transparent as a device, calling attention to the withdrawn stance that distinguishes the chorus from one of the agents. It is as if Euripides decidedly does not want his chorus to be thought of as "one of the actors."

Thus the Euripidean chorus tends to be, not always, of course, but for a higher proportion of the time and to a greater degree, less immediately emotionally engaged in the action. This brings us back to the verb *sunagōnizesthai*. *Agōn* also suggests *agōnia*, the tension and anxiety that a chorus (and an audience) shares with the main agents of the drama. If Aristotle thought of *Oedipus Tyrannus* as a great example of an effective tragedy, he may have appreciated its chorus for its sense of continuous struggle to interpret events and for the forward tension of its songs, even for the perverse tension of its wrong-headed joy just before the truth is revealed. Perhaps his approval of Sophocles' manner has most to do with Sophocles' fuller integration of the emotional stance of the chorus into the emotional dynamic of the plot as a whole. The sense of reversal is not confined to the protagonist of the story, but is shared more widely: in *Oedipus Tyrannus*, for instance, also by the Corinthian messenger and by the chorus. What may have offended Aristotle in much of Euripides was the refusal to maintain or enhance tension, the tendency to relax tension between episodes, as for instance in *Andromache, Hecuba,* and *Medea.* Although this technique seems to be carried furthest by Euripides (unless our samples are seriously misleading), there is at least one early precedent. The third stasimon of *Ajax* (1185–222) falls between the *agōn* of Teucer and Menelaus and the one between Teucer and Agamemnon, while Teucer is temporarily offstage and the threatened body of Ajax is protected by Tecmessa and Eurysaces. This ode does not intensify concern over the fate of the body, but instead deflects attention to the personal wishes and worries of the chorus, now left without Ajax's protection. This is comparable to the personal concerns of the chorus in *Hecuba* expressed between scenes of great grief or tension for Hecuba. Otherwise, the forward tension of Aeschylean and Sophoclean stasima is almost invariable until we reach the end of the century (the odes of *Philoctetes* and *Oedipus Coloneus* have little forward tension). By more often using the chorus to relax tension, Euripides forces upon the audience's attention the contemplative and associative aspect of the choral role and of its own role as interpreter. The stylistic mannerisms of Euripidean lyric tend likewise to dissipate intense emotional involvement with the dilemmas of

Troy), *Tro.* 799 (Telamon), *IT* 392 (Bosporus, allusively), 1089–91 (halcyon), *Hel.* 1106–10 (night-ingale), *Hel.* 1441–5 (ship carrying Helen, elaborately paraphrased), *Phoen.* 226–34 (crags, magic vine, and caves of Parnassus), 801–2 (Cithaeron), 1019–21 (Sphinx).

the characters, although they may still enchant or sweep away the audience with a striking emotionality displaced to a different plane.[123] The audience thus cannot lose itself within the performance once and for all (that is, without being gently nudged or strongly impelled to shift its perspective), nor find with the chorus' help a stable and consistent vantage point from which to experience it.

Relaxation of tension and non-immediate connection are present from *Medea* onward, but Euripidean tendencies toward choral aloofness seem to increase in the last decade of his production. This is the period that gives us the problematic stasima of *Iphigenia in Tauris* and *Helen* so often cited as *embolimon*-like, the casual entrance motivations of *Ion*, *Iphigenia in Aulis*, and *Hypsipyle*, and experimentation with the "foreign chorus." The earliest extant example of the latter is *Phoenissae*, with its Tyrian maidens coincidentally trapped by war in Thebes on their way to Delphi. Their arrival is unconnected to the sympathy they express for Jocasta and the concern they feel for the Thebans as kin descended from the same ancestors, Io and Epaphos. They bring a deep perspective to the background of multiple causation, but they also convey tension about impending developments, though this is muted by the meter, style, and construction of several of the odes. *Bacchae* is often set apart as a play harking back to archaic themes and forms, but the choral role seems to me to fit the tendencies of late Euripides. The Asian bacchants have no attachment to the Theban community; they have little interaction with their putative leader, the disguised Dionysus – even in his human guise, he summons them but does not remain to witness their parodos. They are mostly ignored during the episodes, although realistically a Pentheus who is enraged at his grandfather and Teiresias and the Theban women and the Lydian stranger should also be disturbed by foreign female worshippers gathering in the public space of his city. The chorus of *Iphigenia in Aulis* (still Greek, but "foreign" in their lack of specific communal connection to characters of the drama) goes even farther in the

---

[123] Euripides' lyric style has been analyzed in several different ways, but because the musical accompaniment is lost, it is very difficult to speak usefully of the emotional impact of his choral odes. On a verbal level, Breitenbach 1934 amassed abundant examples of unusual compounds and of pregnant or artificial junctures of nouns, adjectives, and genitive complements. Di Benedetto 1971: 239–72 treated the style of later Euripidean lyric as reflecting a withdrawal from political engagement (by himself and his audience) and an escapist strategy ("evasione verso la poesia bella"), and he related the prettification he detects to trends in other arts (cf. Di Benedetto 1971–74). Kranz 1933 and Panagl 1971 viewed Euripides as under the influence of the so-called New Music and tending toward a "dithyrambic" style in his last decade, but see Csapo 1999–2000 for important qualifications of this approach, arguing that Euripides' embrace of New Music started earlier and that he was a trend-setter rather than a follower.

: connection to the events and the perfunctoriness of their plot. In both *Bacchae* and *Iphigenia in Aulis*, the foreign- us undermines the possibility of choral sympathy for the ʒ. Along with the breakdown in families, polis-society, and here is now the added harshness of further isolation of the universe that fails to provide consolation. The refusal to chorus more tightly may then be a deliberate reflection of a world in which order and sense are hard to discern.

CHAPTER 5

The gods

From Aristophanes to modern times, the role and presentation of the gods in Euripidean tragedy have been the topic of intense discussion and disagreement. At one pole of interpretation, critics suggest that Euripidean tragedy had outgrown the Greek theological tradition and retained the received elements of divine participation in myth either as a separable adjunct, to be dismissed when attention is focused on the real issues of human psychology, or as an ironic exposure of the absurdity or immorality of everyday religious beliefs. At the other pole, Euripidean gods are viewed as provident and potentially merciful in interactions complicated by the blindness and failings of faith of imperfect humans. In between these extremes are many possible gradations. The questions related to this discussion are literary, cultural, and religious, and they include, among others, the following: what is the relationship of a framing divine prologue and epilogue to the dramatic scenes within the frame? To what degree are these framing scenes integrated into the play, or to what degree are they openly marked as distinct from the other scenes? What effect do they have on the audience's interpretation of the actions, behavior, and decisions of the human characters between these frames, and on the audience's assessment of the order or disorder, morality or amorality, of the represented tragic world? Does tragedy's representation of the gods belong, as some argue, to a poetic tradition that really has little to tell us about actual Greek religious practice or belief? Or, alternatively, is tragedy so embedded in the Athenian democracy and its institutions that tragic representation of "religion" should be understood entirely in terms of what one might call "official public piety"? And in general, how shocking or transgressive were tragic characters' individual expressions of criticism or doubt, or their intellectually sophisticated reconceptualizations concerning the gods and divine causation?

In this chapter, I begin with several preliminary propositions or working hypotheses about religious practices and beliefs and tragedy in order to indicate the complexity and difficulty of the topic and the unlikelihood of arriving at a single, simple, and self-consistent formulation of a solution. Then I consider the dialectic of despair and hope or faith within the human characters of the plays, which often varies sharply from character to character and from one situation to another within a single play. This dialectic is significant because it militates against a direct reading of one theological stance as that which is promoted by a play or by Euripides' output in general. Third, I discuss some challenging, idealizing, or speculative prayers to, or statements about divinity that are expressed by Euripidean characters. Then, after a discussion of the gods directly represented by speaking actors in prologues and epilogues, I explore the process of inference by which an audience detects or declines to detect the unseen hand of the gods in what occurs or is reported within the drama. Inferences of this kind make an important difference in how far we regard the action of the plays as psychologically or naturalistically understandable and in how just or unjust, moral or amoral, the universe created by the plays may have seemed to the ancient audience. Finally, a few related conclusions or questions are presented.

PRELIMINARY CONSIDERATIONS ON GREEK RELIGION AND THE DIVINE

The first among the preliminary propositions is that our discussion is about Euripidean tragedy and its presentation of the views and beliefs of human beings who are characters or choruses in the plays. It is not about the beliefs or attitudes of the historical individual Euripides, which are unattainable.[1] To be sure, audiences and scholars who think carefully about what is said and shown on stage will often feel entitled to make inferences about the author who wrote the words and shaped the action, but at best this involves a construction of the implied author of the individual work. It is dangerous, especially in the case of a versatile author like Euripides and a dynamic and variable genre like Attic tragedy, to assume that the construction arrived at from viewing and studying one work will necessarily be valid for another work. When we try to generalize about the tendencies or mannerisms of Euripides, we are speaking metaphorically of a constructed literary personality based on what we conceive to be similar features in the implied authors of various individual works.[2] In regard to beliefs about the gods, some critics

---

[1] Cf. Allan 2000: 236, Schmidt 1964: 220–3, Wildberg 1999–2000: 238.
[2] For the possibility of differently characterized implied authors in different works of one person, see Booth 1983: 71. For the application to drama of the notion of "implied" or "ideal" author considered distinct from "the actual author in his socio-literary role as the producer of the work" see Pfister 1988: 3–4.

in the past (taking their cue from Aristophanes' comedies) have constructed their Euripides as an atheist and others have argued against this characterization, but the questions involved are better discussed in different terms, such as what is the significance of atheistic-sounding statements made by characters in tragedy, both within their dramatic context and within the context of the audience and culture viewing the plays.

Second, in any discussion of "theology" in the archaic and classical Greek context, we must remain aware of the imperfect fit of this concept (as it tends to be understood in modern monotheistic systems) to much of Greek religion.[3] Greek religion is not a religion with an authoritative book or a priestly class with the right to supervise doctrine. It is more fully realized in social practices than in individual thought or belief. The everyday and seasonal experience of religion for most Greeks lay in a recurring routine of dedications, sacrifices, libations, and prayers intended to acknowledge divine power and to appeal for divine good will (and avert divine displeasure), whether for a specifically articulated favor or implicitly for a general continuation of prosperity. This activity involves an implicit (and often vague) "theology": that the gods are powerful both for good and for ill, that they may grant or withhold favor, and that reciprocity may be hoped for but not compelled or guaranteed.[4] Detailed conjectures on the powers and nature of divinity tend to be found in specific intellectual contexts, but are not normally part of ritual action,[5] and there is no widespread indoctrination of explicit propositions about divinity. A small class of intellectuals, beginning with Xenophanes and Heraclitus, make striking pronouncements about the right way to think about divinity, and such discussion proliferates in the sophistic movement of the late fifth century. But even earlier, the archaic and classical poets, through hymns and narratives, often give indirect testimony to less formal, speculative theological thinking, emphasizing the wonder and mystery of divine interactions with humans

---

[3] For recent approaches to Greek religion that emphasize its variety and inconsistency see Versnel 1990, Parker 1996 and 2005, Price 1999. I would like to acknowledge here that my thinking has also benefitted from the unpublished Sather lectures of Henk Vernsel, delivered in Berkeley in early 1999. On general issues of religion in the theater, see Parker 2005: 136–52 (we have come to similar conclusions independently).

[4] On reciprocity see e.g. Yunis 1988, Pulleyn 1997. It is essential to recognize that statements of confidence in the existence of reciprocity between gods and men coexist with the (often submerged?) awareness that the gods act as they please and may or may not actually engage in reciprocal behavior in some particular circumstance (Gould 1985). Pulleyn 1997 occasionally argues that some aspect of the system of Greek prayer would not have "worked" if people were not confident of reciprocity, but this logic ignores the capacity of human beings to hold contradictory beliefs (see below).

[5] Even in most initiations and mystery cults, the key for the celebrants lay in special experiences and revelation rather than in some particular doctrines.

and the inaccessibility of the "mind of Zeus" to human penetration. This kind of speculation is much more at home in poetry than in the relations to divinity embodied in ritual practice, even though there, too, the potential arbitrariness of the gods is carefully acknowledged in the use in prayer of conditionals such as "if it is pleasing to you."

Third, a good deal of traditional scholarship on Euripides has been concerned with the question whether he "believed" in the traditional myths or in the myths he was staging. "Belief" or "non-belief" is the wrong category to apply. The stories of the Greeks about the gods and heroes formed a vast network of variants, a network that was dynamic and creative throughout the archaic and classical period (and later as well). It is the expected role of the Greek poet to reinterpret and extrapolate these stories to suit the occasion, the audience, or a political, ethical, or aesthetic interest. This is as true of Homer, Hesiod, Stesichorus, and Pindar as it is of the Attic tragedians. In the competitive context of Greek poetic performances, each new version seeks to persuade its audience of its capacity to be integrated into the larger system of stories, and its "truth" is mainly a matter of how illuminating and apposite it is in the context in which it is told. All tragedians will have innovated in smaller or larger aspects of the plots they created. Euripides' long career of dramatic production demonstrates that for him the mythological mode was a flexible and enduring arena in which to entertain and move his audience while stimulating them to think about important cultural and ethical issues.

Fourth, in many systems of human belief, there is a large capacity for compartmentalization of beliefs and for toleration of inconsistencies. Thus, in traditional Greek religion one can maintain both that the gods uphold justice and that the gods give both success and suffering (and that suffering is given in larger proportion and is not necessarily justified). The opening of the *Odyssey* provides a strong claim that by their own bad choices men are responsible for the troubles they encounter, but it would be a mistake to interpret all interactions between men and gods in this epic in the light of this claim.[6] Solon's famous *Hymn to the Muses* (poem 13 W) combines in one sequential argument both an endorsement of the justice of Zeus's dispensation and a powerful evocation of humanity's subjection to *elpis* (hope), cataloguing the inability of humans, regardless of their specific skills and the morality of their behavior, to control the end of their actions. Thus, when we compare religious beliefs expressed in tragedy with a reconstruction of the beliefs of the audience, we must acknowledge that the latter did not form a self-consistent or fixed system. And we must also recognize that

[6] See Allan 2006.

the beliefs about divinity that one could espouse in a public assembly or courtroom were a limited selection among the possible beliefs people might espouse in contexts of greater privacy or intimacy or in the hypothetical worlds of poetic fictions.[7]

In addition to the cautions necessitated by the preceding points, it is not easy to define precisely the relation between the poetic representation of the Greek gods and the gods of everyday Greek cult. The gods of drama are presented in a festival context (the Great Dionysia) that is clearly demar- cated from routine life, a festival in which we must also remember the juxtaposition of tragedy, satyr-play, and comedy, each with its somewhat different depictions of divine action and character, not to mention the prayers and myths probably contained in the twenty choral dithyrambs performed at the same festival. The audience of this festival was clearly expected to entertain a multiplicity of world-views, and there was no straightforward correspondence between what they saw and the way they carried on their lives once the festival was over. Moreover, at some level of analysis, the gods in epic and tragedy are a "literary device" (at least in part inherited from a slowly changing tradition) that serves the needs of the narrative and the creation of meaning out of a series of events. As a "literary device" (and in drama often an iconographic and presentational device as well) their contribution can be appreciated even by those who no longer believe in the traditional gods in the same way or by later recipients, such as ourselves, brought up in a monotheistic culture.[8]

We must acknowledge several important distinctions between the gods in traditional verbal and visual narratives and the gods of cult. The gods of tragedy are closely akin to the gods of Homeric epic, who are panhellenic, transcending the separate communities of the Greeks (and Trojans). Most everyday cult practice, in contrast, is extremely localized, with different calendars, aetiologies, ritual requirements, and epithets. To be sure, because of the concrete localization of the plays' geography, tragedy often includes or alludes to localized aspects – Athenian, Theban, Taurian, or whatever is appropriate. Nevertheless, the panhellenic aspect remains strong. Athena of

---

[7] See Parker 1997, who shows that public oratory presents not the norm of Athenian religious belief, but a censored form of speech, with a compulsory optimism.

[8] For various views on the conventionality of the divine apparatus of epic and myth and the possibility of keeping the literary evidence separate from other evidence for "Greek religion," see (for convention- ality or separation) Bröcker 1980, Mikalson 1991; (against, or qualifying) Parker 1997, Sourvinou- Inwood 1997. On Euripidean theology (or theologies) as descendants of the Homeric, see Kullmann 1987, Basta Donzelli 1987, Knox 1991. For interpretation of the gods in tragedy as a poetic technique see, e.g., Schmidt 1964 and Rosenmeyer 1982: 259–83. On the general problem of depictions of gods in ancient literature see also Feeney 1991 and 1998.

Eumenides is founder and protector of democratic Athens, but also the
Iliadic ally of Agamemnon, reconfiguring the traditional ties between her
divine family and the royal family of Argos. In *Antigone* 1115–54, Dionysus is
summoned to give aid as a native son of Thebes, but the god's attachments
to Italy, Delphi, and Eleusis are also evoked. The Taurian Artemis of
Iphigenia in Tauris is also the Artemis who acted at Aulis, the sister of
Delphic Apollo, and the Artemis(es) of Attic cult. The god you see on stage
is mysteriously both the same and not the same as the god you worship in a
completely different local context.

   Also significant is the temporal displacement of the gods as represented in
poetry. Although the Greeks counted a continuum of generations back to
mythic times, and communities or families claimed descent from heroes, they
also had a more or less clear sense of their own separation from the heroic
world. The heroic world was a time of more intimate, frequent, and open
interaction between gods and mortals. The heroes were the product of a
mingling of the two species, a mingling imagined to have ended at a certain
point in history. In that earlier period it was possible for gods to attend a
human wedding, for humans to visit the gods or to be educated by an
immortal being, for exceptionally endowed humans to compete with gods
in strength and skill and to threaten to compete in honor. In some stories, the
gods themselves were still establishing their respective prerogatives as the reign
of Zeus was being consolidated.[9] In the post-heroic world, by contrast, all
interactions are more distant, the human beings are weaker and less able than
the heroic generations, and the major gods have been stabilized into a
complex community. The gods of myth and poetry are involved in stories
of disorder and emerging order, whereas present-day religious practice is
aimed at maintaining an achieved order or equilibrium. Aetiologies and
cult-foundations, often featured at the end of a tragedy, especially in
Euripides, function as references to the more stable present and help the
audience bridge the gap between mythical time and contemporary life, but
such bridging presupposes distance. Tragedy's preference for this distancing
effect of heroic subject-matter has, of course, distinct advantages in allowing
the transfer of the antinomies and strife of contemporary society and politics
to a safe remove, a locus where troubling questions can be posed and the harsh
consequences of crisis can be, ostensibly, confined to others.[10] In *Bacchae*, for

[9] See Clay 1989.
[10] In addition, most tragedies also depict events at a geographical remove from Athens, in Thebes,
Argos, the land of the Taurians, etc. Zeitlin 1990 presents a case for Thebes in particular as an anti-
Athens, a particularly fertile locale for events the Athenians would regard as incompatible with their
ideal self-image.

example, we have displacement in space and time to Thebes in the heroic age as well as a myth of establishment of Dionysiac cult with the typical feature of human resistance to be overcome. For the fifth-century audience itself, however, the same god Dionysus is fully incorporated into the religion of the democratic city of Athens, honored in the very context of the performance with the multiple evolved forms of Dionysiac choral dance as well as with processions, sacrifices, and a spirit of festivity.[11]

Furthermore, through incorporation in narrative, the gods acquire a fuller anthropomorphic psychological personality and a more transparent role in causation than they have in ordinary life. Literary and theatrical gods are also put into relationships of competition, dispute, and alliance with each other in a way that does not commonly arise in cult. The difference of the god-laden literary world is most striking in the matter of causality. Along with the other simplifications and reductions that literary narrative exercises in comparison with real life, Greek heroic narratives usually make causation fuller and more transparent, sometimes even more understandable. In everyday life, in some portion of an agent's deliberations and actions, there will be a basic assumption of autonomous personal agency and no thought of supernatural intervention. Individuals will, of course, have differed in the proportion of their actions recognized to be autonomous in this way, from a very high proportion for the scientifically minded to a very low proportion for the superstitious. Even when the pious or super-stitious do think of what divine forces are involved in their successes and disappointments, there is a good deal of uncertainty. Before the event, one may appeal to a specific divinity, perhaps make a vow to that god. In the event of success, that particular divinity may be thanked or presented with the promised votive offering. But in the event of failure, malevolence is often attributed not to a named individual force, but to *to theion*, "the divine" in general, or to *tuchē*, "fortune."[12] Only in the most severe crises do individuals and communities seek, from oracles or prophets, clarification of

---

[11] On the apparent gaps between the Dionysus of *Bacchae* and the maenadic worship imagined in poetry and in visual representations, on the one hand, and Athenian (and other) cult practices on the other, see Henrichs 1978 and 1990: 257–8, Osborne 1997, Kowalzig 2007.
[12] *Tuchē* is, of course, as often the manifestation of fate or the gods' conscious dispensations or their reflexive "jealousy" as it is a pure chance that cannot be attributed to an origin and that is viewed as the opposite of a discernible supernatural plan involving predictable cause and effect. For the gods and *tuchē* in Herodotus, see Harrison 2000: 99–100, 169–70, and *passim*, and also his ch. 2 for divine *phthonos*. Parker 1997: 155 makes the important point that the sort of resentment or blame that may be expressed in literary representations has no natural outlet in public discourse, except in the funeral oration, where the need not to blame the glorious dead justifies the mention of malignant or unkind anonymous supernatural powers.

the source of malevolence so that it may be appeased. The world of epic and tragedy, in contrast, is much more thoroughly penetrated by divine forces, both anonymous and named.[13] It is a world of concentrated and drastic impulses, where causes of events are more fully accessible and particular deities more readily identifiable. In epic the narrator can tell the audience of the particular god who intervenes at a given moment, while the characters affected are normally unable to put a name to the power that intruded or may not even realize that divine intrusion has occurred. The tragic chorus sometimes has the same sort of authority as the epic narrator in identifying supernatural causes, although (as we saw in the previous chapter) the chorus can also make conjectures that the audience will doubt or deem wrong. Occasionally, even the characters of tragedy may rise to an abnormal confidence in recognizing a divine antagonist, as in the case of Oedipus' naming of Apollo (Soph. *OT* 1329–30) or Phaedra's references to Aphrodite (*Hipp.* 337–47, 401, 725–7). But such is the nature of dramatic presentation that those involved in the action normally know less than the audience that observes them. This discrepancy in awareness can be heightened when, as often in Euripides, a divine character is actually put on stage in a prologue heard by the audience but, of course, unknown to the human characters.

Lastly, whereas a philosophical or monotheistic theology may concentrate on the nature of god *per se*, it is important to remember that in archaic and classical Greece literary gods are part of a system of contrast with human beings. The role of gods in stories is sometimes designed less to establish any particular theological principles or even to assert divine justice than to provide a basic contrast that defines the limitations of the human condition (and the contrast is heightened by the fact that the humans whose limitations are revealed in tragic plots are unusually powerful and successful persons). The contrast of (divine) knowledge and (human) ignorance is fundamental to many tragedies. Efficacy of action is another divine privilege, and the contrast with humans is reflected visually by the use of the upper level (skene-roof) for most divine appearances and by the special form of locomotion provided by the theater crane. The Homeric contrast of the ease of the gods with the desperate plight of humans is carried over into tragedy in the highlighting of the gods' lack of humane pity (as with Athena in Sophocles' *Ajax* or Aphrodite

---

[13] Padel 1992 and 1995 study the language of mental invasion and demonstrate important distinctions between ancient and modern notions of psychology. Nevertheless, I would emphasize that the hypothesis of supernatural invasion is also to be correlated with a rhetorical strategy: it is appealed to in order to deal with the extreme and the uncanny, not the ordinary. Thus, tragedy, as a locus of the extreme and uncanny, does not provide a simple reflection of the range of standard Greek beliefs about the mind and personality.

in *Hippolytus*) or their inaccessibility to the kinds of sympathy, tolerance, and forgiveness available to humans (as with Dionysus at the end of *Bacchae*).

Despite the differences just reviewed, it is not justified to regard the gods of tragedy as *solely* a literary device. As several scholars have recently argued, the theological component of tragedy and other serious Greek literature is still to be regarded as a legitimate concern within the study of Greek religion and not as material that can be neatly bracketed off from other kinds of evidence. Herodotus' claim (2.53) about the role of Homer and Hesiod in institutionalizing Greek religious practice and nomenclature, for example, and the objections raised by intellectual critics (like Heraclitus, Xenophanes, and Plato) against the theological implications of much of Homer, Hesiod, and tragedy guarantee that the Greeks themselves did not accept any clear separation. But the system of Greek religion is complex and not susceptible to a fully rational and self-consistent account, nor should we expect that ancient Greeks were constantly aware of the inconsistencies that scholarly study is able to identify. As a realm of both more transparent causation and more multiple, speculative, and questioning attitudes, literary (and especially dramatic) representations of the gods have the potential to make explicit some of these problems and contradictions.

THE DRAMA OF HUMAN BELIEF

When we turn to the plays of Euripides themselves, instead of looking for a single authorial stance regarding the nature of divinity or even for a self-consistent construction deducible from each single play, we do better to focus attention on the human characters, who are often engaged in a dynamic process, struggling to make sense of their world and their experiences, propounding shifting views about the gods. This struggle to understand within the world of the play is often matched in the audience's own dynamic process of interpreting characters' natures and motivations and of weighing alternative causations. Although the audience has in some ways a privileged position in assessing dramatic events, there are many tragedies, and not only by Euripides, that defer or defeat a final synthesis.

In several plays, a dialectic of hope and despair provides a major source of dramatic tension and shaping: for instance, *Troades*, notorious among critics for its loose structure,[14] acquires one kind of coherence through the dialectical sequence of reactions of Hecuba, Cassandra, and Andromache to repeated blows of misfortune and through the debate they implicitly and

---

[14] See above, pp. 77–9.

explicitly carry on to evaluate their situations, a debate which the incon-
clusive *agōn* between Helen and Hecuba continues. One telltale sign of a
character's despair is criticism of the gods, a poetic motif that goes back to
Homer (e.g. *Il.* 3.365–8, 12.164–5).[15] Like other statements of dramatic
figures, such criticisms must always be evaluated in their particular context,
with attention to who is speaking and in what circumstances and with
comparison to other statements in the same play and the final resolution of
the action. Attention to these details establishes that the complaints and
opinions of human characters are often relativized or subjected to irony
either at once because of the superior knowledge of the audience or over the
course of the play because of the turn of events. Yet there remains a serious
question whether such ironies suffice to render the religion of tragedy fully
normalized and assimilated to traditional piety.[16]

We may begin with a case in which the complaints and doubts of the
characters are clearly recognized by the audience to be based in large part on
misapprehensions: *Iphigenia in Tauris*.[17] In this play, Orestes opens his
expository rhesis in the second scene of the prologue wondering whether
Apollo has "again" led him into a trap by his oracular instruction (77).
Subjectively, this fear is justified by Orestes' long experience of wandering
and intermittent madness. But objectively, the audience has just been
introduced to Orestes' lost sister Iphigenia and can now interpret the last
detail of her dream (53–5) to indicate that the siblings will soon meet. The
audience is likely therefore to feel the force of the story-pattern of
recognition-plots: given the survival of Iphigenia herself, and since the
tradition does not clearly establish that being the victim of a kin-murder
is to be expected as the ultimate fate of Orestes, they will expect the
recognition to lead to some positive result. In addition, Orestes himself
refers to the Athenian destination of the statue he has been instructed to
carry away (90–1): whether or not the audience can yet fully understand the
allusion, which is later explained clearly in the epilogue speech of Athena
(1449–61), this reference to Attic cult of Artemis probably provides another
hint to the audience that the mission will succeed and that Orestes' fears will
not be realized. Running parallel with Orestes' ignorance is Iphigenia's

[15] In particular, there is a literary tradition of critical and challenging prayers: Dale 1963, Labarbe 1980, Heath 1987b: 51, Mastronarde 1994 on *Phoen.* 86–7, Pulleyn 1997: 196–207, Harrison 2000: 109 n. 23; Chapot and Laurot 2001: 48–9, 82–5.
[16] The tendency toward a relatively complete normalization is to be seen in Spira 1960, Burnett 1971, Heath 1987b: 45–64, Lefkowitz 1989, Mikalson 1989 (on which see n. 73 below), Kovacs 1993, Gregory 1999.
[17] The following paragraphs expand on a treatment in Mastronarde 1986. See also Cropp 2000: 31–43.

mistaken interpretation of her dream. The audience can make much more sense than she of the details of the dream, since they can easily read the allusion to the deaths of Agamemnon and Clytemnestra in the collapse of the house, and to the lonely survival of Orestes in the remaining column (46–52). Thus the audience is able to doubt her view that Orestes is already dead even before he comes on stage two minutes later to disprove it. In the following parodos, Iphigenia performs a lament for Orestes that the audience knows is unnecessary (143–235). A few scenes later, she bids farewell to the dream as false when she learns that Orestes is still alive (569). This dismissal, the audience can recognize, is as unfounded as her previous interpretation: it is Iphigenia's reading, not the dream itself, that has been disproved. The parallel between the misapprehensions of the two siblings is made clear by Orestes' following comment that "the so-called wise gods" (*sophoi*, "wise," naturally alludes to Apollo) are no more truthful than dreams (570–1), in veiled reference to his own unjustified (he thinks) trust in his Delphic instruction.[18] In Iphigenia's absence, Orestes can speak more openly, and at 711–15 he asserts that he has been deceived and that Apollo has sent him far off to be rid of him. In reply Pylades defends the oracle and a sense of hope and combats Orestes' hesitation (in other words, he speaks on Apollo's behalf, as Pylades did also in Aeschylus' *Choephori*), and his response verbalizes the audience's position at this moment, as it eagerly awaits the change of fortune (*metabolē*) that the recognition, so long and suspensefully postponed, will bring. Finally, after the recognition, Orestes himself can voice confidence in the confluence of human effort and divine causation: "I believe our project is a concern to divine fortune as well as to ourselves; and if a man is eagerly engaged, the divine, most likely, exerts its strength the more" (909–11). Thereafter the former victims of misapprehension become the manipulators of appearance in duping the Taurian king.

Yet there is no clear sailing for trust in the beneficence of the gods, even in a play of happy outcome like *Iphigenia in Tauris*. Human confusion is not

---

[18] Diggle 1981–94: II.266 expressed suspicion of lines 570–5 but left them in his text with only the mark of corruption in the second half of 573. In the recent editions of Kovacs 1994–2002: IV.208 and Cropp 2000 lines 572–5 are deleted on the suggestion of Cropp. Despite Cropp's reservations about the relevance of "seers" (574) to Orestes' situation, 572–3a are most apposite to the theme of the play, and the veiled language of 575 (ὄλωλεν ὡς ὄλωλε τοῖσιν εἰδόσιν) allows Orestes to speak clearly to the audience but conceal his identity from Iphigenia, so it seems to me these lines were intended for this passage and not incorporated from a different context. One may perhaps argue that after the sharp criticism of divinities, the universalizing pairing of κἀν τοῖς βροτείοις (573) suggests to Orestes the accommodation of assigning the fault to human spokespersons of the gods rather than gods themselves (μάντεων πεισθεὶς λόγοις 574); for such accommodation cf. Soph. *OT* 497–503 (chorus) and 707–9, 723–5 (Jocasta).

simply a result of human weakness, but of entanglements and conundrums in the universe they must live in. Iphigenia's references to Artemis' attitude toward the Taurian cult of human sacrifice provide one indication. In the prologue, the goddess is said to "delight in" (35 *hēdetai*) the custom, but Iphigenia herself implies that the rite is not "fine" (36 *kalon*) and refrains from any more forthright epithet out of fear of the goddess (37). At the end of the first episode, after reviewing the deceit and betrayal at Aulis, she arrives at a crisis of belief (380–91). First she reproaches the "oversubtle distinctions" (380 *sophismata*) made by a goddess who requires ritual purity in other respects but herself "delights in" (384 *hēdetai*) human sacrifice. Then, finding this inconsistency intolerable, she rejects the notion that Artemis could be so "morally insensitive" (386 *amathia*) and declares the story of divine cannibalism within the history of her own family to be "unbelievable" (388 *apista*). Finally, she ascribes the desire for human sacrifice entirely to the Taurians and declares her belief that no god is ever evil (391 *kakon*). It is important to note how this speech grows out of heightened despair and resentment and to observe that during the course of the play Iphigenia's views shift with the circumstances known to her. In the case of Iphigenia's views of Artemis, there is the further double irony that at Aulis the goddess both demanded human sacrifice of Agamemnon (and as far as he and the Greeks were concerned, they performed it for her) and prevented human sacrifice by carrying Iphigenia away to the Taurians – where, however, she has been forced to participate in human sacrifice! Her presence among the Taurians, to whom she tries to confine the scandal of human sacrifice in order to exonerate the goddess, cannot in fact be divorced from Artemis' agency. Moreover, the ritual prescribed by Athena for the new cult at Halai likewise acknowledges that Artemis is still owed the honor of a symbolic substitution for human sacrifice (1458–61). Iphigenia herself later fears that the goddess may resist the theft of the statue ordered by Apollo and prays to her that she will accept the move with good will (995, 1082–8). And when the escape is threatened she appeals to Artemis, asking for forgiveness of the theft and understanding for her loyalty to her brother Orestes (1398–402), again in fear that the goddess may wish to stay among the Taurians and continue to delight in human sacrifice. Such fears presuppose the view of Artemis espoused by the Taurians, since Thoas assumes that the goddess takes an interest in the capture and punishment of the fugitives (1425–46) and the messenger refers to Iphigenia's action as a betrayal of Artemis (1419). In the whole scheme of the play, Iphigenia's purified view of the gods (385–91) cannot be taken as a privileged opinion. It is rather a reflection of the moral idealism in which Iphigenia takes refuge at a particular moment of pain and doubt. Despite the details in the play that tend to focalize the bloodthirsty aspect of Artemis as Taurian and unGreek, this aspect is not merely a projection of barbarian belief: the goddess Artemis is in need of rescue from herself by her brother and in need of the civilizing influence of Athena and Athens.

A second sign of the difficulty of the universe in which the humans of this play operate is provided by the Delphi ode (1234–83).[19] Apart from any other associative relevance of the details of this amusing narrative of the child Apollo's quick action to secure the role (and wealth) of his oracle against a potential threat, this mythic narrative provides an aetiology of the distinction in reliability between Apollo's oracle and dream-prophecy. By Zeus's dispensation, truth is withdrawn from dreams and honor fully restored to the Delphic oracle. This outcome corresponds to the fact that in the play Orestes' doubts of Apollo's instructions are shown ultimately to be unfounded, while Iphigenia is misled by her dream.[20] Part of the human confusion represented in the play is thus structured into Zeus's dispensation, that is, it is an inescapable part of what humans must cope with.

Thirdly, the near failure of the escape (because of a strong sea swell at the mouth of the harbor: 1394–419) may be viewed as evidence that even with the favor of the gods (or of *some* of the gods) human efforts are not assured of success. The theological or cosmological implication of the need for intervention by Athena is that humans are embedded in a world containing multiple forces whose agreement or conflict cannot be relied on or predicted by any means available to humans. An audience is left to wonder whether Taurian Artemis is indeed hostile to the theft/escape, as Iphigenia feared, or whether the messenger is right to detect the opposition of a separate (and up to this point unrelated) agent, Poseidon (1414–15), or whether some other unknown force is in play. Some critics suggest that no such theological inference should be drawn, because the *deus ex machina* is a convention.[21] On this view, the wave is needed to motivate the arrival of Athena rather

---

[19] For discussion of this song, see above, pp. 142–3.
[20] Strictly speaking, we must note that Iphigenia's dream is in fact, like all dreams in tragedy, veridical, containing a symbolism easily interpreted aright by the audience (immediately perceiving that Orestes is the one *surviving* member after the catastrophe at Argos, and later seeing that Iphigenia does indeed perform some ritual preliminaries for a sacrifice that is not completed in the dream or in reality). The problem is that dreams need more interpretation from humans, and such interpretation more easily goes wrong. In addition, it is possible that in "took away truthfulness" (1279) Euripides alludes to the notion of the two gates of dreams (*Od.* 19.560–7), according to which some dreams may be true, but humans have no way to determine which these are.
[21] Spira 1960: 120–1, Matthiessen 1967: 57 n. 4, Lesky 1983: 306 ("suddenly the wind drives it back because Athena must appear"). Strohm 1949: 25 and Burnett 1971: 65 argue that inferences should be drawn from the adverse wind (and Matthiessen 2002: 170 no longer entirely excludes this idea).

than Athena's being needed to undo the threat of the wave. Yet it is proper to insist that Euripides made this particular choice to motivate Athena's intervention. The messenger-speech begins with the assumption that pursuit is perfectly feasible, without any hint of the adverse sea swell: the messenger advises the king to hear the whole story and then consider carefully what pursuit will best succeed (1322–4), and the king agrees that the journey ahead of the fugitives is long enough to allow his forces to catch up with them (1325–6). Thus Euripides could well have introduced Athena and her stopping-action without the adverse wave and without the messenger's speculation about divine hostility, but elected to include these details. Accordingly, a more than minimalist or conventional reading is justified.

The other plays of recognition and rescue often grouped with *Iphigenia in Tauris*, namely *Helen* and *Ion*, can be viewed in a similar light. We may briefly consider only the latter here. In this play, complaints about and criticisms of Apollo are frequently repeated and are strengthened by the agreement of the three separate speakers who utter them.[22] These attacks are indeed relativized in the audience's mind by the ignorance that afflicts the characters. It is unjustified to read the play, as has often been done, as intended mainly as an attack on Apollo; but it is equally questionable to believe that the benevolence and protection of the god are triumphantly asserted.[23] The rebelliousness of the humans derails Apollo's present plan to care for his son's future and threatens in turn the lives of Ion and Creusa. This wayward action arises from the intolerable emotional burden placed on Creusa, and she is not the only figure whose reaction to the situation contributes to the development of events. The chorus feels empathy with Creusa over the god's apparent abandonment of her interest, in contrast to his provision of a son to her husband Xuthus, and this is a major factor leading to their revelation of the secret they have been ordered to keep.[24] The chorus' disobedience prompts Creusa to reveal her past travails and the old servant in turn to prompt Creusa to plot murder.

Apollo's neglect of the burden Creusa bears, his indifference to or ignorance of the human dimensions of his plan, reenacts the neglect of the past – the rescue and nurture of the baby in a way that leaves the mother pained for years by the fear that the infant is dead through her fault. Even

---

[22] Ion, Creusa, and the old servant: *Ion* 252–4, 358 and 355, 365, 367, 370, 384–5, 426, 436–51, 880, 885, 895, 952, 960, 972.
[23] The former view has a long history and is exemplified by Norwood 1953: 236–43 and Rosenmeyer 1963: 105–52, while the latter is promoted by Wasserstein 1940, Burnett 1962 and 1971, and Spira 1960.
[24] See above, p. 120.

though based on misapprehensions, these sufferings are subjectively real to the humans and are lent a decided dramatic weight by their prominence in the fabric of speech and song. There is a tragic gap between the "kindness" and "concern" of the gods and the life lived by those who are favored. Even when the recognition is complete, Ion's lingering intellectual and religious discomfort lead him to want to confront Apollo with a direct question (1546–8). Again there is the option to treat this impulse as simply a plot-device to motivate Athena's arrival, but as in the case of *Iphigenia in Tauris* such a minimalist interpretation is inadequate. Ion's attempt must be given more weight because it continues the pattern of challenging human behavior. The proposed confrontation is parallel to Creusa's earlier attempt to approach the oracle (332–46) and to Ion's speech of "admonition" to Apollo (436–51). While saving Apollo from the embarrassment of reproach, Athena herself acknowledges that reproach would not be an unexpected reaction for the humans (1558). Only after a long exposition of future glories does Athena urge upon Creusa the judgment that "Apollo accomplished all things for the good" (1546–8), which sounds like the extremely favorable assessment of an advocate. In response, Ion has the tact to assert his belief in his paternity and to claim that the truth was not doubtful even before (1608). But Creusa carefully maintains a distinction between past and present attitudes (1609–13, esp. "not praising *before*," "which he *once* neglected," "who was hateful *before*"), a distinction that implicitly rejects Athena's attempted amelioration of the past. The goddess' judgment is oversimplified, adequate perhaps for the gods in their remote and carefree existence, but inadequate to the very different experience of human life.

This kind of analysis of the shifting and competing perspectives of human characters regarding the gods can be applied to plays of other types. Here it suffices to present one more example.[25] *Heracles* provides the supremely tragic instance of the dialectic of human despair and faith in the gods. In the absence of Heracles himself, his father, wife, and children are threatened with execution by the usurper Lycus. There are three interrelated bases for hope in the first part of the play: either Heracles himself may return from the underworld, or Zeus may intervene to protect his suppliants (who are also tied to him specifically by kinship and the obligation created by the "sharing" of Alcmene), or the inevitable cycle of changing fortune in human life may bring an end to Lycus' prosperity and power. Heracles' return could be regarded as a manifestation of Zeus'

---

[25] The example of *Orestes* is treated later in conjunction with the problem of Apollo's final rescue, below, pp. 192–5.

concern, and the power of fortune exists either in competition with or in collaboration with Zeus.[26] Megara and Lycus persuade Amphitryon to abandon his hope in Heracles' return, and the chorus echoes this abandonment in singing an encomiastic dirge for the hero (348–441). With the concession to despair come Amphitryon's sharpest rebukes to Zeus: lines 339–47 charge him with failure as a *philos*, and being "morally insensitive" (*amathēs*) or simply unjust; lines 498–501 assert that many appeals for help have been in vain. And carrying forward this mood of disappointment in the gods is the chorus, which even after the return of Heracles devotes a stanza of the second stasimon to criticism of the way the gods have disposed human life (655–72): they have failed to demonstrate adequate "understanding and wisdom," for they have not provided a clear and reliable distinction between good and bad men, leaving time to foster (immoral) wealth rather than virtue. These criticisms seem to be, for the moment, undercut or refuted. Amphitryon's last prayer to Zeus to give aid before it is too late is answered by Heracles' appearance just a few lines after the old man declares his prayer to be a futile effort. Moreover, Heracles has, in a sense, just been seen to experience the double course of life (the return from Hades) that the chorus desiderated for good men in their song. The chorus itself turns its back on criticism and disappointment in the next song, which accompanies and follows the death of the villain: now the gods do have power, they support the just and punish the unjust, and time itself eventually brings ruin to those who pursue immoral prosperity (772–80). The final words of this theodicy still resound in the air (812–13) when the crane brings into view, extraordinarily (because in mid-play), goddesses who will violently overthrow it. The staging makes visible the externality of the causation, frustrating attempts to detect a psychological or character-based origin for Heracles' madness. Euripides contrives the dialogue of Iris and Lyssa to rule out any interpretation that would see any divine justice in the intervention.[27] Zeus's protection, so long awaited in the crisis of supplication, is henceforth completely absent, giving free rein to Hera's wrath.

More disastrously than in the case of *Iphigenia in Tauris* or *Ion*, the favor of the gods is here shown to be real but so intermittent and unreliable as to render the human condition utterly precarious. The final portion of the play examines how the hero will cope with this precariousness, and human friendship and endurance eventually provide some anchor for continued

---

[26] On the range of meaning of *tuchē* cf. n. 12 above.
[27] *Her.* 846–54, 856 ; cf. too the chorus' reference, in an emendation of the corrupt text at 887, to "unjust Goddesses of Punishment" attacking Heracles.

life. Within the movement toward this conclusion Heracles makes one of
the most famous claims about divinity in the extant plays, rejecting the gods
of poetic myth (who have been active in his whole life and in the events of
this plot) in favor of a purified conception of a divinity of perfect self-
sufficiency, incapable of being liable to the emotional entanglements of lust
and political rivalry (1340–6). These lines, like other expressions of faith and
despair, must be recognized as arising from and colored by the immediate
experiences of the character. They portray a yearning for something that the
represented world of the play denies (and that, this representation implies,
the real world denies). This reflex of optimism is a necessary stage in
Heracles' recovery, but it is not the key to understanding the whole play
or the key lesson of Euripidean theology.

CRITICISM AND SPECULATION

As we have seen in examining the dialectic of hope and despair in several
plays, characters under pressure or suffering greatly are inclined to challenge
the comforting views of "official" piety or a straightforward theodicy. Many
moderns, influenced by their familiarity with religions based on sacred texts,
have tended to view such statements as somehow irreligious or impious. One
need think only of the common view that in Sophocles' *Oedipus Tyrannus*
Jocasta is to be thought "impious" or "frivolous" for what she says about
oracles. But in the ancient Greek tradition, religious ideas are open to
contestation, and anyone who is somehow a religious specialist (like a priest
or seer) has a limited scope of superiority to laymen and does not automatically achieve any wider authority. Protest to or criticism of a god or the gods
lies within an old tradition established in Homer and the Theognidean
corpus, where we find so-called "contesting prayers."[28] Idealizing views that
challenge aspects of the traditional theology implicit in myths and poems are
to be found within the context of routine religious practice, as in the case of
Xenophanes' admonitions about the stories appropriate amidst the libations
and prayers of a symposium (fr. 1 W), or of Pindar's purging of myths in
celebratory songs performed at occasions that included prayer, sacrifice, and
libation (*Ol.* 1.35–53, 9.35–41). Even cosmological speculations were to some
extent an extension of traditional religious ideas, for instance in the personification of principles or in Heraclitus' use of the Erinyes as guarantors of
orderly processes (94 D–K). Treating *Nous* (Mind) as the basic principle

---

[28] See n. 15 above.

(Anaxagoras 13–14 D–K) can be considered an appropriation of earlier ideas about the powerful, planning, inscrutable mind of Zeus.

Reflections of such ideas in Euripidean characters attest both to the *sophia* of the poet (maintaining a high position in the broadening competition for status based on intellectual and verbal skills) and to the ambitions or aspirations of the humans he represents. These ideas ought not to be regarded as in and of themselves suspect or subversive. Euripides stands out, however, because his characters tend to be more analytical and articulate, more inclined toward a thorough rationalism, that is to say, more reflective of the intellectual ferment of his age. This characteristic, however, is at least in part an extension of a traditional prerogative of high-style poetry: the poet's display of *sophia* lies not only in his technical expertise with words and meter or in his representation of moral values and social wisdom, but also in his appropriation of specialized knowledge, whether it be geographical (as in Aesch. *Agam.* 281–311 or *Prom.* 707–35, 790–815, 829–41) or medical (as in *Eum.* 658–61) or anthropological/ sophistic (as in Soph. *Ant.* 332–75). But this appropriation and representation is not an endorsement of any particular speculation. Rather, Euripides' works dramatize crises of interpretation, faith, and intelligibility.

On the nature and behavior of gods, then, Euripidean characters and choruses utter contesting questions or critical statements within a tradition of critique, although the frequency and the style of these remarks are distinctive. The articulate and analytic figures created by Euripides sometimes not only complain but suggest how the universe could have been more intelligently or usefully arranged. In such contexts they may even admonish the gods about preferable behavior, in so-called "nouthetetic prayers."[29]

Some characters protest explicitly that they are not at all blameworthy but nevertheless suffer a grievous fate "from the gods." The most common motif is a phrase like *ouden aitios*, "not at all to blame," such as is used by Hippolytus complaining of his own fate (*Hipp.* 1382–3).[30] Similarly, protest may be voiced against the gods as dispensers of human woe in general or of some particular person's suffering. Thus, the chorus at *Medea* 1112–15 speaks of the early death of children as an ultimate extreme pain inflicted on men by

---

[29] The term (from the Greek *nouthetein* = "advise, admonish") goes back to Dale 1963: 312–13; cf. Mastronarde 1994: 166; to the examples from tragedy one may add Odysseus' prayer to Zeus Xenios in *Cyclops* 354–5.
[30] Cf. *Hipp.* 1146–50 (the chorus is angry at the gods for the suffering of the innocent Hippolytus); *Her.* 1307–10 (Heracles on Hera's persecution); cf. *Alc.* 247 (Admetus on the death of Alcestis).

gods.[31] In *Iphigenia in Aulis* 1402–3, the chorus remarks that whereas Iphigenia's own attitude is noble, the aspect of the situation that derives from *tuchē* and the goddess Artemis "is sick." Many complain of the gods' failure to distinguish clearly and consistently between virtuous and wicked men in the fortunes they mete out to them. For instance, in *Supplices* 610, 612, the semichorus doubts that the gods are just, since the variations in men's fortunes are seen as random.[32] Related to this are the suggestions that the gods have established the laws of existence in a way that conceals vice from ready detection or protects the wicked from punishment. Medea asks why Zeus provided criteria for detecting counterfeit gold, but not for discovering a false man (*Med.* 516–19). The chorus of *Heracles* desiderates a manifest sign of divine support of virtue (655–6); and Ion criticizes the divine laws that provide asylum to the wicked as well as the virtuous (*Ion* 1312–19).

The assumption of the gods' concern and reciprocity is frequently challenged, whether the gods are said not to act at all or to act with frustrating slowness. Alcmene remarks on the slowness of Zeus's help (*Hcld.* 869–70), while Orestes says gods are always slow to act (*Or.* 420). One chorus finds that its comfort in believing the gods care for mortals undermined by the events they observe (*Hipp.* 1104–10, 1120–2); other choruses wonder why Apollo and Poseidon and the other gods abandoned their favored city, Troy (*Andr.* 1009–18 ; *Tro.* 1060–80 ; similarly Hecuba in *Tro.* 1242, 1280–1, 1287–92, 1317). Electra sings that no god hears her cries for justice for her father (*El.* 198–200), and Hecuba says that gods are bad allies to call upon (*Tro.* 469), while, as discussed in the previous section, Amphitryon protests at Zeus's failure to protect his kin and to answer their prayers (*Her.* 339–47, 498–501).[33]

Some of the most striking criticisms of the gods are those in which the human speaker implies or states that the god's behavior is more like that of a hasty, angry, insensitive or stupid (*amathēs*) human being than that of the

[31] Cf. *Hipp.* 725–7 (Phaedra says that Aphrodite destroys her and will be pleased by her death); *Hipp.* 1061 (Hippolytus says he is being destroyed by the gods; *Hel.* 261 (Helen counts Hera as partly responsible for her unhappy life: similarly, Menelaus at 663, Theonoe at 880–6); *Hel.* 1098–1102 (Helen appeals to Aphrodite to cease tormenting her at last); *Phoen.* 352, 379 (Jocasta sees divine action in the ruin of the house of Laius); *Or.* 974 (the chorus says that *phthonos* from the gods and the vote of the people have destroyed the family of Pelops).

[32] Cf. *Phoen.* 1726–7 (Antigone denies that Dike (Justice) pays attention to evil men and punishes bad actions); *IA* 1034–5 (with Diggle's attractive emendation, Clytemnestra says that if the gods are intelligent they reward virtue, while if they are not, there is no point in humans exerting themselves).

[33] Cf. *Hipp.* 1441, where most critics detect at least a slight disappointment or reproach in Hippolytus' comment to Artemis: "you leave with ease an association of long standing." For one god criticizing another god in terms like those used by human characters, see *Tro.* 67–8, discussed below, p. 180.

best sort of human being, who would exhibit self-control, circumspection, pity, and similar qualities. For instance, the servant in *Hippolytus* thinks Aphrodite should be forgiving of Hippolytus' youthful folly "because gods ought to be wiser than mortals" (117–20).[34] The complaint of the messenger in *Andromache* illustrates not only this disappointed expectation, but also the tendency for speakers to cite the ideal that the gods should set an example for good human behavior almost exclusively in contexts where it is found lacking in reality. In *Andromache* 1161–5, very emphatic because they are the conclusion of the rhesis and the last words spoken by this figure, he declares that Apollo, who advises and decides justice for others, himself behaved badly toward Neoptolemus and, "just like a bad man," showed a stubborn remembrance of past wrongs (the vice of *mnēsikakia*). Similarly, in *Ion* 442–4 and 451, Ion argues that as lawgivers the gods should themselves obey the same laws as men, or else they can be blamed for offering the model for human wrongdoing. A similar spirit is evident when Iphigenia cites the inconsistency between Artemis' demand for purity from her worshippers and the impurity of her apparent delight in human sacrifice (*IT* 380–4).

Given the longstanding cultural authority of traditional poetry containing heroic stories, it is natural that mythological exempla should be taken by the Greeks to be models for human behavior – in a selective way, of course, just as the holy books of monotheistic systems are often cited and exploited with a convenient selection that suits the ideological or political goals of the citer. In the critical and competitive atmosphere of fifth-century Greek culture, it is also natural that the artificiality of such selectivity was laid bare in critiques of inconsistency or illogicality (already reflected in Aeschylus at *Eum.* 640–2, where the Furies find it inconsistent that Zeus would support the priority of the claims of a father when he overthrew and imprisoned his own). This is apparent from the controversial use of *a fortiori* arguments of the type "if the gods do X, then it must be all right for humans to do X too." In Euripides, suggestions that men should imitate examples of dubious divine behavior are rejected. When the nurse cites the example of gods afflicted with love and not bothered about it and suggests that Phaedra too should yield to her passion without compunction (*Hipp.* 451–61), the chorus-leader politely rejects this view, but Phaedra condemns it vehemently, and the audience too presumably found it shocking. Helen, another unsympathetic character, cites Zeus's subjection to Aphrodite to

---

[34] Other conditional or regretful references to the wisdom (or lack thereof) of the gods are to be found in *Her.* 347 (Amphitryon), 655–6 (chorus), *Hel.* 851 (Menelaus), *Phoen.* 87 (Jocasta), *IA* 1034–5 (Clytemnestra).

argue that she should be forgiven for being similarly subject to the goddess
(*Tro.* 948–50).[35] *Heracles* 1314–21, however, presents an unusual case:
Theseus, the legendary Athenian king who is somewhat idealized in
many of his tragic appearances,[36] notes that according to poets the gods
violate laws, but rule on and endure after their errors, and so he urges
Heracles to follow this example.[37] Similarly, when Teiresias in *Bacchae*
266–327 praises Dionysus in a way that incorporates rationalistic rewriting
of myth, cosmological principles of wet and dry, and flourishes of rhetorical encomium, I suggest that his position is not to be dismissed as an
impious sophistic distortion of religion: it is rather one of the several
flawed approaches adopted by different voices in the play, but still, in its
way, a creditable effort to uphold tradition and proper behavior through
the analytic powers of the human mind. The famous prayer of Hecuba in
Troades 884–8, whatever may be its allusions to contemporary thinkers,[38]
functions well in the dynamic of Hecuba's hope and despair within the
play. At this moment where she finds some consolation and satisfaction in
the notion that Helen will be punished for the sufferings she has caused,
she invokes Zeus in solemn and dignified terms that do not diminish or
substitute for his traditional divinity, but rather expand it to embrace
speculations about the physical arrangement and operations of the
universe.

Striking statements about the gods were apt to be quoted by later
philosophers and theologians and thus a number have survived as fragments
of lost plays. Without context, however, it is impossible to assess their
significance in the way that is advocated in this chapter. For instance,
Bellerophon in one fragment (286) argues against the view that there are
gods in heaven, but his real concern is that the gods seem not to show
concern for men and support justice, as he believes they should. Later in the
play he tries to fly to heaven to discover the truth, or to chastise or inter-
rogate the gods directly if they exist there. Another line in this play, the
famous "If gods do anything shameful, they are not gods" (fr. 286b.7), again
reflects, presumably, an aspiration for moral clarity, but we have no idea of

---

[35] Cf. fr. 794 of Eur.'s lost *Philoctetes*: probably these are the words of a Trojan speaker (destined to lose
his bid to attract Philoctetes to the Trojan side) who cited the gods as models for "profit-seeking"
(*kerdainein, kerdos* – words of negative connotation).

[36] Mills 1997.

[37] See above, p. 169, for Heracles' idealizing reaction to this suggestion and for the view that his purer
conception of divinity (like that of Iphigenia in *IT*) is undercut by the context of the entire play.

[38] For quotation of the passage and discussion see below, p. 221.

the context, and we know virtually nothing of the overall action of the play and the dialectic of its themes.[39]

It is true, as we observed in the previous section, that many of the speakers of these complaints have only a partial understanding of the overall nexus of events (which the audience may already know, or may gain fuller understanding of as the play proceeds) and a few are premature in despairing of the gods' help or a just outcome. But on the whole they are not unsympathetic characters, their emotional outbursts are humanly understandable and likely to engage the immediate sympathies of an audience, and there is enough residual dissonance at the close of most plays that it would be odd to conclude that the psychic discomfort is entirely a matter of the shortcomings of human understanding, that the gods are indeed consistent, just, and merciful, if only mortals were perspicacious enough to recognize it. Rather, there is revealed a tragic gap between the uncertainty, inscrutability, and amorality of the strongest powers in the universe and the human aspiration for certainty, clarity, and the comfort of comprehensible justice.

SEEN GODS: PROLOGUE GODS

Unseen gods are potentially important in all tragedies: their inferred, suspected, or belatedly revealed or understood interventions contribute to the dynamic of puzzlement and understanding that applies in different ways to characters, chorus, and interpreting audience. In a number of plays, however, divinities are represented visibly as characters of the drama. Such visibility is one of the available conventions for distinguishing the represented world of the performance from ordinary life, and the realm of heroic myth from contemporary history. Visible gods on stage are partly analogous

---

[39] Different editors place fr. 286b variously in their reconstructions, none of which can claim to be compelling; in addition, the text of this fragment is of doubtful coherence: Collard and Cropp 2008a: 289–93, with references to earlier treatments. Another example of the problem of missing context is *Antiope* fr. 210, where Amphion doubts Antiope's claim to have been impregnated by a god disguised in bestial form: this may have occurred before the recognition, and in any case the *deus ex machina*, Hermes, later brings an assertion from Zeus that he did impregnate Antiope. The famous so-called "atheistic" fragment of a play called *Sisyphus* (a cynical exposition of the very perceptive view that religion and the gods are a human construct) cannot be usefully exploited in this discussion, since the authorship is disputed and the context is not available. For the text see Critias *TrGF* I, 43 F 19 or Collard and Cropp 2008b, App. 19, and on the question of authorship see the bibliography cited by Kannicht *TrGF* V.2:658–9 and by Collard and Cropp. We can say that Sisyphus had a very negative character in Greek mythology, was famous for being punished signally by the gods, and will, in fact, in this play most likely have been punished in the end by the gods he denies. Compare with Sisyphus' position the brief traces of rationalizing or sophistic views in Polyphemus' statements about the gods and morality in the satyr-play *Cyclops* (316–17, 336–40, 525–7).

to the gods who appeared observing or inspiring heroes in contemporary sculpture and vase-painting. On the stage, however, the gods are not just observers or helpers, but interact more directly with humans, in the mode of epiphany, and (given the public nature of the represented space of the action) sometimes with a wider audience than would be normal for an epiphany. The example set by epic poetry and by narrative elements in archaic choral poetry must also be taken into account.

Despite the analogies and precedents that make visible gods on stage a culturally expected convention, it is clear that as the genre of tragedy matured it placed limits on such portrayals. In some of Aeschylus' plays gods appear at various points in the action, but in extant Euripides and Sophocles, gods tend to be located at the margins of the action, in the prologue and the exodos. The intervention of Lyssa and Iris in the middle of *Heracles* is all the more shocking because of its exceptional position.[40] Tragedy's interest in human action, human decision-making, and the dramatic force of uncertainty and open-ended struggle can be well served by keeping the gods out of sight and by revealing the disparity of knowledge and power gradually and belatedly. For this generic tendency, we may compare both Aristotle's dislike of *deus ex machina* solutions (*Poetics* 1454b1–6), his depreciation of the visual element (*opsis*: 1450b16–20, 1453b1–11), and perhaps his low ranking of plays involving Prometheus and events in Hades (1456a2–3: a corrupt and obscure passage) as well as Northrop Frye's differentiation of tragedy's high mimetic mode from what he calls "myth" or romance.[41] Finally, the possibility that satyr-plays more commonly featured visible gods as characters of the drama offers a relevant counterpoint to the tragic norm.

The gods who speak Euripidean prologues normally appear in isolation from the human characters, not in interaction with them, as occurs in Sophocles' *Ajax*. In general, the Euripidean prologue-monologue is a device that makes transparent the audience's position as spectators of a representation, inhibiting their total involvement in the performance and their continuous "suspension of disbelief." The sense of full "dramatic illusion" (of total involvement of the represented characters in the fictive world created on stage, without acknowledgment of the presence of an audience in another dimension of space and time) is reached only at the end of the

---

[40] The lost play *Protesilaus* featured Hermes leading the dead hero either to or from reunion with his wife (fr. 646a), and this seems to have occurred within the play, but reconstruction of this play is very uncertain. In addition, *Rhesus* features Athena intervening in the middle of the action.

[41] Frye 1957: 35–43.

monologue. Before that, although there are occasional elements of pathos, the prologue-speaker is preparing the audience for the following action, supplying in a concentrated fashion the background events, identities, and location that could have been supplied (as in the theater of Ibsen or, to some extent, in Sophocles) more gradually and indirectly in the course of the drama, with a greater demand on the interpretive skills of the audience. When the prologue-speaker is a god, the audience's perspective on the unfolding action is significantly affected by the superior knowledge and power of a divinity. The audience shares this superior knowledge and thus is differentiated from the chorus and characters in level of awareness, and the power asserted by the god hangs over the speeches, choices, and actions that the audience subsequently observes.

Because of his involvement in other scenes, the Dionysus of *Bacchae* is a partial exception to the generalizations just made. In the prologue, he announces that he has taken the form of a human devotee and male leader of the Asian bacchants, and in this disguise[42] he interacts with Pentheus and the chorus in several scenes later in the drama (434–518, 604–41, 642–861, 912–76). When he is offstage during the "palace miracle" scene (576–603), his voice is heard from within, and this voice announces itself as that of the god himself (581). At this moment, the audience understands the god and the Lydian stranger are one, but the chorus and Pentheus do not. The final lines of the prologue speech (55–63) also play with this dual identity. The chorus is probably not yet visible, and Dionysus here addresses an unseen group at a distance, which is conventional in Greek drama.[43] In summoning the bacchants to enter and sing and dance in worship of Dionysus, the god uses at one point language implying his divine identity (58–9: "the drums native to the land of the Phrygians, the inventions of mother Rhea and myself").[44] Even so, the interpenetration of the two identities is clear only to the audience, and the chorus, there too, is as unaware as Pentheus is later of who is interacting with them.[45]

---

[42] No other disguised god is known from Euripides; Dionysus may have been similarly disguised in plays by other authors using the motif of resistance to Dionysiac worship, but this cannot be verified from the fragments (Aesch. fr. 61 might be a case); for a disguised Hera deceiving Semele see Aesch. fr. 168 together with Plato *Rep.* 381d.

[43] Taplin 1977: 220.

[44] The other first-person words in the speech (56–7, 62–3) can just as well refer to the pretended identity of the Lydian stranger as to the god himself.

[45] For the technique by which the chorus hears the summons spoken to them but does not register all the specific details heard by the audience, see *Held.* 73, where the chorus responds to the cries for help in 69–72, but is not aware of the full content of those lines (cf. *Tro.* 153; see Mastronarde 1979: 28–30 for the similar technique of partial hearing of a summons called out to those indoors).

Of the extant divine prologues, the most striking, dramatically and
thematically, is that in *Hippolytus*. Apparently, one of the major differences
between this play and Euripides' other (non-extant) treatment of the
Phaedra-Hippolytus story was the appearance of Aphrodite as the prologue-
speaker. In Chapter 4[46] we noted how her speech serves to make the
audience recognize the deficiencies of knowledge affecting the chorus, and
naturally it does the same with regard to the awareness of the characters.
Only the goddess herself can reveal the elements of causation that remain
unknown or obscure to the characters until the end of the play. Although
Phaedra herself can unveil the secret of her passion, she cannot adequately
explain its origin. Her speculation about a familial penchant for disastrous
desire (*Hipp.* 337–43) is plausible, but not supported by the authoritative
voices of Aphrodite and Artemis. In this play, we are given no hint of any
neglect on the part of Theseus. As to the dangerous idleness in Phaedra's
lifestyle (emphasized in an almost Ibsenian reading a century ago by
Wilamowitz),[47] there is very little trace of this in the play itself: allusion
to long gossiping conversations occurs briefly in the context of
behavior Phaedra herself rejects (383–4), and Hippolytus' misconceived
tirade against women evinces a more extreme distrust of any female conversation (645–50). Nor can her delirious desire to share Hippolytus' out-
door activities (208–31) be separated from the longing that has brought her
near to the point of death. Phaedra feels a painful and inexplicable separation between, on the one hand, her sense of herself and her ideals and, on
the other, the desperate longing that has engulfed her. Aphrodite provides
the key to understanding this, emphasizing Phaedra's position as an unwitting tool whose sufferings are so slightly valued by the goddess (47–50).
Thanks to Aphrodite's forthright statements, the audience can appreciate
the exemplary enactment of Hippolytus' policy of resistance to her in the
following scene (88–120), the mixture of authority and subversiveness in the
nurse's speeches, and the blindness that tempers (albeit slightly) the harsh
effect of Hippolytus' tirade against women.

The prologue-speech (*Hipp.* 1–57) invites the audience to understand
Aphrodite's motivation in anthropomorphic terms: honor and violent
protection of honor (*timē, timōria,* 8, 16, 21, 50), settling of accounts with
an enemy (*polemion, echthrous,* 42, 49). Yet the gulf between divine and
human is also clear. The goddess is also a universal force of nature: this is
hinted at in the opening lines and then developed in the choral songs and
the main speech of the nurse (433–81). And the gods are not subject to limit

[46] See pp. 108–9.   [47] Wilamowitz 1891: 48–50 and 1899: 101–3.

(except for the principle of non-interference enunciated in 1328–34), while humans can attract hostility by "thinking too big" (6; the theme is developed more fully in 88–120). Gods cannot be held responsible, and they are frequently exempt from the softer human qualities of empathy, regret, or forgiveness. The goddess' chilling confidence in her own knowledge and efficacy is displayed by the future tenses she uses ("I'll swiftly demonstrate" 9, "I'll avenge on this day" 21–2; "men will say in the future" 33; "I'll reveal … it will come out" 42; "his father will kill the youth" 43–4) and casts a pall over the efforts of understanding and action subsequently undertaken by the characters. Of similar effect is the declaration that turns the door of the palace virtually into the gates of hell for Hippolytus (56–7), for once he enters the skene (after 113) his fate is in fact sealed – when he next emerges, he has heard the secret from the nurse and the sequence of rejection and retaliation is in motion. If Aphrodite appears on the roof rather than on stage-level, the sense of her superiority and control is reinforced visually.[48]

This portrayal answers to the yearning, even the necessity, of conceiving the gods in human form and with human psychology, but also opens space for the recognition that the anthropomorphic appearance and analogy are futile, and a cause of misplaced expectations, as the admonishing prayer of the servant at the end of the next scene (114–20) reveals. An audience can be expected to understand, at some intellectual level, Aphrodite's position, but the forbidding aspects of her role and the fully portrayed anguish of her victims suggest that it is not a position they can be expected easily to admire, adopt for themselves, or share at an emotional level. The opening of this play may usefully be compared to that of Sophocles' *Ajax* (1–133). There, Athena (like Aphrodite) has past slights for which she holds Ajax accountable, but in her interaction with the too-proud and temporarily insane hero, he is shown re-enacting (like Hippolytus) the past slights. Intermediate between the erring hero and the punishing goddess stands the moderate human Odysseus, incapable of enjoying the spectacle of divine power and control that Athena offers him (cf. the role of the servant in *Hipp.*). There, too, the audience is not allowed to be fully comfortable with the position of the goddess.

No other extant Euripidean divine prologue has the same degree of disturbing nakedness of power. *Bacchae* and *Hippolytus* are often paired as examples of the plot-type of god vs. scorner of god and are compared in assessing the problem of Euripides' attitude toward the gods of mythology. Yet in *Bacchae*, Dionysus speaks with much less definiteness about the

---

[48] See above, p. 68 with n. 10.

future course of the play, and his appearance has as much to do with letting the audience in on the secret of his disguise in human form as with making them superior in knowledge to the characters and chorus. Unlike other prologue-gods, he continues to have a visible role in subsequent scenes and (if it is correct to place most of the other prologue-gods on high)[49] he appears on stage-level, walking the streets of Thebes, in token of his adopted human identity and in contrast to the revealed divinity of his epiphany on the upper level at the end of the play. Dionysus declares his goal of recognition and takes responsibility for sending the women of Thebes to revel on the mountains, but in regard to Pentheus (who is first mentioned only late in the prologue) speaks vaguely of demonstrating his divinity and passing on to other Greek cities "after arranging matters here well" (49). Although we may assume that the death of Pentheus was expected by the audience on the basis of general knowledge, the conflict of *theomachos* and god is here presented as yet to be resolved – the key tests for Pentheus await him (and the audience), so that he does not enter already looking on the gates of death, as Hippolytus does. In the conditional phrase in *Bacchae* 50 ("and if the city of the Thebans in wrath seeks to drive the bacchants from the mountain with arms"), Dionysus in fact alludes to the traditional version in which Pentheus died leading an army of men against the Theban maenads. Although the harshness of Dionysus receives criticism later in the play, it is hardly intimated in this prologue.

As discussed earlier,[50] the divine prologue of *Troades* significantly conditions the audience's perspective on the utterances of the characters and the songs of the chorus. Only the audience is capable of deriving any "satisfaction" at the reversal of fortune that the Greeks have merited by their excessive violence. Athena's desire "to hearten the Trojans whom I hated before" (65) is not at all apparent to the suffering Trojans. The insufficiency of this belated divine aid is consonant with a unique feature of this divine prologue. Whereas in other cases the prologue-god hints at or reveals the events about to occur within the play, the revelations of Poseidon and Athena, for the most part, look to the events that follow the end of the play – namely, the storm at sea that will cost many Greeks their lives. One other detail, the fact that Polyxena has already been sacrificed without Hecuba's knowledge (39–40), provides a privileged piece of knowledge for the audience, creating the ironic effect when Hecuba misunderstands Talthybius' deceptively comforting report about her daughter's fate (*Tro.* 260–71). A glimpse into the future after the play is normally one

---

[49] Mastronarde 1990.   [50] See above, pp. 77–8 and 109.

function of the divine epilogue, and the displacement of the revelation in this case to the prologue allows the end of the play to be harsher, more unrelieved and depressing in its impact. Another feature that this scene borrows from the epilogue epiphanies is the critiquing of one god's behavior by another.[51] Poseidon's monologue emphasizes the primary role of Athena in destroying Troy (10, 23–4 (with Hera), 46–7), and he presents himself as motivated by "good will" (6–7) and amenable to cordial relations with his opponent (51–2), evoking Athena's praise of his "gentle temper" (53). He can scarcely believe Athena's new-found interest in the Trojans and wonders "Why do you shift so abruptly from one attitude to another, and hate too much and like <too much> whomever you happen to hate or like?" (66–7). The instability of divine favor (note the verb *pēdān*, "leap about") is a complaint uttered elsewhere by human characters (and such changeability contrasts with a widespread Greek ideal of composure, self-control, consistency, and constancy), and the diagnosis of excess is also not uncommon in human criticism of divine action. To be sure, Athena adequately explains her shift in allegiance (which, as suggested above, effects more destruction in punishment of the Greeks rather than any help or consolation for the surviving Trojans), but Poseidon's initial surprise and disapproval have a lingering effect.

In the other extant divine prologues, the gods assure the audience of an eventual happy outcome. In *Alcestis*, Apollo prepares for the importance of the theme of *xenia* (guest–host friendship) and, through his mention of Asclepius' crime and his debate with Thanatos, takes upon himself the onus of meddling with the processes of life and death. What he tells us of the "gift" to Admetus and of Alcestis' choice, however, is not very detailed and has to be supplemented with later information. The important privileged knowledge conveyed to the audience comes only at the end of the scene, when Apollo ends the stichomythia of failed persuasion with an oracular outburst of future tenses (64–71). The prediction of the restoration of Alcestis conditions an audience's response to all subsequent laments, ironizes the commonplace wisdom that there is no bringing back of the dead, and underscores the ignorance of the mortal characters in their ineffectual plans for the future and their miscommunications. In *Ion*, Hermes informs the audience about the complex (and unfamiliar) background and about the

---

[51] Cf. *Hipp.* 1301–2, 1326–7, 1400 (Artemis on Aphrodite), *El.* 1245–6 (Castor on Apollo), and perhaps *Erech.* fr. 370.59–62 (Athena's rhetorical questions to unseen Poseidon have a reproachful tone); also related is *Ion* 1555–9 (Athena refers to Apollo's avoidance of reproach). Cf. *Rhesus* 938–49 (Muse reproaching Athena).

identities of the unrecognized mother and child who will carry forward the action.[52] Hermes' relation to the characters and events is rather casual, as is his interest in being a spectator of the unfolding events. If most other prologue-gods appeared on high, Hermes' position on stage – he withdraws into a laurel copse near the temple – also shows a more casual, less authoritative relation to the characters. The overall tone is thus more intimate. There is, however, another significance to Hermes' presence, and that is Apollo's absence: it is Hermes who first alludes to the *appearance* of neglect by Apollo (68) that will loom so large in the thoughts and words of Creusa and her associates, and it is Hermes who reports Apollo's plan for Ion and his mother. This information allows the audience both to devalue the accusations of the characters and to pity the ignorance that causes them, and it creates a further interest and dissonance as the audience observes Apollo's plan unravel.

SEEN GODS: EPILOGUE GODS

The epiphany of a god in the exodos of the tragedy (Latin *deus ex machina*, Greek *theos apo mēchanēs*, "god from the crane") is a technique associated especially with Euripides. The technique seems to have been extremely rare in Sophocles: of the seven extant plays only *Philoctetes* has a *deus ex machina*; of the lost plays, *Peleus* and *Athamas* may have had one, but our knowledge of most lost Sophoclean plays is pitifully small. Nevertheless, Euripides was apparently not alone in using this technique among the tragedians of the second half of the fifth century and the fourth century. In joking about how easy the authors of tragedy have it compared to the comic playwright, Antiphanes (fr. 189.13–16 K–A) says "moreover, when tragedians are not able to say any more and are absolutely at an impasse in their plays, they raise up the crane just like a finger, and the audience is satisfied."[53] The device is found in *Rhesus*, apparently a fourth-century tragedy, and the term *apo mēchanēs* had acquired an extended meaning by the time of Aristotle,

---

[52] Hermes may be thought to prefigure the prologue gods of New Comedy who help the audience understand made-up plots of recognition; a prologue god probably fulfilled the same function in one or two other Euripidean plays involving recognition (Apollo in *Alcm. Cor.* fr. 73a ; in *Alex.* the prologue may have been spoken by a god or by Paris' foster father). In other tragedies with recognitions, it suffices to have the parties reveal themselves to the audience in separate scenes of the prologue: *El., IT,* and perhaps *Hyps.*; cf. *Hel.,* when Menelaus appears alone somewhat later in a kind of second prologue (386–436).

[53] Cf. Plato, *Cratylus* 425d: "just as the authors of tragedy, whenever they are at a loss in some way, take refuge in the use of the crane, raising gods aloft." On the disputed meaning of "like a finger" in Antiphanes, see Mastronarde 1990: 291 n. 3 and the notes of Kassel and Austin *ad loc.*

who uses it to refer to an incident of divine intervention in Book 2 of the *Iliad* (*Poetics* 1454b2).[54] The motif of crucial divine intervention in human actions is traditional. In epic, most interventions feature an epiphany before an individual that is hidden from other humans. But the intervention of Athena at the end of the *Odyssey* is close to the pattern found in tragedy: the epiphany is apparent to all, and like many of the tragic examples it is designed to stop a violent action. The divine appearances in the third plays of some Aeschylean trilogies (*Eumenides, Danaides*), although they lack the stereotyped pattern of later examples and are not (at least in *Eumenides*) confined to the exodos, similarly bring an end to violence and have a significant foundational function.

The two most debated aspects of the Euripidean divine epilogue are its relevance to plot construction and its ethical or metaphysical implications. We have considered some of the latter in a previous section.[55] In regard to the former, the usual questions are whether the *deus ex machina* is a solution for poor plot construction – this is the Aristotelian worry that the poet is not doing his job of contriving a sequence of human actions connected by probability or necessity – and whether the technique leads to an ossified form in which the poet sometimes manufactures a crisis to bring on the *deus* (as is sometimes alleged for the wave that stalls the escape in *IT*). Before turning to such questions, we must be clear on the range of functions of the epilogue gods and the variety of the extant examples.

Epiphanies in earlier poetry and myths very commonly have a foundational aspect. Epiphany is similar to consultation of an oracle, except that some epiphanies are completely unexpected encounters and others are in response to prayers. The god may give a foundational gift (such as prophetic or dynastic power to be handed on from generation to generation)[56] or instruct that a cult, festival, or city be established.[57] Of the three tragedians, Euripides is most explicit in tying his plots to the vast fabric of Greek myth and cult. The creative interpretation and invention of the past that take place within the actions of a particular drama are anchored and, as it were, authenticated on the one end by the elaborate genealogical, aetiological, and narrative details of the prologue speech and on the other end by the

[54] Cf. Demosthenes 40.59 (a sole witness appears conveniently "just as if from the crane"); Aristotle *Met.* 985a18 ("Anaxagoras employs Mind like a crane for the creation of the universe").
[55] See above, pp. 165–9.
[56] E.g., Poseidon's meeting with Pelops in Pind. *Ol.* 1.71–87 helps him marry (and thus found dynasties) and earn cult honors at Olympia; Iamus hears the voice of Apollo granting prophetic powers to him and his descendants in *Ol.* 6.57–72.
[57] E.g., the instructions of Demeter to found her Eleusinian cult in *Hom. Hymn. Dem.* 268–74.

references to future cults and foundations at the close of the play, usually foretold by divine speakers from the crane, but insistently conveyed through report of oracles even in plays lacking a *deus ex machina*. This practice carries on an important traditional aspect of Greek public poetry: the acknowledgment and explication of origins in a way that reassures the community of its rootedness in a common past and of the weight of its shared beliefs and rituals. The poet's power to do this is a major part of his *sophia*. In Euripides there supervenes an element of learnedness and cleverness (other aspects of *sophia*) that foreshadows the Hellenistic poets' fascination with aetiologies, but it would be a mistake to undervalue the public and social force of the foundational references incorporated in Euripides' epilogues. Although it has recently been suggested that many such foundational references are Euripidean inventions (and given the paucity of surviving evidence, in many instances we can never be certain they are not),[58] whatever invention may be present is not completely a matter of play or, I think, a source of irony (which might devalue the epilogue's contribution to the drama). Rather, it is more important to recognize the ways in which invention is plausibly grafted onto known versions of myth, known sites and rites, and the tradition of etymological reinterpretation.

The foundational motifs very often refer directly to Attica and Athens. The origin of acquittal by a tied vote in Athenian courts is evoked in both *Iphigenia in Tauris* 1471–2 and *Electra* 1268–9, and although Euripides refuses to adopt Aeschylus' more optimistic and patriotic version of the origin of the Areopagus court and of the cult of the Eumenides/Semnai, he too honors the old court by alluding to its divine origin (*El.* 1258–63) or its divine jurors (*Or.* 1650–2) and to the settling of the Eumenides in Athens (*El.* 1270–2). Cults at Brauron and at the shrine of Artemis Tauropolos at Halae are featured in *Iphigenia in Tauris*, and in *Supplices* shrines (*temenē*) presumably identifiable

---

[58] Dunn 1994 and Scullion 1999–2000; for arguments against Scullion see now Seaford (2009) and cf. Parker 2005: 142 n. 28. As I understand the role of Greek poets in reshaping stories (and I do not think Euripides is radically different from others in the tradition), it would make no sense for a poet to refer to something easily falsifiable by audience knowledge. Any "inventions" are most likely to be reinterpretations or extrapolations that have some point of contact with what the audience knows or has heard before. I cannot review every example here, but will comment on one that Scullion takes to be very compelling. I deny Scullion's premise that the verb ἀπαγγέλλῃ in *Andr.* 1241 must refer to an inscription rather than have a metaphoric sense "announce to the world." The verb is very common in prose and poetry with persons as subjects, and thus any use with a non-human subject, as here and Pindar, *Pyth.* 6.18, is quite strikingly personifying. I know of no evidence of this verb being used for an inscription on a monument. There is, on the other hand, evidence for the metaphorical witnessing of a mythic event by an inanimate object, as in *Hipp.* 979–80, or of an athletic victory, as documented by Bundy 1986: 17 n. 42. The burial of Neoptolemus at Delphi was well known: all Euripides has done is reinterpret its causation and significance for the purposes of this play.

to the audience are mentioned along with a legendary Attic dedication at Delphi and a secret buried knife (1201–12). *Ion* ends in a veritable orgy of imperialistic genealogy, as the future offspring of Ion and the predicted children of Creusa and Xuthus supply the names for the tribes and races of Greece (1575–94).[59] But since the myths of tragedy are mostly panhellenic in nature, the anchoring can also be in non-Attic cults and sites, such as the cult for Medea's murdered children at Perachora (*Med.* 1279–83),[60] or honors for Hippolytus in Trozen (*Hipp.* 1423–7) and for Neoptolemus in Delphi (implicit in the mention of his burial there in *Andr.* 1239–42).[61] Euripides (whether creatively or with some factual basis) has his epilogue gods associate the divinized Helen with her brothers the Dioscuri (*Hel.* 1666–9 and *Or.* 1636–7).[62] The practice of connecting topographical names with heroes is exemplified in the passing mention of the Arcadian village Oresteion (*El.* 1273–5 and *Or.* 1646–7) and the island Helene (*Hel.* 1670–5).[63] In *Andromache* 1243–52, the sufferings of both the Trojans and the noble families of Greece (represented by Peleus' line) are recompensed by the divinely sanctioned founding of the royal dynasty of Molossia, and one suspects that dynastic origins were also foretold by the *deus* in the lost *Archelaus*.

[59] In the lost plays, honors (presumably cultic) were given to Hippolytus by the *deus ex machina* (as we may infer from fr. 446); Athena's speech in *Erechtheus* (fr. 370.77–94) founds shrines and sacrifices for the Hyacinthides and Erechtheus. Even in plays without the *deus*, oracles revealed near the end of the play refer to hero-tombs of Eurystheus (*Hcld.* 1028–36) and Oedipus (*Phoen.* 1703–7), and the shrines and cult of Heracles throughout Attica are explained by Theseus' gift to Heracles (*Her.* 1328–33). Also comparable is the explanation of a shrine on the southern slope of the acropolis given in a prologue by Aphrodite in *Hipp.* 30–3. The Attic connection is also clear in the aetiologies in the middle of *IT* (an unusual position): Orestes describes the Areopagus court, the origin of the ritual of the Choes, and the settling of some of the Furies in Athens (949–69). A topographical aetiology may have been given for the Attic spring of Alope in Eleusis (*Alope* test. iib Kannicht).
[60] See Mastronarde 2002b: 383.
[61] Cf. Hermes' allusion to the hieratic name of Amphion and Zethus in *Antiope* fr. 223.98–9. Scholars also posit an announcement of divine honors for Ino and Melicertes at the end of *Ino* (test. iii Kannicht), and honors for Phaethon at the end of his play (Diggle 1970: 44–6, 178–9); at the end of *Hypsipyle*, Dionysus (fr. 759a.1673) probably revealed the cult name Archemorus for the dead baby Opheltes and alluded to the institution of the Nemean games. The content of *Licymnius* is extremely uncertain, but if it dealt with the death of Argeus at Troy it may have provided an aetiology for the practice of cremation (or, more precisely, of the Athenian military custom: cremation of those who die in war and return of the cremains for funeral and burial at home): Collard and Cropp 2008a: 560.
[62] See Allan 2008 on *Hel.* 1666–9 and Willink 1986 on *Or.* 1635–7. In the lost beginning of the *deus ex machina* speech, Dionysus may have alluded, as in the prologue, to his plan to establish his cult in the rest of Greece.
[63] Cf. also the Theban spring Dirce in *Antiope* fr. 223.80–5 ; other cases can be conjectured, such as Aegeae at the end of *Archelaus* (test. iiia Kannicht), the Hellespont at the end of *Phrixus* A' (test. iib Kannicht), Siris in *Melanippe the Captive* (test. iib Kannicht). Similar to topographical memorials are catasterisms, which apparently were predicted by a god in the epilogue of *Andromeda* (test. iiia Kannicht). Cf. Hecuba 's burial at the Dog's Tomb promontory (*Hec.* 1271–3), predicted from an oracle known to Polymestor.

The superior knowledge of the gods is exploited in the epilogue speeches to bring to the characters (and to the audience, if they are not already aware) recognition of the true state of affairs. There is a certain ethical or emotional satisfaction to be obtained by an audience when it observes the wrongdoers or the sufferers reaching a fuller awareness of what has happened to them – the sort of satisfaction that the end of *Troades* denies and the lonely death of Antigone in Sophocles frustrates. A particularly satisfying instance of this function is found in *Hippolytus*. To complete the movement begun by Aphrodite's prologue, Artemis' epiphany is essential, for only she can tell Theseus what the oath-bound Hippolytus and chorus could not reveal, and only by her revelation can Hippolytus move from a generalized complaint of undeserved suffering from the gods to a specific diagnosis. In *Bacchae*, Dionysus' appearance on high will have been a striking visual confirmation of his claim to divinity, but this has already been well demonstrated in action for the audience and characters, so the god's probable self-revelation in the lost part of his speech may have conveyed more his own exultation (and capacity to change his appearance) than the characters' enlightenment. As discussed in more detail in the next section, an alert spectator of *Ion* may already suspect supernatural manipulation in the salvation of Ion and Creusa from each other. Athena confirms this reading by crediting these events to "the devisings" of Apollo (1564–5) and also tells the characters what the audience has known since the prologue, that Hermes carried the baby from Athens to Delphi at the command of Apollo. In *Orestes*, on the other hand, the audience may be almost as confused as the characters about what has happened to Helen.[64] So Apollo's arrival on the crane with the mute Helen at his side will have been a revelation for both audience and characters, even before he explains that Zeus commanded him to rescue Helen. It is also striking that after all the criticism and doubt of Apollo and the refusal of Tyndareus and the Argive assembly to accept reference of the responsibility to the god, Apollo himself declares that he "compelled" Orestes to commit matricide.[65] An unexpected revelation in the speech of Castor in *Electra* (1280–3) has an ironic effect. He informs the characters and

---

[64] The audience's uncertainty will be greater if one does not accept textual changes that are designed to clarify the (perhaps intentional) confusion: the change of the transmitted aorist verb "was destroyed" (*diōleto*) to imperfect "was being destroyed" (*diōlluto*) in 1512 (West, Diggle) and the seclusion of 1533–36 as inauthentic (Seidensticker, Diggle). I agree with Willink 1986 and Medda 2001 in rejecting those changes.

[65] Cf. below, pp. 192–5. A slighter version of this effect of confirmation is seen in *IT* 1438–41b, when Athena reveals to Thoas that Orestes was sent by Apollo to fetch sister and statue: this recognition contributes to Thoas' acquiescence in the outcome, but also puts a final and positive seal on the theme of whether the oracle could be trusted.

the audience that the Greeks and Trojans fought the Trojan War over an *eidōlon* (a clone-like image of Helen) because Zeus wanted to rid the earth of some human population and that the real Helen was in Egypt all the time. This detail belatedly subverts the whole background of the story, just as other details of the play have subverted the plot-pattern of just revenge.

Comparable to the *deus'* foundational and revelatory powers is the ability to direct or prohibit the human character's present actions or dispose their future. Strong prohibitions accompany the appearance of the *deus* in many cases, as the gods exercise their superior power in stopping the efforts (usually violent ones) of humans. Imminent murder is halted in *Orestes* (also suicide, in this case), *Antiope*, and *Helen*, and pursuit with murderous intention in *Iphigenia in Tauris*. In two cases (*Antiope* and *Helen*), the potential violence is aimed at an invented or minor character, and the intervention is a further element in the author's creation of plot. In both *Orestes* and *Iphigenia in Tauris*, however, what is prevented is a major denial of inherited myth/history.[66] This typical stopping-action of the *deus ex machina* must have been an established technique earlier than *Medea*, for the effect of Medea's appearance on high depends on her assuming not only the position but also the stopping-power (in her command to Jason not to attack the door) and the predictive ability of a god. Orestes tries to appropriate a similar power when he appears above Menelaus in the finale of *Orestes*, but is unable to carry it off, and his raised position is then trumped by the higher position of Apollo on the crane.

Of the positive commands giving dispositions for the characters' imme-diate futures, the instructions to marry (Electra and Pylades in *El.*, *Or.*; Orestes and Hermione in *Or.*; Andromache and Helenus in *Andr.*)[67] are foundational of a dynasty or at least of an aristocratic family, and thus serve, like the cultic references, to tie the conclusion of the newly reconceived slice

---

[66] Additional examples of stopping actions: *Erech.* fr. 370.55–62 (remarkable in that Athena addresses her appeal for cessation to a fellow-god, Poseidon, whose earthquake threatens Athena's war-scarred city); *IT* 1444–5 (before arriving Athena has apparently asked Poseidon to calm the sea for Orestes' escape "as a favor to me"; some in the audience may infer – uncertainly – that Poseidon himself had been blocking the escape before, as the messenger conjectured in 1414–19); *Su.* 1183–8 (Athena delays the departure of Theseus and Adrastus to ensure that solemn oaths of alliance are sworn first); *Ion* 1555–68 (Athena prevents Ion from addressing a challenging direct inquiry to the oracle); perhaps *Theseus*, if a goddess (Athena?) ordered Minos at the end to cease his anger and marry Phaedra to Theseus (test. iiia.14–17 Kannicht).

[67] Cf. also Hermes in *Antiope* fr. 223.100–2, foretelling the marriages of Zethus and Amphion, but this case differs in that neither founded a lasting dynasty and Amphion's marriage to Niobe had a tragic end in the destruction of their many children. This is still a connection to the larger nexus of mythic stories, but the allusion tempers the sense of happiness and success otherwise created by the rescue-and-revenge-plot (cf. Soph. *Phil.* 1440–4, alluding to the impieties that will occur in the capture of Troy).

of heroic legend back to the inherited genealogical tradition. The directions given to Orestes for dealing with the aftermath of the matricide through exile and trial (*El., Or.*) point to the eventual resolution of his troubles and allow the aetiological allusions mentioned above. Exceptionally, attention is paid to the fate of humble characters when Electra's false husband, the farmer of *Electra*, is to be rewarded with wealth in Phocis (*El.* 1286–7), or when Athena in *Iphigenia in Tauris* ensures the return of the chorus of captive Greek women to their homeland and freedom (*IT* 1467–9, prepared for by Iphigenia's promise in 1067–8).

In some cases, the audience might feel that the action directed by the *deus* would have been performed by the characters anyway. In *Supplices*, the insistence of Athena upon an oath of non-aggression introduces a new element just as the Argives were about to depart, but the oath is, in a sense, a further solemnization of the weighty performative utterances of Theseus and Adrastus, asking for and promising eternal gratitude with the gods as witness (*Su.* 1165–79, 1187–95). The use of an oath conforms to the Athenian audience's contemporary practice in concluding treaties, so this detail also contributes to linking the represented action more closely to the ancient viewer's own world (in which either the neutrality or the active alliance of Argos was always important in their hegemonic rivalry with Sparta). In *Hippolytus*, Artemis instructs Theseus to embrace his son and Hippolytus not to hate his father. This is a humane gesture on Artemis' part, softening somewhat the harsh impression created earlier when she browbeats Theseus and promises revenge on Aphrodite's favorite. But it seems clear from the previous dialogue (1403–14) that the final reconciliation of father and son arises as much from their own inclinations as from the divine command. Likewise, in *Ion*, Athena orders secrecy and the continuation of Xuthus' "pleasant deception" (1602), but this is the course upon which Creusa was already prepared to embark (1539–45). The command is addressed to Creusa, but is more needed by Ion, whose yearning for certainty and truth is a potential cause of embarrassment. Athena's endorsement of the deception, however, adds more respectability to Apollo's plan and reduces the chance that Creusa will carry, in the audience's eyes, the onus associated with stereotypical Greek ideas about the deceptive wife.[68]

---

[68] Simply foretelling the future rather than directing specific actions is another way for the *deus* to connect the poet's plot to the known fabric of myth. Thetis promises divinization to Peleus (*Andr.* 1253–8); Castor predicts the translation of Menelaus to the Isles of the Blest (*Hel.* 1676–7); cf. *Erech.* fr. 370.71–4 (Praxithea's daughters become divine Hyacinthids), and possibly *Ino* (if Dionysus as *deus* told that Ino was now the sea-goddess Leucothea). Dionysus foretells a similar translation for Cadmus

The gods

The epilogue gods undoubtedly enjoy the authority of knowledge and power in the ways described so far, but the interpretive and moral authority of these figures is more problematic. First, epilogue gods most often have a particular connection to the characters they address or rescue, whether a previous connection (e.g., Apollo and Orestes in *Or.*), kinship or marriage tie (e.g., Thetis and Peleus in *Andr.*, Castor and Helen in *Hel.*), or city-sponsorship (e.g., Athena with Theseus in *Su.* or with Creusa and Ion in *Ion*). So their stance is rarely that of an entirely impartial witness or judge, and in some cases their partiality may strike the audience fairly forcefully.[69] For example, Artemis is very favorable to Hippolytus and clearly hostile to Aphrodite, and the audience is in a position to contemplate a more balanced view than the one she offers, as will be argued shortly. Second, tragedy depends for its effect on an ambiguity about, or oscillation between, two contradictory impressions: that all that happened had to be and could not have been avoided, and that somehow the disaster was, or should have been, avoidable. The *deus'* speech often weighs in on the side of the fatedness of the events that have occurred, as is evident from the gods' frequent use of words like *to peprōmenon* ("that which is fated") and *moira* ("fate") or their reference to the will of Zeus.[70] This assertion of fatedness is often intended to console the survivors whom the god addresses, and thus to help the audience, too, toward acceptance or resignation after the emotional and moral turmoil of experiencing the tragic action. Occasionally, such statements may also carry a tinge of self-consolation or of apology against the charge of inaction. As usual, however, Euripides shows a wide range of usage. A challengingly extreme instance is Dionysus' invocation of Zeus's

in *Bacchae* 1338–9, but this final disposition is to follow a period of metamorphosis and war that alarms Cadmus and suppresses, for him, any thought of future happiness (1330–7, 1354–62). Athena reveals that the sons of the Seven, with the gods' support, will earn eternal fame as destroyers of Thebes (*Su.* 1213–26). Since the main characters of a tragedy have already faced a mortal or near-mortal crisis in the course of the play, there is not often occasion for an epilogue god to predict the unhappy death of a character outside the frame of the play. This is rather the role of one human taunting another: thus Medea foretelling Jason's death (*Med.* 1386–8), and Polymestor striking back at Hecuba and Agamemnon by predicting their deaths as well as that of Cassandra (*Hec.* 1259–79). (The same motif appears in the satyr-play *Cyclops*: Polyphemus remembers at the end of the play (696–700) an oracle that warned him about being blinded, but to get back at Odysseus adds that the oracle also ordained suffering for the hero.) In two cases, gods refer to the doom of an individual not seen during the play: Aphrodite's favorite (perhaps Adonis is meant) in *Hipp.* 1420–2, and Neoptolemus in *Or.* 1654–7.

[69] For the importance of quasi-aristocratic alliance or *xenia* between gods and heroes in Aeschylus' *Oresteia*, see Griffith 1995. For a similar interpretation of Apollo in *Orestes*, see Griffith 2009.

[70] Cf. *Hipp.* 1327–31 (Aphrodite's will, Zeus's support of the rule of non-intervention), 1434 (the gods' dispensation), 1436 (*moira*); *Andr.* 1268–9 (*to peprōmenon*, Zeus), 1271–2 (the gods' dispensation); *El.* 1247–8 (*moira*, Zeus), 1290 (*peprōmenē moira*), 1301 (*moira, anangkē*); *IT* 1438 (*peprōmenon*), 1486 (*to chreōn*); *Hel.* 1646 (*ou peprōmenoisin … gamois*), 1660–1 (*to peprōmenon*, the gods); *Ba.* 1349 (Zeus), 1351 (*anangkaiōs echei*).

will in the finale of *Bacchae*. Because of a significant gap in the transmitted text, we have lost (except for the first line, *Ba.* 1329) an iambic speech in which Agave must have described her misery and mourned her son. Then Dionysus appeared above, but we lack the opening portion of his speech (perhaps two-thirds or three-quarters of it is missing, while 1330–43 survive). We can thus make only a tentative analysis of the impression the god may have made. In the surviving portion, at any rate, Dionysus' tone seems far from sympathetic. After describing Cadmus' future, he concludes with another assertion of his true godhood as son of Zeus and with a taunting contrary-to-fact condition whose second-person plural verbs lump Cadmus together with the other victims (1341–3: "If you had determined to be prudent then, when you were unwilling to do so, you would be blessed with good fortune, having the son of Zeus as your ally"). The argumentative stichomythia that follows (1344–51) is not paralleled in any other example: only here is the god challenged face to face. Repeating what he had conceded earlier to Agave (1249–50, the god acted "justly, to be sure, but to excess"), Cadmus admits the injustice of his family and its too-late learning, generously including himself among the offenders. But he also declares roundly "you pursue your claim too strongly" (1346) and "gods ought not to be like mortals in wrathful passions" (1348), sentiments that may echo unspoken feelings of many spectators who have witnessed the cat-and-mouse enthrallment of Pentheus after line 810 and observed the horrors of the return of Agave and the laments over Pentheus' torn body. Dionysus' reply to 1348 is "Long ago Zeus, my father, nodded his approval of these events" – which seems in this context an evasion rather than a convincing exculpation, partly because it is Dionysus himself who is here and not some third party (like Castor in *El.* or Athena in *Ion*), and partly because of the sharp contrast with the personal responsibility Dionysus imposed on the humans a few lines earlier. The technique Euripides has adopted here is consonant with the shift of sympathies over the course of the play and with the tragic dilemma it presents – one must both acknowledge Dionysus' divinity and recognize the god's potential for cruel violence and amoral excess.[71]

It is relatively rare for the *deus ex machina* to provide the audience with clear guidance in forming an overall judgment of the represented action. The most striking case is that of *Electra*, where the revulsion felt by Orestes and

---

[71] It would fit the tone of this scene to have Dionysus linger on high as Cadmus and Agave embrace and depart, and deliver *Ba.* 1377–8 (a sort of whining repetition of 1347) in the midst of their exchanges, as the sole manuscript has it. But most editors consider 1351 to be Dionysus' last line (some also assume he departs then) and accept two emendations in 1377 so that 1377–8 may be assigned to Cadmus.

Electra immediately after the matricide is first echoed by the agreement of
the chorus and then validated by the moral judgment expressed by Castor.
This reversal is prepared for by the stichomythia (962–87) in which Electra
must overcome the doubts of Orestes, who at the sight of his approaching
mother feels new scruples about carrying out revenge. Orestes there accuses
Apollo of *amathia* (literally "ignorance, folly," but connoting "moral insensitivity") for commanding matricide in an oracle, and then, reaching for an
explanation that would free the god himself of this charge, wonders whether
the oracle was delivered by a demon usurping the form of the god. Such
criticism and ameliorating speculation are characteristic of many Euripidean
characters in the throes of moral disquiet (as discussed in the previous
section). What sets this instance apart is the echo of the same disquiet in
the more authoritative voice of the *deus*. Unlike Apollo in *Eumenides*, Castor
admits that Orestes' action is just and unjust at the same time ("Just is the
punishment she [Clytemnestra] has received, but you do not act justly"
1244) and applies the same judgment of lack of wisdom, only partly miti-
gated by the aposiopesis in 1245–6 ("Phoebus, Phoebus … but I keep silent,
because he is my lord. Wise god though he is, the oracle he gave you was not
wise"; cf. 1302 "the unwise proclamations of Phoebus' tongue"). This is a
view of the matricide elsewhere confined to the utterances of human
characters (cf. *IT* 570–5, *Andr.* 1036, *Or.* 417).

   In only one other case does the *deus ex machina* give so freely of moral
judgments: *Hippolytus*. Whereas in *Electra*, Castor validates a view toward
which the characters and chorus were already tending, the Artemis of
Hippolytus presents a sequence of varying judgments and betrays a partiality
that the audience may well wish to overcome in seeking a more global view of
the action. Artemis' intervention is different from the usual pattern of
epilogue appearances, for her presence is extended over several scenes with
different configurations, as she first (1283–341) speaks to Theseus alone (and,
unusually, his exclamations are allowed to break up the goddess' rhesis), then
(1342–88) stands by in silence during Hippolytus' aria, and finally (1389–1443)
participates in a three-way stichomythia with Hippolytus and Theseus before
a final rhesis that fulfills the future-directed functions of her role. Artemis
starts from an accusatory position (somewhat comparable to that of Dionysus
in *Bacchae*), heaping on Theseus the charges of unholiness, baseness, haste,
and readiness to be persuaded by obscure or false evidence. At the same time,
she lends her support to the interpretation that sees Phaedra as far from fully
villainous: she concedes to Phaedra a "sort of nobility" (1301–2, echoing
Aphrodite's claim in 47 that Phaedra will die "with good name"), and she
recognizes Phaedra's effort to overcome Aphrodite and the nurse's baneful

role, lending support to the more sympathetic "readings" among those that an audience may try to apply to the sequence of events in the first episode. Likewise, her favorable judgment of Hippolytus' behavior – refusal to be seduced and refusal to break his oath – points away from moralizing interpretations that would suggest that there is something that Hippolytus could have done with in the course of the play that would have saved him from the trap of Aphrodite. In a second movement, however, as if soothed by having forced Theseus to share her pain, Artemis explains how Theseus is deserving of forgiveness, citing the will of Aphrodite and the law of the gods, Theseus' ignorance (which acquits him of the baseness Artemis had shortly before thrown in his face, 1334–5 ~ 1320), and Phaedra's escape from cross-examination. Finally, with Hippolytus himself, she can be very brief in laying the blame for all on Aphrodite (1400, 1406). By combining both blame and understanding or forgiveness in the cases of Theseus and Phaedra, the goddess' words reinforce the audience's own experience of the complex action. Yet both the goddess and Hippolytus seem fixed in a narrower view of the conflict, unable to appreciate the wider themes that the play has placed before the audience: the universality of love and sexuality in the mortal realm, the harsh exclusiveness of Hippoyltus' way of life, his overstepping of human limits in seeking freedom from change and growth and in pursuing a special relationship with a goddess, his role as a pattern of failed transition from youth to full maturity (an ephebe frozen in the transitional state). Artemis thus presents a limited perspective, and this limitation goes hand in hand with her promise of personal revenge, especially since this future violence is juxtaposed to the ritual remembrance of future generations of mortals and to the affecting reconciliation and farewells of father and son, from which the goddess is excluded. This epilogue goddess has undeniable power and authority, yet the very act of appearance before the characters and audience opens up room for evaluation of the *deus ex machina* on the same terms that other speakers in the drama are evaluated. It is this exposure to evaluation that is quintessentially Euripidean.[72]

After this review of the various functions and linkages of the epilogue gods and their potential to provide knowledge and consolation as well as confirmation

---

[72] See above, p. 167, for the reservations both Creusa and an audience may feel about Athena's terse judgment that "Apollo accomplished all things for the good" (*Ion* 1595); in *Su.*, Athena's very positive and untroubled attitude toward the future successful war of the Epigoni evinces an attitude that ignores, or rises inhumanly above, the human dimensions of war so emotionally evoked by many voices within this play. In contrast, the judgment of Castor in *Helen* is unambiguous: in declaring that Theonoe commits no injustice against her brother in trying to fulfill the honorable intentions of their dead father (1647–9, 1656–7), the god endorses the unanimous arguments of the *agōn*-scene.

or unsettling of the audience's judgment, it is suitable to end this section with the problematic case of *Orestes*. The finale of *Orestes* gives the strongest sense of any extant play (the closest comparandum is the nearly contemporary Sophocles' *Philoctetes*) that the decisions of the characters may burst the bonds of tradition, that the creativity displayed with such virtuosity within the course of the drama has taken on a life of its own. Thus the intervention of the god is here felt to be much more controlling from the point of view of the characters and salvific from the point of view of the poet's duty to the tradition. Yet the corrosive treatment of human values and character in the play as a whole, as well as the absence of a dynamic of falling and rising hope or trust in the gods (such as we described earlier for *Iphigenia in Tauris*)[73] may prevent an audience from feeling much satisfaction in the final rescue.

Without being literally a suppliant-drama, *Orestes* nevertheless opens with the children of Agamemnon besieged like suppliants and awaiting help from a more powerful ally.[74] Electra's prologue places all hope in Menelaus, and Orestes first hails the news of his arrival and later supplicates Menelaus for salvation. Apollo, on the other hand, is strongly criticized, through the first quarter of the play, for ordering matricide, and there is little sign of faith in his protection. In a single reference in the prologue, Electra treats as self-evident the injustice of Apollo's command ("What need to speak at length of Apollo's injustice?" (28)), and in the parodos repeats this verdict (163–5: "Loxias, unjust, voiced unjust oracles"); she has despaired of any help from the gods (266–7). Orestes reproaches Apollo for inciting him to matricide (285–7), and responds to Menelaus' puzzlement at Apollo's failure to help by alluding to the slowness of divinity to act (420). Menelaus judges Apollo to be "culpably ignorant" (417 *amathesteros*, "more ignorant [than one ought to be]") of propriety and justice. Exculpatory reference of the crime to Apollo's higher authority is mentioned repeatedly (76 *anapherousa*, 414–16 *anaphorā*, cf. 276, 591–9), and the claim is persuasive to Helen but not persuasive to Tyndareus, and then is not appealed to further (notably, not even in the Argive assembly). The only countervailing sign for the audience that Apollo's support may be present despite the doubt of the human characters is the fact that Orestes' fit of madness ends soon after he follows Apollo's instructions for warding off the Furies, apparently with an imaginary bow.[75]

---

[73] See pp. 162–6 above.   [74] For other aspects of this play, see above, pp. 83–5.
[75] Whether there should be a physical prop present and wielded by Orestes or there are only miming gestures with an unseen bow is disputed (and has been since the scholiasts). I agree with Medda 2001: 90–2 that the bow is imaginary; see also Mastronarde 2002a: 31 n. 44. Among those who assume a real bow is Burnett 1971: 201–3, who makes much of the later mute presence of this unused prop as proof of the culpable lack of faith of the human characters.

After line 599, for over a thousand lines up to Apollo's epiphany, there is only one brief reference to Apollo, at the end of the messenger's speech, and this simply underlines the god's apparent absence: "nor did Phoebus who sits at the Pythian tripod <help you>, but he ruined you" (955–6). Orestes, Electra, and Pylades make no further reference to him, either for criticism or prayer, as if they are sure they have been completely abandoned to their own resources. Their desperate arguments and schemes blur distinctions in ethical and social categories such as noble/ignoble, free/slave, wise/fool, brave/cowardly, sane/insane, just/unjust. Left on their own, they virtually re-enact the crime for which two of them have just been condemned to death, under the delusion that this time they will receive the praise and thanks that the previous murder failed to garner, and the sequence of surprises culminates in the crazy cat-and-mouse dialogue of Orestes and Menelaus (1576–620), in which Orestes gives a final order for murder and suicide just as his uncle seems to have capitulated.

One view of this ending is that an audience is to conclude that the dangers faced by the trio of comrades are their own fault, the result of lack of faith in the promised support of the god: the *deus* then reveals how foolish and weak these mortals are and how wise and beneficent the gods.[76] This interpretation captures an important aspect of the unparalleled black humor or absurdity of the plot of *Orestes*, but it is too generous to the credit of the Olympians. There is no divine prologue or oracle to point from the beginning to the eventual rescue by the god: the only assistance Apollo apparently gave in advance was the instruction on how to ward off the Furies, and there is no indication that Orestes had any hint of an ultimate resolution of his problem. Nor are there prayers to Apollo or criticisms on the count of abandonment that could be shown incorrect by his epiphany. From the point of view of Orestes and his friends, there is only the experience of unexplained delay. Apollo's speech (1625–65) does not address either the question of his delay in taking action or the justification of the matricide. There is, for instance, no appeal to Zeus's will or fate as requiring this unfortunate action, an explanation used by other epilogue gods to console victims or to deflect questioning or resistance.[77] Instead, along with the dispositions for the futures of the characters, the god alludes to two additional stories that emphasize the power (rather than the justice) of the Olympians: the aetiology from the Epic Cycle according to which the destruction of the Trojan War was part of a plan to reduce the heavy population of humans (1639–42); and the death of Neoptolemus at Delphi (1654–7). It is also striking that Orestes welcomes Apollo's rescue by

---

[76] So Burnett 1971: 183–222.   [77] See n. 70 above.

admitting his previous fear that he might have mistaken the voice of a demon (*alastōr*) for that of the oracular god (1668–9). The effect of this allusion to Euripides' own *Electra* 979 ("Could it be that an *alastōr* spoke the oracle, taking the form of the god?") is perhaps to reinforce the theme of Apollo's injustice, so strong in that play and in the first part of this one, and remind us again that Apollo has not addressed it.

The forced quality of Apollo's intervention in *Orestes* is also revealed by the rapid shift in Orestes from holding a sword to Hermione's neck – for apparently he holds it there throughout Apollo's rhesis and removes it only at 1671 – to consenting to marry the girl. Equally jarring is the formulaic wish for prosperity contained in Menelaus' betrothal of his daughter to Orestes. The nobility of Menelaus was called into question earlier by his moral shallowness (371–3), by his sophistic traits of speech and argument, and by his abandonment of his besieged kin. The nobility of Orestes was similarly undercut by the plot against Helen and Hermione and the dialogue with the Phrygian, which showed how little distinction there is between free and noble-born Orestes and the abject non-Greek and unmanned slave. Consequently, there is good reason to wonder whether at least some in the audience found it jarring or absurd when Menelaus consented to Apollo's instructions by saying to Orestes "Being noble yourself and marrying the daughter of a noble man, may you prosper" (1676–7).

We have observed in other plays (especially *Hippolytus*, *Ion*, and *Bacchae*) some dissonance between the epilogue god's point of view and that of the human characters or of the audience. A common approach is to deny, in various degrees, the relevance of the epilogue to the audience's experience of the play. I would prefer to say that while prologues and epilogues are indeed through various techniques marked off as framing elements in the overall structure of Euripidean plays, they should nevertheless not be treated as separable and wholly conventional. Rather, just as the audience is challenged to interpret the other dissonances and discordant voices within the body of a play, they are similarly presented in a divine epilogue with one more perspective, a perspective that is in some ways authoritative and yet simultaneously subject to the same scrutiny and sense of difficulty or *aporia* as other features. Thus in most cases, in my view, the audience ought not to react to the *deus* with disbelief or a feeling that the epilogue does not fit the world of the play.[78] To take a particular example of dissonance, I interpret the superficially pious or orthodox statements made by epilogue gods (such

---

[78] Schmidt 1964 very effectively highlights dissonances between epilogue and preceding scenes and concludes that there is regularly a decided and intended disconnect between the ending and the

as Artemis' generalization about the gods' treatment of the pious and the wicked in *Hipp.* 1339–41, or Castor's about the fate of the noble and of the countless rabble in *Helen* 1678–9, if the elitist claim is not softened by deletion or emendation) as an index of the gulf between the nature of the gods and the condition of mortals: the power, the ease, and the immortality of the Olympians render them unsuited to the appreciation of the complexity of the human condition that is of major interest to tragedy, as it was to Homer. But this gulf exists within a single (puzzling) represented world rather than being a demonstration of a gap between the world represented in most of the play and the world evoked by the divine epilogue.

The *deus ex machina* scene of *Orestes*, however, goes far beyond any other example. The contrast between the human actions, whether completed or intended, and the dispensations delivered by the god are very great. The autonomy of the human agents seems to be undercut to an unusually great degree.[79] Either the intervention has here become a relic of the tragic form, one that cannot bear the weight placed upon it in this extraordinarily deviant plot, or the solution itself must be regarded as absurd, as blackly humorous as the plot it concludes. In either case, the god's presence fails to assert comforting order and to undo the social and ethical decay portrayed in the mortal world of the play. If we do conclude that *Orestes* features a *reductio ad absurdum* of the rescuing divine intervention,[80] this does not entail that interventions in other plays must be so strongly doubted or depreciated. The *deus ex machina* need not have the same moral standing in every example, and different plays may look at the divine role in events in different ways.

UNSEEN GODS: INFERENCE AND UNCERTAINTY

In reaction to the excesses and anachronisms of some interpretations of Euripides that emphasized an ironic stance toward gods and supernatural causation,[81] a number of critics have argued, often with justice, for a more orthodox or traditional view of the gods in Euripidean drama. On the one hand, this involves taking seriously the support that the gods appear to give to characters who exact punishment for violations of key institutions of

preceding action in terms of causation, motivation, and moral complexity. I prefer to see the relationship as more varied from play to play and more problematic and open-ended. On the Euripidean epilogue, see also Dunn 1996.
[79] On some readings, Heracles' dispositions as *deus ex machina* in Sophocles' *Philoctetes* would come close to this effect: Poe 1974.
[80] For a more sympathetic interpretation of Apollo's role as providing reassurance of a different kind through social and material relations (inheritance, marriage) see Griffith 2009.
[81] E.g., Verrall 1895, Norwood 1908.

morality, such as oaths, asylum, and the sanctity of marriage. On the other, it may extend to arguing for the kindness or providence of the divine or to finding a comfortable balancing of deserts at the conclusion of each play, a balancing that confirms the justice of the universe. We are thus again confronted with the problem of how far the "theology" of Euripidean drama can be normalized, that is, shown to match what is taken to be a standard view of Greek piety. In this section, in order to evaluate in one limited area the strengths and weaknesses of such approaches, I shall discuss the process by which audience members construct the presence or participation of an unseen god in an event seen or narrated on the tragic stage.

There is in fact a spectrum of possibilities regarding such inferences of divine participation. At one extreme of this spectrum, the playwright may give very clear guidance. As we saw earlier in this chapter, a god who appears on stage in the prologue has great authority for the audience, setting the conditions for their reception of the following action. Ajax's destruction of the flocks is explained by Athena in Sophocles' play: she intervened to divert his violence to victims other than the ones he intended. The case of Aphrodite in Euripides' *Hippolytus* is partly comparable. Despite the claim of some modern critics that the divine prologue and epilogue of this play are separable and that the action between these conventional frames may be understood in terms of a purely human psychology and social factors, the presence of Aphrodite's speech cannot fail to condition the audience's reception of what follows. An interpretation that insists on completely humanizing the events of *Hippolytus* dismisses not only the prologue and epilogue, but significant elements of the scenes that lie between them.[82]

Of similar authority are at least some statements of seers in tragedy, such as Cassandra's in Aeschylus' *Agamemnon* or Teiresias' in Sophocles' *Antigone*. Somewhat farther down the scale of certainty is the anonymous exhorting voice, a motif of several messenger speeches (*Andr.* 1147, *IT* 1385, *Ba.* 1078–9, Soph. *OC* 1623). Anonymity here is part of the mystery of divine intervention for those experiencing the narrated event, but it is often clear enough to the audience which god is to be assumed to be speaking. The messenger in *Bacchae* in fact adds "to make a guess, it was Dionysus"; the voice in Apollo's temple in *Andromache* is easily assumed to be Apollo himself (and the messenger and Peleus hold him co-responsible), and Apollo is also a logical guess for the audience of *Iphigenia in Tauris*.

[82] See above, p. 114, for the contributions of the chorus and p. 177 on other effects of the knowledge the audience gains from the prologue. For a similar argument see, e.g., Heath 1987b: 52–4.

Indeed, the first-person plural statement of this divine voice (1386–9: "*we have* the objects for which *we* sailed into the inhospitable sea-passage within the Symplegades") suggests retrospectively that Apollo has been with Orestes throughout his journey.[83]

But in other circumstances the process of inference of divine intervention is less secure. We may note first that outside of tragedy there is evidence of disagreement about recognition of specific divine causation or intervention in both Herodotus (e.g., 6.75.3, 6.84) and Thucydides (e.g., 5.104–5, 7.50.4). Similarly, internally to the world of tragedy we can see that different observers adopt different interpretations. In the first scenes of Aeschylus' *Septem*, Eteocles and the chorus have sharply conflicting views on the question whether the gods will intervene in the crisis to protect the city and also differ about what kinds of appeals to them are suitable. In Sophocles' *Antigone*, Creon angrily rejects the chorus' notion that the undetected burial of Polyneices' corpse may be "god-driven" (*Ant.* 78–9), and at this point in the play it is not self-evident that the chorus' view is preferable. Only later, as the action proceeds, is another hint of divine intervention provided in the description of the second burial, and the divine element is thereafter made even more plausible by Teiresias' revelation of the gods' anger. For Euripidean examples we may look to *Medea* 1171–5, where the messenger tells of an old woman who at first incorrectly thinks that the princess has been possessed by Pan or another god, when in fact she is showing the first signs of the operation of Medea's poison, and to *Iphigenia in Tauris* 264–80, where in the first messenger speech one countryman thinks Orestes and Pylades may be gods letting themselves be visible to mortals and a second one, described as *theosebēs* (reverent toward the gods), prays to them, but other witnesses disagree.[84]

Since this range of attitudes is attested both outside literary fiction and internally in the dramatic world, it is reasonable to believe that within the external audience of tragedy as well there will have been different levels of inclination or confidence in making inferences about a divine hand working in the background both in life and in stories. To take the example of *Ion*, it is easy to interpret the oracle given to Xuthus and the coincidence of Ion's

---

[83] Kyriakou 2006: 436–7 argues that the voice is not divine, but human; but her criteria seem to me inappropriate: she holds (1) that it is improbable for a god to use the first-person plural here, and (2) that it is undignified for a god to make the exhortation when the effort called for turns out to be unsuccessful.

[84] At *Her.* 966–7 the messenger reports Amphitryon's incorrect inference that Heracles' mental disturbance is caused by the pollution of the blood he has shed in punishing Lycus (while in *Her.* 1186 Theseus quickly infers that Hera is to blame).

presence at the moment Xuthus leaves the temple as events stage-managed by Apollo, since Hermes has told us of Apollo's intention to arrange this. But what of the ill-omened words of an anonymous slave (1187–9), which prevent Ion from drinking the poison at the celebration of his supposed recognition, and the presence of the thirsty birds (1196–200), which reveals the presence of the poison, or the timely entrance of the priestess (1320–3), which diverts Ion from violence toward his unrecognized mother? The priestess herself credits Apollo for her decision long ago to save the basket in which the baby was found (1346–7) and she asserts that the god now wants Ion to have the means to seek his mother (1352–3). It is not a big step to infer that her arrival is likewise Apollo's will, and in the overall context of the action it is reasonable for an external observer to conclude that Ion's escape from the poisoned drink is owed to divine protection rather than sheer chance. There is also a kind of neat reciprocity between Ion and the birds that encourages such an inference. In the prologue, Ion threatened birds to make them flee, but did not actually shoot his arrows at them, refraining from violence out of reverence for their role in carrying divine messages. In the later scene, the birds die in his stead, thus conveying a message that can be seen as a divine warning.[85] Thus, this much of the case in favor of Apollo's providence seems plausible, though it cannot be insisted that this had to be a universal interpretation among a diverse audience. Furthermore, as argued earlier, Athena's later claim that "Apollo accomplished all things for the good" (1595) can still be regarded, in its context, as open to qualification or doubt.[86]

A few plays presenting more uncertainty about unseen divine interventions deserve some discussion.[87] Since so many of Euripides' tragedies feature gods as characters at the margins of the dramatic action, either in the prologue or in a *deus ex machina* epilogue, the plays in which no gods are seen, such as *Hecuba* and *Medea*, stand out. Of these two, the power of the gods seems more apparent in *Medea* than in *Hecuba*, although both plays leave the intervention or operation of the gods to be inferred by those members of the audience who wish to detect it. Of special interest here are, first, the prominence of the clues within a play that might stimulate or allow an audience to make such inferences and, second, the kinds of intervention that are more or less easily inferred. I would suggest that *events* should be

[85] On the tendency to ascribe divine causation to an event that seems particularly appropriate and so meaningful, compare Aristotle's remarks on the statue of Mitys in *Poetics* 1452a6–10, and cf. Harrison 2000: 236 on Herodotus.

[86] See above, p. 191 and n. 72.

[87] For a list of possible examples of inferred divine action, see Mastronarde 2002a: 44–7.

distinguished in most cases from *decisions* made by major characters. That is, to take an example from outside Euripides, in Aeschylus' *Agamemnon* the safe and rapid arrival of Agamemnon home despite the storm that afflicted and scattered the Greek fleet may properly be seen as a divinely arranged contribution to the complex set of causes that lead to his death: the messenger himself sees a divine hand in the event (*Agam.* 661–6), but the audience is in a position to appreciate the ominous rather than the salvific meaning of the intervention. But when an audience asks itself why Agamemnon is quickly defeated by his wife's persuasion and consents to walk on the precious fabrics (931–44), divine befuddlement of his wits – *atē* – should not be the most prominent or the only explanation that occurs to most viewers.[88] Or, in the case of Sophocles' *Oedipus Tyrannus*, events such as the saving of the baby on Cithaeron, Oedipus' meeting with his father, the plague, the timing of the death of Polybus, and the identity of messenger from Corinth can all be justly inferred to be stage-managed by the gods or fate, but the decisions Oedipus takes during the course of the play to pursue the truth about Laius' death and then about himself need and invite no inference of divine intervention. It is true that in tragedy the audience can often sense a confluence of human impulses and divine purposes, but when the playwrights want an audience to understand that a divinely altered state of perception and thinking is present in a character, there are explicit statements by divine characters or human observers or other conventional indications of madness or trance, such as incoherent speech and uncontrolled gestures.[89]

In the case of *Medea*,[90] Zeus in particular and the gods in general have oversight over oaths and the treatment of *xenoi*, and Jason's suffering may be seen as the destruction that is expected to befall a breaker of oaths, since it is a standard formula that the perjurer risks destruction of himself and his posterity. The early and frequent invocations of Zeus, Themis, and Dike by Medea and her sympathizers support such a reading of Jason's suffering.[91]

---

[88] For the range of causes, symbols, and characterizing traits that come together in the crucial act of treading on the precious fabrics, see Taplin 1978: 78–83; Griffith 1995: 84–5; Sailor and Stroup 1999.

[89] A few examples are Ajax in the prologue of Sophocles' play (1–133: Athena explains how she has already distorted Ajax's perceptions during his imagined attacks on his enemies and how he will not see Odysseus), Phaedra in Euripides' *Hippolytus* (208–49: note the reaction of the nurse, the Doric coloring of Phaedra's anapaests, and her own recognition of her altered mental state), and Pentheus in *Bacchae* (912–76: the mental derangement is prepared for at the end of the previous scene, 850–3, and has already occurred once offstage, as told in 616–41). For offstage madness clearly explained to the audience, cf. *Her.* 822–73 (Iris and Lyssa tell what will happen to Heracles).

[90] The following paragraphs are also incorporated in the Introduction in Mastronarde 2002b.

[91] *Med.* 148, 157, 160, 169–70, 208–9, 332, 516, 764, 1352.

Apart from this, the references to Medea's descent from the sun-god Helios and the invocations of Helios[92] emphasize that god's twofold interest: he is, on the one hand, Medea's progenitor and, on the other, a witness of human action in general and of adherence to or violation of oaths in particular.[93] The repeated naming of Helios earlier in the play prepares for two features of the final scenes. First, the chorus prays to Helios in 1251–60, asking him to avert the killing of his great-grandchildren, and this prayer is not answered.[94] Second, he provides the winged chariot to Medea at the end (1320–2), which is a surprise to the audience and seems a spontaneous intervention, since there is no report of any prayer or request for this aid on Medea's part. The chariot on the crane allows Medea herself to take the position and perform some of the normal functions of the *deus ex machina*.[95] These features of the end of the play reveal clearly that the gods are, in some sense, on Medea's side in her struggle for recognition and revenge.

It is also consonant with Greek religious thought to see the working of the gods, and not blind, random chance, in the arrival of Aegeus at just the moment Medea's plot needs him. Traditional criticism of the so-called Aegeus-episode (*Med.* 663–823) has been preoccupied with the judgment of Aristotle in *Poetics* 1461b19–21: "censure directed at both improbability (*alogia*) and depravity of character (*mochthēria*) is correct whenever, despite a total lack of necessity to do so, a poet uses the irrational (*to alogon*), as Euripides uses Aegeus, or bad character (*ponēria*), as that of Menelaus in <Euripides'> *Orestes*." As discussed in Chapter 3, Aristotle preferred the connection of scenes and events by "probability or necessity," and thus critics of an Aristotelian bent frown upon many plot devices or patterns in Euripides that depend on surprise or on parataxis of parallel or contrasting scenes, although other critics recognize the legitimacy of a variety of dramatic forms. We cannot be sure exactly what Aristotle had in mind in his example of the irrational (it is even possible that he was referring not to *Medea* but to Euripides' *Aegeus*). If he meant that Aegeus' entrance in *Medea* is unnecessary because Medea's escape is later assured by other means, the criticism is ill founded, since the audience has no notion at this point in the play that Helios will provide a flying chariot, and Euripides is in general downplaying the special powers of Medea. More likely, Aristotle had in

---

[92] *Med.* 406, 746, 752, 764, 954.
[93] On this function of Helios see Garvie 1986 on Aesch. *Choe.* 984–6.
[94] On unanswered prayers see Pulleyn 1997: 206–7, Mastronarde 2002a: 37 n. 59 (arguing against Mikalson 1989).
[95] See Cunningham 1954, Mastronarde 1990: 263–6.

mind the lack of motivation of Aegeus' entry. Not only is there no preparation whatever for the entrance of Aegeus in particular, but Aegeus' journey is not intrinsically related either to Corinth or to Medea (it is only at her prompting that he shares with her his uncertainty about the oracle), and he departs with his ignorance uncured (although with more hope about a cure for his childlessness). Euripides has apparently exaggerated the absence of human motivation for Aegeus' convenient arrival. Since the plot of *Medea* is otherwise concentrated and single, Aegeus' arrival stands out more sharply than comparable examples found in plays of looser construction, for instance the arrival of Orestes at *Andromache* 879, the appearance of Evadne at *Supplices* 980, or the arrival of Pylades in *Orestes* 725. Nevertheless, it was open to the original audience to regard Aegeus' arrival not as a matter of blind luck, but as a contrivance of the gods in answer to Medea's pressing needs – a view that Aristotle would have been loath to countenance. Both here in *Medea* and in the equally convenient and unprepared arrival of the Corinthian messenger in Sophocles' *Oedipus Tyrannus*, either one can see the god-like manipulation of time and event by the poet to produce a tragic plot, or one can see the divine intervention that makes the world of the play more organized and transparent than the world of everyday life. The preference for viewing *Medea* as a case of the former and *Oedipus Tyrannus* as a case of the latter reflects a bias toward an organized and somehow "just" world-view (which critics allege is present in Sophocles) and against a chaotic and amoral one – a bias that not everyone need share.

Once it is conceded that the frequent references to the gods and the opportune events in *Medea* point to a theological background that explains the disaster befalling Jason, the question arises whether we should also interpret Medea's own downfall as a punishment brought upon her by the gods, as Kovacs has suggested.[96] Jason refers near the end of the play to an avenging demon (*alastōr*) that pursued Medea from Colchis and brought suffering to him (1333–5). This demon was evoked by Medea's slaying of her own brother on the family hearth (which has been mentioned once earlier in the play at 167 and glancingly alluded to in 257). This is a retrospective analysis by an interested party, so it is unclear how cogent it is to be felt to be, and in any case Jason is applying it to explain his own misfortune, not Medea's. Medea herself laments at a crucial point that "the gods and I have contrived" the situation that demands the death of her children (1013–14). Kovacs has suggested that when Medea plans her scheme of getting at Jason

[96] Kovacs 1993.

through the children and when she overcomes her own objections to it she may be understood to be mentally under the influence of the gods, who are bringing about her punishment at the same time as Jason's. Two objections may be made to such an inference. First, as stated above, the tragedians normally explicitly reveal to the audience when a character is suffering a mental invasion that is controlling his or her perceptions and behavior. Such an indication is lacking in *Medea* at the time when she is making her decisions. The situation is different later when the violent event is occurring: the chorus, shocked and repelled by what Medea is doing, suggests that she embodies an Erinys (1260) and describes her as mentally deranged by wrath (1265–6), and this is a typical reaction of a witness who prefers not to believe that such violence arises from normal humanity. Second, tragedy frequently displays a dovetailing of a character's inclination and desire with the purposes of the god, and this dovetailing involves a rich double motivation rather than one that is reducible simply to divine influence or delusion (*atē*): so with the Aeschylean Eteocles' decision to fight his brother, and Agamemnon's decision to tread on the fabrics at Clytemnestra's persuasion. In the case of Medea, the two sides of the causation are succinctly expressed in 1013–14, but this does not detract from the impression of freedom and voluntariness in Medea's previous or continuing development of her plan, or from the intrinsic quality of the passionate spirit (*thumos*) appealed to in her great monologue (1056, 1079) and of the wrath (*cholos*) cited by the chorus in 1265–6. Medea's citation of the gods in 1013–14 may in fact be interpreted in part as a rhetorical ploy by which Medea steels herself for the deed, just as in the *Iliad* (19.74–144) Agamemnon's retrospective analysis of his *atē* is a face-saving explanation that does not remove his obligation to make amends for his error in the treatment of Achilles. Accordingly, there is hardly a strong sense at the end of the play that Medea is being punished *by the gods* and *for her actions in Colchis*: she has the gods' complicity, and she is on her way to enjoy years of safety and prosperity in Athens. Perhaps some members of the Greek audience may have seen a comfortable moral balance in the ending by ascribing Medea's choices to a divine scheme to make her pay for her past, but the structure of the play, the relative prominence of its various themes and the emotional trajectory of sympathy and revulsion seem to me to invite a less comforting response.

The possibile inferences of divine action in *Hecuba* present somewhat different problems. This is a play which has struck many as presenting a harsh world, where the supernatural is evident mainly in the two ghosts, the visible and pitiful Polydorus and the terrifying Achilles whose epiphany is only reported.[97] A number of critics have concentrated attention on the character of Hecuba herself and concluded that she suffers moral degradation over the course of the play, a degradation symbolized by the prediction at the end that she will be transformed into a dog just before she drowns and becomes memorialized by the topographical landmark called Dog's Sign or Dog's Tomb (*Kynos Sēma*). Several critics have responded with the argument that this moralizing approach is at least in part dependent on modern ethical standards different from those of the Greeks and that Hecuba's revenge, terrible as it may be, is an act of just retribution.[98] The point of interest for the present discussion of inferred divine intervention is what an audience is to make of the reported detail that immediately after the sacrifice of Polyxena the fleet is unable to depart because of the absence of winds (*Hec.* 898–901). A recent suggestion is that the absence of wind is a sign of the gods' displeasure at the human sacrifice offered to Achilles, while the gods' approval of the revenge exacted by Hecuba may be read by an audience from the fact that favorable winds begin to blow just after Polymestor is punished (1289–90).[99] To be sure, the sacrifice of the virgin Polyxena at the beginning of the voyage home from Troy is structurally parallel to the sacrifice of the virgin Iphigenia

[97] The two ghosts have somewhat different status. Achilles appears in epiphany to the Greeks (*Hec.* 37–8, 109–15), which implies the quasi-divine power of a hero worthy of cult. Polydorus is a more ordinary dead person: he has knowledge superior to living humans because in death he has access to what is hidden from the living (this assumption underlies the ancient concept of necromancy), but he engages in a much more limited alternative to epiphany, appearing to his mother in a dream, and it is the power of the gods that arranges the discovery of his body, and perhaps gives him permission to become a dream vision.
[98] The moral deterioration of Hecuba is argued by, e.g., Reckford 1985, Segal 1993. For defense of Hecuba's action as legitimate in the eyes of the Greek audience, see esp. Kovacs 1987a, Burnett 1998: 157–76, and to a lesser extent Gregory 1999. Mossman 1995 steers a middle course between these extremes, in a way more akin to the probing and aporetic stance I argue for in this book (on *Hec.* see pp. 71–3 and 229–34).
[99] Gregory 1999: xxix–xxxi, acknowledging a debt to D. Kovacs. On Gregory's view, the human sacrifice is the free choice of the Greek leaders and not specifically demanded by the ghost of Achilles. This seems to me a very doubtful reading. The demand is first mentioned by Polydorus in 40–1, and Polydorus as a supernatural prologue figure should be taken as an authoritative source for audience knowledge (cf. note 97 above), not as a source that is subject to doubt on the ground that he can offer only his own viewpoint and interpretation as one among others (as Gregory argues). Moreover, when the chorus gives its description of Achilles' demand in 113–15 ("leaving my tomb without a token of honor (ἀγέραστον)"; cf. Polydorus' report in 41: "to receive a precious sacrifice and token of honor (γέρας) for his tomb"), this is most naturally taken as an abbreviation of the fuller details just given by Polydorus (it is a common technique for tragedians not to repeat unnecessarily details that an audience has recently heard), not as a divergent version of the event. That is, an audience does not infer, as Gregory's argument requires, that the chorus has given the entire speech of Achilles and that all he demanded was a *geras* ("prize of honor"), not specifically the human sacrifice of Polyxena. Instead, they assume that the *geras* is precisely the human sacrifice they have heard of, and because they make this assumption they can then understand the immediately following reference to the disagreement over whether to sacrifice the girl at his tomb.

at the beginning of the voyage from Aulis to Troy. Adverse winds played an essential role in the narratives of the earlier event. So one might expect Euripides to strengthen the parallelism by referring to winds that reinforce Achilles' demand. Yet there is in fact no reference to winds in *Hecuba* until line 898, after the discovery of Polydorus' body and the appeal of Hecuba to Agamemnon. The allusions to the demand of the ghost of Achilles establish only that the ghost's appearance and speech caused the Greek fleet to stop its journey (37–9, 111–15). The interval between stopping and decision (this is the third dawn: 32) seems to be mentioned to enhance the pathos of the pitiful abandonment of Polydorus' corpse, described as washed back and forth in the waves of the shore. The interval is also exploited later when Polymestor insincerely explains why he did not come to visit Hecuba earlier: he was inland in the mountains when the Greek fleet arrived and has only now returned to his coastal home (962–7). But the chorus make no reference to the passage of time when they describe the deliberation of the Greeks (116–40). Some audience members may choose to supplement the narrative by assuming that the uncertainty of the Greeks concerning Achilles' demand made them hesitate to act at once, but it is safer to say that the text is not even asking the audience to think about the interval in connection with the sacrifice. The motif of the wind arises later because an interval is needed for Hecuba's revenge (898–901). If one is to make a theological inference from this detail, it should not be a retrospective one concerning the human sacrifice, but a prospective one concerning revenge on Polymestor for the atrocity he committed: the gods are giving Hecuba the time she needs to punish him, and the winds are favorable once the vengeance is completed (1289–90). But such an inference should be considered optional rather than compelling, since the motif of the wind is so sparse within the texture of the play.

It is perhaps useful to compare the references to wind in *Troades*. Poseidon says in the prologue that the Greeks await a favorable wind for home as they are loading their ships with booty (19–20). But after he agrees with Athena to help her attack the fleet, he tells her to get her weapons and await the departure of the fleet (93–4). Soon thereafter it is clear that the chorus and Hecuba expect to depart almost immediately since Greek sailors are moving toward their ships (159–60, 167, cf. 180–1[100]). Cassandra is so eager for the destruction awaiting her enemy that she says "you can't be too

---

[100] The use of oars referred to in *Tro.* 180–1 suggests the standard procedure of rowing away from the shore before raising a mast and sails, and this detail need not be read as a hint that the Greeks will row out against an opposing wind.

quick to watch out for the breeze with your sails" (456). And later, although Menelaus refers to "leisure" allowing him to indulge Hecuba's request for a formal debate, it is clear that some Greek ships are already leaving (1123–7, 1148, 1155). It would not be convincing to make any inferences about the gods from these references to the winds and to the act of departure: they are simply plausible background for the stage-action. So perhaps are the less prominent references in *Hecuba*.

CONCLUSION

The gods in Euripides' tragedies are an integral part of the shaping of the complex and developing experience of the viewing and interpreting audience. Their seen or unseen presence raises the represented world to a different plane from everyday experience. Their pronouncements may have great authority, but also may reveal gaps between the experience of human mortality and a more detached perspective. The shifting viewpoints of the characters (or chorus) about the gods provide a telling dynamic in many plays, revealing the human struggle to reconcile painful experience and uncertainty with longings for clarity and order and aspirations for justice. The audience can often recognize the partiality or error of the claims and critiques voiced by the characters, but will itself at times also be left with a residue of doubt or puzzlement about the overall sense to derive from the conflicting voices and explanations offered by the drama. And from play to play (within a festival or over the years) the interpreting viewer may infer different levels of optimism or despair, different mixtures of divine benevolence and harshness, different impressions of fittingness or discomfort, for both traditional Greek religious ideas and the genre of tragedy easily accommodate such variety and inconsistency.

One thrust of the discussion in this chapter has been to show that, at the same time that the ignorance, misunderstandings, and hasty false conclusions of the human characters are revealed and exploited for dramatic and ethical or metaphysical effect, it is far from easy to adopt a piously optimistic view of the gods in Euripides, a view whereby they uphold justice in a fully comprehensible way and act consistently for human good. But this does not entail that the portrayal of the gods is not in most respects traditional or that it in any way espouses denial of supernatural forces in the universe. Despite the fact that in many contexts (esp. public, ceremonial, and patriotic ones) the Greeks would not want to have said so explicitly, it is inherent in the polytheistic system that the gods have divided interests and loyalties, and this is emphasized or illustrated in Homeric epic and the *Oresteia* as well as in Euripidean plays like *Hippolytus, Andromache, Heracles,* and even *Helen* and *Iphigenia in Tauris.* There are just and beneficent interventions, but there are also interventions of another kind. If in *Heracleidae,* for instance, one chooses to detect some kind of divine favor and justice both in the opportune arrival of Hyllus with his army to join the Athenians against Eurystheus and in the magical rejuvenation of the loyal Iolaus, one must also concede that the divine is responsible for the demand for human sacrifice, since it is made by a consensus of prophetic sources and there can be no question of importing, without any textual clue, the motif of doubt of oracles or the distinction between divine prophecy and prophecy offered by human interpreters. The chorus' reaction to the news is significant: "Are we to believe, then, that when this city is eager to assist the strangers in their need, god does not permit it?" (*Hcld.* 425–6). Human sacrifice was not a reality for the Greeks of Euripides' time, but it was imagined in myth in order to illustrate by reversal and transgression the correct structure of sacrifice (animal is sacrificed by man to god) that prevails in Greek ritual practice. Euripides exploits the motif several times in his work because it allows contemplation of extreme situations of devotion and reciprocity.[101] Whereas in *Phoenissae* Menoeceus atones for a past infringement in order to make the city's future safe, in *Heracleidae* Heracles' daughter seems to be involved in a prospective exchange, her life for future protection. This exchange lays bare the terrifying and ultimately incomprehensible power of divinity: there is reciprocity between gods and men, but the conditions of the exchange are not within human control, as the most optimistic interpretation of human–divine interaction might claim.

Moreover, in the cases of convenient coincidences (as in *Ion*) and the matching of divine designs to human habits and decisions (as in *Hippolytus*), the dovetailing of events and causes is not simply a necessary device of effective storytelling, but a source of wonder and awe (*thauma*), an important motif of mythological narrative that is also an expression of religious experience. One might in fact say that the gods of traditional Greek religion (and tragedy) would be much less interesting, and much less worthy of awe, if they acted in ways that are fully and perfectly understandable.

---

[101] On human sacrifice in Greek religion and myth, see Schmitt 1921, Henrichs 1980, O'Connor-Visser 1987, Hughes 1991.

CHAPTER 6

Rhetoric and character

In Aristophanes' *Frogs*, a recurrent motif in the contrast between the old style of Aeschylus and the new style of Euripides is the connection of Euripides with glib chatter and overrefined logic.[1] The chorus' final assessment[2] associates Euripides with Socrates, in a generalized rejection of the newfangled thought and speech associated, with comic oversimplification, with the intellectual showmen and teachers known as the sophists. The aim of this chapter is to come to terms with some of the issues raised by the obvious pervasiveness of "rhetoric" in Euripidean drama.

Following Aristophanes' lead, a long history of criticism has been concerned with the degree to which the prominence of rhetorical elements affects the notion of character and modifies or inhibits emotional involvement of the audience in the persons and events of tragedy. For some critics it has been a given that rhetoric undermines tragedy or tragic effects because it reduces the element of "spontaneity" and "sincerity" in a character's utterances. Here it will be argued that rhetoric is intrinsic to Euripides' conception of tragedy and that is it often the source of "tragic" effects, in the sense that it exposes to scrutiny the contingency of values and illusory quality of human skills. After some preliminary remarks on what "rhetoric"

---

[1] The key words *lalia* and *stōmulia* are paired in Aeschylus' accusation at *Frogs* 1069: "you taught them to practice chattering and glibness"; other derivatives of the root *lal-* appear with telling force to characterize Euripides and his style in 91, 815, 839, 917, 954, and in 1492 (quoted in next note); likewise derivatives of *stōmul-* are significant in 92, 841, 943, 1071, 1160, 1310. The root *stōmul-* is entirely untragic, while *lal-* is mainly confined to satyr-play (Silenus describing Odysseus in *Cycl.* 315; Soph. fr. 1130.16) and a few tragic passages where humbler characters are rebuked by kings (Creon to the guard in Soph. *Ant.* 320, Theseus to the herald in *Su.* 462; cf. Eur. fr. 1012).

[2] *Frogs* 1482–99 (trans. Henderson 2002): [Strophe, referring to Aeschylus] "Happy the man who has / keen intelligence, / as is abundantly clear: / this man, for his eminent good sense, / is going back home again, / a boon to his fellow citizens, / a boon as well / to his family and friends, / through being intelligent." [Antistrophe, referring to Euripides] "So what's stylish is not to sit / beside Socrates and chatter, / casting the arts aside / and ignoring the best / of the tragedian's craft. / To hang around killing time / in pretentious conversation / and hairsplitting twaddle / is the mark of a man who's lost his mind."

means in relation to Greek tragedy and how Euripides' uses of rhetoric may be distinctive, this chapter will consider the well-attested Greek ambivalence about rhetorical skill and how that ambivalence is reflected and played out in tragedy. Then the discussion will turn to traits of contemporary speculation and intellectual inquiry incorporated in the speeches of tragic figures. Of particular interest is a group of Euripidean characters who may be termed "optimistic rationalists." Such figures, I argue, are tragically caught up in the analysis and verbal articulation of their world, following an impulse Euripides shows to be natural to human beings and to some degree admirable to internal (and presumably external) observers. But they are also involved in actions that show their wisdom and skill to be futile or self-deluding. Finally, the relation of rhetoric to character will be studied. The power of skillfully organized speech and argumentation is often a vehicle for the self-presentation of a settled world-view that is in conflict with a similarly articulated view of another character. Even for such relatively stable characters, however, rhetorical skill is frequently problematized. Such problematization extends even further in other instances, in which I argue that rhetorical skill also acts at times as a force that reinterprets and remakes a variable and inconstant human self.[3]

RHETORIC AND ITS CONTEXT

First, some thoughts about what "rhetoric" means in a discussion of Greek tragedy in its context. Skillfully organized speeches tailored to a particular audience and a particular occasion are present in Homeric epic, far earlier than the emergence of the discipline that the Greeks came to call *technē rhētorikē*, "the art of speaking." Such speeches are an essential tool of the epic genre to involve the listeners in interpretation of the characters' ethical positions, emotional stakes, and intellectual constructs of understanding – how they assume the world to work and how they judge interpersonal relations. Self-presentation and self-justification, remonstrance and praise, persuasion and exhortation all contribute to the exploration of key themes of serious Greek poetry: human and divine causation, responsibility, the nature of excellence and of good sense. Many of the techniques of rhetoric are native to traditional forms of oral discourse and poetry and not an

---

[3] Important discussions relating to the rhetorical element in tragedy in general or Euripides in particular include: Duchemin 1945, Reinhardt 1957 (English version, Reinhardt 2003), Strohm 1957: 3–49, Collard 1975b, Conacher 1981, Goldhill 1986: 222–43, Lloyd 1992, Scodel 1999–2000, Dubischar 2001, Pelling 2000 and 2005. Also relevant to the theme of Euripides' reflections of philosophical and sophistic ideas are Conacher 1998, Allan 1999–2000 and 2005, Egli 2003.

invention of those who explicitly organized and taught the art in the second half of the fifth century. During the course of the fifth century, however, the constant practice of argumentative and persuasive speech in the assembly-meetings of the Athenian *dēmos* and in the courts of the democratic system produced advances in the skills of argumentation and presentation, and an increasing self-consciousness about these skills. In parallel with this advance, and not necessarily in any way dependent on it, the nature of extended speeches in tragedy also changed gradually over time. In the earlier period, in Aeschylus, we find many image-filled, descriptive *tours de force*, sometimes expressive of an almost magical power of control over language: e.g., the clairvoyance of Clytemnestra's beacon speech and her description of the fall of Troy in *Agamemnon* (280–316, 320–50), or the verbal prefiguration of the defeat of the Argive attackers enacted when Eteocles skillfully rebuts their boastful shield-images and threatening words in *Septem* (375–676). But already in Sophoclean plays that are widely considered to be "early" (*Ajax, Antigone*), we find not only a variety of long speeches of self-presentation or self-justification, but also the agonistic form of paired speeches, where the horizontal line of communication (or rather miscommunication or attack) between two speakers is intensified to accentuate as sharply as possible the gaps between the opponents. The rhetorical features for which Euripides is noted were well developed before Gorgias' famous first visit to Athens in 427 as part of a diplomatic delegation from Leontini.[4] Striking argumentation and sophisticated rhetoric are already attested in *Telephus* and *Alcestis* of 438, *Cretans* (probably of similar date), and *Philoctetes*[5] and *Medea* of 431. All that Gorgias did was to carry to a specific extreme some tendencies of style that must have been in the air, not only in Athens (where Euripides and Thucydides and Antiphon reflect them most prominently) but in other cities as well (for a number of the teachers of rhetoric were from Sicily, like Gorgias, and the sophists travelled constantly in their teaching).

When we say that among the tragedians Euripides in particular is "rhetorical," several aspects of rhetoric are involved: (1) a more transparent

[4] Ancient sources allege that in this visit Gorgias stunned and amazed the Athenians, giving them their first exposure to "sophistic" rhetorical techniques: Gorgias 82 A 4 D–K (based on the historian Timaeus).

[5] *Telephus* contained one or two rhetorically striking speeches by Telephus: Cropp in Collard *et al.*1995: 17–21; Collard and Cropp 2008b: 123–7. The most extensive fragment surviving from *Cretans* is Pasiphaë's speech defending her infatuation and intercourse with the bull (fr. 472e). Euripides' *Philoctetes* featured an *agōn* in which a disguised Odysseus, who had won Philoctetes' confidence by claiming to have been mistreated by the Greeks at Troy, had to rebut the arguments of a delegation from Troy, arguing for patriotic loyalty despite any grudge against the Greeks: see Collard in Collard *et al.* 2004: 5–7.

organization of long speeches; (2) the speakers' self-consciousness about structure and about modes of argument; (3) the prominent use of the "argument from probability"; (4) paradox and the pushing of an argument to an unexpected or unconventional extreme; (5) the provision of skillful arguments in support of almost any cause; (6) heavy use of antithesis, in particular involving contemporary preoccupations like nature and custom (*phusis, nomos*) and word/appearance and deed/reality (*logos/doxa, ergon*); and, finally, (7) the virtual universalization of rhetorical skill among characters of different status.

This universalization of rhetorical skill seems indeed to be a major differentiating feature that sets Euripides apart from earlier tragedians.[6] Euripides freely offends against the principle of later rhetorical teaching that holds that the best form of discourse should be tailored to the status and condition of the speaker as assumed by the audience, or the status or condition of which the audience is to be convinced. Aristophanes already makes a joke of this universalization in *Frogs* 948–52:

EUR. Then from the very first lines I wouldn't leave a single character idle,
    but a woman would be speaking in my plays and a slave just as much,
    and a master, and a maiden, and an old woman.
AES. And shouldn't you have been put to death for daring that?
EUR. No, by Apollo. I did it as a democratic gesture.

"Democratic" (*dēmokratikon*) seems to be used by Aristophanes here in the sense of extending to the poor and weak what might otherwise be restricted to the wealthy and strong, but in fact Athenian democracy never went as far as Euripidean tragedy. Speech in most contexts was the privilege of adult male citizens, although free non-citizen males also had venues for formal speech (metics in court, metics and foreigners in symposia, private gatherings, and public festivals). Slaves and women of any age were ideally imagined as excluded from speech except for a subordinate role in very narrow domestic or religious contexts. Tragedy is clearly not in any sense a realistic reflection of everyday life, but a stylized transformation. Choruses can sing elaborate high-style lyrics (and dance elaborate choreography) whether they represent men or women, free or slave, old or young. With few exceptions and only minor variations, the non-mute characters in

[6] Scodel 1999–2000: 132–4. In what we have of Sophocles, *Electra* has the most elaborate formal speeches among female characters, and there is little sign of rhetorical skill among humble characters apart from messengers (except perhaps for the guard in *Antigone*: cf. Griffith 1999: 37, 165, 177). But would our picture be different if we had his *Phaedra, Tereus,* and *Andromeda*? Certainly by late in the fifth century other tragedians beside Euripides were incorporating rhetorical modernism in their style (Ar. *Frogs* 89–91).

tragedy speak in an artificial language that is much the same from speaker to speaker, regardless of status. Even in Sophocles, who (so far as we can tell from the insufficient extant evidence) does not go so far as Euripides, the female figures Antigone and Electra show their extraordinary natures by the arguments they develop and forcefully deliver, and a passive and diffident woman like Deianeira can still deliver a long exposition of her worries or of her decisions. Humble figures who deliver messenger-speeches are endowed with the narrative and stylistic skills authorized by the genre rather than realistically plausible. It is a given of tragedy that conventional forms often override probability and consistency of character-drawing, no matter how much the latter may be aimed for or respected in other ways. So in one sense, Euripides is simply exploiting the conventions of the dramatic genre: effective or impressively stylized communication to the external audience takes precedence over the portrayal of a (socially or culturally) realistic system of internal communication.

But more is, indeed, at stake in Euripides. There are more women's roles, and the self-consciousness of the rhetoric (along with the occasional insistence on referring to the departure from everyday assumptions of propriety) creates a stronger impression of a distinctive anti-realism. The universalization of the rhetorical style increases the polyphony of voices and viewpoints natural to tragedy and lends equal weight to all positions, including those of the weak (including women) and the disreputable (including "villains"), sharpening the disagreements and often making judgment more problematic. The world of discourse in Euripidean drama creates the impression that human beings are naturally articulate, perceptive, analytic, and critical. This is in line with widespread assumptions among Greek thinkers about the uniqueness of speech and reason to the human species, but it also matches some of the key assumptions underpinning democratic "political theory" and the Athenians' self-conception as reflected, for instance, in Thucydides and Aristophanes. What Euripidean tragedy brings, in addition, is tragic doubt: by enmeshing figures with such prominent verbal and analytic skills in the traditional story-patterns of Greek myth, Euripides highlights the gap between understanding and control, showing that man's most prized qualities can be both deceptive and futile.

AMBIVALENCE ABOUT RHETORIC AND THE MODERN

In the cultural wars of the late fifth century, as reflected for instance in several of Aristophanes' plays, the flashier and more self-conscious features of rhetoric are clearly one of the targets of the (conservative) discourse that contrasts the simplicity and uprightness of the past with the decadence and corruption of the present. This was, of course, not the only point of view prevalent in the contemporary society of Euripidean drama, since in certain contexts and before specific audiences even a conservative speaker could espouse the excellence of the present organization of life in the city, the value of effective speaking and argumentation, and the superiority of verbal elegance and eloquence over tongue-tied ignorance or insensitivity.[7] Poetic and other discourses had traditionally contested the nature of human virtue and the nature of manliness. Just as in musical forms, where innovations and elaborations came to be stereotyped as womanish or "Asian" rather than manly or genuinely Greek,[8] so too in verbal skills, especially in some aristocratic contexts, simplicity and honesty were often lauded and their opposites projected upon excluded or abject groups, like "wheedling" women who deceive by verbal trickery as well as attractive appearance, or dishonest tradesmen, or money-making sophists.[9] Similarly, in the later Greek tradition, classicism was often characterized by espousal of a restrained and "pure" style in opposition to an "Asiatic" style, with the same prejudicial accusation of effeminacy and foreignness.[10] The Platonic critique of the sophists has influenced many to accept too easily such negative evaluations, and to ignore the contestation of values and the hypocrisy of many of those who are attacking "sophistic rhetoric." In the interpretation of Euripides, this has sometimes led to what I would consider mistaken evaluations of the reception of rhetorical speeches in the plays.

Within the plays, the condemnation of the dangers of well-wrought speech used in support of immoral or disapproved positions frequently finds expression.[11] Three typical instances may be cited here:

In my view, whoever, being unjust, has a natural talent
at speaking, incurs the greatest penalty.
For being confident that he'll effectively cloak his injustice with verbal skill
he dares to commit any crime. But such a man is not so very clever. (Medea in
reference to Jason, *Med.* 580–1)

---

[7] Cf., for example, Diodotus' insistence on the value of competitive discussion in civic deliberation (Thuc. 3.42).

[8] Csapo 1999–2000, Wilson 1999 and 2003.

[9] On the gendering of deceptive speech as womanly, see Worman 1999, McClure 1999.

[10] See, for instance, the proem of Dionysius of Halicarnassus' *de oratoribus veteribus*.

[11] The linking of verbal skill and deception of course goes back to the traditional opposition between Odysseus and either Ajax or Achilles (*Il.* 9.308–13, Pind. *Nem.* 7.20–30), and traditional poetry itself was liable to the same suspicion of falsehood cloaked in exceptional skill with words (Hes. *Theog.* 26–7, Pind. *Ol.* 1.28–32).

This is the thing that destroys the well-managed cities of men
and their households, arguments that are too seemly.
One should not speak what delights the ears,
but what will make a person fair-famed. (Phaedra in reference to the nurse, *Hipp.*
486–9)

It ought not ever to be the case for mortals
that verbal skill overpowers the actual facts.
Rather, if one has done good, one should speak a good case,
and if one has done evil, the arguments ought to have no solidity. (Hecuba in
reference to Polymestor, *Hec.* 1187–90)

Similar sentiments appear in many other passages.[12]
    On the other side, one also finds confident statements about the
strength or success of an honest case, as in *Hecuba* 1238–9, where the
chorus responds to Hecuba's speech against Polymestor, after an excla-
mation of admiration, with "how upright actions always give mortals the
basis for good arguments." Similarly, the chorus endorses Amphitryon's
speech against Lycus (*Her.* 236–7), and Teiresias says it is easy for a wise
man to speak in opposition to Pentheus' folly (*Ba.* 266–7). Speakers who
desperately need to change someone's mind are quite ready to set a high
value on persuasive speech, as Hecuba does in her appeal to Agamemnon
in *Hecuba* 814–19.[13] The universalization of rhetorical skill in Euripidean
characters introduces irony in a number of passages where verbal skill is
mentioned. Hippolytus' speech before Theseus (*Hipp.* 983–1035) may be
ill suited to persuade Theseus in particular, but despite his own disclaimer
of skill, Hippolytus presents a well-ordered sequence of argumentation
that, in the abstract, is a skillful assemblage of the possible points left to
him so long as he continues to conceal what he has sworn an oath to
conceal. Polyneices in the *agōn* of *Phoenissae* gives a speech (469–96) of
great clarity in structure and arguments, no less "rhetorical" than those of
Eteocles and Jocasta, despite the fact that he uses the proem and conclusion to distinguish himself sharply from those who rely on the elaboration and duplicity of "clever/skilled" speech. The incongruity should
not be applied at the level of individual characterization, to prove that
Polyneices is a hypocrite, but as a more general comment on the one-
sideness, stylization, and contingency of the viewpoints humans espouse
when they make an effort to articulate and generalize their understanding

[12] Cf. *Tro.* 967–8 (chorus reacting to Helen's speech); *Phoen.* 526–7 (chorus reacting to Eteocles'
speech); *Ba.* 268–71 (Teiresias describing Pentheus); *Or.* [907–8], which is probably a Euripidean
couplet from another play; frr. 206, 253, 528, 583, 928b.
[13] Discussed below, pp. 231–2.

f the world.[14] The relevance to Polyneices as an individual should be
understood more in terms of blindness – the inability to recognize that
what he claims is simple and straightforward actually involves complications that undermine his case.

In *Phoenissae*, Eteocles obviously evokes in his speech (499–525) the
contemporary phenomenon[15] of amoral clever young men with sophistic
training, ready to discomfit their traditionally minded elders on any occasion and delighting in scorning cherished beliefs. Yet it is essential to
recognize that modern traits, whether sophistic or intellectualist or philosophically speculative, occur in many kinds of contexts in the mouths of
many different speakers and cannot be universally labeled "sophistic" in the
pejorative sense of that term, with the assumption that such features are
suspect or inevitably produce a negative effect on the audience. As we noted
with regard to religious speculations in the previous chapter, high-style
Greek poetry is a traditional bearer of *sophia*, "wisdom," in its many possible
meanings, including knowledge of inherited information, specialized
knowledge unavailable to laymen, and novel reinterpretation or extrapolation of known traditions. Just as the tragic genre sanctions an overall
uniformity of style for its characters without regard to gender or status, so
the poetic tradition to which it belongs makes room for the incorporation of
the newest forms of *sophia*, including anthropological, political, theological,
scientific, and linguistic speculation. For Euripides, this aspect of human
endeavor and aspiration is just as worthy of portrayal and scrutiny as facility
with speech and argument and exploration of traditional concepts of value.
No instance of the modern, scientific, or sophistic within the plays should
be treated as inorganic or as a private expression of the poet. Each must be
evaluated in terms of speaker and situation and of its role in the dialectic of
viewpoints and ideas that runs through an entire play.

The multivalent potential of arguments with a sophistic tinge is well
illustrated by the *a fortiori* arguments recommending that humans can
justifiably behave a certain way because the gods do.[16] The nurse in
Hippolytus and Theseus in *Heracles* use strikingly similar argumentation
that deserves consideration again here. The nurse cites love affairs of Zeus
and Eos to argue that since the gods do not lose status or hide in shame
because of the unwilling experience of being in love and acting on it,

---

[14] See Mastronarde 1994 on *Phoen.* 469–96, 469–72, and 494–6, as well as on 497–8 for the chorus' use
of the "modern" intellectualist word *suneta*, "intelligible," of Polyneices' speech.
[15] Attested to by Aristophanes (esp. in *Clouds*) and Plato (*Apol.* 23c, *Rep.* 539b-c); cf. Mastronarde
1994: 288.
[16] See above, pp. 172–3.

Phaedra likewise should accept and act upon the desire for Hippolytus that has overcome her (453–61). As explained in the next section, Euripides builds up the moral stature of Phaedra's resistance to her desire by making the nurse speak for a contrasting ethic, and it is clear from the internal reactions of the chorus and Phaedra herself that the external audience is invited to disapprove of the nurse's clever but immoral argumentation. In *Heracles* 1314–21, however, Theseus points to the traditional stories of divine behavior to urge Heracles to be tolerant of the stain that his killing of his family has put upon him. Theseus' rhetorical question "do the gods not still live in heaven and put up with having erred?" (*Her.* 1318–19) is exactly parallel to the nurse's statement "Nonetheless they dwell in heaven and accept their fate of being overcome by the misfortune" (*Hipp.* 456–8), and both follow this up with a rhetorical question demanding that the human character not set himself or herself above the gods. To be sure, in *Heracles*, Theseus' citation of authority, unlike the nurse's, alludes to the motif of the possible deception of poetic stories (1315: "if truly the stories of poets are not false"), and Heracles himself soon rejects the basis of the analogy (1346: "these are the wretched tales of poets"). Nonetheless, it is not at all likely that the use of this argument *per se* is designed to cast any negative light on Theseus, the idealized Athenian king and exemplar in this play of true friendship and rescuing assistance. The argument rather serves to inspire Heracles' own expression of faith and to advance the exploration of the tragic coexistence of the incommensurability of the divine and the human with the human effort to construct the world otherwise.

The "optimistic rationalist" characters of Euripides illustrate best the dramatic importance and the ironies of the incorporation of the modern into tragedy.[17] In contrast to the Euripidean figures like Eteocles who reflect contemporary intellectual culture in such a way as to arouse shock and disapproval, these figures seem to succeed in combining traditional values and intellectual modernity. They believe that the world is orderly and comprehensible and that there are elements in that order which have been fashioned for the good of man. These are basically sympathetic figures, but it is insufficient to be satisfied with such a reaction to them because, in general, the overall context undermines the position of the optimistic rationalist and exposes the futility of even the most refined human constructs of understanding. Three optimistic rationalists will be considered here: Theseus in *Supplices*, Jocasta in *Phoenissae*, and Teiresias in *Bacchae*.

---

[17] The following pages are a revision and condensation of Mastronarde 1986.

The greater part of Euripides' *Supplices* presents a fairly typical story-pattern of political supplication.[18] The wronged parties supplicate a more fortunate state; an internal obstacle is overcome; an external opposition to reception of the suppliants is first expressed in threatening words and then acted out in an armed conflict offstage; the protecting state wins and receives appropriate thanks. All or most of these features can be found in Aeschylus' *Supplices* and (with modifications) *Eumenides*, Euripides' *Heracleidae* and *Supplices*, and Sophocles' *Oedipus Coloneus*. It is not by chance that in four of the five cases the protecting state is Athens, for the Athenians prided themselves on their generous acceptance of refugees and suppliants, even those who had no particular claim to Attic protection.[19] It is especially noteworthy that in *Heracleidae* the sons of Theseus have no hesitation in taking the suppliants' side at once (the difficulty of the oracle comes later as a surprise), and in *Oedipus Coloneus* Theseus almost grants Oedipus' request before hearing it. What happens in Euripides' *Supplices* must be viewed against the background supplied by such examples, and that background suggests that Theseus' initial rejection of the suppliants' request is surprising. Theseus is, for an Athenian audience, usually an ideal king, and there are aspects of this play that perhaps invite the terse ancient judgment "the drama is an encomium of Athens."[20] But the dialectic of viewpoints within the play creates a more nuanced picture.

In his first long speech (195–249), Theseus expresses the view that the workings of the world are fully intelligible, that the gods have provided all the resources necessary for human success and happiness, that the course of human failure and misery can be simply analyzed and fault clearly ascribed. For Theseus (at this point in the play), there is a clear separation between good and bad men, prosperous and wretched men; citizens in a state can be neatly divided into three distinct groups (the greedy rich, the envious poor,

[18] On supplication in general and in tragedy, see Kopperschmidt 1967 and 1971, Gould 1983, Allan 2001: 39–43.

[19] In both *Hcld.* (205–13) and *Su.* (263–4) the claim of kinship is a secondary and reinforcing issue, not the primary motive of the request or the acceptance; contrast Aesch. *Su.*, where the daughters of Danaus first establish a special claim to acceptance by Argos before clinching their case with the threat that their suicide will bring the wrath of Zeus Hikesios ("Zeus of suppliants"). Athenian pride in aiding suppliants is attested by the fact that the aid given to the Argive and Heraclid suppliants is a topos of the state funeral oration (*epitaphios logos*): Lysias 2.7–16; Plato, *Menex.* 239b; [Dem.] 60.8; Hyperides 6.5, cf. Loraux 1986. One may relate to this the Athenian pride in *ponoi* ("toils, hard effort") and in doing *polla* ("many things"): cf. Collard 1975a on *Su.* 577.

[20] The only surviving manuscript of *Su.* contains a remnant of the end of the standard paragraph of prefatory information conventionally ascribed to Aristophanes of Byzantium (see Ch. 1, n. 11): after phrases about the location of the action and the identity of the chorus all that is extant is τὸ δὲ δρᾶμα ἐγκώμιον Ἀθηνῶν. For my doubts about whether such evaluative remarks really go back to Aristophanes, see above Ch. 1, nn. 12 and 25.

too easily swayed by demagogues, and a well-disciplined middle class). Theseus thus combines traditional respect for the gods and their ways with the modern view of human progress and a modern-sounding analytic clarity.[21] Yet the speech's reception must be gauged with attention to its context.[22] The initial movement of the drama is designed to evoke sympathy for the unfortunate Argives, and the scene which follows Theseus' impressive speech reasserts the claims of sympathy and brings a very rapid change of mind. And as already suggested, the suppliant-plot pattern itself, the pretensions of patriotic Athenian myths, and the very stature of Theseus as symbol of Attic unity, civilization, and service to mankind render Theseus' coldly rational refusal a surprising, even shocking, development. Some hesitation in the protector or a minor hindrance imposed from outside may be an expected part of a suppliant-drama, but no one would have expected such a direct and swift refusal from the Athenian king himself. Theseus' speech, optimistic and rational though it is, is undercut by irony and shown to be inadequate to the realities of the tragic world. Beyond this general irony, there are also reversals of specific statements and positions. Aethra provides a more traditionally tragic view of the cyclical workings of human fortune (331). The debate between the Theban herald and Theseus goes further: the herald echoes elements of Theseus' earlier speech, while Theseus now takes an opposite view. It is the herald who now asserts a simple division between what is good and what is bad, criticizes the control of the assembly by the skillful tongue of a villain (423–5, cf. 243), accuses Theseus of aiding bad men and ignoring the judgment of the gods (486–505), and refers to "rashness" and "youth" as causes of disaster in war (508, 580). Theseus, for his part, now speaks differently of the classes of men in a city (408, 433–7; cf. 420–5) and refers to the sufferings of humanity in a manner closer to that of Adrastus (549–55, cf. 176–9). Later in the play, the encomium of the dead warriors (855–917) casts another ironic sidelight on Theseus' initial position. Theseus himself asks for and then supplements the encomium (841–5, 925–31); and the gist of Adrastus' speech is that these men were not, after all, simply bloodthirsty men of sin and violence, but also men of moderation, bravery and public-spiritedness. While some have viewed this surprising praise as a sardonic comment on the insincerity of the

---

[21] Note, for instance, the traditional wisdom in Theseus' rejection of trying to be "wiser than the gods" at 216–18 and in his use of the maxim on the contagion of sinfulness at 226–8, which echoes Aesch. *Sept.* 602–8. For other points see Collard 1975a ad loc.

[22] Cf. Collard 1975a: 131–2, 184–5.

Athenian genre of funeral eulogies for warriors, the challenge may rather be directed to the legibility of human character as simple and consistent.[23]

The Jocasta of *Phoenissae* has the longest speaking/singing role in the play and she dominates its first third. Before the *agōn*, she has been established as the long-suffering but selfless center of the doomed family. Her impossible position is foreshadowed in the stichomythia with Polyneices which leads up to the *agōn*. Even as she brings out Polyneices' love for his fatherland (in preparation for the appeal she will make to him in 568–83), she simultaneously evokes all the ills of exile which drive Polyneices to insist upon his rights. In the *agōn* itself Jocasta is caught between the opposing beliefs and stances of her two sons: Polyneices, an utterly conventional man in his love of kin and country and in his acceptance of aristocratic values, presses the undeniable justice of his claim, while Eteocles, a child of sophistic amoralism, presents a flashy but ultimately selfish and emotional argument for retaining power at all costs. There is virtually no common ground between the brothers, but Jocasta makes a valiant attempt at persuasion, addressing the two in separate appeals in chiastic order and spending more time (as appropriate) reacting to Eteocles' position. Like Theseus, she combines traditional wisdom with sophisticated theorizing about the order of the universe. She values experience (529) and the moderate man's contentment with a sufficiency (554), rejects reckless ambition (531, 567) and greed for more (552–3) and tyranny (549), and assumes the existence of standards of justice and law (523, 548, 549; 538). All of this is quite orthodox and traditional. But there are an equal number of modern or philosophic/sophistic elements in her speech: for example, the prosaic abstraction *Philotimia* (ambitious rivalry) described as a goddess in 532 and, more strikingly, the personification of *Isotēs* (equality) in 536.[24] The speech conveys a construct of an orderly and intelligible universe in which divine powers not only provide mankind with examples but even give them the tools of order. Equality has given men measure and number, and equality is the binding element in nature as well as society. The balance structured into night and day is a service to humanity: that is, both as an example (which Eteocles refuses to follow, 547–8) and as guarantor of the seasons, the order of nature is provided by divine powers for mankind's good.

[23] On this question, see above, p. 82.
[24] Cf. also the connection of night and day with measure and justice (543–7); the universal law stated in 539–40; the emphasis on number and measure (541–2); the oxymoron "happy/prosperous (literally, fortune-blessed) injustice" (*adikian eudaimona*, 549); the form of the "what is?" question in 553 and the hint of the *ergon/logos* antithesis in 557. For parallels to these ideas in philosophic/sophistic contexts see Mastronarde 1994 ad loc.

Humans in turn should feel that they are temporary guardians and users of what is ultimately the gods' (555–7).

Jocasta's speech forms an impressive and intellectually exciting climax of the debate. She surely is meant to win the audience's approval and admiration. But this does not mean that she "wins the debate" in any meaningful sense. Just as the prayers to Zeus (84–7) and the gods (467–8, 586–7) are futile requests for reconciliation and salvation, so Jocasta's lofty beliefs and impassioned argument are without effect, and that is a major tragic point of the scene. In his speech, Eteocles blindly asserts: "Not with arms should Polyneices have come to make a settlement, for speech accomplishes everything that the iron weaponry of enemies can do" (516–17). But both brothers are impervious to persuasion, and at the end of the debate Eteocles says bluntly but more accurately: "No longer is the contest one of words, but the time we spend waiting for battle is wasted in vain: your zeal accomplishes nothing" (588–9). Jocasta's attempt at reconciliation not only fails, but leads to an argument in which the brothers first broach the idea of deliberately seeking each other in battle (621–4).

The Teiresias of *Bacchae* 266–327 shares with Theseus and Jocasta the faith that the gods and the workings of the world can be understood and explained and that mankind is the beneficiary of the divine dispensation. Just as Jocasta assumed that from long experience she could refute Eteocles with wiser words *(Phoen.* 528–30), so Teiresias assumes that wisdom and good speaking can be usefully combined, and the implication is that he himself is doing so in refutation of the rash and mindless eloquence of Pentheus (266–71). As is natural to his encomiastic purpose, Teiresias looks only to the benefits which can be attributed in one way or another to Dionysus. Dionysus supplies the wet principle to balance Demeter's dry; he affords the only cure for cares and troubles; he mediates between man and the other gods; he is even credited with prophecy and helpful panic. The intellectual or sophistic element in Teiresias' speech is displayed especially in his playing with names. Minor evidence of this trait is present in the free choice he offers between the names "Demeter" and "Earth" (275–6) and the implied etymological connection between *mania* ("madness") and *mantis* ("seer") (298–9). But the most sophistic language-play is an integral part of the rationalizing account of the story of Dionysus' birth (286–97). After its modernist features, however, the speech turns toward traditional warnings to Pentheus to recognize the limitations of being human (310–12, 325–7). Like Jocasta, Teiresias can combine traditional values with sophisticated theory.

The dramatic effect of Teiresias' disquisition is hard to gauge. Critics are not agreed about whether or not the preceding Cadmus-Teiresias scene

(*Ba.* 170–209) is humorous and, if it is, how humorous and with what purpose. The answer to these questions must, to some extent, affect an audience's reception of the next scene, although even if the old men have just been ridiculed, the argument with Pentheus may produce a much different effect and challenge the audience to integrate the disparate impressions. Within the speech itself, the ingenuity may be too apparent and too labored to produce the impression of loftiness or sincerity which the speeches of Theseus and Jocasta make. What can be said is that the audience already knows that Pentheus' analysis of Dionysiac worship is incorrect, that the chorus endorses Teiresias' effort, and that the speech is another element in a spectrum of opinions of what Dionysus is and means. This spectrum includes the chorus' joyous, unreflecting acceptance of Dionysus' ecstasy and power (including belief in the tale which Teiresias tries to explain away: 94–8, 523–5); Cadmus' more matter-of-fact worship; Teiresias' intellectualist interpretation of the god; the first messenger's acceptance after witnessing wonders; Pentheus' maligning suspicions and rejection; and Cadmus' and Agave's final expressions of resentment and disapproval. The play as a whole may suggest that the nature of Dionysus justifies many of these attitudes, but that every human effort to come fully to grips with the god is doomed to the failure of partiality or blindness. Whether Teiresias strikes an audience as sympathetic or not, as impressive or not, his viewpoint shares with those of Theseus and Jocasta the feature of inadequacy: Teiresias is not so blind as Pentheus, but the course of events in the play proves that his understanding is not commensurate with the harsh realities of Dionysus' power.

The portrayed conflict of intellectual modernism with traditional beliefs is most striking in the incorporation of rational claims about the gods in tragedy, which were discussed in Chapter 5.[25] This feature is not merely a matter of letting in reforming voices that attempt to purify the gods of the embarrassing features conveyed in traditional stories. It highlights the earnest aspiration of humans for a moral equivalency between divine behavior and the behavior of good human beings, an aspiration frustrated by the full tragic world represented in the plays.

The approach advocated here for interpreting the optimistic rationalists can also guide us toward an interpretation of other insertions of intellectualized or sophistic discourse. A useful example is Hecuba's striking prayer in *Troades* 884–8:

---

[25] See above, pp. 169–74.

O you who carry the earth and who have your seat upon it,
whoever you are, hard to know by conjecture,
Zeus, whether the necessity of nature or the intelligence in men,
I pray to you: for treading with a silent step
you guide all mortal things to justice.

The paradoxical combination in the first line is very closely paralleled in a Hippocratic treatise,[26] and there are suggestions of speculative intellectual cosmologies in "necessity of nature" (*anangkē phuseōs*) and "the intelligence in men" (*nous brotōn*) in the third line. In the second line, although *dustopastos* ("hard to know by conjecture") is a rare word found only in Euripides among classical authors, the concept itself and the accompanying relative clause "whoever you are" are both traditional. A major dynamic of the play up to this point is the variation in reactions to the successive blows of misfortune.[27] The divine prologue presents a grim image of Troy abandoned by its last divine supporter.[28] Just before Menelaus appears to deliver the entrance-speech (860–83) that prompts Hecuba's prayer, the chorus takes as the major theme of its stasimon the abandonment of Troy by the gods who had favored it in the past.[29] Earlier, Hecuba had summoned the gods as witnesses, but as "allies who are bad at the role" (469), and several references had been made to Athena's grudge against Troy (524–41, 560–1, 597–600) and to the reversals of human fortune brought about by the gods (612–13). In the prayer at 884–8, however, Hecuba hails the justice of Zeus because Menelaus has just announced that Helen is to be executed for causing so much suffering and death. This is what changes her attitude so sharply and gives her the confidence to support Helen's request for a chance to defend herself so that she herself may respond in an *agōn logōn*. This confidence is mirrored in and reinforced by the intellectual confidence of the prayer: although she concedes the ultimate unknowability of Zeus, she is able to approach an insight through clever paradox and weighing of alternative possibilities. The rhetorical skill she will show in the *agōn* is prefigured in the prayer, and its solemnity and earnestness are designed to enhance the old woman's stature during this high point of her vicissitudes within the play. It must be very satisfying to an audience, on one level, to see the downtrodden Trojan queen combat the denial of responsibility produced by Helen, traditional object of blame in tragic treatments of the Trojan War, and to hear the gods acquitted of frivolous

---

[26] *De flatibus* 3: "the earth is the basis of this [sc. the air], and this is the vehicle that carries the earth, and nothing at all is empty of this."
[27] See above, pp. 77–9.   [28] See above, pp. 179–80.   [29] See above, pp. 138–9.

complicity. But it is wrong to think that Hecuba "wins" this debate. On another level, a viewer can recognize that Hecuba's pleading is as rhetorical and strained as Helen's. The clues in the text, in my judgment, point clearly to the very outcome that Hecuba fears, that Helen will not be punished at all, but will be reconciled with her husband and live out the fate portrayed in the *Odyssey*. And Hecuba's own arguments for purely human responsibility for the disastrous chain of events are at odds with the divine prologue, the choral odes, and the events staged in the first play of the same trilogy, *Alexandros*, as well as her own statements at 612–13 and 1240–2. The striking prayer is thus an ironic marker of a high point of illusory confidence and futile construction of order.

Unfortunately, just as in the case of many religiously unconventional or "atheistic" statements,[30] many of the other passages that might be collected to show the influx of speculative thought or sophistic ideas into Euripidean tragedy have survived only in the indirect tradition of quotations, so that we have either no sense of the context at all or only a very unreliable one. Even if we know the speaker and have a general outline of the plot of a lost play, we do not have enough detailed information to make the needed judgment of how a view fits into the dynamic of argumentation and characterization over the course of the whole drama.[31]

RHETORIC, AGŌN, AND CHARACTER

(1) Hippolytus *and* Medea: *expressing world-views*

The fullest development of the rhetorical mode in Euripides is, of course, in the characteristic scenes of debate that occur routinely in his plays. The scene-type, the *agōn logōn* ("contest of speeches"), has been studied in detail by several scholars, who have illustrated the formal characteristics and the varieties of configuration of the Euripidean *agōn* and debated the degree to which the *agōn* is or is not integrated into the structure and tone of each drama.[32] Here, I am more concerned to explore the relation of the rhetorical *agōn* to characterization: more specifically, how Euripides uses extended

---

[30] See above, pp. 173–4.
[31] Two especially striking examples lacking context: (for "scientific speculation") *Chrysippus* fr. 839, choral anapaests on the birth of all plant and animal life from Zeus's Aether and Earth, and the dissolution at the end of life into these two elements; (for "sophistic amoralism" on the same lines as later argued by Glaucon and Adeimantus in Plato, *Rep.* 358b–367e) *Ixion* fr. 426a, on having a reputation as a just man while actually committing any acts that bring profit.
[32] See esp. Duchemin 1945, Collard 1975b, Conacher 1981, Lloyd 1992.

speeches to characterize figures through competitive presentation of a world-view, how the contest of arguments is intertwined with a tragic questioning of both the sufficiency of language and the sufficiency of human constructs, and how rhetorical effort at times becomes so powerful as to redefine character or reveal its instability.

Hippolytus provides a good starting-point for observing both the competitive presentation of a world-view through extended speech and the problematization of rhetoric. Critics have well brought out the paradoxes of speech and silence in the play and the simultaneous uncontrolled power and futility of the spoken word.[33] There is, of course, a standard *agōn logōn* between Hippolytus and Theseus in the second half of the play, but equally important are the implicit contests of the first half of the play. Phaedra's great speech of self-presentation (373–430) is intended by her as an uncontested analysis of her situation and of her decision and is designed to demonstrate to herself and the chorus (and to the external audience) the ethical divide that separates Phaedra from unfaithful wives and other persons without high aspirations. The contrasts between this rationally articulate Phaedra of the iambic trimeter rhesis and the Phaedra(s) revealed in previous scenes, namely, the hysterical "lyric" one of 170–266 and the evasive one of the line-by-line exchange of 310–52, are very sharp. While the juxtaposition of the different modes[34] is sanctioned by the formal conventions of the genre, Euripides seems to go farther than others in asking his audience to accept that these modes are capacities within a single person and that the search for any simple unity of *ēthos* is futile.

It is the nurse who turns the second part of the first episode of *Hippolytus* into an *agōn*. In the first part of that episode (176–361), she brings the physically and emotionally afflicted Phaedra into the open air, cannot understand the trance-like utterings her mistress lets escape in the anapaestic exchange, and at the chorus' urging continues to press Phaedra until her desire for Hippolytus is revealed in the stichomythia. The nurse reacts with horror (353–61) and then falls silent as the chorus sings a short lyric in reaction to the shocking truth (362–72) and Phaedra delivers her great speech of self-presentation (373–430). At the end of Phaedra's speech, however, the nurse has recovered from her first reaction, and she now responds with a speech of almost equal length to challenge Phaedra's reasoning and world-view. Like so many speeches in Euripides, the nurse's is a complex blend of traditional maxims and techniques and modern twists.

---

[33] See esp. Knox 1952, Zeitlin 1985, Goff 1990.
[34] For an important discussion of such juxtapositions, see Di Benedetto 1971: 5–72.

The recognition of the goddess' great power (443–50), the acknowledgment of the inevitable mixture of troubles in a human life (471–2), and the emphasis on the commonality of human experiences (439, 459–61) are standard motifs of piety, forgiveness, and consolation, while mythological examples, too, are perfectly traditional (453–6). On the other hand, "modernity" is evident in the self-consciousness of the opening and closing, and in the citation of authorities (451–2, 465–6), and we see skillful rhetorical excess in the ironic inference at 441–2 ("then there will be no profit for those in love with others – or any who will be in the future – if they must die for it"), in the redescription of Phaedra's resistance as an insult to the gods (459–61, 473–5), and in the claim of divine authorization (456–7, 476). The nurse takes the principles of a more flexible, less heroic morality and misapplies them by overlooking or suppressing the specific details of Phaedra's situation: that she is a mortal female and married, and that the object of her desire is her stepson. What is dramatized in this pairing of speeches is the clash of alternative world-views, a clash that may be seen in other *agōnes*, but here there is also the question whether (as the story-pattern and perhaps memory of an earlier version suggest) Phaedra, in her weakened state, may give in to the nurse's persuasion. Euripides clearly raises that issue, since Phaedra refers to the nurse's arguments as "too fine arguments," "pleasing to the ears," and as shameful things "spoken well" (487, 489, 503, 505) and recognizes that she has been predisposed to weakness by her yearning (504–5).

Although spoken in the next episode, the tirade against women that Hippolytus delivers after he bursts into the open air to escape the nurse and her proposition (616–68) should also be read, I suggest, as comprising a virtual *agōn* with Phaedra's speech. Like her speech it purports to analyze the origin of evil in the lives of men, but Hippolytus fastens on woman as the source, projecting upon womankind a uniformity that misses the contrast of attitudes and aspirations that has just been revealed to the audience. Nor can Hippolytus be aware of the ways in which his speech echoes features of Phaedra's, such as disapproval of the facts of the world (386–7, 616–24; cf., however, also the nurse at 459–61), rejection of a particular class of misbehaving women with "I detest" (*misō*) in each case (413, 640), concern about women's conversations (384, 646–7), the problem of *sōphrosunē* (399, 413, 667), and concern with how guilty women face their husbands (415–18, 661–2). On the other hand, at least one rhetorical ploy of the speech is reminiscent of the nurse's: the argumentative self-consciousness of 627 ("by this proof is it obvious that"), followed by the excess of a one-sided interpretation of dowry (628–9, the father pays "in order to be rid of an evil"). Moreover, by projecting Hippolytus' construct of the world, the speech shows clearly how he stands outside of normal society, holding a view that makes him unsuited to any integration within it. Although his misunderstanding of Phaedra's nature is partly the result of his own *idée fixe* and partly the result of the nurse's machinations, Phaedra reciprocates the misunderstanding on a different basis. She is present to one side of the door (upstage) as he delivers his tirade (downstage center, with the nurse close to him), and she hears his speech. She takes in the intense hatred directed at her as much as at the nurse and all women, and the audience will easily infer that she is especially alert to the threat of his watching her confront her husband (661–2), since this matches her own fear of being seen in a shameful light. But when it comes to his statement that he will keep his oath and be silent about what the nurse has told him (656–60), she apparently hears but is unable to credit it, and hence the tragic plot moves forward.[35]

The more explicit, quasi-judicial *agōn* that occurs later in the play is also rich in the ironies of speaking from mistaken assumptions or of arguing before an uncomprehending listener. Yet apart from the miscommunication caused by the false accusation in Phaedra's letter and the oath-imposed silence of Hippolytus himself, the speeches of Theseus and Hippolytus also suggest a deeper, pre-existing gulf between father and son. Theseus accuses Hippolytus of religious charlatanry (948–57). He does not merely allege that Hippolytus has betrayed his ideals; he implies the abnormality and deceit of Hippolytus' whole chosen form of life, mockingly spitting out Hippolytus' favorite words, *sōphrōn* and *akēratos* (949), denying any special relationship with divinity and assimilating his worship to that of suspect non-civic sects. For his part, Hippolytus shows little comprehension of his father's point of view and includes statements in his self-defense that are ill suited to win him over. An apology about lack of skill in speaking, to judge from later private orations and Plato's *Apology*, was a standard topos in Athenian courts for inexperienced speakers (or speakers who wanted to project the *ēthos* of one unaccustomed to litigation). But instead of using the topos in its simple form, Hippolytus gives it an aristocratic (even oligarchic) turn, specifying the audience as "a mob" when he is addressing Theseus alone as father, king, and judge, and claiming the ability to speak well to the few, who are by implication also the wise, since the balancing example is

[35] A few scholars have suggested that Phaedra is not in fact present to hear Hippolytus' speech, but I do not accept this interpretation of the staging and the reassignment of *Hipp.* 669–79 to the nurse that it entails. On this dispute, see Halleran 1995: 200–1, with references to earlier discussions.

"those who are inferior in the eyes of the wise" (988–9). The argument from probability denigrates the beauty of Theseus' wife: "Was her body so superior in beauty among all women [sc. that I was likely to fall in love with her]?" (1009–10). Similarly, the monarchical power that Theseus enjoys (and of which he was an idealized example for the Athenians) is devalued by Hippolytus: "[Can anyone believe that I desired Phaedra] because kingship is welcome to men of good sense? Not at all, since monarchy corrupts the minds of all mortals to whom it is pleasing" (1013–15).[36] If we consider *Hippolytus* as a whole, we may say that it illustrates not only rhetorical contests of self-presentation that allow the audience to observe and interpret the world-views and *ēthos* of four striking characters, but also the frequent futility and moral instability of the verbal skills deployed in the extremities of tragic crises.

The *agōn* in *Medea* impressively dramatizes through rhetoric the fatal gulf between the antagonists of the play. Already as he enters (446–64), Jason gives evidence of the major contrast between himself and Medea: his smug assumption of a natural hierarchy of male over female and of the excellence of his own capacity to plan things out. In contrast, Medea has in previous scenes indicated her view of their relationship as one of equals bound by mutual pledges, and bases her whole argument here on the proper reciprocity (*charis*) to be expected among elite peers. Medea's speech is a small masterpiece of rhetorical invective, combining clear structure and self-consciousness with a justified and controlled display of emotion. The proem (465–74) features strongly emotive terms ("utterly base man," "unmanliness," "shamelessness") and vehement anaphora, but also evinces the analytic in the two explanatory clauses and in the insistence on distinction between terms (469–72). The second section of the speech (475–87) forms a kind of narration (Medea's services to Jason), but incorporates argumentative details (citation of witnesses against Jason in 476–7, comment on her misplaced good will in 485). In the third, directly argumentative section (488–515), Medea exposes the injustice of Jason's return for her favors, with lively variety (direct address, apostrophe to her own hand, ironical suppositions, sarcastic use of positive terms), ending with an echo of the opening of the narration. Finally, there is a typical concluding generalization in the form of an address to Zeus involving a critique of the ways of the world (516–19). Jason's speech answers Medea's in many details.

[36] The transmitted text of 1014 is corrupt, and I follow Barrett 1964 in assuming that the sense must have been more as less as translated here; I do not follow him in his suspicion that 1012–15 might be inauthentic.

Lines 522–5 are a self-conscious opening that carries invective against Medea's vehemence. Medea began with her role as savior (475–6), so Jason in 526–33 first diminishes this role, by attributing sole credit to Aphrodite and assigning Medea's action to compulsion rather than voluntary choice (cf. 483, 488). To Medea's claim of benefactions Jason next opposes (in 534–44) the benefits she has herself received from him. This is the most telling passage for the wide gulf between his understanding of the world and hers and for the challenge of the play to conventional thinking, as Jason takes for granted points that have already been convincingly denied by Medea and the chorus: the superiority of Greece and its laws and justice, the importance of being recognized as "wise/clever," the paramount value of reputation. After a self-conscious transition in 545–6, a long section (547–67) gives an extended reply to Medea's charge of betrayal, as Jason argues that his remarriage demonstrates multiple benefits and virtues. Finally, he reduces Medea's motivation to sexual jealousy alone (568–75), ending in a complaint about the arrangement of the world that answers her conclusion and restates the Hesiodic calumny that women are the source of evil for men's lives (*Theog.* 571–612, *Erga* 57–95). It is noteworthy that the mercantile language of profit, economics, and commerce is used insistently by Jason, in sharp contrast to Medea's more aristocratic concentration on salvation and on traditional values such as loyalty, *philia*, and adherence to oaths. He sees his relationship as one with measurable and finite obligations rather than in terms of the open-ended reciprocity implied by *charis*. Although, as the revenge-plot develops, Medea as revenger takes on more and more traits of her enemy, this *agōn* crystallizes the differences between Medea and Jason, and demonstrates to the audience how committed Jason is to his world-view,[37] a frame of mind that gives Medea an opening for the deception by which she punishes him.

(2) Alcestis *and* Hecuba: *shaping the self*

When we turn next to the confrontation of Admetus and his father Pheres in *Alcestis*, we can observe a tendency that seems to be characteristic of several Euripidean scenes across the full range of his extant oeuvre – the self-propelling impulse of a rhetorical case that seems to carry its speaker far beyond anything he or she previously espoused or recognized. I would suggest that the excess should not be interpreted as lying outside the

---

[37] That is, Jason's rhetoric should be accepted as "sincere" not as a hypocritical evasion of responsibility: cf. von Fritz 1959, and see below, pp. 297–8.

character, nor should it be minimized as simply due to "the rhetoric of the situation" (to use a famous phrase often repeated from A. M. Dale).[38] Rather, such excess should be regarded as a legitimate facet of the dramatic character, one that is revealed or even triggered by the extreme pressure of a hostile *agōn*. The resulting dynamic refashioning of the personality may pose a challenge to an audience's interpretation of character, forcing abandonment of the notion of a readily interpretable and unified *ēthos* and asking the audience to entertain complexity and lack of transparency.

In the third episode of *Alcestis* (606–740), Admetus leaves the palace with the bier conveying his wife's corpse to form a procession to the place of burial with the chorus. But his old father Pheres, the retired king, who had been invited to die for his son but refused, arrives to pay his respects to Alcestis. The old man's opening speech (614–28) is polite and respectful, as he makes himself a partner in his son's mourning and offers strong praise for Alcestis. His attitude becomes much different in the remainder of the scene, after Admetus rejects and blames him. I would argue that the shift in Pheres' position is more a sign of lack of depth and lack of perception in the initial position than evidence of its hypocrisy, and I suggest that it is the impulse of the argument itself that brings the clearer definition of Pheres' stance and thus of his character.

In reply to his father's initial polite approach, as the first half of the paired speeches, Admetus' attack (629–72) relies on two key concepts, *philia* and age. It is as close kin that Pheres comes to share the pain, but Admetus, by making into a mandatory feature of *philia* the ideal that one *philos* should be willing to die for another, regards Pheres' refusal to die for his son as a proof that the *philia* does not exist (hence the inference that he is not really the son of Pheres and his wife). In this argument, Admetus even refers to Alcestis as *othneia*, "an outsider to the family," on the assumption that the insider, Pheres, should have been even more willing to die for him than the outsider. And Admetus also repeatedly suggests that it is more suitable for the old to die than for the young, if a choice is at hand. His claims are indeed logical in terms of Greek ideas of kinship and age. It was an ideal to die in old age leaving behind a living son. But when laid out in a formal argument in favor of willing suicide for the old these claims become shocking. Just as in the plot as a whole the detailed formulation and presentation of the sacrifice of Alcestis for her husband undermine the surface charm of the exemplary tale, so here the impulse to articulate a position clearly and strongly produces the opposite result – a vision that casts routine assumptions into doubt and confuses

---

[38] Dale 1954: xxv.

judgment. For his part Pheres relies on the claim that it is neither an inherited tradition nor even a Greek custom that fathers should die on behalf of their sons: he lists the standard duties of a parent and asserts that he has fulfilled them. In one sense he is correct about Greek custom, since in everyday life such a conscious choice rarely or never arises. But Pheres' argument ignores the complexity of the issue. Among Greek notions about the role of the male in fighting a war is the idea that dying for one's children (and wife and aged parents) is a duty, and loyalty carried to the point of self-sacrifice is also an ideal expressed in stories and maxims. Apollo's intervention has created a unique situation in which various ideals and values, whose inconsistencies or contradictions could be glossed over in most circumstances, have their fault lines painfully exposed, thanks in large part to the rhetorical elaborations that the audience is required to interpret and assess.

This unsettling disruption of definitive judgment is especially characteristic of Euripides, although the same technique can be seen at times in Sophocles (especially, in *Philoctetes*). Sophists were known for their "contrary arguments," "overthrowing arguments," and "double arguments" (*antilogiai, kataballontes logoi, dissoi logoi*), and the *aporia*, agnosticism, or suspension of judgment that is associated with sophistic rhetoric is not far from the state of mind induced by many tragedies, although tragedy complicates the audience's reception by raising such high emotional and physical stakes for the dramatic participants and by inviting the audience to identify with them (at least intermittently) as well as to observe them more objectively. The case of *Hecuba* is worth pursuing in some detail, since there has been so much critical disagreement about the protagonist's moral stature. At one extreme she is viewed as suffering progressive degeneration because of her extreme sufferings and her violence; at the other, her revenge is understood to be more or less normalized by its conformity to widespread Greek notions.[39] Both of these interpretations suffer from excessive attachment to ideals of definitiveness and transparency, when the difficulty of judgment and the incommensurability of human character comprise, I would argue, much of the point of the drama. The interconnections and inconcinnities between the debate of the first part of the play and the rhetorical appeal and judicial *agōn* of the second part are crucial to bringing together the two actions that are often judged with disapproval as being quite separate by critics of an Aristotelian bent.[40]

---

[39] See Ch. 5, n. 98. In what follows I am largely in agreement with the balanced analysis of Mossman 1995.
[40] See above pp. 71–3.

Hecuba's first iambic utterance of the play immediately sets her into the rhetorically agonistic mode. She opens with "Alas! I am now faced, as it seems, with a great contest, full of lamentations and tears" (229–30). Although the topos of the "great contest" (*agōn megas*) often applies to non-verbal situations, and although the description that follows maintains Hecuba's role as *mater dolorosa*, the word *agōn* nevertheless may also remind the audience of more explicit internal acknowledgments of participation in an *agōn logōn*,[41] and the self-referential suggestion is confirmed when Hecuba later uses the phrase "I make this competitive speech/argument" (*tond' hamillōmai logon*, 271). The second half of the short speech (229–37) self-consciously sets the terms for Hecuba to interact verbally with Odysseus, and although there is corruption in the final couplet, the chosen words seem to allude to the practice of questioning and answering for which Socrates was famous and which was also a technique in which the sophists boasted of their ability.[42] The interrogation (239–48) turns out to be quite brief, focused on reminding Odysseus of a past event and extracting his admission that he supplicated Hecuba and used all manner of verbal appeals, so that Odysseus' admission may be the starting-point of Hecuba's rhesis (251–95). Reciprocity (*charis*) is the key idea, yet the speech actually postpones the development of this point. It begins with an indignant question that charges Odysseus with not reciprocating correctly and then almost dismisses the theme as a lost cause, shifting to a generalization about lack of *charis* in all "you politicians." These politicians are accused of not caring whether they harm "their friends" so long as they are saying what meets the approval of the multitude. Indirectly, then, Hecuba is already here claiming that one of the Greek leaders should consider her and hers to be *philoi*. The first full argument in the speech, however, is based on an appeal to justice, *to dikaion* (258–71). Hecuba questions how Polyxena can be the proper object of a retributive slaying desired by Achilles, since the girl herself did nothing bad to Achilles. That is, Hecuba implies that there is some limit of relationship beyond which one should not be held accountable along with other kin: Polyxena should not be made to pay for the acts of her brothers, Hector and Paris. This implication is relevant to Hecuba's own later action of killing Polymestor's sons, but it also meets with an immediate reapplication from Odysseus, who insists that his debt of reciprocity is to Hecuba alone and does not extend to her daughter (301–2).

---

[41] For instances of *agōn* and *hamilla* and similar expressions acknowledging the act of debating, see Lloyd 1992: 4–5.

[42] See, e.g., Plato *Gorg.* 447c5–8, *Prot.* 315c.

Hecuba's appeal for *charis* emphasizes exact payback,[43] and she in fact phrases the request in terms of Polyxena's preciousness to *her* (279–81). In reply, Odysseus cleverly limits his protection to Hecuba's body alone, excluding her feelings. On the other hand, when he speaks of the *charis* due to Achilles or any dead warrior, Odysseus sets no narrow constraint, but speaks as if it is utterly natural to include human sacrifice under the heading of what is due reward (though we are told earlier that the propriety was disputed in the Greek assembly, 118–19, 130–1). Odysseus frames his case in terms of the best course of policy for "cities," and this, along with the appeal to ethnic difference in his peroration (328–31), would have had a strong resonance for the original audience. But again, the clarity and excess of the rhetorical exposition of the case as well as the agonistic setting serve to highlight the uncomfortable fit of the general tenets to particular situations, casting doubt not only on specific beliefs, but on the usefulness of constructing them as universal propositions.

The revenge-action in the second half of *Hecuba* is tied to the sacrifice-action in the first half by the recurrence of the motif of supplication, but it is not only the scenic gesture or its institutional import that binds the parts together.[44] Again the issue of the limits of interpersonal connection is raised as a puzzle. In an unusually long sequence of self-directed speeches delivered away from Agamemnon (736–51), Hecuba first debates with herself whether she has any standing to appeal to Agamemnon: are they enemies to each other (*polemiān* 741, *dusmenes* 745), rendering any request futile? When she does begin her appeal and explains the identity of the corpse, she does not claim any personal hold on Agamemnon's concern, but Agamemnon in fact spontaneously shows sympathy (763, 783, 785) and horror at Polymestor's violation of trust as a host (775).[45] Hecuba's first argument cites universal law and the insult to the gods in Polymestor's action, and climaxes in an appeal for pity based on simple observation of Hecuba's vastly reduced condition (788–811). But Agamemnon draws away, without speaking. Hecuba interprets this behavior as a failure of her first attempt at persuasion, but Agamemnon's withdrawal and silence are not unambiguously readable and could betoken indecision or painful hesitation rather than rejection, as Hecuba so quickly concludes. Assuming failure, however, Hecuba critiques human culture in a passage with multiple levels of irony (814–19):

[43] Note the two *anti-* compounds in 272 and 275 and the repeated forms of *apait-*, "ask back," in 272 and 276.
[44] See above, p. 72.
[45] I take *ō tlēmon* in 775 as an angry apostrophe to Polymestor, but some take it as a sympathetic address to Hecuba (Gregory 1999: 136).

Why then do we mortals toil over and pursue
all other realms of learning in the proper way,
but when it comes to persuasion, which alone has supreme power for mankind,
we don't trouble ourselves particularly to learn it
to its final goal, paying fees for instruction, so that it would be possible on occasion
to persuade others of whatever point one wishes and get their consent as well?

On one level, this analysis divides the heroic world of the play from the contemporary world of the audience, in which some people are in fact paying special attention to the art of persuasion (and sometimes claiming the ability to make any argument successful) and others are paying fees to learn it. Hecuba's tone of regret might be read as implying praise for the actual progress of human arts. At another level, the complaint makes emotional sense (since Hecuba has failed at this point in two desperate appeals, one to Odysseus and one to Agamemnon), but not intellectual sense, since the power of Odysseus' rhetoric was clear both in the Greek assembly as reported and in his speech on stage, and Hecuba herself both before and after this observation makes well-organized and well-argued speeches. The poet has made her, like his other characters, a well-educated speaker of just the kind she seems to want mortals to be. But the overall context shows that Hecuba's hope for proper training is itself utopian: persuasion can never be the sole sovereign power she envisions, for it may exist on both sides of any debate, and its success will still vary and depend on the imponderables of human nature – character, emotion, breadth or narrowness of vision of the speaker and of the audience.

After this interlude of cultural criticism and a renewed acknowledgment of her weakness, Hecuba turns to a more personal argument involving *charis*. Here she again uses the concept of kinship to claim an extension of *charis* from the obvious recipient to a more remote one, as she did earlier with Odysseus. Her daughter Cassandra is now the concubine of Agamemnon. It is a natural association to suggest that a relationship of *charis* may exist between a man and his concubine, based on their sexual union (itself capable of being called *charis*). But in an actual marriage, the interfamilial ties would be much broader, involving an expectation of good will extending to parents, siblings, and other kin of both of the married pair. Thus Hecuba suggests that any *charis* Agamemnon feels toward Cassandra ought to be extended to her, and also to Polydorus. Marking this as her most specific and urgent point with the formula "hear, now" in 833, Hecuba says that Polydorus is to be regarded as a kinsman (*kēdestēs*) for whom Agamemnon will be doing a favor. Yet she is tactfully restrained in making this claim, and in her peroration emphasizes instead the gap in status between Agamemnon ("master, greatest light for the Greeks") and herself ("the old woman") and his obligation to serve justice and punish the wicked (841–5). Hecuba is ultimately successful enough for her purposes. Agamemnon cites pity, the act of supplication, justice, and Polymestor's offense against the gods as grounds for wanting to be of help, and refers to *charis* to Cassandra solely as the motivation he fears the other Greeks will infer if he acts openly. To save himself from this danger, he even tacitly rejects the notion of any tie of his own to Polydorus: "the army counts this man [Polymestor] as a friend and the dead man [Polydorus] as an enemy: if this corpse here is dear/akin *to you*, that is a separate matter and not shared with the army" (858–60).[46]

In the judicial *agōn* that occurs after the blinding of Polymestor and the killing of his sons, Agamemnon serves as arbiter between the Thracian king and Hecuba. Polymestor is an effective first-person narrator of what happened in the tent, but surrounding his narration is an argument that is neither elaborate nor wholly sound. He is a villain who has in fact, for a change, been denied effective rhetoric, although he self-consciously introduces his argument with "hear why I killed him, how rightly and with wise/clever forethought" (1136–7). His ultimate claim is that he killed Polydorus as a favor to Agamemnon (*charis*, 1175), and he labels Polydorus as Agamemnon's enemy at beginning and end of the argument (1138, 1176). But his initial explanation of his reasoning undercuts the claim of service, since he highlights the personal advantage to the Thracians of avoiding any repeat of the Greek assault on Troy (1142–4). Despite these weaknesses, Polymestor's speech nevertheless continues the dialectic on the nature and limits of *charis* and enmity. We find Hecuba enmeshed at the outset of her reply in the shifting nature of human judgment and human ideals. Previously, she wished for supreme persuasive power and faulted mankind for not pursuing this skill sufficiently, but now in her exordium (1187–95) she insists that the tongue should not be stronger than deeds, in a construction that implies that the tongue is in fact stronger. This is similar to the strategy used by Cleon in Thucydides' portrayal of the Mytilene debate: himself a very effective speaker in the Athenian assembly, Cleon attacks the use and enjoyment of opposing

---

[46] In "to you" I follow the text of the manuscripts in *Hec.* 859, accepted by Diggle; many critics, however, prefer Elmsley's emendation "to me," which would make Agamemnon in fact accept Hecuba's stretch of the term *kēdestēs* (Gregory 1999: 147; against her claim that "it would be nonsensical for Agamemnon to phrase Polydorus' φίλος-connection with Hecuba in hypothetical terms," I would cite the similar conditional used argumentatively in *IA* 499–500: "if you [Agamemnon] have any share in the oracles about your daughter, let me [Menelaus] not have a share").

arguments when it suits his policy (3.38). While Thucydides intends his reader to view Cleon in an unfavorable light, in *Hecuba* it seems clear that the balance of an audience's sympathy would be with the Trojan queen and that the audience would tend to welcome Hecuba's admonition rather than view her as hypocritical. In retrospect, or in a more detached portion of the observing mind, however, one may well note the inconsistency as a comment on the fallibility of human constructs of understanding.

Another shift is evident in the theme of *charis*: where Hecuba had striven earlier to establish a claim to *charis* between herself and Odysseus and herself and Agamemnon, she now denies the very possibility of such a relationship between a Greek and a non-Greek (1199–1205). Does an audience infer that Hecuba has learned a bitter and cynical truth from her previous experience, and so has changed her position? Or that she is unscrupulously adopting any position that suits her case – an indication, perhaps, of moral degradation? Or is it better to say that the shifting ground of argumentation is not a problem of individual character but of general human belief, psychology, and behavior under the pressures of severe testing and scrutiny, and that the argument fashions the characters rather than vice versa?

Hecuba's peroration is similarly puzzling. It strongly summarizes the moral claims against Polymestor as if moral standards were utterly clear and it ends with a very blunt admonition, despite the tacked-on disclaimer: "we'll say [sc. if you side with Polymestor] you yourself take delight in evil men, being such yourself. But I do not speak insultingly of my master" (1236–7). An audience member could interpret this in the sense that by speaking so sharply to Agamemnon Hecuba is here assisting the pretense of non-involvement that the king wants to project for his fellow Greeks, in which case there is some insincerity in the lines. I suggest it is better to regard the rhetoric as sincere and to see once again that its excess is built into the nature of the articulate use of language that Euripides portrays as inherent in human beings. The enthusiastic articulation of the view reshapes Hecuba's personality, which is no more (nor less) unstable than anyone else's.

(3) Iphigenia in Aulis *and* Orestes: *instability and self-delusion*

As we have argued in several of the above examples, rhetorical displays contribute to a dialectic in which not only moral positions and assumptions about the world are destabilized, but even the possibility of a self-consistent individuality is brought into question. Even in Sophocles, with figures such as Ajax, Antigone, and Oedipus, who are often thought of as individuals very sure and unwavering in their *ēthos*, the different modes and moments of their self-presentation are seen to undermine any completely intelligible fixity of character. Euripides exploits rhetorical display to intensify such problems of interpretation. Like the sophistic "double arguments" (*dissoi logoi*) that create *aporia*, his plays often offer double visions through the characters' competing speeches. Perhaps the greatest intensification of this technique is seen in the experimental drama on which Euripides was working when he died, *Iphigenia in Aulis*. There are many uncertainties about the coherence and authenticity of the surviving text of this play,[47] but it seems probable to me that the bulk of the first episode is a polished product of Euripides' own hand.[48] In this episode, two formal debates of the brothers Agamemnon and Menelaus are separated by the arrival of news that changes the circumstances: Iphigenia and her mother will soon be in the Greek camp, and their arrival can no longer be prevented. Menelaus enters first, arguing with the messenger to whom Agamemnon had entrusted his second letter to his wife, which Menelaus has intercepted (303–16). When Agamemnon emerges from his tent, an unusual *agōn logōn* begins: the angry line-by-line exchange (317–33) precedes the longer speeches, and the meter is trochaic tetrameter rather than iambic trimeter. Menelaus' first extended speech flows almost seamlessly from this dialogue, which ends with Agamemnon attacking Menelaus' glib tongue and Menelaus attacking his brother's changeable mind and betrayal of friendship.

In the first longer speech by Menelaus, these faults of Agamemnon become the principal topic, as Menelaus uses a circumstantial narration to show two instances. The first (337–49) describes Agamemnon's imperious isolation as chosen leader after the affability and accessibility of his campaign for leadership. Menelaus' hammering repetitions of the word *philos* bring out the selfish or self-regarding aspect of the bond, which is rarely so openly acknowledged. There are topoi on the theme that true friends are those who stick by one in times of adversity, or those who behave with the same loyalty whether one is present or not, near or far. Menelaus' variation, however, displays a curious inversion: "then most of all one should be steadfast toward one's friends, when one is enjoying good fortune and most able to help them" (347–8). The second narration (350–65) presents

---

[47] See Ch. 1, n. 93.
[48] I refer here particularly to the dialogue and longer speeches of Menelaus and Agamemnon (the messenger's speech is much more problematic); I thus do not accept the criterion by which Kovacs 2003 assesses original and later content in this episode, whereby he concludes that *IA* 469–537 are not Euripidean.

Agamemnon's behavior at Aulis, alleging that his ambition overrode all other concerns, that he was pleased and relieved and fully willing to follow Calchas' instruction that Iphigenia be sacrificed. The partiality of Menelaus' argument is obvious, as it puts all its weight on *philia* between the warriors and expresses indignation at the idea of refusing to be murderer of one's daughter. Rhetorical excess is matched to moral self-delusion, as we have seen before. The sententious peroration (366–75) is more problematic in text and authenticity, but some portion of it is probably genuine. The pompous generalization does not contribute directly to the particular argument with Agamemnon, but its presence may show instead the moral obtuseness of Menelaus, as he assimilates this failure of follow-through to political problems of another kind. He also laments the effect on "poor Greece" of not having its chance against the barbarians, introducing in a dubious context a motif that will be taken up later by Agamemnon, and then decisively adopted by Iphigenia.

Agamemnon's reply in this first *agōn* (378–401) opens and closes with self-conscious comments about the brevity, propriety, and self-evidence of what he has to say. He defends his own good sense in reconsidering his decision and accuses Menelaus and the other Greeks of poor judgment or madness, and he briefly condemns the idea of sacrificing his daughter in the very terms that Clytemnestra and Iphigenia will use later (399: "lawless and not just"). This sounds like the speech of a confident man, and of one who smoothly adopts an air of calm and moderation while delivering a stinging rebuke to others. The agonistic setting of rhetorical display has, as it were, given to Agamemnon a more decisive voice than he apparently had in the opening scene of the play, if there is any reflection of genuine Euripides in the image of his tortured doubts about whether to send the second letter or not.

Perhaps there is, however, something mildly off-key or unnatural about this speech, since it is spoken in tetrameters rather than the trimeters that were standard for tragic speeches of this sort.[49] In any case, after the dialogue has settled back into iambic trimeters and word arrives that Iphigenia has arrived at the Greek camp, Agamemnon is shown articulating a much different stance. Euripides clearly alludes to the famous lyric narrative of Agamemnon's dilemma and Iphigenia's sacrifice in the parodos of Aeschylus' *Agamemnon*: the telling details are the yoke of necessity (*Agam.* 218, *IA* 443), the checking of tears (*Agam.* 204, *IA* 451–2), the imagined curse of his daughter (*Agam.* 235–7, *IA* 463–4), and the antithesis of alternatives described in similar terms (*Agam.* 206–8, *IA* 451–2). The difference is that Aeschylus' Agamemnon, once he has decided, is pictured by the chorus as

---

[49] On trochaic tetrameters see n. 55 below.

changed and hardened with boldness, while this Agamemnon is preoccupied with his face or status *vis-à-vis* others, both the Greek mob and his wife and daughter. He no longer speaks of law and justice, but presents himself as outfoxed by the divine power guiding events (a *daimōn* that "proved to be cleverer than my own clever machinations," 444–5). No fewer than eight lines are devoted to a sententious consideration of how his status precludes crying over his troubles, though failure to react with open grief is also shameful. Finally, his passivity is marked by the double use of the phrase "has destroyed me," in 456 of Clytemnestra's arrival and in 467 of Paris' abduction of Helen.

Ironically, once Agamemnon has abandoned his resolve to resist, Menelaus announces in a carefully framed speech (473–503) that he has been won over to the position of Agamemnon's earlier speech. The speech begins with an oath of sincerity, the words backed up by the staged gesture of clasped hands, and it ends with a third explanation of the change of mind (500–3, after 477–9 and 489–90). It is true that Menelaus' shift does not in fact cost him anything, as he is still likely to get what he sought before and now frees himself of some odium in his brother's eyes, and that the speech includes a hint that he might be aware of the futility of his new opinion (498–9: "But if *you* have some involvement with the oracle about your daughter, let *me* have no part in it: I cede my share to you."). Thus, for an audience, a cynical interpretation of his behavior cannot be ruled out.[50] But the way Menelaus continues to resist in the following line-by-line exchange (513–27) points in the direction of "sincerity" instead, in the sense that the whole sequence of speeches and shifts may suggest that the lability of behavior and argument is broadly endemic to human nature and human exploitation of *logos* rather than a character trait limited to a few figures.

Whatever the exact effect of the exchanges of the first episode, the sense of fluidity and instability affects the later verbal confrontations. Clytemnestra's long speech accusing and dissuading her husband (1146–208) contains both allusions to future events known to the audience from other plays and some ad hoc mythological innovation (1148–54),[51] but it also matches Agamemnon's own earlier arguments at a few points, making the alteration of his stance more noticeable. Both exploit the notion that the gods are *sunetoi*, "intelligent," and so will not actually approve foolish or abnormal actions by requiring the suitors to keep their oath to Menelaus or by showing favor to a man who has killed his own daughter (394a–95, 1189–90). And both question why damage to their own family should be endured to benefit

---

[50] This cynical interpretation was already espoused by Erasmus in 1507 (Waszink 1969: 270).
[51] Gibert 2005.

Menelaus' family (396–9, 1201–5). The sharpest change of mind in the drama,
however, is that of Iphigenia,[52] which recapitulates the shifting seen earlier in
Menelaus and Agamemnon. This dramatic coup should, I suggest, be viewed
in terms of a kind of automatism of character-shaping rhetorical elaboration
that asks an audience both to appreciate the noble gesture and suspect that it
involves some self-delusion.

In her final long rhesis at *Iphigenia in Aulis* 1368–401, Iphigenia justifies
her decision to go willingly to be sacrificed by employing many of the same
motifs of bravery, nobility, and fame seen in the cases of other sacrificial
females: Alcestis, the daughter of Heracles in *Heracleidae*, and Polyxena in
Hecuba.[53] Inescapable constraints condition the maiden's decision, but
within those constraints she seeks to accomplish her death "gloriously,"
avoiding "the ignoble" (1376). Her service to Greece will produce "blessed
fame" (1383–4). She rejects "excessive love of life" (1385) and assimilates
herself to the males born to serve a common cause as soldiers (1386–91).
What is striking about the motifs here, however, are the layers of irony that
exist for an audience. One layer derives from the very prominence of the
volte-face between the decidedly unheroic conclusion of Iphigenia's previous rhesis and the tenor of this speech. At 1250–2 she had concluded her
plea for her life with "To enjoy this light of life is the sweetest thing for
mortals, and what lies below is nothing. Only a madman prays to die. It is
better to live miserably [*kakōs*, with an unavoidable hint of "basely"] than to
die nobly." Another layer derives from the positioning of her idealistic
sentiments within the dramatized world of ambition, moral ambivalence,
and irrational desire of the male characters and the unseen Greek army.
A third aspect is the mythological and literary tradition. On the one hand,
that tradition (in the *Oresteia* and in earlier plays of Euripides) reinforces
the competing idea of the impropriety and injustice of the victimization
of Iphigenia, which had also been starkly expressed in earlier scenes by
Agamemnon, Menelaus, and Clytemnestra as well as Iphigenia herself. On
the other, it provides a counterpoint that undermines Iphigenia's argument
for female deference to males. Arguing that she must not cause danger to
Achilles' life for the sake of her own, she states: "This man should not
involve himself in battle with all the Argives, nor die, for the sake of a
woman. A single man is of more value than countless women, as far as

[52] This change of mind was already criticized in Aristotle (*Poetics* 15.1454a31–2) and has been the object
of discussion ever since. Two useful recent contributions (with references to many others) are Foley
1985: 65–105 and Gibert 1995: 202–55.
[53] See pp. 264–70 below for discussion of these examples.

looking on the light of life is concerned" (1392–4). Yet an audience is aware that Achilles will die for the sake of Helen, and before his death he will be in conflict with all the Argives because of Briseis. And since memories of the *Oresteia* were evidently quite alive in the late fifth century,[54] an audience could also think of the important motif there of the death of countless men for the sake of one woman.

Finally, the metrical form of the rhesis, in trochaic tetrameters instead of iambic trimeters, may give Iphigenia's speech a different coloring from the usual formal speech of self-sacrificial resolution. Euripides seems to be experimenting in *Iphigenia in Aulis* with the potential of trochaic tetrameters to modulate the pace and tone of dialogue toward the excited or even the feverish.[55] Earlier, when Menelaus and the old servant enter arguing and physically struggling to wrest sole possession of the letter, the scene begins with iambic trimeter stichomythia (303–16), but when Agamemnon emerges in response to the old man's cries, the argumentative stichomythia between the brothers is in trochaic tetrameters, and the meter carries over into an angry *agōn logōn* (317–401). A few scenes later, the old man's intrusion upon Clytemnestra and Achilles to reveal the true situation also features a shift to trochaic tetrameters (in single-line exchange 855–916, following on the couplet-exchange in iambic trimeters before the old man comes out, 819–54), and the more excited meter then carries over into Clytemnestra's rhesis of supplication to Achilles (900–16). In the scene of Iphigenia's new decision, the trochaic tetrameters begin at 1338 when Iphigenia sees Achilles and a crowd of men approaching in haste, and the dialogue soon turns into rapid shared-line exchange (*antilabē,* the most animated form of dialogue). This *antilabē* (1341–68) is conducted between Clytemnestra and Achilles, since Iphigenia falls silent when the men arrive. After more than twenty-five lines of silence, Iphigenia begins her rhesis in mid-line at 1368, snatching Clytemnestra's turn in the exchange and then maintaining the trochaic tetrameters for over thirty lines. A possible implication of this technique for the audience's reception of the speech is that Iphigenia is swept up emotionally in her new perception that her position is an opportunity for

---

54 Many scholars assume that the *Oresteia* or individual plays from it were reperformed in the last third of the fifth century, providing direct theatrical experience to the audience of Old Comedy for the passages in which Aeschylus was alluded to or quoted, as well as a special resonance for the variations that Sophocles and especially Euripides played on the themes of the Aeschylean classic. For such reperformance see Dover 1993: 23, Olson 2002: 69 (with refs.).

55 On the use of the trochaic tetrameter in tragedy, with references to earlier treatments, see Mastronarde 1994: 319–20.

patriotism,[56] almost in the way that Evadne is shown in *Supplices* carried along to extraordinary action by an extreme interpretation of the ideal of wifely loyalty.[57]

In accepting her fate, Iphigenia uses all the skills of human rhetoric (freely granted, as we have seen, at need to characters of all ages and statuses in Euripidean tragedy) to put the best possible face upon it, thus consolidating her own resolve and attempting to win over Achilles to immediate acquiescence and Clytemnestra to long-term resignation. The ultimate effect of Iphigenia's change of mind is complex: the trajectory of the plot and myth and the motifs of fame, bravery, and service to others may make an audience welcome Iphigenia's solution as generous and idealistic, but it would also be hard to ignore the circumstances and details that imply that the ideals have slipped out of control and are in service to a doubtful goal, and that the human capacity for verbal reasoning is sometimes indistinguishable from the capacity for self-deception.

Iphigenia in Aulis thus thematizes the process of decision-making and the accompanying articulation of reasons and values. Achilles' various speeches perhaps have a role in destabilizing the surface impression of Iphigenia's decision, for he, too, seems to lurch from one idea to the next and expresses uncertainty whether Iphigenia can really live up to what she says when the moment of sacrifice arrives. Unfortunately, several of Achilles' speeches are among the passages about which critics have expressed more serious doubt, so it is dangerous to base an interpretation of Euripidean craft upon them.[58]

The corrosive portrayal of human decision-making and of the articulation of reasoning and values is even more striking in *Orestes*. Again, there is a dialectic of alternative views expressed in different scenes of the play as well as the characteristic Euripidean shifting or destabilizing of the audience's sympathy. In the first movement of the play, Orestes and Electra are presented sympathetically, partly by their own insistence on regret, and partly by the contrast of their misery with the prosperity of Helen and

---

[56] Another possibility to be considered is whether the meter might lend her speech a quasi-oracular authority. Neoptolemus' sudden use of dactylic hexameters in Soph. *Phil.* 839–42 is a clear case of this kind of effect, but with a meter much more naturally associated with the oracular. For the emotional tenor of the meter of Iphigenia's rhesis, compare also Cassandra's trochaic tetrameter conclusion to her argumentative/prophetic farewell rhesis in *Tro.* 424–61 (this is half in iambic trimeter and half in trochaic tetrameter, with predictions of the future in both parts of this speech, and the shift from iambic to trochaic seems to express intensification of emotion and hint at mantic possession, in line with the allusions in this speech to Cassandra's actions and speeches in Aesch. *Agam.*); and the tetrameters of Dionysus (in disguise as the Lydian stranger) in *Ba.* 604–41, where there is an uncanny contrast between the agitation of the Pentheus who is described and the calm the speaking Dionysus claims for himself.

[57] On Evadne see below, pp. 268–9.   [58] See Ch. 8, n. 40.

Menelaus. Orestes is most reasonable when he is on his sickbed, but displays a different sickness, verbal and moral, the more active he becomes in argument and action. Sickness of the tongue is already retrojected to the founder of the family, Tantalus, in the prologue (10). It is the very act of responding to Tyndareus and Menelaus that brings Orestes to alter his initial stance. At the opening of the second episode, Menelaus is very cool and noncommittal in his initial dialogue with Orestes (385–447), and he departs 340 lines later in a similar attitude of caution. For a very short passage in between (481–90), Menelaus speaks more supportively, when the initial challenge presented by Tyndareus induces him to resist and articulate a position. He defends his loyalty to his kin and claims that following his own inclination (against the restrictive cultural norm cited by Tyndareus) is a token of freedom among the "wise." If one point of the episode is to show Menelaus' indecision and weakness, another is to show Tyndareus at the opposite extreme. In his first speech (491–541), he maintains that good and bad (*ta kala … kai ta mē kala*) are obvious to all and that the pursuit of the Furies proves the gods have already condemned Orestes and nothing more need be said. The effective point he makes against vendetta and his praise of *nomos* and legal process appeal to an optimistic view of Greek polis-civilization that would strike a sympathetic chord with the audience. But his view is undercut by the anachronism of the assumption of legal process, by his later vehemence, and by the portrayal of the political realities of the assembly-trial in the later messenger speech.

Whereas speakers like Medea, Jason, Phaedra, and Hippolytus seem in their major *agōn*-speeches to be giving expression to a view of life that has long formed the basis of their behavior, other Euripidean speakers, as we have seen, give the impression of voicing a position almost for the first time, with the dynamism of the argument redefining the character. So here with Orestes in the first episode of *Orestes*. His first long speech (544–601)[59] begins by dismissing the abashed reticence before his grandfather that he had described in detail at the sight of Tyndareus' approach (459–69). The argument proper begins with an admission of the mixed moral nature of his act (546–7), but then concentrates on exculpation, offering a sequence of

---

[59] Both the OCT of Diggle 1981–94 and the commentary of Willink 1986 go too far, in my opinion, in deleting passages of *Orestes* as inauthentic additions. The play was very popular in antiquity in the theater and in schools and there are indeed interpolations in the text, but I would acknowledge fewer than these editors do and agree more often with the editions of West 1987 and Medda 2001. In the speech *Or.* 544–604, I would accept deletion only of 602–4 (the couple 546–7 should be transposed to follow 550).

diverse points. Throughout, Orestes evokes key arguments offered in Aeschylus' *Choephori* and *Eumenides*, but in the first half (551–63), the very brevity of the evocation makes the biological argument (553–4), which was already artificial and indecisive for the human jurors in *Eumenides*, too bald. While the first section ends with another acknowledgment of the godlessness of matricide (563), the second section (564–601) moves in the direction of more confident disavowal of wrongdoing. It begins with the self-conscious introduction "hear how …" that is typical of speakers pushing an extreme point, and ends with the stronger conclusion that the matricide was "well done." Arguments pile up in quick succession: benefit to Greece, keeping women in their place, punishing his mother only when she failed to punish herself, blaming Tyndareus for begetting Clytemnestra, fearing Furies sent by his father for inaction, citing Telemachus and Apollo in succession but to different effects. This style suggests a speaker trying on almost every possible role, some traditional and some novel.[60]

Orestes' argumentation becomes even more excessive after Tyndareus departs at 629 and he is faced with the signs of Menelaus' mental discomfort. Menelaus gives up his internal debate at Orestes' request and implies that this is a moment when speech is better than silence: "go ahead, you're right, sometimes silence can be better than speech, and sometimes speech better than silence" (638–9). But Orestes' proem sounds an odd note: against a tradition in which lack of elaboration and complication in a speech is usually identified with sincerity and truth, he generalizes that long speeches are superior to short ones (640–1). As a whole the speech 640–79[61] explores a legitimate claim to reciprocation, but the extreme formulation of the exchange is again problematic. Orestes openly calls it a swap of one "injustice" for another; makes a frigid comparison of ten years of favor to one day of favor asked in return; and generously declines to ask that Menelaus kill his daughter to make things even with Agamemnon. His use of rhetorical polar opposition for emphasis in 665–8 casts a very self-regarding light on the concept of *philia*: it is common enough to test friends by whether they stick with one in adversity, but here the claim is instead "If you have good fortune, why do you need friends?" (667).[62] The premise of the appeal in 669–72 is

---

[60] Cf. Zeitlin 2003.

[61] I accept the deletion of 663 and 667, but not Diggle's removal of 644–5; 651 can perhaps be kept in its transmitted position, but the transposition that puts it after 657 may be right.

[62] This is also a kind of shameless admission of the reasonableness of behavior that is elsewhere criticized as a moral failing, namely, valuing your friends when you are in need of their help but later failing to show gratitude for their help when you are out of your difficulties (*Peliades* fr. 608).

likewise off-key: Orestes tries to beseech Menelaus in the name of Helen, whom he loves, but his reputation in all of Greece as fond of his wife is in fact often a criticism of his weakness. The final appeal for salvation, offered as a universal human goal, continues a theme set up from the outset of the play, but here it is moving in the direction of the desperate clinging to life by any means that determines the last part of the play. The couplet 644–5 is important to this development, since it carries the roots of the term *philopsychia*, "excessive love of life, cowardice": "I don't mean money [sc. when I ask you to pay my father back what you owe]; it's as good as money if you save my life [*psychē*], the very thing that is the dearest [*philtata*] to me of all I have." The *agōn* sequence ends with Menelaus explaining his decision in 682–716.[63] The sententiousness and lack of exact appositeness (esp. in lines like 694–5, 703) may be interpreted as rhetorical cover for Menelaus' embarrassment at his inability and unwillingness to offer any real assistance. Even while being so evasive and inactive, Menelaus remains committed to his self-presentation as one of the "wise" (695, 710, 716).

Later in the play, the process of debate itself is subjected to severe questioning. The messenger[64] (*Or.* 866–956) comments overtly on the debate in the Argive assembly, which is clearly meant to remind the original audience of contemporary Athenian practice. This speaker's viewpoint is favorable to Orestes and reflective of a humble peasant farmer class that dwells outside the corrupt urban setting. He editorializes about the speakers, the speeches, and their reception, revealing hidden motivations and political maneuvering. Yet his account is not entirely coherent, as he admits that Orestes did not convince the majority "even though he seemed to speak well" (943). The primary meaning of "speak well" in a context like this is "to make a correct argument or suggestion" which the audience accepts as such, but here the majority is not won over. Is this "speaking well" then really a minority opinion of Orestes' friends, or is there a suggestion, based on another common meaning of "speak well," that the assembly approved esthetically or technically of Orestes' speech (as Cleon in Thucydides 3.38 accuses the Athenians of enjoying speeches) but could easily isolate those aspects from the moral or judicial decision before them? A further complication of reception is that the speaker places within his narrative (917–29) another humble farmer like himself, emphasizing his purity of character and wholesomeness as a

---

[63] Four separate deletions (of nine lines in all) are accepted in the OCT, but I would retain all the lines of this speech, believing the defects of style and argument to be deliberately characterizing.

[64] In the messenger speech *Or.* 866–956, I would delete 906–13, 916, and 933; more extensive cuts are favored by Willink 1986 and Diggle 1981–94.

citizen. Yet this speaker is the one with the most extreme view, matching that of Orestes very closely: he declares that Orestes deserves a crown and that the matricide protects the status of husbands and their role as warriors who leave their homes and fight for the city. One way of reading the social and political context of tragedy as relevant to its interpretation might suggest at this point that this is the common-sense view of the Athenian on the street and that accordingly this opinion is particularly validated. Some critics have even suggested that Euripides (here and with the farmer in *Electra*) positively endorses representatives of the humble farming class against the urban populace.[65] To be sure, passages like this do exploit powerful cultural stereotypes of country vs. city and farming vs. trade or handicrafts, but not in a way that leaves the stereotypes unexamined. Here, the onesidedness of the farmer's opinion within the context of competing interpretations and after the repeated admissions of the moral perplexity of the simultaneously just and unjust murder of Clytemnestra ought to cast doubt on any view that simply agrees with the farmer.[66] As with the farmer in *Electra* or the shepherds in *Iphigenia in Tauris* (264–74), the position of the unreflective, decent common man is subjected to some irony. The most balanced opinion in the debate is not that of the "uncorrupt peasant farmer," but that of Diomedes (898–900), who suggests (without elaboration being supplied by the narrative) that the course of piety is not to execute the murderers, but exile them (the position offered as the civilized ideal by Tyndareus in 512–15 before he was exasperated into advocating harsher punishment for Orestes).

The discourse in the episode of mourning and plotting 1018–245 also contributes to the dialectic of viewpoints and values that runs through the play. Here only two points need be considered briefly. First, in 1131–52 Pylades offers his reasoning for the plot against Helen. The justifications are similar to those that were claimed for killing Clytemnestra: Helen is unchaste and an indirect "killer of many." Her unchaste sister was a direct killer of only one man, but Orestes bore a special responsibility to avenge his father, while avenging the multitude of victims of the Trojan War does not fall directly on Orestes and Pylades. The expectation of a warm welcome for the murder flies in the face of the diversity of opinion just shown in the assembly. As we have seen elsewhere, the speaker is endowed with the skill

[65] Most recently Matthiessen 2002: 218; earlier, e.g., Di Benedetto 1971: 193–211.

[66] The problem is recognized by Lloyd 1992: 127–8, who suggests the implication may be that the assembly is such a corrupt venue that it "makes it impossible even for an admirable character to do justice to a case like that of Orestes." I would suggest instead that both the "admirable" character of the quoted speaker and the moral judgment of the reporting character are ironized.

to detect and push hard the possible arguments for a position, but is not endowed with a broad enough perspective or good enough memory to detect the partiality, and hence weakness, of his own case. Second, in 1155–76 Orestes generalizes again on *philia*, but also shifts his view of a noble, free man's death: before the plotting, it was noble and worthy of Agamemnon for them to face their death quietly and bravely, but now that manner of death is called "slavish" and what is worthy of Agamemnon's high status is the murder of Helen and whatever else may give some hope of escaping their sentence.

To sum up, the importance of rhetorical elements in Euripidean drama is at least threefold. First, rhetorical contests of speeches underscore fateful gaps in communication and understanding between characters. Second, the sharpness and excess or exaggeration of intensively developed rhetorical discourse bring to the fore the difficulties of firm judgment, thus marrying sophistic-era *aporia* to the traditional questioning of humans' power to understand and control the course of their actions and lives, and undermining confidence in simple moral universals. And third, the effort of rhetorical formulation of a competing position may at times seem to take on a life of its own and reshape character, revealing the instability of the human soul and restating in late fifth-century terms the ephemeral nature of man.

CHAPTER 7

Women

In previous chapters, we have seen how various techniques and patterns related to structural strategies, the chorus, the gods, and rhetorical speeches serve to draw the audience of Euripidean drama into a dynamic process of inference and interpretation, frequently resulting in reversals of sympathy or destabilization of judgment, inviting exploration of routine assumptions and recognition of complexity and indeterminacy. The representations of women in Euripidean tragedy also contribute to this process in an important way. Women in tragedy have been a fruitful topic for research in recent decades[1] because of the strong impetus toward greater equality of the sexes in Western societies as well as because of the significant shifts in the faculties and student bodies of academic institutions and in the critical theories prevalent in the humanities and social sciences. At the same time, this interest is not merely a sign of our own concerns in the late twentieth and early twenty-first century. Greek culture in general was frequently self-analytic and produced many normative statements on the roles of the sexes as well as on other matters of social and political organization. Euripidean plays in particular (both surviving and lost) contain a greater number of major female roles, they more frequently explore domestic and personal themes, and they show a pervasive engagement with contemporary intellectual trends, among which was the provocative analysis of nature and culture and the questioning of accepted norms, including those pertaining to gender.

The women's roles in tragedy are implicated in the general conundrum of how tragedy functions culturally in its specific social and political setting in democratic Athens in the last third of the fifth century. Many factors make the relationship of the tragic representations of women (as well as representations in other poetic forms, such as comedy, or in other media, such as

---

[1] See especially Foley 1981 and 2001, Loraux 1987, Rabinowitz 1993, Seidensticker 1995, Zeitlin 1996, Wohl 1998, McClure 1999, Pelling 2000: 189–245, Griffith 2001.

vase-painting or sculpture) to the external "reality" complex and indirect. These representations and the ideologies they reflect are predominantly the products of males, for whom Greek maleness is generally taken for granted as the unmarked and unexamined norm; much of the cultural work of structuring their understanding of this male world is managed through representation of others, whether female or non-Greek, i.e., those marked by striking difference from themselves. The strong habit among the Greeks of thinking in binary terms could obscure the existence of multiple facets of personal identity evoked by the various duties and relationships of a human being as citizen, warrior, social friend, political ally, breadwinner, son, brother, husband, or father, or as household manager, daughter, sister, wife, mother, or social friend of other women. In the democracy of fifth-century Athens, women had no direct participation in political affairs and extremely limited formal rights in legal and economic matters.[2] As in many traditional societies, ancient and modern, a woman was expected to be under the supervision and power (and protection) of a male authority (*kurios*), whether a father, brother, husband, or son. In theory, a woman in the household would act either through the male authority or as a subordinate representing the male authority in certain delegated tasks (such as household management). Women are rarely imagined as autonomous agents, and thus (like children and slaves) are thought to be incapable of participating as free human beings in the fullest sense in the exercise of all the virtues valued by society and by dominant social and ethical philosophies.

In stories, however, women are often portrayed as acting with a greater degree of autonomy. Greek myths and their reflections in narratives in epic, tragedy, and other poetry, as well as anecdotes and oral tales such as the ones that Herodotus transmits and adapts, may be read as exploring tensions in the traditional social and familial structures. They both exploit and at times allay the anxieties of those in power (males and the socially dominant classes) about the naturalness and justification of their hegemony. By depicting extremes, crises, and transgressions, tragic representations often reveal the oversimplification conveyed by common polarities and assumptions and suggest a collapse of binary differences. Both the literary tradition and the heroic subject-matter set the women characters in a context that differs substantially from the audience's own society, for instance in social and political structures (kingship, aristocracy, and dynastic families vs. democracy), familial structures (the interstate and interdynastic exchange in many heroic marriages vs. the requirement of marriages within the body

---

[2] See especially Schaps 1977 and 1979, Foxhall 1989, Just 1989.

of citizens in Athens), and customs (*xenia*, concubinage). And there is
further distancing of the representation (of males as well as females) from
the ordinary experience of the audience through the stylization of speech
and song and the use of masks, and for female roles one must add the
convention of impersonation by male performers. These distancing factors
open a safe space for portraying females engaged in extraordinary acts of
"unfeminine" ambition or transgression.

Nevertheless, the similarities of female tragic characters to contemporary
women are also constantly evoked whenever the audience is able to detect a
match between behavior and statements on stage and normative cultural
assumptions. Examples of such linkage include assertions of weakness and
dependency, universalizing statements about proprieties and hierarchies,
and anachronisms.[3] Tragedy demanded of its audience a complex response
that acknowledged both closeness and distance, both similarity to everyday
experience and difference.

In what follows in this chapter I do not attempt to survey or repeat the
full range of the important work on tragedy's exploitation of gender issues
or the impact of gender studies on modern interpretation of tragedy. My
goal is the more limited one of treating a selection of themes that play into
some of the major thrusts of this book, particularly the dialectic of competing viewpoints and judgments, the dynamic and open-ended response
invited from the audience, and the unsettling of familiar assumptions.
Although the representation of women is the primary interest, on many
points it will be helpful or necessary to pay attention to the male side of the
gender polarity.

INDOORS AND OUTDOORS

An important spatial dichotomy structured Greek thinking about the respective roles and natures of males and females.[4] Although there were probably
significant gaps between the ideological norm and real behavior,[5] it was

[3] For instance, tragedy commonly refers to the dowry system more or less as it was known in Athenian
society (the father or other male guardian of the bride is expected to provide a dowry that the woman
brings to the new couple's household), but the epic tradition usually (but not always) assumes the
bride-price system (gifts may be made in both directions between bridegroom and father of the bride,
but the more substantial ones are those with which the bridegroom compensates the father for
surrendering his daughter to him). For anachronisms of this kind, see Easterling 1985.
[4] See in general Padel 1990.
[5] Divergences from the norm could have been related to economic status, age, location in a center of
population or in isolation, and other circumstances, apart from the fact that people in a culture can
simply overlook the dissonance between an accepted norm and real behavior. See Cohen 1989, Pelling

generally assumed in democratic Athens (and in Greek society in general)[6] that the respectable woman belonged indoors and concerned herself only with the household while activity outside the house and concern for the public affairs of the city were the province of the man. By convention, the action of tragedies is imagined as taking place outdoors, in a kind of public plaza that lies in front of the main characters' house (often a palace) or a temple, and the action unfolds mostly in the presence of the chorus, which normally consists of persons from outside the house.[7] Although the dramatic form disarms to some extent the potential scandal of public appearance, there is still a filtered reflection of the proprieties of real life, since it is always open to the playwright to bring this scandal to prominence for a momentary effect. Women who are on stage (that is, outdoors, in public) prominently are in fact usually in the presence of a female chorus. Few tragic heroines are as bold and combative as Aeschylus' Clytemnestra, who toys with the theme of female subservience but in fact dominates the male chorus and her husband, or Sophocles' Antigone, whose outspokenness enrages Creon and provokes the criticism of the male chorus. The opportunity for a Medea or a Phaedra to explicate her crisis and make her decisions in public depends on the identity of the chorus as sympathetic women of the neighborhood. In contrast, it is likely that in Euripides' lost play *Cretans*, which dealt with the consequences of the birth of the Minotaur to Minos' wife Pasiphaë, Pasiphaë herself had relatively little time onstage. The chorus in this play consisted of male priests summoned by Minos, who was upset by the birth. The queen's infatuation with the bull was in the past, and she may not have appeared after her speech unsuccessfully attacking Minos' intention to punish her (fr. 472e).[8] Similarly, in *Alcestis*, there is a noteworthy difference between the tone and subject-matter of the heroine's farewells inside the house, narrated by the servant, and

2000: 189–245; also Jameson 1990a and 1990b (on the lack of archaeological data attesting architectural separation of "women's quarters" from the "men's quarters" in Greek houses) and Schnurr-Redford 1996: 89–98 (on the difficulties in all kinds of evidence relevant to "women's quarters").

[6] Sparta is to some degree an exception: "some degree" because there is little evidence from Spartans themselves, but mainly the (sometimes polemical) comments of other Greeks (cf. Battezzato 1999–2000 on the ideological significance of Dorian dress in Greek tragedy).

[7] Exceptionally, the chorus consists of persons belonging to the household, as in the case of the slave women in Aesch. *Choe.* and Eur. *Phaethon* (and perhaps in one of the *Phrixus* plays, if the slave women addressed in fr. 822 formed the chorus).

[8] See the discussions of Collard in Collard et al. 1995: 53–9, Jouan and van Looy 1998–2003: II.303–20, Collard and Cropp 2008a: 529–33. The gender of the chorus of *Stheneboea*, another play with a notorious unfaithful wife, cannot be determined, but there is little evidence that Stheneboea herself was on stage for very long: possibly she was simply spoken of by her nurse and Bellerophon and then carried on the crane from behind the skene on her way to her death, although some treat fr. 669 as dialogue between Stheneboea and Bellerophon before the flight on Pegasus. See Collard in Collard et al. 1995: 79–83, Jouan and van Looy 1998–2003: III.1–21, Collard and Cropp 2008b: 82–7.

of her own speeches in public before the witnessing chorus of men of Pherae, and any attempt to evaluate Alcestis' feelings about her marriage and her husband should neither ignore the emotions of the report (175–88) nor read too much into the restraint of the onstage speech (280–325).

Euripides exploits the notion that a married woman should not be seen by or converse with males from outside the household. In *Hypsipyle*, Eurydice mourns outdoors before the female chorus and threatens Hypsipyle with execution, but when Amphiaraus, an unrelated male, enters the scene, she veils herself (but does not withdraw indoors) and only uncovers herself after Amphiaraus appeals to his widely known status as a man who is particularly self-controlled (*sōphrōn*).⁹ In *Iphigenia in Aulis* there is an elaborate play of propriety and embarrassment between the married Clytemnestra and the young and socially inexperienced Achilles when they have different ideas of whether they count as strangers or not because of her false belief that he is her future son-in-law (819–52). This mildly amusing misunderstanding serves to characterize Clytemnestra as a well-behaved housewife before she is forced toward her traditional mythic identity by the revelation of her husband's deception and the loss of her daughter.¹⁰ Even in abnormal settings where one might expect the niceties not to prevail, for instance, in a group of enslaved captives, unmarried girls are kept indoors. Thus Polyxena in *Hecuba* and Cassandra in *Troades* are initially located indoors: Polyxena is called out to hear of her impending sacrifice, and Cassandra rushes out in a mock marriage procession when Talthybius comes to fetch her for Agamemnon. Similarly, a temple precinct provides a dramatic setting in which women can properly appear before (some) strangers (as Aethra does in the opening scenes of *Supplices* and as Creusa does in *Ion*), and supplication is also a justification for being in the open (as the title figures are in *Andromache* and *Helen*). Nevertheless, in the group supplication of *Heracleidae* the temple interior is used like a residence: Iolaus and some male children are suppliants at the altar outside, while the female children and Alcmene are initially kept out of sight within.¹¹

⁹ *Hyps.* 874–85 = fr. 757.43–54. The situation in *Electra* is partly comparable. The scene is a lonely outpost in the countryside, a setting in which women presumably had much more freedom of movement than in a concentrated settlement. Thus it is not surprising that the farmer consents to Electra's going forth to fetch water. The *convenances* come back into play, however, when the farmer later finds Electra standing "with young men" (343–4), and his suspicion is allayed only when he is told of the strangers' credentials as associates of Electra's brother.
¹⁰ Her description of her marriage to Agamemnon in *IA* 1148–63 has the same effect: Gibert 2005.
¹¹ There is, to be sure, also a technical reason for this separation in the playwright's need to manage the sharing of roles among three speaking actors, but the thematic reasons remain valid.

Because seclusion is posited as the respectable norm, apologies for appearing in public, or refusals to be restrained from appearance, are standard motifs used to underline the extremity of a situation. In *Phoenissae*, Antigone's seclusion as an unmarried girl is emphasized early in the play so that the later changes in her circumstances and behavior may be more striking.[12] At *Iphigenia in Aulis* 1338–44, Iphigenia wants to withdraw indoors at the approach of strange men and is specifically embarrassed to see Achilles, her putative suitor, but her mother notes "You are in no position for delicacy in the face of present circumstances."[13] The daughter of Heracles in *Heracleidae* apologizes for showing herself (474–5), but Iolaus praises her because she has acted out of concern for her siblings and for himself (476–7). The girl's intrusion on the men's conversation allows her to learn of the oracular demand for virgin sacrifice and so to offer herself as a voluntary victim.

The inside/outside contrast underlines other situations featuring a typically Euripidean reversal of attitude and behavior. In *Heracleidae*, Alcmene initially seems to abide by the rules of female submission. She is within the temple in the first half of the play and comes out only when she hears a shouted summons and suspects a crisis (646–53). Once outside, she tamely cedes the stichomythia on the military situation to Iolaus and the servant, once she knows of Hyllus' whereabouts (664–5: [Servant] "He is positioning and arranging the army he brought with him." / [Alcmene] "This subject is no longer my affair."). When Iolaus departs, she remains on stage as the senior representative of the suppliant family, to interact with messengers and the chorus. Even so, it is surprising, after the attention to proprieties earlier, when Alcmene finally shows herself so vehement and cunning in insisting upon her revenge against Eurystheus, rejecting the admonitions of the servant and of the chorus of aged Athenian males. In the case of Hermione in *Andromache*, on the other hand, public appearance is related to reversal of status and independent action. When she appears before the women of the chorus in the first action of the play, she is confident of her status as wealthy daughter of Menelaus, which in her view entitles her to speak freely. She is a wife running a household in the temporary absence of her husband, but whereas some tragic wives in this position are forced to act on their own largely by external pressures (Deianeira in Sophocles' *Trachiniae*, Phaedra in *Hippolytus*), Hermione

---

[12] Mastronarde 1994: 6 n. 1.
[13] Cf. *Phoen.* 1276: [Antigone] "I am embarrassed to be seen in a crowd." [Jocasta] "Your situation allows no room for shame."

has taken the initiative in using Neoptolemus' absence as an opportunity to get rid of her rival Andromache. Another sign of the aggressiveness of her position is that Hermione speaks of her marital/sexual troubles without the prompting of sympathetic inquirers (hence Andromache's remarks on shamefulness in 238–44).[14] In Hermione's second appearance on stage, however, once she feels her status has been totally undermined by the failure of her plot and the departure of her father, she is out of control, escaping her servants' restraint, tearing off her headdress and letting her robes fly open (802–77). At the end of the lyric iambic exchange the nurse finally refers to the potential shame of Hermione's being seen outdoors (877). Orestes' immediate entrance blocks any further development of the motif: he is both her cousin and someone she can supplicate, so she is freed of the need for restraint or withdrawal.

In some plays the reversal or violation of the norm is even stronger. In *Medea* there is a striking contrast between the distraught "lyric" Medea heard from inside in 96–167 and the self-possessed "iambic trimeter" Medea, who comes out at 214 and holds her position before the door for over a thousand lines before re-entering at 1250 to kill her sons. Her initial emergence is before sympathetic female neighbors, but she stays to face and converse with five males: Creon, Jason, Aegeus, the tutor, and the messenger servant. Abandoned by Jason, she is a woman without a male to represent her interests and thus, as often in the extreme situations of tragedy, must act on her own. Her opening words to the chorus are the reverse of the conventional apology for coming out. Instead she guards against being reproached for staying inside, immediately portraying herself as someone with a public persona and sensitive to the proprieties of social interaction. Medea not only appropriates male discourse and values in this play; she also has a mobility untypical of the female, or at least of a Greek female.[15] It is the new royal bride of Jason who is the secluded female, awaiting his arrival and dying within her own bedchamber (both in Medea's

[14] Perhaps Hermione's confidence and shamelessness are meant to be seen as particularly Spartan traits, but although she proudly emphasizes her Spartan origin a few lines after entry (*Andr.* 151), the invective against Spartans develops later in the play, when she is not present, as Andromache and Peleus confront Menelaus (445–63, 595–601), and it is the aged male Peleus who makes the most sweeping claim that no Spartan female could ever be chaste.

[15] Ethnic difference may account for some of Medea's unique features (which would then not reflect so directly on the women of the Athenian audience's society). There remains a question, however, as to how important Medea's non-Greek status is as compared with her unusual position as one who has participated in heroic adventures, saved men, contracted an oath-bound relationship as an equal, and otherwise appropriates male values and language. On the problem of Medea's "barbarian" status, see Mastronarde 2002b: 22–4.

imagined armed invasion of the bedchamber, 376–85, and in the real murder with poison, 1167–202). Medea's previous movements, from Colchis to Iolcus and from Iolcus to Corinth, are frequently evoked, and at the end she attains the divine locomotion of the theater crane to escape to Athens. In these respects of mobility and detachment from the house, Medea goes far beyond her literary predecessor, Aeschylus' Clytemnestra, who takes over her *oikos* but is also trapped within it, still subject to the Furies that infest it.

In *Hippolytus*, there is an obvious dichotomy between the distant outdoors inhabited by the hero, who trains horses and hunts, and the indoors, the site where Phaedra pines away, ponders human fortune by night, and commits suicide, and where the nurse reveals the queen's love to Hippolytus. The illicit "indoor" topic of Phaedra's passion is brought before the female chorus through a combination of Phaedra's sickness and the efforts of the nurse, but the secret is not yet really public because all who hear it at first are females themselves. Even in front of a female audience Phaedra covers herself out of shame when she realizes that she has openly expressed such unorthodox wishes (239–49). The nurse assures Phaedra of the solidarity of women as sympathetic helpers (293–4) and suggests that disclosure to fellow women is different from an actual "carrying outside" of the matter to men (295–6). Eventually, Phaedra can drop all concealment before the women and deliver her great speech of self-justification (373–430). It is Hippolytus himself who brings the illicit "indoor" topic outside the second time, and Phaedra cannot believe that he will not spread the story farther. This "carrying outside" by Hippolytus is ironic, since he generalizes about (female) servants who "bring outside" the evils that bad women plot inside the house (649–50).[16] In a broader perspective, moreover, the inside/outside distinction is not stable. The two goddesses Aphrodite and Artemis are more similar than different. Artemis has a role inside (as the chorus' allusion to her function as birth-goddess reminds the audience already at 166–9). Aphrodite roams everywhere, not simply in a momentary outbreak caused by Phaedra's illicit dreams of joining Hippolytus' outdoors pursuits or as represented by the bull from the sea, but permanently as a fact of nature. She is latent in the imagery of the meadow whence Hippolytus picks his garland for Artemis (73–87), and she fills all creation (563–4, 1268–82).[17]

The most striking spatial inversion occurs in *Ion*. The Athenian queen Creusa operates in the open, but this is a sacred space and those present with

---

[16] *ekpherousi* in *Hipp.* 650 recalls *ekphoros* in 295.
[17] On these much-discussed themes see esp. Segal 1965, Bremer 1975.

her are all household members, except for Ion, whose connection with the temple and relatively low status make it proper for Creusa to interact with him early in the play. The interior spaces are, in contrast, heavily identified with the male: Apollo leads Creusa to Pan's cave to rape her, the baby Ion is conveyed by Hermes in a closed basket (recalling the container that concealed Erichthonius), Apollo gives his oracle to Xuthus in the temple, and Xuthus had already visited the inner chambers of Trophonius. Ion celebrates his supposed identity within an enclosed tent, and he wants to enter the temple to question the god at the end. It is the goddess Athena who appears publicly above the roof on Apollo's behalf at the end, while the male god, as it were, secretes himself inside the temple. This association of males with enclosure is significant in a play concerned, as Zeitlin and others have shown, with parenthood and identity.[18] The repeated motif of males inside a closed space recalls the traditional image of the woman as womb, as a hollow vessel for bearing offspring to the male, but one that also conceals that offspring and leaves its paternity unclear. In *Ion*, it turns out to be the mother who truly has the power to give Ion his legitimate identity as Athenian king and as symbol of Attic hegemony over the Ionians.

FAMILY AND CITY AND GENDERED MOTIVATIONS

The spatial contrast of indoors and outdoors is matched by the societal contrast of household and city as separate realms for the activities of females and males. Once again, the dichotomy was prevalent in the thinking of many writers and often considered normative, but like other polarities was belied by some details of real life and subjected to exploration, qualification, and reversal in poetic representations. The strong association of the female with the house and family reinforces and is reinforced by other gender stereotypes, such as that women are more attached to their children than are men, that women lack the courage and physical endurance of men, or that women are inferior to men in the ability to deliberate in the way that one must in order to engage in cooperative efforts with comrades or to take on a role within a city or an army. This section considers the various motivations (explicitly cited by characters or reasonably inferred by the Athenian audience) that follow or deviate from such assumptions of differences between the genders.

[18] E.g., Zeitlin 1989 (= Zeitlin 1996: 285–338), Pedrick 2007. On this topic I am also indebted to unpublished work by Melissa Mueller.

In accordance with the belief that women are by nature more nurturing and more naturally attached to childen, protective efforts undertaken on behalf of offspring are extremely frequent on the part of female characters.[19] Male characters who act to protect children, grandchildren, or foster children tend to be old men,[20] but one of the most striking aspects of the Euripidean Heracles in his eponymous play is that he is a male in his prime who openly professes to be "children-loving" (*philoteknos*), a quality often said to be greater in women than men.[21] Although Menelaus in *Andromache* and Agamemnon in *Iphigenia in Aulis* also make efforts on behalf of their daughters, each abandons his daughter's interests in rather shameful circumstances, as fears or other motivations predominate. In *Medea*, Jason claims and believes that his plans for the future are made on behalf of his children, but Medea's accusations and Jason's own self-presentation suggest that other factors are involved as well. At the end of the play, however, his motivation seems purer when he makes a vain effort to save his sons from harm.

There appears to be little difference between women and men characters when there is a lack of the desired offspring. In *Ion*, Creusa and Xuthus are equally eager to remedy their childlessness, and the case of Hermione in *Andromache* is balanced by the case of Aegeus in *Medea*.[22] Female devotion to the family, however, whether the family is that formed by marriage or the natal unit, is very commonly demonstrated by selfless concern to protect or help spouse, brother, or father.[23] A similar strong identification with family or father is also evident in some of the actions that seek revenge (to be discussed shortly). There are fewer examples of such selfless devotion among male characters.[24]

---

[19] Examples (sometimes the motivation is primary, sometimes secondary to other motivations): Alcestis protecting her children from a fatherless life and the dangers posed by a stepmother, Phaedra protecting the reputation of her sons, Aethra concerned about Theseus' good name, Hecuba trying to save Polyxena, Megara trying to save her sons' lives (or save them from ignominy if she cannot), Clytemnestra in *El.* responding to a deceptive call for maternal help; also Andromache, Jocasta, Clytemnestra in *IA*.

[20] Creon in *Med.* (Creon's old age is underlined four times in the messenger speech at 1209–20), Peleus, Iolaus, Amphitryon, Creon in *Phoen.* (his old age is indicated at 968, 995, 1318), Cadmus. Conversely, Pheres makes himself noteworthy by his refusal to count his son's life as more important than his own, and Tyndareus is extremely hostile to his grandchildren: see below, p. 294.

[21] For universalizing uses ("all humans love their children") vs. gendered uses ("women love children more") see Mastronarde 1994: 250.

[22] Cf. Laius as reported by Jocasta in *Phoen.* 13–16.

[23] Loyalty to husband: Alcestis, Evadne, Helen in *Hel.* Acting for siblings: Heracles' eldest daughter in *Hcld.*, Antigone in *Phoen.*, Iphigenia in *IT*, and Electra in *Or.* Devotion to a father: Antigone; cf. Iphigenia in *IT*, who is remarkably well disposed to her father despite his actions at Aulis.

[24] Menelaus in *Hel.*, once the recognition has taken place, matches Helen in spousal devotion. Orestes in *IT* refuses to let Iphigenia die for him and in *Or.* displays first a tender, then a fierce bond with Electra. A somewhat similar kind of selfless devotion with a religious basis may carry some suggestion

Given the heroic subject-matter of tragic plots, the ethic of individual honor is often more prominent in the male characters in tragedy than the social and political ethic of service to the wider community beyond the family. While the male characters may provide a filtered reflection of the rivalries and self-serving efforts of many political leaders (which also provoke the criticism of Thucydides and the poets of Old Comedy), in tragic plots the female figures sometimes serve a positive communal role that would in general be denied to them in contemporary society. Praxithea in *Erechtheus* (fr. 360) is the most extreme example of this, since she delivers a rhetorical speech explaining why she places the needs of the threatened city ahead of the life of her child, and by her agreement to the sacrifice differs sharply from the Creon of *Phoenissae*. Heracles' daughter, likewise, combines concern for the fate of Athens with her service to her family, and Jocasta hopes to save the city as well as her sons. At Aulis Iphigenia arrives in the end at an attitude inspired by service to Greece,[25] and Aethra recommends a course of action that is noble both for her son and for the city. The only male figure whose patriotic impulse seems to reach this level of generous service is the youth Menoeceus in *Phoenissae*, whose plot-role is modeled on that of sacrificial virgins and whose idealism contrasts sharply with the ambition or weakness of other male figures in the play. The patriotic claims of more mature males never seem fully convincing.[26]

Perhaps the most interesting example of the action of a female character impinging on public affairs occurs in *Supplices*. In the conversations of Aethra and her son Theseus we find an idealized alternative to the common attitude that women ought to be silent and have no role in public affairs. The mutual concern of mother and son is evident (87–99, 286–90), as is the

of deviation from ordinary male citizen/warrior status. Hippolytus provides a male example of an unusual commitment to piety, purity, and virginity (for a speculative treatment of his piety see Wildberg 2002); the adolescent Ion serving in the non-political sphere of Delphi is also marked as especially pious and pure in the first part of *Ion*, but he moves into a more adult and political (impure) sphere later in the play. The chorus of priests in *Cretans* was also characterized by an unusual religious commitment (fr. 472), but we do not know how this theme worked in the play as a whole. The similar commitment in virgin priestesses like Theonoe in *Hel.* and the Delphic priestess in *Ion* seems more in tune with gender stereotypes, except that Theonoe's piety has a unique inflection in that she is seen as upholder of her dead father's piety and justice.

[25] See above, pp. 238–40.
[26] In *Hec.*, Odysseus argues that his actions are in service to the army as a *polis*-like body, but the excess of his rhetoric and the sympathy won by Hecuba undercut that patriotic position. The Odysseus of Euripides' *Philoctetes* (frr. 787–9) also presented himself as a servant of the Greek cause, but emphasized and critiqued the self-perpetuating ambition that underlay his willingness to exert toilsome efforts on behalf of the Greeks; moreover, in the lying tale he tells to Philoctetes he reminds the audience of his own use of trickery in the plot against Palamedes (fr. 789d). In *Phoen.*, Creon serves Thebes well by restraining the rash Eteocles in the second episode, but does an about-face in the third episode when Menoeceus' sacrifice is demanded; on his actions in the exodos see below, pp. 295–6.

deference of Aethra (108–9, 293–6), while it is Theseus himself who says that "many wise words come from women too" (294). Like *Heracleidae*, this play dramatizes a supplicatory appeal for Athenian protection and assistance that was a standard mythic-historical example in public oratory used to demonstrate the fearlessness of the Athenians in upholding sacred Hellenic customs and taking on tough opponents. Euripides creates a surprise movement in his version by having Theseus initially reject the suppliants' appeal.[27] Aethra returns the plot to its proper course, by giving visible and then audible expression to pity (causing Theseus to concede that he is not entirely immune to this emotion either, 288), and then by showing tactfully the issues of piety, honor, courage, and national pride that are implicated in the decision. The rest of the play gives wide scope for the lamentation of the chorus of Argive mothers for their lost warrior-sons, enacting the kind of public grief that the Athenian public funeral for the war-dead perhaps discouraged, or at least contained,[28] and Evadne, the widow of one of the fallen Seven Argive champions, goes even farther than the chorus in a personal enactment of grief through suicide. Aethra, however, embodies the behavior expected of citizen women by the official discourse of the polis: to bear male citizens to fight for the city and to send them off willingly into danger. Theseus alludes to this when he asks "What will hostile people say of me, when you who bore me and feel fear on my behalf are the first to bid me to undertake this task?" (343–5). Aethra's good advice about public action is thus aligned with an idealization of her citizen-mother role.

   Other motivations that we might expect to be gendered as masculine on the basis of the contemporary Athenian world of the plays are concern for fame and honor and the creation or maintenance of extrafamilial bonds, such as guest-friendship (*xenia*), personal friendship (*philia*), and mutual favor and obligation (*charis*). Fame and honor are considered in more detail in the next section. For extrafamilial connections there are many male examples from Admetus and Heracles in *Alcestis* to Orestes and Pylades in *Orestes*.[29] But the high-status women of the heroic age provide tragic figures who are not always restricted by the limitations that would hold in contemporary society. Medea, unlike Jason, assimilates their marriage to a partnership of equals, and with Aegeus she is both a suppliant and a co-equal exchanging favors. Hecuba, too, tries somewhat unconvincingly to claim mutual obligation first with Odysseus and later with Agamemnon, as

---

[27] See above pp. 216–18.   [28] See Foley 2001: 21–55.
[29] Cf. Theseus and Heracles in *Her.*, Demophon and the relatives of Heracles in *Hcld.*, Orestes and Pylades in *IT*.

we saw in Chapter 6,[30] and the pre-existing relation of *xenia* with Polymestor allegedly survives the death of Priam and his sons and can be used to lure him to his punishment.

Revenge-actions reflect the second part of the traditional duty to help one's friends and harm one's enemies.[31] Especially for male figures, to take action against an enemy is often closely linked to maintaining one's honor and status, and both males and females try to harm enemies in order to defend the interests of their kin. Yet such actions are frequently morally ambiguous. In some cases, the balance of justice seems relatively clear and the agent is easily viewed as punishing a wrongdoer while defending justice, divine or universal laws, or the rights of suppliants.[32] More often, there is some moral complication: the situation is not what it appears to be to the agent, or the punitive action turns out to be no less transgressive than the provocation. In *Hippolytus*, Theseus wrongly believes he is punishing a miscreant, and in *Ion* the young man pursues an apparently justified punishment until he learns that the criminal is his mother. Agamemnon in *Hecuba*, Menelaus in *Troades*, Tyndareus in *Orestes* are all flawed avengers or punishers because of mixed motives, blindness, or moral inflexibility.[33] At the opposite end of the spectrum from the "just" acts of revenge are the threats and acts that are portrayed as villainous from the start.[34] Eurystheus appears at first to belong in this category, although an audience's impression of him probably improves at the end of *Heracleidae* because he has a chance to present his case and he promises a benefit to Athens, and because Alcmene is so fierce.

Tragic women who seek violent revenge are often acting directly because they have no male kin surviving or present to act on their behalf or on behalf of their family.[35] Medea and Hecuba in *Hecuba* are the clearest examples of this. Their violence falls upon unsuspecting male victims and yet is also condemned as typically female: this reflects the contradictory assumptions that women are more devious, spiteful, and untrustworthy than men and

[30] See above, pp. 229–34.   [31] See in general, e.g., Blondell 1989, Burnett 1998.
[32] In the political suppliant-plays *Hcld.* and *Su.*, Demophon and Theseus conduct "just" wars, and in the former, Iolaus' narrated action of pursuing and capturing Eurystheus fits this pattern. Heracles and Amphitryon justly entrap and kill the villain-figure Lycus in *Her.* Compare in satyr-play the vengeance taken by Odysseus for the killing of his comrades: again in this respect, Odysseus is very close to a figure from tragedy (acting to live up to his reputation: *Cycl.* 198–202, 693–5) and is free of the buffoonery seen in Silenus and Polyphemus.
[33] Cf. Orestes in *El.* and *Or.*, and Eteocles and Polyneices in *Phoen.*
[34] Cf. Menelaus and Orestes in *Andr.*; plot-required villains or blocking figures like Lycus, Thoas, and Theoclymenus also belong here.
[35] See Foley 2001: 161–3 for this principle as it applies to surviving daughters and sisters.

that women are too weak to be a danger to men. In both cases, the audience
is invited to feel that the avengers are initially or partially justified in seeking
to exact vengeance, but over the course of each play the heroine's actions
and arguments lose the audience's sympathy or create revulsion. The
vengeful Electra in *Electra* differs from Medea and Hecuba in that her
male champion has finally appeared and also in that, when the usual shift of
perceptions and sympathies develops late in the play, she herself shares the
revulsion at what has been done. As with the male avengers, some female
characters plan violence that is less ambiguously perceived as unjust, as, for
example, in Phaedra's lying accusation of Hippolytus.[36]

We noted a little earlier some instances in which the actions of
women characters impinged on the public sphere in a beneficial way.
Revenge-actions, too, may entail a female intrusion into the public sphere,
but in a negative way. Hecuba's punishment of Polymestor might have been
perceived by the Greek army as contrary to their communal interests, as
Agamemnon fears (*Hec.* 858–63), but by being the judge in a mock trial he
is able to determine that such a view does not prevail. Medea's murder of the
king and princess damages the Corinthian community, but Jason reports that
the danger will come from the clan of Creon (*Med.* 1301–5), not the city as a
whole.[37] Perhaps the most striking instance is that of Alcmene, the mother of
Heracles, in *Heracleidae*, who pursues revenge against the captive Eurystheus
with a striking independence at the end of the play. Unlike a Medea or a
Hecuba, Alcmene is not a woman without male support: she has received the
protection of the Athenian kings and people and also has family champions in
her grandson Hyllus and in Heracles' nephew Iolaus, both of whom have
survived the battle with the Argives. Yet she insists on acting against
Eurystheus before any powerful males, whether Athenian or her own relatives,
can arrive to forestall her. In previous scenes of the play, as noted above,[38] her
behavior and speech were quite in accord with cultural norms limiting the
female. Thus, when she later suddenly takes on the role of a strong-willed
woman who defies the instructions of male authorities and promotes a violent
trangression of custom, she diverges sharply from her own previous role, from
the manner of her male counterpart Iolaus, and from the idealized behavior of
the self-sacrificing virgin daughter of Heracles. Her killing of the captive
Eurystheus is, however, advantageous to the interests of the Athenians, and

[36] Cf. Hermione's attempt against Andromache and her son, Electra's later actions in *Or.*, and possibly
Eurydice's treatment of Hypsipyle in *Hypsipyle* (and Dirce's of Antiope in *Antiope*).
[37] In addition, one may feel that the Corinthian community's reaction has already been compromised
by the complicity of the chorus of local women: see above, p. 119.
[38] See above, p. 251.

the transgression is conveniently retrojected upon an agent who is both female and non-Athenian.[39]

Apart from revenge actions that become ambiguous or cause revulsion, the motivations that are likeliest to be associated with unsympathetic characters are those that aim most transparently for a personal advantage, such as wealth (Polymestor), sexual satisfaction (Theoclymenus, Menelaus initially in *IA*, Laius in *Chrysippus*, Macareus in *Aeolus*), or political power (Lycus, Eteocles, Menelaus in *Or.*). Wealth and political power seem to be motivations that are gendered as male,[40] but the Greek stereotype held that women were naturally weak when faced with the challenge of sexual desire while men were more capable of self-control. So for a man to be acting because of erotic desire, or to be accused of that, entails a defect of manly virtue, and Menelaus indeed had a traditional reputation as less warlike and so less "male" than other heroes, as did Paris, whose role Theoclymenus takes in *Helen* in the re-enactment of deception by a false marriage to Helen. Some lost plays showed women who were shamelessly seeking sexual satisfaction,[41] but this motivation is not found in pure form in the extant plays. The extant Phaedra does not seek consummation of her desire, as the onus of approaching Hippolytus is transferred to the nurse acting without her consent. Helen's transgression is always in the past (as is Clytemnestra's). Even in *Troades*, when Helen's behavior is most explicitly condemned, it is also defended by alternative interpretations, and her sexual guilt is eliminated in *Helen*. Hermione's motivation is more complicated than the sexual insatiability of which Andromache at one point accuses her (*Andr.* 218, 229).

Finally, the impulse toward self-preservation is delicately balanced between being an acceptable motivation and being blameworthy depending on the circumstances and perhaps partly on gender. Sympathetic characters who are in peril are hardly to be criticized for trying to save themselves from death or distress. But in fact most such characters are female and suppliants.[42] Orestes, Pylades, and Menelaus join the heroines of *Iphigenia in Tauris* and *Helen* in seeking escape and salvation, and this does not seem

[39] The degree of complicity or tacit consent on the part of the chorus of Athenians is unclear because of damage to the text at the end of the play. See Wilkins 1993: xxx–xxxi, 193.
[40] Only Clytemnestra in Aeschylus appears to be a woman who relishes political power, in accordance with her "heart of manly counsel" (*Agam.* 11) and domination over her "co-tyrant" lover Aegisthus.
[41] Stheneboea in *Stheneboea* and Phaedra in the lost *Hippolytus*; the reconstruction of *Cressae* is much too uncertain to say anything about Aerope (Collard and Cropp 2008a: 516–19, with references to other discussions).
[42] Andromache, Electra in the first part of *Or.*, Megara, Creusa when taking asylum on the altar, Helen in *Helen*, Iphigenia in *IT* and, until her volte-face in *IA*.

unmanly in this type of plot.[43] Supplicating men, however, are generally old men, like Iolaus and Amphitryon. Perhaps the fact that Telephus, a free elite male in his prime, took asylum at an altar was another strikingly unusual aspect of a scene that we know stuck in the public mind for the bold gesture of using the baby Orestes as a hostage.[44] It is easy, however, for self-preservation to be recast as cowardice. Megara does this in arguing with Amphitryon in the opening scenes of *Heracles*, and the young women accepting sacrifice, to whom we turn next, project a refusal to do so as cowardly, appealing to a masculine concept of bravery. Adult male figures in fact find it hard to avoid the charge of unmanliness when they strive too hard to stay alive. This is evident in Admetus and Pheres in *Alcestis*, and by implication applies to Orestes and his mirror-figure the Phrygian eunuch in the last part of *Orestes* (1506–28).

WOMEN, FAME, AND COURAGE

Both in their relation to space and in their relation to motivations, male and female figures reflect cultural stereotypes in a way that is complicated by the conventions of drama, the displacement of the action to the heroic world, challenging reversals, and contradictions or inaccuracies embedded in the simple polarities with which the Greeks (and others) like to think. Against the background of such variations, I now turn to the representation of women's fame and courage in Euripidean tragedy. A major aspect of the self-definition of fifth-century Athenian male citizens resided in the notion of the incapacity of normal Greek women for the male virtues of bravery and physical endurance and for the citizen's virtues of good judgment and leadership. Women were imagined as warriors only when transposed to the level of divinity (as in the case of Athena) or when exiled to the wild sphere outside civilization as the Greek city-state understood it (as in the myth of the Amazons). In the Athenian democracy, in the paradoxical formulation of Thucydides' Pericles, woman's proper "fame" or "glory" is a negative thing, absence of improper behavior and absence from mention by others (Thuc. 2.45.2): "if I must say anything on the subject of female excellence to those of you who will now be in widowhood, it will be all comprised in this brief exhortation. Great will be your glory (*doxa*) in not falling short of your

[43] For possible qualification see below, pp. 286–7 and 302–3.
[44] The scene was parodied by Aristophanes both in *Acharnians* in 425 and in *Women at the Thesmophoria* in 411, and the image of Telephus on the altar with sword in one hand and baby in the other was repeated by vase-painters (Taplin 2007: 205–10).

natural character; and greatest will be hers who is least talked of (*kleos*) among men whether for good or for bad."[45] Social historians have noted that in fact respectable living women of citizen status were not referred to by name in most public contexts.[46]

A woman could be praised for keeping to her place as a woman and doing well what patriarchal ideology expected of her. Even in court cases, though named only as daughter or wife or mother of a named male, a woman could be referred to as meeting all male expectations of good female behavior. Once again, however, the realm of heroic myth offers a representation of human life and action that need not conform in any simple way to social ideologies prevalent in the audience's present-day culture. In myth, the names of women are important. They are examples of approved and disapproved behaviors, and they are founding mothers of distinguished lineages that explain the past and present of Greek communities. In tragedy, accordingly, stronger terms of renown can be used, and women often make a claim to honor. In *Troades* 636–83, Andromache makes a remarkable argument about the ironic result of her *eudoxia*, the "good repute" she earned even among the Greeks by doing all that is expected of a woman who is *sōphrōn* ("prudent, self-controlled, chaste").[47] What might have been an advantage for a widow in real Athenian society is transposed into a disadvantage in the heroic world because of its location within a war of conquest and captivity and because of the prominence of the idealizing motif of spousal loyalty beyond death. A similar notion that a wife can acquire fame by being *sōphrōn* is deployed by Electra when she attacks Clytemnestra (*El.* 1080–5) for failing to take advantage of the excellent opportunity to differentiate herself from her sister Helen. Creusa even construes her concealment of the shameful secret of illicit childbirth as part of her having engaged in "contests of virtue" in the eyes of her husband and the world, a contest she sees no point in carrying on after her husband's apparent betrayal (*Ion* 859–69).[48]

---

[45] The Crawley translation. For some cautions against treating this statement as a simple truth about Athenian culture, see Pelling 2000: 189–91.

[46] Schaps 1977. For collection and discussion of many ancient testimonia to women's roles and rights, see Just 1989.

[47] See the discussion of this passage in Pelling 2000: 189–94. Andromache is being used as an extreme example, but even here being well behaved does not entail a complete self-effacement within the family: "I knew the matters in which I ought to have victory over my husband and the matters in which I ought to cede the victory to him" (655–6).

[48] A more extreme rhetorical development of the idea that such concealment is virtuous is seen in Pasiphaë's argument that Minos is responsible for the shame that has come upon his household, since she concealed "the divinely caused stroke of fortune" while he revealed it to the world (fr. 472e.29–33).

The most complex and paradoxical exploration of the notion that "fame" accrues to the woman who avoids all reproach in her role as wife and mother is seen in *Hippolytus*. The prologue goddess Aphrodite announces rather cryptically that in the completion of her scheme of revenge on Hippolytus, Phaedra "will die with good repute (*eukleēs*), but all the same will die" (47). Phaedra's concern for her "good repute" (*eukleia*) is a leitmotif in her deliberations and her final fateful decision, but, differently from Aphrodite, she believes that her reputation will be preserved only if the truth never comes out.[49] As the play approaches its end, Aphrodite's prediction seems puzzlingly inaccurate. Theseus has not in fact been shown "the matter" in its real shape, and Phaedra is "of good repute" in her death only in his eyes, while the audience, like the chorus, knows her full shame, not only her illicit desire but the deception by which she caused the death of an innocent man. Soon, however, in an ironic union of opposites, Artemis herself provides the fulfillment of Aphrodite's declaration "I'll show the matter to Theseus" (42), and she transfers the important achievement of "dying with a good name" to Hippolytus (1299), although she also confirms Aphrodite's claim about Phaedra by acknowledging the latter's resistance as "in a certain manner nobility" (1300–1) and excusing her failure as unwilling (1305). The eternal memorialization of Phaedra's love in Trozenian cult (1429–30), promised as an honor for Hippolytus, might seem the final proof that women like Phaedra can have nothing but bad fame, no matter what her own intentions and no matter what Aphrodite claims. But the story to be told includes Phaedra's noble resistance, just as Euripides' own play does, and perhaps an audience, aware of the contradictory aspects of Phaedra's fame, is meant to be left with a more nuanced view.

The renown claimed by females in tragedy can in fact be much more similar to male glory than in the examples considered so far. As early as Sophocles' *Antigone* we find a tragic heroine claiming fair fame for herself in her defiant service to her brother against the dictates of male authority (*Ant.* 502–4, 694–5). The ideas of gender-conflict and gender-competition are very prominent in this play,[50] but, tellingly, these ideas occur not in Antigone's statements but in Creon's, reflecting a male anxiety rather than a female aspiration, and in Ismene's, reflecting a contrasting acquiescence in female subordination. In Euripides, in contrast, although there are

---

[49] *Hipp.* 423, 489, 687, 717. Phaedra's belief that her resistance to her illicit desire is admirable gives the nurse an opening to prise out her secret (329–32).
[50] Clytemnestra in Aesch. *Agam.* does not make such prominent claims to personal fame, although she delights in her power and victories over males and superiority to their doubts and distrust.

of course males hasty to reject any suggestion of being defeated by women, it is sometimes the female characters themselves who are represented as expressing awareness of a competition of genders. The play *Medea* is the most striking case, since the character Medea appropriates a wide range of images and terms from the male spheres of battle and athletics and insists firmly on her honor and glory (*kleos*) in terms that recall heroes like Achilles and Ajax.[51] In the same play, the female chorus, for its part, uses Jason's betrayal to combat a one-sided poetic tradition. When they explain in the first stasimon that they would have replied to misogynistic male song if they had been granted the poetic skill to do so, they are, in the very act of singing as a tragic chorus, already exercising that skill (at least notionally, since the actual singers behind the masks are male). There are, however, few characters comparable to Medea in her aggressive competitiveness. There is a little of this quality in Agave in *Bacchae* when she is under the sway of Dionysiac possession. She glories in the success of her hunt and uses the term *aristais* ("best, bravest") for herself and her sisters and *aristeia* ("bravest achievement in battle") for her own prime role in killing the lion who is really her own son Pentheus (*Ba.* 1179–80, 1199, 1204–9, 1233–9). The collapse of distinctions that is typical of Dionysiac power is also illustrated by Agave's suggestion that Pentheus should mimic his mother's example and learn to hunt well (*Ba.* 1252–5). Elsewhere, as mentioned above and discussed further below, several female characters insist they must live up to the example set by their male relatives. Agave's suggestion of imitation in the other direction is strikingly abnormal. But more is involved than just male vs. female modes of action, for the Dionysiac and the female are here as elsewhere aligned with nature against culture. In 1205–9 the civilized (male) technologies of hunting, nets and javelins with their throwing loops, "the worked products of the spear-manufacturers," are rejected, since Dionysus has empowered the women to use their bare hands. Similarly, in 1236–7, Agave points out that she has abandoned her cultural role, weaving (the emblem of women's role indoors in the household), and moved on to "greater pursuits, hunting wild beasts by hand."

In a less transgressive manner, unmarried girls in tragedy who voluntarily face death routinely lay claim to glory. The examples in *Heracleidae*, *Hecuba*, and *Iphigenia in Aulis* invite the question whether there is anything challenging to the male audience in such claims or whether any possible challenge is disarmed by other motifs, such as service to family and service to

[51] Knox 1977 and Bongie 1977 are clear exponents of this aspect of the play and have been echoed in many subsequent analyses. The evidence is summarized in Mastronarde 2002b: 18–20, 36.

the community. In *Heracleidae*, after the Athenians agree to protect the suppliants who are being pursued by Eurystheus, they consult oracles in advance of the expected war and find that the gods demand the sacrifice of a well-born virgin as a precondition for divine favor in the coming war. When the unnamed eldest daughter of Heracles[52] explains in detail her willingness to be the needed voluntary virgin sacrifice, she uses the familiar heroic choice between living ignobly or dying nobly, which was also evoked in praise of dead Athenian soldiers (Thuc. 2.42.4, Lysias 2.62). The girl is clearly serving the interests of her family as well as those of the *polis* that has given her family protection. She indicates her adherence to conventional propriety when she apologizes for appearing in public (474–7) and declares that her goal if she stayed alive would be the normal gender-defined one of being married and bearing children (523–4). On the other hand, as the child of the paradigmatically courageous hero Heracles, she views herself as living up to legitimate expectations in volunteering to be sacrificed and in preferring a noble death to an ignoble life. She uses the standard terms of bravery and cowardice, with emphasis on the opprobrium to be avoided: "flee from" (506), "ridicule" (507), "cowardly" (510, 519), "dishonorable" (513), "love life too much" (518, 533), "betray" (522), "contrary to my worth" (526). One index of her resolve is her sense of shame at an imagined reproach of some anonymous future witness: "And will I not be ashamed if someone may say 'Why have you come here with your suppliant branches when you are yourselves too much in love with life [i.e., behaving like cowards]?'" (516–18). This is a reminiscence of a famous epic expression of the warrior-ethic, Hector's fateful lines at *Il.* 22.105–6, "I feel shame before the Trojans and the trailing-gowned women of Troy, lest someone ever say …" The unusual phrase "stand by the slaughter" (*paristasthai sphagēi* 502), with the victim as subject, may be meant to evoke the notion of the good soldier in the hoplite rank, the comrade-by-one's-side (*parastatēs*) whom the ephebe in his traditional oath swears not to betray.[53] Using positive terms as well, the girl already counts herself among the ethically elite (*chrēstoi*, 510) and declares herself "notable" (*episēmos*, 527) and will now "leave her life with fair fame" (534). Her exemplary bravery, acknowledged by both her male interlocutors, Iolaus and Demophon, gives her the authority to instruct and admonish others in her farewell speech (574–95).

---

[52] Often called Macaria in the later mythographic tradition and in discussions of *Hcld.*; it is possible that this name was assigned to her in the lacuna at the end of Euripides' play (Wilkins 1993: 193), but earlier in the play she is just Heracles' daughter.

[53] For the ephebic oath see Rhodes and Osborne 2003: 440–9 (no. 88). The maiden uses the same verb in *Hcld.* 589–90: "I did not fail to stand by you [my siblings]."

Through the emphasis on her kinship with Heracles and the presentation
of an extraordinary situation of need and divine command, the anonymous
maiden is virtually portrayed as an honorary male. Rather than challenging
male assumptions, this character feeds off them to establish her own status,
and can be welcomed as an a fortiori example for males in the audience: if a
young girl can reason like that and act like that, then they themselves should
be capable of similar bravery. It is interesting to compare to Heracles'
daughter the only male self-sacrificial victim in extant plays, Menoeceus
in *Phoenissae*. Within that play, Euripides signals that he has modeled the
incident on a familiar Athenian myth about an oracle-induced sacrifice of a
maiden, the daughter of Erechtheus and Praxithea, and many scholars have
concluded that Menoeceus is an invented figure.[54] Menoeceus is treated by
the oracle and by his father Creon as not fully adult, indeed in a sense not
fully male, since the oracle stipulates that the victim be not only unmarried
but not even betrothed to be married. Nevertheless, Menoeceus projects
himself into the ranks of adult warrior-males by rejecting survival,
using the same language of cowardice, shame, baseness, and betrayal
(*Phoen.* 993–1012).

When the sacrifice of Hecuba's daughter Polyxena is demanded by the
ghost of Achilles in *Hecuba*, the Trojan princess reasons in very similar
terms, but her courageous gesture is divorced from the feminine motivation
of service to the family, for she cannot construe her death upon Achilles'
tomb as a debt to her city or her family or as an act that saves others. Her
eagerness to die derives rather from her conviction that she can no longer
"live well" in accordance with her self-image as a royal princess with high
expectations: she insists on living up to the status she believes her family
position has conferred on her. Evoking the same traditional heroic models
as the daughter of Heracles, Polyxena says "If I shall not show myself eager
to die, I'll be exposed as a base and cowardly woman" (347–8), using the
terms *kakos*, "base, cowardly," and *philopsychos*, "too fond of one's life,
cowardly," and she rejects "meeting a shameful fate in a manner that
besmirches my worth" (374). In the messenger speech, Polyxena is quoted
using the term *eukardiōs*, "with courageous spirit" (549), and the Greek
observers award her the same term in 579–80, "the young woman who was
exceedingly courageous and most brave in spirit." Hecuba, too, uses strong
terms of approbation in her final assessment of her daughter's behavior (592,
597–8): *gennaios* ("noble"), *esthlos* ("noble-born, excellent"), *chrēstos*

---

[54] I support this view in Mastronarde 1994: 28–9, with reference to some discussions that favor the
alternative, that this sacrifice has a pre-Euripidean origin.

("virtuous"). In one sense, as with the daughter of Heracles, Polyxena's bravery is no threat to assumptions of masculine viewers, since she can demonstrate such qualities only in an extreme situation, and she may even be accepted as an a fortiori example to inspire male viewers to face dangers bravely. We should also recognize that Polyxena's arguments and language are tailored to reinforce important cultural norms strongly valuing freedom over slavery.

On the other hand, there is also a sense in which, within the world of the play, Polyxena does compete with her male observers and even puts them to shame. She keeps the sacrificial attendants from seizing her, she makes the sacrificer himself reluctant (566, "unwilling and willing at the same time"), and she causes some observers to call each other "most base" (577) for not responding adequately to her bravery. Perhaps it is in the light of such competition and reversal that one should interpret Polyxena's striking and much-debated gesture of laying bare her chest before her executioners (558–65). Several divergent interpretations have been proposed in recent studies, ranging from detection of "pornography" to allusion to Amazons.[55] The described gesture may indeed have had multiple and conflicting resonances for the contemporary audience. Here I would highlight one that is aligned with fifth-century notions about the body and gender.[56] While Polyxena is still alive and has any power at all over her situation, she expresses defiance of her sacrificers' status, and claims special status for herself, by ignoring the taboo on public female nudity. She thus behaves more like a male youth than a young woman and seizes control of her status. Respectable male nudity, as seen in the *kouros* statue or in Greek athletics, is plausibly understood as a token of the free citizen's bodily integrity, self-control, and fitness for his duties. In artistic representation, male nudity is also a marker of the heroic. A similar point is suggested by Polyxena's invitation to Neoptolemus to strike her in the chest, since for a soldier killed or wounded in battle, a wound in front is beautiful and honorable as a proof

[55] Gregory 1999: 112–13 summarizes several approaches. Cohen 1997 shows that the unveiling of the female breast in artistic depictions may be a sign of violence being done to the woman and even, especially with Amazons, an indication that death is imminent. The important difference here is that Polyxena does this voluntarily, while the baring occurs accidentally for the dying Amazons. Polyxena's case also differs from the accidental disrobing of maenads (caused by the movements of dancing), the voluntary baring of the breast of old women in supplication to their sons, and the voluntary baring directed erotically to a single male (Helen and Menelaus). See also Michelini 1987: 158–70; Scodel 1996. The term "pornographic gesture" is used by Rabinowitz 1993: 106, but although there is an admixture of eroticism and voyeurism in the scene, the term "pornography" relies too heavily on modern extensions of the meaning of that term.

[56] Cf. Stewart 1997: 24–42, 118–24.

that the warrior did not turn and flee. In these ways Polyxena seems to intrude forcefully on male prerogatives. Yet the girl (or Euripides) also manages to have it both ways: in her dying movement she maintains the proprieties of female bodily concealment, depriving the observers of any advantage after her death, when she is truly powerless (568–70).

The third example of the sacrificed maiden is the Iphigenia of *Iphigenia in Aulis*, whose final long rhesis (1368–401) has already been discussed in Chapter 6 in terms of the power of rhetoric to reshape character or to produce self-delusion.[57] When Iphigenia reveals her new resolve, she employs many of the same motifs of bravery, nobility, and fame to justify her sudden decision to go willingly to be sacrificed. She seeks to accomplish her death "gloriously," avoiding "the ignoble" (1376), and rejects "excessive love of life" (1385). She expects to receive "blessed fame" (1383–84) for her service to Greece, and she assimilates herself to the males born to serve as soldiers (1386–91).

Of the three sacrificed virgins we have considered, Polyxena is the one who offers the most defiant appropriation of male terms of reference and thus competes most challengingly with the males around her. Her case is also distinct in that her sacrifice does not entail a service to others to whom she owes allegiance or gratitude, so that her willingness demands an even higher level of courage and self-esteem (her conviction of what she owes to her conception of herself). The daughter of Heracles is far more comfortably adopted into the system of gender hierarchy. Iphigenia's own final speech also suggests accommodation within that system by its emphasis on the lesser value of women compared to warrior men, and any challenge must be supplied on her behalf by the audience struggling to integrate its response to the play, weighing the girl's idealism against the cynicism and instability of the world around her.

The language of fame and nobility, with the concomitant motifs of "not betraying" and avoiding cowardice, is also significantly exploited when a married woman character dies for her husband, and here too the idea of competition between the genders may arise. In the cases of Evadne in *Supplices* and Alcestis in her name-play, the motif of "not betraying" is especially strong, but here the rejected betrayal is within the family rather than connected to the polis or a larger community, as the ideal of spousal loyalty is pushed to its limit. In *Supplices*, Evadne has escaped from her home in Argos and reached the Attic location on her own, already a violation of norms (1038–44). She leaps upon the funeral pyre of her

[57] See above, pp. 238–40.

husband in a transport of grief, but also in a hypertrophy of the spousal
virtue of loyalty. Although the text of her aria (990–1030) is corrupt at
several points, it is safe to assume that she refers to the good fame she seeks,
to her refusal to betray her spouse, and to the sincere emotional attachment
of a noble wife (1015, 1024, 1029–30). In her exchange with her father Iphis
(1045–71) she sees her act as "glorious" (1055) and "unheard of" (1057) and a
source of "fair victory" (*kallinikos*, 1059, an epithet associated with athletic
victory and the hero Heracles), and claims she will outdo all other women
not in the socially approved qualities cited by her father ("Do you mean in
the works of Athena [sc. weaving] or in good sense [sc. modesty and
obedience]?" 1062), but in "virtue" (*aretē* 1063), which here must connote
both the bravery to welcome death and intense loyalty to her husband.
Similarly, while her father recommends the concealment of silence because
he finds such an idea abnormal, Evadne insists that all should learn of her
deed (1066–7). The notion of "dying together" with one's dear ones is
evidence of the close analogy of intrafamilial kinship-ties, even of female
and male, with the ties of male comradeship (*hetaireia*) and military solidarity. The familial version is a traditional motif in narratives, embracing
unfulfilled wishes or promises, actual suicides, and distorted variations.[58]
The expression of ultimate loyalty is found both in the daughters of
Erechtheus and Praxithea who commit suicide to fulfill a pact with their
sacrificed sister and in Pylades who, in *Orestes*, insists on joining his friend in
death (although neither of them ultimately kills himself). The idealized view
of the marriage-tie exemplified in the Evadne episode coexists in Greek texts
and society with hierarchical views that depreciate the female's worth and
her capacity for ethical activity. The brief treatment in *Supplices* is unusual
for its concentration of male-centered terms and open rejection of norms of
female subordination and invisibility.

   Whereas Evadne insists on joining her husband in death, Alcestis is ready
to die to save her husband from death. Often, such an offer of one-for-one
substitution is briefly dramatized as an option that is not really allowed;[59]
but *Alcestis* presents the bittersweet working out of such a substitution.
Alcestis herself uses the language of non-betrayal (180, 282–90). One sign of

---

[58] E.g., wishes: *Od.* 20.61–82 (Penelope's wish for death if Odysseus is lost); *Hel.* 293, 833–40; suicide:
Phoen. 1283, 1458–9, 1578, Laodamia in *Protesilaus* (Collard and Cropp 2008b: 71–3), Soph. *Trach.*
719–23 (the motive of loyalty is mixed with the idea that it is intolerable to live on with the shame of
having caused Heracles' death); distorted variation: Aesch. *Choe.* 894–5, 904 (Orestes' jeering demand
that Clytemnestra die with her lover Aegisthus).
[59] Thus older relatives of sacrificial victims say they would happily offer themselves instead: *Hec.* 385–8,
Hcld. 453–7, *Phoen.* 968–9; cf. *IT* 1004–6, *Andr.* 406–20.

the difficulties that arise in this situation and of Admetus' imperfect understanding of his situation is that he uses the same term of Alcestis' imminent
death when he says "don't betray/abandon me" (275). It is, to be sure, a
traditional motif of lamentation that the survivor complains to the dead that
they have abandoned or betrayed the survivor;[60] but the idea jars here
because Alcestis' "not betraying her husband" is also her willingness to die
for him.[61]

   Alcestis once refers to herself as "the best" or "an excellent" wife and
mother (324–5). The term *aristos* could convey simply "excellent of its kind"
and not evoke an excellence that appropriates or competes with male values.
But in the course of the play, it emerges that Alcestis' virtue is indeed in
competition with that of Admetus. The motif of the "best wife" is first
introduced by the chorus at 83–4, then asserted by both the chorus and the
serving woman in 150–6 (with the addition of the terms "glorious" (*eukleēs*)
and "surpassing" (*hyperbeblēmenēn*)), and *aristē* is repeated five times more
(235, 241, 442, 742, 899). The notion of gender-competition enters subtly at
first when Pheres claims that Alcestis' act has made the condition of
all women "more fair-famed" (623–4): this implies the traditional
male-centered assumption that women have no fame or only ill fame (like
the paradigmatic Helen and Clytemnestra). Admetus himself makes the
competition explicit, as he contrasts his parents with Alcestis when he
accuses his father of cowardice and failure to avail himself of "a noble
contest" (*kalon agōna* 648). But Pheres easily turns the tables on his son
and throws back at him the same comparison with Alcestis: "You dare to
speak of my lack of spirit, you utter coward, when you have shown yourself
inferior to a woman?" (696–7).[62] Pheres' barb strikes its target, for in
Admetus' speech of recognition (935–61) he admits to the loss of his status,
imagining the indignant public comment "Does he think he is a man?" and
echoing language used of and by Alcestis (955–7 "shamefully," "did not
dare," "lack of spirit," "has fled from death"). In *Alcestis*, the audience is
asked both to enjoy the fairy tale and to perceive its insufficiency as a
representation of human life, and the implicit competition for virtue
between Alcestis and Admetus reveals fault lines in the ethics of loyalty
and bravery, while the frustration of Alcestis' altruistic intent highlights the
difficulty of all human endeavor.

[60] Alexiou 1974: 182–4.
[61] The same verb *prodounai* is addressed to Alcestis by Admetus twice without an explicit object, in 202 (reported) and in 250, where the meaning is possibly "give up" rather than "abandon [sc. me]," but even with the former meaning the echo contributes to the ambiguity of this motif.
[62] The *agōn* between Admetus and Pheres is discussed more fully above, pp. 227–9.

MISOGYNISTIC SPEECH

Speakers in tragedy make many statements that reflect the male-centered construct of the female as the other or the polar opposite of the desired model of (male) humanity: emotional and uncontrolled rather than rational and self-controlled, naturally closer to raw nature than to organized culture, prone to concealment and deception rather than openness and honesty. This hierarchy based on superiority of the male is conveyed not only in words, but in aspects of plot structure and outcome, and it is assumed or expressed not only by male speakers but by female speakers. Nevertheless, this discourse of gender difference is at times destabilized by the complications of motivation, situation, and rhetorical context that are typical of tragedy and especially of Euripidean tragedy. When Hippolytus utters his tirade against all women in *Hipp.* 616–68, any thoughtful member of the audience will note that Hippolytus is not aware of all the circumstances, either on the purely human level (the contrast in ethics between Phaedra and the nurse, the points in which Phaedra herself agrees with Hippolytus, Phaedra's efforts at self-control – backhandedly acknowledged by Hippolytus later in 1034) or on the supernatural level (Aphrodite's anger and will). Jason's similar, briefer complaint in *Med.* 569–75 is likewise blocked from full endorsement (for at least some viewers) by the prior build-up of the case that Jason has been unjust and unfaithful to a solemn pledge and by the sophistic style of his speech as a whole.

Female characters themselves often endorse the male-centered constructs of the female as inferior or more suspect. In her first speech to the chorus (*Med.* 214–66), Medea provides an analysis of the condition of women that strongly challenges cultural norms and that applies broadly to ordinary women, indeed more appropriately to other women than to her own case.[63] Nevertheless, at the emphatic conclusion of her speech, when she appeals for the chorus' silence regarding her as-yet-unformulated plan to punish her husband, she utters the gnome (263–6): "In other matters a woman is full of fear, without courage for warlike valor and unequipped to face the weaponry of battle; but when she is in fact wronged over her marriage-bed, no other mind is more disposed to deadly violence." This generalization relies on the assumption that women are more uncontrollably swayed by sexual matters than are men, the same idea later exploited by Jason in the complaint just referred to (*Med.* 569–73): "You women carry things so far that you think everything is perfect if the marriage-bed is successful, but if, conversely, any adversity befalls that relates to the bed,

[63] For the details, see Mastronarde 2002b ad loc. and Pelling 2000: 198–203.

you consider what is finest and dearest to be most hateful." Some listeners in the Athenian audience might do no more than accept that Medea is voicing the accepted traditional "wisdom" prevalent in society; or from a modern perspective one would say that the male author has unreflectively put the male-centered gnome into his female character's mouth. But other listeners, even in antiquity, may have perceived some disjunction between Medea's other claims of competition with or equality with the male and this admission. Such a disjunction may invite a psychological or a rhetorical interpretation, or both. Psychologically, Medea is so intent on establishing and maintaining her heroic status that she may be, here and elsewhere, envisioning "all that is female as despicable."[64] Rhetorically, Medea is striving to evoke and strengthen solidarity between herself and the chorus, and so tailors the maxim to her audience of ordinary women (assumed more easily to share the cultural stereotype), even though this involves glossing over the difference of her own history and situation. A similar reading can be entertained for *Medea* 407–9: "In addition, we are by nature women, completely without resources for noble actions, but the most skilled contrivers of every form of harm." Here the appropriation of a misogynistic principle is not directed strategically to the internal audience, but seems rather a bitter and defiant ventriloquism of the male view, since it refers back with "noble actions" (*esthla*) to the displays of valor on which men pride themselves (248–52), but from which women are excluded by the restrictive conditions of their lives, leaving them only with the arena of "evils" (*kaka*, that is, underhanded and ignoble actions) in which to compete. In both these passages,[65] it does not appear that Euripides is simply echoing the cultural stereotype innocently, although some would still argue that in spite of any questioning or irony the end result of the plot would bear out the fears encapsulated in the stereotype. In any case, Medea makes an even more clearly self-conscious use of the stereotypes when she plays the "weak woman" in deceiving Jason in the fourth episode (866–975). Scenes like this one and the parallel scene of Clytemnestra verbally overpowering Agamemnon in Aeschylus' *Agamemnon* display the contradiction within the gender-constructs of the Greeks: on the one hand, women are assumed to be mentally inferior to men; on the other, their capacity for clever deception of unsuspecting and unperceptive males is also held against them.

[64] Foley 2001: 264–5.

[65] In a third passage, *Med.* 384–5, the transmitted *sophai* would make the statement about ability with drugs and poisons apply to all women, but the emendation *sophoi* (masculine plural form used by a female speaker of herself, by a common tragic idiom) limits the statement to Medea herself and is preferable here: Mastronarde 2002b ad loc.

Phaedra comes close at several points to sharing Hippolytus' opinions about women, but unlike him is always ready to make distinctions. Her analysis of the human failure to enact the good that is recognized (*Hipp.* 375–87) is cast in universalizing masculine plurals and posits "the fine and noble" (*to kalon*) as the proper aim in life, which is the aristocratic or heroic goal. Nevertheless, when she lists the pleasures that divert humans from the pleasure of "the fine and noble,"[66] the items evoke either possible complaints about women or qualities associated more strongly with women. "Long conversations and leisure, a pleasant evil" suggests vaguely what Hippolytus is more explicit about later, women's gossipy and potentially seductive conversations (645–50),[67] and *aidōs* is both a quality expected of women and one involved in Phaedra's concession to the nurse's pressure (335). Critics who have favored a fully psychological interpretation of Phaedra believe that all these terms are particularly apt for her own situation (she is, on this view, the bored upper-middle-class housewife with nothing better to do), but in fact she herself believes she has distanced herself from such temptations, and if they are crucial in her downfall, she is blind to this fact.[68] More likely, the match between the first two and the traditional accusation voiced by Hippolytus is designed to mark Phaedra's will to distinguish herself from the fallible and erring women of the cultural stereotype. She recognizes the stereotype as prevalent (406–7: "I also realized that I am a woman, an object of hatred for all"), but believes, unlike Hippolytus, that not all women are the same, that there are both good women and bad women. She no more believes that all women are justifiably "an object of hatred to all" than that all well-born women are corrupt, though she assigns special significance to the sins of the well-born, as providing a bad example for other women. The statements and actions of Phaedra's nurse also have an ambivalent relationship to misogynistic discourse. On the one hand, through her role in the development of events the nurse seems to embody the charge of Hippolytus that servants act as go-betweens, and Phaedra herself repeatedly acknowledges (in rejecting) the shameful temptation offered by the nurse. Moreover, the nurse herself endorses, in an emphatic position at the conclusion of her speech (478–81),

---

[66] The interpretation of 382–7 is much disputed. In my view, 382–3 implies that *to kalon* is a pleasure in Phaedra's eyes, and I take *dissai*, "double," in 385 to refer to *aidōs*, "shame," and not to *hēdonē*, "pleasure" (the latter is the view of Kovacs 1980).

[67] Compare Andromache in *Tro.* 651–2 and Hermione in *Andr.* 930–53 (discussed below).

[68] Compare Deianeira: in Soph. *Trach.* 438–49 she sincerely acknowledges the power of love and says she will not "fight with Eros" (I do not regard this as a speech of deception), but this assertion reflects blindness to the way her intentions will evolve under the pressure of the situation, for she shortly thereafter does "fight with Eros" by trying to regain Heracles' love.

the idea of a gendered expertise in dangerous scheming and magic. On the other hand, the examples with which she tries to persuade Phaedra offer gods and males as the models to follow in managing and living with sexual peccadilloes (451–69), as if it goes without saying that such erotic fallibility is universal, just as the power of goddess is ubiquitous (447–50).

Both Medea and Phaedra's nurse provide examples of the connection of scheming with the female, and this stereotype, though it, too, is embedded in many plays, also depends on a selective acknowledgment of the tradition of stories and of "reality."[69] In escape deliberations,[70] it is almost always the female partner in the dialogue who arrives at the clever and successful plan. If we trace only the word *mēchanē* ("device, scheme") and words of the same root, we can observe that these are used by Medea of her scheme against Jason (*Med.* 260) and by Artemis of the nurse's ploy in approaching Hippolytus against Phaedra's will (*Hipp.* 1305). Andromache makes a tellingly offhand comment to the slavewoman who is to carry her message to Peleus: "you might find many devices, for you're a woman" (*Andr.* 85). The chorus, the messenger, and Ion all refer to the scheme to poison Ion with this term (*Ion* 1116, 1216, 1326). Goddesses, too, are associated with this root: Poseidon uses it of Athena's device of the Trojan horse (*Tro.* 10), Iris uses it of Hera's scheme to persecute Heracles (*Her.* 855), and Helen uses it of Hera's method of frustrating Paris' desire with the phantom Helen (*Hel.* 610). Although these passages resonate with a pejorative cultural stereotype, there are in fact twice as many instances of the *mēchanē* root applied to men in Euripides, and although some of the usages are neutral (as is also Phaedra's use in *Hipp.* 331 of her efforts to overcome her desire), there is often a connotation of disapproval, as frequently in *Andromache* in reference to Menelaus and Orestes (66, 447, 549, 995, 1116).

Misogynistic maxims and judgments fill a long section of the anthology of Johannes Stobaeus entitled "Criticism of women" (4.22g), and Euripidean passages account for over half of the sixty-six extracts. Striking as some lines from lost plays are, they cannot contribute much to our discussion since we lack sufficient knowledge of their context. There was a noteworthy debate on misogyny in *Melanippe the Captive*, from which we have fr. 493 attacking women and fr. 494 defending them (usually assumed to have been spoken by Melanippe). It is frustrating not to know more of

---

[69] For the theme in general and its assocation with the female see Detienne and Vernant 1978; obvious counterexamples are Odysseus, Sisyphus, Autolycus, and in historiography or anecdote the notion of the clever Greek bamboozling the unsuspecting non-Greek (Hall 1989: 80, 122–3; Mastronarde 2002b: 301).

[70] See below, p. 287.

this, but at least these extracts again indicate that other plays incorporated both traditional misogynistic discourse and arguments against it, dramatizing a contestation of values rather than any simple endorsement.

Leaving aside such fragments, we may conclude this section by considering some speeches in *Andromache*, a play that features a number of parallels and reversals of situation and argument.[71] In the first part of the play, the confrontation of Andromache and Hermione presents a concentration of negative gender-related stereotypes spoken by women themselves. It is noteworthy that Andromache confronts Hermione and Menelaus in sequence and not together, creating two different contexts, a more private one (in the presence of the female chorus) in which the women speak of marriage and sex (147–272), and a more public one (with Menelaus and his male attendants and her captive son) in which Andromache speaks of public issues (justice, her duty to her son) and comments on the public reputation of Menelaus and the Spartans (309–463). Hermione's invective against Andromache (155–80) exploits the hierarchies that posit Europe's superiority to Asia and Greeks' to barbarians: women from Asia are more skilled in drugs (159–60), and barbarians lack a *nomos* to prevent incest and other odd couplings, such as Andromache's with the son of the killer of her previous husband (170–6). The anti-barbarian rhetoric is undercut already by the preceding build-up of sympathy for Andromache and the unflattering aspects of Hermione's boastful opening lines. Her repeated recourse to it in the following line-for-line argument (234–60) comes across as bluster, and at 244 Andromache delivers a telling rejoinder ("both there [in non-Greek lands] and here shameful things involve shame"), while the end of the play confirms the propriety of the linkage of Andromache's blood and Neoptolemus' in the Molossian dynasty. Hermione's specific charge of incest and kin-murder is likewise an ironic one when alleged by a member of the family of Atreus, and she will end up marrying the murderer of her current husband.

Andromache, for her part, counsels subservience to a husband, but also engages cultural stereotypes (183–231). She uses an example of Thracian customs in a kind of *reductio ad absurdum* (215–18). The unstated milder scenario implied by the Thracian example is that it is simply Greek *nomos* that a husband alienated by his wife may turn to another woman, and thus Hermione is rebelling against this practice by trying to kill the rival rather than to amend her own behavior to win her husband back. The rhetorical

---

[71] See above, pp. 74–7. For discussions of the speeches of Andromache and Hermione see McClure 1999: 158–204, Allan 2000: 118–48.

question asks whether, if she were transported to Thrace, land of royal polygamy, Hermione would kill all the other wives of her husband. To do so (and by implication simply if she kills the one concubine Andromache) would create such a strong model of sexual incontinence (*aplēstia lechous*, literally "inability to be filled or satiated by the bed") that the charge would besmirch all women (compare the opposite logic at *Alc.* 623–4: Alcestis' nobility brings better fame to all women). Andromache then concedes that "we women suffer this disease in a worse form than males do," but adds that "we have guarded against it well" (220–1). Andromache next tries to enforce upon Hermione the propriety of silence about "a shameful subject" (236–42), but Hermione objects that marital matters are of prime importance for women. Andromache accepts this generalization, but again tries to assert a distinction that will differentiate proper female behavior from improper: "yes, that is so, *if* we women are experiencing them well (or, alternatively, dealing with them well); but otherwise, these matters are not fine (*kala*)." The strongest statement reflecting an essentially male-centered view is the condemnation of woman as dangerous expressed when Andromache criticizes the arrangement of the world in the concluding lines of the episode (269–72): "It is outrageous that for savage serpents some god has created cures to help mortals, but when it comes to something more savage than a viper or fire, no one has yet discovered a curing drug to use against woman." This has the sweeping universality characteristic of speakers like Hippolytus and Jason, although in context it is clearly intended by its speaker not to be a universal reproach, but only to apply to violent women like Hermione.[72]

Andromache, then, a sympathetic character, is represented as a "good woman," one who sees virtue in overcoming or resisting the faults that are "natural" to the female and in complaisantly making the best of whatever her husband has to offer.[73] Within the sharp antagonism of the *agōn* of *Andromache*, the heroine differentiates herself as strongly as possible from Hermione on the specific issue between them. As in the examples discussed in Chapter 6 in which the rhetoric (re)shapes character dynamically, here too the position taken seems surprising and extreme. Andromache

[72] The harshness is reduced if *Andr.* 273 is retained as genuine, since "against woman" would then be "against a bad woman," but it is most likely that 273 was added later for the very purpose of softening the sweeping statement.
[73] Another female figure supporting the assumption of the prevalence of bad behavior among women is Clytemnestra in *IA* 1162–3: "it is a rare attainment for a man to get a wife like this [sc. a good one such as I have been up to now]; it's not a rare thing to have a bad (*phlauran*) wife." This utterance is part of Euripides' strategy of maximizing the contrast between this Clytemnestra before the incident at Aulis and the Clytemnestra of the standard tradition.

apostrophizes her dead husband and, suggesting a mythological past for which there is no other evidence (and thus it was probably created *ad hoc* by Euripides) asserts that for Hector's sake she even went along with his love affairs (*xunērōn*, "I shared in the love") and "often" gave her breast to Hector's bastards, winning her husband's attachment by her "virtue" (222–7). Critics have been at odds about how this claim would have gone over with Euripides' audience. While it may be excessive to judge it, with Michelini,[74] as so "over the top" that it momentarily destroys the audience's engagement with Andromache's cause, the boast is unusual enough in the specificity of *xunērōn* and the inclusion of "often" to make a complete normalization of reception (as if it were entirely comparable to known examples)[75] not fully plausible. Again, Euripidean rhetoric is asking for a complex response: admiration for the exquisite pointedness of the argument and for the speaker's impulse to be of service to the one she loves and to offer an alternative to the injustice of Hermione's position, combined with awareness that a norm has been exceeded and that rhetoric runs out of the control of the speaker and easily becomes similar to self-delusion.

Later in the play, misogynistic commonplaces become prominent again in a paradoxical form when Hermione herself offers self-justification and admonition (920–53). Leading up to this rhesis is a dialogue of Orestes and Hermione in which their shared assumptions about a woman's place are clear (896–919). Orestes treats it as a self-evident surmise that the trouble in which Hermione finds herself is connected to her marriage: "for a woman who does not yet have children, what trouble could there be except in regard to the bed?" (904–5). Likewise, he advances the question-and-answer dialogue by surmising that another woman is involved, that the rival is Andromache, and that Hermione has contrived against her rival something "of the sort a woman would" (907–11). The close matching of assumptions and easy progress of the exchange may be understood as inspiring Hermione's confidence in Orestes and thus prompting her rhesis, and the rhesis in turn is to be interpreted on one level as a self-presentation aimed at Orestes, designed to rehabilitate Hermione into a prudent woman in his eyes. She blames "the visits of bad women to my house" (930) for her mistakes and echoes Andromache's arguments from probability: in 938–42, she asks essentially "what did I have to worry about from her?" just as in 192–204 Andromache had asked rhetorically what she could have gained by trying to displace Hermione. But Hermione's rhetoric also aims at a wider

---

[74] Michelini 1987: 92–4. [75] Gregory 1999–2000: 67–9.

audience, since in her lengthy peroration she offers an admonition to all
married men of good sense.

Never, never (for I shall say it more than once)
ought husbands who have any sense
to allow women to pay visits to a wife in the home.
For these are the teachers of evils.
One assists in corrupting the marriage for some profit,
while another who has strayed wants the wife to share this sickness with her,
and many do it out of wantonness. And from these causes
men's households suffer. Therefore, carefully guard
the gates of your houses with closed doors and bars,
because the visits of women from outside
accomplish nothing healthy, but many ills. (*Andr.* 943–53)

    This is the sort of admonition that one would expect to hear from a male
voice: Hippolytus offers a characteristically extreme version in *Hipp.* 645–50
("it ought to be the rule that no attendant go in to see a woman, one should
establish as their housemates only mute biting beasts"). For at least some of
the Greek audience, however, the advice itself and the misogynistic construct behind it will be destabilized by the incongruity of the speaker of the
advice and by the effort required to incorporate this version of events (with
Hermione spurred on by the cutting comments of visiting women) into the
situation the viewer has constructed from the information in the first half of
the play (where Hermione seems an arrogant Spartan princess, unlikely to
interact with the local ladies). Again, one may wonder whether effective
rhetoric has slipped over into self-deception. The dishonesty would be
neatly matched by that of Orestes, who reveals in 959–63 that he already
knew the details that he seemed so sympathetically to surmise in the earlier
dialogue.
    In this context of the characters' contesting claims about the nature
and role of women, it is interesting to note the brief statements that the
chorus-leader contributes after each lengthy speech. Such statements are
often gnomic or irenic, sometimes indecisive, and were perhaps not always
fully attended to in the theater. But by representing the reaction of an
internal audience, they may hint at one kind of reaction a speech might
provoke in the external audience. At 181–2, after Hermione's first speech
with its anti-barbarian charges against Andromache, the chorus-leader
comments that the female mind is given to jealousy and is hostile to rivals.
She follows Andromache's reply not with any comment on it, but with a
polite appeal to Hermione to make peace (232–3). The choral songs express
sympathy for Andromache but also (in 464–93) disapproval of a situation in

which two women are rivals in one house. Despite this sympathy, after Andromache's first speech to Menelaus, the chorus-leader gives a critical judgment: "you have spoken to excess, as a woman addressing a man ... and the prudence of your mind has overshot the mark" (364–5).[76] After Hermione's admonition to husbands, the chorus-leader comments in terms of female solidarity and concealment of troubles (954–6): "You have spoken too critically against your own kind. / This is, to be sure, understandable in your case, but all the same, / women ought to put the best face on women's troubles." The choral tendency toward moderation, face-saving, and peace-making thus highlights the intensity of feelings and vehemence of argument displayed by the individual characters and points to the external audience's difficult task of balancing identification and distance, and of settling on any firm judgment in the lively dialectic presented by the drama. In these examples from *Andromache* as well as in the other aspects of the representation of women in Euripidean tragedy, it is clear that generalizations about gender are as much exposed to questioning and qualification as any other values and rules normally accepted without nuance in cultural constructs of hierarchy and order.

---

[76] The sense of the final words is very uncertain, and there may be a line missing between the two clauses; among other possible interpretations are "prudence has departed from your mind" and, with a subject supplied in a lost line, "your intensity has driven good sense from your mind"). There is a similar comment on excess when the chorus-leader refers at 726–7 to the uncontrolled anger of old men in response to Peleus' invective against Menelaus, although in the following choral ode the chorus praise Peleus very strongly.

CHAPTER 8

Euripidean males and the limits of autonomy

In discussing the topics related to women characters in the previous chapter, it was frequently necessary to refer to male characters for comparison, since in ancient Greece (as in other cultures) the prevalent thinking about women featured so many polarities contrasting the two genders, and women were often defined by their lack of or deficiency in qualities ascribed to (free, Greek, adult) men. One of the commonplaces in discussions of the normative discourse about women and men is that the true man has a high degree of autonomy (controlling his own body and actions) while a woman lacks autonomy. This can also be expressed by the claim that males can be "subjects" while women are normally "objects." Recent scholarship has made good progress in moving beyond such a sharp contrast and exploring possible areas of subjectivity and more autonomous agency in the women represented in Greek drama and in the women of Attic society.[1] My purpose in this chapter is to examine the other side of the gender contrast by exploring how the autonomy and agency of male figures are portrayed in Euripidean tragedy. Tragedy in general is frequently about failure, frustrated intentions, and destruction; and tragedy routinely questions the efficacy of all human intention and agency, setting it against a background of fate and divine will and thus following in the footsteps of Homer and other earlier poets who presuppose in their story-telling traditional religious beliefs about man's inferiority to the gods in power and understanding. It is no surprise, therefore, that blocked intentions are so much a part of the Euripidean dramatic world.[2]

Late fifth-century Athenian assumptions about masculinity were conditioned by a long, mainly aristocratic tradition of selective emulation of the

[1] E.g., Wohl 1998, Foley 2001, Griffith 2001, Goff 2004.
[2] In some plots, one may even say that the frustration is extended to divine agents. The clearest example is Apollo in *Ion*, but one may also consider Artemis (*Hipp.* 1328–34) and Castor (*El.* 1298–302) and note the limited effect of Zeus's apparent salvation of Heracles' family (*Her.* 827–9).

heroes as depicted in poetry and oral stories, with extensions and adaptations of heroic ideals for the purposes of contemporary conditions, such as the democratic political system and the role of imperial power. We already noted in previous chapters that those who took the straightforward man of action (an Achilles, Heracles, or Ajax) as a primary model for masculinity could interpret eloquence, persuasion, and rhetorical skill, or cleverness, resourcefulness, and cunning, as markers of a failure of masculinity or indeed as "feminine" traits that undermine a true man's status and fame.[3] Some interpreters hold that competition for status was so definitive of full masculinity that any retreat from aggressive self-defense was likely to arouse disapproval in an Athenian male audience. It may be granted that the ideal of the democratic citizen as physically inviolable and autonomous and capable of being a subject (that is, of legitimately initiating and executing actions) was something that clearly distinguished the Athenian citizen in ideological terms from non-Athenian males within (and outside) the city, from women, and from slaves. Nevertheless, in interpreting Attic tragedies we need to avoid the assumption that cultural views on issues like masculinity and autonomy were monolithic and uncontested and that they univocally determined how a dramatic character or a dramatic action was to be read by a Greek audience. While it is important to be aware of the perceptual filters through which the ancient audience interpreted speech and action, if the operation of such perceptual filters is applied too crudely and inflexibly understood, we risk merely reasserting the validity of a particular viewpoint, a viewpoint that usually represents the bias and the aspirations of one dominant sector of the society, or (even more narrowly) of that sector in its normative public discourse, a discourse that need not apply strictly in other contexts. A further danger is that we might ignore the inconsistencies and contradictions that are inherent in any culture, and so posit a completely self-consistent and harmonious culture, and thus replicate in another form the idealizing and totalizing error of an old-fashioned "classicism."

The Athenians valued both aggressive and irenic qualities in each other, and the ordinary democratic citizens could be suspicious and resentful of their wealthy and "well-born" fellow-citizens while simultaneously admiring and craving their splendor and leadership.[4] Social life entails a similar complexity, for a person is involved, over time and at the same time, in a

---

[3] See p. 212 above.
[4] For various aspects of the negotiation of relative positions and status between the elite and the ordinary citizens, see Ober 1989, Griffith 1995 and 2005a, Wilson 2000.

number of positions and identities, with different constraints and powers, and with different positions in a hierarchy of status. Stories and dramas invite the recipient to observe and experience vicariously a range of positions, and the multiplicity of an individual's own experiences of power and dependency, equality and inequality allow her or him to identify with the other as well as with the like, and with the subjected as well as with the dominant. Tragedy in particular provides an arena of fantasy or alternative experience that invites the audience to identify temporarily with figures of many statuses (slave and free, Greek and non-Greek, elite and humble, male and female).[5]

Since we are about to discuss dramatic figures as agents, it is appropriate to note that both the concept of the "person" or "self" and the concept of "agency" are fraught with philosophical difficulties. The concept of the "self" or of a unitary personal identity has been challenged, especially in postmodern theories. In feminist critiques, in particular, there have been a variety of efforts to come to terms with how gender identities are constructed and with how one is to carve out any room for autonomy and legitimate agency once the powerful forces of ideological and cultural norms have been recognized. Of course, the methodological and metaphysical problems are much greater when we are dealing with real human beings rather than with characters in literature. Literary and dramatic "character," of course, has its own problems,[6] but it is a limited representation governed by certain conventions and ellipses, engaging the reader or audience in processes of interpretation similar, but not identical, to those applied in everyday life to the conundrum of human behavior. In a tragedy, a fixed and somewhat consistent reference point is provided even for a fractured, mobile, incomplete or enigmatic identity by the mask, the name, and often the underlying narrative of the genealogical and mythological tradition known to the audience and invoked by the poet. Figures in serious Greek literature, particularly in Homer and tragedy, can be seen as what Bernard Williams called "centres of agency": they are shown in the epic or the drama to have beliefs, desires, and purposes, and they manifest the "basic conceptions of action for human life: the capacities to deliberate, to conclude, to act, to exert oneself, to make oneself do things, to endure."[7] This is an appropriate rough definition for our purposes, because it includes deliberative and conative aspects that are especially important in looking at

[5] Griffith 2005b.
[6] Cf. Gould 1978, Goldhill 1986: 168–98, Blondell 1989: 16–25, Easterling 1990, Gill 1996.
[7] Williams 1993: 40.

tragic characters, for whom speech often predominates over physical action and whose exertions often fail to produce the desired result.

In the previous chapter, we considered similarities and contrasts in purposes and motivations between male and female figures in Euripidean tragedy, as well as the relation of the two genders to inside and outside, to household and city, and to fame and bravery. There the primary interest was the female. In this chapter it will be the male (although comparison with the female will be made at a few points).[8] Here we will be interested primarily in the significant actions that contribute to the chain of causation that moves a plot from beginning to end[9] and in the failed or frustrated intentions that are significant for their lack of effect. "Actions" must be given a broad sense, but it is proper to take account of distinctions that were often made in normative discourse: some are "actions" in the narrower sense of physical effort requiring physical strength (which, if present in Greek tragedy, will normally be reported as having occurred offstage), but others (much more typically) are verbal efforts – argument or persuasion, deceit and trickery. Since failure is so common, it is also revealing to ask whether a character has failed through ignorance, through the opposing action of another character, or through divine intervention. Plot-type or story-pattern is often an important determinant of the nature of the action available to the characters and of the opportunity for success.

To structure the discussion, it will be helpful to adopt a classification by social and age status. Like almost all societies, Greek society ascribed different capacities, tendencies, and cultural roles to persons not only according to gender but also according to social class and to sexual development. Class is generally reflected in Greek tragedy by the difference between anonymous humbler figures and the elite named figures, who are individuals known

---

[8] For females as agents, see esp. Foley 2001; also Rabinowitz 1993, Wohl 1998.

[9] Thus I am considering for the most part the actions within the dramatic time of the play itself. In Euripides, the antecedent actions that brought about the situation as it is at the start of each play are mainly revealed in the scenes of the prologue, especially the monologue that begins his plays. Typically, human male agency, along with divine agency, predominates in the antecedents of a drama. For instance, in *Alcestis* the fate that ordains an early death for Admetus, the hospitable treatment Admetus gives to Apollo, and Apollo's "gift" of the opportunity for a substitution to prolong Admetus' life all set up the situation. In reaction to these circumstances, Admetus accepts the offer and canvasses his kin for a volunteer, and his parents refuse to help, while Alcestis accepts the sacrifice instead. Alcestis' decision is vital to the initial situation, but arises only in response to the actions of others. In lost plays like the *Hippolytus Veiled* or *Stheneboea*, a woman may have had a more significant role in creating the initial situation, but this is uncommon in the extant plays, where figures like Hecuba, Iphigenia, and Creusa are victims of men or divine agents. The most female-determined initial situation is that in *Andromache* (Hermione has plotted to bring Menelaus to Phthia during her husband's absence so as to kill her rival; Andromache has secreted her son and sought refuge at an altar), but the more remote antecedents derive from the actions of males (Menelaus, Neoptolemus).

from the mythological tradition or newly grafted onto it. The named figures are clearly the focus of the audience's attention, and three age-classes[10] are of interest when considering these figures as agents: adolescents or those in the "ephebic"[11] stage, men in their physical prime (normally married with children), and old men.[12] For unmarried youths in Attic society the transitional status could be stretched out over several years, since for males marriage was often postponed to the age of about thirty; but in myths young heroes tend to come of age, embark on adventures, and get married within a compact time-frame. The onset of old age was not easy to define for men: some indications were physical decline, withdrawal from warrior status or political power, and the existence of grandchilden or at least of grown-up sons taking independent action.

The humbler figures in tragedy include the messengers, nurses, and attendants of various kinds. Some of these are identified as slaves, some as free, and in some cases their status is indeterminate, but (in the monarchic and aristocratic world of the heroes) clearly subordinate. For the most part, these subordinate figures act either as extensions of the named characters who command them or as reporters of information to which the major characters must respond.[13] Like the chorus, the humble characters can make a very valuable contribution to the polyphony of dramatic voices, often offering a moderate viewpoint that contrasts with the intensity of the main characters.[14] At times, however, the humble characters are crucial to plot

[10] I do not consider here child-characters, who are usually silent extras; they contribute to pathos in several plays by being victims (or expressing bereavement, in *Alc.*), but do not themselves deliberate or take action. See Kassel 1954.

[11] Although the extent of "ephebic training" in Athens in the fifth century is uncertain (the organized ephebate we hear of in written sources probably originated in the second half of the fourth century), rites of passage for adolescent males were known in other Greek cities and clearly had analogies in traditional myths about young heroes like Perseus, Orestes, Theseus, and Pelops. Such myths and rites associate youths with several possible inversions or liminal states (typical of a liminal stage in a rite of passage), among which are hunting, deception, and the use of disguise. See P. Vidal-Naquet 1968 and 1986, Winkler 1990, Hesk 2000: 85–122.

[12] This tripartite structure is reflected in Greek legal and military systems (in eligibility for different offices and in different forms of military service) and is also taken for granted in Greek studies of human behavior, as can be seen in Aristotle's generalizations about the young and the old (marked by various excesses and deficiencies) as differing from the (unmarked) adults in their prime (*Rhet.* 2.12–14, 1389a3–90b13). The age-classes for females are analogous: unmarried but newly sexually mature girl (in Athenian society generally given in marriage as soon as possible), married woman capable of bearing children, and post-menopausal old woman.

[13] Cf. the Argive herald in *Heracleidae* 55–287 who, as representative of the absent persecutor Eurystheus, physically attacks the suppliants and argues at length for their surrender; the Theban herald in *Supplices* 399–584 is similar, except that he attempts no physical action.

[14] E.g., in *Hippolytus* the old servant admonishes both Hippolytus and Aphrodite in 88–120, and the messenger defends Hippolytus' reputation and advises Theseus not to be harsh to his dying son (1249–54, 1261–4).

development. Male servants provide several important examples.[15] In several cases, the long-standing loyalty of the servant to the family is cited as a justification for these actions, so that even when taking the initiative these subordinates are viewed as extensions of the interests of their masters, an idealizing view of the attitude of slaves that is common in tragedy.[16] Because they are used by the playwright for the advancement of the plot, most of the humble agents are successful in carrying out what they attempt,[17] but the audience is not heavily invested in these figures in and of themselves. Only a female servant, the nurse in *Hippolytus*, comes close to the status of a figure whose feelings might be of interest to the audience. Despite her deceptiveness and her crass morality, the nurse does care for Phaedra and wants above all to keep her alive, and the way her intentions backfire, in that her actions make Phaedra more desperate and precipitate her active suicide, is a typically tragic motif that echoes the experiences of the major characters.[18]

UNMARRIED YOUNG MALES

Young males of an age that might be considered "ephebic," unmarried and just entering on the responsibilities of adulthood, are of natural interest in both Greek myths and tragic plots because the youths' experiences illustrate the possibilities and dangers of a key life-transition and provide models for initial testing in the realm of political or familial responsibility, in the

---

[15] Cf. the servant in *Alcestis* 747–860, who, apart from confirming for the audience the painful social awkwardness of the situation created by Admetus' insistence on hosting Heracles, informs Heracles of the real situation so that he decides to rescue Alcestis; the old man in *Electra* 487–698, who brings about the recognition, guides Orestes to Aegisthus, and carries the message that lures Clytemnestra into a fatal trap; the old man in *Ion* 725–1047, who urges Creusa to take vengeance and later tries to carry out the poisoning (1171–216); the old servant in *Iphigenia in Aulis* 855–95, who reveals the truth about the false marriage to Clytemnestra and Achilles.

[16] The same motivation of loyalty in *Hel.* 1640–1 is cited when someone blocks Theoclymenus' attempt to go indoors to harm his sister, but it is disputed whether this is the chorus-leader or a male servant: see Kannicht 1969: II.422–5, Allan 2008: 338. Women servants, at least in the extant plays, are less likely to contribute to the causal chain (but cf. the slave in *Andr.* who takes the risk of carrying a plea for help to Peleus). The nurse in *Hipp.* is the female servant who is most influential on the course of action (see above, pp. 69, 223–4). As in the case of the old man in *Ion*, one function of the nurse figure in this version is to assume the onus for something shameful, the approach to Hippolytus, so that Phaedra may maintain a greater admixture of sympathy and understanding in the judgment of the audience. In both cases, the moral status of the elite figure is improved to some degree at the expense of the servant figure.

[17] In one case of failure (of the old man's attempt to poison Ion in *Ion*), this outcome is no real surprise to an audience, given Hermes' predictions in the prologue, and it conforms to the viewers' desire to see mother and son recognize each other.

[18] This case is somewhat comparable to that of the Corinthian messenger in Soph. *OT* (treated by Aristotle as exemplary in his discussion of *peripeteia*, *Poetics* 11.1452a24–6).

earning of personal status, and in the formation of friendships and alliances with other males, especially their age-mates.[19] In respect to the latter, the figures of Orestes and Pylades became one of the prime examples in antiquity of loyalty between friends.[20] Euripides' *Iphigenia in Tauris* gave a major impetus to this motif in its portrayal of the pair. After Iphigenia proposes to her unrecognized brother that she could arrange for his safe release if Pylades remains as sacrificial victim, Orestes insists on being the one to face his doom among the Taurians so that Pylades can return home alive (597–608). Pylades, for his part, is reluctant to accept the exchange and to survive without his friend (674–86). Later, Orestes extends this theme of loyalty when he rejects the notion that he might escape without Iphigenia (1004–11). These verbal declarations of resolve are matched by physical action when the two youths prove their manly worth, both when spotted alone at the seashore by the herdsmen and when defending their ship against Thoas' men during the escape. These violent physical actions are necessarily offstage events narrated by messengers (301–33, 1366–85), and they reflect well on the spirit of the two youths even though the first action does not prevent their capture and the second is not fully successful until Athena intervenes as *dea ex machina*.[21] While on stage, Orestes' only significant actions affecting the progress of the plot are verbal. When he initially refuses to reveal his name to the priestess (499–504), this action serves the plot by retarding the recognition in a typical way, but it also suggests the character's keen sense of honor and dishonor. Later, he clinches his acceptance by his sister as truly her brother by speaking of the tokens of

---

[19] Young females are also at a key life-transition and this is frequently reflected in tragic roles in the motif of marriage (Andromeda in *Andromeda*, Hermione at the end of *Andr.* and *Or.*, Electra at the end of *El.*, *IT*, and *Or.*, Antigone in *Phoen.*, the offstage princess in *Med.*) or of death as a substitution for marriage (the sacrificed virgins in *Hcld.*, *Hec.*, *IA*; or Cassandra as fatal bride of Agamemnon in *Hec.* and *Tro.*; on this motif see Seaford 1987, Rehm 1994). Unmarried girls who are raped by gods and bear children are featured in *Alope*, *Auge*, *Danae*, and *Melanippe the Wise*, and the same motif lies in the past of the plays in which the mothers are recognized by the children they abandoned long ago (*Antiope*, *Hypsipyle*, *Melanippe the Captive*). In the absence of marriage, the unmarried girl may show a particularly close tie to the natal family, especially to a father or brother (Antigone in *Phoen.*, Theonoe in *Hel.*, Electra in her plays, Iphigenia in *IT*). The Electra of *El.* is the most strikingly ambiguous young female: she shares "ephebic" qualities with Orestes in that she is in an extended liminal state between virginity and marriage (and refuses to attend the festival of Hera, which had distinct roles for unmarried girls and for married women: see Zeitlin 1970), she dwells in a lonely outlying district, and she engages in deception; but she also manipulates her mother by appealing for help after childbirth and speaks strongly on behalf of the proprieties of male and female roles (931–51, 1068–75).

[20] The pair appears in all three tragedians, and Pylades is regularly depicted along with Orestes in visual representations from classical vase-painting to Roman sarcophagi (*LIMC* s.vv. Orestes and Pylades).

[21] See above, pp. 165–6.

his family's history that were depicted in Iphigenia's childhood weaving or stored out of sight in the maiden-chambers of the palace (808–26).

Orestes meets with success in the end, as the plot-type requires, but that success is not entirely his own doing or in his own control. It depends on the support of his comrade Pylades, the joint participation of his sister,[22] the acceptance of her clever plan, the use of deceit (in a scene in which Orestes is silent), and an element of divine favor. The escape scheme in particular suggests the insufficiency of open physical action that is one possible ideal of mature masculinity. To the degree that Orestes is regarded as an ephebic figure in a liminal phase of his maturation, the use of deception is fitting. Nevertheless, it is his sister who turns out to be the most effective agent in the escape plot. Just as Helen does in the closely parallel sequence of action in *Helen* 1032–89, Iphigenia develops the plan for escape after her male partner's plans are rejected as impractical (1017–51). The pattern follows gender stereotypes, since the men propose violence or other physical action, while the women think of a deception (*dolos*) in which most of the pretence has to be carried out by the female partner acting a role.[23] Thus *Iphigenia in Tauris* is a good example of a tendency seen in many Euripidean plays: the main characters are relatively weak as individuals and are shown engaged in a world in which they must negotiate a complex situation in cooperation with, or even dependency on, others and also hope for the uncertain favor of the gods.[24]

Revenge-plots are another type in which successful action based on deception is to be expected. In *Electra*, Orestes can again be thought of as in a quasi-ephebic status: he operates in the countryside and not in town, "disguises" himself from his sister, and uses stealth against both victims. The collaboration of Electra is essential, whereas here the other ephebic youth, Pylades, is a silent presence, much different from the Pylades of *Iphigenia in Tauris* or *Orestes*.[25] Several of the important steps leading (unintentionally)

[22] Iphigenia's dogged pursuit of extracting information from the captives makes possible the recognition, and she carries off the entire deception of Thoas while Orestes is a silent and veiled presence; gender norms are restored during the actions described in the messenger speech, since Iphigenia is carried aboard the ship by her brother (in the same way that the stolen statue of Artemis is, thus marking the parallel between Orestes' rescue of his sister and Apollo's rescue of his) and her participation is limited to the verbal one of a reported prayer (*IT* 1398–402).
[23] See above, p. 274. There is a similar sequence of rejected suggestions of a male interlocutor followed by the adopted scheme of a female character in the revenge-plot in *Ion* 970–1038, but there the scheme is carried out by the old slave.
[24] See pp. 163–6 above.
[25] He maintains the silence that characterizes the Aeschylean Pylades except when the latter briefly breaks so significantly into speech to seal Clytemnestra's fate (Aesch. *Choe.* 900–2). In *El.*, the prompting function has been shifted to Electra.

to the recognition and revenge are due to the humble farmer (who rashly, in Electra's view, invites the strangers inside for hospitality) and the old man (summoned because of the need for hospitality, but then crucial in the recognition and the revenge-plot). Orestes himself is noteworthy for his passivity, caution, and concealment, especially evident first when he withholds his identity from Electra beyond the point where he knows it is safe to reveal it to her, and later when he lurks in the house as he awaits his mother, who is manipulated by the old man and Electra rather than by Orestes himself as in Aeschylus' *Choephori* or Sophocles' *Electra*. The plan for one killing comes from the old man (612–39), for the other from Electra (646–62). Offstage, however, as described by the messenger (774–855), Orestes is a successful deceiver and avenger and shows enough authority to persuade the attendants of Aegisthus to acknowledge him as the legitimate lord of his household. Once back onstage, nevertheless, he reverts to uncertainty before the matricide (962–87) and falls into repentence immediately after it (1177–232). Orestes is thus portrayed as uncomfortable both in his traditional mythological role of avenger of his father and in his social role of young adult attempting to prove himself ready for independent action. In a striking challenge to aristocratic ideas of male achievement,[26] neither birth nor divine favor has helped him live up to expectations.

Orestes offers the latest Euripidean variation on the young hero. In this play, it is striking how the efforts of the main characters are constantly frustrated and how by the end the element of ephebic idealism seen in *Iphigenia in Tauris* is carried *ad absurdum*. The mutual affection and loyalty of Orestes, Electra, and Pylades are displayed without irony in their earlier interactions (1–315 and 729–806). After the condemnation of the siblings at the trial, however, the motif of sticking together even unto death alludes to and distorts the versions seen in *Iphigenia in Tauris*.[27] Soon, moreover, Pylades and Electra have developed a plan for all to survive by kidnapping Hermione and killing Helen. Orestes spends much of his time engaging in a series of futile speeches, before Menelaus, Tyndareus, and the Argive assembly.[28] The display of warrior status is here directed against eunuchs and women. Among so many failed efforts, Orestes is successful against the

---

[26] Cf. *El.* 367–90, in which Orestes himself comments on the unreliability of assumptions based on birth and other traditional criteria of worth or superiority. On the problem of the authenticity of various sections of this speech, see Cropp 1988:123–6, with references to other discussions.

[27] Cf. *IT* 1007–8 ~ *Or.* 1039–40 (Electra asks Orestes to kill her; he refuses with the same reason he used to insist he would not leave Iphigenia behind in danger of her life), *IT* 674–99 ~ *Or.* 1069–97 (Pylades insists he must die with Orestes even though he is not condemned to death).

[28] See above, pp. 240–5.

Phrygian slave,[29] and he temporarily halts Menelaus' assault on the door. But the finale apparently shows him unable or unwilling to complete the negotiations with Menelaus and then stopped on the brink of murder and arson by Apollo.[30] Orestes is not simply an ephebe who makes the wrong choices. He is a noble youth who uses all the right terms of freedom, nobility, and bravery, but the system of values to which he appeals is exposed as being in a state of collapse.

In terms of the motifs identified as particularly "ephebic," Hippolytus is the figure who most typically fits certain parts of the pattern: he is a hunter, is associated with the wild outdoors, and is alienated from political and domestic society. On the other hand, he is not at all associated with disguise or deception (although accused by Theseus of these faults). Nevertheless, his story can be regarded as the exemplary tale of an adolescent who fails to make the transition to adulthood: by his attachment to Artemis, he tries to freeze himself in time and in social/sexual development, but the conditions of mortal life allow no such permanence of status, and the goddess symbolizing sexual generation, a necessary concomitant of change and mortality, destroys him. In his actions within the play, Hippolytus is characterized by refusal: refusal to pray to Aphrodite at the prompting of the old servant (the warning figure), refusal of the nurse's overtures, refusal to abandon his oath of silence. Although the first of these reflects a disastrous attitude, the latter two are the marks of his integrity, allowing him to be awarded heroic fame for being truly noble. In his speech-acts, Hippolytus is generally unsuccessful. His initial prayer to Artemis is effective in an ironic sense, since his wish "may I reach the end of my life in just the condition in which I began it" (*Hipp.* 87) will be fulfilled by his imminent death. His dismissal of Aphrodite echoes the sort of past speech for which the goddess now pursues him. His tirade against women is based on a misjudgment of Phaedra's intentions and contributes to Phaedra's decision to lay a false accusation of rape against him.[31] His self-defense before Theseus is futile and ill adapted to its recipient.[32] Only the speech-act of forgiveness at the end is truly effective. Even in the messenger's narration, Hippolytus' physical action of trying to control his horses fails, as does his pathetic address to them ordering them to stop (1219–26, 1240–1). The frustration of action and the futility of speech we observe in Hippolytus are shared by Phaedra and

---

[29] At least on the assumption that Orestes does shepherd the slave back into the palace (cf. 1510, 1524); but Willink 1986: 330–1 argues that he in fact abandons this intention at *Or.* 1526 and lets the slave go off to tell Menelaus what is happening (see also Medda 2001: 314–15 on this problem).
[30] See above, pp. 191–5.   [31] See above, p. 253.   [32] See above, pp. 225–6.

Theseus, whose only effective utterances, in the letter and the curse (856–90), are unjustly destructive ones. The play thus achieves a consistent and terrifying portrayal of the tragic conditions of human existence.

Pentheus, the other youth who clashes fatally with a god, has moved into an adult role as king of Thebes, and as such he exhibits the bluster and violence characteristic of several tragic rulers. His apparent political control of affairs is demonstrated by the arrest and imprisonment of some maenads and of the foreign stranger (Dionysus in disguise). But these accomplishments are quickly and easily undone by Dionysus. Although after the "palace miracle" Pentheus briefly continues to threaten to lead military forces against the maenads (*Ba.* 778–809), he soon loses all initiative and free will and succumbs to the suggestion that he don female garb and spy on the maenads. Pentheus' immaturity is revealed both on the political level (by his blustering entrance, his threat to Teiresias, and the first messenger's fear to speak openly) and on the psychological level (by his frequent reference to the imagined sexual misbehavior of the maenads and by his agreement to Dionysus' suggestion that he would like to see the maenads).[33] His inflexibility and his blindness to the evidence reported to him go hand in hand with the portrayal of hyper-masculine behavior, as seen in his mockery of the stranger's effeminate appearance and insistence on control of and superiority to women. Thus he offers a different model of failed maturation as a male and human being.[34]

The efficacy or ultimate success of ephebic figures is correlated to the plot-type. In the recognition-play *Ion*, the adolescent Ion moves from being a slave (a status here dignified somewhat by the fact that it is temple slavery) to free, from non-citizen living in Delphi to citizen living in Athens, from anonymous orphan to legitimate heir of the rulers of Athens through his living mother, Creusa. Although the conclusion is a happy one for Creusa and Ion, as agents the humans are no more perceptive and successful than in many plays with bleaker outcomes, and (as discussed earlier) wondrous chance or wondrous divine manipulation determines the actual result of

[33] For the former cf. *Ba.* 210–22, 345–51, 668–71; for the latter *Ba.* 222–5, 234–8, 314–18, 353–4, 453–9, 487, 686–8, 811–16, 1059–62.

[34] A comparable theme of the political failure of young king or leader is evident in Eteocles and Polyneices in *Phoen.* Although Polyneices is in fact married (a given of the myth of the Argive expedition against Thebes), it is clear that the brothers are within just a few years of their coming of age (*Phoen.* 63), have struggled with their new leadership of their family (prompting Oedipus' curse), and now strive to establish or maintain an honorable elite status of independent wealth and power. While the curse of their father and Laius' disobedience before that certainly underlie the events of the play, the beliefs and desires of the two sons mesh perfectly to bring about the final disaster.

events and decisions.[35] Young heroes gaining brides provided leading roles in a few lost plays. These are based on the mythic pattern of a brave youth daring to wrest or rescue a daughter from a possessive or threatening father. The success of such young men requires courage and the favor of assisting divinities, and perhaps at times deception.[36]

Orestes in *Andromache* and Theoclymenus in *Helen* may be viewed as transgressive examples of the motif of young man seeking bride. In *Andromache*, instead of taking a daughter away from a cruel or dangerous father, Orestes abducts (or rescues) the unhappy wife of his enemy, whom he is also shortly to murder. In both actions he successfully uses deception, verbal in the case of Hermione and verbal and physical (slanderous rumors and ambush) in the case of Neoptolemus. The criticism of Apollo by the chorus, the messenger, and Peleus align this action of Orestes with his previous matricide, also ordered by Apollo, the god of ephebes.[37] This portion of the plot of *Andromache* thus seems to offer a bitter twist on the traditional pattern and yet another variation on the problematic coming-of-age of Orestes. In *Helen*, on the other hand, Theoclymenus is a non-Greek king and serves as the villain in the plot, so he is naturally depicted as using his authority in a violent and oppressive way, falling short of the moral stature of his late father and his sister Theonoe, who outdoes him in imitating her parent and caring for the memory of his virtue. Moreover, Theoclymenus is a second Paris, hoping to snatch Helen from her true husband, and he falls prey to Helen's deception when she takes advantage of this hope. The failures that the Egyptian king experiences as an agent undermined from so many sides (by his sister, by Helen and the unarmed Menelaus, and by the chorus-leader[38]) are all justly deserved, and do not reflect as negatively on comfortable assumptions of masculine superiority and power as in the case of Orestes, since Theoclymenus is non-Greek.[39]

[35] See above, pp. 197–8. In *Phaethon* we have another youth, this time on the brink of marriage, discovering his divine father, but with a disastrous result; unfortunately, the fragments do not provide us enough clues about how Phaethon's character and motivations were worked out in the full play: see Diggle 1970, Collard *et al.* (1995) 195–200, Collard and Cropp 2008b: 191–6.
[36] Cf. *Oenomaus*, featuring Pelops and Hippodameia (Collard et al. 2004: 133–43, Collard and Cropp 2008b: 25–6), and *Andromeda*, featuring Perseus and Andromeda (Collard and Cropp 2008a: 124–9). Sophocles also wrote plays of these titles. Deception is involved in a standard version of Pelops' defeat of Oenomaus, but it is impossible to say whether or how Euripides used this motif.
[37] See above, pp. 76–7. [38] Or his servant: see n. 16 above.
[39] Achilles of *IA* might also be considered here. In the text as we have it, Achilles comes across as an awkward mixture of inexperience, idealism, pride, and self-absorption, but many of Achilles' lines are under strong suspicion of being post-Euripidean, so it is risky to analyze his motivations and character in too much detail. He may have been (in part?) an idealistic youth operating in a world of more

OLD MEN

Male characters who are identified as old (with terms like *presbus*, *gerōn*, *geraios*, *polios*) are hardly to be expected to be major physical agents, since for the Greeks old age implies a significant diminution of physical powers, as is clear from the lamentations of aged choruses in both tragedy (*Heracles*, Aeschylus' *Agamemnon*) and comedy (Aristophanes' *Wasps*) and the portrayal of the difficult physical movements of various aged characters. This weakness may be viewed as a return to early childhood, since the old sometimes need to be led by the hand, as a child is led by a slave tutor, or they regularly use a staff for support.[40] The weakness of old age is a particularly important motif in the first half of *Heracles*: Amphitryon and the chorus complain of it (228–35, 268–72, 312–15); both are loyal to Heracles and his family but unable to act against the tyrant and his youthful henchmen, and they are left with only words or song as a mode of resistance. In tragedy, however, speech itself may be powerful in the external communication system, appealing to the audience for approval or sympathy, or in the internal communication system, persuading or deceiving another character. Although Lycus mocks Amphitryon for having only words that cannot forestall his actions (238–9), the old man's oral articulation of resistance is essential to several dramatic goals. In the prologue and first episode, he balances the despair of Megara and prepares for the later exploration by Heracles and Theseus of suicide, heroism, and despair. The praise of Heracles that he delivers (170–205) sharpens an audience's sense of the unfairness of Hera's intervention and makes it difficult to accept Hera's perspective on what Heracles' actions have merited from the gods. He challenges Zeus in a manner that heightens the shock when, after his criticism of the god's neglect seems to have been refuted by Heracles' miraculously timely return, the rescuer turns into destroyer.[41] Amphitryon's speech has a brief moment of internal efficacy when, as Heracles' agent, he deceives Lycus into entering the house to meet his punishment (701–33), but after the disaster he is reduced to lamentation and the sympathetic informing of his ruined son, and he is sidelined in the decisive final debate.

---

cynical, ruthless, or fallible adults, like the young Menoeceus in *Phoen.* (see above, p. 266), but he seems to be trapped by the same compulsiveness of the traditional outcome of the myth that undercuts the efforts of the other figures in this play.

[40] Cf. *paidagōgein* in *Hcld.* 729, *Ba.* 193; for the staff as a regular prop for old characters or choruses of old men, cf. Mastronarde 1994: 579–80.

[41] See above, pp. 167–9.

Iolaus in *Heracleidae* is initially similar to Amphitryon. He, too, is a suppliant protecting young children and unable to resist superior physical strength on his own. But his words (1–15, 26–30) articulate themes of loyalty, service to the family, and nobility, and these values far outweigh any questions one may raise about his relation as citizen to the city of Argos.[42] Iolaus' themes of service and loyalty in fact set the terms of the alignment of the Athenians and the Heraclids against the Argives and are effective in winning the support of Demophon (and thus of the Athenians). The same motifs are then echoed in the declaration of the daughter of Heracles that she must volunteer herself for sacrifice (500–34, 574–96). On the other side, the old man's impotence is again obvious in his physical collapse at the departure of the girl for sacrifice (602–4). And that impotence becomes a matter of humor when he later insists on going to the battlefield with borrowed armor that he cannot himself carry and is led by the hand by an attendant (720–47). In a typically Euripidean reversal, however, Iolaus' will to fight turns out to be no laughing matter. Apparently as a reward for his justice and loyalty, the gods answer his prayer for one day of rejuvenation and he is able to chase down and take captive the arch-enemy Eurystheus (849–63). Thus, through a wondrous gift of divine favor, he matches the successful military effort enacted offstage by the younger males (Hyllus, Demophon, and their respective troops). The weak old man is an ideal vehicle for the reversal of expectations that is so dear to tragic drama, and is comparable in this to the apparently weak, oppressed women characters who turn out to be strong enough to exact revenge from males.[43]

Peleus in *Andromache* presents a similar case, although the arc of his role is the reverse of Iolaus'. The slave woman who assists Andromache in the prologue suggests that Peleus is too old to be of any help even if he answers the summons (80). He later arrives with only a single attendant.[44] Nevertheless, his arrival and commands freeze the action during the long verbal confrontation with Menelaus (577–714), and his presence proves so authoritative that he personally removes the captives from the control of

---

[42] Mendelsohn 2002: 74–85 suggests that there would be something suspect for the male Athenian viewer in the fact that Iolaus has fled from his native city with his family, as if he has thereby exhibited a culpable failure of civic values. This seems to me very unlikely. Civic ideals are only one category of values within which males operate, and the Athenians did not disrespect the values motivating Iolaus' flight or necessarily find unusual the pragmatic act of going into exile to avoid execution at the hands of rivals or enemies (Socrates' failure to go into exile was the unexpected choice).

[43] Cf. Oedipus in Soph. *OC*, and for oppressed females Medea and the Hecuba of *Hec.*

[44] The only sign of an attendant is the command to a singular addressee in *Andr.* 551 "lead me on (more) quickly"; possibly this is just the slave woman sent to summon him.

those who detain them and he unties Andromache's bonds. This triumph over Menelaus, who either has a number of his own attendants or has been commanding the slaves of Neoptolemus' household, is provocatively unrealistic, underlining the weakness of Menelaus and the inherent strength of Peleus and his family, which is also celebrated in the choral ode that follows this episode. Peleus' performance echoes, but outperforms, the strength that Andromache expressed in her forthright speeches to Hermione and Menelaus, despite their power over her body. This idealized victory of the virtuous is counterbalanced in the exodos (1047–288), however, by the helplessness and grief of Peleus. There, the old man can only react to the report of his grandson's treacherous death. That is a more typical tragic role for the aged,[45] although Peleus' situation is somewhat redeemed by the assurances of Thetis *ex machina*.

Tyndareus in *Orestes* has a comparably efficacious role, but in a much darker light, since his effort to avenge his murdered daughter Clytemnestra pits him against his own grandchildren.[46] He arrives with the expected mute attendants, who lead him on and off (474, 629), and faces down a weak Menelaus (his son-in-law), who only briefly tries to justify loyalty to Orestes in the stichomythia 482–90 and then does not participate any further in the dialogue with the old man. Menelaus' retreat is a little more seemly here than in *Andromache* because it is delayed until after the old man's withdrawal from the scene, but it is clear enough that Tyndareus' threats have been effective. And later the messenger's report reveals that the old man has fulfilled his promise to see that the Argive assembly votes to condemn his grandchildren, Orestes and Electra (915). As we saw in Chapter 6,[47] in his verbal confrontation with Orestes, Tyndareus' attitude is without nuance, and his vehemence is unrelieved, or, by the end of his appearance, heightened. His ultimate purpose, however, is finally blocked by Apollo's intervention.[48]

---

[45] Old men as mourners: Amphitryon in *Her.*, Iphis in *Su.*, Oedipus in *Phoen.*, Cadmus in *Ba.*, and probably Merops in *Phaethon*.

[46] Old men are less frequently agents of revenge than old women. Cf., in addition to Tyndareus, Amphitryon in *Her.* (but he is clearly subordinate to Heracles), Oedipus in Soph. *OC* (vengeance through his curse and refusal to return to Thebes). Among old women characters we find Hecuba in *Tro.* using speech to get vengeance on Helen (but this effort is abortive since she will not really be punished: see pp. 221–2), and actual physical vengeance in the case of Hecuba in *Hec.* (see pp. 72–3) and Alcmene in *Hcld.* (see pp. 259–60), though the killing of Eurystheus is to be completed after the end of the play.

[47] See above, p. 241.

[48] Another old man in conflict with his younger kin is Pheres in *Alcestis*, who attacks Admetus only after being provoked. Though he is an unsympathetic figure, he has a key effect in planting the seed for Admetus' recognition. See above, pp. 228–9.

Concern for and protection of the younger members of a family are the factors common to the roles of most of the older males, while the lack of these attributes marks characters like Tyndareus and Pheres as particularly harsh.[49] Iphis in *Supplices* is perhaps the extreme case of a minor character defined by the loss of his kin. Earlier parts of this play develop the contrast between the women – the mourning mothers and Aethra (who is motivated in part by pity) – and the warlike males, especially in Theseus' cold first reaction to the supplication for aid, in his control of the funerals, and in the civic-military memorialization of the Seven in Adrastus' funeral oration. The episode featuring Evadne and Iphis reverses the gender roles and destabilizes the distinctions. As we saw earlier,[50] Evadne co-opts male language and heroizes her suicide upon her husband's pyre, while her father Iphis is the image of helpless weakness, wishing he had never begotten children at all.

The concern of men for offspring is also an important motif in *Medea*, where it applies to the mature males Aegeus (who does not yet have any) and Jason (who is devastated by his loss) and to the older male Creon.[51] The king of Corinth is motivated especially by concern for his daughter when he exiles Medea (283, 327, 329), and Medea's appeal on behalf of her children exploits Creon's natural affection to win the reprieve of one day that she needs for her revenge (340–7). Later, it is the hold of the daughter's affection over Creon that is the key to Medea's sending of the poisoned gifts (941–5, 1154–7). Creon's affection leads him to embrace his daughter's corpse and cause his own death, as his conventional wish "may I die with you" is gruesomely fulfilled despite Creon's struggle to extricate himself from the corpse's embrace (1204–20).[52] Like Jason, Creon finds his plans for the future wrecked by Medea.

In the complex action of *Phoenissae*, the Theban Creon has a more varied role than most figures who are old men.[53] He appears first as as a patriot and counselor, loyal to the "tyrannical"[54] regime of Eteocles, but embodying prudence and caution in opposition to Eteocles' rashness in planning to

[49] On this motivation, see p. 255 above. Possibly Hellen was a harsh old man in *Melanippe the Wise*, where he apparently urged his son Aeolus to destroy the exposed twin babies (not known at that point to be the children of his granddaughter Melanippe): Collard and Cropp 2008a: 569–71; for an image probably reflecting this play with a "fierce-looking" Hellen see Taplin 2007: 193–6.
[50] See above, pp. 268–9. [51] For Creon's age, cf. *Med.* 1209–20.
[52] The Creon of *Phoen.*, also an older male, likewise acts at crucial points to protect his sons.
[53] Creon's role is less varied if one accepts some of the deletions that have been proposed by many scholars in the text of *Phoen.* The points I make here rely on a form of the text that does not accept so many deletions: for discussion see Mastronarde 1994, with references to many earlier treatments, and Medda 2006.
[54] Cf. *Phoen.* 506, 523–5, 549, 560–1.

defend the city from assault (706–47). The defense strategy turns out to be
Creon's, not Eteocles', in a deliberate reversal of the achievement of Eteocles
in Aeschylus' *Septem*. On the other hand, he is merely a passive recipient of
Eteocles' "testamentary" orders about what is to be done if Oedipus' curse is
fulfilled and both brothers die (757–77). In the third episode (834–1018), his
patriotism gives way before his love of his youngest child Menoeceus, and
Creon plans to send him away to safety. His choice thus echoes on another
level the entanglements and difficulties of duties to city and duties to kin
that are explored throughout the play. The boy frustrates this plan by
deceiving his father, so that Creon appears as a stricken mourner in the
fifth episode (1308–31). In the exodos (1582–1736), the role of civic leader
reemerges. If the main lines of this disputed passage are accepted as
Euripidean, then Creon reverts to his traditional role of unjustly denying
burial (as previously explored in *Supplices*, in Sophocles' *Antigone*, and in
Athenian funeral orations) and also exiles Oedipus. Here, too, his actions do
not project full autonomy and efficacy. He cites the public good to explain
his decrees about Polyneices and Oedipus, but also refers the responsibility
to others, Eteocles and Teiresias. He is forceful enough to withstand
Antigone's objections to these two acts, but gives up on the planned
marriage between Haemon and Antigone to protect his surviving son
from the threat that Antigone will kill him if she is forced to marry instead
of accompany her father into exile.

Of the old men characters, then, a few do indeed carry their intentions
through to fruition, but the only one who comes close to full success is the
unpleasant Tyndareus of *Orestes* (but his effort to punish his grandchildren is
ultimately blocked by Apollo, the saving *deus ex machina*). Iolaus succeeds in
winning protection from the Athenians, but loses his young cousin to
human sacrifice, and then in a final miracle wins rejuvenation from the
gods. The brief successes of Amphitryon and Peleus soon yield to violent
reversals of fortune. Creon (in *Medea*), Oedipus, and Iphis are little more
than victims of others. From the perspective of a narrow definition of
masculinity that emphasizes physical vigor, aggression, and competition
for personal honor, one might claim that the elderly male is feminized,
that is, limited to words in place of action, preoccupied with children and
family, and frequently shown mourning. But on a more expansive view of
masculinity, one might say that in the heroic world, with its assumption of
kingship and a pre-democratic polis, males who retire from the youthful
activity of war are thrown back on the household and naturally develop sides
of their being that were secondary, but not necessarily absent, in their prime.
In either event, the old men provide a version of the "other" through which

the playwright can evoke pathos and the audience can vicariously experience marginality and vulnerability, with occasional moments of unexpected triumph.

So far, we have considered the marked age-categories, those who are not yet fully mature and fully incorporated into the status that could be regarded as the fulfillment of a natural end (*telos*) and those who have declined from it. The unmarked class is what is left in between, mature men, usually married and the parents of children. Mature male figures in tragedy bear a divided identity: on the one hand, they are elite males who, to a greater extent than the aged or the ephebic, operate and compete in the public realm, maintaining honor and status and attempting actions to help friends and harm enemies; on the other hand, they lead a household and are involved in differentiated relations with wives and children (and possibly elderly parents). An adult male is ideally imagined as enjoying freedom of action and authoritative power. But a generic feature of Greek tragedy is that it commonly explores extreme situations in which freedom and power are constrained by ignorance, illusion, and bad judgment or limited by fate or divine will. In many of the plot-types favored by the tragedians, the norm of the tragic world is to fail in some key aspiration or effort, often spectacularly and fatally. The failures of major male figures in tragedy are not merely a matter of portrayal of an overstepping traditional aristocracy being destroyed to make room for the more democratic society of the contemporary world of the audience.[55] These failures offer to all a "religious" lesson of the superior power of forces outside human control and of the insufficiency that distinguishes mortal from god.

A good starting-point for consideration of the mature male figures is Jason in *Medea*, who suffers a complete undoing of his plans. Acting independently of Medea, he contracts an elite alliance with the royal family of Corinth by marrying the only child of the king. He presents this as a carefully calculated plan to bolster his future, and it is preferable to accept his self-presentation as sincere (and cold-hearted, morally obtuse, and deluded) rather than as a hypocritical defense created for the sake of his debate with Medea.[56] Medea exploits Jason's self-confidence and stereotypical thinking when she acts out the part of the weak female and echoes his claim of foresight, so that Jason's own *ēthos* is a vital causative factor in

---

[55] Seaford 1994 and 2007.   [56] See above, pp. 256–7.

facilitating the disaster. By the end, he has no tie to the Corinthians, no bride or prospect of future offspring, and Medea has utterly erased her marriage with him by destroying the children born of it. The tragedy reveals that Jason's autonomy is severely limited. As a male agent, he must concern himself with his status vis-à-vis other males and communities (such as the kin of Pelias and the city of Iolcus): these concerns condition the antecedents of the play and the insecurity that makes him want the tie to Creon and Corinth. His identity as a family man also imposes constraints, or consequences for ignoring such constraints. Medea's pride, anger, cunning, and deception are forces that Jason is shown to be unequipped to resist. Medea is an unusually successful agent, outperforming the three males who interact with her.[57] But, equally important (and this is characteristic of Greek tragedy, even in Euripides), the gods are always capable of frustrating a man's power to act effectively. There are ample indications in *Medea* that Jason has offended the gods by violating his oaths and abandoning the obligations he entered into by supplicating Medea and establishing a kind of peer-to-peer relationship of *xenia* with her.[58] It is the intersection of Jason's *ēthos* and choices, Medea's determination to uphold her status, and divine interest in punishing transgression that makes *Medea* an effective tragedy not only in terms of Medea herself, the primary figure of the drama, but also in terms of Jason, who has the secondary role.

The Theseus of *Hippolytus* is unusual in his fallibility. As a national hero and founder of civic institutions, Theseus is often portrayed in an idealistic light: this is particularly true of Sophocles' *Oedipus Coloneus* and largely true for Euripides' *Heracles* and *Supplices*.[59] In *Hippolytus*, Theseus is entangled in the same human ignorance that makes Phaedra and Hippolytus suffer. It is not surprising that he gives credence to the deceptive deathbed testimony of his wife, and the deadly outcome becomes inevitable because of the supernatural force of the wish/curse that he utters before even the chorus can react to the first revelation of Phaedra's accusation (874–92). Theseus uses his power as king and father to exile his son. But it is not just his mistake about the true facts of the situation that corrupts his agency. There is a suggestion of haste both in the quickness with which the curse is invoked (891–2, 899–901) and the refusal of any delay for further consideration of Hippolytus' claim of innocence (1036–7, 1051–9), and Artemis

---

[57] Mastronarde 2002b: 8–12.   [58] See above, pp. 199–200.
[59] Mills 1997; see above, pp. 173, 215. It is possible, however, that some lost plays may have been less flattering: Sophocles' *Phaedra*, Euripides' other *Hippolytus*, plays entitled *Peirithous* by Achaeus and Critias.

reproaches Theseus harshly on these points (1321–4) before offering the consolation that this was, after all, Aphrodite's doing (1325–8). Moreover, as discussed earlier,[60] the *agōn logōn* demonstrates an underlying alienation between father and son, who espouse quite different values and who each distrust the lifestyle adopted by the other: on Theseus' side, this is reflected in his suspicions of Hippolytus' religious practices and his demeaning references to non-civic cults and charlatanism. Theseus acts to avenge the alleged wrong to his wife and to reassert his own status within the family and in the eyes of all Greece, which knows him as a punisher of the wicked and godless (976–80). These are proper elite, male motivations, but in a tragic world they do not lead to a happy result.

Admetus is another mature male character whose aspirations are largely foiled, but as is characteristic of *Alcestis* in general, his experience is full of paradox. Prior to the time of the play, his excellent performance of the duties of hospitality won Apollo's favor and the "gift" of foreknowledge of his time of death and the opportunity to provide a substitute. During the play, this same impulse to be an accommodating host results in Heracles' favor of rescuing Alcestis from death. But, as we have seen earlier,[61] Admetus' status as a respectable male is strongly challenged by the appropriation of terms of bravery and loyalty by Alcestis herself and the application of those terms to Alcestis by others, as well as the realization that his survival may be branded as a proof of cowardice.[62] Moreover, even Admetus' prime virtue becomes problematic. Apollo's favor causes a rift with Admetus' parents: however unattractive Pheres may be in the *agōn*-scene, his son hardly comes off much better when he renounces his mother and father, failing one of the principal duties of Greek morality (*Alc.* 636–47, 662–8). The chorus and Heracles agree that Admetus' concealment of the death of Alcestis from his *xenos* is outside the norm and causes offense even as it pays extreme honor (551–2, 561–2, 816, 822, 832–3, 855–60). When Heracles turns the tables on his host and engages in the charade of depositing "a woman" with him, entrusting

---

[60] See above, pp. 225–6.   [61] See above, p. 270.

[62] It is ironic that Alcestis herself contributes to diminishing the value of her gift of life to her husband and in setting up Admetus' failure. She requests that Admetus promise not to marry again and subject their children to the dangers of a hostile stepmother (299–319), apparently a new idea at that moment, for it reverses the assumption she made in her earlier reported speech (181–2: "some other woman will possess you [the bed]: she couldn't be more chaste than I, but perhaps more fortunate"). In response, Admetus forswears not only remarriage, but all pleasures of festivity, and not merely for a year of mourning, but forever, thus apparently expanding the promise to permanent celibacy. In Greek society the decision not to remarry and have more children (328–35) need not imply celibacy, since the status of concubine served precisely the function of sexual companionship without marriage or offspring. But abstinence from sympotic feast and music (343–7) and substitution of a statue as bedmate (348–56) do appear to promise that.

her only to his own hands, Admetus is browbeaten into virtually betraying his promise to Alcestis.[63] On one level, the male hero of this play gets off easy: through his powerful male friends, he delays the time of his death and does not even lose his wife. But the play as a whole demonstrates the necessity and importance of the condition of human mortality and reveals the strains and failings, within an extreme situation, of the supposedly straightforward values of friendship, gratitude, and loyalty.

The mature males discussed so far are entangled in conflicts between relations within their families and their status in the public realm. The next group of characters to be considered might be called the "unidealized political leaders." Although such figures tend to get their way in the end, Euripidean tragedy does not present a very flattering portrait of this sort of male achievement.[64] In *Hecuba*, we see both Odysseus and Agamemnon interacting with the title figure. As elsewhere in Euripides (in the lost plays *Philoctetes* and *Palamedes*), Odysseus is the model of an ambitious politician, not aspiring to the highest position, but pleased to serve the army and its leaders in any way that will reflect well on his intelligence and fame. The chorus' chanted (anapaestic) narrative of the Greek assembly (*Hec.* 130–40) credits Odysseus with the decisive intervention in the debate over the ghost's demand for human sacrifice, and he appears on stage to fetch Polyxena. In his debate with Hecuba,[65] Odysseus evokes patriotic ideals very familiar to the Athenians, but in a context where the means toward the end are questioned and where the coldness and calculation of Odysseus are clearly less sympathetic than the desperation of Hecuba or the noble resolve of Polyxena. Agamemnon is likewise portrayed in the light of contemporary political leadership. His view is defeated in the assembly that debates the sacrifice, and later his sympathy for Hecuba and his judgment that Polymestor deserves punishment are constrained by his need to avoid the criticism of his fellow Greeks (850–63). Thus, Agamemnon expresses allegiance to traditional moral values (justice, piety, respect for supplication, pity for the wretched), but does not have the heroic sense of self-worth and

---

[63] There is, of course, an unending debate in the scholarship on *Alcestis* about Admetus' character and whether or how seriously he "betrays" Alcestis in the final scene: see esp. Burnett 1965, Michelini 1987: 41–9, 325–9, Rabinowitz 1993: 67–99, Gregory 1991: 19–49. My view is that the play is not primarily about Admetus' individual character, that the play designedly invites shifting and contradictory responses, and that the "betrayal" at the end must be read in the immediate context of Heracles' browbeating and deception and the overall context of failed human intentions and confusion of normal values.

[64] Much the same can be said of some political leaders in Homer (Agamemnon's poor leadership skills in *Iliad*), Aeschylus (Agamemnon in *Agam.*), and Sophocles (Agamemnon and Menelaus in *Ajax*).

[65] See above, p. 231.

self-sufficiency that would impel him to ignore the opinion of others. Moreover, even if an audience may feel that Polymestor deserves to lose his trial-debate with Hecuba, viewers are aware of the dishonesty of Agamemnon's position when he pretends to be an impartial judge in a dispute he supposedly comes to as an outsider. A similarly politicized portrayal occurs in *Iphigenia in Aulis*, where Agamemnon initially struggles to disentangle himself from his political ties and claims a right to make an autonomous decision about his own immediate family.[66] But as in *Hecuba*, he can imagine accomplishing this only by acting in concealment, and once he knows that his daughter is already approaching the camp, he abandons the effort and considers himself compelled to carry through with the planned sacrifice. His weakness as an agent is demonstrated further when he simply returns to the deception he had initiated against Clytemnestra and Iphigenia, and then abandons the lie only when directly confronted by them.

The most successful male agents are those who have the function of rescuers in a plot of positive outcome. Thus, Heracles in *Alcestis*, although initially deceived by Admetus and allowed to behave inappropriately until the servant tells him of the real situation, has no trouble accomplishing his goal thereafter. He is, however, a unique hero who in his adventures and labors repeatedly surpasses the limits of normal human action and thus can play an almost divine saving role, without suggesting that ordinary mortals in the audience can aspire to anything similar or that the kind of reprieve from suffering granted to Admetus can easily be repeated. This deficiency in human exemplarity must be one reason why Heracles was more commonly a figure in satyr-plays and comedies than in tragedies, and his role in *Alcestis* is one element in which this "tragedy" performed as fourth in its tetralogy does show affinity to the satyr-play genre.[67] The Theseus of *Supplices* and his son Demophon (paired with a silent brother Acamas) in *Heracleidae* are likewise effective agents on behalf of suppliants and Greek custom. We have noted earlier, however, Theseus' unusual initial rejection of the suppliants' plea and the importance of his mother Aethra in *Supplices*,[68] and Theseus endures a sort of correction from another female figure when the goddess Athena insists that an oath be extracted from the Argives, whereas he had intended to rely on a noble-minded faith in the informal force of *charis*, a reciprocal sense of gratitude and favor that is not to be too precisely quantified or qualified. Demophon's action on behalf of the children of Heracles is temporarily stalled by the intervention of an oracle calling for the

---

[66] See above, pp. 236–7.   [67] See above, pp. 55–7.   [68] See above, pp. 256–7.

sacrifice of a maiden as a precondition for victory. Again, the divine sets a limit on the autonomy of human agents, and a female, the eldest daughter of Heracles, makes a crucial contribution to end the impasse.

The Menelaus of *Helen* also functions as a rescuer and is parallel to the ephebic Orestes in *Iphigenia in Tauris*, the play with which *Helen* shares so much structural and thematic similarity. But in the late plays of Euripides it is even harder than in the earlier ones to find a vigorous, confident, and successful male agent. The tradition made Menelaus a deficient hero from the beginning, as a "soft" fighter, too attached to his wife, and politically in the shadow of his brother. Nowhere in extant tragedy (including Sophocles' *Ajax*) does he cut an impressive figure, and in Euripides outside of *Helen* he has small roles marked by bluster and weakness.[69] In *Helen*, his appearance in rags, his lack of success with the slave woman who answers the palace door, his befuddlement at what she says of Helen's presence, and his inability to accept Helen's declaration of her identity all suggest a figure who cannot be taken with full seriousness. Moreover, the entire set-up of the situation postulates that Menelaus has been fighting for an illusion for seventeen years, making him, along with all the Greeks and Trojans, the sad victims of a divine deception. In the appeal to Theonoe, an odd *agōn* in which the two speakers represent the same position, Menelaus speaks second (947–95), after Helen (894–943). Despite the self-conscious rhetoric of the opening and close of his speech, in which he distinguishes himself from Helen's womanly appeal (which uses supplicatory posture and tears), Menelaus is in the same condition of dependency as his wife and has to use basically the same arguments (justice, what Proteus would have done), although he ornaments his delivery (and perhaps saves face) by apostrophizing Proteus in his tomb and Hades (962–74) rather than addressing Theonoe directly for the central part of his appeal. The only new element is the threat of using physical force against Theoclymenus or of committing suicide on the tomb, which mixes male and female modes of behavior.[70] Once Theonoe's cooperation is assured, however, there is more room for positive action. Just as the recognition and reunion of the separated siblings in *Iphigenia in Tauris* put them in a position to take charge of events, so here

---

[69] In *Andr.*, he is a Spartan resisted by Andromache and foiled by the old man Peleus. In *Tro.*, the audience understands that the punishment Menelaus assesses against Helen will never be carried out (see above, p. 222). In *Or.*, he offers only clever language and evasions in his first appearance, fails to appear at the assembly trial of Orestes, and at the end engages in a futile dialogue of failed capitulation. In *IA*, finally, he intervenes importantly to prevent Agamemnon's letter from reaching Clytemnestra and then joins his brother in the flip-flop of positions in the complicated *agōn logōn* (see above, pp. 235–7).

[70] For the threat of suicide, cf. the Danaids in Aesch. *Su.* 455–67.

Helen and Menelaus, once reunited and freed of illusions, can appropriate the role of creating illusion and can make Theoclymenus a new Paris in order to escape. As we have noted before, the male hero does not come up with the needed plan, but has it suggested to him by Helen after he proposes various impractical alternatives.[71] Menelaus does, however, have an effective speaking role in the ruse (1250–92), unlike the silent Orestes in *Iphigenia in Tauris*, and comports himself well in the battle to commandeer the ship as described by the messenger (1537–612). That narrative also does something to restore the conventional gender roles of husband and wife, as Menelaus plays the leading part: he sees that his Greek crewmates join the voyage, he gets the sacrificial animal on board, he slaughters it, prays, and wins a victory over the Egyptian crew. Menelaus thus is noticeably transformed by the reversal of his previous ignorance and separation from the true Helen: his new clothes restore something like true heroic status, and are a visual token of his new capabilities for effective action.

As we have seen, the rescue-plot by its nature tends to put on display successful actions by male figures, and in a case like *Helen* the final result also confirms or restores the social, political, or heroic status of the male. Yet divine favor and assistance may be involved in the process in more or less explicit ways. In *Heracles*, the initial rescue-plot is subordinated to a complex doubling and reversal that depend on a hostile divine intervention,[72] presenting the strongest possible challenge to the notion of the male hero's control of his life and achievements. Unlike the callous and violent Heracles of Sophocles' *Trachiniae*, the hero of Euripides' play is domesticated, referring strikingly to his affection for his children, although there is no diminution in credit for an extraordinary course of successful labors and service to the gods and religion. As a result, Heracles in this play can become exemplary in an *a fortiori* sense: if the male hero of strength *par excellence*, who is also a loyal family man, ally of civilization and justice, and closely tied to the highest god, can suffer such a total reversal, no mortal can be confident that piety and decency will earn an appropriate reward.[73] One quintessentially tragic limiting factor for male agents is the divine, or, in other terms, the very structure and nature of the universe as imagined in

---

[71] See above, p. 287.
[72] Aspects of the play's structure and the role of the gods in it have been treated above, pp. 69–71, 167–9; see p. 255 on Heracles' love of his children.
[73] Compare the a fortiori exemplarity of Oedipus in Soph. *OT*, despite his extraordinary situation: if the one man who solved the Sphinx's riddle, the man who is regarded as most successful in his interactions with the supernatural, can in fact be so ignorant of his identity and of the terrible hollowness and impurity of his success, then the gulf between divine knowledge and intention and human blindess is so great that no mortal can hope to understand and control his destiny.

tragic drama, which thus carries on a traditional world-view at odds with the assumptions of confident autonomy and vigorous purposeful activity fostered in the Athenian democracy in its imperial age. In the final movement of *Heracles*, language and argument are the tools that Theseus and Heracles employ in determining how to cope with the aftermath of disaster. Theseus had been prepared to help Heracles as a military ally, but it is too late for that (nor had Heracles needed such help to deal with Lycus). Instead, he offers expostulation and consolation to dissuade Heracles from his initial decision that suicide is the best response to the pollution and shame of what he has done. Heracles, in resisting part of Theseus' argument, arrives at a formulation that allows him to live on, even though it involves a blind faith in pure divinity that is belied by the events of the play.[74] Thus, what these heroes of action rely on in the resolution of this play are human social and civic institutions (loyal friendship and the honors and cult awarded to Heracles in Attika) and human creativity in articulating rationales (even illusory ones) for interpreting and living in their world.

THE DEFICIENT HERO

In *Frogs*, Aristophanes has his character Aeschylus convey the claim that Aeschylean drama represented heroes of impressive grandeur who could properly serve as models for a "true" manhood characterized by action rather than speech and by simplicity rather than versatility and cleverness. Euripides' males, by contrast, are said to be whiners, glib talkers, individuals reduced in inward confidence and outward decorum by adversity. An orthodox view of characterization in Greek tragedy holds that Sophoclean characters, too, are more heroic, Euripidean more realistic and in some cases de-heroized or anti-heroic. Sophocles himself is supposed to have said, according to Aristotle, *Poetics* 25.1460b34, that "he himself made the characters of the sort they ought to be while Euripides made them as they actually are." Now that we have reviewed some of the variations in the way Euripides' plays represent the efforts of male figures, it is useful to ask how much they differ from at least the Sophoclean males (since Sophocles was producing plays throughout the years that Euripides was active).

The intransigent heroic temper of Sophoclean figures famously described by Bernard Knox[75] involves the isolation of the hero from others, that is, a heightened autonomy, self-confidence, and self-satisfaction, qualities that often verge on setting the hero apart from human society. So one area of

[74] Cf. above, pp. 168–9; Mastronarde 1986.   [75] Knox 1964.

difference between Sophocles and Euripides may lie in the way in which the characters interact with others in the plays. The major Sophoclean characters perhaps tend to define themselves more through acts of rejection and refusal, but we noted above how often Hippolytus engages in refusal, and Pentheus, too, is a figure who isolates himself in his own distorted perception of what is happening around him. Women characters are far more numerous and significant in Euripides than in the extant Sophoclean plays, and males in Sophocles do not interact so frequently or directly with female agents as do many males in Euripides. So another point of difference is that at least some Euripidean male agents are more embedded and entangled in their social relations with their families and societies. Yet for all Ajax's aloofness from his dependents and the Greek army, he is strongly motivated by shame and, whether he sets out deliberately to deceive or not, tailors the language of his penultimate speech (*Ajax* 646–92) to spare the feelings of Tecmessa and the chorus of his sailors. These differences are more a matter of degree and frequency than of exclusive either/or choices, and there are several areas of continuity. Sophoclean males such as Heracles, Ajax, Oedipus, and Creon also operate in conditions of ignorance and misjudgment, misconceiving the nature of the action they are pursuing. In the case of the Heracles of *Trachiniae*, manly physical achievement is deconstructed as potentially bestial and too easily intertwined with uncontrolled *erōs*, while the safeguarding of honor is carried too far in Ajax. Success for Sophoclean male agents is also related to plot-type, for Orestes is a successful avenger (although in this *Electra* his character is not developed at length and his role is dwarfed by that of Electra), and Theseus is a successful rescuer and protector in *Oedipus Coloneus*. In that play, Oedipus, too, is a kind of successful old man, an apparently weak and helpless figure who reveals unexpected power and resists and punishes his enemies. Haemon and Neoptolemus are problematic ephebes, struggling with their first interventions in public affairs, negotiating their emulation of or separation from their fathers: Haemon dies in the effort, and Heracles' warning about piety at the end of *Philoctetes* reminds an audience that Neoptolemus' moral success on this occasion does not mean he has arrived at a stable good character. Moreover, various political types are embodied – and more often with negative than with positive features – in Sophocles: the two Odysseuses, the three Creons, and Menelaus and Agamemnon. Although Sophoclean speakers do not use the self-conscious style of rhetoric we associate with Euripides, major male figures do use discourse skillfully and powerfully: not only the old Oedipus in *Oedipus Coloneus*, whose chief power is in words, but Creon in *Antigone* and even the man-of-strength, Ajax.

Thus, much of what we see in the major male figures in Euripides has some analogy in Sophocles. But many Euripidean males stand out as less self-confident and more given to doubt and painful analysis, particularly analysis before the fact: consider the Odysseus of the prologue of Euripides' *Philoctetes* (frr. 787–9) compared to the one in Sophocles' version, or the differences in the depiction of Orestes in the two *Electra* plays. We have also observed that the Euripidean males are less autarkic, more engaged in their social connections, particularly with women. These differences come across as more "realistic," that is, more like "ourselves" in our ordinary weaknesses and complexities. Accordingly, in antiquity as well as in modern times, audiences and readers perceive grandeur in many Sophoclean figures. But Euripidean drama deliberately refuses to sustain grandeur unmixed if it is present or to project it in the first place. By refusing to offer the simple and the uniform, Euripides leaves the audience with a more unrelieved aware-ness of the contingency of values and of the illusory nature of constructions of order and sense.

The differences between male agents and female agents in tragedy often match the stereotypical cultural assumptions of the contemporary society, and cultural assumptions about action vs. speech and active youth vs. weak old age are reflected as well. But such reflections are neither simple nor unproblematic. Tragedy often depicts paradoxical reversals. Typically male values and motivations (*philia, xenia, charis, timē*) are scrutinized and chal-lenged, clear distinctions may collapse, and disaster may result from pursuit of what seems to conform to approved values. Through blindness or misjudg-ments, males often create the crisis in which, on the day represented in the play, females are compelled to react in challenging and dangerous ways. In their own efforts, ephebic-aged youths and mature males as well as old men are more often than not frustrated in their intentions and actions. Although speech is most often the tool of the weak and old, it is a very important element of the tragic performance and of the formation of the audience's reading of the events, and in interesting cases it is also an important tool of the active mature male, as with Heracles and Theseus in *Heracles* (and Theseus in *Supplices*). Moreover, many of the most striking successes of male agents (as of female agents) depend on divine favor or support or on collaborating and interlocking efforts of comrades both male and female, high and low. Most important, only in certain specific plot-types is success to be expected, while in the majority of plot-types the point of the story is the presentation of frustration and failure, the traditional acknowledgment of the insufficiency of the human mind and human effort against the conditions of human life, as personified in many plays by the gods.

Conclusion

Since it has been one of the major aims of the preceding chapters to argue for the great variety of Euripides' oeuvre and of his techniques, for the divergent and shifting positions represented within the dramatic world of each play and the associated split or shifting judgments made by an interpreting viewer, and for the indeterminacy and uncertainty (*aporia*) frequently induced by the plays, it is slightly antithetical to present final conclusions. Nevertheless, some sort of coda is desirable for such a long enterprise, and it may suitably begin with the point made in the preface, that this book gathers together some topics that struck the author as important and challenging, but does not aim to be exhaustive or definitive. Among the topics omitted, Euripides' treatment of the mythographic tradition is surely a fascinating one, both in individual details and in general, but the huge gaps in the evidence make it both difficult and highly speculative to develop any arguments. Just as we have extant an infinitesimal portion of the fifth-century tragedies and dithyrambs in which Euripides and his audience regularly heard a very wide range of mythological stories repeated or modified, so too the earlier sources of myth (non-Homeric epic, archaic choral poetry, the oral traditions that each community had in connection with its local cults and festivals and its foundation and genealogies) can no longer be recovered adequately. To arrive at even speculative conclusions, the discussion would reach a level of complexity and obscurity that is beyond the scope of this book.

Reflections of the "political," in its broadest sense, would also provide another worthy topic. This would entail, among other things, discussion of monarchy and its inflections as tyranny or idealized kingship or kingship coexisting with the power of an assembly; of aristocratic/oligarchic vs. egalitarian values; of the relation of the individual to the state (or soldier to the army); of hierarchies of status and rights; of war and interstate relations; and of civil strife, political rivalry, and healthy and unhealthy forms of debate, judicial process, and political leadership. Several of these topics have in fact been touched on, at least briefly, in various chapters of this book. For instance, aristocratic values were relevant in connection with genre, the chorus, rhetoric, women, and men; hierarchies in connection with the chorus, women, and men; judicial process in connection with the rhetorical *agōn*.

The relation of tragic plots to ritual patterns (by which I mean not as veiled reflections of Dionysiac or other origins, but as evocations of patterns embodied in contemporary rites familiar to Euripides' Athenian audience) is another topic that I have not deemed suitable for the present book. On this topic, too, the background evidence is scanty and difficult to interpret and sometimes to locate firmly in time. At least some patterns are of a very general nature and common both to ritual and myth and to good story-telling. Thus it becomes hard to perceive when the ritual pattern was strongly evoked for Euripides' audience and when the force of the similarity had become significantly diluted for them because of the many extant instantiations of the pattern.

Finally, at an early stage I had contemplated attempting a general treatment of Euripides' verbal style, but that topic seemed not to fit with those included here and also to be aimed at a somewhat different audience, inasmuch as I have made an effort to make most of this study accessible to readers who may not know Greek.

One of the major motifs of this book has been the continuities of Euripidean drama with the earlier poetic and tragic tradition. Even as Euripides experiments and extends boundaries, we have been able to highlight continuities, with Homer, choral lyric, and Aeschylus and even Sophocles, in the range of story-patterns adopted, in structural strategies, in aspects of the choral voice and the use of exemplary myth, in the human struggle to understand divine power and its effects on events, and in self-presentation through speech. Unsurprisingly, given the intellectual developments and cultural ferment of the second half of the fifth century as well as the inherently agonistic and innovative approach to genre that characterizes Greek poetic production, there is more self-consciousness about the poetic and tragic tradition in Euripides, and evidently an expectation that the audience will also be more self-conscious about that same tradition. More than this, however, some techniques of Euripidean drama (for instance, related to the chorus, rhetoric, prologue and epilogue gods) suggest that the formal and stylistic choices themselves are aimed at making the audience more fully aware of the continual and sometimes challenging process of interpretation that is imposed on them by the performance. Such self-consciousness about epistemological issues is in tune with the contemporary delineation and analysis of professions and scientific disciplines seen in the sophists, medical writers, and others.

This increased self-consciousness, however, must not be confused with any form of optimism or rationalism, in the sense that Euripides himself or the thrust of his dramas displays confidence in the intelligibility of man and his world, as the Aristophanic-Nietzschean caricature assumed. Euripides is interested in representing such attitudes within his dramas, but does not do so in such a way as to prove their accuracy or efficacy. The crises of faith and intelligibility that had traditionally been represented in tragedy (as in famous choral passages of Aeschylus' *Agamemnon* and Sophocles' *Antigone*) are made even sharper as they become more explicit and are shared more frequently by the main characters in Euripides. Similarly, social and political tensions are brought to the surface more often in Euripides (at least, to judge from the extant plays and from the passages excerpted in later anthologies), but the dramatic form gives a license to explore avant-garde or unorthodox opinions without commitment. Euripidean plots and characterization remain inextricably embedded in their social and political milieu. Strikingly unorthodox statements can be found about the hierarchy of the genders, about social class, about slaves and non-Greeks. Their presence may induce or compel greater openness to alternative views and contribute to a process of unsettling a viewer's complacent confidence in conventional mores. On the other hand, these elements coexist with reflections of the society's norms. For instance, many male characters, as we have seen, may be judged to fail to live up to the claims of their elite status, but the background assumption of the importance of aristocratic values of honor and fame persists, and such values are often celebrated by choruses and adopted by women and by figures of humbler status. Greek chauvinism may be tweaked in various ways by the representation of confrontations between Greeks and non-Greeks, but in other details Greek superiority is reinforced by the ultimate triumph of the Greeks over gullible or militarily inferior non-Greeks. An ironic light is occasionally thrown on Athenian patriotic themes or political practices, but elements bolstering Athenian hegemony and pride are even more common, especially in the aetiologies.

Although I have tended to emphasize at several points the way Euripides often denies a firm ground for settled judgment or provokes awareness of contradictions, it is proper to recognize as well the manifold pleasures and satisfactions that the audience of a Euripidean tragedy could enjoy even in the absence of a sense of certainty and comfort. The whole complex of performance elements was profoundly important to the immediate experience. No matter how much readers and scholars try to conjure up in their mind's eye an imagined staging of what they read, the effect pales before the real visual and aural experience in three dimensions, where one appreciates the costuming/masking (and the limited décor), the vocal and gestural skills of the actors and choruses (with effective modulations of tone, volume, and rhythm), the choreographed movements on stage and in the orchestra, and the musical accompaniment of the *aulos*-player. A second sort of pleasure derived from creative use of heroic myth in tragedy. The spectator could both enjoy recognizing the familiar elements in story and character and take delight in being surprised, amused, or intrigued by variations and novelties. When we detect allusions (such as those to the *Oresteia* in *Medea*, *Electra*, *Iphigenia in Tauris*, and *Orestes*), we are limited to a feeble imitation of such pleasures because we cannot reproduce the position of a spectator who was immersed in the "song culture" and surrounded by reminders of gods and heroes in particular sites and in statuary and images and who saw dozens of tragedies over a period of years.

A different emotional and intellectual pleasure is offered by the release of tension related to ignorance or uncertainty. In Greek tragedy this release is more often focalized in the characters of the drama than in the audience; but even though the spectator often knows the truth or the outcome from the beginning, some satisfaction arises in the spectator when a character is freed from ignorance. The overall shape of a play or particular moments in it may evoke intellectual pleasure of the kind that Aristotle discusses in Chapter 9 of *Poetics*. Aristotle himself emphasizes the learning and recognition of universal patterns that emerge from a tightly constructed sequence of scenes which follow upon each other with causal chains of "probability or neces- sity." I argued in Chapter 3, however, that there are other patterns – mirroring and repetition and juxtaposition – that can also be perceived as significant, providing a similar sense of recognition, albeit requiring more effort from the interpreter.

Even in dark and unsettling plays, Euripides sometimes provides moments that produce a pleasure that might be termed moral, the pleasure of admiration. The reconciliation of father and son at the end of *Hippolytus* has often been valued as such a moment, and any manifestation of an ideal or extreme of generosity, bravery, or sympathy in a dire situation will have a similar potential – not only, for example, a self-sacrifice like that of the daughter of Heracles in *Heracleidae*, but also the tender sympathy of Amphitryon and the friendship of Theseus at the end of *Heracles*. Finally, there are two diametrically opposed pleasures to consider. On the one hand, there is the delight in fantasy which derives from putting oneself, momen- tarily and in a safe context, in the positions of figures who may be radically different from oneself, thinking their thoughts and feeling their emotions. On the other hand, there is an enjoyment that comes from the safety of the context, the status of the spectator as a survivor, and perhaps in some ways a beneficiary, of the tragic story, as the allusions to survivals and memorials in the present-day world suggest.

All of these types of pleasure were available to the audience from Euripidean tragedy (and in general from other contemporary tragedies). Side by side with these pleasures the spectators could experience less comfortable mental and emotional effects, and I have repeatedly suggested that such effects differed between Euripides and others more in degree than in kind. The most general term for this other effect is *aporia*, the sense of being at a loss, unsettled, uncertain, with no obvious way out. Tragic *aporia* is fostered in many ways. The inherent variety and generic mixing of tragedy require a more versatile response on the part of the audience, and open structures invite more probing efforts at inference and interpretation. The insistent alternation between intense engagement with the positions and emotions of the dramatic figures and a more withdrawn and reflective viewpoint may be unsettling in itself and may also impress on the viewer the need to evaluate a complex situation. Likewise, the second-order analysis or commentary that is internalized in the speeches of the characters, on topics like rhetoric or politics, reminds the audience of their own processes of interpretation and the conflicting attractions of different viewpoints. The evocation of alternative versions of a story also serves as a reminder that there are competing interpretations. A similar contestation of viewpoints arises from any clashes between a human perspective and a divine perspective, and from the reversals and deconstructions of ethical terms and values induced by dialectical argumentation over the course of a play.

In sum, Euripidean tragedy, probably to a greater degree than other Greek tragedy, imposes on its viewer and interpreter a significant burden of *aporia* and compels a thoughtful recipient to acknowledge difficulty and uncertainty, to perceive the fragility of cherished structures and values, and to accept the insufficiency of man, whether in isolation or in a social and political group. We should recognize in this not an opposition between an intellectual tradition and a religious one, but rather a marriage of the two. The common factor is the need to know one's limits, to gain the wisdom that comes from accepting doubt, uncertainty, and ignorance. This theme has a strong resonance in the Greek philosophical and intellectual tradition, with its critique of, and struggle to get beyond appearances, sense perception, and received conventions.

But it is also an expression of a Greek form of religious piety – not the arrogant piety of "true believers," scriptural literalists, and dogmatic theologians, but the humble and modest piety of those who yearn and seek and doubt, knowing there is something they cannot comprehend and control.

Bibliography

Achelis, T. O. (1913) *De Aristophane Byzantio argumentorum fabularum auctore.* Jena.

Aélion, R. (1983) *Euripide, héritier d'Eschyle.* Paris.

(1986) *Quelques grands mythes héroïques dans l'oeuvre d'Euripide.* Paris.

Alexiou, M. (1974) *The Ritual Lament in the Greek Tradition.* Cambridge.

Allan, W. (1999–2000) "Euripides and the Sophists: society and the theatre of war," in Cropp *et al.* 1999–2000: 145–56.

(2000) *The* Andromache *and Euripidean Tragedy.* Oxford.

(ed.) (2001) *Euripides. The Children of Heracles.* Warminster.

(2005) "Tragedy and the early Greek philosophical tradition," in Gregory 2005: 71–82.

(2006) "Divine justice and cosmic order in early Greek epic," *JHS* 126: 1–35.

(ed.) (2008) *Euripides. Helen.* Cambridge.

Arnott, W. G. (1981) "Double the vision. A reading of Euripides' *Electra*," *G&R* 28: 179–92.

(1984–85) "Alcuni osservazioni sulle convenzioni teatrali dei cori Euripidei," *Dioniso* 55: 147–55.

(1996) Alexis: The Fragments. *A Commentary.* Cambridge Classical Texts and Commentaries 31. Cambridge.

Arthur, M. (1977) "The curse of civilization: the choral odes of *Phoenissae*," *HSPh* 81: 163–85.

Assaël, J. (2001) *Euripide, philosophe et poète tragique.* Louvain.

Bacon, H. H. (1994–95) "The chorus in Greek life and drama," *Arion* ser. 3, 3(1): 6–24.

Bain, D. (1977) *Actors and Audience. A Study of Asides and Related Conventions in Greek Drama.* Oxford.

(1981) *Masters, Servants and Orders in Greek Tragedy. A Study of Some Aspects of Dramatic Technique and Convention.* Manchester.

Barchiesi, A. (2001) "The crossing," in *Texts, Ideas and the Classics*, ed. S. J. Harrison, Oxford: 142–63.

Barker, A. (1984) *Greek Musical Writings*, vol. I: *The Musician and his Art.* Cambridge.

Barlow, S. A. (1981) "Structure and dramatic realism in Euripides' *Heracles*," *G&R* 29: 115–25.

(1986) *Euripides. Trojan Women.* Warminster.

(1996) *Euripides. Heracles.* Warminster.

Barrett, W. S. (ed.) (1964) *Euripides. Hippolytus.* Oxford.

Basta Donzelli, G. (1987) "Euripide: una coscienza alla prova," in *La coscienza religiosa del letterato pagano*, ed. Basta Donzelli *et al.* U. di Genova, Pubblicazioni del Dip. di archeol., filol. class. e loro tradizioni, n.s. 106. Genova: 27–49.

Battezzato, L. (1999–2000) "Dorian dress in Greek tragedy," in Cropp *et al.* 1999–2000: 343–62.

(2003) "I viaggi dei testi," in *Tradizione testuale e ricezione letteraria antica della tragedia greca*, ed. L. Battezzato. Amsterdam: 7–31.

(2005) "Lyric," in Gregory 2005: 149–66.

Behler, E. (1986) "A. W. Schlegel and the nineteenth-century *damnatio* of Euripides," *GRBS* 27: 335–67.

Bierl, A. (1991) *Dionysos und die griechische Tragödie: politische und "metatheatrische" Aspekte.* Classica Monacensia 1. Tubingen.

Blackman, D. (1998) "Archaeology in Greece 1997–1998," *Archaeological Reports* 44: 16–17.

Blondell, R. [writing as M. Whitlock Blundell] (1989) *Helping Friends and Harming Enemies. A Study in Sophocles and Greek Ethics.* Cambridge.

Boedeker, D. (1991) "Euripides' *Medea* and the vanity of ΛΟΓΟΙ," *CP* 86: 95–112.

(1997) "Becoming Medea: assimilation in Euripides," in Clauss and Johnston 1997: 127–48.

Bond, G. W. (ed.) (1981) *Euripides. Heracles.* Oxford.

Bongie, E. B. (1977) "Heroic elements in the *Medea* of Euripides," *TAPhA* 107: 27–56.

Booth, W. C. (1983) *The Rhetoric of Fiction.* 2nd edn. Chicago.

Breitenbach, W. (1934) *Untersuchungen zur Sprache der Euripideischen Lyrik.* Tübinger Beiträge zur Altertumswissenschaft, Heft 20. Stuttgart.

Bremer, J. M. (1975) "The meadow of love and two passages in *Hippolytos*," *Mn* 28: 268–80.

Brink, C. O. (1963) *Horace on Poetry. Prolegomena to the Literary Epistles.* Cambridge.

(1971) Horace on Poetry. The *Ars Poetica*. Cambridge.

Bröcker, W. (1980) *Poetische Theologie.* Wissenschaft und Gegenwart. Geisteswissenschaftliche Reihe 62. Frankfurt.

Brumoy, P. (1730) *Le Théâtre des Grecs.* 3 vols. Paris.

Bundy, E. L. (1986) *Studia Pindarica.* Berkeley.

Burian, P. (ed.) (1985a) *Directions in Euripidean Criticism. A Collection of Essays.* Durham, North Carolina.

(1985b) "Logos and pathos: the politics of the *Suppliant Women*," in Burian 1985a: 129–55.

(1997a) "Myth into *mythos*: the shaping of the tragic plot," in Easterling 1997a: 178–208.

(1997b) "Tragedy adapted for stages and screens: the Renaissance to the present," in Easterling 1997a: 228–83.

Burkert, W. (1966) "Greek tragedy and sacrificial ritual," *GRBS* 7: 87–121.

Burnett, A. P. (1960) (as A. Pippin) "Euripides' *Helen*: a comedy of ideas," *CP* 55: 151–63.
(1962) "Human resistance and divine persuasion in Euripides' *Ion*," *CP* 57: 89–103.
(1965) "The virtues of Admetus," *CPh* 60: 240–55 (abbreviated version in Segal 1968: 51–69).
(1971) *Catastrophe Survived. Euripides' Plays of Mixed Reversal*. Oxford.
(1973) "*Medea* and the tragedy of revenge," *CP* 68: 1–24.
(1985) *The Art of Bacchylides*. Cambridge, Mass.
(1998) *Revenge in Attic and Later Tragedy*. Berkeley.
Buxton, R. G. A. (1985) "Euripides' *Alcestis*: five aspects of an interpretation," *Dodone (Philologia)* 14: 75–90.
Calame, C. (1994–95) "From choral poetry to tragic stasimon: the enactment of women's song," *Arion* ser. 3, 3(1): 136–54.
(1997) *Choruses of Young Women in Ancient Greece. Their Morphology, Religious Role, and Social Functions*, trans. D. Collins and J. Orion. Lanham, Md.
(1999) "Performative aspects of the choral voice in Greek tragedy: civic identity in performance," in Goldhill and Osborne 1999: 125–53.
Cambiano, G., Canfora, L., and Lanza, D. (eds.) (1996) *Lo spazio letterario della Grecia antica*, v. 3: *Cronologia e bibliografia della letteratura Greca*. Rome.
Cameron, A. (2004) *Greek Mythography in the Roman World*. New York.
Canevet, M. (1971) "Aspects baroques du théâtre d'Euripide," *Bulletin de l'Association Guillaume Budé*, ser. 4. 2: 203–10.
Cartledge, P. (1997) "'Deep plays': theatre as process in Greek civic life," in Easterling 1997a: 3–35.
Casolari, F. (2003) *Die Mythentravestie in der griechischen Komödie*. Orbis antiquus, Bd. 37. Münster.
Castellani, V. (1991) "The value of a kindly chorus: female choruses in Attic tragedy," in *Women in Theatre (Themes in Drama, 11)*, ed. J. Redmond. Cambridge: 1–18.
Chalk, H. H. O. (1962) "APETH and BIA in Euripides' *Herakles*," *JHS* 82: 7–18.
Chapot, F., and Laurot, B. (2001) *Corpus des prières grecques et romaines*. Recherches sur les rhétoriques religieuses 2. Turnhout.
Clauss, J., and Johnston, S. I. (eds.) (1997) *Medea. Essays on Medea in Myth, Literature, Philosophy, and Art*. Princeton.
Clay, J. S. (1989) *The Politics of Olympus. Form and Meaning in the Major Homeric Hymns*. Princeton.
Cohen, B. (1997) "Divesting the female breast of clothes in classical sculpture," in *Naked Truths: Women, Sexuality, and Gender in Classical Art and Archaeology*. ed. A. O. Koloski-Ostrow and C. L. Lyons. London: 66–92.
Cohen, D. J. (1989) "Seclusion, separation, and the status of women in classical Athens," *G&R* 36: 3–15.
Collard, C. (ed.) (1975a) *Euripides. Supplices*. Groningen.
(1975b) "Formal debates in Euripides' drama," *G&R* 22: 58–71 (reprinted in Mossman 2003: 64–80).
(ed.) (1984) *Euripides. Suppliant Women*. Warminster.
(ed.) (1991) *Euripides. Hecuba*. Warminster.

Collard, C. and Cropp, M. (eds.) (2008a) *Euripides. Fragments: Aegeus-Meleager* (= Loeb Classical Library, Euripides VII). Cambridge, Mass.

(2008b) *Euripides. Fragments: Oedipus-Chrysippus, Other Fragments* (= Loeb Classical Library, Euripides VIII). Cambridge, Mass.

Collard, C., Cropp, M., and Gibert, J. (eds.) (2004) *Euripides. Select Fragmentary Plays*, vol. II. Warminster.

Collard, C., Cropp, M., and Lee, K. H. (eds.) (1995) *Euripides. Select Fragmentary Plays*, vol. I. Warminster.

Conacher, D. J. (1967) *Euripidean Drama. Myth, Theme and Structure.* Toronto.

(1981) "Rhetoric and relevance in Euripidean drama," *AJPh* 102: 3–25 (reprinted in Mossman 2003: 81–101).

(1988) *Euripides. Alcestis.* Warminster.

(1998) *Euripides and the Sophists. Some Dramatic Treatments of Philosophical Ideas.* London.

Connor, W. R. (1989) "City Dionysia and Athenian democracy," *C&M* 40: 7–32.

Conte, G. B. (1994) *Genres and Readers. Lucretius, Love Elegy, Pliny's Encyclopedia.* Baltimore, Md.

Cousland, J. R. C., and Hume, J. R. (eds.) (2009) *The Play of Texts and Fragments. Essays in Honour of Martin Cropp.* Mnemosyne Supplement 314. Leiden.

Craik, E. (1988) *Euripides. Phoenician Woman.* Warminster.

Croally, K. (1994) *Euripidean Polemic. The Trojan Women and the Function of Tragedy.* Cambridge.

(2005) "Tragedy's teaching," in Gregory 2005: 55–70.

Cropp, M. (1981) "τί τὸ σοφόν;" *BICS* 28: 39–42.

(ed.) (1988) *Euripides. Electra.* Warminster.

(ed.) (2000) *Euripides. Iphigenia in Tauris.* Warminster.

Cropp, M., and Fick, G. (1985) *Resolutions and Chronology in Euripides. The Fragmentary Tragedies.* BICS Suppl. 43. London.

Cropp, M., Lee, K., and Sansone, D. (eds.) (1999–2000) *Euripides and Tragic Theatre in the Late Fifth Century* (= *ICS* 24/25, 1999–2000). Champaign, Illinois.

Csapo, E. (1999–2000) "Late Euripidean music," in Cropp *et al.* 1999–2000: 399–426.

(2004a) "The politics of the new music," in *Music and the Muses. The Culture of Mousike in the Classical Athenian City*, ed. P. Murray and P. Wilson. Oxford: 207–48.

(2004b) "Some social and economic conditions behind the rise of the acting profession in the fifth and fourth centuries BC," in *Le Statut de l'acteur dans l'antiquité grecque et romaine*, ed. D. Hugoniot, F. Hurlet, and S. Milanezi. Tours: 53–76.

Csapo, E., and Miller, M. C. (eds.) (2007a) *The Origin of Theater in Ancient Greece and Beyond. From Ritual to Drama.* Cambridge.

(2007b) "General introduction," in Csapo and Miller 2007a: 1–38.

Csapo, E., and Slater, W. J. (1995). *The Context of Ancient Drama.* Ann Arbor, Mich.

Cunningham, M. P. (1954) "Medea ἀπὸ μηχανῆς," *CP* 49: 151–60.

Dale, A. M. (1954) *Euripides. Alcestis.* Oxford.

(1963) "Note on Euripides: *Helena* 1441–50," *Maia* 15: 310–13.

Davidson, J. (2005) "Theatrical production," in Gregory 2005: 194–211.

Dawe, R. D. (1984) *Sophoclis Tragoediae* I. Leipzig.

Dearden, C. (1999) "Plays for export," *Phoenix* 53: 222–48.

Del Corno, D. (1995) "Esperimenti di drammaturgia tragica nel teatro ateniese," in *Studia classica Iohanni Tarditi oblata II*, ed. L. Belloni, G. Milanese, and A. Porro. Milan: 843–56.

Denniston, J. D. (1939) *Euripides. Electra.* Oxford.

Detienne, M., and Vernant, J.-P. (1978) *Cunning Intelligence in Greek Culture and Society*, trans. J. Lloyd. Atlantic Highlands, N.J.

Di Benedetto, V. (1971) *Euripide. Teatro e società.* Torino.

(1971–74) "Il rinnovamento della lirica dell' ultimo Euripide e la contemporanea arte figurativa," *Dioniso* 45: 326–33.

Diggle, J. D. (ed.) (1970) *Euripides. Phaethon.* Cambridge.

(1981–94) *Euripidis Fabulae.* 3 vols. Oxford Classical Texts. Oxford.

Dillon, J. M. (1997) "Medea among the Philosophers," in Clauss and Johnston 1977: 211–18.

Dodds, E. R. (1960) *Euripides. Bacchae.* 2nd edn. Oxford.

Dover, K. J. (1993) *Aristophanes. Frogs.* Oxford.

Dubischar, M. (2001) *Die Agonszenen bei Euripides: Untersuchungen zu ausgewählten Dramen.* Drama Beiheft 13. Stuttgart.

Duchemin, J. (1945) *L'Agôn dans la tragédie grecque.* Paris.

Dunbar, N. (ed.) (1995) *Aristophanes. Birds.* Oxford.

Dunn, F. (1994) "Euripides and the rites of Hera Akraia," *GRBS* 35: 103–15.

(1996) *Tragedy's End. Closure and Innovation in Euripidean Drama.* Oxford.

Dyson, M. (1988) "Alcestis' children and the character of Admetus," *JHS* 108: 13–23.

Easterling, P. E. (1977) "The infanticide in Euripides' *Medea*," *YClS* 25: 177–91.

(ed.) (1982) *Sophocles. Trachiniae.* Cambridge.

(1985) "Anachronism in Greek tragedy," *JHS* 105: 1–10.

(1990) "Constructing character in Greek tragedy," in *Characterization and Individuality in Greek Literature*, ed. C. B. R. Pelling. Oxford: 83–99.

(1994) "Euripides outside Athens: a speculative note," *ICS* 19: 73–80.

(ed.) (1997a) *The Cambridge Companion to Greek Tragedy.* Cambridge.

(1997b) "A show for Dionysus," in Easterling 1997a: 36–53.

Easterling, P. E., and Muir, J. V. (eds.) (1985) *Greek Religion and Society.* Cambridge.

Edwards, A. T. (1993) "Historicizing the popular grotesque: Bakhtin's *Rabelais* and Attic Old Comedy," in *Theater and Society in the Classical World*, ed. R. Scodel. Ann Arbor, Mich.: 89–117.

Egli, F. (2003) *Euripides im Kontext zeitgenössischer intellektueller Strömungen.* Beiträge zur Altertumskunde 189. Munich.

Elliott, R. C. (1962) "The definition of satire: a note on method," *Yearbook of Comparative and General Literature* 11: 19–23.

Else, G. F. (1967) *The Origin and Early Form of Greek Tragedy.* Cambridge, Mass.

Elsperger, W. (1908) *Reste und Spuren antiker Kritik gegen Euripides.* Philologus Supplementband 11(1). Gottingen.

Ewans, M. (1995) *Aischylos. The Oresteia.* London.

Fairweather, J. A. (1974) "Fiction in the biographies of ancient writers," *Ancient Society* 5: 231–75.

Fantuzzi, M. (2004) "Performance and genre," in M. Fantuzzi and R. Hunter, *Tradition and Innovation in Hellenistic Poetry.* Cambridge: 1–41.

Feeney, D. (1991) *The Gods in Epic. Poets and Critics in the Classical Tradition.* Oxford.

(1998) *Literature and Religion at Rome. Cultures, Contexts, and Beliefs.* Cambridge.

Firpo, L. (1963) "Kaspar Stiblin, Utopiste", in *Les Utopies à la Renaissance. Colloque international (avril 1961). Université Libre de Bruxelles, Travaux de l'Institut pour l'étude de la Renaissance et de l'Humanisme,* 1. Brussels, Paris: 107–33.

Fitton J. W. (1961) "The *Suppliant Women* and the *Herakleidai* of Euripides," *Hermes* 89: 430–61.

Foley, H. P. (1981) "The conception of women in Athenian drama," in *Reflections of Women in Antiquity,* ed. H. P. Foley. New York and London: 127–68.

(1985) *Ritual Irony: Poetry and Sacrifice in Euripides.* Ithaca, New York.

(1989) "Medea's divided self," *ClAnt* 8: 61–85.

(2001) *Female Acts in Greek Tragedy.* Princeton.

(2003) "Choral identity in Greek tragedy," *CP* 98: 1–30.

Foxhall, F. (1989) "Household, gender, and property in classical Athens," *CQ* 39: 22–44.

Friedrich, R. (1996) "*Everything to do with Dionysos? Ritualism, the Dionysiac, and the tragic,*" in Silk 1996: 257–83.

Frischer, B. D. (1970) "*Concordia discors* and characterization in Euripides' *Hippolytus,*" *GRBS* 11: 85–100.

Frye, N. (1957) *The Anatomy of Criticism. Four Essays.* Princeton.

Fusillo, M. (1992) "Was ist eine romanhafte Tragödie? Überlegungen zu Euripides' Experimentalismus," *Poetica* 24: 270–98.

Garvie, A. F. (1986) *Aeschylus. Choephori.* Oxford.

Gelzer, T. (1985) "Μοῦσα αὐθιγενής. Bemerkungen zu einem Typ Pindarischer und Bacchylideischer Epinikien," *MH* 42: 95–120.

Genette, G. (1986) "Introduction à l'architexte," in Genette and Todorov 1986: 89–159.

Genette, G., and Todorov, T. (eds.) (1986) *Théorie des genres.* Paris.

Gentili, B. (1988) *Poetry and its Public in Ancient Greece. From Homer to the Fifth Century,* trans. A. T. Cole. Baltimore, Md.

Gibert, J. (1995) *Change of Mind in Greek Tragedy.* Hypomnemata 108. Gottingen.

(1997) "Euripides' 'Hippolytus' plays: which came first?" *CQ* 47: 85–97.

(2005) "Clytemnestra's first marriage: Euripides' *Iphigenia in Aulis,*" in Pedrick and Oberhelman 2005: 227–48.

Gill, C. (1983) "Did Chrysippus understand Medea?" *Phronesis* 28: 136–49.

(1996) *Personality in Greek Epic, Tragedy, and Philosophy. The Self in Dialogue.* Oxford.

(2005) "Tragic fragments, ancient philosophers and the fragmented self," in McHardy *et al.* 2005: 151–172.

Goff, B. (1990) *The Noose of Words. Readings of Desire, Violence, and Language in Euripides' Hippolytus.* Cambridge.

(1999–2000) "Try to make it real compared to what? Euripides' *Electra* and the play of genres," in Cropp *et al.* 1999–2000: 93–105.

(2004) *Citizen Bacchae. Women's Ritual Practice in Ancient Greece.* Berkeley.

Goldhill, S. (1986) *Reading Greek Tragedy.* Cambridge.

(1987) "The Great Dionysia and civic ideology," *JHS* 107: 58–76 (also in Winkler and Zeitlin 1990: 97–129).

(1991) *The Poet's Voice. Essays on Poetics and Greek Literature.* Cambridge.

(1994) "Representing democracy: women at the Great Dionysia," in Osborne and Hornblower 1994: 347–69.

(1996) "Collectivity and otherness – the authority of the tragic chorus: Response to Gould," in Silk 1996: 244–56.

(1997) "The audience of Athenian tragedy," in Easterling 1997a: 54–68.

(2000) "Civic ideology and the problem of difference: the politics of Aeschylean tragedy, once again," *JHS* 120: 34–56.

Goldhill, S., and Osborne, R. (eds.) (1999) *Performance Culture and Athenian Democracy.* Cambridge.

Gould, J. (1978) "Dramatic character and 'human intelligibility' in Greek tragedy," *PCPhS* 24: 43–67.

(1983) "Hiketeia," *JHS* 93: 74–103.

(1985) "On making sense of Greek religion," in Easterling and Muir 1985: 1–33.

(1996) "Tragedy and collective experience," in Silk 1996: 217–43.

Gregory, J. (1977) "Euripides' 'Heracles,'" *YClS* 25: 259–75.

(1979) "Euripides' *Alcestis*," *Hermes* 107: 259–70.

(1986) "The power of language in Euripides' *Troades*," *Eranos* 84: 1–9.

(1991) *Euripides and the Instruction of the Athenians.* Ann Arbor, Mich.

(ed.) (1999) *Euripides. Hecuba.* Atlanta, Ga.

(1999–2000) "Comic elements in Euripides," in Cropp *et al.* 1999–2000: 59–74.

(ed.) (2005) *A Companion to Greek Tragedy.* Blackwell Companions to the Ancient World. Oxford.

Griffin, J. (1977) "The Epic Cycle and the uniqueness of Homer," *JHS* 97: 39–53.

(1998) "The social function of Attic tragedy," *CQ* 48: 39–61.

Griffith, M. (1983) *Aeschylus. Prometheus Bound.* Cambridge.

(1990) "Contest and contradiction in early Greek poetry," in Griffith and Mastronarde 1990: 185–207.

(1995) "'Brilliant dynasts': power and politics in the *Oresteia*," *ClAnt* 14: 62–129.

(1998) "The king and eye: the rule of the father in Greek tragedy," *PCPhS* 44: 20–84.

(1999) *Sophocles. Antigone.* Cambridge.

(2001) "Antigone and her sisters: voicing/embodying women in Greek tragedy," in *Making Silence Speak. Women's Voices in Greek Literature and Society*, ed. A. Lardinois and L. McClure. Princeton: 117–36.

(2002) "Slaves of Dionysos: satyrs, audience, and the ends of the *Oresteia*," *ClAnt* 21: 195–258.

(2005a) "Authority figures," in Gregory 2005: 333–51.

(2005b) "The subject of desire in Sophocles' *Antigone*," in Pedrick and Oberhelman 2005: 91–135.

(2008) "Greek middle-brow drama (Something to do with Aphrodite?)," in *Performance, Reception, Iconography. Studies in Honour of Oliver Taplin*, ed. M. Revermann and P. Wilson. Oxford: 59–87.

(2009) "Orestes and the in-laws," in *Bound by the City. Tragedy and Sexual Difference, and the Formation of the Polis*, ed. D. McCoskey and E. Zakin. Albany, New York: 275–330.

(in press) "Satyr-play and tragedy face to face, from East to West," in *Pronomos. His Vase and its World*, ed. E. Hall and O. Taplin. Oxford.

Griffith, M., and Mastronarde, D. J. (eds.) (1990) *Cabinet of the Muses. Essays on Classical and Comparative Literature in Honor of Thomas G. Rosenmeyer*. Atlanta, Ga.

Griffiths, E. (2006) *Medea*. London.

Grube, G. M. A. (1941) *The Drama of Euripides*. London.

Günther, H. C. (ed.) (1988) *Euripides. Iphigenia Aulidensis*. Bibliotheca Scriptorum Graecorum et Romanorum Teubneriana. Leipzig.

Guggisberg, P. (1947) *Das Satyrspiel*. Zurich.

Guillén, C. (1971) *Literature as System. Essays toward the Theory of Literary History*. Princeton.

Guthke, K. S. (1968) *Die moderne Tragikomödie. Theorie und Gestalt*. Gottingen.

Hall, E. (1989) *Inventing the Barbarian. Greek Self-Definition through Tragedy*. Oxford.

(1997) "The Sociology of Athenian tragedy," in Easterling 1997a: 93–126.

(1998) "Ithyphallic males behaving badly: or, satyr drama as gendered tragic ending," in *Parchments of Gender. Deciphering the Bodies of Antiquity*, ed. M. Wyke. Oxford: 13–37.

Halleran, M. R. (1985) *Stagecraft in Euripides*. London.

(ed.) (1995) *Euripides. Hippolytus*. Warminster.

Hamilton, R. (1985) "Slings and arrows. The debate with Lycus in the *Heracles*," *TAPhA* 115: 19–25.

Hanink, J. (2008) "Literary politics and the Euripidean *Vita*," *CCJ* 54: 115–35.

Harrison, T. (2000) *Divinity and History. The Religion of Herodotus*. Oxford.

Hartung, J. A. (1843–44) *Euripides Restitutus*. 2 vols. Hamburg.

Hauptman, I. (1992) "Defending melodrama," in Redmond 1992: 281–9.

Heath, M. (1987a) "*Iure principem locum tenet*: Euripides' *Hecuba*," *BICS* 34: 40–68.

(1987b) *The Poetics of Greek Tragedy*. London.

Heilman, R. B. (1968) *Tragedy and Melodrama. Versions of Experience*. Seattle, Washington.

Henderson, J. (1991) "Woman and the Athenian dramatic festivals," *TAPhA* 121: 133–47.

(ed.) (2002) *Aristophanes IV. Frogs, Assemblywomen, Wealth*. Cambridge, Mass.

Henrichs, A. (1978) "Greek maenadism from Olympias to Messalina," *HSPh* 82: 121–60.

(1980) "Human sacrifice in Greek religion: three case studies," in *Le Sacrifice dans l'antiquité*, ed. J. Rudhardt and O. Reverdin [Fondation Hardt, Entretiens 27]. Geneva: 195–235.

(1984) "Loss of self, suffering, violence: the modern view of Dionysus from Nietzsche to Girard," *HSPh* 88: 205–40.

(1990) "Between country and city: cultic dimensions of Dionysus in Athens and Attica," in Griffith and Mastronarde 1990: 257–77.

(1994–95) "'Why should I Dance?': Choral self-referentiality in Greek tragedy," *Arion* ser. 3, 3(1): 56–111.

(1996) "Dancing in Athens, dancing on Delos: some patterns of choral projection in Euripides," *Philologus* 1996: 48–62.

Herington, C. J. (1985) *Poetry into Drama. Early Tragedy and the Greek Poetic Tradition.* Berkeley.

Hesk, J. (1999) "The rhetoric of anti-rhetoric in Athenian oratory," in Goldhill and Osborne 1999: 201–30.

(2000) *Deception and Democracy in Classical Athens.* Cambridge.

Hofmann, H. (ed.) (1991) *Fragmenta Dramatica. Beitrage zur Interpretation der griechischen Tragikerfragmente und ihrer Wirkungsgeschichte.* Gottingen.

Hose, M. (1990–91) *Studien zum Chor bei Euripides.* 2 vols. Beiträge zur Altertumskunde, Bd. 10, Bd. 20. Stuttgart.

(2008) Euripides. *Der Dichter der Leidenschaften.* Munich.

Hose, M., *et al.* (2005) "Forschungsbericht zu Euripides (I) 1970–2000," *Lustrum* 47: 7–740.

Hughes, D. D. (1991) *Human Sacrifice in Ancient Greece.* London.

Hunter, R. L. (1983) *Eubulus. The Fragments.* Cambridge Classical Texts and Commentaries 24. Cambridge.

Iser, W. (1978) *The Act of Reading. A Theory of Aesthetic Response.* Baltimore, Md.

Jacobs, F. C. W. (1798) *Charakter der vornehmsten Dichter aller Nationen; nebst kritischen und historischen Abhandlungen über Gegenstände der schönen Künste und Wissenschaften, von einer Gesellschaft von Gelehrten.* Nachträge zu Sulzers Allgemeiner Theorie der schönen Künste, Bd. 5.2. Leipzig.

Jameson, M. H. (1990a) "Private space and the Greek city," in *The Greek City from Homer to Alexander,* ed. O. Murray and S. Price. Oxford: 171–95.

(1990b) "Domestic space in the Greek city-state," in *Domestic Architecture and the Use of Space. An Interdisciplinary Cross-cultural Study,* ed. S. Kent. Cambridge: 92–113.

Jauss, H. R. (1982) *Towards an Aesthetic of Reception.* Minneapolis, Minn.

Jens, J. (ed.) (1971) *Die Bauformen der griechische Tragödie.* Poetica Beiheft 6. Munich.

Johnson, W. R. (1970) "The problem of the counter-classical sensibility and its critics," *CSCA* 3: 123–51.

Jones, J. (1962) *On Aristotle and Greek Tragedy.* London.

Jouan, F., and van Looy, H. (1998–2003) *Euripide VIII. Fragments.* 4 vols. Paris.

Just, R. (1989) *Women in Athenian Life and Law.* New York and London.

Käppel, L. (1992) *Paian. Studien zur Geschichte einer Gattung.* Untersuchungen zur antiken Literatur und Geschichte 37. Berlin.

Kaimio, M. (1970) *The Chorus of Greek Drama within the Light of the Person and Number Used.* Societas Scientiarum Fennica, Commentationes humanarum litterarum. Helsinki.

322 *Bibliography*

(1988) *Physical Contact in Greek Tragedy. A Study of Stage Conventions.* Annales Academiae Scientiarum Fennicae, ser. B, 244. Helsinki.

Kamerbeek, J. C. (1966) "Unity and meaning of Euripides' *Heracles*," *Mn* 19: 1–16.

Kannicht, R. (ed.) (1969) *Euripides. Helena.* 2 vols. Heidelberg.

(1996) "Zum Corpus Euripideum," in ΛΗΝΑΙΚΑ: *Festschrift für C. W. Müller*, ed. C. Mueller-Goldingen and K. Sier. Beiträge zur Altertumskunde 89. Stuttgart and Leipzig: 21–31.

Kassel, R. (1954) *Quomodo quibus locis apud veteres scriptores graecos infantes atque parvuli pueri inducantur describantur commemorentur.* Wurzburg (reprinted in his *Kleine Schriften.* Berlin 1991: 1–73).

(2005) "Fragments and their collectors," in McHardy *et al.* 2005: 7–20 (translation of "Fragmente und ihre Sammler" in Hofmann 1991: 243–53).

Kitto, H. D. F. (1961) *Greek Tragedy. A Literary Study.* 3rd edn. London.

Knox, B. M. W. (1952) "The Hippolytus of Euripides," *YClS* 13: 1–31 (reprinted in Knox 1979: 205–30; abbreviated version in Segal 1968: 90–114].

(1964) *The Heroic Temper. Studies in Sophoclean Tragedy.* Berkeley.

(1970) "Euripidean comedy," in *The Rarer Action. Essays in Honor of Francis Fergusson*, ed. A. Cheuse and R. Koffler. New Brunswick, N.J.: 68–96 (reprinted in Knox 1979: 250–74).

(1977) "The *Medea* of Euripides," *Yale Classical Studies* 25: 193–225 (reprinted in Knox 1979: 295–322).

(1979) *Word and Action. Essays on the Ancient Theater.* Baltimore, Md.

(1991) "Divine intervention in Euripidean tragedy," in *Studi di filologia classica in onore di Giusto Monaco.* Palermo: I.223–30.

Kopperschmidt, J. (1967) *Die Hikesie als dramatische Form. Zur motivischen Interpretation des griechischen Dramas.* Tubingen.

(1971) "Hikesie als dramatische Form," in Jens 1971: 321–46.

Kovacs, D. (1980) "Shame, pleasure and honor in Phaedra's great speech (Euripides, *Hippolytus* 375–87)," *AJPh* 101: 287–303.

(1987a) The Heroic Muse. Studies in the *Hippolytus* and *Hecuba* of Euripides. Baltimore.

(1987b) "Treading the circle warily. Literary criticism and the text of Euripides," *TAPhA* 117: 257–70.

(1993) "Zeus in Euripides' *Medea*," *AJPh* 114: 45–70.

(1994) *Euripidea.* Mnemosyne Suppl. 132. Leiden.

(ed.) (1994–2002) *Euripides.* 6 vols. (Loeb Classical Library). Cambridge, Mass.

(2003) "Toward a reconstruction of *Iphigenia Aulidensis*," *JHS* 123: 77–103.

Kowalzig, B. (2007) "'And now all the world shall dance!' (Eur. *Bacch.* 114): Dionysus' choroi between drama and ritual," in Csapo and Miller 2007a: 221–51.

Kranz, W. (1933) *Stasimon. Untersuchungen zu Form und Gehalt der griechischen Tragödie.* Berlin.

Krumeich, R., Pechstein, N., and Seidensticker, B. (eds.) (1999) *Das griechische Satyrspiel.* Texte zur Forschung 72. Darmstadt.

Kullmann, W. (1987) "Deutung und Bedeutung der Götter bei Euripides," in *Mythos. Deutung und Bedeutung*, ed. W. Kullmann *et al.* Innsbrucker Beitr. zur Kulturwissenschaft. Dies Philologici Aenipontani 5. Innsbruck: 7–22.

Kurke, L. (1998) "The cultural impact of (on) democracy: decentering tragedy," in *Democracy 2500: Questions and Challenges*, ed. I. Morris and K. Raaflaub, Archaeological Institute of America, Conference and Colloquia Papers. Dubuque, Iowa: 155–69.

Kyriakou, P. (ed.) (2006) *A Commentary on Euripides' Iphigenia in Tauris*. Untersuchunen zur antiken Literatur und Geschichte 80. Berlin.

Labarbe, J. (1980) "La prière 'contestataire' dans la poésie grecque," in *L'Expérience de la prière dans les grandes réligions*, ed. H. Limet and J. Ries. Louvain-la-neuve: 137–48.

Lee, K. J. (1976) *Euripides. Troades*. London.
  (1996) "Shifts of mood and concepts of time in Euripides' *Ion*," in Silk 1996: 85–109.
  (1997) *Euripides. Ion*. Warminster.

Lefkowitz, M. R. (1979) "The Euripides *Vita*," *GRBS* 20: 187–210.
  (1981) *The Lives of the Greek Poets*. Baltimore, Md.
  (1989) "Impiety and atheism in Euripides' dramas," *CQ* 39: 70–82.

Leinieks, V. (1996) *The City of Dionysos. A Study of Euripides' Bakchai*. Beiträge zur Altertumskunde 18. Stuttgart.

Lenting, J. (1819) *Euripidis Medea*. Zutphen.

Lesky, A. (1983) *Greek Tragic Poetry*, trans. M. Dillon (of *Die tragische Dichtung der Hellenen*, 3rd edn. Gottingen 1972). New Haven, Conn.

Ley, G., and Ewans, M. (1985) "The orchestra as acting area in Greek tragedy," *Ramus* 14: 75–84.

Lloyd, M. (1984) "The Helen scene in Euripides' *Troades*," *CQ* 34: 303–13.
  (1985) "Euripides' *Alcestis*," *G&R* 32: 119–31.
  (1986) "Realism and character in Euripides' *Electra*," *Phoenix* 40: 1–19.
  (1992) *The Agon in Euripides*. Oxford.
  (ed.) (1994) *Euripides. Andromache*. Warminster.

Lloyd-Jones, H., and Wilson, N. G. (eds.) (1990) *Sophoclis Fabulae*. Oxford.

Lolos, G. G. (1997) "'Σπήλαιον ἀναπνοὴν ἔχον ἐς τὴν θάλασσαν': το Σπήλαιο του Ευριπίδη στη Σαλαμίνα," *Dodone (hist)* 26(1): 287–326.

Longman, G. A. (1959) "*Gnomologium Vatopedianum*: the Euripidean section," *CQ* 9: 129–41.

Lonsdale, S. H. (1993) *Dance and Ritual Play in Greek Religion*. Baltimore, Maryland.

Lopez Eire, A. (2003) "Tragedy and satyr-drama: linguistic criteria," in Sommerstein 2003a: 387–412.

Loraux, N. (1986) *The Invention of Athens. The Funeral Oration in the Classical City*. Cambridge, Mass.
  (1987) *Tragic Ways of Killing a Woman*. Cambridge, Mass.
  (1990) "Kreousa the Autochthon: a study of Euripides' *Ion*," in Winkler and Zeitlin 1990: 168–206.

Ludwig, W. (1954) *Sapheneia. Ein Beitrag zur Formkunst im Spätwerk des Euripides*. Tubingen.

Luppe, W. (1972) "Die Zahl der Konkurrenten an den komischen Agonen zur Zeit des Peloponnesischen Krieges," *Philologus* 116: 53–75.

MacDowell, D. M. (ed.) (1971) *Aristophanes. Wasps*. Oxford.

Mastronarde, D. J. (1975) "Iconography and imagery in Euripides' *Ion*," *ClAnt* 8: 163–76 (reprinted in Mossman 2003: 295–308).

(1979) *Contact and Discontinuity: Some Aspects of Speech and Action on the Greek Tragic Stage*. University of California Publications: Classical Studies 21. Berkeley and Los Angeles.

(1983) "Review article: Euripides' *Heracles*," *Échos du Monde Classique/Classical Views* 12, n.s. 2: 93–116.

(1986) "The optimistic rationalist in Euripides: Theseus, Jocasta, Teiresias," in *Greek Tragedy and its Legacy: Essays presented to Desmond Conacher*, ed. M. Cropp, E. Fantham, and S. Scully. Calgary: 201–11.

(1988) *Euripides. Phoenissae*. Leipzig.

(1990) "Actors on high: the skene-roof, the crane, and the gods in Attic drama," *ClAnt* 9: 247–94.

(ed.) (1994) *Euripides. Phoenissae*. Cambridge Classical Texts and Commentaries 29. Cambridge.

(1998) "Il coro euripideo: autorità e integrazione," *QUCC* 60: 55–80.

(1999) "Knowledge and authority in the choral voice of Euripidean tragedy," *Syllecta Classica* 10: 87–104.

(1999–2000) "Euripidean Tragedy and Genre: the terminology and its problems," in Cropp *et al.* 1999–2000: 23–39.

(2002a) "Euripidean tragedy and theology," *SemRom* 5: 17–49.

(ed.) (2002b) *Euripides. Medea*. Cambridge.

(2009) "The Lost *Phoenissae*: an experiment in reconstruction from fragments," in Cousland and Hume 2009: 63–76.

Matthiessen, K. (1967) *Elektra, Taurische Iphigenie und Helena. Untersuchungen zur Chronologie und zur dramatischen Form im Spätwerk des Euripides*. Hypomnemata 4. Gottingen.

(1974) *Studien zur Textüberlieferung der Hekabe des Euripides*. Bibliothek der klassischen Altertumswissenschaften, n. F., 2. Reihe 52. Heidelberg.

(1989–90) "Der Ion – eine Komödie des Euripides?," in *Opes Atticae. Miscellanea philologica et historica Raymondo Bogaert et Hermanno Van Looy oblata*, ed. M. Geerard, J. Desmet, and R. Vander Plaetse (= *Sacris Erudiri. Jaarboek voor Godsdienstwetenschappen* 31): 271–91.

(2002) *Die Tragödien des Euripides*. Zetemata 114. Munich.

(2008) *Euripides. Hekabe*. Berlin.

McClure, L. (1999) *Spoken like a Woman. Speech and Gender in Athenian Drama*. Princeton.

McDermott, E. (1989) *Euripides' Medea. The Incarnation of Disorder*. University Park, Pa.

McHardy, F., Robson, J., and Harvey, D. (eds.) (2005) *Lost Dramas of Classical Athens. Greek Tragic Fragments*. Exeter.

Medda, E. (2001) *Euripide. Oreste*. Milan.

(2005) "Il coro straniato: considerazioni sulla voce corale nelle *Fenicie* di Euripide," *Prometheus* 31(2): 119–31.

(2006) *Euripide. Le Fenicie*. Milan.

Meijering, R. (1985) "Aristophanes of Byzantium and scholia on the composition of the dramatic chorus," in *ΣΧΟΛΙΑ. Studia ad criticam interpretationemque textuum Graecorum et ad historiam iuris Graeco-Romani pertinentia D. Holwerda oblata*, ed. W. J. Aerts *et al*. Groningen: 91–102.

(1987) *Literary and Rhetorical Theories in Greek Scholia*. Groningen.

Mendelsohn, D. (2002) *Gender and the City in Euripides' Political Plays*. Oxford.

Meridor, R. (2000) "Creative rhetoric in Euripides' *Troades*: some notes on Hecuba's speech," *CQ* 50: 16–29.

Michelini, A. N. (1987) *Euripides and the Tragic Tradition*. Madison, Wisc.

(1999–2000) "The expansion of myth in late Euripides," in Cropp *et al*. 1999–2000: 41–57.

Mikalson, J. D. (1989) "Unanswered prayers in Greek tragedy," *JHS* 109: 81–98.

(1991) *Honor Thy Gods. Popular Religion in Greek Tragedy*. Chapel Hill, N.C.

Mills, S. (1997) *Theseus, Tragedy, and the Athenian Empire*. Oxford.

Moretti, J.-C. (1999–2000) "The theater of the sanctuary of Dionysus Eleuthereus in late fifth-century Athens," in Cropp *et al*. 1999–2000: 377–98.

Morwood, J. (2002) *The Plays of Euripides*. London.

Mossman, J. (1995) *Wild Justice. A Study of Euripides' Hecuba*. Oxford.

(ed.) (2003) *Oxford Readings in Classical Studies. Euripides*. Oxford.

Most, G. (2000) "Generating genres: the idea of the tragic," in *Matrices of Genre. Authors, Canons, and Society*, ed. M. Depew and D. Obbink. Cambridge: 15–35.

Mueller-Goldingen, C. (1985) *Untersuchungen zu den Phönissen des Euripides*. Palingenesia 22. Stuttgart.

Mullen, W. (1982) *Choreia: Pindar and Dance*. Princeton.

Murray, G. (1947) *Greek Studies*. Oxford.

Nesselrath, H.-G. (1990) *Die attische Mittlere Komödie. Ihre Stellung in der antiken Literaturkritik und Literaturgeschichte*. Untersuchungen zur antiken Literatur und Geschichte, Bd. 36. Berlin and New York.

(1993) "Parody and later Greek comedy," *HSCPh* 95: 181–95.

Nestle, W. (1901) *Euripides: der Dichter der griechischen Aufklärung*. Stuttgart.

Newton, R. M. (1985) "Ino in Euripides' *Medea*," *AJPh* 106: 496–502.

Norwood, G. (1908) *The Riddle of the Bacchae. the Last Stage of Euripides' Religious Views*. Manchester.

(1953) *Greek Tragedy*. 4th edn. London.

Ober, J. (1989) *Mass and Elite in Democratic Athens. Rhetoric, Ideology, and the Power of the People*. Princeton.

O'Brien, M. J. (1964) "Orestes and the Gorgon," *AJPh* 85: 13–39.

O'Connor-Visser, E. A. M. (1987) *Aspects of Human Sacrifice in Euripides*. Amsterdam.

Olson, S. D. (2002) *Aristophanes. Acharnians*. Oxford.

Oranje, H. (1984) *Euripides' Bacchae. The Play and its Audience*. Mnemosyne Suppl 78. Leiden.

Osborne, R. (1997) "The ecstasy and the tragedy: varieties of religious experience in art, drama, and society" in Pelling 1997: 187–211.

Osborne, R., and Hornblower, S. (eds.) (1994) *Ritual, Finance, Politics. Athenian Democratic Accounts Presented to David Lewis.* Oxford.

Padel, R. (1974) "Imagery of the elsewhere: two choral odes of Euripides," *CR* 24: 227–41.

(1990) "Making space speak," in Winkler and Zeitlin 1990: 336–65.

(1992) *In and Out of the Mind. Greek Images of the Tragic Self.* Princeton.

(1995) *Whom Gods Destroy. Elements of Greek and Tragic Madness.* Princeton.

Page, D. L. (1934) *Actors' Interpolations in Greek Tragedy. Studied with Special Reference to Euripides'* Iphigeneia in Aulis. Oxford.

Panagl, O. (1971) *Die 'dithyrambischen stasima' des Euripides.* Vienna.

Papadopoulou, T. (2005) *Heracles and Euripidean Tragedy.* Cambridge.

Parker, L. P. E. (2007) *Euripides.* Alcestis. Oxford.

Parker, R. (1996) *Athenian Religion. A History.* Oxford.

(1997) "Gods cruel and kind: tragic and civic theology," in Pelling 1997: 143–60.

(2005) *Polytheism and Society at Athens.* Oxford.

Pattoni, M. P. (1989) "La sympatheia del coro nella parodo dei tragici greci: motivi e forme di una modello drammatico," *SCO* 39: 33–82.

Patzer, H. (1962) *Die Anfänge der griechischen Tragödie.* Schriften der Wissenschaftlichen Gesellschaft an der Johann Wolfgang Goethe-Universität Frankfurt am Main, Geisteswissenschaftliche Reihe 3. Wiesbaden.

Pechstein, N. (1998) *Euripides Satyrographos: ein Kommentar zu den Euripideischen Satyrspielfragmenten.* Beiträge zur Altertumskunde 115. Stuttgart.

Pedrick, V. (2007) *Euripides, Freud, and the Romance of Belonging.* Baltimore, Md.

Pedrick, V., and Oberhelman, S. (2005) *The Soul of Tragedy. Essays on Athenian Drama.* Chicago.

Pelling, C. (ed.) (1997) *Greek Tragedy and the Historian.* Oxford.

(2000) *Literary Texts and the Greek Historian.* London.

(2002) "Tragedy, rhetoric, and performance culture," in Gregory 2005: 83–102.

Pfister, M. (1988) *The Theory and Analysis of Drama* (trans. of *Das Drama,* Frankfurt 1977). Cambridge.

Pickard-Cambridge, A. W. (1927) *Dithyramb, Tragedy and Comedy.* Oxford.

(1962) *Dithyramb, Tragedy and Comedy.* 2nd edn, rev. T. B. L. Webster. Oxford.

(1988) *The Dramatic Festivals of Athens.* ed. J. Gould and D. M. Lewis. 2nd edn (1968), with supplement and corrections. Oxford.

Platter, C. (2006) *Aristophanes and the Carnival of Genres.* Baltimore, Md.

Poe, J. P. (1974) *Human and Divine Justice in Sophocles' Philoctetes.* Mnemosyne Suppl. 34. Leiden.

Pöhlmann, E. (1995) "Der Chor der Tragödie an den Grenzen der Bühnenkonventionen des 5. Jh.," in E. Pöhlmann, *Studien zur Bühnendichtung und zum Theaterbau der Antike.* Studien zur klassischen Philologie, Bd. 93. Frankfurt am Main: 63–72.

Pohlenz, M. (1930) *Die griechische Tragödie.* Leipzig and Berlin.

(1954) *Die griechische Tragödie.* 2nd edn. Gottingen.

Porter, J. R. (1994) *Studies in Euripides' Orestes.* Mnemosyme Suppl. 128. Leiden.

(1999–2000) "Euripides and Menander: *Epitrepontes*, Act IV," in Cropp *et al.* 1999–2000: 157–73.

Price, S. (1999) *Religions of the Ancient Greeks*. Cambridge.

Pucci, P. (1980) *The Violence of Pity in Euripides' Medea*. Cornell Studies in Classical Philology 41. Ithaca, N.Y.

Pulleyn, S. (1997) *Prayer in Greek Religion*. Oxford.

Rabinowitz, N. (1993) *Anxiety Veiled: Euripides and the Traffic in Women*. Ithaca.

Radt, S. L. (1991) "Sophokles in seinen Fragmenten," in Hofmann 1991: 117–35.

Rawson, E. (1970) "Family and fatherland in Euripides' *Phoenissae*," *GRBS* 11: 109–27.

Reckford, K. J. (1985) "Concepts of demoralization in the *Hecuba*," in Burian 1985a: 112–28.

Redmond, J. (ed.) (1992) *Themes in Drama 14: Melodrama*. Cambridge.

Redondo, J. (2003) "Satyric diction in the extant Sophoclean fragments: a reconsideration," in Sommerstein 2003a: 413–31.

Rehm, R. (1994) *Marriage to Death. The Conflation of Wedding and Funeral Rituals in Greek Tragedy*. Princeton.

Reinhardt, K. (1957) "Die Sinneskrise bei Euripides," *Eranos-Jahrbuch* 26: 279–313 (reprinted in his *Tradition und Geist: gesammelte Essays zur Dichtung*, ed. C. Becker. Gottingen 1960: 227–56).

(2003) "The intellectual crisis in Euripides," in Mossman 2003: 16–46 (English version of Reinhardt 1957).

Revermann, M. (1999–2000) "Euripides, tragedy and Macedon: some conditions of reception," in Cropp *et al.* 1999–2000: 451–67.

(2006) "The competences of theatre audiences in fifth- and fourth-century Athens," *JHS* 16: 99–124.

Rhodes, P. J. (2003) "Nothing to do with democracy: Athenian drama and the polis," *JHS* 123: 104–19.

Rhodes, P. J., and Osborne, R. (2003) *Greek Historical Inscriptions 404–323 BC*. Oxford.

Ritter, F. (1861) "Sieben unechte schlussstellen in den tragödien des Sophokles," *Philologus* 17: 422–36.

Rivier, A. (1972–73) "En marge *d'Alceste* et de quelques interprétations récentes," *MH* 29: 124–40 and 30: 130–43.

Roberts, D. (1987) "Parting words. Final lines in Sophocles and Euripides," *CQ* 37: 51–64.

Rode, J. (1971) "Das Chorlied," in Jens 1971: 85–115.

Rosenmeyer, T. G. (1963) *The Masks of Tragedy*. Austin, Tex.

(1981) "Drama," in *The Legacy of Greece. A New Appraisal*, ed. M. I. Finley. Oxford: 120–54.

(1982) *The Art of Aeschylus*. Berkeley.

(1985) "Ancient literary genres: a mirage?," *Yearbook of Comparative and General Literature* 34: 74–84.

Roselli, D. K. (2007) "Gender, class and ideology: the social function of virgin sacrifice in Euripides' *Children of Herakles*," *ClAnt* 26: 81–169.

Rossum-Steenbeek, M. van (1998) *Greek Readers' Digests?: Studies on a Selection of Subliterary Papyri.* Mnemosyme Suppl. 175. Leiden.

Roux, J. (1970–72) *Les Bacchantes.* 2 vols. Paris.

Ruck, C. (1976) "Duality and the madness of Herakles," *Arethusa* 9: 53–75.

Rusten, J. S. (1982) "Dicaearchus and the Tales from Euripides," *GRBS* 23: 357–67.

Rutherford, I. (2001) *Pindar's Paeans. A Reading of the Fragments with a Survey of the Genre.* Oxford.

Saïd, S. (1985) "Euripide ou l'attente déçue: l'exemple des *Phéniciennes*," *ASNP* ser. 3, 15(2): 501–276.

Sailor, D., and Stroup, S. C. (1999) "ΦΘΟΝΟΣ Δ᾽ ΑΠΕΣΤΩ: the translation of transgression in Aiskhylos' *Agamemnon*," *ClAnt* 18: 153–82.

Sansone, D. (1978) "The *Bacchae* as Satyr-Play?" *ICS* 3: 40–6.

Sauzeau, P. (1998) "'La Grèce entière est le tombeau d'Euripides.' Vie, mort et immortalité des poètes tragiques: quelques réflexions sur l'imaginaire biographique et sur la caverne d'Euripide," *CGITA* 11: 59–101.

Schadewalt, W. (1926) *Monolog und Selbstgespräch. Untersuchungen zur Formgeschichte der griechischen Tragödie.* Neue Philologische Untersuchungen 2. Berlin.

Schaps, D. M. (1977) "The woman least mentioned: etiquette and women's names," *CQ* 27: 323–30.

(1979) *Economic Rights of Women in Ancient Greece.* Edinburgh.

Schlegel, A. W. (1809) *Vorlesungen über dramatische Kunst und Literatur.* Heidelberg. (Eng. trans.: *A Course of Lectures on Dramatic Art and Literature*, 1815).

Schlegel, F. (1794a) *Von den Schulen der griechischen Poesie.*

(1794b) *Über die weiblichen Charaktere in den griechischen Dichtern.*

(1795–97) *Über das Studium der griechischen Poesie* (Eng. trans.: *On the Study of Greek Poetry*, trans. Stuart Barnett. Albany, N.Y. 2001).

(1798) *Geschichte der Poesie der Griechen und Römer.* Berlin.

(1815) *Geschichte der alten und neuen Literatur. Vorlesungen, gehalten zu Wien im Jahre 1812.* Vienna. (Eng. trans.: *Lectures on the History of Literature, Ancient and Modern*, partial (J. G. Lockhart) 1818, complete 1859).

Schlesinger, E. (1966) "Zu Euripides' *Medea*," *Hermes* 94: 26–53 (abbreviated English trans. "On Euripides' *Medea*" in Segal 1968: 70–89).

Schmidt, W. (1964) *Der Deus ex machina bei Euripides.* Tubingen.

Schmitt, J. (1921) *Freiwilliger Opfertod bei Euripides. Ein Beitrag zu seiner dramatischen Technik.* Religionsgeschichtliche Versuche und Vorarbeiten 17(2). Giessen.

Schorn, S. (2004) *Satyros aus Kallatis: Sammlung der Fragmente mit Kommentar.* Basel.

Schnurr-Redford, C. (1996) *Frauen im klassischen Athen: sozialer Raum und reale Bewegungsfreiheit.* Berlin.

Schwering, W. (1916–17) "Die Entstehung des Wortes tragicomoedia," *IF* 37: 139–41.

Schwinge, E.-R. (1968) *Die Verwendung des Stichomythie in den Dramen des Euripides.* Bibliothek der klassischen Altertumswissenschaft, 2. Reihe 27. Heidelberg.

Scodel, R. (1980) *The Trojan Trilogy of Euripides*. Hypomnemata 60. Gottingen.

(1996) "Δόμων ἄγαλμα: virgin sacrifice and aesthetic object," *TAPhA* 126: 111–28.

(1999–2000) "Verbal performance and Euripidean rhetoric," in Cropp *et al.* 1999–2000: 129–44.

(2007) "Lycurgus and the state text of tragedy," in *Politics of Orality*, ed. C. R. Cooper. Orality and literacy in ancient Greece 6 = Mnemosyne Suppl. 280. Leiden: 129–54.

Scullion, S. (1999–2000) "Tradition and invention in Euripidean aitiology," in Cropp *et al.* 1999–2000: 217–33.

(2002) "'Nothing to do with Dionysus': tragedy misconceived as ritual," *CQ* 52: 102–37.

Seaford, R. (1981) "Dionysiac drama and the Dionysiac mysteries," *CQ* 31: 252–75.

(1984) *Euripides. Cyclops*. Oxford.

(1987) "The tragic wedding," *JHS* 107: 106–30.

(1994) *Reciprocity and Ritual. Homer and Tragedy in the Developing City-State*. Oxford.

(1996) "Something to do with Dionysos – tragedy and the Dionysiac: response to Friedrich," in Silk 1996: 284.

(2000) "The social function of Attic tragedy: a response to Griffin," *CQ* 50: 30–44.

(2001) *Euripides. Bacchae*. Rev. edn. Warminster.

(2007) "From ritual to drama: a concluding statement," in Csapo and Miller 2007a: 379–401.

(2009) "Aitiologies of cult in Euripides: a response to Scott Scullion," in Cousland and Hume 2009: 221–34.

Segal, C. (1965) "The tragedy of the *Hippolytus*. The waters of ocean and the untouched meadow," *HSPh* 70: 117–69 (reprinted in his *Interpreting Greek Tragedy. Myth, Poetry, Text*. Ithaca, N.Y.: 1986).

(1970) "Shame and purity in Euripides' *Hippolytus*," *Hermes* 98: 278–99.

(1971) "The two worlds of Euripides' *Helen*," *TAPhA* 102: 553–614.

(1982) *Dionysiac Poetics and Euripides'* Bacchae. Princeton.

(1991) "Euripides' *Alcestis*: female death and male tears," *ClAnt* 11: 142–57.

(1992) "Admetus' divided house: spatial dichotomies and gender roles in Euripides," *MD* 28 (1992) 9–26.

(1993) *Euripides and the Poetics of Sorrow. Art, Gender, and Commemoration in Alcestis, Hippolytus, and Hecuba*. Durham, N.C.

(ed.) (2001) *Euripides. Bakkhai*, trans. R. Gibbons. Oxford.

Segal, E. (ed.) (1968) *Euripides. A Collection of Critical Essays*. Englewood Cliffs, N.J.

Seidensticker, B. (1982) *Palintonos Harmonia. Studien zu komischen Elementen in der griechischen Tragödie*. Hypomnemata 72. Gottingen.

(1995) "Women on the tragic stage," in *History, Tragedy, Theory. Dialogues on Athenian Drama*, ed. B. Goff. Austin, Tex.: 151–73.

Selden, D. (1994) "Genre of genre," in *The Search for the Ancient Novel*, ed. J. Tatum. Baltimore: 39–64.

Sharp, W. (1992) "Structure of melodrama," in Redmond 1992: 269–80.

Sheppard, J. T. (1916) "The formal beauty of the *Hercules Furens*," *CQ* 10: 72–9.

Silk, M. S. (ed.) (1996) *Tragedy and the Tragic. Greek Theatre and Beyond.* Oxford.

Silk, M. S., and Stern, J. P. (1980) *Nietzsche on Tragedy.* Cambridge.

Smith, W. D. (1966) "Expressive form in Euripides' *Suppliants*," *HSPh* 71: 151–70.

Snell, B. (1953) "Aristophanes and aesthetic criticism," in B. Snell, *The Discovery of the Mind. Greek Origins of European Thought,* trans. T. G. Rosenmeyer. Oxford: 113–35.

Solmsen, F. (1934) "*Onoma* and *Pragma* in Euripides' *Helen*," *CR* 48: 119–21.

Sommerstein, A. H. (2002) "Comic elements in tragic language: the case of Aeschylus' Oresteia," in *The Language of Greek Comedy,* ed. A. Willi. Oxford: 151–68.

(ed.) (2003a) *Shards from Kolonos. Studies in Sophoclean Fragments.* Le Rane: Collana di Studi e Testi 34. Bari.

(2003b) "The anger of Achilles, mark one: Sophocles' *Syndeipnoi*," in Sommerstein 2003a: 355–71.

Sourvinou-Inwood, C. (1997) "Tragedy and religion: constructs and readings," in Pelling 1997: 161–86.

(2003) *Tragedy and Athenian Religion.* Lanham, Md.

Spira, A. (1960) *Untersuchungen zum Deus ex machina bei Sophokles und Euripides.* Kallmünz.

Stevens, P. T. (1956) "Euripides and the Athenians," *JHS* 76: 87–94.

(ed.) (1971) *Euripides. Andromache.* Oxford.

Stewart, A. F. (1997) *Art, Desire, and the Body in Ancient Greece.* Cambridge.

Stinton, T. C. W. (1990) *Collected Papers on Greek Tragedy.* Oxford.

Stockert, W. (ed.) (1992) *Euripides. Iphigenie in Aulis.* 2 vols. Wiener Studien, Beiheft 16(1–2). Vienna.

Strohm, H. (1949) *Euripides. Iphigenie im Taurerlande.* Munich.

(1957) *Euripides: Interpretationen zur dramatischen Form.* Zetemata 15. Munich.

Sutton, D. F. (1973) "Supposed evidence that Euripides' *Orestes* and Sophocles' *Electra* were prosatyric," *RSC* 21: 117–21.

Taplin, O. (1977) *The Stagecraft of Aeschylus. The Dramatic Use of Exits and Entrances in Greek Tragedy.* Oxford.

(1978) *Greek Tragedy in Action.* London.

(1984–85) "Lyric dialogue and dramatic construction," *Dioniso* 55: 115–22.

(1986) "Fifth-century tragedy and comedy: a synkrisis," *JHS* 106, 163–74.

(1993) *Comic Angels and Other Approaches to Greek Drama through Vase-Paintings.* Oxford.

(2007) *Pots and Plays: Interactions between Tragedy and Greek Vase-Painting of the Fourth Century B.C.* Los Angeles.

Thalmann, W. G. (1993) "Euripides and Aeschylus: the case of the *Hekabe*," *ClAnt* 12: 126–59.

Thummer, E. (1986) "Griechische 'Erlösungsdramen,'" in *Im Bannkreis des Alten Orients. Studien zur Sprach- und Kulturgeschicthe des Alten Orients und seines Ausstrahlungsraumes Karl Oberhuber zum 70. Geburtstag gewidmet,* ed. W. Meid and H. Trenkwalder. Innsbrucker Beiträge zur Kulturwissenschaft, Bd. 24: 237–59.

Trenkner, S. (1958) *The Greek Novella in the Classical Period.* Cambridge.

Verrall, A. W. (1895) *Euripides the Rationalist. A Study in the History of Arts and Religion.* Cambridge.

(1905) *Essays on Four Plays of Euripides. Andromache, Helen, Heracles, Orestes.* Cambridge.

Versnel, H. (1990) *Inconsistencies in Greek and Roman Religion I. Ter Unus. Isis, Dionysos, Hermes. Three Studies in Henotheism.* Studies in Greek and Roman Religion 6(1). Leiden.

Vidal-Naquet, P. (1968) "The black hunter and the origin of the Athenian ephebeia," *PCPhS* 14: 49–64.

(1986) *The Black Hunter. Forms of Thought and Forms of Society in the Greek World.* Baltimore, Md.

Vietor, K. (1986) "L'histoire des genres littéraires," in Genette and Todorov 1986: 9–35.

Voelke, P. (2001) *Un Théâtre de la marge. Aspects figuratifs et configurationnels du drame satyrique dans l'Athènes classique.* (Le Rane: Collana di Studi e Testi 31). Bari.

von Fritz, K. (1959) "Die Entwicklung der Iason-Medea-Sage und die Medea des Euripides," *Antike und Abendland* 8: 33–106 (repr. in his *Antike und moderne Tragödie: neun Abhandlungen.* Berlin 1962: 322–429).

Walsh, G. B. (1977) "The first stasimon of Euripides' *Electra*," *YClS* 25: 277–89.

Wasserstein, F. M. (1940) "Divine violence and providence in Euripides' *Ion*," *TAPhA* 71: 587–604.

Waszink, J. H. (ed.) (1969) *Euripidis Hecuba et Iphigenia in Aulide*, ed. D. Erasmus (1506 and 1507), in *Opera Omnia Desiderii Erasmi Roterodami* I:1. Amsterdam. 193–359.

Webster, T. B. L. (1967) *The Tragedies of Euripides.* London.

Weinberg, B. (1961) *A History of Literary Criticism in the Italian Renaissance.* 2 vols. Chicago.

West, M. L. (1987) *Euripides. Orestes.* Warminster.

(1989) "The early chronology of Attic tragedy," *CQ* 39: 251–4.

Whitman, C. (1951) *Sophocles. A Study in Heroic Humanism.* Cambridge, Mass.

(1974) *Euripides and the Full Circle of Myth.* Cambridge, Mass.

Wilamowitz-Moellendorff, U. von (ed.) (1891) *Euripides. Hippolytos.* Berlin.

(1895) *Euripides Herakles.* 3 vols. 2nd edn. Berlin.

(1899) *Griechische Tragoedien.* Bd I. Berlin.

Wildberg, C. (1999–2000) "Piety as service, epiphany as reciprocity: two observations on the religious meaning of the gods in Euripides," in Cropp *et al.* 1999–2000: 235–56.

(2002) *Hyperesie und Epiphanie: ein Versuch über die Bedeutung der Götter in den Dramen des Euripides.* Zetemata 109. Munich.

Wiles, D. (1997) *Tragedy in Athens: Performance Space and Theatrical Meaning.* Cambridge.

Wilkins, J. (1993) *Euripides. Heraclidae.* Oxford.

Williams, B. (1993) *Shame and Necessity.* Berkeley and Los Angeles.

Willink, C. W. (1986) *Euripides. Orestes.* Oxford.

Wilson, P. J. (1996) "Tragic rhetoric: the use of tragedy and the tragic in the fourth century," in Silk 1996: 310–31.

(1999) "The *aulos* at Athens," in Goldhill and Osborne 1999: 58–95.

(2000) *The Athenian Institution of the Khoregia. The Chorus, the City and the Stage.* Cambridge.

(2003) "The sound of cultural conflict: Kritias and the culture of *mousike* in Athens," in *The Cultures within Ancient Greek Culture. Contact, Conflict, and Collaboration,* ed. L. Kurke and C. Dougherty. Cambridge: 181–206.

Winkler, J. J. (1990) "The ephebes' song: *tragoidia* and *polis.*" in Winkler and Zeitlin 1990: 20–62.

Winkler, J. J., and Zeitlin, F. (eds.) (1990) *Nothing to Do with Dionysos?: Athenian Drama in its Social Context.* Princeton.

Wohl, V. (1998) *Intimate Commerce. Exchange, Gender, and Subjectivity in Greek Tragedy.* Austin, Tex.

Wolff, C. (1968) "Orestes," in Segal 1968: 132–49.

(1973) "On Euripides' *Helen,*" *HSPh* 77: 61–84.

(1992) "Euripides' *Iphigenia among the Taurians*: aetiology, ritual, and myth," *ClAnt* 11: 308–34.

Worman, N. (1999) *The Cast of Character. Style in Greek Literature.* Austin, Tex.

Wright, M. (2005) *Euripides' Escape Tragedies. A Study of Helen, Andromeda and Iphigenia among the Taurians.* Oxford.

Young, D. C. C. (1970) "Pindaric criticism," in *Pindaros und Bakchylides,* ed. W. M. Calder III and J. Stern. Wege der Forschung 134. Darmstadt: 1–95.

Yunis, H. (1988) *A New Creed. Fundamental Religious Beliefs in the Athenian Polis and Euripidean Drama.* Hypomnemata 91. Gottingen.

Zacharia, K. (1995) "The marriage of tragedy and comedy in Euripides' *Ion,*" in *Laughter Down the Centuries,* vol. II. Annales Universitatis Turkuensis, ser. B, tom. 213. Turku: 45–63.

(2003) *Converging Truths: Euripides' Ion and the Athenian Quest for Self-Definition.* Mnemosyne Suppl. 242. Leiden.

Zeitlin, F. (1970) "The Argive festival of Hera and Euripides' *Electra,*" *TAPhA* 101: 645–69.

(1985) "The power of Aphrodite. Eros and the boundaries of the self in the *Hippolytus,*" in Burian 1985a: 52–111.

(1989) "Mysteries of identity and designs of the self in Euripides' *Ion,*" *PCPhS* 35: 144–97.

(1990) "Thebes: theater of self and society in Athenian drama," in Winkler and Zeitlin 1990: 130–67.

(1991) "Euripides' *Hekabe* and the somatics of Dionysiac drama," *Ramus* 20: 53–94 (revised in Zeitlin 1996: 172–216).

(1996) *Playing the Other. Gender and Society in Classical Greek Literature.* Princeton.

(2003) "The closet of masks: role-playing and myth-making in the *Orestes* of Euripides," in Mossman 2003: 309–41 (reprint of *Ramus* 9 (1980): 51–77).

Zimmermann, B. (1992) *Dithyrambos: Geschichte einer Gattung*. Hypomnemata 98. Gottingen.

Zuntz, G. (1955) *The Political Plays of Euripides*. Manchester.

(1958) "Contemporary politics in the plays of Euripides," *Acta Congressus Madvigiani*. International Congress of Classical Studies, Proceedings II: I.155–62 (reprinted in *Opuscula Selecta*. Manchester 1972: 54–61).

(1960) "On Euripides' *Helena*: theology and irony," in *Euripide*, ed. O. Reverdin. Entretiens Hardt 6. Geneva: 201–41.

Index of names and topics

a fortiori argument
  from behavior of a heroine, 266, 267
  from behavior of an exemplary hero, 303
  from divine behavior, 172, 214
Achaeus, *Peirithous*, 298
Achilles, 32, 36, 76, 113, 139, 264, 281
  in *Hec.*, 33, 72, 144, 202, 230, 266
  in *IA*, 43, 135, 141, 238, 239, 240, 250, 251, 285
Admetus, 29, 101, 108, 122, 124, 131, 170, 180, 227, 228, 257, 261, 270, 283, 285, 294, 299, 301
Adrastus, 40, 125
  in *Su.*, 34, 51, 80, 81, 82, 96, 186, 187, 217, 295
Aegeus
  in Bacchylides, 98
  in *Med.*, 30, 117, 118, 137, 200, 252, 255, 257, 295
Aegisthus
  in Aesch. *Agam.*, 115
  in Aesch. *Choe.*, 100, 115, 269
  in *El.*, 34, 120, 285, 288
Aeolus, in *Melanippe the Wise*, 295
Aerope, 260
Aeschylus, 11, 18, 26, 27, 50, 53, 87, 89, 103, 115, 131, 134, 142, 207, 209, 239, 249, 253, 308
  Aetnaeae, 53
  Agamemnon, 65, 66, 67, 100, 101, 103, 107, 115, 196, 199, 236, 240, 260, 272, 292, 300
    choral odes, 123, 149, 309
  Argo, 53
  as character in Arist. *Frogs*, 23, 24, 207, 304
  Choephori, 34, 58, 65, 67, 84, 98, 103, 105, 125, 163, 242, 249, 288
    chorus, 115
  chorus, 102
  contrasted with Euripides, 2, 68, 100, 148, 207
  Cressae, 53
  Danaides, 182
  Eumenides, 59, 66, 84, 96, 142, 182, 183, 216, 242
    chorus, 102
  gods portrayed on stage, 175
  Heracleidae, 112

Oresteia, 45, 60, 66, 67, 84, 85, 142, 188, 205, 238, 239, 310
Persae, 45, 50, 66
Prometheus Bound, *see* anonymous, *Prometheus (Bound)*
Prometheus Pyrkaeus, 55
Prometheus Unbound, *see* anonymous, *Prometheus Unbound*
Septem, 50, 100, 197, 296
  choral odes, 123
Supplices, 66, 96, 216
Aethra, 34, 80, 81, 96, 217, 250, 255, 256, 295, 301
aetiology, 309
  and poetic skill, 22, 183
  at end of a tragedy, 158, 187, 193
  in choral myth, 122, 124, 165
  in prologue, 182
affirmation of values, 20
Agamemnon, 79, 103, 132, 139, 158, 163, 164, 192, 242, 245, 250
  in Aesch. *Agam.*, 115, 199, 202, 272, 300
  in *Hec.*, 33, 72, 120, 188, 204, 213, 231, 232, 233, 234, 257, 258, 259, 286, 300
  in *IA*, 42, 135, 143, 235, 236, 237, 239, 250, 255, 301
  in *Iliad*, 202, 300
  in Soph. *Ajax*, 150, 300, 305
  prayer to his ghost in *Or.* and Aesch. *Choe.*, 85
Agathon, 49, 88, 127
Agave, 42, 87, 189, 220, 264
age status, 28, 283
agency, 149, 159, 164, 280, 282, 298
agōn (logōn), 76, 80, 117, 150, 162, 209, 213, 218, 221, 222–45, 270, 276, 299, 302, 308
agōn-scene, 78, 191, 299
aidōs, 108, 135, 273
Ajax, 212, 264, 281
  in Soph. *Ajax*, 66, 75, 150, 178, 196, 199, 234, 305
akolouthia, 127
alastōr, 194, 201

Alcestis, 29, 75, 107, 131, 180, 228, 238, 250, 255,
　　268, 269, 276, 283, 285, 299
Alcman, *First Partheneion*, 91
Alcmene
　　in *Hcld.*, 31, 86, 171, 250, 251, 258, 259, 294
　　in *Her.*, 167
Alexandrian scholars, 2, 3, 5, 46, 57
Alexis, 6
amathia, 164, 171, 190, 192
Amazons, 261, 267
Amphiaraus, 82, 125, 250
Amphion, 174, 184, 186
Amphis, 5
Amphitryon, 35, 71, 168, 171, 172, 197, 213, 255, 258,
　　261, 292, 294, 296, 310
anachronism (within the tragic world), 241, 248
Anaxagoras, 3, 182
Anaxandrides, 6
Andromache
　　in *Andr.*, 32, 75, 76, 84, 104, 111, 113, 131, 132,
　　　　186, 252, 255, 259, 260, 274, 275, 276, 277,
　　　　278, 283, 293, 302
　　in *Tro.*, 36, 78, 79, 138, 161, 262, 273
Andromeda, 286, 291
anonymous
　　Life of Aeschylus, 52
　　Prometheus (Bound), 26, 65, 66, 78, 102
　　Prometheus Unbound, 53, 65
　　Rhesus, 4, 26, 175, 181
Antigone
　　in *Phoen.*, 40, 171, 251, 255, 286, 296
　　in Soph. *Ant.*, 66, 68, 114, 115, 149, 185, 211, 234,
　　　　249, 263
antilabē, 239
antilogiai, 229
Antiope, 174, 259
Antiphanes, 5
Antiphon, 209
antithesis, 69, 210, 218, 236
anti-war themes, 13, 77
Aphrodite, 135, 143, 172, 227
　　in *Hipp.*, 31, 68, 108, 114, 160, 172, 177, 178,
　　　　185, 187, 190, 196, 253, 263, 271, 284,
　　　　289, 299
Apollo, 17, 90, 158, 171, 182
　　in Aesch. *Eum.*, 85, 102, 190
　　in *Alc.*, 29, 57, 107, 122, 124, 131, 180, 229,
　　　　283, 299
　　in *Alcm. Cor.*, 181
　　in *Andr.*, 75, 76, 132, 138, 172, 196, 291
　　in *El.*, 111, 190
　　in *Ion*, 38, 110, 166, 167, 180, 181, 185, 187, 198,
　　　　254, 280
　　in *IT*, 37, 73, 142, 162, 163, 164, 165, 185,
　　　　196, 287

　　in *Or.*, 41, 84, 120, 180, 185, 188, 192, 193, 194,
　　　　195, 242, 289, 296
　　in Soph. *OT*, 116, 160
Apollophanes, 6
aporia, 194, 229, 235, 245, 307, 311
apostrophe (by chorus), 114, 130, 131, 133, 138, 139,
　　140, 141, 143, 144, 149
apotropaic statements by choruses, 96, 114, 124,
　　134, 136
apraktos, 146
archē kakōn, 123, 124, 131, 134, 140, 144, 149
Archemorus, 184
Archilochus, 92
Argeus, 184
argument from probability, 210, 226, 277
Arion, 51, 92, 98
aristocratic values, 18, 19, 212, 218, 225, 227, 273,
　　280, 284, 288, 307, 309
Aristophanes, 1, 2, 3, 6, 12, 23, 24, 26, 44, 45, 48,
　　52, 57, 127, 149, 153, 155, 207, 210, 211, 214,
　　261, 304, 309
　　Acharnians, 1, 261
　　Aeolosicon, 5
　　Clouds, 1, 24, 214
　　Frogs, 1, 2, 23, 24, 44, 48, 49, 207, 304
　　Peace, 1
　　Wasps, 292
　　Women at the Thesmophoria, 1, 261
Aristophanes of Byzantium, 4, 8, 216
aristos, 264, 270
Aristotle, 1, 2, 3, 8, 9, 11, 16, 25, 26, 27, 45, 46, 51,
　　52, 54, 57, 58, 63, 65, 88, 93, 106, 119, 126,
　　145, 147, 148, 150, 175, 181, 198, 200, 284,
　　285, 304
　　Poetics, 1, 2, 11, 25, 46, 58, 63, 88, 146, 147, 310
Aristoxenus, 2
Arsenius of Monembasia, 9
Artemis, 129, 143, 171
　　Attic cult in *IT*, 162, 164, 183
　　in a lost ending of *IA*, 42
　　in *Hipp.*, 60, 68, 108, 114, 171, 177, 180, 185, 187,
　　　　188, 190, 195, 253, 263, 274, 280, 289, 298
　　Taurian cult, 73, 128, 158, 164, 165, 172
Asclepius, 107, 122, 180
Astyanax, 36, 79, 138, 139
atē, 149, 199, 202
atheism, 2, 155, 174, 222
Athena, 143, 182, 261
　　in Aesch. *Eum.*, 66, 84, 157
　　in *Erechtheus*, 180, 184, 186
　　in *Ion*, 38, 110, 167, 180, 185, 186, 187, 189, 191,
　　　　198, 254
　　in *IT*, 37, 162, 164, 165, 185, 186, 187, 286
　　in *Rhesus*, 175
　　in Soph. *Ajax*, 160, 178, 196, 199

Athena (cont.)
  in *Su.*, 34, 186, 187, 188, 301
  in *Theseus*, 186
  in *Tro.*, 36, 78, 79, 109, 139, 179, 204, 221, 274
Athenian state copies of tragedies, 5
Atreus, 74, 134, 140, 275
Autolycus, 274
autonomous agents
  men as, 304
  women as, 247, 280
Axionicus, *Phileuripides*, 6

Bacchylides, 22, 65, 91, 98
  poem 15, 17
  poem 17, 17, 92
  poem 18, 17, 92, 98
barbarian, as antithesis of Greek, 72, 74, 96, 165, 236, 252, 275, 278
beginning of evils, *see archē kakōn*
Bellerophon, 173, 249
biographical tradition, 1, 3, 4, 8, 9
bow, imaginary or actual in *Or.*, 192
bravery, 217, 238, 240, 261, 265, 266, 267, 268, 269, 270, 283, 289, 299
Brumoy, Pierre, 11

Cadmus
  in *Bacchae*, 42, 59, 87, 125, 187, 189, 219, 255, 294
  in *Phoen.*, 40, 124
caesura, 50
Capaneus, 34, 83
Cassandra, 123, 131
  in Aesch. *Agam.*, 107, 115, 196, 240
  in *Hec.*, 34, 188, 232, 286
  in *Tro.*, 36, 78, 79, 138, 161, 204, 240, 250, 286
Castelvetro, 10, 11
Castor
  in *El.*, 180, 185, 189, 190, 280
  in *Hel.*, 187, 188, 191, 195
catasterisms, 184
character, *see ēthos*
  rhetoric and, 207
characterization, 2
charis, 19, 72, 226, 227, 230, 232, 233, 234, 257, 301, 306
children characters, 284
chorēgia, 17, 19
choregic system, *see chorēgia*
chorēgos, 19, 77, 95
chorou melos, 88
chorus
  and knowledge, 89
  Aristotle's views, 2
  as collective body, 19
  authority of choral voice, 89, 90–106

complicity with violence, 119, 120, 129, 259, 260
connection and relevance of songs, 126–45
contrasted with elite characters, 20
entering the skene suggested but not realized, 96, 118, 120, 144
female, 100, 101, 102, 103, 105, 249, 250, 253, 264, 275
identification of theater audience with, 89, 98–106
ideological functions of, 89, 95, 99
last words, 97, 105
level of knowledge, compared to audience, 106–14
marginal status, 99, 101
moral and interpretive authority, 114–21
privilege of higher level of knowledge, 112
sympathy, 117, 119, 127, 147, 151, 152, 278
withdrawal from participation in action, 99, 115, 121, 149, 150
Chrysippus (Stoic philosopher), 8
Cicero, 10
citizen elders (as chorus), 100, 101, 104, 115
class, social, 17, 19, 283
classical, the classical, 48, 61, 62, 64, 127, *see also* classicism
classicism, 52, 54, 63, 65, 281
  German, 11, 52
  Greek, 8, 212
Cleisthenes (tyrant of Sicyon), 51
Cleisthenic reforms (Cleisthenes of Athens), 15
closed form, 64, *see also* open form
Clytemnestra, 85, 121, 142, 163, 242, 244, 260, 270, 294
  in Aesch. *Agam.*, 68, 115, 202, 209, 249, 260, 263, 272
  in Aesch. *Choe.*, 269, 287
  in Aesch. *Oresteia*, 253
  in *El.*, 34, 111, 121, 139, 255, 262, 285
  in *IA*, 43, 135, 141, 143, 171, 172, 236, 237, 238, 239, 240, 250, 255, 276, 285, 301, 302
collapse of distinctions, 264, 306
Collin, Rudolf, 9
colloquialism, 50
comedy
  as a genre, 4, 17, 21, 46, 50, 51, 52, 55, 58, 59, 60, 157, 246, 292
  as source of biographical details, 3
  Euripides parodied or alluded to in, 5
  Middle Comedy, 6
  New Comedy, 6, 181
  Old Comedy, 20, 50, 57, 94, 239, 256
competition of genders, 263–70, 272
complaints about the gods, 87, 162, 166, 170, 171, 172, 174, 180, 185, 227
contesting prayers, 162, 169

contradictions, inherent in values and norms, 229, 261, 272, 281
courage, relation to genders, 261–70
cowardice, 87, 115, 243, 261, 265, 266, 268, 270, 299
Creon
in *Med.*, 30, 117, 136, 252, 255, 259, 295, 296, 298
in *Phoen.*, 40, 255, 256, 266, 295
in Soph. *Ant.*, 65, 66, 68, 114, 115, 197, 249, 263, 305
in Soph. *OC*, 66, 305
in Soph. *OT*, 97, 305
Creusa, 38, 109, 120, 129, 166, 167, 181, 184, 185, 187, 191, 250, 253, 255, 260, 262, 283, 285, 290
Critias, *Peirithous*, 298
criticism of the gods, 153, 162, 166, 168, 169, 170, 171, 179, 180, 185, 190, 193, 226
cult-foundations, 158

Danaids, 66, 126, 302
daughter of Heracles (Macaria), 31, 86, 206, 238, 251, 255, 256, 259, 265, 266, 268, 293, 302, 310
decadence, associated with Euripides or newer styles in music, etc., 11, 13, 26, 212
deception, 69, 73, 74, 110, 113, 120, 136, 142, 143, 146, 187, 212, 215, 227, 250, 260, 263, 271, 272, 273, 284, 286, 287, 289, 291, 298, 300, 301, 302
decline (of the tragic genre), 14, 53, 88
deconstructive criticism, 14
decorum, 3, 8, 26, 48, 54, 56, 58, 146, 304
Deianeira, 66, 67, 100, 103, 211, 251, 273
democracy
democratic values and ideologies, 307
democracy, Athenian, 15–21
democratic values and ideologies, 45, 89, 95, 99, 153, 210, 211, 249, 261, 304
Demophon, 31, 257, 258, 265, 293, 301
despair, dialectic of hope and despair, 111, 154, 161, 167, 169, 173, 205, 292
destabilization
of audience interpretation, 69, 82, 240, 246
of norms, 83, 234, 271, 278, 295
deus ex machina, 2, 69, 78, 82, 85, 106, 113, 165, 174, 175, 181, 182, 183, 184, 186, 187, 188, 189, 190, 191, 193, 194, 195, 198, 200, 286, 294, 296
see also epilogue gods
diaulos, 70
Dicaearchus, 2, 7
Didymus, 4, 8
Dio Chrysostomus, 7
Diocles, 6

Dionysia
Great or City, *see* Great Dionysia
local, 26
Dionysiac power or possession, 21, 26, 42, 264
Dionysius of Halicarnassus, 52
de oratoribus veteribus, 212
Dionysus
Dionysian aspects of drama and theatrical festivals, 17, 21, 55, 60, 102
Dionysian origins of drama, 21
dramatic performances at festivals of, 17
festivals of, 92, 93 *see also* Dionysia, Great Dionysia
in Athenian cult, 51, 55, 91, 159
in *Bacchae*, 41, 87, 110, 125, 128, 140, 151, 159, 161, 173, 176, 178, 184, 185, 188, 189, 190, 196, 219, 240, 264, 290
in disguise in lost plays, 176
in *Hypsipyle*, 184
in *Ino*, 187
in Soph. *Ant.*, 116, 158
myths of triumph over persecutors, 60
polarities associated with, 21
Dioscuri, 184
in *El.*, 35, 121
in *Helen*, 39, 113
Diphilus, 6
Dirce
character in *Antiope*, 259
spring in Thebes, 140, 184
disguise, 60, 61, 125, 128, 151, 176, 179, 284, 287, 289, 290
dissoi logoi, 70, 229, 235
dithyramb, 17
Arion, 92, 98
choral performance at Great Dionysia, 15, 17, 21, 55, 91, 92, 104, 157, 307
dithyrambos, 17, 92
divine prologue, 107, 109, 153, 160, 174–81, 193, 196, 221
in Menander, 109
dolos, see deception
Donatus (commentator on Terence), 10
double movement or focus (plot structure), 68, 69, 70, 71, 72, 73, 74, 104
double plot (Aristotelian term), 58, 61
doxa, 210, 261
dramatic illusion, 52, 94, 175
dreams (prophetic), 73, 111, 142, 144, 162, 165
dustopastos, 221

educational system and practice, 7, 22, 24, 25, 54, 147
Electra
in *El.*, 35, 86, 111, 121, 128, 139, 171, 186, 189, 250, 259, 262, 286, 287

Electra (cont.)
 in *Or.*, 41, 83, 85, 86, 120, 186, 192, 240, 255, 259,
  260, 286, 288, 294
 in Soph. *El.*, 211, 305
elpis, 111, 156
embolima, 49, 88, 126, 141, 146, 151
ephebe, 191, 265, 284, 285, 286, 287, 288, 289, 290,
  291, 297, 302, 305, 306
Epictetus, 8
epilogue gods, moral and interpretive authority
  of, 188–91
epiparodos, 131
epiphany, 90, 114, 175, 179, 181, 182, 185, 193,
  202, 203
episodic, 77, 80, 82
epitome(s), 4, 6, 9, 27
Erasmus, 9, 237
Erechtheus, 123, 266, 269
ergon, 210, 218
Eriphus, 5
Eros, 114, 115, 135
erōs, 54, 305
escape deliberations, 274
escape scheme, 287
escape wish, 135
Eteocles
 in Aesch. *Se.*, 100, 197, 202, 209, 296
 in *Phoen.*, 8, 40, 213, 215, 218, 219, 256, 258, 260,
  290, 295
ethical first person, 133, *see also* first person
ethnic difference, 231, 252
ēthos, 4, 13, 15, 207, 223, 225, 226, 228, 235, 282, 297
Eubulus, 5
eudoxia, 262
eukleēs, 263, 270
eukleia, 263
Euripidean triad, 7
Euripides
 Aegeus, 5, 101, 103, 200
 Aeolus, 5, 103, 260
 Alcestis, 4, 26, 29–30, 46, 55, 56, 57, 59, 75, 101,
  107, 127, 130, 180, 209, 227–9, 249, 257,
  261, 269, 270, 283, 284, 294, 299, 300, 301
  chorus, 122
 Alcmeon A', 103
 Alcmeon A' or B', 5
 Alcmeon B', 103
 Alexandros, 78, 181, 222
 Alope, 103, 286
 Andromache, 7, 32–3, 74–7, 84, 97, 104, 105, 111,
  127, 131, 140, 150, 172, 186, 188, 196, 206,
  250, 251, 255, 258, 274, 275–9, 283, 285,
  286, 291, 293, 302
 Andromeda, 5, 103, 286, 291
 Antiope, 5, 101, 103, 259, 286

Antiope (*deus ex machina*), 186
Archelaus, 101, 103, 184
Auge, 5, 286
Bacchae, 5, 41, 101, 105, 125, 128, 151, 158, 161,
  176, 178, 185, 189, 190, 194, 196, 264, 290
Bellerophon, 6, 101, 103
cave on Salamis, 3
Chrysippus, 6, 260
Cresphontes, 101, 103, 127
Cressae, 103, 260
Cretans, 6, 101, 103, 209, 249, 256
criticism of his art, 2, 3, 8, 12, 52, 127, 147,
  200, 238
Cyclops, 10, 26, 55, 57, 59, 120, 174, 188
Danae, 6, 103, 286
Electra, 9, 34, 67, 86, 104, 111, 127, 181, 186, 187,
  244, 250, 255, 258, 259, 286, 287, 306, 310
  chorus, 121, 128
  deus ex machina, 187, 189, 190
Erechtheus, 6, 71, 81, 101, 103
Hecuba, 7, 9, 33–4, 71–3, 86, 105, 119, 124, 127,
  143, 145, 150, 198, 202–5, 229–34, 238, 250,
  256, 258, 264, 266, 286, 293, 294, 300
Helen, 6, 38–9, 50, 56, 59, 61, 73–4, 100, 125,
  128, 166, 181, 206, 250, 260, 291, 302, 303
  deus ex machina, 186
 Great Mother Ode, 151
Heracleidae, 30–1, 57, 71, 86, 101, 128, 206, 216,
  238, 250, 257, 258, 259, 264, 265, 286, 293,
  301, 310
Heracles, 35–6, 69–71, 72, 83, 100, 101, 111,
  167–9, 171, 175, 206, 214, 261, 292, 298,
  303, 310
Hippolytus (extant), 4, 31–2, 60, 66, 68–9, 96,
  97, 98, 104, 105, 108, 111, 113, 119, 127, 131,
  161, 172, 177, 178, 185, 187, 190, 194, 196,
  206, 214, 223–6, 251, 253, 258, 263, 285, 298
Hippolytus Veiled (lost), 4, 103, 105, 119, 177,
  260, 283, 298
Hypsipyle, 103, 127, 128, 181, 250, 259, 286
  chorus, 151
 in Aristophanes, 1
Ino, 103, 187
Ion, 6, 38, 58, 105, 109, 114, 120, 129, 151, 166,
  168, 180, 184, 185, 187, 188, 189, 194, 197,
  206, 250, 253, 254, 255, 256, 258, 285, 290
Iphigenia in Aulis, 1–43, 67, 71, 104, 123, 129,
  140, 235–40, 250, 255, 256, 260, 264, 268,
  286, 291, 301, 302
  chorus, 101, 121, 125, 151
Iphigenia in Tauris, 2, 37, 56, 59, 61, 73–4, 111,
  113, 125, 128, 158, 162–6, 167, 168, 181, 186,
  192, 196, 206, 260, 286–7, 288, 302, 310
  Delphi Ode, 142, 143, 149, 151, 165
  deus ex machina, 183, 186, 187

Ixion, 6
Licymnius, 184
Medea, 4, 6, 7, 8, 30, 96, 104, 105, 150, 151, 198, 199–202, 209, 252, 255, 264, 286, 295, 297, 310
   agōn logōn, 226–7
   allusion to *deus ex machina* convention, 186
   chorus, 116–19, 128, 131
Melanippe the Captive, 101, 103, 274, 286
Melanippe the Wise, 286, 295
Meleager, 6
Mysi, 6
Oedipus, 6
Oenomaus, 6, 291
Orestes, 4, 6, 7, 40–1, 46, 67, 83–5, 86, 104, 120, 127, 167, 185, 186, 188, 192–5, 200, 240–5, 257, 258, 269, 287, 288, 294, 296, 302, 310
   deus ex machina, 186
Palamedes, 103, 300
Peliades, 6, 103
Phaethon, 103, 249, 291, 294
   chorus, 129
Philoctetes, 6, 101, 103, 209, 300
Phoenissae, 4, 6, 7, 8, 10, 39–40, 67, 71, 80, 101, 105, 121, 127, 128, 141, 151, 206, 213, 214, 218–19, 251, 255, 256, 258, 266, 286, 290, 292, 294, 295
   song cycle, 124
Phoenix, 6
Phrixus, 249
Polyidus, 6
Protesilaus, 6, 103, 175, 269
Rhesus, see anonymous, *Rhesus*
Scyrii, 101, 103
Stheneboea, 249, 260, 283
Supplices, 34, 57, 80–3, 88, 96, 124, 128, 183, 187, 191, 215, 216, 240, 250, 256, 258, 268, 294, 295, 296, 298, 301
Telephus, 101, 103, 209
Troades, 36, 77–9, 97, 100, 105, 109, 124, 128, 138, 161, 179, 185, 204, 250, 258, 260, 286, 294, 302
Eurydice, 250, 259
Eurystheus, 112
   in *Hcld.*, 31, 87, 184, 206, 251, 258, 259, 265, 284, 293, 294
Eusebius, 16
Evadne, 34, 82, 201, 240, 255, 257, 268, 295
exemplum, mythic, 65, 91, 92, 93, 108, 114, 122, 126, 139, 148, 149, 172, 224, 257
exodos, 75, 175, 181, 182, 294, 296
extradramatic position
   chorus, 89, 113, 114, 121
   prologue-speaker, 122

fame and honor, relation to genders, 257, 261–70
family and city, as separate realms for women and men, 254–61
farmer
   in *El.*, 121, 187, 244, 250, 288
   messenger in *Or.*, 243
   speaker in assembly in *Or.*, 243
Favorinus, 8
Filelfo, 9
first person, choral, 132, 135, *see also* ethical first person
formalism, 14, 22
foundation (of cult, custom, or dynasty by *deus ex machina*), 182–4, 186
funeral orations (at Athenian public rites for war-dead), 81, 295, 296
Furies
   in Aesch. *Eum.*, 102, 172
   in Aesch. *Oresteia*, 253
   in *Or.*, 40, 84, 192, 193, 241, 242

geloion, 51, 62
genre, 44–62
geras, 203
ghosts, status and knowledge, 203
gnome(s), 7, 22, 91, 126, 132, 133, 134, 143, 271
gnomic statements, 7, 9, 23, 91, 107, 130, 134, 135, 146, 278
gnomological tradition, 6, 7, 9
gods
   anthropomorphic features, 159, 177, 178
   as a literary device, 157–61
   inferred actions in tragic plots, 195–205
Gorgias, 45, 209
Great Dionysia, 5, 15, 17, 20, 26, 45, 50, 52, 54, 55, 77, 91, 92, 95, 157, *see also* Dionysia
guard, in Soph. *Ant.*, 210

Haemon
   in *Phoen.*, 296
   in Soph. *Ant.*, 115, 305
hamartia, 64
Hector, 79, 230, 265, 277
Hecuba
   in *Hec.*, 10, 33, 71–3, 86, 119, 124, 143, 144, 150, 184, 188, 203, 213, 229–34, 255, 256, 257, 258, 259, 266, 283, 293, 294, 300
   in *Tro.*, 36, 77, 78, 79, 109, 138, 161, 171, 173, 179, 204, 220, 221, 283, 294
Hegel, G. W. F., 47
Heinsius, Daniel, 11
Helen, 123, 129, 135, 140, 141, 144, 186, 237, 239, 260, 262, 267, 270
   in *Hel.*, 38–9, 73, 74, 79, 138, 142, 184, 188, 255, 260, 274, 287, 291, 302

Helen (cont.)
  in *Or.*, 41, 84, 85, 121, 184, 185, 192, 194, 240,
    243, 244, 288
  in *Tro.*, 36, 78, 109, 138, 162, 172, 221
Helene (island), 184
Helenus, 186
Helios, 200
Hellen, in *Melanippe the Wise*, 295
Hellenistic scholars, *see* Alexandrian scholars
Hera, 70, 71, 168, 180, 274, 292
Heracles, 31, 138, 259, 265, 269, 281
  in *Alc.*, 29, 56, 107, 257, 285, 299, 301
  in *Her.*, 35, 70, 71, 105, 111, 124, 167, 169, 173,
    215, 255, 257, 258, 274, 292, 294, 303, 306
  in *Prom. Unbound*, 65
  in satyr-plays and comedies, 301
  in Soph. *Phil.*, 86, 305
  in Soph. *Trach.*, 60, 66, 86, 100, 303, 305
Heraclitus, 155, 161, 169
Hermes
  in *Hel.*, 39
  in *Ion*, 38, 109, 180, 185, 198, 254, 285
Hermione
  in *Andr.*, 7, 32, 75, 76, 113, 131, 251, 255, 259,
    260, 273, 275, 276, 278, 283, 286, 291, 294
  in *Or.*, 41, 85, 121, 186, 194, 286, 288
Herodotus, 65, 92, 159, 197, 198, 247
heroic temper (of the Sophoclean hero), 304
Hesiod, 156, 161, 227
hetaireia, 269
hierarchy, social, 18, 48, 62, 147, 226, 248, 268,
    269, 271, 275, 279, 282, 307
Hippodameia, 291
Hippolytus, 31, 68–9, 87, 108, 119, 122, 135, 170,
    171, 177, 178, 184, 185, 187, 190, 213, 215,
    223, 224, 225, 241, 253, 256, 259, 260, 263,
    271, 273, 274, 276, 278, 284, 285, 289,
    298, 305
historicism, 14, 15
Homer, 2, 6, 19, 24, 49, 54, 58, 65, 156, 157, 160,
    161, 162, 169, 195, 205, 208, 280, 282,
    300, 308
  Iliad, 58, 67, 143, 182, 300
  Odyssey, 51, 58, 60, 67, 109, 143, 156, 182, 222
Homeric Hymn to Apollo, 142
honors
  cultic, 184
  divine, 184
hubris, 116
humble (non-elite) characters in tragedy, 19, 68,
    187, 210, 211, 243, 282, 283, 284, 285, 288
  forming chorus, 96, 134
Hyllus
  in *Hcld.*, 31, 206, 251, 259, 293
  in Soph. *Trach.*, 86, 98

hypothesis, 7, 9, 46, 75, *see also* prefatory material,
    epitome(s)
Hypsipyle, 125, 128, 250, 259

Ibsen, Henrik, 13, 176
identification, of audience with protagonists, 93
impersonation, 98, 122, 128, 248
implied author, 27, 154
indoors and outdoors, as gendered contrast,
    248–54
Ino, 184
intellectual inquiry (incorporated in
    tragedy), 208
interpretation, effort required of audience for, 23,
    87, 93, 116, 145, 228, 235, 246, 282
interrogation of values, 19, 20
Iolaus, 31, 59, 112, 206, 250, 251, 255, 258, 259, 261,
    265, 293, 296
Iole, 114, 126
  in Soph. *Trach.*, 67
Ion (in *Ion*), 38, 110, 120, 129, 166, 167, 171, 172,
    181, 184, 185, 187, 188, 197, 254, 256,
    274, 290
Ion (the rhapsode), 24
Iphigenia, 203
  in Aesch. *Agam.*, 115, 149
  in *IA*, 2, 43, 135, 141, 143, 171, 235, 236, 238, 239,
    240, 251, 256, 260, 268, 283, 301
  in *IT*, 37, 73, 74, 113, 128, 140, 142, 162, 163, 164,
    165, 172, 173, 187, 255, 260, 283, 286,
    287, 288
Iphis, 82, 269, 294, 295, 296
Iris, 70, 71, 112, 168, 175, 199, 274
isēgoria, 95
Ismene
  in Soph. *Ant.*, 263
  in Soph. *OC*, 66
isonomia, 95

Jason
  ephebic hero, 73
  in *Med.*, 30, 116, 118, 134, 137, 186, 188, 199, 201,
    212, 226, 241, 252, 255, 257, 259, 264, 271,
    272, 274, 276, 295, 297
Jocasta
  in *Phoen.*, 39, 151, 171, 172, 213, 215, 218, 219,
    220, 255, 256
  in Soph. *OT*, 116, 163, 169
juxtaposition (in structuring a drama), 64, 66, 72,
    74, 77, 80, 85, 87

kataballontes logoi, 229
katharsis, 25
kēdeutēs, 146
kleos, 19, 262, 264, 309

knowledge
    extradramatic prescience of chorus, 99, 112,
      113, 117
    superior position of spectators, 89, 99, 107, 109,
      162, 176, 179
kurios, 247

Laius, 149, 171, 199, 255, 290
    in *Chrysippus*, 260
Laodamia, 269
Lenaea, 5, 26, 52, 54
Libanius, 7
logos, 210, 218, 237
loyalty
    of slaves to masters, 285
    to friends or kin, 70, 83, 84, 164, 227, 229, 235,
      240, 241, 262, 268, 270, 286, 288, 292, 293,
      294, 299, 303
Lycurgus, 5
Lycus, 35, 70, 71, 112, 120, 167, 197, 213, 258, 260,
    292, 304
lyric style, 2, 151
Lyssa, 70, 71, 112, 168, 175, 199

Macareus, 260
Macaria, 265, *see* daughter of Heracles
Macedonia, 5
males
    mature men as agents, 297–304
    old men as agents, 292–7
    young men as agents, 285–91
Margites, 58
Marmor Parium, 16
marriage
    destiny of young females, 250, 286
    of Peleus and Thetis, 125, 135, 141
Marxian interpretation of tragedy as an
    institution, 18
masculinity, 280, 287, 296, 304
mass vs. elite, 44, 89, 101, 281
mēchanē (crane), *see* theater crane
mēchanē (scheme), 274
Medea, 30, 86, 116, 117, 118, 119, 125, 126, 134, 137,
    171, 184, 188, 197, 199, 200, 201, 212, 226,
    241, 249, 252, 255, 257, 258, 259, 264, 271,
    274, 293, 295, 297
    acting like a *deus ex machina*, 186
    used as an example by philosophers, 8
Megara, 35, 71, 112, 168, 255, 260,
    261, 292
Melanchthon, Philip, 9
Melanippe, 274
    in *Melanippe the Wise*, 295
Melicertes, 184
melodrama, 61

Melos, Athenian conquest of, 77
Menander, 6
Menelaus, 267
    in *Andr.*, 75, 76, 252, 255, 258, 274, 275, 279,
      283, 293, 302
    in *Hel.*, 73, 74, 96, 113, 138, 171, 172, 181, 187,
      255, 260, 291, 302
    in *IA*, 43, 135, 235, 236, 237, 239, 260, 302
    in *Or.*, 2, 41, 84, 85, 120, 186, 192, 194, 200, 240,
      242, 260, 288, 289, 294, 302
    in Soph. *Ajax*, 150, 300, 305
    in *Tro.*, 79, 109, 205, 221, 258, 302
Menoeceus, 7, 40, 206, 256, 266, 292, 296
merē, 88
Merops, 294
metabolē, 163
Minos, 128, 186, 249, 262
Minturno, 11
mirroring elements in drama, 65, 68, 69, 70, 72,
    77, 79, 87
misogynistic maxims, 274
misogynistic speech, 271–9
mnēsikakia, 172
Mnesimachus, 5
moira, 188
muthoi, 22
myth
    Euripides' belief in, 156
    in choral dithyrambs at Great Dionysia, 157
    in non-tragic choral lyric, 22, 51
    in pre-tragic choral lyric, 91, 92, 93, 307
    in the poetic tradition, 48, 247
    in tragic choral lyric, 112, 122–6, 130, 133, 140,
      149, 165
    providing serious subject-matter for tragedy, 51,
      54, 55, 56, 262
mythographers, 6, 265
mythography, 4, 7
mythological depth, 66, 83, 144

Nauplius, 113
Neoptolemus
    in *Andr.*, 32, 75, 76, 111, 113, 132, 138, 172, 184,
      193, 252, 275, 283, 291, 294
    in *Hec.*, 267
    in Soph. *Phil.*, 66, 86, 146, 305
    in *Tro.*, 79
Neoptolemus of Parium, 146
New Music, 2, 104, 151
Nicochares, 6
Nietzsche, Friedrich, 12, 309
Niobe, 186
nomos (law, custom), 210, 241, 275
nomos (musical), 104
non-betrayal, 265, 266, 268, 269

non-immediate connections (of choral songs), 130, 131, 133, 137, 140, 141, 148, 151
nouthetetic prayers, 162, 170, 178
nurse
  in Aesch. *Choe.*, 58
  in *Andr.*, 252
  in *Hipp.*, 69, 108, 172, 177, 190, 199, 213, 214, 223, 224, 225, 253, 260, 263, 271, 273, 274, 285, 289
  in *Med.*, 7, 118, 123

Odysseus, 79, 212, 274, 300
  in *Cyclops*, 55, 120, 170, 188, 207, 258
  in Eur. *Phil.*, 209, 256, 306
  in *Hec.*, 33, 72, 144, 230, 232, 234, 256, 257, 300
  in Soph. *Ajax*, 178, 305
  in Soph. *Phil.*, 66, 305
Oedipus
  in Aesch. *Se.*, 149
  in *Phoen.*, 40, 124, 184, 290, 294, 296
  in Soph. *OC*, 66, 78, 216, 293, 294, 305
  in Soph. *OT*, 67, 86, 97, 116, 136, 160, 199, 234, 303, 305
Oenomaus, 291
oikonomia, 63
old age, 31, 101, 228, 284, 292, 306
open form, 64, 77, 80, 85, 87, *see also* closed form
Opheltes, 184
opsis, 175
optimistic rationalist, 80, 208, 215–20
oracles (in plays without *deus ex machina*), 183
orchestra (*orchēstra*), 54, 94, 98
Oresteion, 184
Orestes, 286
  baby in *Telephus*, 75, 261
  ephebic hero, 284
  in Aesch. *Choe.*, 58, 103, 115, 269
  in Aesch. *Eum.*, 66, 102
  in *Andr.*, 75, 76, 111, 113, 132, 201, 252, 258, 274, 277, 278, 291
  in *El.*, 34, 86, 111, 121, 139, 187, 189, 258, 285, 286, 287, 288, 306
  in *IT*, 37, 73, 74, 111, 128, 142, 162, 164, 165, 184, 185, 186, 197, 255, 257, 260, 286, 287, 302
  in *Or.*, 40, 83, 84, 85, 86, 120, 171, 185, 186, 187, 188, 192, 193, 194, 240, 241, 242, 243, 244, 255, 257, 258, 261, 288, 294, 302
  in Soph. *El.*, 305, 306
organic unity, 11, 26, 63, 65, 67, 86, 93, 147

parastatēs, 265
Paris, 39, 74, 135, 141, 144, 149, 230, 237, 260, 274, 291, 303
  Judgment of, 123, 129, 131, 140, 144

parodos, 88, 107, 108, 111, 113, 114, 118, 121, 127–9, 130, 137, 143, 151, 163, 192, 236
parrhēsia, 20, 95
Pasiphaë, 209, 249, 262
pathos, 77, 82, 118, 145, 176, 204, 297
Peisistratus, 16
Peleus, 79, 135, 139, 141
  in *Andr.*, 7, 33, 75, 76, 84, 111, 124, 132, 184, 187, 188, 196, 252, 255, 274, 279, 285, 291, 293, 296, 302
Pelops, 74, 123, 149, 171, 182
  ephebic hero, 284
  in *Oenomaus*, 291
Pentheus
  in *Bacchae*, 42, 87, 110, 123, 125, 136, 140, 151, 176, 179, 189, 199, 213, 219, 240, 264, 290, 305
  leading an army against maenads, 179
peprōmenon, 149
Perachora, 184
performative utterances, 91, 130, 187
Pericles, 261
peripeteia, 285
Persephone, myth of descent and return, 60
Perseus
  ephebic hero, 73, 284
  in *Andromeda*, 291
Phaedra, 31, 68–9, 86, 104, 108, 114, 119, 128, 135, 149, 160, 171, 172, 177, 190, 199, 213, 214, 223, 224, 225, 241, 249, 251, 253, 255, 259, 263, 271, 273, 274, 285, 289, 298
  in Eur. *Theseus*, 186
  in lost *Hippolytus*, 119, 260
Phaethon
  in *Hipp.*, 122, 136
  in *Phaethon*, 129, 184, 291
pharmakos, 97
phaulon, 51, 62
Pheres, 29, 108, 227, 228, 255, 261, 270, 294, 295, 299
Philetaerus, 6
philia, 70, 72, 121, 227, 228, 236, 242, 245, 257, 306
Philippides, *Phileuripides*, 6
Philoctetes (in Soph. *Phil.*), 66
philopsychia, 243
philopsychos, 266
philos, 70, 84, 168, 228, 230, 235
philoteknos, 255
Philyllius, 5
phusis, 210
Pindar, 22, 51, 65, 91, 92, 93, 112, 156, 169
  relevance of myth in, 93
pity and fear (Aristotelian concept), 25, 54, 93

Plato, 10, 24, 26, 45, 49, 63, 161, 212
  Apology, 225
  Laws, 25
  Republic, 25
plot-motifs, 6, 53
plot-type, 27, 28, 51, 52, 53, 57, 178, 283, 287, 290,
  297, 305, 306
Plutarch, 8, 10
Polydorus, 33, 71, 144, 145, 202, 232
Polymestor, 33, 72, 86, 119, 144, 184, 188, 203, 213,
  230, 231, 233, 234, 258, 259, 260, 300
Polyneices, 125
  in *Phoen.*, 8, 40, 128, 213, 218, 258, 290, 296
  in Soph. *Ant.*, 197
  in Soph. *OC*, 66
  in *Su.*, 82
Polyxena
  in *Hec.*, 33, 36, 71, 72, 124, 143, 145, 203, 230,
    238, 250, 255, 266, 267, 268, 300
  in *Tro.*, 77, 79, 179
Porson's Law, 50
Poseidon, 171, 182
  in *Erechtheus*, 180, 186
  in *IT*, 165, 186
  in *Tro.*, 36, 77, 109, 179, 204, 274
Praxithea, 81, 187, 256, 266, 269
prefatory material, 1, 4, 7, 8, 56
priamel, 126, 129, 130, 148
priestess, Delphic (*Ion*), 38, 198, 256
proagōn, 57
probability or necessity, 2, 3, 25, 26, 63, 64, 66, 72,
  127, 182, 200, 310
Prodicus, 3
professionalization (of actors, musicians, poets),
  18, 45, 92
prohedria, 16
Prometheus, 78, 97, 175
  chorus of Oceanids, 97
prosatyric, 56, 57
Pylades, 286
  in Aesch. *Choe.*, 85, 287
  in *El.*, 35, 186, 287
  in *IT*, 37, 128, 163, 197, 257, 260, 286, 287
  in *Or.*, 4, 41, 84, 85, 121, 186, 193, 201, 244, 257,
    269, 287, 288

Quintilian, 7, 9

rationalism
  characters portrayed as rationalists, 170, *see also*
    optimistic rationalist
  Euripides interpreted as a rationalist, 13
  rationalist approach to myth, 173
realism, 2, 13, 26, 61, 104, 108, 118, 151, 210, 211,
  304, 306

reception, 1
  in Renaissance, 9–11
reciprocity
  between gods and men, 60, 155, 171, 206
  between men, 19, 72, 226, 227, 230
recognition as plot element, 67, 73, 74, 120,
  128, 162, 166, 167, 285, 286, 288,
  290, 302
religion, civic, 17
Renaissance poetic theory, 10, 11, 54, 59, 127
rescue-action, 70, 73, 74, 83, 112, 141, 166,
  186, 303
resolutions (metrical), 50
revenge-plot, 67, 71, 84, 85, 186, 227, 231, 258, 259,
  260, 287, 288
reversal
  as element of plot structure, 52, 54, 60, 72, 75,
    77, 111, 275, 303
  of attitude or judgment, 82, 116, 121, 150, 190,
    217, 246, 251, 293, 303
  of norms or stereotypes, 254, 261, 267, 306
  of treatment in a previous version, 296
rhesis, 117, 126, 162, 172, 190, 194, 223, 230, 238,
  239, 268, 277
rhetoric, 85, 207–45, 311
  ambivalence about, 211–14
  and character, 28, 222–45, 268, 276
  and self-delusion, 236, 238, 240, 268,
    277, 278
  approach to decorum, 146
  arguments, 76, 79
  cleverness, 2, 202, 224, 243
  education, 7, 210
  excess, 84, 224, 231, 234, 236, 242, 245, 256, 262
  formal speeches, 77, 86, 173, 212, 226, 229, 230,
    234, 245, 246, 256, *see also agōn (logōn)*
  invective, 226
  problematization, 223
  reshapes character, 223, 234, 238, 241, 245,
    268, 276
  rhetorical theorists, 46
  self-consciousness, 54, 209, 210, 211, 224, 226,
    227, 230, 233, 236, 242, 302, 305
  self-propelling force, 227, 238, 245, 277
  skill, 8, 10, 78, 123, 150, 208, 210, 221, 232, 233,
    240, 272, 278, 281
  universalization of, 210, 211, 213, 240
  sophistic, 212, 229
  technique, 7, 208
rhetorical question, 136, 180, 215, 275, 277
ritual patterns, 308
romantic tragedy, 59, 61
romanticism
  German, 11, 47
  model of the individual character, 61, 67

sacrifice
  human, 37, 40, 73, 164, 172, 203, 204, 206,
    231, 296
  of a virgin, 31, 33, 36, 43, 141, 143, 149, 203, 251,
    256, 265, 266, 268, 286, 300, 302
  self-sacrifice, 229
  voluntary, 228, 238, 261
sacrifice-action, 71, 231, 293
Sannyrion, 6
Satyros, 4
satyr-play, 4, 17, 21, 26, 46, 53, 54–7, 58, 60, 157,
    175, 301
satyr-plays of Euripides, 57
Scaliger, 10
scheming, associated with the female, 274
Schlegel, Friedrich and August, 12,
    47, 63
scholia, scholiasts, 1, 2, 4, 8, 9, 10, 52, 63, 88, 127,
    145, 147, 192
Schopenhauer, Arthur, 12
secrecy, choral agreement to maintain, 96
self-preservation as an ambiguous motivation,
    260, *see also philopsychia*
Semele, 42, 114, 125, 126, 176
semiotics, 14
Shaw, George Bernard, 13
shift of audience sympathy, 53, 68, 86, 87, 189,
    240, 259
Sidney, Sir Philip, 10
sightseers, chorus as, 101, 125, 129
Silenus, 55, 56
  in *Cyclops*, 120, 207, 258
Simonides, 51
Sisyphus, 274
Sisyphus (by Euripides or Critias?), 174
skene-roof, site of most divine appearances, 68,
    160, 178, 179, 254
Socrates, 2, 3, 12, 24, 207, 230, 293
soldiers (as chorus), 101
Solon, 49, 99, 156
sophia, 45, 48, 170, 183, 214
sophists, 2, 23, 155, 207, 209, 212, 229, 230
Sophocles, 13, 18, 24, 26, 27, 48, 53, 54, 87, 88, 94,
    96, 103, 115, 131, 134, 175, 239, 308
  Aegeus, 52
  Ajax, 66, 75, 101, 148, 160, 196, 209,
    300, 302
    god in prologue, 175
  Andromeda, 52, 210, 291
  Antigone, 45, 53, 58, 65, 66, 68, 97, 100, 101, 104,
    114, 115, 148, 185, 196, 197, 209, 263,
    296, 309
  Athamas, 53, 181
  Atreus, 52
    chorus, 102, 148

  contrasted with Euripides, 2, 3, 7, 8, 11, 52, 61,
    63, 66, 68, 86, 88, 100, 103, 104, 108, 127,
    146, 147, 148, 149, 150, 176, 181, 210, 211,
    234, 304, 305
  Electra, 34, 59, 67, 86, 103, 148, 210, 288, 305, 306
  Ichneutae, 55, 57
  lost plays, 52
  Madness of Odysseus, 53
  Manteis, 53
  Nausicaa, 53
  Niptra, 53
  Oedipus Coloneus, 53, 66, 67, 78, 101, 148, 150,
    216, 293, 294, 298, 305
  Oedipus Tyrannus, 53, 61, 65, 66, 86, 97, 101, 107,
    115, 146, 148, 150, 169, 199, 201, 285, 303
  Oenomaus, 53, 291
  Peleus, 53, 181
  Phaedra, 210, 298
  Philoctetes, 53, 66, 86, 101, 146, 148, 150, 181, 192,
    229, 305
    chorus, 120
    deus ex machina, 195
  Tereus, 52, 210
  Trachiniae, 60, 66, 67, 86, 97, 103, 105, 148,
    251, 303
  Triptolemus, 53
  Tyro, 53
sophos, 22, 163
sōphrōn, 225, 250, 262
Sparta, 76, 187, 249, 252, 275, 278, 302
spoudaion, 48, 51, 62
stereotypes, cultural, 244, 254, 256, 261, 272,
    275, 287
Stesichorus, 51, 156
Stheneboea, 249, 260
Stiblinus, Gasparus, 10
stichomythia, 118, 126, 180, 189, 190, 218, 223, 239,
    251, 294
Stobaeus, 7, 274
stopping-action (of *deus ex machina*), 166, 182, 186
story-pattern, 27, 51, 52, 54, 56, 60, 62, 67, 99, 110,
    162, 211, 216, 224, 283, 308
Strattis, 6
structuralism, 14
sunagōnizesthai, 146, 147, 150
suppliant, 31, 32, 70, 75, 80, 83, 112, 141, 167, 192, 216,
    250, 251, 257, 258, 260, 265, 284, 293, 301
suppliant-action, 70, 80, 82
suppliant-drama, 19, 67, 101, 137, 192, 217, 258
suppliant-plot, 80, 217
supplication, 34, 66, 72, 73, 75, 93, 113, 128, 168,
    231, 233, 239, 250, 295, 298, 300
  political, 216, 257
survival of chorus, representing communal
    survival, 97, 105

Talthybius
  in *Hec.*, 33, 72, 124
  in *Tro.*, 36, 77, 79, 179, 250
teaching, tragedy as, 20
technē, 24
technē rhētorikē, 208
Tecmessa, 150, 305
Teiresias
  in *Ba.*, 42, 59, 125, 151, 173, 213, 215, 219, 290
  in *Phoen.*, 40, 296
  in Soph. *Ant.*, 65, 196, 197
Telephus, 75, 209, 261
Teles, 8
tension
  forward tension (of choral song), 130, 150
  relaxation of, 142, 143, 145, 150, 151
Terence, 10
tetrameters (trochaic), 235, 236, 239
Thanatos (in *Alc.*), 56, 57, 180
thauma, 206
theater crane (typically for divine locomotion),
    112, 160, 168, 181, 185, 200, 253, *see also deus
    ex machina*
thematic relevance (of choral songs), 89
Theoclymenus, 39, 142, 258, 260, 285, 291, 302
Theognidean corpus, 169
theomachos, 179
Theonoe, 39, 74, 138, 171, 191, 256, 286, 291, 302
Theseus
  ephebic hero, 284
  epics about, 58
  in Eur. *Theseus*, 186
  in *Her.*, 36, 70, 173, 184, 197, 214, 257, 292, 304,
    306, 310
  in *Hipp.*, 31, 69, 114, 119, 177, 185, 187, 190, 213,
    223, 225, 258, 263, 284, 289, 298
  in Soph. *OC*, 216, 305
  in *Su.*, 34, 80, 81, 82, 186, 187, 188, 215, 216, 218,
    219, 220, 255, 256, 258, 295, 301, 306
Thespis, 16
Thetis, 135, 140, 141
  in *Andr.*, 32, 76, 113, 133, 188, 294
Thoas, 164, 185, 258, 286, 287
Thomas Magister, 9
Thucydides, 197, 209, 211, 233, 256, 261

Thyestes, 74, 123, 140
Timaeus (the historian), 209
timē, 19, 95, 177, 306, 309
tragic hero, assumption of focus on single
    character, 64
tragic, the tragic, 15, 26, 46, 47, 62
tragicomedy, 58, 61
tuchē, 159, 171
Tyndareus, 41, 84, 120, 185, 192, 241, 242, 244, 255,
    258, 288, 294, 296
Tzetzes, John, 56

Verrallism, 13
villain, 53, 55, 61, 68, 70, 71, 86, 114, 120, 168, 211,
    217, 233, 258, 291

weaving, 143, 264, 269, 287
winds
  adverse winds at Aulis, 204
  adverse winds in *Hec.*, 203
  in *Tro.*, 204
women
  as nurturing or protecting offspring, 255
  associated with the scheming, *see* scheming
  devotion to family, 255
  in the audience at the Great Dionysia, 16
  intruding into public sphere, 259
  playing communal role in tragic plots, 256
  rhetorical skill, *see* rhetoric, skill,
    universalization of
  seeking revenge, 258

xenia, 72, 101, 180, 188, 248, 257, 298, 306
Xenophanes, 155, 161, 169
xenos, 199, 299
Xuthus, 38, 110, 120, 166, 184, 187, 197,
    254, 255
Xylander, Guilielmus, 9

Zethus, 184, 186
Zeus
  dispensation of, 165
  in *Her.*, 70, 167, 171, 280, 292
  inscrutable mind of, 156, 170, 221
  will of, 60, 142, 188, 189, 193

Index of passages cited

Aeschylus
Agamemnon
11: 260
204: 236
206–8: 236
218: 236
235–7: 236
248: 115
280–316: 209
281–311: 170
320–50: 209
355–487: 115
471–4: 134
473–4: 125
661–6: 199
757–62: 134
931–44: 199
1072–330: 107
1296–304: 115
Choephori
306–509: 85
585–662: 148
855–69: 120
872–4: 100, 115
894–5: 269
900–2: 287
904: 269
935–71: 130
1061: 115
Eumenides
64: 85
640–2: 172
658–61: 170
fr. 168: 176
fr. 61: 176
Septem
375–676: 209
602–8: 217
677–719: 115
720–91: 149
Supplices
455–67: 302

Alcaeus
42 L–P: 140
Anaxagoras
13–14 D–K: 170
anonymous
Prometheus
526–35: 134
707–35: 170
790–815: 170
829–41: 170
894–7: 134
Rhesus
938–49: 180
Antiphanes
fr. 189.13–16 K–A: 181
Archilochus
114 W: 134
Aristophanes
Acharnians
10: 2
Birds
786–9: 55
Clouds
1365: 2
fr. 161 K–A: 2
Frogs
89–91: 210
91: 207
92: 207
815: 207
839: 207
841: 44, 207
849–50: 44
892–4: 44
892: 44
917: 207
939–44: 44
943: 207
948–51: 44
948–52: 210
949–50: 44
954: 44, 207

346

971–9: 24
976–91: 44
1008–10: 23
1009–10: 24
1034–6: 24
1043–51: 44
1043–52: 44
1054–5: 23
1069–71: 44
1069: 207
1071: 207
1078–81: 44
1084–6: 44
1160: 207
1203: 44
1301–2: 44
1310: 207
1327–8: 44
1331–63: 44
1471–8: 44
1482–99: 207
1491–9: 44
1492: 207
Women at the Thesmophoria
389–428: 24
Aristotle
EE
1244a10: 8
EN
1110a28: 8
1136a11: 8
1142a2: 8
1167a32–4: 8
Met.
985a18: 182
Poetics
1448b24–49a6: 51
1448b38–49a2: 58
1449a19–21: 57
1450b16–20: 175
1451a23–35: 58
1451b25–6: 106
1452a24–6: 285
1452a6–10: 198
1453a30–5: 54
1453a30–9: 58
1453b1–11: 175
1454a31–2: 238
1454b1–6: 175
1454b2: 182
1456a2–3: 175
1456a25–32: 146
1456a27–32: 127
1456a29–30: 88
1460b33–4: 2

1460b34: 304
1461b19–21: 200
Ch. 9: 2, 310
Ch. 13: 2, 64, 65
Ch. 14: 2
Ch. 15: 2
Ch. 16: 2
Ch. 18: 2
Ch. 25: 2
Pol.
1227a19: 8
Rhetoric
1389a3–90b13: 284
1405b5–25: 52
Aulus Gellius
Noctes Atticae
15.20: 3

Bacchylides
5.79–92: 49

Critias(?)
Sisyphus
43 F 19: 174

Demosthenes
40.59: 182
60.8: 216
Dictys Cretensis
5.16: 10
Dio Chrysostomus
Orat. 18.6: 7
Orat. 52.15: 52
Dionysius of
Halicarnassus
de imitatione
II fr. 6.2.10–11: 52

Euripides
Alcestis
64–71: 107, 180
83–4: 270
83: 107
112–30: 107
112–18: 107
118: 107
119–20: 107
121–30: 107
124–6: 107
127–9: 122
150–6: 270
175–88: 250
180: 269
181–2: 299
202: 270

Euripides (cont.)
213–37: 130
235: 270
241: 270
247: 170
250: 270
275: 270
280–325: 250
282–90: 269
299–319: 299
324–5: 270
328–35: 299
435–75: 131
442: 270
455–9: 107
551–2: 108
568–605: 131, 140
568–87: 124
569–605: 140
588: 124
600–3: 108
604–5: 113
606–740: 228
614–28: 228
623–4: 270, 276
629–72: 228
636–7: 299
648: 270
662–8: 299
696–7: 270
742: 270
747–860: 285
840–54: 107
861–934: 131
899: 270
935–61: 270
962–1005: 131
962–72: 107
962: 133
969–72: 107
973–5: 107
976–7: 134
982: 107
985–90: 107
986: 107
993: 107
Alcm. Cor.
fr. 73a: 181
Alope
test. iib: 184
Andromache
49–55: 111
80: 293
85: 274
117–46: 113

147–272: 275
151: 252
155–80: 275
181–2: 278
183–231: 275
192–204: 277
215–18: 275
218: 260
220–1: 276
222–7: 277
229: 260
232–3: 278
234–60: 275
236–42: 276
238–44: 252
269–72: 276
273: 276
274–308: 131, 140
274–92: 123
293–308: 123
309–463: 275
331: 274
364–5: 279
406–20: 269
445–63: 252
447: 274
464–93: 131, 278
465: 133
469–70: 134
492–3: 113
511–67: 138
549: 274
551: 293
565–6: 138
572–6: 75
573–4: 75
577–714: 293
595–601: 252
726–7: 279
765: 75
766–802: 111, 121, 132
768: 133
785: 125
790–801: 124
791: 132
802–77: 252
820–78: 75
879: 201
891–5: 75
894–5: 75
896–919: 277
904–5: 277
907–11: 277
920–53: 277
921–3: 75

938–42: 2, 7
943–53: 278
954–6: 279
959–63: 278
995: 274
1009–18: 171
1009–46: 132
1009: 138
1022: 132
1028: 132
1036: 132, 190
1042: 132
1047–1288: 294
1116: 274
1117: 75
1123: 75
1147: 196
1156: 75
1161–5: 172
1239–42: 184
1241: 183
1243–52: 184
1253–8: 187
1260–2: 113
1268–9: 188
1271–2: 188
1284–8: 106
Andromeda
   test. iiia: 184
Antiope
   fr. 210: 174
   fr. 223.80–5: 184
   fr. 223.98–9: 184
   fr. 223.100–2: 186
Archelaus
   test. iiia: 184
Bacchae
   49: 179
   50: 179
   55–63: 176
   88–103: 125
   94–8: 220
   120–34: 125
   138–92: 106
   170–209: 59,
     220
   193: 292
   210–22: 290
   222–5: 290
   234–8: 290
   266–327: 173, 219
   266–71: 219
   266–7: 213

   309: 219
310–12: 219
314–18: 290
325–7: 219
345–51: 290
353–4: 290
434–518: 176
453–9: 290
487: 290
519–75: 140
519–29: 125
521: 141
523–5: 220
539–44: 123
561–4: 122
576–603: 176
598–9: 122
604–61: 176
604–41: 240
616–41: 199
642–861: 176
668–71: 290
686–8: 290
778–809: 290
810: 189
811–16: 290
850–3: 199
862–911: 136
877–81: 136
897–901: 136
912–76: 176, 199
1059–62: 290
1078–9: 196
1179–80: 264
1199: 264
1204–9: 264
1205–9: 264
1233–9: 264
1236–7: 264
1249–50: 189
1252–5: 264
1329: 189
1330–43: 189
1330–7: 188
1338–9: 188
1341–3: 189
1344–51: 189
1347: 189
1349: 188
1351: 188, 189
1354–62: 188
1377–8: 189

Euripides (cont.)
  Bellerophon
    fr. 286: 173
    fr. 286b: 174
    fr. 286b.7: 173
  Chrysippus
    fr. 839: 222
  Cretans
    fr. 472: 128, 256
    fr. 472e: 209, 249
    fr. 472e.29–33: 262
  Cyclops
    198–202: 258
    270–2: 120
    315: 207
    316–17: 174
    336–40: 174
    354–5: 170
    525–7: 174
    693–5: 258
    696–700: 188
  Electra
    87: 111
    192–7: 111
    194–5: 121
    198–200: 111, 171
    343–4: 250
    352: 121
    367–90: 288
    432: 141, 149
    432–86: 139
    432–88: 124
    440: 139
    451: 139
    479–80: 140
    482–6: 121
    483–6: 111
    487–668: 285
    612–39: 288
    646–62: 288
    669–746: 123, 140
    700: 141
    745–6: 121
    774–855: 288
    931–51: 286
    962–87: 121, 190
    979: 194
    1060–99: 121
    1068–75: 286
    1080–5: 262
    1147–64: 130
    1168: 121
    1177–1232: 121
    1183–4: 121
    1201–5: 121

    1224: 121
    1244–6: 190
    1245–6: 180
    1247–8: 188
    1258–63: 183
    1268–9: 183
    1270–2: 183
    1273–5: 184
    1280–3: 185
    1286–7: 187
    1290: 188
    1298–1302: 280
    1301: 188
    1302: 190
    1357–9: 105
  Erechtheus
    fr. 360: 81, 256
    fr. 370.55–62: 186
    fr. 370.59–62: 180
    fr. 370.71–4: 187
    fr. 370.77–94: 184
  fr. 206: 213
  fr. 253: 213
  fr. 446: 105
  fr. 528: 213
  fr. 583: 213
  fr. 928b: 213
  fr. 1012: 207
  Hecuba
    32: 204
    37–9: 204
    37–8: 203
    40–1: 203
    59–67: 72
    109–15: 203
    111–15: 204
    113–15: 203
    116–40: 204
    118–19: 231
    130–40: 300
    130–1: 231
    229–30: 230
    229–37: 230
    239–48: 230
    251–95: 230
    258–71: 230
    271: 230
    272: 231
    275: 231
    276: 231
    279–81: 231
    301–2: 230
    328–31: 231
    347–8: 266
    374: 266

385–8: 269
438–40: 72
444–83: 143
444: 149
482–3: 143
499–502: 72
549: 266
566: 267
568–70: 268
577: 267
579–80: 266
592: 266
598–9: 266
627–8: 144
629–49: 123, 124
629–57: 143
631–4: 144
640: 144
644–6: 144
753–61: 231
763: 231
775: 231
783: 231
785: 231
788–811: 231
814–19: 213, 231
833: 232
841–5: 233
850–63: 300
858–63: 259
858–60: 233
859: 233
898–901: 203, 204
905–52: 144
914–51: 124
962–7: 204
1023–34: 120
1042–3: 144
1056–60: 72
1058–9: 72
1136–7: 233
1138: 233
1142–4: 233
1175: 233
1176: 233
1187–90: 213
1187–95: 233
1199–1205: 234
1236–7: 234
1238–9: 213
1254–79: 73
1259–79: 188
1259–74: 86
1261: 10
1271–3: 184

1289–90: 203
1293–5: 105
1293: 106
Helen
1–315: 288
137–42: 113
214–26: 123
261: 171
293: 269
361–2: 134
385: 96
386–436: 181
528–760: 138
610: 274
663: 171
729–806: 288
761–1106: 138
767: 113
833–40: 269
851: 172
880–6: 171
894–943: 302
947–95: 302
962–74: 302
1032–89: 287
1098–1102: 171
1106–10: 150
1107–64: 138, 140
1126–31: 113
1151–4: 138
1250–92: 303
1301–68: 141
1301–51: 126
1355–7: 142
1368: 142
1441–5: 150
1470–5: 122
1495–1511: 113
1537–1612: 303
1640–1: 285
1646: 188
1647–9: 191
1656–7: 191
1660–1: 188
1666–9: 184
1670–5: 184
1676–7: 187
1678–9: 195
1688–92: 106
Heracleidae
1–15: 293
26–30: 293
55–287: 284
69–73: 176
73–119: 96

Euripides (cont.)
205–13: 216
357–60: 134
425–6: 206
453–7: 269
474–7: 265
474–5: 251
476–7: 251
500–34: 293
502: 265
506: 265
507: 265
510: 265
513: 265
516–18: 265
519: 265
522: 265
523–4: 265
526: 265
527: 265
533: 265
534: 265
574–96: 293
574–95: 265
589–90: 265
602–4: 293
608–29: 134
646–53: 251
664–5: 251
680–747: 59
701–8: 112
706–7: 112
720–47: 293
729: 292
748–50: 149
813–17: 87
849–63: 112, 293
869–70: 171
892–927: 121
909–18: 124
926–7: 134
1028–36: 184
1053: 106
Heracles
170–205: 292
228–35: 292
236–7: 213
238–9: 292
268–72: 292
312–15: 292
339–47: 168, 171
347: 172
348–441: 138, 168
357–8: 112
359–429: 124

425–9: 112
498–501: 168, 171
562–4: 70
631–2: 70
637–700: 112, 134
655–6: 171, 172
655–72: 168
662: 70
701–33: 292
734–48: 120
763–814: 112, 121
772–80: 168
812–13: 168
815–21: 112
822–79: 199
827–9: 280
846–54: 168
855: 274
856: 168
966–7: 197
1016–18: 122, 126
1021–2: 122, 126
1101–4: 70
1102: 70
1186: 197
1214–27: 70
1307–10: 170
1314–21: 173, 215
1315: 215
1318–19: 215
1328–33: 184
1340–6: 169
1346: 215
1424: 70
1425–6: 70
1427: 106
Hippolytus
1–57: 177
21: 68
30–3: 184
42: 263
47: 68, 190, 263
47–50: 177
57: 68
73–87: 253
87: 289
88–120: 177, 284
113: 178
114–20: 178
117–20: 172
121–30: 128
131–40: 128
141–69: 108, 128
148–50: 68
155–60: 108

166–9: 253
170–266: 223
176–361: 223
208–49: 199
208–31: 177
239–49: 253
255–7: 171
293–4: 253
295–6: 253
295: 253
310–52: 223
329–32: 263
331: 274
335: 273
337–47: 160
337–43: 177
362–72: 223
364–5: 134
373–430: 223, 253
375–87: 273
382–7: 273
383–4: 177
384: 224
386–7: 224
399: 224
401: 160
406–7: 273
413: 224
415–18: 224
423: 263
433–81: 177
439: 224
441–2: 224
443–50: 224
447–50: 274
447–8: 68
451–61: 122, 172
451–52: 224
451–69: 274
453–61: 215
453–6: 224
456–8: 215
456–7: 224
459–61: 224
465–6: 224
471–2: 224
473–5: 224
476: 224
478–81: 273
486–9: 213
487: 224
489: 224, 263
503: 224
504–5: 224
505: 224

525–64: 114, 143
525–9: 114, 134
545–62: 126
563–4: 68, 253
575–80: 96
616–68: 224, 271
616–24: 224
627: 224
628–9: 224
640: 224
645–50: 177, 273, 278
646–7: 224
649–50: 253
650: 253
656–60: 225
661–2: 224
667: 224
669–79: 225
687: 263
717: 263
725–7: 114, 160
732–75: 135
732–4: 135
738–41: 122
748–51: 123
752–63: 108
752–3: 149
856–90: 290
874–92: 298
891–2: 298
899–901: 298
948–57: 225
976–80: 299
979–80: 183
983–1035: 213
988–9: 226
1009–10: 226
1012–15: 226
1013–15: 226
1034: 271
1036–7: 298
1051–9: 298
1061: 171
1102–50: 134
1104–10: 171
1111–19: 134
1120–2: 171
1146–50: 170
1219–26: 289
1240–1: 289
1249–54: 284
1261–4: 284
1268–82: 114, 130, 143, 253
1272–3: 68
1283–1341: 190

Euripides (cont.)
1283: 68
1299: 263
1300–1: 68, 263
1301–2: 180, 190
1305: 263, 274
1314–21: 122
1320: 191
1321–4: 299
1325–8: 299
1326–7: 180
1327–31: 188
1328–34: 178, 280
1334–5: 191
1339–41: 195
1342–88: 190
1347–88: 69
1382–3: 170
1389–1443: 190
1400: 180, 191
1403–14: 187
1406: 191
1420–2: 188
1422: 68
1423–7: 184
1429–30: 263
1434: 188
1436: 188
1441: 171
1446–61: 310
1462–6: 98, 105
Hippolytus Veiled
fr. 370.77–94: 184
Hypsipyle
752h.40: 125
874–85 = fr. 757.43–54: 250
fr. 752g.18–31: 126
fr. 753c: 125
fr. 759a.1673: 184
IA
164–230: 129
178–84: 123
231–302: 129
303–16: 235, 239
317–401: 239
337–49: 235
347–8: 235
350–65: 235
366–75: 236
378–401: 236
382–90: 135
394a–95: 237
396–9: 238
399: 236
443: 236

444–5: 237
451–2: 236
456: 237
463–4: 236
467: 237
469–537: 235
473–503: 237
477–9: 237
489–90: 237
498–9: 237
499–500: 233
500–3: 237
513–27: 237
543–89: 129, 134
554–7: 134
573–89: 123, 141
585–6: 135
751–800: 135, 143
757–61: 122
785–6: 134
794–7: 122
819–52: 250
819–54: 239
855–916: 239
855–95: 285
900–16: 239
1034–5: 171, 172
1036–97: 135, 141
1036–79: 125
1062–75: 141
1080–97: 141
1146–1208: 237
1148–54: 237
1148–63: 250
1162–3: 276
1189–90: 237
1201–5: 238
1250–2: 238
1338–44: 251
1338: 239
1341–68: 239
1368–1401: 238, 268
1368: 239
1376: 238
1383–4: 238
1385: 238
1386–91: 238
1392–4: 239
1402–3: 171
Ino
test. iii: 184
Ion
68: 181
184–218: 126
184–237: 114

184–7: 129
231–6: 129
252–4: 166
332–46: 167
355: 166
358: 166
365: 166
367: 166
370: 166
384–5: 166
426: 166
436–51: 166, 167
442–4: 172
451: 172
452–516: 140
452–509: 138
452–91: 109
452–7: 122
469–70: 110
470: 110
493–509: 109
666–7: 120
676–724: 110
685: 110
699–705: 110
720: 120
723–4: 123
725–1047: 285
752–60: 120
859–69: 262
880: 166
885: 166
895: 166
936–69: 122
952: 166
960: 166
970–1038: 287
972: 166
985–1017: 122
1048–1105: 110
1048–60: 120
1090–8: 110
1099–1105: 110
1116: 274
1171–1216: 285
1187–9: 198
1196–1200: 198
1216: 274
1229–49: 120, 130
1312–19: 171
1320–3: 198
1326: 274
1346–7: 198
1352–3: 198
1539–45: 187

1546–8: 167
1555–68: 186
1555–9: 180
1558: 167
1564–5: 185
1575–94: 184
1589–94: 110
1595: 191, 198
1602: 187
1608: 167
1609–13: 167
1619–22: 105
IT
1–66: 128
35–7: 164
46–52: 163
53–5: 162
67–122: 128
77: 162
90–1: 162
123–46: 128
142–235: 163
143–235: 111
191–201: 123
233–4: 142
264–74: 244
264–80: 197
301–33: 286
380–91: 164
380–4: 172
385–91: 164
392: 150
394–8: 122
407–21: 111
411–21: 142
423: 122
435–7: 122
435–8: 113
499–504: 286
537: 113
569: 163
570–5: 163, 190
570–1: 163
597–608: 286
674–99: 288
674–86: 286
711–15: 163
808–26: 287
811–26: 122
909–11: 163
949–69: 184
995: 164
1004–11: 286
1004–6: 269
1007–8: 288

Euripides (cont.)
  1017–51: 287
  1067–8: 187
  1082–8: 164
  1089–1152: 140
  1089–91: 150
  1098–1102: 122
  1234–83: 126, 142, 165
  1234–82: 111
  1235: 141
  1279: 165
  1322–4: 166
  1325–6: 166
  1366–85: 286
  1385: 196
  1386–9: 197
  1394–1419: 165
  1398–1402: 164, 287
  1414–19: 186
  1425–46: 164
  1438–41b: 185
  1438: 188
  1444–5: 186
  1449–61: 162
  1458–61: 164
  1467–9: 187
  1471–2: 183
  1486: 188
  1491: 164
Ixion
  fr. 426a: 222
Medea
  1–6: 123
  96–167: 252
  111–14: 117
  113–213: 137
  148: 199
  157: 116, 199
  160: 199
  163: 116
  165: 117
  167: 201
  169–70: 199
  182–3: 117
  206–7: 117
  208–9: 199
  214–66: 137, 271
  214: 252
  248–52: 272
  257: 201
  260: 274
  261: 117
  262: 117
  263–6: 271
  267: 117

283: 295
327: 295
329: 295
332: 199
340–7: 295
358–63: 117
364–409: 117
376–85: 253
384–5: 272
406: 200
407–9: 272
410–45: 117, 136
446–64: 226
465–74: 226
469–72: 226
475–87: 226
475–6: 227
483: 227
488–515: 226
488: 227
516–19: 171, 226
516: 199
522–5: 227
526–33: 227
534–44: 227
545–6: 227
547–67: 227
568–75: 227
569–75: 271
569–73: 271
580–1: 212
627–62: 117, 134
627–35: 134
633–52: 134
663–823: 117, 200
663–763: 137
746: 200
752: 200
764: 199, 200
811–18: 137
824–65: 117, 121, 137
866–975: 272
941–5: 295
954: 200
976–1001: 117
1013–14: 201
1019–80: 117
1056: 202
1079: 202
1081–1115: 118,
  125, 143
1112–15: 170
1154–7: 295
1167–1202: 253
1171–5: 197

1204–20: 295
1209–20: 255, 295
1236–50: 117
1250: 252
1251–92: 118, 130
1251–60: 200
1260: 202
1265–6: 202
1275: 118
1279–83: 184
1282–9: 126
1301–5: 259
1320–2: 200
1333–5: 201
1352: 199
1386–8: 188
1415–19: 106
Melanippe the Captive
    fr. 493: 274
    fr. 494: 274
    test. iib: 184
Orestes
    1–210: 83
    1–724: 83
    10: 241
    28: 192
    71–131: 84
    76: 192
    163–5: 192
    211–315: 83
    266–7: 192
    276: 192
    285–7: 192
    371–3: 194
    385–447: 241
    414–16: 192
    417: 190, 192
    420: 171, 192
    459–69: 241
    474: 294
    481–90: 241
    482–90: 294
    491–541: 241
    512–15: 244
    544–604: 241
    544–601: 241
    546–7: 241
    551–63: 242
    553–4: 242
    563: 242
    564–601: 242
    591–9: 192
    629: 242, 294
    638–9: 242
    640–79: 242

640–1: 242
644–5: 242, 243
651: 242
657: 242
663: 242
665–8: 242
667: 242
669–72: 242
682–716: 243
725–1097: 84
725: 201
729–806: 134
807–43: 123, 134
819–21: 120
823–5: 120
866–956: 243
898–900: 244
907–8: 213
915: 294
917–29: 243
943: 243
955–6: 193
974: 171
1018–1245: 244
1039–40: 288
1069–97: 288
1085–97: 84
1098–1690: 84
1104: 121
1131–52: 244
1153–4: 121
1155–76: 245
1225–45: 85
1305–10: 123
1353–65: 130
1361–5: 123
1506–28: 261
1510: 289
1512: 185
1524: 289
1526: 289
1533–36: 185
1537–48: 130
1539–40: 121
1545–8: 121
1576–1620: 193
1625–65: 193
1635–7: 184
1636–7: 184
1646–7: 184
1650–2: 183
1654–7: 188
1668–9: 194
1671: 194
1676–7: 194

Euripides (cont.)
  Peliades
    fr. 608: 242
  Phaethon
    63–101 = fr. 773.19–58: 129
    68–70 = fr. 773.23–6: 114
    93–4 = fr. 773.49–50: 114
  Philoctetes
    fr. 787–9: 256, 306
    fr. 789d: 256
    fr. 794: 173
  Phoenissae
    13–16: 255
    63: 290
    84–7: 219
    86–7: 162
    87: 172
    196–7: 128
    226–34: 150
    248: 122
    352: 171
    379: 171
    408–25: 122
    467–8: 219
    469–96: 213, 214
    469–72: 214
    494–6: 214
    497–8: 214
    499–525: 214
    506: 295
    516–17: 219
    523–5: 295
    523: 218
    526–7: 213
    528–30: 219
    529: 218
    531: 218
    532: 218
    536: 218
    538: 218
    539–40: 218
    541–2: 218
    543–7: 218
    547–8: 218
    548: 218
    549: 218, 295
    552–3: 218
    553: 218
    554: 218
    555–7: 219
    557: 218
    560–1: 295
    567: 218
    568–83: 218
    586–7: 219

    588–9: 219
    621–4: 219
    638–89: 141
    706–47: 296
    757–77: 296
    767–7: 122
    801–11: 123
    801–2: 150
    834–1018: 296
    846: 94
    968–9: 269
    968: 255
    991–1018: 7
    993–1012: 266
    995, 255
    1019–21: 150
    1019–66: 141
    1026: 141
    1276: 251
    1283: 269
    1284–1307: 130
    1308–31: 296
    1318: 255
    1458–9: 269
    1578: 269
    1582–1736: 296
    1595–1614: 122
    1703–7: 184
    1720–1: 94
    1726–7: 171
  Phrixus
    fr. 822: 249
  Phrixus A'
    test. iib: 184
  Protesilaus
    fr. 646a: 175
  Stheneboea
    fr. 669: 249
  Supplices
    1–777: 80
    87–364: 80
    87–99: 256
    108–9: 257
    131–61: 122
    176–9: 217
    195–249: 216
    216–8: 217
    226–8: 217
    243: 217
    263–4: 216
    286–90: 256
    288: 257
    293–6: 257
    294: 257
    331: 217

343–5: 257
399–584: 284
399–597: 80
408: 217
420–5: 217
423–5: 217
433–7: 217
462: 207
486–505: 217
496: 83
508: 217
549–55: 217
577: 216
580: 217
610: 171
612: 171
628–9: 122
634–751: 80
639: 83
786–91: 81
822–3: 81
833–6: 122
838–917: 81
841–5: 217
855–917: 217
861: 83
925–31: 217
934: 83
955–89: 81
980–1113: 82
980: 201
990–1030: 269
1038–44: 268
1045–71: 269
1087–91: 82
1165–79: 187
1183–8: 186
1187–95: 187
1201–12: 184
1213–26: 188
1232: 106
Theseus
   test. iiia.14–17: 186
Troades
   1–47: 77, 180
   10: 274
   19–20: 204
   39–40: 179
   48–97: 78
   51–3: 180
   65: 78, 179
   66–7: 180
   67–8: 171
   77–94: 109
   93–4: 204

153: 176
159–60: 204
167: 204
180–1: 204
260–71: 78, 79, 179
260: 79
294–461: 79
365–405: 79
365–7: 78
406–7: 78
424–61: 240
456: 205
462–5: 96
469: 171, 221
469–70: 78
472–510: 138
516–67: 124
524–41: 221
560–1: 221
568–779: 79
597–600: 221
612–13: 221, 222
619–31: 78
624–5: 79
630–83: 79
636–83: 262
651–2: 273
655–6: 262
701–5: 79
706–9: 79
775–6: 78
782–6: 79
799–859: 138
799–858: 78
799: 150
814: 139
817: 139
843: 109, 139
856–7: 139
860–83: 221
884–8: 173, 220
948–50: 173
967–8: 213
1053–4: 109
1053–9: 109
1060–1117: 78
1060–80: 171
1062: 109
1077: 109
1100–17: 109
1107–8: 109
1114: 109
1123–7: 205
1126–8: 79
1148: 205

Euripides (cont.)
1155: 205
1240–2: 78, 222
1242: 171
1269–71, 79
1280–1: 78, 171
1287–92: 171
1317: 171
1332: 106

Gorgias
82 A 4 D–K: 209
82 B 23 D–K: 25

Heraclitus
94 D–K: 169
Herodotus
1.23: 92
2.53: 161
5.67: 51
6.75.3: 197
6.84: 197
Hesiod
Catalogue of Women
fr. 10a.20–4: 110
Erga
57–95: 227
Theog.
26–7: 212
571–612: 227
Homer
Iliad
3.365–8: 162
9.308–13: 212
12.164–5: 162
19.74–144: 202
22.105–6: 265
Odyssey
8.382–468: 49
19.560–7: 165
20.61–82: 269
Homeric Hymn to Apollo
146–76: 91
187–206: 90
Homeric Hymn to Demeter
268–74: 182
Horace
de arte poetica
318–26: 146
Hyperides
6.5: 216
hypothesis Eur. *Alc.*,
46, 56
hypothesis Eur. *Or.*, 46

Libanius
progymn.
11.22: 7
Lysias
2.7–16: 216
2.62: 265

Pindar
Nemeans
7.20–30: 212
Olympians
1.28–32: 212
1.35–53: 169
1.52–3: 134
1.57–72: 182
1.71–87: 182
9.35–41: 169
Pythians
1.1–12: 90
6.18: 183
9.79–83: 112
11.50–4: 134
Plato
Apology
23c: 214
Cratylus
425d: 181
Gorgias
447c5–8: 230
Ion
540d–1b: 24
Laws
700–1: 49
Menexenus
239b: 216
Protagoras
315c: 230
Republic
358b–367e: 222
381d: 176
539b–c: 214
Plautus
Amphitryo
59–63: 59
pseudo–Aristotle
Problemata
19.48: 146

Quintilian
Inst. orat.
10.1.66–68: 7

Sappho
fr. 137 L–P: 49

Sch. Arist.
  Acharn.
    443: 127
Sch. Eur.
  Alc.
    962: 147
  Hippolytus
    1102: 147
  Med.
    823: 147
  Or.
    1691: 147
  Phoenissae
    1019: 127
    1053: 127
Sch. Soph.
  Ajax
    596a: 127
    1205: 127
  OT
    596a: 127
Solon
  13 W: 156
Sophocles
  Ajax
    1–133: 178, 199
    596–645: 149
    646–92: 305
    693–718: 116, 130
    1185–1222: 150
  Antigone
    211–22: 116
    278–9: 197
    320: 207
    332–75: 114, 115, 148, 149, 170
    373–5: 134
    502–4: 263
    582–625: 114, 115, 149
    694–5: 263
    766: 65
    781–800: 114, 115
    944–87: 116
    1091: 65
    1115–54: 116, 158
    1270: 116
  Electra
    145–52: 122
    472–515: 149

    1384–97: 130
    fr. 1130.16: 207
  Oedipus Coloneus
    1556–78: 130
    1623: 196
  Oedipus Tyrannus
    408–62: 136
    463–512: 136
    497–503: 163
    707–9: 163
    723–5: 163
    863–910: 116, 148
    863–72: 134
    896: 99
    911–30: 116
    1086–1109: 107, 116
    1186–1222: 116
    1329–30: 160
    1524–30: 97
  Philoctetes
    676–729: 113
    839–42: 240
    1440–4: 186
  Trachiniae
    438–49: 273
    496–530: 149
    719–23: 269
    723–30: 100, 115
    947–70: 130
    1275–8: 98
Stobaeus
  4.22g: 274
Suda
  s.v. Εὐριπίδης: 3, 5, 16
  s.v. Ἀρίων: 92, 98

Thucydides
  2.42.4: 265
  2.45.2: 261
  3.38: 234, 243
  3.42: 212
  5.84: 77
  5.104–5: 197
  5.114–16: 77
  70.50.4: 197

Xenophanes
  fr. 1 W: 169